THE CIVIL LAW

IN

SPAIN AND SPANISH-AMERICA,

INCLUDING

Cuba, Puerto Rico and Philippine Islands,

AND THE

SPANISH CIVIL CODE in force, annotated and with references to the CIVIL CODES of

MEXICO, CENTRAL AND SOUTH AMERICA,

WITH

A History of all the Spanish Codes, and Summary of Canonical Laws, of the Principal Fueros, Ordenamientos, Councils and Ordenanzas of Spain from the Earliest Times to the Twentieth Century, including

THE SPANISH, MEXICAN, CUBAN AND PUERTO RICAN AUTONOMICAL CONSTITUTIONS,

AND

A HISTORY OF THE LAWS OF THE INDIES — RECOPILACION DE LEYES DE LOS REYNOS DE LAS INDIAS,

BY

CLIFFORD STEVENS WALTON,

Doctorando, University of Madrid, Licentiate of the University of Havana, Member of the Bar of the Supreme Court of the United States and of the Bar of the District of Columbia, Associate of the Institut de Droit Internacional, and Corresponding Member of the Sociedad Geografia y Estadistica de Mexico.

THE LAWBOOK EXCHANGE, LTD.
Clark, New Jersey

ISBN 978-1-58477-245-3

Lawbook Exchange edition 2003, 2016

The quality of this reprint is equivalent to the quality of the original work.

THE LAWBOOK EXCHANGE, LTD.
33 Terminal Avenue
Clark, New Jersey 07066-1321

Please see our website for a selection of our other publications and fine facsimile reprints of classic works of legal history:
www.lawbookexchange.com

Library of Congress Cataloging-in-Publication Data

Walton, Clifford Stevens, 1861-1912.
The civil law in Spain and Spanish-America : including Cuba, Puerto Rico, and Philippine Islands, and the Spanish Civil code in force, annotated and with references to the civil codes of Mexico, Central and South America ... / by Clifford Stevens Walton.
p. cm.
Originally published: Washington, D.C. : W.H. Lowdermilk & Co., 1900.
Includes bibliographical references and index.
ISBN 1-58477-245-X (cloth: alk. paper)
1. Civil law—Spain. 2. Civil law—Latin America. 3. Civil law—Philippines. I. Title.

K623 .W35 2002
346.46—dc2l

Printed in the United States of America on acid-free paper

THE CIVIL LAW

IN

SPAIN AND SPANISH-AMERICA,

INCLUDING

Cuba, Puerto Rico and Philippine Islands,

AND THE

SPANISH CIVIL CODE in force, annotated and with references to the CIVIL CODES of

MEXICO, CENTRAL AND SOUTH AMERICA,

WITH

A History of all the Spanish Codes, and Summary of Canonical Laws, of the Principal Fueros, Ordenamientos, Councils and Ordenanzas of Spain from the Earliest Times to the Twentieth Century, including

THE SPANISH, MEXICAN, CUBAN AND PUERTO RICAN AUTONOMICAL CONSTITUTIONS,

AND

A HISTORY OF THE LAWS OF THE INDIES—RECOPILACION DE LEYES DE LOS REYNOS DE LAS INDIAS,

BY

CLIFFORD STEVENS WALTON,

Doctorando, University of Madrid, Licentiate of the University of Havana, Member of the Bar of the Supreme Court of the United States and of the Bar of the District of Columbia, Associate of the Institut de Droit Internacional, and Corresponding Member of the Sociedad Geografia y Estadistica de Mexico.

WASHINGTON, D. C.:
W. H. LOWDERMILK & CO.
1900.

J. B. LYON COMPANY
PRINTERS AND BINDERS
ALBANY, N. Y.

PREFACE.

At the beginning of the Twentieth Century, the student does not find himself so fully enlightened with the modern development of law and the facilities for the study of jurisprudence, that he cannot profit by an investigation of ancient legislation and institutions, and occasionally discover in far distant ages some useful information for these practical times.

In the Aryan household of three thousand years ago, we are surprised to encounter a corporation, the existence of the paternal power, and rights of succession; in Greece, ideas entertained about the State which would do credit to a much later civilization. Rome, with her highly developed municipal system, attempted to establish a representative government in Southern Gaul as early as 418 A. D., and the much vaunted Anglo-Saxon jury system was tried and rejected by her over a thousand years ago. Much abused Spain was the first European nation to publish a code of commerce; she possessed and exercised a writ of *habeas corpus* (*manifestacion*) in Aragon before America was discovered; and Gothic democratic principles were there developed and exercised more liberal than those recognized in any monarchy of to-day, and, being evolved with time, formed the basis of the Republic of Iceland, the Magna Charta of England, and the American Declaration of Independence.

In presenting this work to the public, if the author contributes anything of interest on the history of law in Spain and Spanish-America or incites the student to become better acquainted with Spanish jurisprudence and institutions his reward will be ample.

History has been freely quoted, as its study is essential to comprehend ancient legislation and institutions and to give the student a better idea of the conditions and requirements existing in remote times.

The difficulties encountered and the labor involved in such a work can be appreciated to some extent by considering the period of time covered, and the fact that no other country of Europe has been so prolific in legislation as Spain, whose language, customs and laws have been observed over a larger geographical area than those of any other nation.

At the beginning of the Nineteenth Century, it was estimated that the general and provincial codes already published embraced something like one hundred thousand different enactments; and since that time, marked by the disintegration of the body of their laws and the modern scientific classification of legislation, the number of codes, laws, amendments and revisions issued are bewildering.

In giving a summary of the ancient codes of the Peninsula, some new material has been discovered and other matters treated for the first time, which throw considerable light on Spanish laws and institutions, such as the Gothic Code of Euric or of Tolosa, observed by the Goths prior to the Fuero Juzgo, tending to clear up a long pending controversy as to the date of application of the latter code, the influence and effect of Canonical Law, the Councils of Toledo, and the Arabic dominion upon Spanish jurisprudence.

Considerable attention has been given to the interesting laws of the Indies — *Recopilacion de Leyes de los Reynos de las Indias* — inasmuch as they, supplemented by the laws of the mother country, formed the jurisprudence of Spanish-America for some three hundred years and are essential to the student who wishes to become familiar with the laws and customs of Latin-America as well as of interest to persons who seek information in regard to land and mining grants in the Indies.

Upon the Spanish-American colonies gaining their independence, during the Nineteenth Century, the changes in jurisprudence have not been so marked as might be supposed. In political and administrative law the new states have largely followed the institutions of the United States of America, but their private law is that of Spain, amended on the lines of the Code Napoleon.

The Latin-American Commercial Codes are, in general, based on the commercial laws of Spain.

The Civil Code of 1889, while not entirely satisfactory to Spain on account of the peculiar conditions existing in the Peninsula and the conflict between the so-called common law and statute or provincial legislation, is, aside from these differences, a most excellent code, representing some twenty-four hundred years' development of the Roman Civil Law or from the Twelve Tables of Rome until the present time. An eminent French jurisconsult, A. Leve, who recently translated the Civil Code into French, pays a high tribute to it, declaring that it is more scientific than the Code Napoleon.

A few of the leading authorities to whom the author is indebted are as follows:— On Primitive Times and the Goths,— Tacitus, Dahn, Masdeu, Vandoncourt, Sempere, Lafuentė (the first volume alone being considered impartial).

Arabic Language, Customs and Institutions,— Gayangos, Dosy, and the professors of Arabic, Codera, Simonet, Cardenas, in the Universities of Madrid, Granada, and Seville, also Lerchundi of Tangier.

Ancient Aragon,— Zurita, Mariani, Matheu, Robertson.

Navarre,— De Gurrea, Lagreze (Fr.).

On the Indies,— De las Casas, Solorzano, Ulloa, Muñoz, Vega, Perez y Lopez, Calvo, the latter brings the legislation down to recent times.

Mexico,— Bandelier and Morgan, Solis, Beleña, Dublan and Lozano.

On Administrative Law,— Posada, Azcarate, Freixa, Romero Giron, Santamaria.

Canonical Law,— Tejada y Ramiro, Andres, Morales, and Escriche.

Civil Law and Code,— Antequera, Hinojosa, Comas, Sanchez Roman, Amandi, Falcon, Scævola.

Commercial Law,— Reus y Garcia, Abella, Manzana, Armas y Saenz.

Criminal Law and Procedure,— Du Boys, Pacheco, Montero, C. Becarra (It.), Ortolan (Fr.), Valdes Rubio.

Mortgage and Notarial Laws,— Santamaria, Morell, Oliver y Esteller, Zarzoso (forms).

Military and Naval Laws,— Almirante (Guide and Dictionary), Garcia y Hernandez, Romero y Villanueva.

Municipal Fueros and Town Charters,— Valdelomar, and Muñoz y Romero.

Provincial Laws,— Lecanda (Vizcaya), Vadillo (Navarre), Castells y de Bassols (Catalonia), Gil Berges (Aragon).

CLIFFORD S. WALTON.

WASHINGTON, D. C.

TABLE OF CONTENTS.

CHAPTER II.

BOOK FIRST.

PERSONS.

BOOK SECOND.

PROPERTY, OWNERSHIP, AND ITS MODIFICATIONS.

PRELIMINARY PROVISION.

BOOK THIRD.

DIFFERENT WAYS OF ACQUIRING OWNERSHIP.

PRELIMINARY PROVISION.

BOOK FOURTH.

OBLIGATIONS AND CONTRACTS.

CHAPTER II.

CHAPTER III.

CHAPTER IV.

HISTORICAL INTRODUCTION.

Il faut eclairer l'histoire par les lois, et les lois par l'histoire.—Montesquieu.

Some writers, taking a passage from Josephus as a basis, have affirmed that Tubal Cain, son of Japhet and grandson of Noah, was the first man to discover and settle in Spain, and it is related "that he governed it in a mild and just way." Others refer to a chapter in Genesis in which Tharsis, son of Javan and grandson of Japhet, is mentioned among those who went out to people the Isles of Nations, after the confusion of tongues at the tower of Babel, and name him as the discoverer of Spain, and state that he gave his name to the Tharseya Islands, which was the origin of the Spanish nation.

It appears, according to leading authorities, that the Iberians were the primitive inhabitants of Spain whose eastern part they occupied, and, from the most authentic data, it is deduced that they came from the *Indo-escitical* tribes, nomadic shepherd warriors, who, from *India escitica,* migrated as far as the western extremities of Europe. Some historians maintain that the Iberians entered the Peninsula from Africa, instead of from the North.

The learned Vandoncourt, continuing the investigations of Bayer, Schlozer, and Adelung, concerning the origin of the nations of Europe, makes the Iberians the aborigines of Spain. Many hold that the language of these people is the one spoken to-day by the Vascs or Euskares, while other erudites and authors of note assure us that the Iberian tongue was Hebro-Phenician or a dialect of the Hebrew from which they claim the Spanish language has acquired at least one-third of its words.

The Basques, who still occupy an isolated position both in origin and language among the peoples of Europe, pride themselves on being the descendants of the Iberians, and, from ancient times to the present day, have not only preserved their former vigor and unclassified language but also their customs and independence, surviving Roman, Gothic and Moorish domination.

The Celts, " the men of the forest," at an uncertain date invaded the country and a long struggle ensued between them and the Iberians (Iberi, Ebro) or " men of the river," which ended in the final reconciliation and partial mingling of the two tribes in the Celtiberian nation, the Iberian element predominating, although the Celts, as usual, gave their names to many places.

The Celtic tribes embraced the Cantabrians, Asturians, Vascones, Galicians, and Lusitanians, and their subsequent settlement seems determined, but it has long been disputed whether the Celts existed in Spain, prior to their appearance in Gaul, or emigrated from Gaul to Spain. Ruins found in different parts of the Peninsula indicate that druidical worship was observed by them.

The more numerous Iberians extended from Gibraltar through parts of Andalusia, Valencia, Murcia and Aragon to the Pyrenees, and the blended Celtiberians occupied the center of the Peninsula, on the border land between the two nations.

If faith be given to such authorities as Justin and Pomponius Mela, the history of Spain definitely commences in the sixteenth century B. C., in which epoch the Phenicians arrived in Spain. Guided by the spirit of adventure and trade, they did not possess at first the idea of conquest, but of trading and of exploiting Spanish mines, and for that purpose upwards of about two hundred colonies were established, according to Strabo, commencing with Gadir (Gades or Cadiz), founded before Rome, and Hispalis (Sevilla), Cŏrduba (Cŏrdova), Malaca (Malaga), and Abdera (Adra) which were the most important.

The Guadalquivir was the principal artery of Phenician commerce and they took out such riches from the country that, according to Aristotle, the anchors and other parts of their vessels were made of silver, and they used the same metal for ballast. At Coruña, they reared a tower in honor of Melcarth; at Cadiz a showy temple to the same god, erecting in it two magnificent brass columns, the ruins of which were discovered, about the middle of the last century, on the beach at Cadiz upon a marked fall of the waters; which fact, no doubt, became associated with the tradition of the formation of the Straits of Gibraltar and the Pillars of Hercules.*

Besides extensive trade and developed industries, the information given us by the Jesuit Masdeu supports Strabo in the statement that, during the fifteenth century B. C., the Phenician colonists already had laws, histories in verse and poems demonstrating an advanced civilization. During the tenth century B. C., Greeks came to Spain from various places: the Rhodians, proceeding to the coast of Catalonia, founded the city of Rodas (Rosas), and afterwards occupied the four Balearic Islands, calling two of them *Gymnasias* and the other two *Pitiusas.*

About the year 700 B. C., Greeks from Zante founded Saguntum in Valencia. The Phocaens, coming from Massilia (Marseilles) to establish closer trade relations with the natives of the country, founded Ampurias, where, as well as at Rosas, a temple was erected to Diana Ephesus, the most worshiped deity of paganism. Diánio (Dénia) in Valencia was one of their principal colonies. Later on they occupied the most important towns in Granada and those near the Ebro river which was the most important artery of their trade.

The Greek colonies left a more complete record of their legislation and political organization than the Phenicians; their laws were generally founded upon an excellent sense of justice, and possessed many notable features, including a permanent publicity inflicted on violators of the laws. Their government, similar to that of the Greeks at Massilia, had as a fundamental institution a Senate or Supreme Body consisting of 600 members who had to be citizens of a nobility established at least three generations, and were required to have descendants; they received the title *Timucos* and their office was permanent. The executive power was confided to three presidents appointed by the Senate, and the administration of justice was entrusted to fifteen magistrates who were also Senators.

Returning to the history of Carthaginian Spain, it is found to begin with the arrival of the Barca factions in Baetica (Andalusia).

* These two brass columns have often been confounded with the Pillars of Hercules, names given to the two mountains Calpe and Abila, which designated the extremities of Africa and Europe, and which were then believed to mark the extreme ends of the habitable earth.

Three hundred years before the wealth of Cadiz having excited the envy and hostility of the natives, its Phenician citizens called in the aid of Carthage and her Numidian allies who soon overran much of the country and made it a dependency of the great south Mediterranean city.

In 237 B. C., Hamilcar Barca landed at Cadiz with a large army, after having conquered the northern coast of Africa as far as the ocean. In eight years he had overcome the west and south of Spain, but the confederated chiefs of Vettones succeeded in defeating him, and he was drowned in the passage of the Guadiana.

Hasdrubal, his son-in-law, with a rare union of vigor and humanity, soon greatly extended the dominion of the Carthaginians with his fifty-six thousand men and two hundred elephants. He built the city of Carthage Nova (Carthagena), which became a great commercial, maritime, and military outpost full of fortifications and arsenals. The frightened Greek colonies implored the aid of the Roman senate against the Carthaginian power. A treaty stipulated the independence of these colonies, and fixed the limits of the growing Carthaginian empire, but Hasdrubal, feeling himself strong in the affections of the people and finding himself firmly intrenched at Carthagena, resolved to break the treaty, and would have done so, had not the dagger of an assassin put an end to his life.

Hannibal, son of Hamilcar, a young man of twenty-five, was chosen by the army to succeed Hasdrubal; and now he saw a chance to show at last the eternal enmity which his father had made him swear against the Romans.

The admirable portrait left by Livy is a pregnant individualization of one of the great men of antiquity. In the same lucid and impassioned pages the memorable story of the siege of Saguntum, the ally and funeral offering of Rome to the vengeance of the Carthaginians, still glows with eloquence after the lapse of twenty centuries.

The great struggle between Rome and Carthage had now begun. During the second Punic War, in 218 B. C., Cneius Scipio came over to Spain and soon got possession of the eastern coast from Carthagena to the Pyrenees, but in 211 he perished, having been preceded by his brother Publius, who underwent the same fate together with his army. In the brilliant and moving pages of

Plutarch, their successor, Publius Cornelius Scipio (210), is seen landing in Spain with eleven thousand men, capturing Carthagena with immense booty, gaining all hearts by his politic magnanimity, conquering Cadiz, founding Italica near Seville, and dividing the country into two great provinces, Hither and Further Spain. Cato was sent thither as consul in 195 B. C., and that system of minute and merciless plundering was inaugurated by which Spain, the first and richest of all the great Roman colonies, was transformed into the market garden of Rome.

The revolt of Viriatus, the shepherd chieftain of the Lusitanians, who for more than eight years (140–148 B. C.) defied the whole power of Rome, showed even more than innumerable rebellions and outbreaks from decade to decade, how difficult it was to break the free and spirited population to a foreign yoke. Numantia, equally a Celtiberian city, resisted with the energy of despair the encroachments of Rome, and only fell before sixty thousand men and Scipio Aemilianus, another of that remarkable family whose names are so gloriously and dismally connected with the subjugation of Spain. Saguntum, Numantia and Saragossa — three sieges of world-wide celebrity — testify to that impassioned strength and fortitude, which in religion as in war, two thousand years ago as now, have always formed the foundation of the Spanish character.

The revolt of Sertorius, a Roman exile dreaming of the independent sovereignty of Spain, occurred twenty years after the siege of Numantia and was crushed by Pompey and Metellus after eight years of furious and difficult encounter.

The most remarkable of all the quarrels espoused by the Peninsula was that of Pompey and Caesar. Caesar triumphed, and has left a record of the contest in his inimitable commentaries. Under Augustus Spain was declared the perpetual tributary of the empire, and for the first time, after two hundred years of sanguinary strife, the dominion of Rome showed itself beneficent and tolerable. A regular administration was introduced; the country, to facilitate its control and organization, was divided into three provinces (Baetica, Tarraconensis, and Lusitania); wise and humane laws were established, protecting the inhabitants; magnificent roads, bridges and aqueducts were built; and graceful altars smoked in honor of the father and liberator of Spain.

Tiberius, to whom altars burned and whom medals immortalized, exemplified in Spain the epigram of the great historian. Caligula, Nero, Galba, and Otho caressed and spurned the Peninsula according to the needs of the moment. Under Vespacian the persecution of the Jews broke out, and a colony of the wretched exiles was planted in Spain and settled at Merida: they afterwards filled the history of the country with their intrigues, miseries, and oppressions.

Trajan and Hadrian were both Spaniards, born at Italica, and were loved and honored by the people for the well-being and tranquillity enjoyed by the land under their vigorous but appreciative administration. Antoninus and Marcus Aurelius (sprung from a noble Spanish family sojourning in Rome) gave Spain the happiness that needed no history; and under them it reached the culminating point, after which there is continual decline. A band of Suevi crossed the Pyrenees in 270 A. D., and ravaged the provinces for some time. The reigns of Diocletian and Constantine were important to Spain, more particularly from a religious point of view. Crushed by imposts, stripped of its communal rights, devoured by the thousand fiscal agents of the new Rome of the Bosphorus, its social system dissolved, its magistrates became almost universally corrupt, and it took refuge, as a last resort, in the arms of the clergy. Christianity seemed to have penetrated into Spain about the time of Nero. The Spaniard attributes its introduction to St. James the greater (Santiago). Originally persecuted by the polytheists, the new religion increased step by step until it took its seat on the imperial throne in the person of Constantine. The council of Illiberis in Spain, held about 306 A. D., is claimed to be the earliest great western church council on record, and here were fixed, after the fashion of an austere orthodoxy, the rites, ceremonies, and dogmas of the Spanish church, nineteen years before the council of Nicæa (325). Constantine had divided Spain into seven provinces (Lusitania, Baetica, Galicia, Carthageniensis, Tarraconensis, the Balearic Isles, and Tingitania on the African coast), and with these the ecclesiastical provinces corresponded. The bishops dwelling in the capitals of these provinces, Merida, Seville, Braga, Carthagena, Saragossa, Palman, and Tangier took the name of the *metropolitans*. Of these the metropolitan of Toledo — substituted for Carthagena,—

owing to the fact that the celebrated parliament councils were held there, gradually assumed pre-eminence, and at length acquired the primacy of Spain. The heresies of Arianism and Pricillianism — the former introduced by the Gothic conquest, and the latter by an eloquent and voluptuous Spanish priest — agitated the country until Pricillian was put to death (384) and the Goths embraced Catholicism under Recared.

Vestiges of antiquity, chiefly utilitarian, still show the blossoming of art in Spain under the empire. The ruins of the palace of Augustus at Tarragona; the arch of Bara raised by Trajan; the splendid bridge of Alcantara, believed by the Moors to have been raised by genii; the less celebrated bridges of Evora, Calatrava, and Salamanca; the aqueducts of Seville, Tarragona, and Avora, and the stupendous aqueduct bridge at Segovia; the wonderfully preserved theatre at Saguntum; the famous mosaic of Italica; and the baths, porticoes, and ruins of many sorts, attest the grandeur ot the Roman civilization. The country was intersected by unequalled roads, some of which still exist. Spain, even to-day, is full of reminders of the grandiose scenic displays of ancient times, combats of gladiators, chariot races, gymnasiums, amphitheatres, bull fights; and we are told that Diocles, the Lusitanian charioteer, was victorious two thousand five hundred and twenty-six times in the races.

A noble literary efflorescence revived in Spain the waning lustre of Roman intellectual life. Posterity can but do honor to the illustrious works of Seneca, Lucan, the Plinys, Martial, Quintilian, Pomponius Mela, Silius Italicus, Florus, and Columella.

It is necessary to confess that there is nothing certain about the laws by which the first founders of Spain were governed before its invasion by the Carthaginians; it would appear that they had no written laws, and that they undoubtedly were governed by those of custom and by arbitrary decrees founded on equity and justice. It is believed that the Carthaginians would have begun at least by introducing their system into the provinces which they ruled, but even this conjecture is not altogether fixed, if the short time is considered that their government lasted, during which they were agitated by continual wars.

The Romans succeeded the Carthaginians in their sway over Spain, and the former, as soon as they completed the conquest of all the provinces, introduced in them their language, customs and legislation.

Upon the advance of the Huns from Central Asia to Western Europe, during the latter part of the fourth century A. D., a general migration of the barbaric tribes of Europe took place: The Vandals, Alans, Silingi, and Suevi, all appeared to have entered the Spanish Peninsula about the same period: The Vandals remained but a few years, then crossed the straits into Northern Africa where the tribe became extinct. The word "Andalusia" is derived from their language.

The western part of Spain was settled by the Suevi of whom, prior to their migration with the Vandals and the Allemans or Alans to the Peninsula, about 409 A. D., but little is known. For many years the Peninsula lay helpless before their depredations, and their power was enabled to maintain itself for nearly two centuries, owing to the impregnable cliffs and gorges amid which they lived and thrived. Wretched Hispania between these two Germanic peoples — Goths and Suevi — was indeed "ground to pieces as between two millstones." The conversion of the Suevi to Catholicism in 560 A. D., and the final amalgamation of the Suevi and the Goths, under Leovigild in 585, obliterated forever all lines of distinction between the rival institutions, though it has often been suggested that the noticeable differences between Portuguese and Spaniard may have arisen from the fact that the ancient Lusitania was the abode of the Suevi, while the Goths spread themselves over the remainder of the Peninsula. As late as the time of Philip II, *Suevosos, los Sevosos,* is said to have been a nickname given by the Castilians to the Portuguese.

The Arabs had entertained the idea of invading Spanish soil for some time, and, although they attempted it during the reign of that sturdy and vigorous ruler Wamba, they were not successful until the time of Roderic, 711 A. D. Their victory on the Guadalete was so complete and their subsequent movements so rapid that scarcely three years were necessary for them to establish the crescent throughout the Peninsula, save in the rugged heights of the Pyrenees where the Spaniards, united in a common cause, formed nuclei of resistance against the Moslems (718) and led on by Pelayo, their first king, gained a victory over the Moors at Covadonga which, being followed up by other successes, enabled them to establish the small kingdom of Oviedo, the first territory acquired by the Spaniards during the reconquest. Spain, except the northern provinces,* was made a dependency of the caliphate of Bagdad, and Cordova became the capital of a separate caliphate, founded in 756 by Abderrahman, the last of the Ommyiade dynasty.

The war between the Spanish and the Moors lasted nearly eight hundred years. It was a war for fatherland and for religion. The Arabs founded a flourishing Empire in Spain, and established one of the first schools in Europe for the arts and sciences. Their schools were frequented by Christians and Jews who lived under their dominion, and they were treated with kindness and generosity.

The Spaniards continued to wage war with an ineradicable fanaticism against the Moslems. In the middle of the ninth century they reached the line of the Duero; towards the end of the eleventh century that of the Tagus; in 1085 they reconquered their old capital Toledo. At the beginning of the twelfth century, the Christians occupied one-half of the country — Leon, Castile, Aragon, and Navarre,— each of which formed an independent kingdom. Soon, however, Castile and Aragon assumed a prominent position, increasing both by uniting other Christian provinces and by conquering Mohammedan territories. Castile acquired Leon in the beginning of the thirteenth century, and conquered Murcia, Estremadura, Cordova, Seville, and Cadiz. Aragon acquired Catalonia and Valencia, and conquered the Balearic Isles, Sardinia, Sicily, and even Naples. At last a union of the two kingdoms took place in 1469 by the marriage between Ferdinand V, the Catholic king of Aragon (1479–1516), and Isabella, queen of Castile (1474–1504), though each of them continued to rule independently in their respective kingdoms. Meanwhile the war

* It appears that the Roman institutions and language were never received in the Asturias and Biscayne Mountains, and that it was here that the Spaniards lost the purity of the Latin tongue. About 914 A. D., the followers of Pelayo established their Capital at Leon, and during this time the Spanish nation and language were founded, the language being the result of a combination of Latin and Visigothic; the Visigothic was never a written language in Spain. The oldest documents in Spanish, known to be authentic, date from the reign of Alfonso VII, the Charter of Oviedo in 1145 A. D., and the confirmation of the Charter of Aviles in 1155. Spanish does not appear to have existed in written form earlier than 1100 A. D. Spanish poetry can be traced back nearly as far as 1155, the oldest poem, The Cid, dating about 1200.

was carried on successfully against the Moors. After their defeat at Tolosa, in Sierra Morena, in 1212, they had only Cordova and Granada left, and in 1492 they lost their last possession, Granada, to Ferdinand and Isabella, and became a subjected race, whose extirpation was effected by degrees.

Under the reigns of Ferdinand and Isabella, Charles the First, and culminating in that of Philip the Second, Spain arose to the height of her power and glory, becoming by far the most powerful nation in Europe, and the mistress of the greater part of the New World which she controlled down to and including the early part of the nineteenth century.

SPANISH-AMERICA.

The French revolution of 1789, the Constitutional Cortes of Cadiz of 1812, and the success of republicanism in North America were precursors of the revolt of Spain's colonies which was aided not a little by the writings of Montesquieu, Voltaire, Rousseau, and others of that school.

In briefly narrating the overthrow of Spanish dominion in her American colonies, the conquest and settlement of the country is not referred to, as unlike the history of Spain, the explorers and colonists were Spaniards who brought with them their laws and customs which were established in the country and, by an observance of some three hundred years, have left a lasting impression.

The first great change to be noticed in their political system and legislation was to be wrought by their independence which in South America proper, that is from the Isthmus of Panama to Cape Horn, was accomplished mainly by two great military geniuses, Martin and Bolivar, assisted by Sucre and other able and distinguished lieutenants. José de San Martin, born in Yapeyú, in 1778, a small town of the Argentine Republic, on the borders of Paraguay, operated in the southern part of South America, and Simon Bolivar, born in Caracas, the capital of Venezuela, on July 25, 1783, covered the northern portion of that continent. Both belonged to distinguished families of Spanish descent, and both had received a military education in Spain and had served with distinction in the Spanish army, having flown to their country's assistance when they heard that independence had been proclaimed. Bolivar was of an impulsive and reckless disposition, and suffered, therefore, many serious defeats, while San Martin, being a much more cautious man, was never defeated.

Buenos Ayres or the Argentine Republic, as it is now called, had not only practically established her independence in 1813, after the decisive battles of Tucuman, fought on September 24, 1812, and Salta, on February 20, 1813, although she formally declared her independence only in 1816, but had also driven the Spaniards from Uruguay and Paraguay, and had assisted the adjoining provinces of Upper Peru, which had also rebelled against Spain. The Argentine Republic was, therefore, the base of operations against the Spanish government in the southern portion of South America, and her capital, Buenos Ayres, was the only capital on the continent which, once occupied by the patriots, was never recovered by the Spanish. Peru was at the time, after Mexico, the main seat of Spanish power in America, and the viceroy of Peru sent frequent expeditions not only to subdue the insurgents of Upper Peru, which was a comparatively easy task, but also against those of Buenos Ayres, who suffered serious defeats in Vilcapujio on October 1, 1813, and in Ayouma on November 14th of the same year, after having obtained an important victory at San Elezario in 1813. San Martin was for some months commander of the Argentine army in Upper Peru during 1814, and he soon became satisfied that the war could not end until a mortal blow was given to the Spanish power in Peru, and he realized that the only effectual way to accomplish that end was to march from Chile to Peru by the Pacific. He was, therefore, transferred, at his own request, to the Province of Cuyo, at whose capital, Mendoza, which commanded the main pass of the high cordillera dividing Argentina from Chile, he organized and disciplined his army, availing himself of the assistance of the Chilean patriots who flocked to his banner, among them being O'Higgins, who subsequently took such a leading part in public events in Chile.

On January 17, 1817, San Martin's army left Mendoza and crossed the high cordillera by the Uspallata pass, an undertaking accomplished in the face of the enemy, and which may well be compared with the crossing of the Alps by Hannibal, centuries before, when he invaded Italy. While in Chile San Martin defeated the Spanish army at Chacabuco on February 12, 1817, which permitted him to occupy Santiago, the capital of that country. The viceroy sent from Lima another army of Spanish veterans, which was defeated by San Martin at Maipo, near Santiago, on April 5, 1818, thus achieving the independence of Chile, and putting the Spanish viceroy at Lima on the defensive.

The governments of the La Plata Provinces and Chile had agreed by a treaty signed at Buenos Ayres on February 5, 1819, to send a joint expedition of their forces to liberate Peru; but before the expedition started a revolution broke out in the Argentine Provinces, necessitating the return of the Argentine army from Chile, and instructions were sent to San Martin to hasten back. San Martin, realizing that if he went back to Buenos Ayres the cause of independence would be seriously jeopardized, made up his mind to disobey his instructions, and he resigned his command, but was recognized as general-in-chief by his army at Rancagua, in Chile, and finally appointed general-in-chief of the joint Chilean-Argentine expeditionary army by the Chilean government. Before San Martin left Chile for Peru, the Argentine government had been overthrown, anarchy prevailing there, and he found himself, therefore, without a government or nation to back his force, but he acted as general-in-chief of the combined army, both by the appointment of the Chilean government and by the act of Rancagua. San Martin knew that he could not march to Peru overland, and he, therefore, concentrated all his efforts to assist in providing Chile with a navy which would clear the Spanish armada from the Pacific.

The geographical position of Chile, a long and narrow strip of land bounded by the Cordilleras on the east and bordering on the Pacific Ocean, made it indispensable for her to have a navy. It is extraordinary how, being the poorest and the last of the Spanish crown American colonies, she could under the able leadership of O'Higgins, a Chilean patriot of Irish descent, and while she was carrying on her war of independence against Spain, improvise a navy, a task in which she was very substantially assisted by San Martin and the Buenos Ayres government with the man-of-war "Intrepid," lost at the capture of Valdiva on February 3, 1820, by Lord Cochrane. By September, 1818, O'Higgins had procured five men-of-war, manned by raw recruits with little or no naval discipline, and a few English and Americans who could not speak

Spanish. These he put under the command of Colonel Manuel Blanco Encalada, who had previously served in the Spanish navy, and who attacked the frigate "Maria Isabel" on October 28, 1818, while she was under the protection of the forts at the port of Talcahuano, and captured that vessel, as well as five Spanish transports, with seven hundred Spanish soldiers. The enlarged Chilean navy was placed under the command of dashing Lord Cochrane, a very distinguished admiral of the British Royal Navy, then under a cloud at home, who took service under the Chilean flag, attacked and defeated the Spanish navy at the port of Callao, capturing the flagship "Esmeralda," and so established Chilean naval supremacy in the Southern Pacific among the American Republics.

In that navy, consisting of nine men-of-war and sixteen transports, San Martin left Valparaiso for the Peruvian coast on August 20, 1820, with an army of four thousand one hundred and eighteen men, of which two thousand three hundred and thirteen were Argentines and one thousand eight hundred and five Chileans. Eighteen days later he landed in Peru near the city of Pisco, to the south of Lima. The viceroy had over twenty-three thousand men under his command, which he could concentrate against San Martin, and it required great generalship and skillful manœuvering to baffle the Spanish army. After remaining a month and a half at Pisco, and sending a portion of his army to the interior to raise the people in favor of independence, San Martin sailed with the remainder of his army, on October 29, 1820, to Ancon, a port twenty miles north of Lima. When the Spanish army was being concentrated against him there he moved again, on November 8, having possession of the sea, to Huacho, about seventy miles north of Lima, thus severing the communication of the viceroy with his northern provinces. In the meantime, the principal towns of Peru began to join the independent cause, and even a portion of the native army of the viceroy joined San Martin. The viceroy was thus forced to evauate Lima on July 6, 1821, and it was forthwith occupied by San Martin.

San Martin clearly foresaw the great unrest and political turmoil which the adoption of republican institutions would necessarily entail upon the new nations, as they were not prepared for a form of government which requires an enlightened people, capable of self government, and he therefore, as well as the Argentine government under Pueyrredon, favored the establishment of a monarchy, Bolivar, on the other hand, being decidedly for a republican form of government.

San Martin was not to accomplish by himself his final object, as that task was reserved to Bolivar. In 1822 San Martin's condition in Peru was difficult, as his army had been considerably reduced by hard service and sickness, he having only eight thousand five hundred men, many of them raw recruits, while the viceroy had in Upper Peru about nineteen thousand men who could be easily concentrated in a comparatively short time. San Martin thought it necessary, therefore, to have the assistance of Bolivar to give a speedy finishing blow to the Spanish dominion in Peru, and he proposed to meet Bolivar. They met in Guayaquil on July 26 and 27, 1822.

No authentic report of that interview has ever been published, and this has given rise to many surmises about its objects and results. From the events which preceded and followed the same, and from a letter written soon afterward by San Martin to Bolivar on August 29, 1822, and his conversations with friends, there is room to form an idea of what took place at the meeting. San Martin offered Bolivar to serve under his orders, if he would go with his victorious armies to Peru; but his proposal was not accepted, Bolivar saying that he could not leave Colombia without permission from the Colombian Congress, and he only agreed to send one thousand five hundred men of his army to aid San Martin. It is well known that San Martin and Bolivar differed greatly in their views on many subjects relating to the work that they both had undertaken. The difference of opinion between the two regarding the government of the new states was another factor which contributed to prevent their acting in accord. One cause of irritation between them was the question of the port of Guayaquil, which San Martin thought ought to belong to Peru, or be decided by negotiations between the Colombian and Peruvian governments, while Bolivar had already annexed it to Colombia. San Martin understood that he was in Bolivar's way, and sincerely wishing the success of the cause of independence, proved himself a true patriot and a great man, preferring to sacrifice his future, and decided to withdraw from his field of operations leaving his competitor alone with the sole responsibility for the course of future events.

San Martin consequently returned to Peru, where he had previously convoked a national congress to organize the country, and on the very day when congress met, on September 20, 1822, he resigned his command in Peru and sailed for Chile.

Bolivar's career was still more eventful. He fought the Spanish both in Venezuela and New Granada with varying success from 1810 to 1817, as often crushed and defeated as victorious, and twice being obliged to fly from the country and take refuge in foreign lands. Finally he asserted his supremacy, and at the battle of Boyacá, fought on August 7, 1819, he achieved the independence of New Granada and captured Bogota, its capital, while at Carabobo, fought on June 24, 1821, he achieved the independence of his native land, Venezuela, having previously occupied its capital, Caracas.

Bolivar, like San Martin, realized that his success could not be permanent, as long as the Spaniards were in possession of the neighboring countries, and more especially Peru, the principal Spanish stronghold in South America, which they used as a base of attack against the new nationalities, and he, therefore, decided to attack them first in Ecuador and eventually go to Peru. Both armies, each from opposite ends of South America, converged on Peru with the same object in view, of putting an end to the Spanish domination. He consequently marched his army to Ecuador and defeated the enemy at Bomboná on April 7, 1822, and achieved the independence of that country at the battle of Pichincha, fought on May 24, 1822.

As San Martin predicted, the patriots' army in Peru was defeated after he left the country, both at Torata and Moquegua. After those defeats and the destruction of the army organized by Peru, under General Santa Cruz, the Peruvian government made a treaty with Colombia on April 12, 1823, for the purpose of having the assistance of six thousand troops, and finally after the country had fallen into anarchy, Bolivar made his appearance in Lima, where he was hailed as the liberator of the country, the Peruvian congress appointing him, by decree dated at Lima on August 10, 1823, Dictator and Liberator of Peru, thus giving him entire civil and military control over the country, and realizing San Martin's prediction.

Bolivar, in full charge of the combined Peruvian, Chilean, and Argentine armies, as well as the whole of the Colombian army, marched against the Spaniards in Upper Peru, and fought and defeated at Junin, on August 6, 1824, a cavalry division, the flower of the Spanish army, and gave the finishing blow to the Spanish domination in South America, at the battle of Ayacucho, on December 9th of the same year, where Bolivar's army was commanded by Sucre.

When the enormous difficulties are considered that the liberating armies had to contend with, traversing immense distances in a difficult and broken country, without railways or even wagon roads, having often to transport their artillery on mule back, without any commissariat or money to pay the army, and often even without arms or ammunition, it is really wonderful what was accomplished.

In Mexico, as in all the other Spanish colonies, the war of independence had begun in 1810, and it terminated on September 27, 1821, when Iturbide entered the City of Mexico with his victorious army, although the war had been practically ended when the Spanish Viceroy O'Donaju signed with Iturbide at the city of Cordova on August 24, 1821, a treaty in which he recognized on behalf of the Spanish government the independence of Mexico.

In what is now called Central America the people remained under the Spanish government without any attempt to proclaim independence, very likely because they thought they could not cope with the power of the Spanish viceroy in Mexico. When they heard of Iturbide's success, however, they proclaimed their independence and annexation to Mexico on September 15, 1821. They seceded from Mexico in 1823, and established then, and not until then, the Central American confederation, under the name of the United Provinces of Central America, a confederation which lasted until 1839, when each of the five states became an independent nation.

On March 8, 1822, when Mr. Monroe asked Congress to recognize the independence of the Spanish colonies in America, Mexico, the Central American States, New Granada, Venezuela, Buenos Ayres, Paraguay, Uruguay, and Chile had fully accomplished their independence, and in Ecuador and Peru independence was practically accomplished, as Bolivar's army was then fighting under General Sucre in Ecuador, and the Spanish viceroy had evacuated Lima on account of San Martin's manœuvres after July 6, 1821. The independence of Bolivia, or Upper Peru, as it was then called, had been practically accomplished when San Martin invaded Chile in 1817.

CUBA AND PUERTO RICO.

It was not until the close of the nineteenth century, four centuries after Columbus had unfurled the Spanish colors on Cuban soil, that this emblem was destined to be lowered in the Western Hemisphere.

Attempts to secure the independence of Cuba, commencing with that of Bolivar in 1823, and recurring in 1826, 1828, 1848, 1851, when Lopez and Crittenden lost their lives, the ten-year insurrection of 1868–78, and that of 1884, were alike doomed to failure.

The revolution, so long and carefully planned by Marti and begun in February, 1895, however, was to be successful, owing to the intervention of the United States, by declaration of war April 25, 1898, which resulted in the Philippine Islands and Puerto Rico being ceded to the former government by the treaty of Paris, December 10, 1898, and the Cubans given a chance to demonstrate to the world their capacity for self-government and independence.

PART FIRST.

PRELIMINARY.

The historical study of the laws of Spain begins, in reality, with the establishment of the Goths in that country, under Athaulf, about the year 414 A. D. However, a general review of the history of primitive times, and of the dominion of Phenicians, Greeks, and Carthaginians, and especially of the Romans, is necessary as a basis for such study.

The policy of tolerance observed by the Goths from their entrance into Spain, either through an understanding with the Roman authorities or from an instinctive sentiment of respect for the superior Roman culture, produced the legislation of castes, symbolized by the Code of Euric or of Tolosa, and by the Code of Alaric or *Breviarium Aniani.* Under these two legislative systems, conquerors and conquered lived until the end of the seventh century within the same territory and under one supreme authority, but with complete independence as to religions, laws, customs, and tribunals.

The rapid decline of the Roman Empire, the consequent disregard of her interests in Spain, and the natural tendency towards assimilation of the two people, living together, culminated in the conversion of Recared to Catholicism at the Third Council of Toledo. This marked a new regime in the legislative life of the Peninsula, the outgrowth of which was the formation of the *Fuero Juzgo,* during the reign of Chindasvint, afterwards corrected by Recesvint, Ervigio, and promulgated by Egica.

The Gothic Monarchy fell before the strength of the Mohammedan armies. Although the Moors became the masters of the greater part of Spain, they did not completely subdue it, owing to the heroic efforts of a band of Spaniards commanded by Pelayo, who, by his victory at Covadonga, laid the basis of the national restoration and thereby wrote the first page of that remarkable struggle which continued during eight centuries.

This exceptional state of affairs, produced by constant warfare, could not but affect legislation, substituting for its prior aspect of uniformity that of the most extensive diversity. This was a logical consequence of granting special privileges in every direction to bring about the necessary combination of all the social elements, each one helping, according to its strength, in the great work undertaken to recover the national territory. From these causes originated the *fueros* of the nobility, with their excessive privileges in the shape of *señorios* and feuds; as, for example, the *Ordenamiento de las Cortes de Nájera,* and the *Fuero Viejo.* From the same origin came the *fueros* of localities or provinces, the municipal *fueros,* such as those of Léon, Cuenca, Sepulveda, and others, which later came to be a powerful dike against the disorders of the nobility and a firm bastion to re-establish the prestige of the crown.

After the reconquest had become well advanced and with it the national unity better assured, Ferdinand III, known as the Saint, appreciating the necessity of making thorough legislative reforms, undertook the task, but death prevented the accomplishment of his project and the completion of this work was solemnly commended to his son, Alfonso X, known as the Wise, who, with better desires than fortune, endeavored to accomplish it, forming during his reign the legal works known as the *Fuero Real, Especulo,* and *Partidas.*

Notwithstanding this commendable effort, the differences of opinion which prevailed about legislative reforms, the vested interests endangered, and perhaps the triumph of the arms of Sancho IV, in the War of Succession, carried on against the Infantes de la Cerda, were all causes which prevented this work being completed until Alfonso XI formed his famous *Ordenamiento* at the Cortes of Alcalá de Henares in 1348. There the order of prelation among the different legal bodies was for the first time established in Spain and important reforms in Spanish laws were made, including that of the Code of *Siete Partidas.* This important event gave this period of the history of Spanish legislation a marked, critical and transitive character.

The successors of Alfonso XI were not competent to continue his great work, and, if the publication of the *Fuero Viejo* (skillfully disguised from its original and exclusive nature of a nobiliary code by dispositions of common law which gave it the appearance of a general code), be excepted, we do not find any notable changes in the legislative and governing powers until the time of Ferdinand and Isabella.

The necessity of reforming and harmonizing so many scattered and contradictory legislative elements was not overlooked by these zealous monarchs to whose reign so many remarkable achievements were accorded by destiny,— the end of the reconquest, the re-establishment of the royal authority, and the discovery of a New World. They commended to Alonzo Dias de Montalvo, a distinguished jurisconsult of their time and judge in their council, the compilation of the laws, which order he carried into effect under the title of the *Ordenanzas Real de Castilla* or Royal Ordinances of Castile, also known as the *Ordenamiento de Montalvo,* but which was accomplished in such an inefficient manner that it did not deserve the royal approval.

Repeated petitions to the Cortes by the attorneys of towns and cities, constantly denouncing the harm done to the administration of justice by the multiform and antagonistic conditions of Spanish laws, caused the publication of the *Leyes de Toro* or Laws of Toro at the Cortes, which took place in the city of Toro in the year 1505, in order to proclaim Doña Juana, "la Loca," as Queen of Spain.

Though these compilations furnished no definite and convenient solution of the legislative anarchy, and though the necessity of reforming the laws of the country became more and more urgent, other legal works were successively published, such as the *Nueva Recopilacion* of the time of Philip II, in the year of 1567; the *Novisima Recopilacion* during the reign of Carlos IV, in the year 1805, and its supplement in 1808, with a *Coleccion de Autos,* given by the Council corresponding to the period of time elapsed between said two collections by which the first one was enlarged. Such measures augmented instead of decreasing the chaotic condition of Spanish legislation, because they left in force all the prior compilations and added new elements to the already numerous ones which constituted it. To this ever-present necessity for legislative reform, the influence of the doctrines of the French revolution, and the transcendental national fact of the war for independence, gave a new aspect. Differing from what, until then, had been the confusing practice of attempting to modify Spanish law as a whole, the authorities proceeded to unify each branch separately; following this system in the codification of the Mercantile Law, of the Penal Law, and of the Civil and Criminal Laws of Procedures, lastly came the pretended codification of the Civil Law which, with a partial character in respect to Castile and even incomplete in relation to the so-called *derecho comun* or common law of the same, was carried on by the promulgation of the Civil Code of 1889. This unification did not happen to the Administrative Law, which, on account of its changeable nature, was not susceptible of codification, nor to the civil law, regarding which the divers provincial laws now in force presented great opposition; nevertheless, both were considerably augmented and bettered, first by some successful reforms of ancient laws, not altogether in agreement with the spirit of the present time, secondly, by the publishing of other new ones growing out of a superior civilization, and lastly by the Civil Code.

Summary.

The history of the Spanish Law may be summarized under six headings, as follows:

1. The Primitive Period, corresponding to the dominion of the Phenicians, Greeks, Carthaginians, and Romans (sixteenth century B. C. to 414 A. D.).
2. The Visigothic Epoch, or from the invasion of the northern barbarians, and the independence of legislation, as marked in the Gothic Code of Euric or of Tolosa, and in the Roman Code of Alaric or Breviarium Aniani, until the reign of Egica (414–687).
3. The Hispano-Gothic Period, characterized by the fusion of the laws of castes into a political and juridical unity by the promulgation of the Fuero Juzgo as a general code (687–700 to 711).
4. The Saracenic Invasion and the period of statute or foral laws, in which the legislation comprises a mere collection of singular and independent privileges, like those granted to the nobility and towns, dictated under the necessities of the Reconquest (711 to 1255).
5. The re-establishment of Roman Laws, by sanctioning of the Fuero Real, Partidas, etc., and the conflict and confusion pro-

duced by subsequent legislation and the attempt to harmonize and unify the diverse legislation of the country (1255 to 1810).

6. The Modern Epoch, marked by the disintegration of the body of Spanish laws and the scientific reclassification thereof (1810 to 1900).

CHRONOLOGICAL TABLE.

Phenician Dominion, on the southern coast of Spain, from the sixteenth century to 238 B. C.

Greek Dominion, on northeastern coast of Spain and in the Balearic Islands, from the tenth century B. C.

Carthaginian Dominion, from 237 to 210 B. C.

Roman Dominion, from 210 B. C. to 414 A. D.

Visigothic Dominion, from 414 to 711.

Arabic Dominion, from 711 to 1492.

Reconquest begun by Pelayo, 718 to 1492.

Union of Castile and Aragon by the marriage of Ferdinand and Isabella in 1469.

Discovery of the New World, 1492.

Independence of Buenos Ayres or Argentine Republic, July 9, 1816.

Independence of Chile, April 5, 1818.

Independence of New Granada (Colombia), August 7, 1819.

Independence of Venezuela, June 24, 1821.

Independence of Mexico, August 24, 1821.

Independence of Central America, September 15, 1821.

President Monroe's Message to Congress, asking for the recognition of the independence of the Spanish colonies, March 8, 1822.

Independence of Ecuador, May 24, 1822.

President Monroe's Message enunciating the Monroe doctrine, December 8, 1823.

Independence of Peru, December 9, 1824.

Cuban Insurrection begun, February 24, 1895.

War Declared between the United States and Spain, April 25, 1898.

Peace Protocol signed, August 12, 1898.

Treaty of Peace signed, December 10, 1898.

President McKinley's Message, manifesting the attitude of the Administration in respect to the Philippines, Puerto Rico, and Cuba, December 5, 1899.

CHAPTER I.

Elements Which Have Influenced the Civil Law in Spain.

Spanish Civil Law was influenced in its development principally by four powerful elements, to wit: (1) Roman, (2) Germanic, (3) Canonical, including the Councils of Toledo, and (4) Arabic, aside from the natural law, and the undefined influence of the tribes which inhabited the Iberian peninsula in the early history thereof; and, in recent times, it has been influenced by scientific law, foreign legislation, and doctrinal resolutions of jurisprudence as a result of the sentences of the Supreme Tribunals of Justice.

The people who inhabited the peninsula prior to Roman dominion left no marked influence on the legislation on account of the short periods they inhabited the country.

Rome, on the other hand, introduced into Spain her religion, laws, customs, language, and civilization.

Neither the ruin of the Western Empire, upon the success of the Northern barbarians, nor the Arabic domination was sufficient to displace the authority of the Roman laws, whose existence was not only respected in Spain by the Goths and by the Arabs but received from the former a new sanction, and were made the basis of a code.

The Visigoths, finally, came to substitute the unity of legislation for that of castes, and notwithstanding that the Fuero Juzgo was inspired by and based on Gothic laws and customs, they sought in the fundamental Roman laws for institutions unknown to the Goths, such as the law of testaments or wills, and adapted from them laws with which they had grown familiar.

The Code of Partidas, a faithful transcript of the Roman law, was later on given a preference on account of its recognized merit and its extensive general doctrines which applied to all persons and things, and finally the Roman law came to be considered as supplementary law in some of the important territories of Spain, such as Catalonia and Navarre.

THE ROMAN ELEMENT.

In the development of law, the household was the starting point out of the union of which arose villages or tribes, and, finally, from the union of tribes or towns arose the state.

It was by the confederation of a group of villages that Rome was constituted, eventually centralizing within its walls the political power of the world. The distinguishing feature of early Roman institutions, municipal law, owes more to Italy than to Greece (where the idea of the state as an independent city was entertained) in view of the fact that Italian cities were usually smaller than those of Greece and showed a greater willingness to unite in confederations.

Rome, in its origin, was only a municipality, a corporation, and the government of Rome was merely the aggregate of the institutions which were suited to a population confined within the walls of the city: these were municipal institutions, but this is not the case with Rome only, for if we turn our attention to Italy, at this period, we find around Rome nothing but towns; that which was then called a people was simply a federation of towns, and the Latin people was a federation of Latin towns.

When Rome extended itself, she conquered or founded towns; it was against towns that she fought; with towns that she contracted alliances; it was also into towns that she sent colonies, and the history of the conquest of the world by Rome is the history of the conquest of a great number of towns.

In Gaul, in Spain, there was met nothing but villages, at a distance from which the territory was covered with marshes and forests, and if the character of Roman roads is examined you will find great roads which reach from one city to another; the multiplicity of minor roads, which now cross the country in all directions, was then unknown; there is nothing resembling that countless number of villages, country seats and churches, which have been scattered over the country since the middle ages. Rome has left little but immense monuments, stamped with the municipal character, and destined for a numerous population collected in one spot, and from whatever point of view the Roman world is considered its almost exclusive preponderance of towns, and social nonexistence of the country is manifest.

The great extension of the Roman dominion, during the period of more than a century (B. C. 264–146) comprised by the three

Punic wars, led to many important changes in legal and political institutions.

The political relations of some of the new countries acquired were determined by treaties, but the greater number were reduced to the condition of provinces (*e. g.,* Sicily, Sardinia, Cisalpine Gaul, Illyria, Spain, and Carthage), placed under the direct surveillance of Rome, and governed by Roman magistrates, according to the terms of the *lex plebiscitum, or senatus-consultum* which established them, and regulated the greater or less amount of privileges enjoyed. The soil of the province belonged by right of conquest to the Roman people, the actual holders paying a tax for its use, and as these holders were subjects or tributaries, not citizens, they also paid tribute in the form of a personal tax.

Within the provinces, *colonias, municipia, praefecturae,* etc., were established free from both personal and land tax, and possessing more or less the rights of citizenship according to the constitution of each.

At first, the *comitia* at Rome specially appointed magistrates for the provinces, but after four such provincial prætors had been created, the system was adopted of sending consuls and prætors, on the expiration of their duties at Rome, as governors to the provinces under the title of pro-consuls or pro-prætors, and the four provincial prætors remained the first year at Rome without special jurisdiction, but assisting their colleagues.

When the term of office of a consul at the head of an army in the field had expired, he was frequently retained at his post by a *lex curiata,* which made him a representative of the consul nominally for a year, though this term was usually prolonged through the influence of party intrigue. In this way originated the provincial governors, to whom the civil administration was also confided, and who bore the title of pro-consul, if they were military commanders, otherwise pro-prætors. They were assisted by *legati proconsulis* (deputies whose number only was determined by the senate), and *questors* of the public treasure, sent direct from Rome. The judicial functions were performed by *recuperatores,* and the taxes were collected by the vicious system of farming, and for a time the knights claimed the exclusive privilege of being selected as *publicani.*

About 418 A. D., a singular idea suggested itself to one of the Roman emperors; he desired to discover whether, in hope of general liberty, a confederation — a system analogous to modern representative government,— would not better defend the unity of the Roman Empire than despotic administration. The most favorable territory, southern Gaul, was chosen for the experiment, and careful preparations were made for the purpose.

The provinces and the towns refused the benefits; no one would nominate the deputies; no one would go to Arles; centralization and unity were contrary to the primitive character of their society; the local and municipal spirit reappeared everywhere, and the impossibility of reconstituting a general society or body politic became evident. The towns confined themselves, each to its own walls and its own affairs, and the empire fell because none wished to be of the empire, because citizens desired to be only of their own city. Thus, at the fall of the Roman Empire, the same condition is manifested that existed in the cradle of Rome, namely, the predominance of the municipal form and spirit. The Roman world had returned to its original status; towns had constituted it; it dissolved, and towns remained.

In the municipal system we see what ancient Roman civilization has bequeathed to modern Europe; that system was very irregular, much weakened and far inferior, no doubt, to what it had been in earlier times; but, nevertheless, it was the only real, the only constituted system which had outlived all the elements of the Roman world.

Of the Roman Empire there remained, properly speaking, nothing but the municipal system. It had happened, from the vexations of despotism and the ruin of the towns, that the *curiales,* or members of the municipal bodies, had become discouraged and apathetic; on the contrary, the bishops, and the body of priests, full of life and zeal, offered themselves for the superintendence and direction of all matters. It would be wrong to reproach them for this or to tax them with usurpation; it was all in the natural course of things; the clergy alone was morally strong and animated; they became everywhere powerful.

The marks of this revolution are visible in all the legislation of the emperors of this period. If you open the Code, either of Theodosius or Justinian, you will find numerous regulations which remit municipal affairs to the clergy and bishops, and a tendency towards more humane laws, and other evidences of the changes which Christianity was working in jurisprudence and legislation of this period.

Constantine initiated a uniform administration for the whole vast empire. Spain and Gaul formed one of the four divisions into which the immense agglomeration fell. The twenty-five military colonies, formed of the citizens and soldiers who enjoyed on foreign soil all the rights of the mother country, kept Spain in subjection during the imperial period; forty-nine *municipia,* with privilege of self-government, came next in order among the graduated cities; then the cities of the Latin Law, peopled by families from Latium, who, without the right of Roman citizenship, could acquire this right after they had held certain magistries; then the six free cities (*immunes*), having their own laws and magistrates, and exempt from the usual imperial burdens; and, last, the allied cities, and the tributary cities (*stipendiarae*), which were heavily burdened with the task of feeding Rome and furnishing supplies for carrying on the government. A throng of petty communal republics, however, soon arose,— always a characteristic feature of Spanish administrative life,— and, by paying the regular imposts, were left free to govern themselves. Under Antoninus all the subjects of the empire were proclaimed Roman citizens.

JURIDICAL ORGANIZATION.

The judicial organization of Roman Spain included (1) judicial concourses and (2) judicial councils.

The first were known as *consejos judiciales* or *tribunales colegiados,* presided over by the governors of the provinces and composed of experts in the law to take cognizance of different classes of appeals in matters of certain importance; these assemblies were not permanent, but met periodically.

They did not exist in all the provinces, and, on this account, those that were formed were known as judicial concourses of which there were forty in Spain, as follows: In Lusitania; in Mérida, Béjar and Santarén; in Tarragona, Zaragoza, Cartagena, Luna, Astorga, Braga and Lugo; in Baética, Seville, Cadiz, Cordoba and Ecija.*

* Pliny's Nat. Hist.. Book 3, chap. 1.

These councils, temporary in character, similar to the concourses, were not analogous to those of similar classification in the Visigothic reign, as they were neither so free nor possessed so much authority on account of their limited objects, being constituted simply to represent the emperor in remedying the evils of administrative and economical complications, and finally did not have the mixed character of civil and religious councils which the latter included.

As particular laws of the time can be cited provincial laws and edicts: the former were similar to special charters which were given to towns at the time of their becoming subject to Roman dominion in which the limitation of each was defined as well as all or some of the rights of Roman citizenship,— as an example of this can be cited the Law of Gallia Cisalpina, recently discovered, by which the inhabitants of this province were granted the privileges of citizenship and the right of suffrage: the latter were nothing more than an imitation of those published in Rome by prætors and other magistrates, since the officials appointed to positions in the provinces, before leaving Rome, with the assistance of eminent jurisconsults, formed their edicts comprising civil, processal and administrative laws, and published them upon arrival at their destinations.

As examples of special laws of cities and municipalities can also be cited those discovered on the tablets of Malaca* which occurred in 1851, comprising the laws of that municipality and of Salpensa,† as well as those on the celebrated bronzes of Osuna,‡ discovered in 1870, which contain some laws of a Roman colony.§

---

* Found on a bronze discovered in a tile-kiln in Malaga, and published in 1853. It contains a fragment of the municipal law given Malaca by an emperor of the Flavian family in the first century, A. D.

† Found on a bronze, at the same time as above, and containing a fragment of a municipal law given to Salpensa by Domitian in the same period.

‡ The fifth table, with interpolations, found under similar conditions to above, covering a period from 123 to 134 A. D., and published in Malaga in 1873. These bronzes are in the Museo Loringiano at Malaga.

§ Municipal corporations are of greater antiquity in Spain than in any other European country, except Italy. Robertson's History of Charles V, vol. I, sec. 3, note 34.

ROMAN CODES WHICH INFLUENCED SPANISH JURISPRUDENCE.

The Gregorian and Hermogenian Codes.

Papirius Justus, under Marcus Aurelius, and Paul, under Caracalla, published summaries of imperial constitutions, and in the period between Diocletian and Constantine, the two jurisconsults, Gregorianus and Hermogianus, collected, chronologically arranged and annotated the most important rescripts of the emperors, from Septimus Severus to Diocletian and Maximian, 196 to 296 A. D. These collections were without legislative authority, but formed the models for the codes of Theodosius and Justinian, and as rescripts of Valentinian and Valens are asserted to have found a place in the code of Hermogenian; his date ought perhaps to be 364 A. D., but this is doubtful, as also whether the same jurisconsult was author of the Epitome of Law, arranged in the order of the Perpetual Edict, of which abstracts are found in the Digest.

Theodosian Code.

Theodosius II, in 429 A. D., directed a commission, under the presidency of the prætorian prefect Antiochus, to collect the imperial constitutions which had appeared subsequently to the Hermogenian and Gregorian Codes.

This work, of which the greater part is now extant, was completed in nine years, and was published simultaneously in the west under the authority of Valentinian III. It was to be the sole source of imperial law and was divided into sixteen books, and these subdivided into titles, with the imperial constitutions, from Constantine to Theodosius II, chronologically distributed under them. The first five books, arranged in the order of the edict, contained the *jus privatum;* the rest include the different magistracies, military, criminal, fiscal, and ecclesiastical matters, public works and games, etc. In order to maintain the general agreement of the laws of the two empires after the promulgation of the code, it was arranged that the *novellae,* or new constitutions, subsequently published, should not acquire binding force until they also appeared in the other empire; but this practice was discontinued after a time, and the projected new code of Theodosius never appeared with the constitutions in their entirety, but contained only such extracts from the Gregorian and Hermogenian, and his own code, and from the works of the jurists, as should represent the actual living law.

The Gregorian, Hermogenian, and Theodosian Codes were revised and modified by Justinian A. D., 528–529, and the result was known under his name.

In order to extract the spirit of the laws, the Pandects and the Institutes were published in 533 A. D.

These, together with the Justinian Code, constituted the Roman system of civil jurisprudence which has largely formed the basis of Spanish law.

ROMAN LAWS PUBLISHED BY THE GOTHS.

The barbarians, who settled in Gaul, Spain, Africa and Italy, did not interfere with the existing Roman law, but the legislation became *personal* or of castes, instead of territorial, *i. e.,* each individual was judged according to the laws and customs of the nation to which he belonged. After a short period, several barbarian kings published collections of Roman laws by the side of the *leges barbarorum,* or national laws and customs, mostly of Germanic origin, peculiar to themselves.

Breviarium Alaricianum or Aniani.

The Visigothic king, Alaric, intrusted a commission of Gothic jurisconsults of which Count Goyaric was president, with the compilation of the Breviarium Aniani from existing Roman legislation. This work was revised and approved by bishops and magnates, nominated from the different provinces of Spain, who assembled in the year 506, according to the most authentic data, in Adur (now Aire, France). Alaric decreed that only the copies signed by the chancellor, Anianus, should be authentic, and Goyaric sent authorized copies to the provincial authorities accompanied by the *Commonitorium,* in which curious information of the history of this code is given, but which is lacking in some copies and is badly mutilated in others.

The work is known under different names, such as *Lex Romana, Liber legum, Auctoritas Alaritii regis, Lex Theodosii, Commonitorium,* and *Breviarium Aniani.*

The integral elements of this collection from the Roman law are the Constitutions of the Emperors together with the writings of Roman jurisconsults, although some doubt has been thrown about this point on account of the numerous alleged editions of Anianus which are not authentic, and whose contents vary.

Considering the editions of the codes which are the most meritorious, to-wit, San Galo, Lugdunense, Real Parisiense, number 215, Monaceuse de Wurtburgo, Guelpherbytano, and the Epítome of Aegidio, it can be stated that the Code of Alaric contained something of the sixteen books of the Theodosian Code, of the Novelas of the Emperors Theodosian, Valentinian III, Marcian, Majorian and Severo, some fragments of the Institute of Gayo; the first five books of the Sentences of Paul; thirteen titles of the Gregorian Code; two titles of the Hermogenian; and a small fragment of the Answers of Papinian.

This code was in force in Spain for nearly two centuries, until the definite formation of the Fuero Juzgo, or until the beginning of the reign of Egica in 687, and the promulgation of the notable law (8a, tit. 1, book 2 of the Fuero Juzgo) which prohibited the use of other than Gothic laws.

At the present time four principal editions of this Code can be cited (there having existed some sixteen in all), to-wit: An edition of Petu Egidio, at Lorayna in the year 1517, under the direction of Charles V of Germany and First of Spain, of which copies are rare; that of Almeric Bouchard, printed in Paris in 1525, which comprises other compilations, which is less rare; that of the Monk Juan Sicard, at Basilea, in the year 1528; and one of Canciani at Venice in 1789.

THE GERMAN ELEMENT.

It was natural that the Goths upon their settlement in Spain should lose much of their primitive customs and character as a nomadic people, and should endeavor to break off the relations and overcome the subordination of the inhabitants of the Peninsula to Roman influence by establishing a new nationality and introducing their customs and laws. These were reduced to writing, first in the Code of Euric or of Tolosa and afterwards in that of the Fuero Juzgo, thus presenting a German element which dominated the country in the aspect of a truly national law, and which had a marked influence on Spanish civil legislation.

The latter remarkable and original Code, the Fuero Juzgo, had for its basis a multitude of institutions purely Germanic, such as property of the conjugal community (*gananciales*), and advantages (*mejoras*) which even to-day are of much importance in Spanish civil legislation. The origin of the individual and martial spirit which inspired the nobiliary and municipal fueros and influenced the legislative element is also essentially German.

THE VISIGOTHS.

In many respects the career of the Goths is strikingly different from that of any other nation of historic renown. In the earliest times they were living near the Baltic and Vistula, and, subsequently, about 180 A. D., they migrated South. For three hundred years, beginning with the days of Tacitus, their history consists of little else than a dreary record of barbarian slaughter and pillage, but, a century afterwards, the Goths had become the most powerful nation in Europe, one of their two kings was seated on the throne of the Cæsars, a wise and beneficent ruler, and the other was reigning over Spain, and the richest part of Gaul.

Of the religion of the Goths in their heathen days we know but little. Their native historian tells us that they worshipped certain beings called Anses, and this word is plainly the same as Aesir (plural of Ass or Ans), the name which the Scandinavians applied to the greater gods of their mythology, and undoubtedly their customs and religious observances were similar to those of other tribes of Northern Europe.

While the Visigoths were originally idolaters, yet, when they came in contact with Roman civilization, they became Arians and so remained until they adopted Catholicism in the time of Recared.

The Goths possessed an alphabet of their own, the letters of which were called " runes " but they do not appear to have had any extensive written literature or laws. In their heathen days, they used no more convenient writing material than boards and wooden staves, on which their inscriptions were carved, and it is not likely that the great bulk of the people knew how to read and write. The word " rune " literally means a secret or mystery, and that shows that the art of writing was looked upon with superstitious awe as a sort of half-miraculous endowment. Very likely the knowledge of it was kept carefully in the hands of the priesthood, or some learned caste. The Goths used their runes for inscribing the names of their dead heroes on their tombstones, and for marking their swords and jewels with the owner's name. Their wise men wrote witchcraft spells to hang up in the people's houses to drive away bad spirits or to bring good luck. Sometimes, perhaps, a new law might be carved in wood or stone to be handed down to later ages; letters were sent from one chief to another about matters too weighty to be trusted to word of mouth; or the poet might now and then call in the aid of the rune-man to preserve the memory of one of his songs. There were undoubtedly some rude attempts at history writing, such as we have in the early part of the Saxon Chronicle — brief memoranda of events put down at the time, saying that "such a king died; So-and-so was made king; Goths fought with Gepids; Gepids were beaten, with great slaughter; this or that chief was killed." But all this is more or less uncertain, as only one or two Gothic inscriptions, and those very short ones, have been preserved. From the Goths, however, the Runic alphabet passed to the kindred nations dwelling near the Baltic, and it is found on hundreds of tombstones and memorial pillars in Scandinavia, Iceland, and the British Isles.

The Gothic people had many noble qualities, frequently acknowledged, even by their enemies, and which are proved by many incidents in their history: they were especially brave, generous, patient under hardships and privation, and chaste and affectionate in their family relations.

The only great reproach, which the Roman writers bring against them, is that of faithlessness to their treaties, a charge frequently made by civilized peoples against barbarians and one for which the barbarians often had good reason. In the flush of victory, it is said they were excessively cruel, but on the other hand, there is nothing in their history more remarkable than the humanity and justice exercised by them towards the nations whom they conquered, and there are many instances of record where Romans sought refuge from the oppressions of their own rulers under the milder sway of the Goths.

About the year 200 A. D., while still living on the north shore of the Black Sea, the Gutans or Goths divided themselves into two great branches, the Thervings and the Greutungs. However, these two people had also other names, which are much better known in history: the Thervings were called Visigoths (*i. e.,* West

Goths), and the Greutungs, Ostrogoths (East Goths), which names were applied, at first, owing to the relative positions which the two divisions then occupied, one east, and the other west of the Dniester and the designations became lasting in history.

After the Goths had conquered the south of Europe, the Visigoths migrated further westward to Gaul and Spain, while the Ostrogoths settled in Italy.

The Visigoths appear to have been a people superior in many respects to the Ostrogoths, and while the latter were subdued by the dreaded Huns, the scourge of Europe, and subsequently united with them against their own kinsmen, still they never subdued the Visigoths; and in the great battle of Chalons (451), one of the decisive contests in the history of Europe, the Romans and Alans, allies of the Visigoths, were driven from the field, and it was only due to the remarkable bravery and skill of the Visigoths that the day was saved and the Huns under Attila were finally and completely worsted, losing one hundred and sixty thousand men.

The defeat of the Visigoths at the hands of the Arabs in Spain and the downfall of the Visigothic monarchy were undoubtedly due to the refining influence of the Roman civilization and the conversion of the Visigoths to Catholicism, which diverted them from their previous martial career.*

As has been noticed, the inhabitants were driven into the mountain fastnesses of Northern Spain by the Saracenic invasion, and here the Visigoths and Spaniards were drawn more closely together by a common religion and a common hatred of the infidels, and, by their united efforts for freedom, finally became blended into one nation.

In all the uprisings of the Christians against the Moors, and in the last great struggle which ended in the overthrow of the infidel dominion, men with Gothic names are conspicuous as leaders, and it even may be said that, but for the Gothic element in the Spanish people, the chivalry of Castile would never have existed, and Spain, until to-day, might have remained under Mohammedan rule.

---

* It is well to note here that in ancient Greece and Italy, the city became the centre of social and political life; while in countries inhabited by the Teutons, the idea of the city was foreign to the genius of their institutions. They were Nature's children, and at home wherever they chanced to be, either in the forests of Northern Europe, or on the banks of the Danube, Tiber, or Tagus.

To determine the origin of the Visigoths, how this people passed from a nomadic and errant life to a sedentary one, and the effects of its shocks on Roman civilization, is a task extremely difficult on account of the little data which exists on these points, and on account of the diverse opinions sustained about the same by different writers.

Their customs brought new elements of life to the country, distinct from those which formed Roman civilization, exercising a signal influence on the Spanish mode of living and which to-day, even after the lapse of time, are noted in various customs and institutions.

The distinctive characteristics of these people were intense individuality and esteem for personal bravery.

They were ruled by a monarchy, whose chief was a leader who, above everything else, prided himself on his prowess in the chase and in combat; he was assisted by assemblies, composed of all citizens who were capable of bearing arms in defense of their firesides. Slavery was tolerated, but limited to conquered enemies, whose lives were spared; property acquired in matrimony was considered as property of both husband and wife. Fathers were permitted to exercise control over their sons, but this authority terminated when the latter were able to protect themselves, and the sons generally became useful members of society at the age of fifteen years.

The Visigothic reign demonstrated that, up to this period, the German customs were largely influenced by individual principles and the personality of its subjects.

In the opposition of the Visigothic culture to the Roman, it was natural that the Visigothic should lose some of its primitive character, and that Spaniards should also forget some of the principles which formed the Roman education. In regard to the personality of the Visigoths, it, no doubt, caused the Spaniards to respect the former people, their uses, and customs, as well as their religion, and even their laws. So that in the earliest times of the Visigothic monarchy, there existed in Spain two conditions of culture, two religions, and two distinct systems of laws, one pertaining to the conquered Spaniards and the other peculiar to the conquering Visigoths. This period of the judicial history of Spain is characterized by the existence of legislation of castes or races.

It is not strange that in the commencement of the Visigothic reign, it was difficult to define the social character of the monarchy; but, with time, it became established on a solid basis, and acquired power and refinement in the diverse elements which constituted that society.

There were four elements constituting the Visigothic reign: the royalty, the clerical party, the nobility, and the people.

The nobility among the Visigoths was formed by the descendants of the first chiefs and from it came the king, whom it alone elected, at first, but afterwards in conjunction with the clerical party, so that it always exercised much power in the government of the state.

The great influence which the nobility exercised in the Visigothic monarchy and the large number of landed estates which they owned, were the seed which, with time, produced Spanish feudalism.*

The legislative union of the Visigoths and Spaniards was a most important factor in blending the two elements which formed the kingdom, especially, since, by the conversion of Recared, the religious differences which separated them were laid aside. Some time before Chindasvint occupied the throne, there were some tendencies manifested towards procuring the unity of the laws, gaining more force and vigor with time. At this period, as has been seen, there were in force in the Visigothic monarchy two bodies of laws, springing from different sources and having diverse characteristics, the Gothic Code of Euric or of Tolosa, and the Roman Code of Alaric or Breviarium Aniani; and in order to bring about a unity of the laws, which was rendered so necessary by the union of the two peoples, there was compiled the Fuero Juzgo, with the character of a single legal code, applicable to all.

---

* Some germs of feudalism are to be encountered in primitive Spain, besides the religious institution of *Soldurios*, of which Strabo, V. Maximus and Plutarch speak.

The bronze of Lascuta, engraved 189 B. C., published in Paris in 1867, and to be found in the Louvre, demonstrates that a state of feudalism existed on the estates of a Spanish prince in Ibera de Asta before that date.

Catalonia was a feud of France at the beginning of the reconquest of the Moors, and so remained until the eleventh century; the county of Castile also early bore this relation to the kings of Leon, and Galicia, Algarbes and Portugal were feuds. See the Fuero Juzgo, book V, tit. 7, in recognition of feuds.

GOTHIC CUSTOMS AND LAWS.

In respect to the customs and laws of the Goths, Tacitus states that their kings were elected by the nobility, but their captains for their valor.

The power of the kings was neither absolute nor perpetual, and their captains, when they showed themselves to be brave and the first to engage in combat, governed more by the example of their valor and the respect that it won than by the authority of their office.

In matters of state princes determined affairs of less importance, and those of greater weight were considered in a general assembly by all who were considered capable of bearing arms.

They came together to treat of public affairs on certain days, as when a new or full moon occurred; time was not counted by days, as at present, but by nights.

Any person could answer another in their assemblies, even though a crime imposing death was involved.

Penalties were prescribed in conformity with crimes; traitors and those who deserted to an enemy were hanged to a tree.

For crimes of less importance, the convicted were condemned to forfeit a certain number of horses or sheep.

The princes were also elected in the same assemblies which administered justice in the villages and hamlets; there took part in these one hundred representatives chosen from among the common people, and they served in an executive and administrative capacity as well as courts of justice. When peace had lasted a long time and they found themselves unoccupied, many of the younger nobles joined other nations at war, as they abhorred tranquillity, and when there was no war, the Goths spent considerable time at the chase; but they also were addicted to idleness, and devoted much time in feasting and sleeping, as no strong and warlike people were much inclined to work, but usually left the care of the house, farm and fields, to women, old men, and weak members of the family.

None of the German people inhabited neighboring cities, nor suffered that their houses should be adjoining: they lived divided and apart from one another where it most pleased them, in the forests, near the water, or in the fields.

Like the Hindoos, they strictly guarded among themselves the laws of matrimony, which above everything else gave commendation to their customs, and among the barbarians in general almost all of them were contented with one wife. If it were not so with their chiefs, this was not on account of corrupt tendencies, but only of the desire to increase their kin, and to leave heirs to their property and rights.

The wife brought no dower, the husband gave it to her. At the beginning of the marriage life the wife was advised of all things, and did not think of her own freedom but, as a companion, shared the work and dangers of the husband. A woman's chastity protected her and there were few cases of adultery among so many people; the wife guilty of such offense was punished and then committed to the husband, who, after cutting off her hair in presence of relatives, ejected her in a nude condition from his house.

Wills or testaments were unknown to them, as they were to other early people whose customs and practices rendered them unnecessary.

In default of sons, the daughters were the first to inherit, and then the uncles first on the father's and secondly on the mother's side.

They considered it inhuman to deny their house to any person, and set before strangers the best that they could provide according to their state and condition; and when they could no longer do so, their visitors were taken to the house of a friend where they could be well cared for.

Gold and silver were unknown to them, and they did not know what it was to give or take interest, nor to increase their fortunes by usury.

As has been noticed, the policy of the first Visigothic kings in Spain was of the greatest tolerance towards the conquered, not only respecting the religion and the customs of the natives, but also permitting them to be governed by Roman laws and respecting their organization of tribunals.

Theodoric, for example, that enlightened king of the Ostrogoths, in assuming authority over Italy, is purported to have said to the Romans—"that other kings made their conquests at the ruination of the conquered people, but that he, on the contrary, desired that they might congratulate themselves on the benefits of his domination."

His government was marked by few radical changes, and by that human and tolerant policy observed in Spain by the Visigoths which is in harmony with the present practice of civilized nations.

Upon the settlement of the Visigoths in Spain, they established their capital at Toledo, and the higher state of Roman civilization which they met gradually had a marked effect on their customs and laws: all the nobles were supposed to take a part and to assist the king in resolving important matters under the name of *Officio Palatino* — a reunion of the nobles for such purposes, which bore a resemblance to the *Aula regia* of the Roman emperors.

The reunion of Visigothic people at court received the name of *curia,* and its members *curiales* or *palaciegos,* which must not be confused with the Roman *curia* and *curiales,* nor with the assistants in the administration of justice, who are still called *curiales.*

Among those charged with the functions of the government and jurisdictions of provinces and cities of the kingdom, were dukes, counts, and *gardingos.*

It was often difficult to distinguish between the political, judicial and military character and acts of such officials.

The political constitution of the Visigothic nation was an elective and moderate monarchy, first under the *Officio Palatino* and afterwards by the Councils of Toledo, but the second acted in conjunction with the first, from which latter the king still selected the dukes, counts and *gardingos* to whom he confided the government of the provinces and cities.

The Visigoths, principally with the assistance of the dukes, counts and *gardingos* who constituted a judicial hierarchy, completed the system, first with the *vicarios,* judges named by counts in civil affairs, and the *thinfados,* intrusted with civil and criminal affairs, superior to the *vicarios* but inferior to the *gardingos,* who had commands in the army under the counts. Besides there were *vilicos* or governors of hamlets, and the *pacis adsertors* who were judges nominated by the king to intervene in certain affairs and reconcile the parties, duties somewhat similar to those of municipal judges or justices of the peace to-day.

The mode of procedure was simple: the parties verbally set forth their complaints, produced their proof, and decision was rendered, from which appeal lay to a duke or count, while from the latter a further appeal could be taken to the king.*

The judges were required to follow the law strictly, and where it was silent to refer the matter to the king.†

They were also limited to eight days in which to decide suits, unless a holy-day intervened, under a penalty of paying all costs and damages; and they had power to compel parties and witnesses to appear before them.‡

The responsibility of judges was strictly enforced; if a judge made an erroneous decision, he was compelled to pay the injured party double the amount involved, and if he was unable to do so, he was punished with fifty lashes; but if his decision was affirmed on appeal, he received from the appellant an amount equal to the condemnation.

Suitors also had the right to challenge judges without assigning reasons therefor: a judge could, however, exempt himself from corporal punishment by making oath that the error arose from ignorance, and was not the result of favor or solicitation.§

The modes of proof admitted both documentary and oral evidence, and, when such was lacking, sworn testimony of the principals was required.

Witnesses were carefully examined, and perjury was severely punished; the perjurer, besides making an indemnity for the injury done, was disqualified as a witness in the future, and sometimes became the slave of the person against whom he testified. Inciting to give false testimony was similarly punished.||

After the time of Recared, the bishops were charged to protect the poor and to watch over the administration of the law, and, to this end, could suspend such judges as were unfaithful and incompetent.¶

Murder was punished with death, and aiders and abetters received two hundred lashes, had their heads shaved, were condemned to pay five hundred sueldos, and in default of this payment became slaves of the deceased man's heirs. The criminal laws, in some respects, followed the principle of the Lex talionis,

* Fuero Juzgo, book 2, tit. 1, law 22.
† Id., prelim. title, law 2.
‡ Id., book 2, tit. 1, laws 17 and 20.
§ Id., book 2, tit. 1, laws 19, 22.
|| Id., book 2, tit. 4, law 6.
¶ Id., book 2, tit. 28, law 28.

except in the more serious injuries inflicted by deadly weapons, when a punishment greater in degree might be imposed.*

In the matter of procedure, the Visigothic laws were the most advanced of the times, as can readily be seen by examining the Fuero Juzgo.

THE CODE OF EURIC OR OF TOLOSA.

At the beginning of the Visigothic reign, it has been observed that this people was ruled by their own laws, and that the conquerors in carrying out a spirit of tolerance permitted the Romans to continue under their former laws, later known as the Code of Alaric or Breviarium Aniani.

Following the conquest of the Peninsula, the Visigoths, on account of their changed conditions and of the vast territory which they acquired, realized the necessity of reducing their laws to written form.

Euric (466–484) in whose reign such conditions existed, was, according to the better opinion of expounders of law, the first to give written laws to the Visigoths. This has been confirmed by San Isidore,† the Archbishop D. Rodriges, and the Bishop of Burgos, D. Alonso of Cartagena, who assures us that the Code of Euric was approved in the junta of Próceres, convened for this purpose in Arles, although Marichalar and Manrique believed that this is confused with the junta in Aire which approved the Breviarium Aniani.

The Code of Euric or of Tolosa (from the name of the town where it was published), or *Lex Wisigothorum de Euric*, was little known until recent times, and for the discovery of some fragments of it we are indebted to the Benedictines of San German.‡

* Fuero Juzgo, book 6, tit. 5, law 12.

† Crón. Wisig., no. 19.—P. Flores, vol. 6, Esp. Sag.—Arz. D. Rod., Cron. of Cardeña, book 2, chap. 10.—Alons. de Cartag., Anacephalæosis, chap. 16. St. Isidore of Seville, born in Cartagena 570, and who died in Seville in 639, was one of the wisest and most learned men of the age, the author of Hispana or Isidoriana, and one of the founders of ecclesiastical law. His *Origines* served as an encyclopædia of jurisprudence, and of all other sciences.

‡ The discovery of the Laws of Euric, the West Goth, has deprived the Lex Salica of its claim to be the oldest extant statement of Germanic custom. Pollock and Maitland's History of the English Law, vol. 1, p. 6, 1899.

Euric's laws are sufficient to remind us that the order of date among these *Leges Barbarorum* is very different from the order of barbarity. Scandinavian laws that were not written until the thirteenth century, will often give us

It appears that these monks in working on a palimpsest of San Jeronimo, discovered marks of the ancient writing. An investigation was begun, and by the use of restoratives, some chapters of the *Lex Wisigothorum* of Euric were discovered which later, in 1839, Kunst was preparing to publish when he died.

This work was continued by Pertz and finally completed and published in 1847 by Blume under the title of *Reccaredi Wisigothorum Regis antigua legum collectio. Ex membranis diletitiis regiae parisiensis bibliotecae restitutam adjecta vulgata legum Wisigothorum lectione.*

The collection discovered includes from three paragraphs prior to chapter 277 up to chapter 326, of which only thirty-five are completed and intelligible.

This work includes not only Visigothic laws in force until the promulgation of the Fuero Juzgo, which embraces many of them, but also Roman legislation, such as the contract of purchase and sale, security, donation, loans, commodatum, deposit, testamentary successions, etc., unknown to the Goths but which were undoubtedly introduced by clerical influence, and little observed at the time by the Visigoths.

THE CANONICAL ELEMENT.

The progress of the civilizing influence of Christianity in the Middle Ages elevated human personality out of its former abject condition, and the power which the Church gained thereby and the superior culture of its priesthood inspired and stimulated the people to great activity, resulting in a remarkable advance in the enlightenment of humanity and exercising a powerful influence over legislation.

In Spain the clergy in the Councils of Toledo taking an active part in legislative matters gave the canonical element a fixed place in the Spanish civil law.

---

what is more archaic than anything that comes from the Gaul of the fifth or the Briton of the seventh, and, on the other hand, the mention of Goths in Spain should remind us of those wondrous folk-wanderings and of their strange influence upon the legal map of Europe. The Saxon of England has a close cousin in the Lombard of Italy, and modern critics profess that they can see a specially near kinship between Spanish and Icelandic law. Ficker, Untersuchungen zur Erbenfolge, 1891–1895; Ficker, Ueber nähere Verwandschaft zwischen gothisch-spanischem und norwegisch-isländischem Recht, 1888, ii, 456 ff.

The councils and the kings legislated together in the Visigothic period and, consequently, the theocratic spirit reflected itself in the Fuero Juzgo.

One after another the Spanish legal works gave evidence of this truth in dedicating a large part of their dispositions to religious matters and to the rights of the clergy. The denial of juridical capacity to heterodox persons; the severity of the penal laws prescribed for the repression of crimes against the Faith; the regulation of matrimonial affairs at first wholly by the doctrine of Tridentina and the royal cedula of Philip II, and, subsequently by the royal decree of February 9, 1875, and by the Civil Code; placing the family under the exclusive authority of the Church, until recent times; making the record of birth answer for the civil status of those born; matrimony depending upon the certification from parochial registry, and death upon that of ecclesiastical interment, all these illustrate the great influence which canonical law has exercised over civil law in Spain up to the present time.*

A SUMMARY OF CANONICAL LAW.

Canonical law is a collection of canons and ecclesiastical laws or rules established by the Church in relation to matters of faith and for discipline. It is classed as written and unwritten, the latter being also divided into traditional and customary.

The first and fundamental basis of ecclesiastical law is the Holy Bible, *la Sagrada Escritura,* which is composed of the Old and New Testaments whose authority was fixed in the Council of Trent.

The canons are nothing more than the resolutions of the Councils, the *decretos* or *decretales* of the Pope, and the sentences and opinions of the Holy Fathers, collected and adopted in the book of canonical law.

The body of canonical law contains six collections, to-wit: the

* In common-law countries, little attention is usually given to the study of canonical law, and there appears to be a tendency to overlook the principles which have been taken from it and embodied in the common law.

Ecclesiastical law was an element in English jurisprudence only to the extent that the King and Parliament received and adopted it, and, in this manner, it entered common-law institutions and is to-day the basis of the law of marriage and divorce, registry of births and deaths, interments, separation, testamentary law, alimony, execution and proof of wills, and of the law of intestacy.

decreto of Gracian, the *decretales* of Gregory IX, the sixth of Boniface VII, the Clementinas, the Extravagantes of Juan XXII, and the common Extravagantes.

The *decreto* of Gracian comprises various canons of Councils, sentences of the Holy Fathers, civil and capitulary laws of the Kings of France which were published in 1151.

Canonical law is also divided into ancient and modern law.

The ancient is of the Eastern Church and of the Western Church, while the collection of ancient laws of the Eastern Church includes:

1. Those attributed to Stephen, Bishop of Ephesus, which comprises one hundred and sixty-five canons collected from the five private councils of Ancira, Neocesarea, Gangres, Antioch and Laodicea, and from the general councils of Nicæa and Constantinople.

2. The first collection increased to three hundred and seven canons, by including those of the general councils of Ephesus and Calcedonia.

3. The same augmented by one hundred and two canons of the Council of Trulano or Quinsexto, by twenty-one of the Council of Sardica, one hundred and thirty-two of that of Carthage and one hundred and sixty-one taken from the works and epistles of the Greek bishops and fathers, and eighty-five apostolic canons.

4. The previous collection increased by twenty-two canons of the second Council of Nicæa.

In the ninth century, this collection was weakened by adding seventeen canons taken from the two councils improperly convened by Focius, Patriarch of Constantinople.

5. The collection of imperial constitutions and canons of Focius, or the union of the canons and civil laws of the Emperors confirming the ecclesiastical laws, the work of Focius who collected and arranged four hundred and forty canons under fourteen titles.

The ancient collection of the Western Church embraces:

1. The canons of the Councils of Nicæa and Sardica, to which were afterwards added those of the general council of Constantinople, and the canons of the five private ones held in the East, of one hundred and sixty-five of which mention was made in the first collection noted.

2. The collection of Dionisius el Exiguo, a Sicilian monk, including the one hundred and sixty-five canons above referred

to, fifty of the Apostles, twenty-one of Sardica, twenty-seven of Calcedonia and one hundred and thirty-eight of the African Councils, making altogether four hundred and one. Adrian I delivered this collection with some additions to Charles the Great, and it received the name of *Collectio Adriana* and *Codex Canonum.*

3. The collection, made by the same Dionisius el Exiguo, of one hundred and eighty-seven *decretales* from the time of Pope Siricio to Anatasio II inclusive.

4. The ancient Spanish collection or ancient code, as it was called in the first council of Braga, composed, it is believed, of various canons of Nicæa, Sardica, Arles, and certain national ones.

5. The collection of Martin Bracarense, entitled *Capitulos de los Sinodos orientales recopilados por Martin, Obispo de Braga,* believed to have been published about 580.

6. The Gothic-canonical collection attributed to San Isidore, Archbishop of Seville.

This collection embraces the canons of the first four mentioned general councils, the five private ones of the Eastern Church, already referred to, those of Sardica, nine of Africa, seventeen of France, thirty-six Spanish and one hundred and three *decretales* of various pontiffs.

This valuable collection was translated by Don Juan Tejada y Ramiro in 1859, and forms a most important work for students of canonical law.

7. The collection of the French Church, composed largely of canons of the Oriental Church collection, before referred to, which were received by Charles the Great from the Pope Adrian.

8. The *Breviarium canonum,* a collection of the African Church, published in the sixth century by the deacon of Carthage, Fulgencius Ferrando.

9. The *Concordia canonum,* the canons which the Bishop Cresonius, in the eighth century, compiled and arranged together with the pontifical *decretales.*

10. The *falsas decretales,* a collection published in the ninth century, subsequent to 829 by one Isidore Mercator or Peccator.

This collection contains various authentic and important documents taken from the Spanish collection, from that of ancient Gallicius and from Dionisius el Exiguo, and some false collections invented by the author in imitation of San Isidore, and apparently in order to support the pretensions of the court at Rome to the supremacy of the temporal power. They form part of the *decreto* of Graciano.

11. The *Capitulares de los Reyes francos,* the *Nomo* canons published by the kings of France with the assistance of the magnates and the bishops reunited in synods or assemblies, similar to the Councils of Toledo.

In 827, the Abbot Ansegiso collected them, and in 845 there were added to them three more books by a deacon of Maguncea, called Benito, to whom has been improperly attributed the authorship of the *falsas decretales.*

12. The collection of the Abbot of Abadia of Prum, Reginon, published subsequent to 906 for the use of the German Church. This collection includes canons of various councils, *decretales,* true and false, sentences of the Holy Fathers, the *Breviarium* of the Gothic chancellor Anianus, and chapters and laws of the Brugundians and Ripurarians.

13. The collection of Abbon, Abbot of Fleury, published at the end of the tenth century, composed of the chapters, of laws of the Justinian codes, councils and *decretales.*

14. The *decretal* of Burcard, Bishop of Worms, published at the beginning of the eleventh century, composed of numerous canons taken from the Roman Penitentials of Theodore and Beda.

Modern canonical law of the Western Church is composed of the collections which are enumerated at the beginning of this article:

First, The *decreto* of Gracian.

Second, The *decretales* of Gregory IX, which comprise five books and principally embrace the decisions or rescripts of the Popes from Alexander III to Gregory IX, who confirmed and published them in 1230.

The Third Collection is called the Sixth of the *decretales* or of Boniface VIII, because it was added as an appendix or supplement to the five books of Gregory IX. It contained the constitutions subsequent to Gregory IX, those of the Popes who followed him, and also those of Boniface, who was its author and who published it in 1298.

The Fourth Collection bore the name of Clementinas because Clement V composed it, partly from the canons of the Council of Vienna and in part from his own constitutions; but this, on account of Clement V's death, was not published until 1317, by his successor Juan XXII.

The Fifth Collection did not contain more than twenty constitutions of Juan XXII, who died in 1334, and its date of publication is not known.

The Sixth Collection is called the *Extravagantes comunes* and includes the constitutions of different Popes who lived before and after Juan XXII.

Besides the collections mentioned in the time which intervened between the publication of the *Decreto* of Gracian and the *Decretales* of Gregory IX, there were compiled ten collections which, if not all done by public authority, enjoyed great credit among the private ones. Seven of these have been published, the first five being consecutively numbered, while of the remaining five three remain unedited.

THE COUNCILS OF TOLEDO.

The Councils of Toledo were in their origin ecclesiastical councils, national synods of Spain, which existed before the Visigothic invasion, as proof of which can be cited, among others, the celebrated one of Iliberis, whose canons were the admiration of the fathers who met in the general councils in Nicæa.

Moreover, before the conversion of Recared, two councils, the First and Second, were held in Toledo, which were occupied in considering religious affairs only.

Undoubtedly the high character, religious fervor and progressive spirit shown in these councils had much to do with the conversion of Recared (586–601) early in his reign before the Third Council, upon which these councils acquired the mixed character of religious and political assemblies, and the clergy gained a direct participation in State affairs and in legislation.

In the Third Council, regulations were prescribed as to the vows to be taken by widows in respect of a new marriage. Marriages were forbidden between Jews and Catholics. Jews were forbidden to buy Christian slaves and to fill public offices to the prejudice of Catholics, manumissions performed by prelates gave complete liberty to slaves and their descendants and the right of church patronship.

During the Fourth Council, over which San Isidore presided, great influence was gained by the clergy in all affairs; they secured exemption from taxation and taking part in public works, bishops were clothed with authority to watch over, to advise and to correct judges and high officials, numerous dispositions as to the Jews were prescribed, as well as laws for the election of kings, the form of proceedings and the penalties for the improper exercise of office, etc.

The dispositions of the Council constituted a kind of tacit pact between the Church and the Throne as to a mutual and reciprocal understanding in respect to power, which may be found included in the preliminary title of the Fuero Juzgo.

In the Fifth and Sixth Councils, during the time of Chintila who owed his election to the bishops, the clerical party increased its power, privileges and exemptions, and severer laws against the Jews were promulgated.

The Seventh Council, convened in the reign of Chindasvint, was marked by a reaction against the power of the Church in reducing the privileges and correcting abuses of the clergy which had become open and notorious.

Important legislative changes took place, in the abolition of the Roman law and the promulgation of a general law for both the Visigoths and the conquered people, which formed the basis of the Fuero Juzgo.

Recesvint convoked the Eighth Council which completed the fusion of the two peoples and resulted in a legislative unity: Marriages were sanctioned between Goths and Romans, agreements against hereditary successions were considered, the rights of bishops and magnates to elect kings were confirmed, and an extreme persecution of the Jews was tolerated.

The Ninth, Tenth and Eleventh Councils limited the prelates to consider matters properly within their spheres, and much of the royal prerogatives and sovereign power which they had previously exercised, was assumed once more by the king owing to the discreet action of Wamba, in whose reign these councils took place.

A reaction took place in the Twelfth Council under Ervigio, and the Church regained much of the lost power and obtained many new prerogatives; licenses and evils which Wamba and his well-disciplined forces had abolished or held in check were again rampant, and the Jews became more oppressed than ever.

The Thirteenth, Fourteenth and Fifteenth Councils convened also in the time of Ervigio, enacted few important measures and continued to antagonize the followers of Wamba.

Among the most important laws considered were a reduction of taxes, and a prohibition of the widows of kings to contract new marriages.

The Sixteenth and Seventeenth Councils in the time of Egica were especially noted for the cruel measures devised against the Jews. They were expelled from their homes throughout the land, their wives and children were reduced to slavery, and the children upon reaching seven years of age were torn from their parents and placed under Catholic instruction.

Bishops and abbots exclusively composed the primitive Councils, but after the conversiòn of Recared, these also included the nobility.

The monarch convoked the Council which first considered religious matters, and later affairs relating to the temporal order; the king submitted the latter to the council for its discussion in a kind of discourse or message called *tomo régio.*

The resolutions of the Councils were called canons and referred either to the religious order or to the civil order.

In the first case they enjoyed complete authority, but in the second, the Monarch had to approve them, and he could alone, if he thought advisable, dictate laws on public affairs without consulting the Councils.

THE FUERO JUZGO.

The Fuero Juzgo is known under the following names: *Codes Legum, Liber Gothorum, Lex Wisigothorum, Liber Judicum,* and *Fori Judicum;* the latter title was corrupted into Fuero Juzgo at the beginning of the thirteenth century by which name it is now generally known.* Its origin coincides with the earliest history of the Gothic people and in it are the laws sanctioned by Euric and his successors, but it was not definitely compiled until the sixteenth Council of Toledo, during the reign of Egica (687–700),† a high-minded monarch, who directed the systematic arrangement of the multitude of laws including those of Euric, Recesvint, and Ervigio,

* The Spanish Academy has in recent times made searching investigations in the different archives of Spain to throw more light on the subject for the purpose of publishing an edition of this work. Many ancient and valuable manuscripts were found, viz., one in the archives of Murcia, six in the Escorial, some from the Church of Toledo, one from the college of Bartholomy, and a number from private sources.

† Opinion of Mariana,— Ensayo historico-critico sobre la legislacion, vol. 1, p. 41.

omitting many which did not harmonize with the times, or which were already derogated and in contradiction to others deserving, by their advance and wisdom, greater attention and preference. This collection is, without doubt, the one of that epoch. The opinion of Ambrosius Morales, strengthened by that of Lardizabal, is very weighty on this particular point: this author assures us that, at this Council of Toledo, the book of Fuero Juzgo was compiled. This evidence naturally leads us, without the need of any philological help, to the conclusion that it was written in Latin; since it was initiated when that was the language in use; one of the strongest reasons being that the Council of Toledo took upon itself to handle the matter, the majority of its members being bishops of the Church, at that time the depositary of learning and the art of illumination; and lastly because it was finished by an assembly which, like all bodies of that kind, published its resolutions in that language, the only one accepted by the Church to give practical form to all the declarations of its authority.

The system adopted in this Code to make known the large number of different matters embraced, does not adhere to any regular plan, and the laws which form it are in disorder, because, although they are assembled in order of subjects, and divided into books, and these into titles, a regular order of exposition is not followed; it seems as if the compilers, on forming a determined method of procedure, had later abandoned the plan, deeming it impossible to carry it to the end with all the details involved.

The Fuero Juzgo is composed of a preliminary title and twelve books which contain fifty-four titles, subdivided into five hundred and seventy-eight laws, of which one hundred and eighty-three are attributed to Euric and Leovigild, one hundred and twenty-four to Sisenand and San Isidore, one to Recared, three to Sisebut, sixty-four to Chindasvint, one hundred and fifty-two to Recesvint, five to Wamba, eight to Ervigio, and nineteen to the Councils of Toledo.

The preliminary title treats of the election and duties of monarchs and their subjects and includes the public law of the Visigothic Monarchy formed in the Fourth Council of Toledo. Although imperfect, this title includes in reality one of the earliest written constitutions of Europe, in which are recognized principles more liberal than those known to any modern monarchical constitution.* It expressly declares, among other things, that the people have the right to depose their kings when the latter fail to do their duties, which provision was often carried into practice.†

Book I is entitled "*De instrumentis legalibus*" in Latin, and "*Del facedor de la ley et de las leyes*" in Spanish. It treats of the lawmaker and the law, under two titles.

The law declares the concurrence of certain circumstances whose simple conception causes us to form a high opinion of the Visigoths, such as the application of clear and manifest justice, suitable to the time and place of its promulgation, dignified, honest, practical, equal in its application, and without prejudice, either as to tribunals or as to persons.

"*E reluze cuemo el sol en defendiendo á todos*" ‡ and instructive and moral, "*e ama iusticia, y es maestra de vertudes, é vida de tod el pueblo.*" §

The student will be surprised at the modern principles embraced in these laws; they are especially noted for their common sense and practical application and would, in some respects, serve as good examples for legislators of the present age.

Book 2 is entitled "*De Negotiis Causarum*"—"*De los Juicios y Causas.*" Under five titles it continues to treat of the laws, amendments, and interpretations, stating that the laws are applicable to all the inhabitants of the territory; of judges, their powers and attributes; of suits and procedure, including retroactive laws and prescribed actions; of written and oral testimony; and of the execution of last wills and testaments.

Book 3 is entitled "*De ordine Conjugali*"—"*De los Casamientos é del las Nascencias*" and under six titles treats of marriages, of births, and the offenses against chastity, divorce, and the marriage relations.

In order to facilitate the fusion of the two peoples, it authorized marriages between the invaders and the Romans, and in cases of adultery the German law was followed which punished the guilty person severely, even to delivering the latter to the injured

* Many of the leading principles of modern constitutions are recognized as Teutonic in their origin.

† In the observance of this law, the chief justice of Aragon, upon the administration of the oath of office to a new king, is related to have said:

"We who are equal to you, and who together are more than you, require this oath." Zurita — Anales de Aragon, and La Navarre Francaise.

‡ Book 1, tit. 2, law 3.

§ Book 1, tit. 2, law 2.

one for his own punishment; it even permitted the innocent party to slay the guilty one and to confiscate the latter's property.

Book 4 is entitled "*De ordine Naturali*"—"*Del Linaje Natural,*" and under five titles treats of relationship and the laws of descent and inheritance, the rights and duties of guardians, orphans, and the administration of estates.

They, like the Hindoos, recognize the distinction between natural and juridical persons, and cited the Roman axiom "*de que no todos los hombres son personas, ni todas las personas, hombres.*"

They also observed the division of children, born during the life and after the death of the father, and required that a child must have lived ten days and have been baptized in order to be considered legally born.*

Posthumous children were subject to similar conditions and rights of elder children.†

Persons under fifteen years of age were minors, and orphans were provided for.‡

Book 5 is entitled "*De transactionibus*"—"*De las Avenencias é de las Compras,*" and comprises seven titles, of which the first treats of gifts to churches and of ecclesiastical property, the second and third of donations, and the remaining of the contracts of exchange, sales, deposits, commodatum, pledges, and manumission. Most of these contracts recognize the principles of the Roman law, but some have a resemblance to those of India.

Mortgages and pledges are not distinguishable and are designated by the common name "*penno.*"

Only the owner could give his things in pledge, and by his free will. The pledgee was liable to a fine of double the value where he constrained the pledgor to make the pledge; the creditor was the custodian of the thing pledged but could not use it, and ten days after the pledge period had expired, it permitted the debtor, without appearing in court, to sell the article, after appraisal by the creditor and three good men.§

Book 6 is entitled "*De Sceleribus et Tormentis*"—"*De los Malfechos, é de las Penas, é de los Tormentos,*" and under five titles treats of various crimes, penalties therefor, and infliction of punishment.

---

* Book 4, tit. 2, law 18.
† Id., tit. 2, law 20.
‡ Id., tit. 3, law 1.
§ Book 2, tit. 5, law 8; id. 5, tit. 6, laws 1, 2, 3, and 4.

Criminal responsibility is declared personal but is not visited on descendants, except as to the civil responsibility.

The death penalty was inflicted in certain cases and sentences were publicly executed.*

Book 7 is entitled "*De Furtis et Fallaciis*"—"*De los Furtos é de los Engannos,*" and under six titles treats of punishment of thieves, robbers, kidnappers, forgers and counterfeiters.

Book 8 is entitled "*De Illatis violentiis et damnis*"—"*De las Fuerzas é de los dannos, é de los quebrantamientos*" and under six titles the subject of penalties is continued with respect to forcible entry and taking possession of other persons' property, or doing injury thereto contrary to law.

Book 9 is entitled "*De Fugitivis et de refugientibus*"—"*De los siervos foidos é de los que se tornan,*" and under three titles treats of fugitive slaves, also of fugitives from military service, and of ecclesiastical asylums.

Book 10 is entitled "*De divisionibus et annorum temporibus atque limitibus*"—"*De las particiones, é de los tiempos, é los annos, é de las lindes,*" and under three titles treats of the division of lands, the use thereof by owners and tenants, leases, prescription, and determining and fixing the boundaries.

The division made of territory between the Visigoths and the conquered people was in the proportion of two-thirds for the former and one-third for the latter, except that lands not already divided were to be shared equally.

The principal means of acquiring ownership of lands were: 1. By occupation; 2. By accession; 3. By prescription; 4. By succession on account of death.

Occupation by the Visigoths partook of a military aspect in conformity with the warlike character of these people, and with their partiality for hunting and fishing.†

Accession was of three classes:

(a) By building; (b) By planting; (c) By sowing, subject to conditions as to good faith and ownership, similar to those found in the present Spanish Civil Code.

Prescription was a subject for which the Gothic laws had special regard, and was considered under two classes:

(a) Common prescription of thirty years; (b) Extraordinary prescription of fifty years.

* Books 6, 7, and 8.

† Book 8, titles 4 and 5.

The first class applied to the acquisition and loss of personal rights, as well as of dominion even though it belonged to the King, provided he should have knowledge of the prescription.*

The second was applicable only to the division of lands between the Goths and Romans, and to property of minors. Churches and monasteries were not subject to prescription, nor did it apply to persons out of the country or imprisoned.†

Book 11 is entitled "*De aegrotis atque mortuis, et transmarinis negotiatoribus*"—"*De los fisicos é de los mercaderes de ultramar, é de los marineros*"—under three titles and treats, first of the rights and duties of physicians and of sick persons; secondly of penalties for violating cemeteries; and thirdly of maritime commerce.

There are only four laws under the third head, two of which are of little interest, referring to penalties for doing certain prohibited acts, while the others relate to annulling sales improperly made, and provide for trying foreign merchants by special judges.

Book 12 is entitled "*De removendis pressuris, et omnium haereticorum omnimodo sectis extinctis*"—"*De devedar los tuertos, é derraigar las sectas é sus dichas*"—and under four titles, the last of which is a duplicate, treats of the impartial administration of the law by the judges, directs them in criminal cases to mitigate punishments when offenders are poor and ignorant and prescribes heavy penalties for exactions and unnecessary expenses; of the power of bishops over alcaldes; of the Jews; of the relations of the Jews to the Christians, and among the harsh provisions of the law to which this race were subjected; it was prescribed "that no Christian should shelter or defend a Jew."

This unfortunate persecution of the Spanish Jew seems to have been fostered from before the Gothic invasion until it culminated in the disastrous expulsion of the Jews from Spain, during the reign of Ferdinand and Isabella, through the great influence of the Inquisitor-General Torquemada who is said to have coerced Isabella, much against her own convictions, into signing the decree of expulsion.

In the thirteenth century, the Fuero Juzgo appeared translated into common or vernacular Spanish by order of San Ferdi-

* Book 10, tit. 2, law 3 (see the celebrated usage *Omnes causae* of Cataluña), and id. laws 4 and 5.

† Book 4, tit. 3, law 2; book 5, tit. 1, law 5; book 10, tit. 2, laws 1 and 7.

nand, and was declared to be the law of the territory of Cordoba. Its legal authority was not the same as in the eighth century.

The battle of Guadalete (711 A. D.), the disastrous result of which brought so many and radical changes to Spain, also affected the destiny of this legal work, which was swept aside by the tumultuous current of local legislation, born out of the dreadful chaos of the reconquest.

Its influence was weakened but not extinguished; it was from the beginning accepted as law at those places where a tenacious resistance was made to the advance of the Moors; and in the Asturias first, as later in Leon, Navarre and Castile, it governed as the only law until the new customs and habits, and, above all, the necessity of encouraging the hope of a reward in the struggle made it necessary to grant peculiar privileges or *fueros* to the territories conquered by the Christian army.

In this way its use gradually declined until at last, in 1241, it was, with few exceptions, confined to the towns of Cordoba, or rather to the towns of Andalusia; although it was always the object of special consideration at the Court of the Kingdom, and above all by Alfonso X, and by his son Don Sancho, who ordered its observance at Talavera, without distinction, between Mos-Arabians and Castilians.

It was thus preserved until the reign of Alfonso XI, who published the *Ordenamiento de Alcalá* in order to harmonize the contradictory elements of law, plunged into the most frightful confusion by the extraordinary liberality of his ancestors.

The author of the *Ordenamiento de Alcalá* endeavored to relegate it to the inferior position of a fuero, but its merit and value were so highly regarded that both monarchs and tribunals preferred it to the Fuero Real and Leyes de Partidas, in spite of the declarations made concerning the Laws on Prelation as to the relative importance of the different codes, disregarding the Fuero Juzgo.*

---

* Of foreigners, Montesquieu (Esprit des Lois, 1, b. 28, chap. 7), Mably and Robertson (Histoire de Charles V, introd., No. 32, s. 3), Cujaccius (De-Feudis, b. 2, tit. 11), and others, perhaps often with insufficient knowledge or examination, criticise the code.

Such scholars as Guizot (Curso de Historia de la civilización europea, leccion 3a), Gibbon (Decline and Fall of the Roman Empire, chap. 28, vol. 4), Savigny (Revue Francaise, 1828, No. 6, p. 202), the critic Sempre, Ferrand, Legrand, and d'Clussi, besides the learned Spanish author Francisco Martinez Marina, praise and extol its virtues.

Evidence of its worth is furnished in the reign of Charles III by the important decision of the Council, published in 1779, upon reference of a case from the Chancery of Granada; it was ordered that a law from this code should be applied in preference to another law from the Partidas, and it was held that *"as said Law of Fuero Juzgo is not derogated by any other, you should abide by it on determining on this or similar business, without attaching much importance to those from the Partidas."*

By decision of the Council, its authority exceeds that of those two Codes, and the legal force of this last disposition cannot be denied.

After this decision, no dispute can be had about the existence to-day of the Gothic-Spanish legislation. Although its application may be limited or rare, part of the Fuero Juzgo is included in the later collections, and while other portions do not entirely harmonize with the social, juridical, and political spirit of the epoch, many of its laws can be found, in some form, in the present Spanish Civil Code.

Its influence on modern law has been large and transcendental, and it has been a firm basis for Spanish jurisprudence, which has resisted the influence of opposing civilizations; neither subsequent laws, nor the most carefully selected opinion have been able to obscure the wise precepts and philosophical maxims contained in its pages. This Code is perhaps the most famous, the most important, and the most regular and complete of all the bodies of law, formed after the fall of the Roman Empire; the one which has the highest standing among those of its time. In it are found the germs of many of the great political principles which long years afterwards were proclaimed by far advanced nations.*

Various editions of the Fuero Juzgo have been published; those worthy of especial mention are: That of Peter Pithou, in Paris, in 1579; one of P. Andrés Escoto and Lindembrog in Germany; and another of Canciani in 1660, reprinted in 1792; of D. Juan Antonio Llorente, with preliminary introduction and index, in Madrid, in 1792, and the one of the Royal Spanish Academy of 1815, which is probably the most perfect of all, as it was made

---

* In the Gothic customs were embodied principles and morals from which in time were evolved the constitutional basis of the Republic of Iceland, the Magna Charta of England, and the American Declaration of Independence.

with the assistance of the Codes of Vigilan, the most ancient of which was the one written in 976 by the monk Vigila and his assistants Sarracin and García, all of the monastery of Albelda in Rioja from which it took the name of Albeldense.

THE ARABIC ELEMENT.

The origin of the Arab race, like that of many others, is a matter of conjecture. Some writers basing their reasons on Hebrew records have included the entire nation under the titles of Ishmael and Joptan, and Mohammedan evidence on the subject can have little more weight than the Jewish from which it is believed to be derived.

A race of southern origin appears to have been the first one that history recognizes in control of Arabia, and the oldest and principal one of the Arabic monarchies was that of Yemen, the seat of its government being on the site of the abandoned town of Mareb, in the extreme south, which afterwards was removed to Sanaá.

The Yemenite kings, descendants of Kahtan, and Himyar, "the dusky," a name suggesting African origin, and each bearing the surname of "Tobba," a word of African etymology, signifying "powerful," are said to have reigned, with few dynastic interruptions, for about two thousand five hundred years, governing nearly all the Peninsula.

Arabic chroniclers state that they subdued the whole of central Asia, reached the boundaries of China, and had in an early age overrun northern Africa. That they possessed a vigorous and partially civilized government is attested by the literary and architectural relics of the times.

Their sovereignty was overthrown 529 A. D. by an Abyssinian invasion, and was re-established 603 A. D. as a dependency of the Persian Empire, until 634, when it was finally absorbed by Mohammedan conquest.

The race was composed of two branches; the "Arab" or pure race of the south, and the Mostareb of the north, probably of Asiatic origin.

The Arabs were idolators of celestial bodies up to the time Mahomet appeared among them. By his genius, bravery and good policy, with great difficulties, he overcame their religion and taught his followers to believe in one soul, an eternal and all powerful God, the Creator of heaven and earth and of all that is in them. He commanded the use of certain practices of ablution and purification, enjoining likewise daily prayers, almsgiving and religious pilgrimage to the Temple of Alharem.

Mahomet finally reunited the previously disconnected tribes, and imbued his followers with a fanatical zeal for Islam, inspiring them with the most ardent desire for its extension throughout the world.

Before the appearance of Mahomet, the Arabs were accustomed to compute their years from the Ethiopian Wars, in which the grandfather of Mahomet totally routed the King of Ethiopia, but after the celebrated Hegira, the flight or retirement of Mahomet and his followers from Mecca to Medina Yatrib on July 16, 622 A. D., they began to count their years from that important event.

At this time Mahomet was about fifty years of age, and he died in the eleventh year of the Hegira. Upon his death, the chief Moslemah chose six electors from their number and by these men were subsequently selected the first five Khalifs and successors of Mahomet.

It was due to the marshalship of General Muza Ben Noseir, a soldier of much capacity and many endowments, that the innumerable tribes of Barbary were finally brought into subjection; and the permission of the Khalif Walid or Abulabas having been obtained, the invasion of Spain was attempted by Muza ordering General Taric Ben Zeyad (the one-eyed), a captain of great renown, to debark on the southern coast of Andalusia with a select body of cavalry to reconnoitre the country in which a Christian of Tanja (Tangiers) acted as his guide.

The first invasion took place about 710 A. D., and was so successful and met with such little resistance that a general invasion of the country was planned which was carried forward with much zeal and haste, the invading army landing on Green Island (now nearly submerged) opposite Algeciras. Taric fortified himself on Gibraltar, then called Gebal Taric or Mount Taric in his honor, and, according to the statement of Xerif Edrix, burnt his ships to deprive his troops of all hope of flight.

Seventeen hundred Christians opposed the landing of Taric on the mainland but were, after several skirmishes, put to flight, as likewise the flower of the Gothic cavalry sent against them by King Roderic, and the country was rapidly overrun by the Moslems in every direction.

Roderic succeeded in getting together an army of ninety thousand men on the plains of Sedonia with which to oppose the invaders, but although the Goths outnumbered four to one, the trained and hard troops of Taric, they, owing to the degenerating influence of Roman life with which they had come in contact, had lost much of their natural prowess and old time martial vigor, and, although not lacking in bravery, their skill and endurance were not equal to the test.

After three days of a fiercely contested and sanguinary conflict on the Guadalete Roderic and his principal chiefs were killed, and his army routed the last of July, 711 A. D. This battle marked the downfall of the Goths, and led to the rapid subjection of Spain, save the Asturias and the Biscayne Mountains, to Moslem dominion.

Conde states that that "the conditions imposed on the conquered nation were such that the people found consolation rather than oppression in the presence of the conquerors; and when they compared their then fate with that which they had previously endured, could not fail to consider the change a fortunate one.

"The free exercise of their religion, a careful preservation of their churches from all injury, the security of their persons, with the unimpeded enjoyment of their goods and possessions,—such were the first returns which they received for their submission to the stranger, and for the tribute (a very moderate one) which they paid to their victors.

"But there was yet more; the fidelity of the Arabs in maintaining their promises, the equal-handed justice which they administered to all classes, without distinction of any kind, secured them the confidence of the people in general, as well as of those who held closer intercourse with them: and not only in these particulars, but also in generosity of mind, and in amenity of manner, and in the hospitality of their customs, the Arabians were distinguished above all other people of those times."

ARABIC DOMINION.

The Spanish-Arabs possessed no special civil and municipal codes. The Khalif, his Viceroys or Amirs ruled largely by precepts of the Koran, which served in all Mohammedan countries both for law and gospel.

Arabian annalists take great pleasure in recording brilliant acts of justice, generosity and forgiveness in the administration of particular Khalifs, but these shine as the voluntary actions of an autocrat who was supreme and who often might have been guilty of injustice by following his own caprices or one-sided opinions, especially as fixed grounds of administration were wanting. Under the great expounders of the Koran, a system of political ethics was attempted; and that can hardly be called a despotic dominion which in practice must govern itself by religious laws read in every mosque; expounded by the Friday preachers, taught in schools; and, by divine authority, made quite as binding upon the governors as upon the governed.

Starting with the supremacy of the Khalif, the system of government included the appointment of *Ulemas* or wise men — the Moslem Witenagemot,— a body which in later days contained three classes,— the *Imams,* who were the chief ministers of religion; the *Muftis,* who expounded the law; and the *Kadis* or dispensers of justice.

The provinces, generally seven in number, were intrusted to the care of *walis* or governors, who reported, at stated times, to the central government, but who often, like the Roman proconsuls, aspired to independent authority, and thus gave a momentum to the decline of Arabian power in the Peninsula.

The department of justice was intrusted, under the special vizier, to numerous judges or *kadis,* who were possessed of extraordinary powers.

Law courts and juries as existing to-day were unknown.

There were two tribunals, the great and the small *shortah,* the head of each being called *sahíbu,* and the *sahíbu* of the great *shortah* could investigate and punish offenses committed by people of the highest degree, including princes of the blood.

The head of the small *shortah* only had cognizance of crimes and misdemeanors committed by the lower classes.

Thus justice was administered "in the gates," upon an elevated seat, surrounded by guards. Each party to any suit could plead his own cause before the *kadi* or *sahib,* but the head of the household was supreme in cases affecting wives and children.

The power of the judges grew to be fixed and irreversible, and Ibn Sa'id tells that "whenever a judge summoned the Khalif, his son, or any of his beloved favorites to appear in his presence as a witness in a judicial case, whoever was the individual summoned would appear in person,— if the Khalif, out of respect for the law; and if a subject, for fear of incurring his master's displeasure."

The authority of the kadis took cognizance of all offenses against morality, and they could punish any offender with death.

Among the Eastern Arabs, and probably in Spain, a first theft was punished by the loss of the left hand and by plunging the stump into boiling tar or oil; a second, by cutting off the left foot; a third, the right hand; a fourth, the right foot; at last, by death.*

Among these officers of justice was one in each town called the *mohtesib,* whose duty it was, as it is that of a similar officer *mohtesib aga* to-day in Turkey, to daily ride through the shops and markets, with an attendant carrying a pair of scales; he regulated weights, measures, and prices, and punished false weights and measures, and attempts at extortion, with great severity.

The Arabs held women in little regard; their appreciation of the weaker sex is expressed in their proverb "Consult a woman, and then do just the opposite of what she tells thee." They had no place in the moral and spiritual world, and were only of value from the physical point.

The condition of women among the Spanish-Arabs, however, continued to improve and was better than that existing in the Orient. The marriage contract might only be verbal, but the better classes confirmed it before the kadi, and for them the ceremonies of betrothal and espousal were formal and elaborate.

A wife might be twice divorced and twice taken back, even without consulting her wishes; but if divorced a third time, she could not be taken back without her consent.

The Koran and the Sunneh prescribe a table of kinship and affinity within which a man was forbidden to marry, not unlike that prescribed by the Church of England.

---

* Observe similar penalties inflicted on the American Indians. Las Casas' Destruction of the Indies.

The number of wives permitted to a Moslem by the Koran was four (most of them exceeded this number), and they might be either of his own faith, Christian, or Jewess, but no Mohammedan woman could marry any one but a Mohammedan.

Appointments to office among the Moors were independent of favoritism. The best men, suitable for positions on account of their learning, energy and honesty, were selected from the rich class, or made rich in advance, as no salaries or fees were paid, so that there might be no temptation to dishonesty or corruption, and the great desire of all public officers appears to have been to gain an extended reputation for wisdom, dignity and probity.

In the regulation of agriculture and the irrigation of lands for that purpose, no nation has ever possessed more just and beneficial laws than the agrarian edicts of the Spanish-Arabs; evidences of which still exist in parts of Spain, especially in Valencia where, when the Moors were driven out, King Jayme, who was wise enough to appreciate their great skill and progress in irrigation, decreed that "water should be taken and used in the order that was established of old, and was customary in the times of the Saracens."

In Granada when Ferdinand and Isabella planted their standard on the Alhambra, they recognized that, however they persecuted their enemies, it was good policy to preserve their admirable system of irrigating canals, and those who consented to change their faith were guaranteed protection in the enjoyment of their estates and irrigation rights and customs, some of which are embraced in the present irrigation code of Granada.

The influence which the Arabic invasion and dominion exercised over Spanish legislation was extraordinary and lasting. It can be reduced to four heads:

First. The destruction of the national union and the creation over the ruins thereof of numerous small nationalities or new states, such as the kingdoms of the Asturias, Léon, Galicia, Pamplona, Sobrarbe, Ribagorza and Aragon, and the counties of Castile and Barcelona.

Second. The disregard of existing laws, on account of changed conditions, and the influence which the active social classes acquired by virtue of their needed support, sought for by the Crown, and stimulated and rewarded by the Monarchy throughout the reconquest.

Third. The consequent destruction of legislative unity and the creation of a multiplicity of legislation, which inspired not only a diversity of territories or states, but of social classes in them, through the granting of privileged laws to the nobility and clergy and of special charters to the popular or municipal element.

Fourth. The preservation of certain Arabic customs and laws, especially those relating to agrarian and irrigation privileges and rights.

THE RECONQUEST PERIOD.

The invasion of the Saracens brought to the Spaniards and to all Europe new days of trouble with all the brutal instincts of war and intolerance. Jurisprudence disappeared in the waging of a religious struggle which lasted nearly eight centuries, and this same struggle, together with the sentiments and passions which it awoke and the institutions over which it threw its shadows, changed the destinies of humanity, giving life to a new civilization as distinct in its tendencies as in its causes.

The *Fuero Juzgo* continued, nevertheless, to be the law of the Spaniards even after the catastrophe at Guadalete.

The Spaniards and Goths took refuge in the mountain fastnesses of the Asturias and Biscayne Mountains to commence there the reconquest, naturally preserving the traditions and laws of the Gothic monarchy, and thus it is that the *Fuero Juzgo* was continually the "fuero" (the law) of the crown of Léon, the first kingdom which was formed after the Saracenic invasion.

As the reconquest progressed, the necessities of society changed, and the Visigothic laws were found insufficient to govern the country and people in this perpetual state of war with Saracens, because there was arising a new monarchy, with new conditions and elements, out of the ruins of the old one.

The monarchy of Alaric did not resemble that of the people of the Spanish Marca led on by Pelayo against the Arabs who then held possession of the country.

The Gothic government was a monarchy that was established over the Spanish provinces of the Roman Empire; certain of its power, although it preserved a personal system of castes between conquerors and conquered, it had a tendency to join the two peoples into one and to create an independent kingdom united by the ties of a common interest, and from the beginning to form a system of laws which all should share alike. It resembled less the liberal monarchy which began in the time of Recared, and which rested at its foundation on the power of the national assemblies which commenced under the name of the Councils of Toledo.

A conquering race like that of Alaric, had nothing in common with the Spanish people who, making war against the Arabs, were moving to and fro against the power of the new conquerors.

A nation which did not profess the same religion as the subjects of Recared and his successors, could not resemble the people of Léon and Castile who, united by a religious bond, fought in the name of God and the Fatherland against a dominant people who professed the Mussulman faith. In this interminable struggle, it was the varied fortune of war which decided the fate of the people who were seeking emancipation.

The Gothic and Spanish races became separated, each community and each individual making war independently on his own account, and consequently, as they continued to drive the Arabs towards the interior of the monarchy, each community, each captain of guerrillas was proclaiming independence, accordingly giving his orders and forming a system of government appropriate to the moment.

The nobles (*hijos-dalgos*) and the grandees (*ricos-omes*) who waged war against the Arabs took possession of communities, recaptured and disposed of the same almost as sovereigns. The councils which followed extended their jurisdiction over the Saracens, proclaiming also their dominion and independence. Others established abbeys and monasteries among the people whom they governed, and this was the beginning of the nobility of Castile, the origin of councils and communities, free towns or *los pueblos de behetria* and monasteries, each with its seigniory, with its laws and fueros and with its jurisdiction over the territory conquered. These different aristocracies, independent of one another, governed by different uses and laws, were united by no other ties than that of a common dependency upon the Crown.

The various fueros and codes, which were in effect in those times under different monarchs and counts of Castile, were born from many different sources; the famous *Becerro de las Behetrias,* the *fueros municipales,* the military fueros or those of the (fijos) *hijos-dalgos,* and over all these was formed the *Fuero Viejo* of Castile.

FUEROS.

From the success of the Saracenic invasion until the convening of the Cortes of Alcalá of Henares and the Ordenamiento of Alcalá, or from 712 until 1348, the legislation of Spain is known as the local or foral period on account of the multiple aspect which legislation assumed during that time.

This period is especially marked by the power and influence gained by the nobility and the great number of fueros granted.

Broadly speaking, the word "fuero" comprises uses or customs, local law, privileges, exemptions or franchises authorized by public power to diverse classes or districts.*

In a more precise sense it has had and has to-day many different meanings. In olden times and especially in the language of the middle ages the following were called fueros:

1. The compilations of general law codes such as the *Fuero Juzgo,* the *Fuero-Real,* etc.

2. The uses and customs, which, consecrated by a general and constant observance, came to acquire, in course of time, the force of unwritten law.

3. The letters of privileges, exemption from payment of certain taxes, the granting of gifts, mercies, enfranchisements and liberties.

4. *Las cartas pueblas* or charters to build towns by which the owner of the land made a contract with settlers as colonists relating to the conditions under which they should cultivate and use it, and which were generally reduced to the payment of a certain tax or to the acknowledgment of vassalage.

5. The instruments or deeds of donation executed by any lord or proprietor in favor of any private persons, churches or convents, granting them any lands, possessions or districts with annexed exemptions and privileges.

6. Declarations made by magistrates about penalties and fines imposed and the cases in which the penalties of the Fuero Juzgo should be applied.

---

* Marina considers "fuero" in five different meanings, not including the processal use of the word. Ensayo Hist. Crit. on Leg., vol. 1, book 4, No. 1.

7. Municipal fueros or letters given by kings and lords which embraced ordinances, civil, criminal, administrative, political, and processal laws to strengthen the communities of towns and cities, to constitute them into municipalities and to insure them a just and moderate government in harmony with the constitution of the kingdom.

In a Juridical Sense.

8. The place of holding a court of justice.

9. Judgment, the jurisdiction and power of judging, in which sense it is said that such a cause or suit belongs to the *fuero ecclesiastico,* if it belongs to the jurisdiction of the Church; that it belongs to the *fuero secular* if it comes under the secular jurisdiction; and that it is of *mixto fuero* (*mixti fori*), if it belongs to both jurisdictions.

10. The tribunal of the judge to whose jurisdiction the criminal or the defendant may be subjected is called *fuero competente.*

11. The district or territory within the limits of which each judge exercises his jurisdiction.

Fuero, considered in the sense of jurisdiction or place of judgment, is divided into common and special or privileged.

Fuero ordinario or common fuero is the authority for investigating and the place where all civil and criminal suits are tried, excepting those which belong to special or private courts of justice or tribunals; and *fuero especial ó privilegiado,* or special or privileged fueros, is the authority for investigating and the place where the civil or criminal lawsuits of certain classes only are tried.

There are several kinds of privileged or special fueros; as for instance, fuero of the Church, military fuero, fuero of the navy, commercial fuero, municipal fuero, etc.

The *fuero ordinario* or common fuero also comprises all of the suits and classes of persons which have not obtained an express exemption from it; and the special or privileged fueros are mere exceptions and not theretofore extended to any other persons or suits than those for which the law has provided.

Fueros under a nobiliary aspect comprised two institutions, *señorios* (seigniories) and *feudos* (feuds), the former of which some have confounded with the well-known meaning of the latter.

Señorio in Spain was not an institution exclusively of the nobility as it lacked the elements of fealty and vassalage and pertained to different classes as an outgrowth of the reconquest; it was exercised by the king, nobility, clergy and the people as well.

There were four classes of *señorios: solariego, abadengo, behetria* and *realengo,* each marked by peculiar privileges or exemptions.

MUNICIPAL FUEROS.

The extent of the estates and the great influence acquired by the nobility and clergy, at this period, seriously threatened the royal power and prerogatives. This condition was fortunately counteracted by special legislation, the *fueros municipales* or municipal fueros which strengthened a new power in the state,— the democratic charters of the people. Municipal fueros, however, had previously existed, but from this time on they became an increasing and important factor in checking the encroachments of the aristocracy.

It is quite generally conceded that the first of these granted was the Fuero of Léon, authorized by Alfonso V in 1020.

Among the earliest are also those of Nájera, authorized by Sancho, Mayor of Navarre, and confirmed in 1076 by Alfonso VI when that city was incorporated in Castile; that of Logroño in 1095 by the same monarch; and that of Sahagún by Alfonso VI in 1085 and 1096 which was curtailed by Alfonso VII in 1152 on account of the too liberal prerogatives granted to the monastery of that town.

In the twelfth century may be cited the fueros of Alcalá of Henares in 1114; Toledo, Salamanca and Escalona in 1118 by Alfonso VII, Molina in 1154, and Palencia, Haro, Zamora and Cuenca in 1181, 1187 and 1190, respectively, by Alfonso VIII.

The municipal fueros are much inferior to the Fuero Juzgo as a scientific collection of laws; they represent legislation caused by an extreme and unnatural condition of affairs, growing out of the unsettled times, and were a necessity at that period to obtain the support of different localities in the great work of the reconquest.

They may also be considered as the restoration and development of the laws of the primitive tribes which populated the Iberian Peninsula, recognizing as they did uses and customs of long standing.

There is no complete work on this subject; the one of Juan de la Reguera Valdelomar considers many of the fueros of Castile, Léon, Asturias, Galicia, Sepúlveda, Córdoba and Seville; the collection of municipal fueros and *cartas pueblas* of Castile, Léon, Aragon and Navarre by Thomas Muñoz y Romero; works on the subject by the Madrid Academy of History, Aureliano Fernandez-Guerra, Feliciano Callejas, and Julian Sanchez Ruano, also a general work by the French jurisconsult Albert Du Boys.

FUERO OF HIJOS-DALGOS (HIDALGOS).

This code, which is also known under the name *Ordenamiento de Nájera y Fuero de las Fazañas y alvedríos y de las costumbres antiguas de España,* is essentially a nobiliary code, including the clergy as well as the nobility. On account of the numerous and influential classes to which it applied, it came to be recognized as more in the nature of a general code than its name would signify.

The elements which constituted this work were the usages and customs of Castile, the *fazañas* or *facimientos* and the *alvedríos,* the second of which included the sentences or judgments as a result of litigation, and the third the decision of arbitrators.

Original copies of the code are not extant and many of its original laws appear to have been suppressed; as a result little of its contents are known, excepting what is contained in title 32 of the Ordenamiento of Alcalá.

FUERO VIEJO DE CASTILLA.

Many of the laws which should form part of the Fuero of the Hijosdalgos belong to another legal collection, known as the Fuero Viejo or Ancient Code of Castile which dates from 1212.

This work, believed to have been framed in the Cortes of Nágera, and attributed to Sancho Garcia, is based largely on the *fazañas** of the nobility of that period, many of the laws of the Ordenamiento of the Cortes of Nágera, and the fueros of some of the towns and cities, like Sepúlveda, Logrono, Granon and others.

During this epoch, the feudal principle was evolved in Spain, and in order to regulate it and to keep it within certain bounds, the

* Fazañas, sentences given in suits.

Fuero Viejo of Castile, the Fuero of Albedrios,* and the *fazañas* were published.

The Fuero Viejo originated with the nobility, who, on account of the alarm which they felt at the increasing power of the other classes, demanded of the king that their fueros be confirmed. Alfonso X, instead of acceding to their demands, ordered that their fueros be collected and unified and, in the meantime, permitted them to exercise their customary privileges until the publication of the Fuero Real.

This caused much opposition from the nobility, and in order to conciliate them, Peter I reformed the Fuero Viejo, added new dispositions, and in 1356 promulgated it as a general code.

As better known in the edition of Asso and Manuel, it is composed of five books, classified under thirty-three titles, comprising two hundred and twenty-nine laws.

Book 1 treats of public law, king's prerogatives, rights of vassals, rules of combat, feudal laws, etc.

Book 2 treats of penal laws.

Book 3 treats of the organization of tribunals, laws of procedure, etc.

Book 4 treats of civil law, principally of contracts, prescription, public works on lands, and possession.

Book 5 continues the subject of civil institutions, dowry, donations between husband and wife, protection of orphans, disinheritance, illegitimate children, etc.

The most notable edition of this Code was published by Asso and Manuel in 1771. The works of Pidal in his *Adiciones al Fuero Viejo* and Manrichalar and Manrique in their *Historia de la legislacion Español,* are also deserving of mention.

NOTE.—As to the obsoleteness of this Code, see Nov. Recop., book 3, tit. 2, law 3.

* Fuero of Albedrios, laws of arbitration.

CHAPTER II.

Fuero Real.

At this period of Spanish history, it is worthy of notice that each province, city and town was governed independently by special laws, and that any citizen could decide to live by himself and independently of all others. In one section the Fuero Juzgo was in force, in other parts the Fuero Viejo, and in some places neither the one nor the other, while Castile with its conglomeration of beliefs, institutions, and rival interests offered the spectacle, not of a people united by common ties but of a disorganized monarchy and a disruptured society which was beginning to dissolve on account of the shock of so many antagonistic elements.

In this state of affairs, the necessity was more manifest than ever that society should be organized under a system of laws common to all and under a government which was to the utmost the personification of the general welfare. Alfonso X, the Wise, comprehended perfectly the necessity, and, with this object in view, in 1255 published the *Fuero-de las Leyes,* commonly known as the Fuero Real, and also known under the names, *Fuero del libro, Fuero de la Corte, Fuero Castellano, Fuero de Castilla, Libro de los Concejos de Castilla* and *Flores de las leyes.*

The Fuero Real is a collection of laws, fueros, and uses of the Castilian monarchy of the epoch in which it was published. It is a code of the Middle Ages which then satisfied society and the necessities of the times, which reflected the spirit and customs of the thirteenth century, a work of immediate application and of national character, acceptable and important as a monument of Spanish jurisprudence and of no less interest as a historical monument for the study of those distant times, not well understood even up to the present age.

The Fuero Real is divided into four books, comprising seventy-two titles and five hundred and forty-five laws.

Book 1 treats principally of religious and political matters, of public offices, attorneys, under the designation of *voceres, procuradores,* etc.

Book 2 considers the subject of procedure, evidence, judgments, appeals, etc.

Book 3 embraces civil law, marriages, donations, legacies, partitions, successions, guardianships, contracts, etc.

Book 4 treats of penal laws, Jews, Saracens, interments, navigation, etc.

There are three editions of this Code; one by Montalvo, in 1500, another by the Academy of History of Madrid in 1836, and still another to be found in the collection of codes of La Publicidad.

ESPÉCULO.

The second code attributed to Alfonso X is the Espéculo,* which appears to have been formed in the Cortes of Palencia about 1258, and which includes many of the laws of Justinian, canonical laws from the Decretales, recognized public principles of that period, and some of the municipal fueros of Léon and Castile. It is analogous to the Partidas. The Espéculo comprises five books, divided into fifty-four titles including six hundred and fifty-seven laws.

Book 1 treats of the legislative power, and the laws, and contains various dispositions in relation to the religious order.

Book 2 considers the political constitution of the kingdom.

Book 3 treats of public law, and the greater part is given up to the military service.

Books 4 and 5 consider judicial organization and procedure.

The Madrid Academy of History issued an edition of the Espéculo in 1836.

ORDENAMIENTO DE LAS TAFURERIAS.

Is a collection of forty-four laws, promulgated in 1276 by Alfonso X, which are of little importance to-day, except from a historical standpoint.

They were devised to regulate and correct the evils of gaming of that age.

---

* Espéculo is from the Latin word *speculum,* or reflector of the laws.

LEYES DEL ESTILO.

This work, which embraces two hundred and fifty-two laws of the time of Ferdinand IV (1295–1312) contains many provisions relating to and explanatory of the Fuero Real, and treats principally of procedure, rules, forms, customs and practices in conducting suits, entering appeals, etc., also of contracts and testaments.

It is essentially a code of practice, the greater part of which is to be found in the Novisima Recopilacion. It was not compiled officially, but by observation and usage acquired legal sanction.

A private edition was published by Cristobal de Paz of Salamanca, early in the seventeenth century.

THE ORDENAMIENTO OF ALCALÁ.

Was published in 1348 under the name *Ordenamiento Real de Alcalá,* and embraces the laws of the Cortes of Ciudad-Real or *Leyes de Villareal,* those formed in the Cortes of Segovia, those of the Ordenamiento of Nájera and others formed in the Cortes of Alcalá in 1348.

The collection consists of thirty-two titles including one hundred and twenty-five laws, the first fifteen of which relate to procedure, the next three to contracts, the nineteenth to testaments, the following four to crimes, penalties and usury, the twenty-fourth to weights and measures, and the remainder to penalties, taxes and tolls, meaning of certain words, prescription of civil and criminal jurisprudence, order of prelation of the codes, duels, the custody of castles and fortresses, vassalage, and the last to the observance of the Ordenamiento of Alcalá.

An edition of this collection was published by Asso and Manuel in 1774, and on the same subject can be cited the History of Legislation by Manrichlar and Manrique, and a discourse by Pastor and Huerta.

ORDENANZAS REALES DE CASTILLA OR ORDENAMIENTO DE MONTALVO.

This collection of laws, also known under the names of *Ordenamiento Real* and *Leyes de los Ordenamientos,* was formed by Alonzo Diaz Montalvo, a distinguished jurisconsult during the reign of Ferdinand and Isabella; it consists of eight books, divided into one hundred and fifteen titles, including one thousand one hundred and thirty-three laws.

The first book, comprising twelve titles, treats of religious matters; the second, of twenty-three titles, is occupied with political laws, judicial organization, and administrative affairs; the third book, of eighteen titles, considers laws of procedure; the fourth, of eleven titles, treats of caballeros, hidalgos, and exemptions; the fifth, of fourteen titles, embrace matrimony, successions, contracts, and other general provisions of civil law; the sixth, under three titles, of the administration and collection of public revenues; the seventh, under five titles, of municipal government; and the eighth, under nineteen titles, embrace penal legislation.

There have been numerous editions of this collection, the first being published in Huete in 1484, and the last in the collection of La Publicidad in 1872.

LEYES DE TORO.

The laws of Toro are in no sense a code; they were formed in the Cortes of Toledo in 1502, which had for its object to explain, to correct defects and to supply omissions in existing legislation, which on account of so many independent enactments had fallen into great confusion.

This work is not arranged under any general plan, lacks titles and methodical order, the eighty-three laws embraced following one after another without regard to subject-matter.

One of the most notable features of this body of laws is the recognition and restoration of certain Germanic elements of law, *gananciales* or property of the conjugal society, and *mejoras* or advantages are treated of at some length, while the subject of *mayorazgos* or right of succession of the first-born is a new feature of legislation.

The Leyes de Toro are largely devoted to civil law, little attention is paid to procedure, and the last seven laws consider penal legislation. Asso and Manuel, in speaking of these laws, stated "that they were so highly thought of at the time of their publication that they took a first place among those of the kingdom." It appears that no official editions of these laws have been published for the reason that they are included in the Nueva and Novisima

Recopilacion. Commentaries on the collection by Cifuentes, Antonio Gomez, Llamas and Molína, and Pacheco (continued by Gonzales and Serrano) deserve mention.

THE PARTIDAS.

The famous laws of the Partidas wrought a radical change, a revolution, in Spanish laws and jurisprudence.

This renowned work was taken largely from the Roman laws, which laws, sometimes translated and the decrees literally copied and published in the spirit of the doctrines of the Italian school, formed a code destined to obscure the municipal codes, to stifle the spirit of localism and feudal anarchy which was controlling the legislation and customs of Castile. The Partidas, on account of its excellency as a doctrinal work, above all other codes, was naturally the work which greatly attracted the attention of jurisconsults.

It was made the object of general study by men dedicated to the legal profession, a subject for thoughtful men which soon made it the jurisprudence and common law of Spaniards, and which was recommended by all learned writers, in spite of the difficulties and obstacles with which it had to struggle from the day of its publication. The result was that it impressed the stamp of unity and strength upon the monarchy which, until then, it had not possessed since the invasion of the Arabs.

The celebrated laws of the Partidas are considered as an admirable work of the wisdom and philosophy of the age in which they were published; but it is not alone under the aspect of a code and of the rules which ought to govern in a work of this class that the merit of this compilation should be judged. Under such an aspect it is much inferior to the Fuero Juzgo and the Fuero Real.

The Siete Partidas is a work of law, the most complete treatise of jurisprudence which had been published up to that time; and it was not only a highly scientific work but one of immediate and necessary application for the society for which it was intended.

In those times the history of Rome, and above all, the study of its laws and practices was the favorite subjects for the investigations of the wise men of Europe and its schools. They read and interpreted the sayings and sentences of the most celebrated jurisconsults; they praised their works, and Alfonso X showed the greatest admiration for this kind of study. He was recognized as one of the leading wise men of his time, the Justinian of Spanish jurisprudence, and demonstrated his wisdom by giving to posterity his work of the Siete Partidas, the most notable code of that age.

The title, Siete Partidas, was not the original name of this work, which was first known as the *Libro de las Leyes* or *Fuero de las Leyes.*

The names *Posturas* and *Septenario* attributed to it appear to have little foundation in fact, and the word *Siete* was afterwards prefixed on account of the work being divided into seven parts.

The work was begun in 1256, but as to its date of completion there is uncertainty, some claiming that it was published in 1263; the name Partidas was not officially given to it until 1347 by Alfonso XI.

The theoretical legal force of this Code is determined by law I, tit. 28 of the Ordenamiento of Alcalá, reproduced in law I of Toro, and to be found also in the Nueva and Novisima Recopilacion. It is considered as supplemental law which is applicable after the preceding codes and the Nueva and Novisima Recopilacion, but in practical use it has a wider scope on account of the inapplicability of many of the old fueros.

This work is divided into seven parts, each commencing with one of the letters of its author's name, Alfonso, and has one hundred and eighty-two titles comprising two thousand four hundred and seventy-nine laws.

The First Partida embraces twenty-four titles, and treats in the first two of the natural law, and the laws of usages and customs, and in the remaining twenty-two, of the Holy Catholic faith, religious doctrines and canonical laws. In it may be seen the extraordinary power exercised by the Pope and clergy of this period.

The Second Partida comprises thirty-one titles on public law, the first eleven of which treat of the prerogatives of the crown, duties of the monarch to his family, officers and subjects, and religious observances, the next nine of the duties of the people towards the sovereign, and the remaining titles of military captives and ransoms, public education, professors, organization of studies, etc.

The Third Partida treats, under thirty-two titles, first of justice and the benefits of its wise administration, the next twenty-seven treat of the judicial organization and rules of procedure, and the last five of dominion, prescription, possession and servitudes. Nearly all its provisions are Roman law.

The Fourth Partida is divided into twenty-seven titles and is dedicated to civil law, principally on family relations, while the last seven consider feudalism, relations between lord and vassal, and a dissertation on friendship which has little logical sequence with what precedes it.

The Fifth Partida comprises fifteen titles taken from the Roman civil law on the subjects of obligations and contracts, including loans, deposit, commodatum, sales, partnerships, mortgages and pledges.

The Sixth Partida, under nineteen titles, continues the subject of civil legislation, the first fifteen treating of testaments, codicils, of heirs, successions, executors, intestates and partitions, and the last four of minors, orphans, tutorships, curators, etc.

The Seventh Partida treats of penal legislation under thirty-four titles, with a termination explaining the meaning of certain words and rules. While defective in some particulars, this partida is considered as the most advanced legislation of the times on criminal laws. There have been numerous editions of this Code published, from time to time, the earliest being that of Montalvo in 1491, and the one that is most highly prized of Gregorio Lopez, published under royal authority in Salamanca in 1555, of which a copy was deposited in Simancas.

The edition of 1807 by the Spanish Academy of History is inaccurate, and in a decision of the Supreme Court of March 27, 1860, it was decided that in case of a conflict between this edition and that of Lopez, the latter should prevail.

LA NUEVA RECOPILACION.

This compilation, which was sanctioned by Philip II, in 1567, comprises all the laws which were not considered abrogated, published since the Fuero Real and Partidas, some of the laws of the Fuero Juzgo, of Estilo, of Montalvo, almost all those of the Ordenamiento of Alcalá, the Laws of Toro, and subsequent ones, including, in a separate book, the *Autos Acordados* or *Pragmaticas, Cédulas, Ordenes,* and *Decretos* of the Supreme Court up to the year 1745.

The Nueva Recopilacion embraces three thousand three hundred and ninety-one laws, divided into nine books, under two hundred and fourteen titles.

Book 1 treats, under twelve titles, of religious matters.

Book 2 consists of twenty-five titles and considers public officials of the Supreme Court, the judges of the Courts of Chancery of Valladolid and Granada, and certain court details.

Book 3, embracing nineteen titles, considers the organization and duties of various tribunals and other offices of a political and judicial character, also rules for the exercise of certain professions, and important provisions on the jurisdiction of the tribunal of commerce of Bilbao. (See Book 9, tit. 2 of Nov. Recop.)

Book 4, under thirty-three titles, is devoted to the civil law of procedure.

Book 5 treats, under twenty-five titles, of civil institutions, including marriages, successions and contracts.

Book 6, comprising twenty titles, considers the diverse political conditions of Spaniards, their rights and duties, the court and ambassadors, fortifications, mines, taxes, etc.

Book 7, also embracing twenty titles, treats of city councils and towns, municipal franchises, administration, and disconnectedly of nautical matters, etc.

Book 8 considers, under twenty-six titles, penal laws and procedure.

Book 9, under thirty-four titles, treats of royal revenues, taxes, frauds, etc.

The Autos Acordados comprise one hundred and ten titles and one thousand one hundred and thirty-four laws.

The Nueva Recopilacion instead of making existing legislation more intelligible, for which purpose it was undertaken, had the opposite tendency.

LA NOVISIMA RECOPILACION.

Strictly speaking, this is neither a civil, commercial, political, penal, religious nor processal code, yet it embraces material on all these subjects, as well as police regulations for the City of Madrid.

On account of the defects of the Nueva Recopilacion, the necessity for a complete codification of the laws had long been realized, and finally Charles IV intrusted Juan de la Reguera Valdelomar, an official of the court of Granada, with this task, which was completed in 1802, within the short period of two years. It has been much criticised, especially by Marina in his *Juicio critico de la*

Novisima Recopilacion, and is commented upon by Reguera in his *Extracto de la Novisima Recopilacion.* Considering the age in which it was compiled, it is much inferior to the Fuero Juzgo which preceded it by eleven centuries, and to the Partidas of six centuries before.

Its legal force is determined by Royal Decree of July 15, 1805, which renders these laws superior to all preceding legislation. However, its effect was to render Spanish legislation more confusing than ever, as it left intact the order of prelation of codes, provided in law 1 of Toro, and law 28, tit. 1 of the Ordenamiento of Alcalá. Only one edition of this compilation has been officially issued, that of 1805, entitled *Novisima Recopilacion de las leyes de España,* composed of six volumes, five of which were printed at that time, and the sixth, which contained the supplement, in 1829.

The elements of this code are substantially those of the Nueva Recopilacion, arranged under a different plan with some laws suppressed and later ones added. It consists of twelve books, three hundred and forty titles, and four thousand and twenty laws.

Book 1, under thirty titles, treats of the church, its property, rights, and officials, and observers of the Faith.

Book 2, under fifteen titles, considers ecclesiastical jurisdiction.

Book 3, under twenty-two titles, treats of the king, succession to the crown, royal decrees, the palace, and the court.

Book 4, under thirty titles, embraces the subject of royal jurisdiction and of the Supreme Court of Madrid.

Book 5, under thirty-four titles, treats of the courts of chancery and the audiencias.

Book 6, under twenty-two titles, relates to nobles, their privileges, vassals, knights, fueros, foreigners, military service and tribunals, obligations, and taxation.

Book 7, under forty titles, treats of civil government, political and economical questions of cities and towns.

Book 8, under twenty-six titles, considers the sciences and the arts, and educational institutions.

Book 9, under twenty titles, treats of commerce, maritime courts, money and mines.

Book 10, under twenty-four titles, is taken up with contracts, successions, marriages, and other matters of a civil nature.

Book 11, under thirty-five titles, treats of civil procedure.

Book 12, under forty-two titles, considers criminal law and procedure.

The supplement, including the three indices of the above compilation, is divided into twelve books of seventy-five titles, comprising one hundred and twenty-two laws; it embraces laws published in 1805 and 1806, and some of the ordinances omitted in the compilation, and was ordered published in 1808, but was not issued until 1829.

The original object was to have a series of supplements published periodically, embracing the subsequent laws, but this scheme was never realized.*

COLLECTIONS AND DIGESTS OF LAWS FROM 1807 TO THE MODERN CODES.

From September 24, 1810, to September 14, 1813, all laws enacted in Spain were compiled in four volumes and are known as *Colección de decretos y ordenes de las Cortes,* the title of which was changed, upon the return of Ferdinand VII to power, to *Decretos del Rey D. Fernando VII.* This collection was increased to six volumes by March 7, 1820. From this latter date until 1823, six more volumes appeared under the first name mentioned.

Laws promulgated from 1823 until 1833 were published with an introduction entitled *Decretos del Rey Nuestro Señor Don Fernando VII y Reales Ordenes,— Resoluciones y reglamentos generales expedidos por la Secretaría del Despacho universal y Consejo de S. M. Muerto el Rey.*

From 1833 to 1846 this collection was called the *Collección de las leyes, decretos y declaraciones de las Cortes y de los Reales decretos, Ordenes y Reglamentos generales expedidos por los respectivos Ministerios,* and in 1846 took the name *Colección legislativa,* which it has since retained, and to which have been added the decisions of the Supreme Court and those of the Council of State which are still being so published.

The period from 1807 until 1810, which was not included in the first collection cited, has been covered by the work of José Indalecio Caso in the form of a general index.

One of the best private collections of laws of this period, and the

* The ancient codes of Spain were published in full, in two volumes, in Madrid, in 1885, by Marcello Martinez Alcubilla.

one generally used, is that of Casas y Moral, entitled the *Recopilación legislativa de España desde* 1810*á*1859; also can be mentioned the *Diccionario jurídico-administrativo,* by a society of lawyers under the direction of Carlos Massa Sanguineti; and, especially, the excellent and complete work of Marcelo Martínez de Alcubilla, *Diccionario de la administration español,* which is systematically arranged both by dates and by subjects, and of which the fifth edition is the latest and best. This compilation is now being issued one volume annually, and covers all branches of law enacted.

For convenient reference the compilations of the modern civil and penal laws, annotated in two volumes, by Medina y Maranon, are recommended.

TABLE OF KINGS.

Visigothic Kings.	A. D.
Alaric I . . . . 382 to	411
Athaulf	415
Sigric	415
Wallia	420
Theoderic I	451
Thorismund	454
Theoderic II	466
Euric	484
This king, after conquering the Suevi and other races, is considered the founder of the monarchy.	
Alaric	507
Gesaleic	510
Amalaric	531
Theudis	548
Theudisel	549
Agila	554
Athanagildo	567
Leova I	572
Leovigild	586
After destroying the barbarians that still remained in the country, he was the first king who ruled over the whole of the Peninsula.	
Recared I	601
Summoned the 3d Council of Toledo, renounced Arianism, and became the first Catholic king of Spain (587).	
Leova II	603
Witteric	610
Gundemaro	612
Sisibut	621
Recared II	621

Visigothic Kings (continued).	A. D.
Swintila	631
Sisinand	635
Tulga	640
Chindasvint	650
Recesvint	672
Wamba	680
Ervigio	687
Egica	701
Witiza	709
Don Rodrigo	711
The Moors entered Spain and defeated Don Roderic at the battle of Guadalete, who disappeared there. The Moors occupied in the two following years almost the whole of the Peninsula, and governed under the dependence of the Kaliphs of Damascus.	

Moorish Rulers in Spain.

Amirs dependent on the Kaliphs of Damascus	711–715
Independent Kaliphate established by the Ummeyah family, the capital being Cordova	755–1009
Kings of Taifas, governors of the provinces which declared themselves independent during the last Kaliphate, Hischen II	1009–1090

Moorish Rulers in Spain (continued). A. D.

The Almoravides from Africa established themselves in the Moorish territory of the Peninsula 1090–1157

The Almohades conquered the Almoravides 1157–1212

Kings of Granada. The Moorish domination is reduced to the kingdom of Granada, 1226–1492

The rule of the Moors in Spain ends in 1492, at the conquest of Granada.

Kings of Asturias, Leon, and Castile.

Pelayo (the re-conquest begins) . . . . 718 to 737
Favila 739
Alonso I, el Catolico 757
Favila I (fixes his Court at Oviedo) 768
Aurelio 774
Silo 783
Mauregato 788
Bermudo I, el Diacono 795
Alonso II, el Casto 843
Ramiro I 850
Ordoño I 866
Alonso III, el Magno 910

Divided the kingdom of Galicia, Leon, and Asturias, among his sons, the three following kings.

Garcia 913
Ordoño II 923
Fruela II 924

Ordoño fixed his Court at Leon, and here end the named kings of Asturias.

Alonso IV, el Monje 930
Ramiro II 950
Ordoño III 955
Sancho I, el Craso 967
Ramiro III 982
Bermudo II 999
Alonso V, el Noble 1028
Bermudo III 1037

The territory of Castile, which formed a separate state, governed by *Condes*, passed to Doña Sancha and Don Fernando I, who entitled themselves Kings of Castile and Leon.

Kings of Asturias, Leon, and Castile (continued). A. D.

Fernando I and Doña Sancha . . 1065
Sancho II, el Fuerte 1073
Alfonso VI 1108
(Conquered Toledo in 1085.)
Doña Urraca 1126
Alfonso VII, el Emperador 1157

At his death the kingdoms of Castile and Leon are divided among the six following kings:

Sancho III (Castilla) 1158
Fernando II (Leon) 1188
Alfonso VIII (Castilla) 1214
Alfonso IX (Leon) 1230
Enrique I (Castilla) 1217

Doña Berenguela, who abdicated the crown of Castile in favor of her son, Fernando III, who inherited also the crown of Leon, from his father, Alfonso IX.

Fernando III, King of Castile and Leon 1252

He conquered Cordova, Jaen, and Seville.

Alonso X, el Sabio 1284
Sancho IV, el Bravo 1295
Fernando IV, el Emplazado . . . 1312
Alonso XI 1350
Pedro I, el Cruel 1369
Enrique II, el Bastardo 1379
Juan I 1390
Enrique III, el Doliente 1407
Juan II 1454
Enrique IV, el Impotente 1474
Doña Isabel, la Catolica 1504
Fernando V, de Aragon 1516
Doña Juana, la loca 1555
Felipe I, el Hermoso (first king of the House of Austria) 1505
Carlos V, Emperador 1558
Felipe II 1598
Felipe III 1621
Felipe IV 1665
Carlos II 1700
Felipe V (first king of the house of Bourbon) abdicated in 1724
Luis I 1724
Felipe V 1746
Fernando VI 1759
Carlos III 1788
Carlos IV, abdicated 1808
Fernando VII 1833
Isabel II, dethroned 1868
Provisional Government 1871
Amadeo, abdicated 1873

Kings of Asturias, Leon, and Castile (continued). A. D

Spanish Republic 1873
Alfonso XII . . . . 1875, died 1886
Cristina, Regent (Alfonso XIII) . . . .

Kings of Navarre.

The inhabitants of Navarre began the reconquest from the middle of the eighth century. Their rulers were called condes, or kings, until Sancho Abarca widened the territory; from that time they are always called kings of Navarre.

Sancho Abarca . . . . 980 to 994
Garcia III 1000
Sancho III, el Mayor 1038
Garcia IV 1057
Sancho IV 1076
Sancho Ramirez V 1092

This king, and the two that follow, were likewise kings of Aragon.

Pedro I 1106
Alfonso, el Batallador 1134
Garcia Ramirez IV 1150
Sancho VI, el Sabio 1194
Sancho VII, el Fuerte 1234

Here begin the kings of the House of Champagne.

Teobaldo I 1253
Teobaldo II 1270
Enrique I 1273
Juana I 1304

On her marriage with Philip le Bel, Navarre passed to the House of France.

Luis Hutin 1316
Felipe le Long 1320
Carlos I, de Navarra, IV, de Francia 1329
Juana II 1343
Carlos II, d'Evreux 1387
Carlos III 1425
Doña Blanca y Juan I 1479
Francisco Febo 1483
Catalina 1512

Fernando V, of Navarre, took possession in 1512 of Navarre, and it was then incorporated with Castile.

Kings of Aragon.

Aragon belonged to the kingdom of Navarre until Sancho III gave it to his son Ramiro. A. D.

Ramiro I . . . . 1035 to 1063
Sancho I 1094
Pedro I 1104
Alfonso I, el Batallador 1134
Ramiro II, el Monje 1137

Aragon and Cataluña are united.

Petronila 1162
Alfonso II 1196
Pedro II 1213
Jaime I, el Conquistador 1276
Pedro III 1285

Sicily is united to Aragon.

Alfonso III 1291
Jaime II 1327
Alfonso IV 1336
Pedro IV 1387
Juan I 1395
Martin 1410
Fernando, el de Antequera. . . . 1414
Alfonso V 1458
Juan II 1479
Fernando, el Catolico.

Aragon passes to the crown of Castile.

Counts of Barcelona.

In the eighth and ninth centuries Cataluña belonged to Charlemagne and his successors. Wilfredo was the first independent Conde.

Wilfredo, el Belloso . . . 864 to 898
Borrell I 912
Suniario 917
Borrell II and his brother Miron 992
Ramon Borrell 1018
Ramon Berenguer I 1025
Ramon Berenguer II 1077
Berenguer and Ramon Berenguer III 1113
Ramon Berenguer IV 1131

Ramon Berenguer V married Doña Petronila de Aragon, and this kingdom was incorporated with the Condado de Cataluña.

Contemporary Sovereigns.

The periods have been selected during which leading events in Spanish history have occurred.

A. D.	Spain.	England.	France,	Popes.
800	Alonso II el Casto	Egbert	Charlemagne	Leo III.
877	Alonso III el Magno	Alfred	Louis II.	John VII.
996	Ramiro III.	Ethelred II	Hugh Capet	Gregory V.
1075	Sancho II	William the Conqueror.	Philip I.	Gregory VII.
1155	Alfonso VII	Henry II	Louis VII	Adrian IV. Breakspeare.
1245	San Fernando X.	Henry III	St. Louis	Innocent IV.
1345	Alfonso XI.	Edward III	Philip VI	Benedict VI.
1360	Pedro el Cruel	Edward III	John II	Innocent VI.
1479	Isabel la Catolica	Henry VII	Charles VIII.	Innocent VIII.
1516	Fernando de Aragon	Henry VIII	Francis I.	Leo X
1516	Carlos I	Edward VI	Henry II	Paul III.
1556	Felipe II	Elizabeth	Charles IX	Pius IV.
1644	Felipe IV	Charles I	Louis XIV	Innocent X.
1705	Felipe V	Anne	Louis XIV	Clement XI.
1760	Carlos III	George III	Louis XV	Clement XIII.
1788	Carlos IV.			
1808	Fernando VII	George III	Napoleon I	Pius VII.
1833	Isabel II	Victoria (1833–1886)	Louis-Philippe / Napoleon III.	Gregory XVI. and Pius IX.
1868	Prov. Government			
1873	Republic		French Republic	Leo XIII.
1875	Alfonse XII			
1886	Cristina, queen-regent			

The date Era on old inscriptions prevailed in the Roman dominions, and arose from the date of the particular payment of taxes, *aes, aera.* It commenced in the fourth year of Augustus Caesar. To make the Era correspond with the *Anno Domini,* thirty-eight years must be added, thus: A. D. 1200 is equivalent to Era 1238. The Moorish Hegira commences from Friday, July 16, A. D. 622 — Era 660. The New Style was introduced by Gregory XIII into Spain in 1582. October 5, of the Old Style, was then called October 15. This must be remembered, for the New Style was only introduced into England in 1751.

TABLE OF ANCIENT CODES.

Year.	Tables.	Books.	Titles.	Laws.	Vols.
466–485.	Code of Euric or of Tolosa	....	....	....	....
506.	Breviarium Aniani	....	....	....	....
687–700.	Fuero Juzgo	12	55	578	1
1212.	Fuero Viejo	5	33	229	1
1255.	Fuero Real	4	72	545	2
1258.	Especulo	5	54	675	5
1263.	Siete Partidas	7	182	2479	4
1300.	Leyes de Estilo	....	....	252	1
1348.	Ordenamiento de Alcala	7	32	125	1
1490.	Ordenamiento Real	8	115	1133	2
1502.	Laws of Toro	....	....	83	1
1567.	Neuva Recopilacion	9	214	3391	2
1680.	Recopilacion de Indias	9	218	6474	3
1745.	Autos Acordados	9	110	1134	2
1805.	Novisima Recopilacion	12	330	4020	4

[Continued at end of book.]

PART SECOND.

CHAPTER I.

The Civil Law in Spain.

From the fall of the Empire all Roman laws were comprised in their civil codes, a confused mass of canonical, political, administrative, mercantile, penal, and processal laws, but, by the lapse of time, influenced by the constant law of progress, a complete decomposition was to result and out of this heterogeneous combination, each branch had to emancipate itself: the independence of one after another assisting in this regeneration.

As Christian truths and influence became more universally observed, and civil and religious societies were established and supported by temporal and ecclesiastical power and secular legislation, there naturally resulted the emancipation of canonical legislation first of all.

This movement facilitated the separate and early establishment of the penal laws more promptly than others on account of the recognized necessity and the frequency of their application in the establishment of law and order.

Commercial relations made great strides and became more extensive and, consequently, assumed an important position in the eyes of the law. Contracts were abbreviated and made more practical than the cumbersome formalities of the civil law provided, with the result that the mercantile law came into an independent existence.

The modern legislative spirit, awakening with the philosophical movement at the end of the eighteenth century, initiated a new phase in public law, which became known, in general: 1 — as interior, and, 2 — as exterior law, the first being classed as political, and as administrative law, political law treating of the organization of public powers, and administrative law of the relations between the governing officials and the governed; the second or exterior law treated, first, of public international law which considered matters and relations between foreign states, and second, of private international law which had for its object to fix the rights and duties of the subjects of a country residing in a foreign land.

All these causes separated the general body of laws before existing and made the decomposition mentioned necessary.

In Spain similar vicissitudes in the civil law have been observed, as well in the Fuero Juzgo as in the municipal laws, including, in the so-called civil law, a collection of juridical precepts of very diverse origin and dispositions:* in the Fuero Real and principally in the Partidas are still observed the temporal law united with the canonical.

At the beginning of the nineteenth century by virtue of the great spirit of codification which characterized it, there was separated from the civil law the foreign elements which contaminated its true nature.

The mercantile law which had to emancipate itself from the *Consulado del Mare* and the *Ordenanzas de Bilbao* became a complete commercial code in 1829.

The principle of national sovereignty having become proclaimed in France, there resulted the representative system, and, consequenly, these doctrines extended their influence to Spain, and, being aided by the success of the War for Independence, the Constitution of 1812 was promulgated, emancipating with it political as well as administrative law.

The same succeeded with penal law; the unfortunate attempt of 1822 to restore it successively recurred with better success in 1848, in 1850 and in 1870. The laws of procedure also came from this common base, together with provisional regulations for the administration of justice, and the organic law of the tribunals.

Thus discarding from the Spanish civil law foreign subject-matter, it reduces itself, in fact, to common law (*derecho común*), and to local, statutory or provincial law (*derecho foral*).

Usually common law is understood as the law of Castile, and local law as that which has governed or is in force in Aragon, Catalonia, Mallorca, Navarre, Valencia and some parts of the Vascongada provinces.

---

* Modern critics profess that they can see a specially near kinship between Spanish and Icelandic laws. Pollock and Maitland, History of the English law, vol. 1, p. 6.

This classification, though generally accepted, is not exact.

On account of the Saracenic invasion, it has been noticed that the unity of the destroyed monarchy was substituted by numerous small nationalities, which in their own way aided in the reconquest, one of which, although more extensive than the others, was Castile, but all existed independently with their own legislation, on which account as well as for other reasons, its legislation, strictly speaking, ought to be called by its provincial name or Castilian.

The laws abolishing señorios, those of desvinculación, of intestate successions, mortgage, matrimony, interdiction, civil registry, and many others which could be cited, are not peculiar to Castile but are Spanish in every conception of the word, and, consequently, in strict logic should be called common law as well as those laws dictated from the time of Philip the Fifth which concluded with autonomic legislation of almost all the provinces. Finally, it is to be noticed that the Spanish civil law has never been codified in the true meaning of the word.

The Partidas is a legal collection of laws which nearest approaches a codification but there is not yet a general code, much less a complete civil one, because the different branches of the law form a part of it.

In defining the Spanish system of legislation, in general, it may be said that it comprises a collection of compiled and codified laws, and that it continues as such, even after the partial codification of the civil law by which, until the present, the so-called common law is alone referred to, besides which there are a multitude of laws still subsisting.

THE CONSTITUTIONS OF SPAIN.

The first constitution of Spain was framed, during the enforced absence of Ferdinand VII, in the Cortes which was summoned and met in Cadiz in 1810, then one of the few cities unoccupied by foreign soldiers.

This constitutional Cortes was a popular body, made up of loyal and representative Spaniards, and it was convened to give a regular government and to maintain national independence in place of the disorganized state of affairs growing out of the Peninsular war. This representative Cortes promulgated the Constitution of 1812 which was received as the fundamental law of the land, and which, notwithstanding some errors, kept constantly before the people the one great principle of making the throne subordinate to the law.

The Cortes, which consisted only of one body, was intrusted with the government of the realm in subjection to the Constitution in recognition of that democratic principle that sovereignty resides in the people; the personal inviolability of the monarch was neutralized, so far as proper, by the direct responsibility of his ministers, and there were guards and checks which secured the rights of all classes from the encroachments of prerogative and power.

The Cortes, during its short term, reformed many abuses and established much that was wise, liberal and of promise.

The first act of Ferdinand, upon his restoration to power in 1814, was to overthrow the Constitution, forswear the oath he had voluntarily taken to support it, and to imprison and to drive into exile the faithful servants who had been loyal to him and to the best interests of the country.

The constitutional system was revived in 1820 and there was a brief struggle to maintain it, when France, through the influence of the Holy Alliance and the co-operation of other States, invaded Spain and by armed intervention put down the Constitution of 1812.

Canning's attitude in respect to the South American revolutions gave moral support to the American Monroe doctrine, and led to the opposition shown by Great Britain to the high-handed act of France, which attitude was further supported by England's recognition of the independence of several of the Spanish-American countries.

Ferdinand VII concluded his disastrous reign in comparative peace. He married a fourth wife, Maria Cristina of Naples, in 1829, and soon afterwards issued a "Pragmatic Sanction" abolishing the Salic law* in Spain in anticipation of the birth of a daughter and to exclude his brothers and their heirs from the throne. The birth of Isabel II in 1830 justified these precautions. She was proclaimed queen upon the king's death in 1833, with Cristina as regent, which led to the Carlist war, headed by Don Carlos, a brother of the deceased king.

Cristina was compelled to rely upon the liberals, and to conciliate them by the grant of a Constitution, the *estatuto real,* which established two chambers in the Cortes, chosen by indirect election.

This Constitution, influenced by Louis Philippe of France, failed to satisfy the advanced liberals, and the Cristinos became divided into two parties, the *Moderados* and the *Progresistas,* and the latter or progressive party by force of arms caused the revival of the Constitution of 1812.

In the constitutional Cortes of 1837 another organic law was adopted which had the sanction of both of the above political parties, and this Constitution was less democratic than the previous one, and, therefore, found more favor in the eyes of the nobility.

It retained the two chambers, originated by the "*estatuto real,*" suffrage was restricted, and the king was vested with veto power, and had the authority to convoke and dissolve the Cortes, a substantial voice in making new laws, and many of the details in the Constitution of 1812, improper for such an instrument, were eliminated.

In 1839, Espartero put an end to the Carlist war and, upon the flight of Cristina, as the head of the Progresistas, became regent in her stead until his downfall in 1843, and the accession of Isabella II at the age of thirteen.

The Constitution of 1845 was adopted under the auspices of Narvaez and the Moderado party, and the royal prerogatives were

---

* The famous clause in the Salic Law, by which, it is commonly said, women are precluded from succession to the throne, and which alone has become known in course of time as the Salic Law, is the fifth paragraph of chapter 59, in which the succession to private property is regulated.

not disregarded in its provisions. While many more rights and privileges than formerly granted were apparently secured to the citizens, they will be found upon careful examination to be dependent upon clauses of limitation which are confusing; for example, article 2 provides that "all Spaniards may print and publish their ideas freely without previous censorship, *but with subjection to the laws;*" and article 7, "No Spaniard shall be detained or imprisoned, or kept from his domicile, nor shall his house be forced, *except in those cases and in that manner which the laws may prescribe.*"

The Cortes was composed of two chambers, and the senators were appointed by the Crown and were unlimited, a wise precaution for the Crown in case the king lacked a majority. They were required to have certain qualifications, similar to provisions contained in the Constitution of 1876.

A deputy or representative could be chosen for every district having thirty-five thousand inhabitants, except the colonies, which in 1837 lost the right of representation in the Cortes which they had enjoyed under the Constitutions of 1812–20.

Deputies were required to have a yearly income of six hundred dollars from real property or to pay fifty dollars a year in direct taxes.

Notwithstanding the prescribed representative system and the safeguards on paper, the government could on any occasion return a majority in its favor with little effort, so great was its power.

In 1869, subsequent to the exile of Isabel II, the national Cortes was convoked for the purpose of establishing a permanent form of government, and a committee of fifteen, the republican deputies being excluded, were chosen to draw up a constitution.*

* The birth of the two new political parties, the Conservatives and the Liberals, date from this period, and as nearly all Spanish-American countries have to-day similarly designated parties, founded on similar lines, the most excellent differentiation of these parties by Senor Sagasta, the late premier and one of the leading statesmen of Spain, is given herewith:

"The separation and difference between the Conservative and the Liberal parties takes root in the Revolution of 1868. Before that date the lines of separation of the political parties were founded neither in principle nor doctrines, public men occupying themselves with preparing for the downfall of Isabel II, which they considered indispensable to the establishment of a liberal and parliamentary *regime* in Spain. After the triumph of the Revolution of 1868 and the proclamation of the constitutional monarchy in 1869, the politics of the parties were founded on democratic principles, which are generally called individual rights. Since that date, the parties recognizing the constitutional monarchy, have been formulated and defined, so that to-day

The restoration of a monarchical form of government, with constitutional guarantees, was clearly provided, as well as freedom of the conscience, and the principle was recognized that "all governments derive their just powers from the consent of the governed;" a senate, council of state and other new features were added.

Deputies from Cuba, however, were not again admitted to the Cortes until after the adoption of the Constitution of 1876.

---

they are not only perfectly distinguished, but each has a clear and definite program. We may, therefore, classify the Conservative and Liberal parties as the two grand nuclei of political forces, around which, as occurs in England, the different tendencies of Spanish politics are grouped. In this way the Conservative party has already absorbed a great part of the Reactionaries. Those have entered into it who give more importance to religious peace than to the form of government; that is, those who are called Ultramontanes, and have separated from the Carlists. Equally figures within the Conservative party, or at its side, the remnant of the old Moderate party, which was overcome in 1868. On the other hand are collected in the Liberal party those Republicans who give preference to principles over forms of government, and who strive to give efficiency to those principles by co-operation with the Liberal party. In the same attitude are found those other liberal elements the advocates of which, without being defined by a political organization, yet rely upon legal means for the triumph of their ideas and opinions. Among these may be included the Free-traders, a large part of those called Socialists, and especially the Labor party.

"At the extremes of both the great parties are two groups of real importance in the country, who accept neither reforms nor legal methods of procedure, and whose reliance is upon force to accomplish the triumph of their ideals. These are the Carlists, on the extreme right, and the Red Republicans, on the extreme left.

"Conservatives and Liberals sustain the constitutional monarchy with equal energy, there being on this point no essential difference between the Constitutions of 1869 and 1876. Both likewise defend the rights and guarantees of individual liberty, of property, of free speech, of liberty of the press, and of establishing associations. These rights are confirmed in all the constitutions, and it is in the methods of guarantees that the difference between the parties begins. It is the aspiration of the Liberal party to commit the complete guarantee of liberty and of the electoral system to the courts of justice, while the Conservative party is inclined to exercise a guardianship over all these rights by means of administrative authorities and of ministerial power. It is in this diverse tendency that the distinction between the two parties originates and the difference of program is born. In its platform the Liberal party affirms the development and accomplishment not only of what are termed public liberties, which are conceded by all, but the evolution of democratic principles as proclaimed by the Revolution of 1868. * * * The Conservative party has in reality no program confronting that of the Liberal. Its attitude is expectant, and, so to speak, negative. It does not recognize the urgency of any great reforms or great legislative measures, except as concern the finances, and the organization of the military forces — questions which belong to no party, and the solution of which appertains specially to no one political group. Given this attitude, the Conservative party is reduced to opposing the reforms of the Liberal party, but at the same time it declares itself disposed to accept them if practice demonstrates their advantage, and in any way to respect legal solution to which co-operation is

Alfonso, son of Isabel II, was heralded to Spain from his exile upon the failure of the Republic,* by a *pronunciamiento* which was opportune and popular, and the government which he set up, although not chosen by the Cortes, was accepted as legitimate.

The liberal Constitution of 1869 was discarded and that of 1845 accepted as Isabel II in her abdication, in various acts under the latter, had assented to the succession of Alfonso, her son.

Under the guiding hand of one of the most eminent of Spanish statesmen, the late Antonio Cánovas, many reforms were inaugurated which laid the foundation of the Constitution of June 30, 1876. This Constitution which continues in force provides for a hereditary monarchy, confined to the late Alfonso XII and his descendants. Under it the king is inviolable, he exercises the executive power, while the legislative power is vested in the king and the Cortes.†

---

given by an intelligent and active discussion. There is, therefore, no other difference than that of grade and conduct. Essential differences and opposing plans do not exist, except that in the application and the development of each of the questions indicated an opposition between the two parties may be formed at any moment. What remains to be stated will make clear this point.

"Although the two great lines of action which constitute the policy and purpose of the Liberal party have been traced, yet for a fuller understanding it is necessary to call attention to two points of view, which, although not formulated, define and characterize its tendency, inasmuch as they relate to the complete and historical policy of Spain.

"One of these refers to the connection between Church and State, the basis for many years of struggles and revolutionary movements. The Liberal party, which has affected disamortization and the suppression of tithes, has lately succeeded in marching in perfect agreement with the Holy See and restoring an understanding, for a long time disturbed, between the State and the Church. Any idea of the separation of the two powers is foreign to the policy of the Liberals. On the contrary, in the harmony of the two powers, the party seeks the complete re-establishment of peace in Spain, and a change in the opinions and conduct of the clergy, who, after having been ultramontane, now begin, under the intelligent action of Leo XIII, to separate themselves completely from politics, and to devote themselves to their purely spiritual mission. This transformation of the clergy is too beneficial for the Liberal party to ignore, or to allow it to excite any difficulty which might reproduce the worst periods of modern Spanish history."

* Republicanism has been a failure in Spain for lack of republicans. The late ex-president Castelar, who was one of the most ardent and capable expounders of republicanism, when questioned, a few years before his death, as to his changed attitude in support of the throne, is related to have said that the Spanish people have acquired many of the privileges and rights for which he had struggled so long, and that the time was not yet ripe for them to appreciate and to exercise self-government.

† In Spain, legislation is often accomplished, during a recess of the Cortes, by a royal decree, a legislative act, by which also the Constitution may be suspended or abrogated, and there is no remedy except by an election or by a pronunciamiento, as courts of last resort, with original or appellate juris-

A Senate and House of Deputies compose the Cortes and it meets annually. Representatives from Cuba were again admitted in 1878.

The king convokes, suspends, or dissolves the Cortes, appoints the presiding officers of the Senate, and nominates cabinet ministers, through his prime ministers.

Local self-government is allowed to the various provinces, districts, and communes,* and while the Catholic religion is maintained as that of the state, private Protestant services are allowed.

---

diction, to afford adequate relief when constitutional rights have been disregarded, do not exist in Spain. The decisions of the Supreme Court are only of a recommendatory nature, and not binding on the legislative or sovereign power, which is the case with corresponding courts in most European countries.

* By the organic law of 1871, the country is divided into departments, each department into *arrondissements*, and each *arrondissement* into cantons. The canton is an aggregate of rural communes or parishes.

CONSTITUTION OF THE SPANISH MONARCHY.*

TITLE I.

Spaniards and their rights.

1. The following are Spaniards: (1) Spaniards born in Spanish territory. (2) The children of a Spanish father or mother, even though born outside of Spain. (3) Foreigners who have obtained naturalization papers. (4) Those who, having obtained said papers, have acquired a residence in any town of the Monarchy.

The citizenship (*calidad*) of a Spaniard is lost through acquiring that of a foreign country or by accepting an office from another Government without the permission of the King.

2. Foreigners may unrestrictedly establish themselves in Spanish territory and exercise therein their industry or devote themselves to any profession, for the discharge of which the laws do not require diplomas of proficiency issued by the Spanish authorities.

Those who are not naturalized cannot fill, in Spain, any office which carries with it authority or jurisdiction.

3. Every Spaniard is obliged to defend the country with his arms when called upon to do so by law, and to contribute, in proportion to his means, to the expenses of the State, province and municipality.

No one is compelled to pay a tax which is not passed by the Cortes or by the corporations legally authorized to impose it.

4. No Spaniard nor foreigner can be detained, except in the cases and in the manner prescribed by law.

Every person detained shall be placed at liberty or turned over to the judicial authorities within the twenty-four hours following the arrest.

Seventy-two hours after having been turned over to the Judge of competent jurisdiction, the person arrested shall be either set at liberty or remanded to prison.

The decision which may be rendered shall be communicated to the person interested within the same period.

* Promulgated June 30, 1876, and extended to Cuba and Puerto Rico, April 7, 1881.

5. No Spaniard can be arrested without an order from a competent Judge.

The warrant of commitment shall be ratified or annulled, after having heard the person presumed to be guilty, within the seventy-two hours following the commitment.

Every person detained or imprisoned, without the legal formalities having been complied with, or except in the cases provided for in the Constitution or by law, shall be set at liberty at his own request or at that of any other Spaniard. The law shall determine the summary mode of procedure in such cases.

6. No person shall enter the domicile of a Spaniard or of a foreigner residing in Spain without his consent, except in the manner and in the cases expressly prescribed in the laws.

The search of papers and effects shall always take place in the presence of the person interested or in that of a member of his family, and in their absence, in the presence of two witnesses, residents of the same town.

7. Administrative authorities can neither detain nor open correspondence intrusted to the mails.

8. Every warrant of imprisonment, search warrant or order for the detention of correspondence, shall state the reasons for the action.

9. No Spaniard can be compelled to change his domicile or residence, except by virtue of an order of a competent authority and in the cases prescribed by law.

10. The penalty of confiscation of property shall never be imposed, and nobody can be deprived thereof except by a competent authority and for sufficient cause of public utility, always after the proper indemnity has been paid.

Should this requisite not precede, the Judges shall protect, and, in a proper case, restore the possession to the person whose property has been taken.

11. The Apostolic Roman Catholic religion is that of the State. The nation binds itself to maintain the worship and its agents.

No one shall be disturbed in Spanish territory on account of his religious opinions nor for the exercise of his respective worship, reserving the respect due the Christian faith.

Nevertheless, no other ceremonies or public manifestations shall be allowed, but those of the State.

12. Everybody is free to select his profession and to learn it in the manner he may deem fit.

Every Spaniard may establish and support establishments for instruction or education, in accordance to law.

The State shall issue professional diplomas, and shall establish the conditions to be filled by those desiring to obtain them, and the manner in which they are to prove their proficiency.

A special law shall determine the duties of professors and the rules to which teaching in institutions of public instruction, supported by the State, provinces or towns, are to be subject.

13. Every Spaniard has a right:

To freely express his ideas and opinions, either by word or in writing, making use of the press or of any other similar means, without being subject to previous censorship.

To assemble pacifically.

To associate with one another for the ends of human life.

To address individual or collective petitions to the King, to the Cortes and to the authorities.

The right of petition cannot be exercised by any kind of armed force.

Nor shall it be exercised individually by any person forming part of an armed force, except in accordance with the laws of their institution, in so far as it may be related thereto.

14. The laws shall contain the proper rules in order to assure Spaniards a mutual respect of the rights granted them in this title, without conflicting with the rights of the Nation nor with the essential powers of the public authority.

Said laws shall also determine the civil and criminal liability to which the Judges, authorities and officials of all kinds who attempt to violate the rights enumerated in this title shall be subject.

15. All Spaniards are eligible for public employments and offices, according to their merit and capacity.

16. No Spaniard can be tried nor sentenced except by the judge or court of competent jurisdiction, by virtue of the laws existing before the crime was committed, and in the manner prescribed in the same.

17. The guaranties mentioned in articles 4, 5, 6 and 9 and in the first, second and third paragraphs of article 13, cannot be suspended in the entire Monarchy nor in a part of it, except temporarily and by means of a law, when necessary for the security of the State, under extraordinary circumstances.

Only in case the Cortes should not be in session and in a serious case and of well-known urgency, can the Government, under its responsibility, order the suspension of the guaranties referred to in the foregoing paragraph, submitting said order to the approval of the Cortes as soon as possible.

But in no case shall more guaranties than those mentioned in the first paragraph of this article be suspended.

Neither military nor civil officials are permitted to establish other penalties than those previously prescribed by law.

TITLE II.

The Cortes.

18. The power to make laws is vested in the Cortes with the King.

19. The Cortes are composed of two co-legislative bodies, having similar powers: The Senate and the Congress of Deputies.

TITLE III.

The Senate.

20. The Senate is composed of: (1) Senators in their own right. (2) Senators appointed for life by the Crown. (3) Senators elected by the corporations of the State and by the persons paying the highest taxes, in the manner prescribed by law.

The number of Senators in their own right and for life cannot exceed 180.

There shall be the same number of elective Senators.

21. The following are Senators in their own right:

The sons of the King and of the immediate successor to the Crown, who have attained their majority.

The grandees of Spain who are such in person, who are not subjects of any other power and who prove that they have an annual income of 60,000 pesetas, derived from real property of their own, or from rights enjoying the same legal consideration.

Captains-General of the Army and the Admiral of the Navy.

The Patriarch of the Indies and Archbishops.

The President of the Council of State, the Presiding Judge of the Supreme Court, the President of the Court of Accounts of the Kingdom, of the Supreme Council of War and that of the Navy, after having filled their office for two years.

22. Spaniards can only be appointed Senators by the King or elected by the Corporations of the State and highest taxpayers, who belong to any of the following classes:

1. President of the Senate or of the Congress of Deputies.
2. Deputies who have belonged to three different Congresses or who have exercised the deputation for eight Legislatures.
3. Ministers of the Crown.
4. Bishops.
5. Grandees of Spain.
6. Lieutenant-Generals of the Army and Vice-Admirals of the Navy and after two years' service.

7. Ambassadors, after two years' active service, and Ministers plenipotentiary after four years'.

8. Councillors of the State, *Fiscal* of the Council of State, and *ministers* and *fiscales* of the Supreme Court and of the Court of Accounts of the Kingdom, Councillors of the Supreme Council of War and of the Navy, and the Dean of the Court of Military Orders after two years' service.

9. Presidents or Directors of the Royal Spanish Academies, of History, of Fine Arts of San Fernando, of Mathematics, of Physics, of Natural Science, of Moral and Political Science and of Medicine.

10. Academicians by number of the said corporations, who are in the first half of the roll of their class; General Inspectors of the first class of the Corps of Road, Mine and Forest Engineers; regular professors in the universities, provided they have been in their category in active service for four years.

The persons included in the foregoing categories must furthermore enjoy an income of 7,500 pesetas, derived from their own property, or from salaries from employments which cannot be lost except for causes legally proven, or by pension, retirement or suspension with a salary.

11. Those who for two years previous possess an annual income of 20,000 pesetas or who pay 4,000 pesetas in direct taxes into the Public Treasury, provided they also have a title of the Kingdom, or have been Deputies to the Cortes, provincial deputies or mayors in the seat of a province or in towns having more than 20,000 souls.

12. Those who at any time before the promulgation of this Constitution have filled the office of Senator.

The persons who, in order to be Senators, should at any time have proven that they had a certain income, may, on becoming Senators in their own right, prove it, in order that it may be computed, by means of a certificate of the Registry of property showing that they still possess the same property. The appointment of Senators by the King shall be made by special decrees, and there shall always be stated therein, in accordance with the provisions of this article, on what title the appointment is based.

23. The conditions necessary to be appointed or elected a Senator may be changed by a law.

24. The elective Senators shall be renewed by half every five years and in full when the King dissolves this part of the Senate.

25. Senators cannot accept any appointment, promotion (unless by strict seniority), title nor decorations, during the sessions of the Cortes.

The Government may, nevertheless, appoint them to any commission within their profession or category required by the public service.

The office of Minister of the Crown is excepted from the provisions contained in the first paragraph of this article.

26. In order to take a seat in the Senate it is necessary to be a Spaniard, to have attained the age of thirty-five years, not to be subject to any pending criminal prosecution, nor disqualified to exercise political rights, and to have his property free from attachment.

TITLE IV.

The Congress of Deputies.

27. The Congress of Deputies shall be composed of the persons appointed by the electoral boards, in the manner determined by law. At least one Deputy shall be appointed for every 50,000 inhabitants.

28. Deputies shall be elected and may be re-elected indefinitely, by the means established by law.

29. In order to be elected a Deputy it is necessary to be a Spaniard, and a layman, of age, and in the enjoyment of all civil rights. The law shall determine with what kind of functions the office of Deputy is incompatible, and the cases of re-election.

30. Deputies shall be elected for five years.

31. Deputies upon whom the Government or the Royal Family confers a pension, office, promotion (not strictly by seniority) commission with salary, honors and decorations, shall discontinue in his office without the necessity of any declaration whatsoever if within the fifteen days immediately following his appointment he informs the Congress that he has declined the favor.

The provisions of the foregoing paragraph do not include Ministers of the Crown.

TITLE V.

Sessions and powers of the Cortes.

32. The Cortes shall assemble every year. The King shall convene, suspend and adjourn the sessions, and dissolve the elective part of the Senate and the Congress of Deputies, either separately or simultaneously, under the obligation, in such case, to reassemble the body or bodies, dissolved, within three months.

33. The Cortes must necessarily be convened upon the vacation of the Crown, or when the King should become incapacitated in any manner whatsoever for the Government.

34. Each of the two co-legislative bodies shall draw up the respective regulations for their proceedings, and shall be the judges of the qualifications of their respective members and the legality of their election.

35. The Congress of Deputies appoints its President, Vice-President and Secretaries.

36. The King appoints for each Legislature from among the Senators, the President and Vice-Presidents of the Senate, and the latter elects its Secretaries.

37. The King opens and closes the Cortes in person or through the Ministers.

38. One of the co-legislative bodies cannot meet without the other doing so also; a case in which the Senate discharges judicial duties is excepted.

39. The co-legislative bodies cannot deliberate together, except in the presence of the King.

40. The sessions of the Senate and of the Congress of Deputies shall be public and only in cases of a private nature may secret sessions be held.

41. The King and each of the co-legislative bodies shall propose laws.

42. Laws relating to taxes and to the public credit shall first be presented to the Congress of Deputies.

43. The resolutions in each of the co-legislative bodies shall be passed by a plurality of votes; but in order to pass laws a majority of all the members constituting the body must be present.

44. If one of the co-legislative bodies should refuse to pass a project of law or the King should refuse to sanction it, another project of law relating to the same object cannot be presented during that Legislature.

45. Besides the power of enacting laws, the Cortes, with the King, shall have powers:

1. To receive the oath of the King, of the immediate successor to the Crown and to the Regency or of the Regent of the Kingdom, to preserve the Constitution and the laws.

2. To elect a Regent or Regency of the Kingdom and to appoint a guardian for the King, should he be a minor, when prescribed by the Constitution.

3. To enforce the liability of the Secretaries, who shall be impeached by the Congress and tried by the Senate.

46. Senators and Deputies shall have immunity for their speeches and votes in the discharge of their office.

47. Senators cannot be indicted nor arrested without a previous resolution of the Senate, unless they may be found *in flagrante*, or the Senate should not be in session; but in every case notice shall be given to this body as soon as possible, in order that it may decide what would be done. Nor shall Deputies be indicted or arrested during the sessions without the permission of the Congress, unless they are found *in flagrante;* but in such case, and in case of indictment or arrest when the Cortes are not sitting, notice shall be given as soon as possible for its information and action. The Supreme Court shall take cognizance of criminal causes against Senators and Deputies in the cases and in the manner prescribed by law.

TITLE VI.

The King and his Ministers.

48. The person of the King is sacred and inviolable.

49. The Ministers are liable.

No order of the King can be carried out if not countersigned by a Minister, who, through this act alone, becomes liable.

50. The power to enforce the execution of laws is vested in the King, and his authority extends to all that relates to the preservation of public order in the interior and to the security of the State from without, in accordance with the Constitution and the laws.

51. The King sanctions and proclaims the laws.

52. He has the supreme command of the Army and Navy and disposes of the military and naval forces.

53. He grants military grades, promotions and rewards, in accordance to law.

54. It is also the duty of the King: 1. To issue decrees, regulations and instructions which may be necessary for the execution of the laws. 2. To see that justice is speedily and fully applied in the entire Kingdom. 3. Grant pardons to law breakers in accordance to law. 4. To declare war and make and ratify peace, afterwards informing the Cortes in writing thereof. 5. Direct the diplomatic and commercial relations with other powers. 6. To supervise the coining of money, on which his bust and name shall be placed. 7. Decree the inversion of funds devoted to each one of the branches of the administration within the budgets laws. 8. Confer civil offices and grant honors and titles of all kinds in accordance to law. 9. Unrestrictedly appoint and remove the Ministers.

55. The King requires authorization by a special law: 1. To alienate, assign or exchange any portion of Spanish territory. 2. To annex any other territory to the Spanish territory. 3. To admit foreign troops into the Kingdom. 4. To ratify treaties of offensive alliance, special commercial treaties, those containing stipulations of giving subsidies to any foreign power and all those which might individually bind Spaniards. In no case shall the secret articles of a treaty repeal the public ones. 5. To abdicate the Crown in favor of his immediate successor.

56. The King, before contracting marriage, shall inform the Cortes, for whose approval the marriage contracts and stipulations shall be submitted, and which must be the object of a law.

This rule shall also be observed with regard to the immediate successor of the King.

Neither the King nor his immediate successor can contract marriage with a person who is excluded from succession to the Crown by law.

57. The allowance of the King and of his family shall be fixed by the Cortes at the beginning of each reign.

58. The Ministers may be Senators or Deputies and take part in the discussions of both co-legislative bodies; but they shall have the right to vote only in the one to which they belong.

TITLE VII.

Succession to the Crown.

59. The legitimate King of Spain is Alfonso XII, of Bourbon.

60. The succession to the throne of Spain shall follow the regular order of primogeniture and representation, the prior line always being preferred to the subsequent ones; in the same line the nearer degree to the one more removed; in the same degree the male to the female, and in the same sex the person having the greater age to the one having the lesser.

61. After the lines of the legitimate descendants of Alfonso XII, of Bourbon, are extinguished, his sisters, his aunt, the sister of his mother, and their legitimate descendants, and those of his uncles, the brothers of Fernando VII, should they not be excluded, shall succeed in the order established.

62. If all the lines mentioned should extinguish, the Cortes shall make new designations, in the manner most advisable for the Nation.

63. Any doubt of fact or right which may arise in the order of succession to the Crown, shall be decided by a law.

64. The persons who may not be capable to govern, or should have done anything by which they deserve to lose the right to the Crown, shall be excluded from the succession by a law.

65. When a female reigns, the Prince consort shall not take any part in the Government of the Kingdom.

TITLE VIII.

The minority of the King and the Regency.

66. The King is a minor until he attains the age of sixteen years.

67. When the King is a minor, the father or the mother of the King, and in their absence, the relative nearest in line of succession to the Crown, according to the order established in the Constitution, shall immediately enter upon the duties of the Regency, and shall discharge them until the King attains his majority.

68. In order that the nearest relative may exercise the Regency, he must be a Spaniard, have attained the age of twenty-one years and not be excluded from the succession to the Crown. The father or the mother of the King may exercise the Regency only during the time they remain widowed.

69. The Regent shall take an oath of allegiance to the King and to preserve the Constitution and the laws, before the Cortes.

Should the Cortes not be in session, the Regent shall call them at once, and in the meantime he shall take the said oath before the Council of Ministers, promising to repeat it before the Cortes as soon as they meet.

70. Should there be no person entitled to the Regency, said Regency shall be appointed by the Cortes, and shall be composed of one, three or five persons.

Until this appointment is made, the Kingdom shall be temporarily governed by the Council of Ministers.

71. Should the King become incapacitated to exercise his authority and the incapacity should be recognized by the Cortes, the Regency shall be exercised, during the obstacle, by the first-born son of the King, if over sixteen years of age; in his absence by the consort of the King, and in the absence of the latter, by those called to the Regency.

72. The Regent and the Regency, in a proper case, shall exercise all the authority of the King, in whose name the acts of the Government shall be published.

73. The person designated in the will of the deceased King shall be the guardian of the King who is a minor, provided said person is by birth a Spaniard; should none have been designated, the father or the mother shall be the guardian, during the time they remain widowed. In their absence a guardian shall be appointed by the Cortes; but the charges of Regent and guardian of the King can be vested only in the father or mother of the latter.

TITLE IX.

The administration of justice.

74. Justice shall be administered in the name of the King.

75. The same Codes shall govern in the entire Monarchy, without prejudice to the changes determined by the laws on account of special circumstances.

There shall be but one law for all Spaniards in ordinary, civil and criminal suits.

76. The power to apply the laws in civil and criminal suits is vested exclusively in the superior and inferior Courts, and they cannot exercise any other functions but those of judging and seeing to the execution of the sentences.

77. A special law shall determine the cases in which previous authorization from the authorities or their agencies necessary in order to institute actions before the ordinary courts.

78. The laws shall determine the superior and inferior Courts which there shall be, their organization, their powers, the manner of exercising them, and the qualifications the members of the same are to have.

79. Trials in criminal matters shall be public, in the manner determined by the laws.

80. Associate Justices and Judges shall be irremovable and cannot be removed, suspended nor transferred except in the cases and in the manner prescribed by the organic law of Courts.

81. Judges are personally liable for every infraction of the law they may commit.

TITLE X.

Provincial Deputations and Municipal Councils.

82. In every province there shall be a Provincial Deputation elected in the manner determined by law and composed of the number of members designated therein.

83. In towns there shall be Mayors and Municipal Councils. The Municipal Councils shall be appointed by the residents, to whom the law grants this right.

84. The organization and duties of the Provincial Deputations and Municipal Councils shall be governed by their respective laws.

Said laws shall conform to the following principles: 1. Government and direction of the private interests of the province or of the town by the respective corporations. 2. Publication of the budgets, accounts and resolutions of the same. 3. Intervention of the King, and in a proper case of the Cortes, to prevent the Provincial Deputations and the Municipal Councils to go beyond the limits of their powers to the prejudice of general and permanent interests. 4. Determination of their powers with regard to the budgets, in order that the provincial and municipal budgets may never be in opposition to the tax system of the State.

TITLE XI.

Taxes.

85. Every year the Government shall submit to the Cortes a general budget of expenses of the State for the following year, and the plan of ways and means to cover the same, as well as the accounts of the accounting and application of the public funds, for their examination and approval.

Should it not be possible to pass upon them before the first day of the following fiscal year, the budgets for the previous year shall govern, provided the same may have been discussed and passed upon by the Cortes and sanctioned by the King.

86. The Government requires authority by means of a law to dispose of property of the State and to contract loans on the credit of the Nation.

87. The public debt is under the special protection of the Nation.

TITLE XII.

The military force.

88. The Cortes shall, every year, fix the permanent military force of the Army, as well as of the Navy, on the recommendation of the King.

TITLE XIII.

The Government of the Colonial Provinces.

89. The Colonial Provinces shall be governed by special laws; but the Government is authorized to apply to them, with the modifications it may deem advisable and informing the Cortes thereof, the laws enacted or which may hereafter be enacted for the Peninsula.

Cuba and Puerto Rico shall be represented in the Cortes of the Kingdom in the manner determined by a special law, which may be different for each of the two provinces.

Transitory Article.— The Government shall determine when and in what manner the representatives to the Cortes from the Island of Cuba are to be elected.

CHAPTER II.

THE MODERN CIVIL CODE OF SPAIN.*

The Spanish Civil Code, promulgated by Royal Decree of July 31, 1889, which is in force in Spain, Cuba, Puerto Rico, and the Philippines, notwithstanding the recent changes, is the basis of civil law in those Islands.

It owes its origin to the constitutional Cortes of Cadiz which, on February 5, 1811, approved the resolution of Deputy Espiga y Gadea to codify the most important branches of the Spanish laws. In furtherance of this project, a committee of the most distinguished men of the times was appointed in 1813 to accomplish the work, but, unfortunately, the violent reaction of 1814, the return of Ferdinand VII to the Spanish throne, suppressed these preparations.

Upon the establishment of a second constitutional regime in 1821, another committee of equal importance attempted to carry into effect the project of a civil code, part of which was published, but it was not concluded on account of the reaction in 1823.

Private interest kept the purpose alive, notwithstanding the opposition in official circles, and jurisconsult Don Pablo Gorosabal became the first to publish a project; another was later formulated by the celebrated public officer, Don Manuel Maria Cambronero, which was completed by other jurisconsults in 1836 and officially presented to the Cortes in 1839, but no action was taken in respect to it by the legislative power.

By Royal Decree of August 19, 1843, a general committee on codes, made up of twenty-four eminent men, was appointed, and subsequently another committee of six succeeded to the work and the latter, in 1851, laid before the government the project of a civil code, and this was printed and is now known as "The Project of 1851."

---

* This code was recently translated into French by the eminent jurisconsult A. Levé, of France, who pays a high tribute to it, claiming that it is more scientific than the Code Napoleon.

The committee fixed six general "bases" for the codification which was afterwards divided into sections.

This project was published, from time to time, to facilitate the examination, study and criticism of the codification and to induce the different tribunals, authorities, boards of lawyers, universities and persons interested to make suggestions and recommendations.

It is difficult to appreciate the difficulties encountered in this work and the prejudices overcome without studying the local or foral laws of Spain, peculiar to each province, and Spanish jurisprudence and political institutions.

The project, to which reference is made, consisted of three books: The first treats of persons; the second of the things; and the third of the modes of acquiring property.

In 1880, some bases were presented to the Cortes which the civil section of the Committee on Codes was to consider in the compilation of a civil code.

It appears that the public authorities were doubtful about the proceedings to be followed in reference to the formation of a code, and, to such an extent was this true that the Minister of Grace and Justice, Don Manuel Alonso Martinez, presented to the Chambers the first two books of the code, together with the bases referred to, in a completed condition.

Sometime later the Minister of Grace and Justice, Don Francisco Silvela, presented to the Cortes other new bases upon which to form a civil code. It is worthy of notice that so much importance was given to the enterprise by the public, in general, that the "Royal Academy of Jurisprudence and Legislation" convened a juridical congress in which the most important matters of the Spanish civil law were discussed, and some conclusions were reached.

In the meanwhile the Committee on Codes continued its works, and divergent schools were developed in respect to the schemes to be followed.

Some jurists, in fact, contended that the unification of the laws should be accomplished, which idea was tenaciously opposed by the representatives of provinces which possessed statute laws (*forales*), who did not desire the annulment of the special legislation of the same; while others maintained that, to avoid the inconveniency of such opposition, as many codes should be made as legislations of a special civil nature existed in Spain.

These were not the only opinions sustained on this matter; there were some jurists who thought it easier to arrive at the codification in a partial way, that is, by the publication of special laws on certain matters of law; opinions which did not determine the difficulties presented to the enterprise, and offered on the contrary the danger of new struggles amongst the representatives of the different sections, every time they should try to decide any of the matters which affected the legislation relating to statute laws.

Even among those who thought it preferable to have only one codification, different tendencies existed, because, some advocated that a code should be formed, in which (not taking into account each particular institution), the scientific principles of all should be included: this scheme was exposed to great dangers, because the legislator could not include all states or conditions of being of the country for which he legislated, but had to keep in mind the ideal of the law in the matter, the traditions, habits and customs of the people; in a word, the historical elements of the same. Others desired that the principles of modern civil codes of other countries should be brought to Spain, which idea had the inconveniency of bringing to Spain principles which were altogether uncommon to the laws. Still others thought that a code of general character should be compiled for Castile which would abolish all dispositions on particular statute laws, and, according to others, a comparative study of each one of these different legislations should be made, so as to give a general character to the one thought to be the best.

Lastly, some jurisconsults thought that it was neither opportune nor possible to transfer the legislation of Castile to the sections where statutory laws existed or to bring such legislation to Castile, but that it was necessary to carefully study the civil law, not only within the Castilian legislation, but within each one of the provinces to ascertain the good which was found in them with regard to each institution, and cast such parts afterwards into a common mould by which proceeding the code would have been accepted by everybody, because it would not have any opposition to the character and tendencies of the legislations which have existed in our country.

From what has been said it can be deduced how difficult the position was in which the compilers of the code found themselves, when each one of the different opinions mentioned opposed others.

Nevertheless, the earnest desire felt by all of disregarding matters of form and the system of the same, etc., in order to form a legal entity in which all dispositions of civil law in force should be considered finally overcame the difficulties.

The tenacity with which the provinces guarded their local laws and customs is illustrated, for example, in articles 10, 12, and 13 of the Civil Code.

Article 1976 of the Code provides that:—"All the legal compilations, uses, and customs which constitute the common civil law in all matters which are the object of this Code are hereby abrogated and they shall remain without force or effect, either as direct obligatory laws or as supplementary law. This provision shall not apply to the laws which have been declared in force by this Code." This disposition contains, therefore, the principal exceptions, one in reference to the laws declared in force by the Code, and the other relative to the legal compilation anterior to the Civil Code but in reference to matters which are not treated in it.

The first question about this matter is that of determining how the Civil Code abrogates the legal dispositions anterior to its publication and relative to matters unfolded in the same; for in reality, the dispositions to which said article refers also treat of matters not unfolded by the precepts of the Code.

If the intention of the compilers of the Civil Code was to abrogate all anterior legal works, they should have expressed their desire in a clear way, saying that they were abrogated, and remained without any legal strength or value; but from the moment the distinction by subject-matter was established by them, the difficulty then is to determine the true sense in which such phrase was to be used.

In fact, taking the word *matter* in a broad sense, all laws anterior to the Code were abrogated by the final disposition of this one, but the result should be less, if by *matter* all and each one of the dispositions explained in detail by it were to be understood, and more reduced still, if with such a word they wanted to mean the different subjects each question can embrace. So, for instance, taking the word *matter* in its second sense, all the laws in opposition should have been abrogated in respect to the latter ones, which are altogether different from this institution; and taking said word in its last sense, only a few laws which should legislate on certain points of the same should have been.

It can be deduced from this that it is not sufficient to recur to the old legal bodies to fix the precepts which rule after the publication of the Civil Code, but it is necessary to pay attention to the order of prelation of the same, established by the laws of Toro, and by the " Nueva and Novisima Recopilacion."

On the other hand it being understood by article 1976, that the derogatory disposition referred to is not applicable to the laws by it declared in force, a good many dispositions assume such a character. Among others can be cited that of June 17, 1870, about Civil Registry, those about waters, mines, intellectual property, laws on mortgages, on hunting and fishing; notarial legislation; law on obligatory sale on account of public welfare, etc. All this as it is easily understood, comes to augument the confusion produced by the final dispositions of the Civil Code, which is still greater, if we bear in mind that this one recognizes legal force to the local customs on those points to which its precepts make no reference, under which aspect they subsist; among others, the regulations and local customs, on partition walls, etc.

From what has been already said, and without further discussion on the matter, it can be deduced that the final disposition of the Civil Code, far from satisfying the general desire of the Spaniards of having all the positive civil rights compiled within one legal body, constitutes, on account of the extension of its conception, a true juridical enigma.

It should also be noted that until now no work has been done to accomplish what has been ordered by the law of the bases on foral legislation. According to said law, the Government, previously considering information of the Committee on Codes, should present to the Cortes and as an appendix to the Civil Code, the statutory laws which should be retained in each one of the provinces or territories where they are now existing.

The day on which such work shall be accomplished, it will be seen, and perhaps on account of the several civil laws of general character now existing, that the differences which separate the Castilian from the legislation of the provinces are not many.

If the conflicting differences between the local and common law, peculiar to Spain and which have little force in Cuba, Puerto Rico and the Philippines, are eliminated from the Spanish Civil Code, and a few amendments in harmony with United States institutions are substituted for the provisions which relate to monarchical institutions, there would result, in the opinions of those familiar with the subject, a most excellent code suitable for the people of Puerto Rico and the Philippines.

PROVINCIAL OR LOCAL LAWS, NOT ABROGATED BY THE CIVIL CODE, AND THEIR ORDER OF PREFERENCE.

Order of preference of the legal measures in the civil laws of Aragon, Mallorca, Catalonia, Navarre and Viscaya, after the promulgation of the Civil Code.

Articles 12, 13, 1976 and 16 of the Civil Code, are bases for their determination, and are as follows:—

"Art. 12. Provisions under this title in as far as they determine the effects of the laws, statutes, and general rules for their application, are binding in every province of the Kingdom. The provisions contained in title 4, Book 1, are similarly binding.

"In all other matters, the provinces and territories, in which local law (*derecho foral*) is in force, shall preserve it, for the present, in its entirety without suffering any alteration in its existing juridical regime, whether written or customary, by the publication of this code which shall be enforced only as supplementary law in default of that which may be considered as such supplementary law by their special laws.

"Art. 13. Notwithstanding the provisions of the preceding article, this Code shall go into effect in Aragon and in the Balearic Islands at the same time as in the provinces, not under local law, in so far as it may not oppose those provisions, local or customary, which are actually in force."

Article 1976 is cited here only in so far as it repeals the provisions of the Castilian law, but not those of the local law.

Article 16 says: "In matters which are governed by special laws, the deficiency thereof shall be supplied by the provisions of this Code:" which means that the Civil Code shall govern also as first suppletory law in all countries governed by local laws, in so far as matters are concerned which may have been the subject of special laws, such as the Water laws, Mining laws, Intellectual, Industrial, etc., property, and which, according to the said article 16, are still in force.

According to said bases, as appears from the foregoing provisions, the order of preference of the different legal measures in each of the provinces, where local laws are in force from the time of the promulgation of the Civil Code, is as follows:—

FIRST. ARAGON.

1. Preliminary title of the Code, in so far as its provisions determine the effects of laws, and of statutes and general rules for their application; and Title 4, Book 1, of the same, in the provisions it contains relating to marriage.

2. General Laws of the Nation, published subsequently to the Royal Decree of April 3, 1711, in which the Civil law of Aragon was again sanctioned, unless it is stated therein that they do not affect the local laws of Aragon.

3. The local laws of Aragon, and the Compilation of 1547.

4. The *Observancias,* that is, the uses and customs, compiled in 1407.

5. Natural reason or equity.

6. The Civil Code, in force since May 1, 1889, as suppletory law, "in so far as it may not oppose those provisions, local or customary, which are actually in force"

SECOND. BALEARIC ISLANDS. (Ancient Kingdom of Mallorca.)

1. The preliminary title of the Civil Code and Title 4 of Book 1 of the same, in the terms mentioned for Aragon.

2. Laws subsequent to the Royal Decree of November 28, 1715.

3. The Royal Ordinances and Privileges (*Reales Pragmaticas y privilegios*) applied from ancient times in said territory.

4. The usages, customs and constitutions of Catalonia.

5. The Civil Code, in force since May 1, 1889, as suppletory law, and "in so far as it may not oppose those provisions, local or customary, which are actually in force."

THIRD. CATALONIA.

1. The preliminary title of the Civil Code and Title 4 of Book 1, of the same in the terms aforementioned.

8

2. The general laws subsequent to the decree of *Nueva Planta,* unless it is stated therein that they do not affect the local laws.

3. The *Ustages,* Constitutions, *Capitulos or Actos de Corte, Pragmaticas, Concordias, Sentencias reales* and *arbitrales,* which constitute the *Recopilacion* of the Catalonian law.

4. The Ecclesiastical law, in the order of preference of its respective measures, as first special suppletory law.

5. The Roman Civil Law, also with its respective preference, also as special suppletory law of the second order.

6. The Civil Code, in force since May 1, 1889, as last suppletory law, in the absence of the two preceding which are specially of the legislation of Catalonia; excepting the provisions of article 16 with regard to the matters governed by special laws of general application to the entire Peninsula, with regard to which and to the other elements of the same the Code will have a prior, preferred and to a certain extent exclusive place in the suppletory law, in the territory of Catalonia.

FOURTH. NAVARRE.

1. The preliminary title of the Civil Code and Title 4 of Book 1 of the same, in the terms aforementioned.

2. The laws of this century, passed in general session of the Cortes, which are applicable to Navarre, according to the law of August 16, 1841.

3. The laws enacted subsequent to the *Novisima Recopilacion* of Navarre.

4. The *Novisima Recopilacion* of Navarre.

5. The general laws of Navarre and their amendments. (*Amejoramientos.*)

6. The Roman Law, as first special suppletory law.

7. The laws of *Partida,* as second special suppletory law.

8. The Civil Code, in force since May 1, 1889, as general and subsidiary suppletory law to the two preceding, which are the special ones; with the exception aforementioned, with regard to article 16 of the Civil Code, with regard to the matters governed by special laws, enacted for the entire Peninsula.

FIFTH. VIZCAYA. (Territory.)

1. The preliminary title and Title 4 of Book 1 of the Civil Code, in the terms mentioned in the preceding orders of preference.

2. The general laws subsequent to October 25, 1839, unless they contain an exception leaving the local laws in force.

3. The *Coleccion de Fueros,* denominated *Privilegios, franquezas y libertades de los caballeros hijos-dalgo del Muy Noble y Muy Leal Señorio de Vizcaya.*

4. The law of Castile, prior to the Code, as special suppletory law in this foral region.

5. The Civil Code, in force since May 1, 1889, as general and subsidiary suppletory law to the previous special one, with the aforementioned exception with regard to Catalonia and Navarre, with respect to article 16 of the Code, as to the matters which are governed by special laws enacted for the entire Peninsula.

THE
SPANISH CIVIL CODE

IN FORCE IN

SPAIN, CUBA, PUERTO RICO

AND

THE PHILIPPINES

ROYAL DECREE.

Upon the proposal of the Minister of Colonies (Ultramar), approved by the Council of Ministers;

In the name of my August Son, the King D. Alfonso XIII, and as Queen Regent of the Kingdom,—

I decree the following:—

Article 1. The Civil Code in force in the Peninsula, enacted in conformity with the provisions of the law of May 11, 1888, and approved by Royal Decree of the 24th instant, is hereby extended to the Islands of Cuba, Puerto Rico, and the Philippines.

Art. 2. This Code will go into effect in the aforesaid Islands twenty days after its publication in the official papers of the same.

Art. 3. In harmony with the provisions of art. 1 of the same Code, the laws shall go in force in the Colonial provinces, twenty days after their promulgation, it being understood that this shall be considered as made the day on which their insertions in the official papers of the Islands terminate.

Given at San Ildefonso, the thirty-first day of July, 1889.

MARIA CRISTINA.

The Minister of the Colonies,

MANUEL BECERRA.

CIVIL CODE.

[The laws on which the different chapters and subjects are based are cited in footnotes, and references to Spanish-American civil codes in notes under the corresponding articles; the following abbreviations are used: Arg.—Argentina, Col.—Colombia, Guat.—Guatemala, Mex.—Mexico, Uru.—Uruguay.]

PRELIMINARY TITLE.

*Laws, their effect, and general rules for their application.**

Article **1.** Laws shall be binding in the Peninsula, the adjacent Islands, the Canaries, and African territory, subject to Peninsular legislation, twenty days after their promulgation, if it is not otherwise provided in them.

The promulgation is understood to be made upon the day of the termination of the insertion of the law in the (Official) Gazette.

Col. 11, 12; Chile, 6, 7, 8; Uru. 1; Peru, 1; Guat. 1; Mex. 2.

2. Ignorance of the law does not excuse from compliance with the same.

Arg. 20; Col. 9; Chile, 8; Uru. 2; Mex. 21.

3. Laws shall not have a retroactive effect, unless the contrary is provided in them.

Arg. 3; Col. 13; Chile, 9; Guat. 2; Uru. 7; Mex. 5.

4. Acts executed against provisions of law are null, except in the cases in which the same law orders their validity.

---

* Digesto, book 1, tit. 3, laws 22, 42; id., book 21, tit. 2, law 6; id., book 5, tit. 5, law 3; id., book 22, tit. 6, law 9. Codigo, book 1, tit. 18, law 10; id., book 6, tit. 32, law 2; id., book 1, tit. 14, laws 5, 7, 14. Instituciones, book 5, tit. 2, par. 9. *Auto acordado del Consejo de Castilla*, 1767; id., Oct. 24, 1785. Constitution of 1812, art. 156. Royal Order, Sept. 22, 1836. Law of Nov. 28, 1837, Royal Orders of May 4, 1838, and Sept. 14, 1839. Royal Decree, March 9, 1851, arts. 1, 2, 3. Fuero Juzgo, book 2, tit. 1, law 3. Fuero Real, book 1, tit. 6, law 4. Part 1, tit. 1, laws 20, 21; id. 5, tit. 14, law 31. Nov. Recop., book 3, tit. 2, law 2. Fuero Juzgo, book 2, tit. 1, laws 1, 2. Part. 3, tit. 14, law 15; id. 5, tit. 11, laws 28, 38; id. 6, tit. 9, law 32; id. 5, tit. 1, law 9. Nov. Recop., book 10, tit. 1, laws 6, 7, 17; id., book 3, tit. 2, law 11. Penal Code, art. 368. Part. 1, tit. 1, law 15.

Rights conceded by the laws may be renounced, provided they are not contrary to public interest or order, or prejudicial to a third person.

Arg. 18, 19; Col. 6, par. 2, 15; Chile, 10, 11, 12; Peru, 7; Mex. 7.

5. Laws are abrogated only by other subsequent laws, and the disuse or any custom or practice to the contrary shall not prevail against their observance.

Arg. 17; Mex. 8, 9; Peru, 6; Uru. 9, par. 1; Guat. 6, 11; Col. 8; Chile, 2.

6. Any tribunal which refuses to give sentence on the pretext of silence, obscurity, or insufficiency of the laws shall incur responsibility therefor.

When there is no law exactly applicable to the point in controversy, the custom of the place shall be applied, and, in default thereof, the general principles of law.

Arg. 15, 16; Guat. 17; Col. 25 to 32; Chile, 19 to 27; Peru, 8, 9, 11; Uru. 15.

7. If, in the laws, months, days or nights are referred to, it will be understood that months have thirty days, days twenty-four hours, and nights from the setting to the rising of the sun.

If the months are designated by their names, the number of days which they respectively contain shall be computed.

Arg. 23 to 29; Col. 67; Chile, 48.

8. Penal laws, police laws, and those of public security are binding on all those who reside in Spanish territory.

Arg. 1; Col. 18; Chile, 4; Peru, 4.

9. Laws relating to family rights and obligations, or to the status, condition, and legal capacity of persons are binding on Spaniards, even when residing in a foreign country.

Arg. 6, 7, 8; Col. 19; Chile, 15; Mex. 13.

10. Personal property is subject to the laws of the nation of the owner; real property to the laws of the country in which it is situated.

Nevertheless, legal and testamentary successions, in respect to the order of succeeding as well as to the amount of the successional rights and the intrinsic validity of their provisions, shall be regulated by the laws of the nation of the person whose succession is considered, whatever may be the nature of the property and the country in which it may be found.

Biscayans, although they may reside in towns, shall continue to submit, in respect to the property they possess in the level lands, to law 15, title 20 of the Fuero of Vizcaya.

Arg. 10, 11; Col. 20; Chile, 16; Mex. 14, 18; Peru, 33, 34, 35; Guat. 5.

11. The forms and solemnities of contracts, wills, and other public instruments are governed by the laws of the country in which they are executed.

When such instruments are authorized by diplomatic or consular officials of Spain in a foreign land, the solemnities required for their execution by Spanish laws shall be observed.

Notwithstanding the provisions of this, and the preceding article, prohibitive laws concerning persons, their acts or property, and those which have for their object the public order and good morals, shall not become ineffective by laws or sentences dictated or by regulations or conventions agreed upon in a foreign country.

Arg. 12; Col. 21; Chile, 17, 18; Guat. 13; Uru. 6; par. 1; Peru. 40, 679.

12. Provisions under this title in as far as they determine the effects of the laws, and general rules for their application are binding in every province of the Kingdom. The provisions contained in title 4, book 1, are similarly binding.

In all other matters, the provinces and territories, in which local law (*derecho foral*) is in force, shall preserve it, for the present, in its entirety without suffering any alteration in its existing juridical *regime*, whether written or customary, by the publication of this Code, which shall be enforced only as supplementary law, in default of that which may be considered as such supplementary law by their special laws.

13. Notwithstanding the provisions of the preceding article, this Code shall go into effect in Aragon and in the Balearic Islands at the same time as in the provinces, not under local law, in so far as it may not oppose those provisions, local or customary, which are actually in force.

14. In accordance with the provision of article 12, what is established in articles 9, 10, and 11, respecting persons, acts and property of Spaniards in a foreign land, and that of foreigners in Spain, is applicable to persons, acts, and property of Spaniards in territories or provinces having different civil legislation.

15. Family rights and obligations, those relating to the status, condition, and legal capacity of persons, and those of testamentary or intestate succession, declared in this Code, are applicable:

1. To persons born in common law (*derecho comun*) provinces or territories of parents subject to local law, if the latter, during the minority of the children, or the same children within the year following their majority or emancipation, declare it is their will to subject themselves to the Civil Code.

2. To the children of a father, and, if he does not exist or is unknown, of the mother belonging to provinces or territories subject

to common law, even when born in provinces or territories where local law is in force.

3. To those who, proceeding from provinces or territories having local law, should have gained a residence in places subject to common law.

For the effects of this article, a residence will be gained, by a residence of ten years in provinces or territories subject to common law, unless the interested party, before the termination of this period, manifests his will to the contrary; or by a residence of two years, whenever the interested party manifests this to be his will.

Both manifestations should be made before a municipal judge for the corresponding inscription in the Civil Registry.

In every case, the wife shall follow the condition of the husband, and the children, not emancipated, that of their father, and, in his default, that of their mother.

The provisions of this article are of reciprocal application to Spanish provinces and territories having different civil legislation.

16. In matters which are governed by special laws, the deficiency thereof shall be supplied by the provisions of this Code.

Col. 10; Chile. 4.

BOOK FIRST.

PERSONS.

TITLE I.

*Spaniards and foreigners.**

Article **17.** The following are Spaniards:

1. Persons born in Spanish territory.

2. Children of a Spanish father or mother, although they may have been born out of Spain.

3. Foreigners who have obtained letters of naturalization.

4. Those who, without them, have gained a residence in any place in the Monarchy.

Peru, 30; Chile, 56; Arg., Mex., Guat., Col., refer to Constitution.

18. Children, while they remain under the parental power (*patria potestad*), have the nationality of their parents.

In order that those born of foreign parents in Spanish territory may enjoy the benefits granted to them by No. 1 of article 17, it shall be an indispensable requisite that the parents declare, in the manner and before the official specified in article 19, that they choose, in the name of their children, Spanish nationality, renouncing any other.

Arg. 3.

19. Children of a foreigner, born in Spanish dominion, should declare, within the year following their majority or emancipation, if they desire to enjoy the quality of Spaniards which article 17 concedes to them.

Those who are in the Kingdom shall make this declaration before the official in charge of the Civil Registry of the town in which they reside; those who reside in a foreign land, before one of the consular or diplomatic agents of the Spanish government; and those who are in a country in which the government has no agent shall address the Spanish Minister of State.

Mex. 2, 3.

---

* Digesto, book 1, tit. 5, laws 7, 19, 24; id., book 50, tit. 1, laws 22, 38, par. 3; id., book 50, tit. 1, law 16; id., book 50, tit. 22, law 3. Codigo, book 50, tit. 16, law 131; id., book 12, tit. 1, law 13. Constitutions of 1812, art. 5; of June 18, 1837, art. 1; of May 23, 1845, art. 1; of June 6, 1869, and art. 1 of June 30, 1876. Law of Civil Registry, arts. 101, 102, 103, 104, 105, 106, 107, 108, 109, 112. Constitutions of June 18, 1837, art. 1; of May 23, 1845; of June 6, 1869, and of June 30, 1876, art. 1, par. 2. Royal Decree, Nov. 17, 1852, art. 1. Nov. Recop., book 6, tit. 11, law 9.

20. The quality of a Spaniard is lost by acquiring naturalization in a foreign country, or by accepting employment from another government, or by entering the armed service of a foreign power without permission of the King.

21. A Spaniard who loses this quality by acquiring naturalization in a foreign country can recover it, upon returning to the Kingdom, by declaring before an official in charge of the Civil Registry of the domicile which he elects that such is his will, in order that the official may make the corresponding inscription therein, and by renouncing the protection of the flag of such country.

22. A married woman follows the condition and nationality of her husband.

A Spanish woman who marries a foreigner, shall, upon dissolution of the marriage, recover Spanish nationality by fulfilling the requisites expressed in the previous article.

Peru, 41.

23. Any Spaniard, who loses this quality by accepting employment of any other government, or by entering the armed service of a foreign power without the King's permission, shall not recover Spanish nationality without previously obtaining the royal authorization.

24. Any person, born in a foreign country of a Spanish father or mother, who may have lost Spanish nationality on account of the parents having lost it, may also recover it by complying with the conditions prescribed by article 19.

25. In order that foreigners who have obtained letters of naturalization or gained a residence in any place in the Monarchy may enjoy Spanish nationality, they have to previously renounce their former nationality, swear to the Constitution of the Monarchy, and inscribe themselves as Spaniards in the Civil Registry.

26. Spaniards who change their domicile to a foreign country, where they may be considered as natives without other conditions than that of residence in it, in order to preserve their Spanish nationality, shall be required to manifest that such is their will before the Spanish diplomatic or consular agent who shall inscribe them in the Registry of Spanish residents, as well as their consorts, if they are married, and any children which they may have.

27. Foreigners enjoy in Spain the rights which the civil laws concede to Spaniards with the exception of what is provided in article 2 of the Constitution of the State or in international treaties.

Peru, 32, 33; Guat. 51.

28. Corporations, institutions, and associations recognized by law and domiciled in Spain shall enjoy Spanish nationality, provided they possess the character of juridical persons in accordance with the provisions of the present Code.

Associations domiciled in a foreign land shall have in Spain the consideration and rights which treaties or special laws may determine.

Mex. 45; Guat. 46.

TITLE II.

Birth and extinction of civil personality.

CHAPTER FIRST.

*Natural persons.**

Article **29.** Birth determines personality; but the conceived child is considered as born for all the effects favorable to it, provided that it be born with the conditions which are expressed in the following article.

Col. 90; Chile, 74; Peru, 2, 3; Arg. 70; Mex. 12.

30. For civil effects, the fœtus shall only be considered as born when it may have a human figure and shall live twenty-four hours entirely separate from the mother (*seno materno*).

Col. 90; Chile, 74; Guat. 22; Peru, 4; Arg. 70.

31. Priority of birth, in case of double parturition, gives to the first born the rights which the law recognizes in primogeniture.

Peru, 8.

32. Civil personality is extinguished by the death of a person.

Minority, insanity or imbecility, state of being deaf and dumb, prodigality, and civil interdiction are only restrictions upon juridical personality. Those who are in any of these conditions are susceptible of rights and even obligations when such rights or obligations arise from the facts or the relations between the property of the incapacitated and a third person.

Arg. 103, par. 1, 56, par. 2; Col. 94; Chile, 74; Peru, 12 to 17, 28.

33. If there is doubt, between two or more persons called to succeed each other, which of them has died first, he, who alleges the prior death of one or the other, shall be obliged to prove it; in default of proof, it will be presumed that they both died at the same time,

---

* Fuero Juzgo, book 4, tit. 2, laws 18, 19, 20. Part. 4, tit. 23, law 3; id., 6, tit. 6, laws 3, 6. Fuero Real, book 3, tit. 6, law 3. Part. 4, tit. 6, law 5. Toro, law 13. Law of Civil Marriage, art. 68. Part. 7, tit. 33, law 12.

and the transmission of rights from one to the other will not take place.

Arg. 109; Col. 95; Chile, 79.

34. In respect to the presumption of the death of an absent person and its effects, the provisions of title 8 of this book shall rule.

CHAPTER II.

*Juridical persons.**

Article **35.** The following are juridical persons:

1. Corporations, associations, and institutions of public interest recognized by law.

Their personality begins from the very moment in which, in accordance with law, they shall have become validly constituted.

2. Associations of private interests, whether they may be civil, mercantile, or industrial, to which the law concedes proper personality, independent of that of each one of the associates.

Arg. 33, 39, 45; Guat. 44, 45; Col. 663; Chile, 545; Mex. 43.

36. The associations, to which No. 2 of the previous article refers, shall be governed by the provisions relative to the contract of association, according to the nature of the same.

Guat. 47; Col. 635; Chile, 547.

37. The civil capacity of corporations shall be regulated by the laws which have created or recognized them, those of associations by their statutes, and those of institutions by the rules of their establishment, duly approved by administrative authority, when such requirement is necessary.

Guat. 46; Col. 636; Chile, 548; Arg. 31; Mex. 45.

38. Juridical persons can acquire and possess property of every class, as well as contract obligations and enforce civil and criminal actions, in conformity with the laws and rules of their constitution.

The Church shall be governed, in this particular, by what has been agreed between both powers; and the establishments of instruction and beneficence by the provisions of the special laws.

Arg. 41; Col. 643; Chile, 556; Mex. 799.

39. When corporations, associations, and institutions have ceased to act, because of the expiration of the periods during which they should legally exist, or by having realized the ends for which they were constituted, or because it has become impossible to apply to

* Digesto, book 46, tit. 1, law 22.

such ends the activity and the means at their disposal, their property shall receive the application which the laws or their statutes or the clauses of their foundation have assigned to them in anticipation of such cases.

When nothing has been previously established, the property shall be applied to the realization of similar purposes in the interests of the region, province, or municipal district which should have principally reaped the benefits of the extinguished institutions.

Arg. 48, 50; Col. 649; Chile, 561.

TITLE III.

*Domicile.**

Article **40.** For the enforcement of the rights and the fulfillment of civil obligations, the domicile of natural persons is the place of their ususal residence; and, in certain cases, that determined by the Law of Civil Procedure.

The domicile of diplomatic residents, who by reason of their duties in a foreign land enjoy the rights of extra-territoriality, shall be the last domicile which they had when in Spanish territory.

Col. 78; Chile, 50; Peru, 44 to 50; Arg. 89; Guat. 60; Mex. 26; Uru. 25.

41. When neither the law which has created or recognized them, nor the statutes or rules of their foundation shall fix the domicile of juridical persons, it shall be understood that they have it at the place where their legal representation is established or where they exercise the principal functions for which they were established.

Arg. 90; Guat. 70; Col. 86; Uru. 37.

TITLE IV.

Marriage.†

CHAPTER FIRST.

General provision.

SECTION FIRST.

Forms of marriage.

Article **42.** The law recognizes two forms of marriage, the canonical which all who profess the Catholic religion should contract, and

* Municipal law, Oct. 2, 1877, arts. 12, 13; Law of Civil Procedure, arts. 64 to 69; Supplement to Nov. Recop., law 2, tit. 26, law 7.

† Digesto, book 4, tit. 3, law 22, par. 7; id., book 23, law 57, par. 1; id., book 23, tit. 2, law 39; id., book 24, tit. 3, law 22, par. 8; id., book 47, tit. 10, law 2; id., book 48, tit. 5, law 11, par. 3. Codigo, book 5, tit. 15, law 8; id., book 5, tit. 17, law 8, pars. 4, 5; id., book 8, tit. 47, law 9. Novela, 117, chap.

the civil, which shall be celebrated in the manner provided in this Code.

Arg. 167, 183; Guat. 119; Col. 113, 140; Chile, 117, 118; Peru, 156; Uru. 87, 89.

SECTION SECOND.

Provisions common to both forms of marriage.

Article **43.** Future espousals do not cause obligation to contract marriage. No tribunal shall entertain a complaint in which their fulfillment is claimed.

Guat. 114, 105; Col. 110, 111; Chile, 98, 99; Arg. 116; Mex. 160; Peru. 120 to 131; Uru. 85.

44. When the promise has been made in a public or private document by a person of age, or by a minor, assisted by the person whose consent is necessary in order to celebrate the marriage, or when the banns have been published, the one who refuses to marry, without just cause, shall be obliged to indemnify the other party for the expenses which he or she may have incurred by reason of the promised marriage.

An action in order to recover the indemnity for expenses, to which the previous paragraph refers, can be exercised only within a year counted from the day of the refusal to celebrate the marriage.

Col. 112; Chile, 100; Peru, 123, 124, 125, 135; Arg. 169.

45. Marriage is forbidden:

1. To the minor who has not obtained consent and to a person of age who has not asked the advice of the persons to whom it pertains to authorize one or the other, in the cases provided for by law.

2. To the widow, during the three hundred and one days following the death of her husband, or before child-birth if she should have been left pregnant, and to the woman whose marriage may have

---

14; id., 117, chap. 7. Part. 3, tit. 2, law 5; id., 4, tit. 2, laws 1, 7; id., 4, tit. 4, law 17; id., 4, tit. 3, laws 1, 5; id., 4, tit. 9, law 2; id., 4, tit. 11, law 23; id., 4, tit. 12, law 3; id., 4, tit. 13, laws 1, 13; id., 4, tit. 17, law 3; id., 5, tit. 4, law 50; id., 6, tit. 3, laws 5, 7; id., 7, tit. 4, law 50. Nov. Recop., book 10, tit. 1, laws 11, 12, 13; id., book 10, tit. 2, laws 4, 5, 18; id., book 10, tit. 20, law 10. Fuero Juzgo, book 3, tit. 1, laws 2, 8; id., book 3, tit. 2, law 1; id., book 3, tit. 4, law 1; id., book 8, tit. 2, law 2; id., book 3, tit. 1, laws 2, 5, 6, 13, 14; id., book 3, tit. 2, laws 4, 6. Fuero Viejo, book 5, tit. 1, laws 1, 2. Rescripts, March 23, 1776; April 10, 1803. Sentences, May 12, 1866; Sept. 28, 1880; October 10, 1861. Royal Decree, Dec. 26, 1790. Toro, laws 47, 49, 82. Laws June 20, 1862, arts. 12, 13, 15, par. 182, art. 13, last par.; June 20, 1852, arts. 1, 2, 3, 4, 5, 6. Law of Civil Marriage, June 18, 1870, art. 4, number 5, arts. 6, 44, 45, 47, 48, 49, 50, 53, 54, 55, 79, 81, 82, 87, 88, 89, 90, 94, 97.

been declared null, under the same circumstances and limitations, to be counted from her legal separation.

3. To the guardian and his or her descendants with respect to persons whom such guardian may have or may have had under charge, until the guardianship has terminated and the accounts of the same have been approved, except in the cases where the father of the person, subject to guardianship, has authorized the marriage in a will or in a public instrument.

Mex. 165, 174; Uru. 106, 111; Col. 117, 173, 140; Chile, 107, 128, 116; Guat. 122, 129, 199; Peru, 146.

46. The consent, referred to in No. 1 of the preceding article, ought to be granted to the legitimate children by the father; in his default, or where he is impeded, the power to grant it devolves, in this order, upon the mother, the paternal and maternal grandparents, and, in default of all of them, upon the family council.

Recognized natural children or children legitimated by royal concession should ask such consent of those who have recognized or legitimated them, of their ascendants, and of the family council, in the order stated in the preceding paragraph.

Adopted children shall ask such consent of the adopting father, and, in his default, of the persons of the natural family upon whom it may devolve.

Other illegitimate children should obtain the consent of their mother, when she is lawfully known, that of the maternal grandparents, in similar cases, and, in default of the above, that of the family council.

It pertains to the heads of foundling institutions to give consent for marriage to those educated therein.

Guat. 125, 126; Col. 116, 117, 118, 119, 120; Chile, 107; Arg. 169; Peru, 147, 148, 152; Uru. 106, 109; Mex. 172.

47. Children of age are obliged to ask the advice of the father, and, in his default, of the mother. If they should not have obtained it, or it should be unfavorable, the marriage cannot be celebrated until three months after the petition is made.

48. The consent and the favorable advice for the celebration of a marriage should be proven, upon the latter being asked, by a document authorized by a civil or ecclesiastical Notary or the Municipal Judge of the petitioners domicile.

When the consent has been asked in vain, the lapse of time, to which the preceding article refers, shall be proven in the same manner.

Peru, 149; Col. 117; Guat. 140.

49. None of those called to give their consent or advice is obliged to make known the reasons for granting or denying it, nor is there any remedy against such dissent.

Arg. 170; Col. 121; Guat. 128; Chile, 112; Peru, 150, 151.

50. When, notwithstanding the prohibition of article 45, the persons comprehended within it get married, their marriage shall be valid; but the contracting parties, without prejudice to the provisions of the Penal Code, shall remain subject to the following rules:

1. The marriage shall be understood as contracted with the absolute separation of property, and each consort shall retain the dominion and administration of that which belong to him or her, making as his or her own all the fruits, although with the obligation of proportionally contributing to the support of the marriage charges.

2. Neither one of the consorts shall receive from the other anything by donation or by will.

The provisions of the two preceding rules shall not apply in the cases of No. 2 of article 45, when dispensation has been obtained.

3. When one of the consorts is a minor, not emancipated, he shall not receive the administration of his property until he attains majority.

In the meantime, he shall only have a right to support which shall not exceed the net income from his property.

4. In the cases of No. 3 of article 45, the guardian shall, besides, lose the administration of the property of the ward during her minority.

Col. 124; Chile, 114; Peru, 155; Arg. 177; Guat. 138; Mex. 176.

51. Civil or canonical marriage shall produce no civil effects, when either one of the consorts is already lawfully married.

Guat. 120; Peru, 142; Mex. 163; Col. 140; Chile, 103.

52. Matrimony is dissolved by the death of one of the consorts.

Peru, 134; Uru. 171; Col. 152; Chile, 123; Arg. 219.

SECTION THIRD.

Proof of marriage.

Article **53.** Marriages, celebrated before this Code went into effect, shall be proven in the manner established by the former laws. Those contracted afterwards shall be proven only by the certification of the record of the Civil Registry, unless the books thereof have not existed or have disappeared, or a question is pending before the courts, in which cases all kinds of proof are admissible.

Uru. 40, 41; Arg. 179.

54. In the cases referred to in paragraph second of the previous article, the constant possession of the status of the parents, united to the certifications of the births of their children as legitimate ones, shall be one of the means of proof of the marriage of the parents, if it is not shown that one of the two was bound by another previous marriage.

Uru. 49; Arg. 179.

55. A marriage contracted in a foreign country, where such acts are not subject to a regular or authenticate registration, may be proven by any of the means of proof admitted by law.

Arg. 179.

SECTION FOURTH.

Rights and obligations between husband and wife.

Article **56.** The consorts are obliged to live together, to be faithful to and mutually help each other.

Uru. 127; Guat. 149, 151, 152; Col. 176; Chile, 131; Peru, 177, 174; Mex. 198; Arg. 184, 185.

57. The husband is obliged to protect the wife and the latter to obey the husband.

Guat. 150; Mex. 201; Peru, 175; Uru. 128; Arg. 185.

58. The wife is obliged to follow her husband wherever he may establish his residence. The tribunals, nevertheless, may, with just cause, exempt her from this obligation when the husband changes his residence beyond the seas or to a foreign country.

Guat. 151; Arg. 187; Peru, 176; Col. 178; Chile, 133; Uru. 129; Guat. 151.

59. The husband is the administrator of the property of the conjugal society, except when stipulated to the contrary, and that provided in article 1384.

When he is under eighteen years of age, he cannot administer without consent of his father, and, in his default, without that of the mother, and, in default of both, without that of his guardian.

Neither can he appear in a suit in court without the assistance of said persons.

In no case, until he has attained majority, can the husband, without the consent of the persons, mentioned in the preceding paragraph, borrow money, burden nor alienate the real property.

Uru. 130; Col. 180; Chile, 135; Guat. 162; Peru, 180, 181; Mex. 205; Arg. 186.

60. The husband is the representative of his wife. She cannot, without his permission, appear in a suit by herself or through an attorney.

Nevertheless, she does not require such permission to defend herself in a criminal proceeding, or for bringing suit or defending herself in suits with her husband, or when she may have obtained habilitation in conformity with what the law of Civil Procedure may provide.

Peru, 179, 184, 185, 186; Uru. 131, 132; Arg. 188; Guat. 153, 156; Col. 182; Chile, 136; Mex. 206, 212.

61. Neither can the wife, without the permission or power of her husband, acquire (property) by an onerous or lucrative title, alienate her property or bind herself, except in the cases and with the limitation established by law.

Peru, 182; Uru. 134; Arg. 189; Col. 182; Chile, 137; Mex. 207.

62. Acts, executed by the wife, contrary to the provisions of the preceding articles, are null and void, except when they involve things which by their nature are destined for the ordinary consumption of the family, in which case, purchases made by the wife shall be valid.

Purchases of jewels, furniture and precious objects, made, without the permission of the husband, shall only be confirmed when he may have consented that his wife should have the use and enjoyment of such objects.

Uru. 141; Arg. 190; Col. 192; Chile, 147; Guat. 148.

63. The wife, without permission of the husband, can:

1. Execute a will.

2. Exercise the rights and fulfill the duties which pertain to her in respect to legitimate and recognized natural children whom she may have had by another, and in respect to the property of the same.

Col. 182; Chile, 139; Guat. 155, 165; Arg. 191; Mex. 413.

64. The wife shall share the honors of the husband, except those which may be strictly and exclusively personal, and shall retain them as long as she does not contract a new marriage.

65. Only the husband and his heirs can claim the nullity of the acts executed by the wife without competent permission or authorization.

Uru. 144; Guat. 163; Arg. 192; Peru, 187; Mex. 214.

66. What is established in this section is understood without prejudice to the provisions of the present Code, about absence, incapacity, prodigality, and interdiction of the husband.

Mex. 211.

SECTION FIFTH.

Effects of nullity of marriage and divorce.

Article **67.** The civil effects of petitions and decrees about the nullity of marriage and about divorces can only be obtained before the ordinary tribunals.

Mex. 166, 168; Peru, 138; Chile, 168, 103; Arg. 202; Guat. 166.

68. After the petitions, which are referred to in the preceding article, are interposed and admitted, the following provisions shall be adopted during the pendency of the suit:

1. To separate the consorts in every case.
2. To place the wife under protection in the cases and in the form provided by the Law of Civil Procedure.
3. To place the children under the care of one or both of the consorts, as may be proper.
4. To provide for the support of the wife and the children who do not remain under the power of the father.
5. To decree the necessary measures to prevent the husband, who may have given cause for the divorce, or against whom the petition for nullity of the marriage has been instituted, from causing injury to the wife in the administration of her property.

Mex. 266; Col. 157, 158; Guat. 167, 173, 182, 183, 184, 185, 188; Peru, 204, 203, 202, 201, 205, 206, 207; Arg. 203, 205, 211, 213.

69. Marriage contracted in good faith produces civil effects, although it may be declared null and void.

When good faith has existed on the part of one of the consorts alone, it shall produce civil effects only as to this one and the children.

Good faith is presumed, if the contrary is not shown.

When bad faith has existed on the part of both consorts, the marriage shall only produce civil effects in respect to the children.

Col. 148, 150; Arg. 230, 231, 232; Uru. 183; Guat. 192; Mex. 302, 303, 304; Peru. 170, 171.

70. When the nullity of the marriage has been finally decreed, the sons over three years of age shall remain under the care of the father, and the daughters under the care of the mother, if there should have been good faith on the part of both consorts.

When good faith may have existed on the part of only one of the consorts, the children of both sexes shall remain under this one's power and care.

When both are guilty of bad faith, the court shall decide as to the disposition of the children in the form provided for in paragraph second of No. 2 of article 73.

The sons and daughters, under three years of age, shall remain under the care of the mother, in every case, until they complete this age, unless on account of special reasons the sentence has disposed otherwise.

Arg. 213; Uru. 174; Col. 149; Mex. 306 to 308.

71. The provisions of the first and second paragraphs of the preceding articles shall not be effective, if the parents, by common agreement, shall provide otherwise for the care of the children.

72. The final decree of nullity shall produce, in respect to the property of the marriage, the same effects as the dissolution by death; but the consort who has acted in bad faith shall have no rights to the profits of the conjugal society (*gananciales*).

When both have acted in bad faith, that shown by one shall be a set off against the other.

Mex. 2180, 2181, 2195, 2196; Uru. 186.

73. A decree of divorce shall produce the following effects:

1. The separation of the consorts.

2. The children to remain or be put under the power and protection of the innocent consort.

When both are guilty, a guardian shall be provided for the children in conformity with the provisions of this Code.

Nevertheless, when the decree has not provided otherwise, the mother, in every case, shall have in her care the children under three years of age.

Upon the death of the innocent consort, the guilty one shall recover the parental power and his or her rights, when the cause which gave origin for the divorce should have been adultery, violence to the person, or grave acts of contumely (*injurias graves*).

When the causes are different, a guardian shall be appointed for the children.

The deprivation of the parental power and of its rights shall not exempt the guilty consort from the fulfillment of the obligations which this Code imposes upon him or her in respect to the children.

3. The guilty consort shall lose all that may have been given or promised him or her by the innocent one or by any other person in consideration for such one; and the innocent consort shall keep all that he has received from the guilty one, being able, besides, to claim forthwith all that may have been promised by the guilty one.

4. The separation of the property of the conjugal society, and the loss of the administration of that of the wife, if the husband should possess it, and is the one who gave cause for the divorce.

The retention by the innocent husband of the administration, if he should have it, of the property of the wife who shall only have the right to be supported.

Col. 166; Chile, 174; Guat. 165, 182, 183, 184, 172, 173, 174; Peru, 208, 210, 202, 212, 209, 213; Uru. 162 to 170.

74. Reconciliation determines the suit for divorce and leaves, without subsequent effects, the decree dictated in respect thereto; but the consorts must give notice of it to the tribunal who has or may have cognizance of the suit.

The effects of the decree shall subsist in respect to the children, without prejudice to the provision of the preceding article, when it is founded on the attempt or connivance of the husband or of the wife to corrupt the sons or to prostitute their daughters, in which case, if the sons and daughters still continue under the parental power, the tribunals shall adopt convenient measures in order to protect them from corruption or prostitution

Mex. 268, 271, 273, 276; Peru, 216, 217; Chile, 178; Col. 167; Arg. 218; Guat. 179, 180.

CHAPTER SECOND.

*Canonical marriage.**

Article **75.** The requisites, form, and solemnities for the celebration of canonical marriages shall be governed by the provisions of the Catholic Church and of the Holy Council of Trent, accepted as laws of the Kingdom.

Uru. 87; Chile, 117; Peru, 156; Arg. 167.

76. Canonical marriage shall produce all the civil effects in respect to the persons and property of the consorts and their descendants.

Arg. 167, 168.

77. A municipal judge or other state official shall be present at the act of celebration of the canonical marriage with the sole object of verifying the immediate inscription of it in the Civil Registry.

For this object, the contracting parties are obliged to give notice in writing to the respective Municipal Judge, twenty-four hours, at least, before the day, hour, and place where the marriage is to be cele-

* Fuero Real, book 3, tit. 1, law 7. Partidas 4, tit. 10, law 7. Nov. Recop., book 1, tit. 1, law 13. Royal Decree, Feb. 9, 1875, par. 1, art. 5, par. 1, art 1, par. 1, art. 2. Royal Order, Feb. 19, same year, approving precepts for execution of preceding decree, arts. 2, 4. Precepts, Feb. 19, 1895, for the execution of the decree dated 9 of same month and year, art. 5. Council of Trent, session 24, Bull of Bonifacio XIV, *Satis vobis*.

brated, incurring, if they do not do so, a fine of from five to eighty pesetas.

The Municipal Judge shall give a receipt for the notice from the contracting parties. Should he decline to give it, he shall incur a fine, which shall not be less than twenty nor exceed one hundred pesetas.

The celebration of the canonical marriage shall not be proceeded with without the presentation of said receipt to the parochial priest.

If the marriage is celebrated without the presence of the Municipal Judge or his representative, notwithstanding that the contracting parties may have advised him of it, the transcription of the certificate of the canonical marriage to the Civil Registry shall be done at his expense, besides he shall pay a fine which shall not be less than twenty nor exceed one hundred pesetas. In this case, the marriage shall produce all its civil effects from the moment of its celebration.

If the contracting parties should be to blame for not having given notice to the Municipal Judge, they can remedy the defect, asking for the inscription of the marriage in the Civil Registry.

In this case, the marriage shall produce no civil effects, except from its inscription.

78. Those who contract canonical marriage *in articulo mortis* shall give notice to the official in charge of the Civil Registry, at any time whatever prior to its celebration, and prove, in any manner whatever, that they have fulfilled this duty.

The penalties imposed upon contracting parties who omit this requisite shall not be applicable to the case of marriage *in articulo mortis,* when it is shown that it was impossible to give timely notice.

In every case, in order that the marriage may produce civil effects from the date of its celebration, the sacramental certificate shall be inscribed in the Registry within ten days next following.

79. The secret marriage of conscience, celebrated before the church, is not subject to any formality of the civil order, neither shall it produce civil effects, except from the moment of its publication by virtue of its inscription in the Registry. This marriage shall, nevertheless, produce civil effects from its celebration, if both contracting parties, of common accord, shall ask the bishop who may have authorized it for a copy of the entry made in the secret Registry of the bishopric, and shall directly send it, with the proper secrecy, to the *Direccion General* of the Civil Registry asking for its inscription.

For this purpose the *Direccion General* shall keep a special and secret Registry with the necessary precautions that the contents of such inscriptions may not be known, until the interested parties ask that they may be given publicity by transferring the same to the Municipal Registry of their domicile.

80. The cognizance of suits for nullity and divorce, in case of canonical marriages, belong to the ecclesiastical tribunals.

Arg. 201; Peru, 138.

81. When a suit for divorce or nullity of marriage is commenced before the ecclesiastical tribunal, it belongs to the civil tribunal to dictate, upon the petition of the party interested, the dispositions referred to in article 68.

Guat. 166; Arg. 202, 203.

82. A final decree for nullity or divorce of canonical marriage shall be inscribed in the Civil Registry, and shall be presented to the ordinary tribunal in order to ask for its execution as to the part relating to civil effects.

Guat. 168.

CHAPTER THIRD.

*Civil marriage.**

SECTION FIRST.

Capacity of contracting parties.

Article **83.** The following cannot contract marriage:

1. Males, until they have attained the full age of fourteen, and females until they have attained the full age of twelve.

Marriage contracted by person under puberty shall, nevertheless, be *ipso facto* validated, without the necessity of an express declaration, if a day after having arrived at the legal age of puberty, they should have lived together without having brought suit against its validity, or if the woman should have conceived before the legal age of puberty, or before having established such suit.

2. Those who were not in the full exercise of their reason at the time of contracting marriage.

3. Those who suffered from physical, absolute, or relative impotency for the purposes of generation, prior to the celebration of the marriage, in a patent, perpetual or incurable manner.

4. Those ordained *in sacris* and those professed in an approved

* Law of Civil Marriage, arts. 4, 6, 7, 9, 11, 12, 13, 14, 15, 16, 17, 18, 19, 20, 21, 22, 23, 24, 25, 26, 31, par. 1, 33, 35, 37, 38, 41, 42, 43, 56, 83, 85, 86, 92, last par. 93. Regulation of the same law, Dec. 13, 1870, art. 37, 40, 41, 42, 44, 45, 46, 48, par. 2, number 9, 49, 57. Part. 4, tit. 1, law 1; id. 4, tit. 2, law 5; id. 4, tit. 10, law 4. Novela, 122, chaps. 8, 9; id. 117, chap. 9.

religious canonical order, bound by a solemn pledge of chastity, except those who may have obtained the corresponding canonical dispensation.

5. Those that are already lawfully married.

Mex. 164, 281, 280, 63; Peru, 141, 142; Uru. 90; Guat. 120.

84. Neither can the following contract marriage between themselves:

1. The ascendants or descendants by legitimate or natural consanguinity or affinity.
2. Collaterals by legitimate consanguinity up to and including the fourth degree.
3. Collaterals by legitimate affinity up to and including the fourth degree.
4. Collaterals by natural consanguinity or affinity up to and including the second degree.
5. The adopting father and mother and the adopted; the latter and the surviving consort of the adopters, and the adopters and the surviving consort of the adopted.
6. The legitimate descendants of the adopter with the adopted, while the relation of adoption lasts.
7. Adulterers who have been condemned by a final sentence.

Those who have been condemned as authors or author and accomplice of the death of the consort of any of the parties.

Guat. 120; Uru. 90; Peru, 142; Mex. 163.

85. The government, with just cause, can, on petition of a party, dispense the impediment included in No. 2 of article 45; the third and fourth degrees of collateral relationship by legitimate consanguinity; the impediments growing out of legitimate or natural affinity between collaterals, and those referring to the descendants of the adopter.

SECTION SECOND.

Celebration of marriage.

Article **86.** Those who, in conformity with article 42, desire to contract marriage in the manner determined in this Code, shall present to the Municipal Judge of their domicile a declaration signed by both contracting parties, in which appears:

1. The names, surnames, ages, professions, domiciles or residences of the contracting parties.
2. The names, surnames, professions, domiciles or residences of the parents.

Certificates of birth and of the status of the contracting parties, the consent or advice, if required, and dispensations, when necessary, shall accompany this declaration.

Guat. 139, 140; Col. 126 to 129.

87. Marriages shall be celebrated personally or by a proxy to whom a special power has been granted; but the presence of the contracting party who is domiciled or resides in the district of the Judge who is to authorize the marriage shall always be necessary.

The name of the person with whom the marriage is to be celebrated shall be expressed in the special power, and such power shall be valid if, before its celebration, the person so authorized should not have been notified in an authentic form of the revocation of the power.

Guat. 136, 143.

88. When the Municipal Judge, selected for the celebration of the marriage, should not be at the time (of the district) of both contracting parties, two declarations shall be presented, one before the Municipal Judge of each contracting party, expressing which of the two Judges they have chosen for the celebrations of the marriage, and, in both courts, the proceedings which are established in the following articles shall be observed.

89. After the petition has been ratified by both parties, the Municipal Judge shall order that edicts or proclamations shall be posted for fifteen days announcing the pretension with all the details, indicated in article 86 and requiring those who have information of any impediment thereto to denounce it.

Similar edicts shall be sent to the Municipal Judge of the towns in which the interested parties have lived or been domiciled, during the last two years, requiring that they be posted in the place of the holding of their public court for the period of fifteen days, and that, after the lapse of this time, they should be returned with a certification of said requisite having been fulfilled and whether or not any impediment has been denounced.

Uru. 91, 92.

90. Soldiers in active service who may intend to contract marriage shall be dispensed from publishing such edicts outside of the place where they reside, if they present certificates that they are unmarried, issued by the commanding officer of the military body to which they belong.

91. When the interested parties are foreigners, and have not resided two years in Spain, they shall prove, by a certificate in due form given by competent authority, that in the territory where they have had their domicile or residence, during the last two years, publication has been made of the marriage which they intend to contract with all the solemnities which are required in said place.

92. In all other cases, the government can dispense with the publication of the banns on account of serious causes, properly approved.

93. Notwithstanding what is provided in the preceding articles, the Municipal Judge shall authorize the marriage of a person who is in imminent danger of death, whether he is domiciled in the place or is a transient.

This marriage shall be considered as conditional, until the previous single status of the contracting parties be legally established.

94. Paymasters of war vessels and captains of merchantmen shall authorize marriages which are celebrated on board (ship) in imminent danger of death.

These marriages shall also be considered as conditional.

95. The provision of the preceding article is applicable to the commanders of military bodies in the field in default of a Municipal Judge, respecting members of the same who intend to celebrate marriage, *in articulo mortis.*

96. When the fifteen days, which are referred to in article 89, have elapsed without any impediment having been denounced, and the Municipal Judge has no knowledge of any such, he shall proceed with the celebration of the marriage in the manner and form prescribed in the Code.

When a year elapses from the publication of the banns without the marriage taking place, the marriage shall not be celebrated without a new publication.

97. When, before the celebration of the marriage, any person should appear opposing it and alleging a lawful impediment, or the Municipal Judge should have knowledge of any such, he shall suspend the celebration of the marriage, until the truth or falseness of the impediment is established in a final sentence.

98. All those who have knowledge of a pretension of a marriage are obliged to denounce any impediment known to them.

Such denouncement having been made, it shall be transmitted to the Public Attorney, who, if he finds any legal foundations therefor, shall establish opposition to the marriage.

Only private parties who may have an interest in preventing the marriage shall by themselves formalize the opposition, and in both cases such opposition shall be followed in conformity with the Law of Civil Procedure, giving it the form of an incidental question (*tramitacion de los incidentes*).

Uru. 93.

99. When, by a final sentence, the alleged impediments are declared false, he, who taking them as a basis formalized in his name the opposition to the marriage, remains obliged to make indemnity for damages and injuries.

Uru. 95.

100. The marriage shall be celebrated by the contracting parties appearing before the Municipal Judge, or one of them and the person to whom the absentee may have granted a special power to represent him, accompanied by two witnesses of lawful age and without legal impediments.

Forthwith, the Municipal Judge, after reading articles 56 and 57 of this Code, shall ask each one of the contracting parties if they persist in the resolution to celebrate the marriage, and if he must actually perform it; and, if both reply affirmatively, he shall draw up the act of marriage with all the circumstances necessary to make it appear that the requirements, provided in this section, have been complied with.

The act shall be signed by the Judge, the contracting parties, the witnesses and the Secretary (clerk) of the Court.

Consuls and vice-consuls shall exercise the functions of Municipal Judges in marriages of Spaniards, celebrated in foreign countries.

Guat. 143, 144, 145; Uru. 96.

SECTION THIRD.

Nullity of marriage.

Article **101.** The following marriages are null:

1. Those celebrated between persons to whom articles 83 and 84 refer, except in cases of dispensation.
2. Those contracted by error as to the person, or by compulsion or serious fear which avoids the consent.
3. Those contracted by the abductor with the abducted, while the latter is in the former's power.
4. Those which are celebrated without the intervention of a competent Municipal Judge or of the person who must authorize it in his place, and without the presence of the witnesses, required by article 100.

Mex. 280, 289, 180, 184, 191; Peru, 160, 161, 162, 163, 165, 144; Uru. 175, 176; Col. 140; Guat. 191.

102. The action to ask for the nullity of the marriage belongs to the consorts, to the Public Attorney, and to any persons whatever who may have interest in it.

The cases of abduction, error, force or fear are excepted, in which cases only the consort, who may have suffered from it, can exercise it; and that of impotency, in which the action belongs to one or the other consort and to the persons who may have an interest in the nullity.

The action lapses, and the marriage shall be confirmed, in their respective cases, when the consorts having lived together during six months after the error has disappeared or after the force or the cause of the fear has ceased, or if, after the abducted party having recovered liberty, he or she should not have interposed a demand for nullity during said term.

Guat. 144; Peru, 164; Mex. 285, 287, 290, 292, 293, 295, 288.

103. The civil tribunals shall take cognizance of the suits for nullity of marriages, celebrated in conformity with the provisions of this chapter, shall adopt the measures, indicated in article 68, and shall give sentence definitely.

Arg. 277; Guat. 169, 191.

SECTION FOURTH.

Divorce.

Article **104.** Divorce only produces the suspension of the life in common of the consorts.

Mex. 239; Arg. 198, 205, 209; Peru, 191; Guat. 165; Col. 152.

105. The legitimate causes for divorce are:

1. Adultery on the part of the wife, in every case, and on the part of the husband, when public scandal or disgrace of the wife results from it.

2. Personal violence actually inflicted or grave acts of contumely (*injurias graves*).

3. Violence exercised by the husband over the wife in order to oblige her to change her religion.

4. The proposal of the husband to prostitute his wife.

5. The attempts of the husband or wife to corrupt their sons or to prostitute their daughters, and the connivance in their corruption or prostitution.

6. The condemnation of a consort to *cadena perpetua** or to *reclusion perpetua.*†

Mex. 240, 242, 246; Peru, 192; Uru. 148; Arg. 204; Guat. 170.

---

* To perpetually wear chains and be confined outside of the Islands of Cuba and Puerto Rico (P. C. 104).

† To be perpetually imprisoned at forced labor within or without the Islands of Cuba and Puerto Rico (P. C. 108).

106. Only the innocent consort can petition for divorce.

Col. 156; Uru. 149; Mex. 262; Arg. 204, 226, 227.

107. The provision of article 103 shall be applicable to suits for divorce and their incidents.

TITLE V.

Paternity and filiation.

CHAPTER FIRST.

*Legitimate children.**

Article **108.** Children, born after one hundred and eighty days next following the celebration of marriage, and before three hundred days next following its dissolution, or the separation of the consorts, shall be presumed legitimate children.

Against this presumption no other proof shall be admitted than that of the physical impossibility of the husband to have had access to his wife, during the first one hundred and twenty days of these three hundred next preceding the birth of the child.

Guat. 200, 202; Mex. 314, 315; Arg. 240, 246; Uru. 190, 192.

109. A child shall be presumed to be legitimate, even though the mother should have declared against its legitimacy, or should have been condemned as an adulteress.

Uru. 193; Arg. 255; Guat. 203.

110. The child, born within one hundred and eighty days next following the celebration of a marriage, shall be presumed to be legitimate, if any of the following circumstances exist:

1. If the husband knew, previously to the marriage, that his wife was pregnant.

2. If he, being present, has consented that in the record of the birth his name should be given to the child delivered by his wife.

3. If he has expressly or tacitly recognized the child as his own.

Uru. 191; Arg. 253; Guat. 212; Mex. 318.

111. The husband or his heirs can disavow the legitimacy of the child, born after the expiration of three hundred days next following the dissolution of the marriage or the actual legal separation of the

* Digesto, book 1, tit. 5, law 12; id., book 1, tit. 6, law 6; id., book 2, tit. 4, law 5. Part. 3, tit. 14, law 9; id. 4, tit. 23, law 4; id. 4, tit. 14, law 2. Nov. Recop., book 10, tit. 5, law 2. Law of Civil Marriage, arts. 56, 57, 58, 59.

consorts; but both the son and the mother shall also have a right to verify, in such cases, the paternity of the husband.

Uru. 74; Arg. 250; Guat. 201; Mex. 317.

112. The heirs can contest the legitimacy of the child only in the following cases:

1. If the husband has died before the expiration of the term fixed for instituting his action in court.
2. If he dies after presenting the complaint and without having withdrawn it.
3. If the child was born after the death of the husband.

Uru. 196; Mex. 323; Arg. 258; Guat. 209, 208.

113. The action to contest the legitimacy of the child shall be instituted within two months next following the inscription of the birth in the Registry, should the husband be in the same place, or, in certain cases, (if) any one of his heirs (should be present).

When they are absent, the term shall be three months if they reside in Spain, and six (months) if without Spain. When the birth of the child has been concealed, the term shall commence to be counted from the date of the discovery of the fraud.

Mex. 320; Arg. 258; Guat. 208; Uru. 195.

114. Legitimate children have the right:

1. To bear the family names of the father and the mother.
2. To receive support from the same, from their ascendants, and, in certain cases, from his brothers in accordance with article 143.
3. To the *legitime* and other successional rights recognized in them by this Code.

Arg. 265, 3, 565; Guat. 237; Mex. 218.

CHAPTER SECOND.

*Proofs of the filiation of legitimate children.**

Article **115.** The filiation of legitimate children is proven by the record of the birth, inscribed in the Civil Registry, or by an authentic instrument, or a final sentence in the cases to which articles 110 to 113 of the preceding chapter refer.

Guat. 223; Arg. 263; Uru. 40; Mex. 332.

116. In default of the documents, stated in the preceding article, filiation shall be proven by the constant possession of the status of a legitimate child.

Mex. 332; Uru. 48.

* Law of Civil Marriage, arts. 61, 62, par. 1.

117. In default of the records of birth, authentic documents, a final sentence, or possession of status, legitimate filiation may be proven by any other means, provided there is a commencement of proof in writing coming from both parents, either conjointly or severally.

Mex. 338.

118. The action to claim its legitimacy belongs to the child during all its life and shall be transmitted to its heirs, should it die during minority or be a lunatic. In such cases, the heirs shall have a term of five years for instituting the action.

The action already instituted by the child is transmitted by its death to the heirs, if it has not before become void.

Mex. 341, 342, 343; Uru. 200; Arg. 257; Guat. 221, 222.

CHAPTER THIRD.

*Legitimated children.**

Article **119**. Only natural children can be legitimated.

Natural children are those born out of marriage of parents who, at the date of the conception of the child, could have married with or without dispensation.

Uru. 202; Arg. 311, 324; Mex. 352, 358; Guat. 260.

120. Legitimation may be obtained.

1. By the subsequent marriage of the parents.
2. By Royal Concession.

Guat. 258; Mex. 353; Uru. 203; Arg. 311.

121. Children can only be considered as legitimated by a subsequent marriage, when they have been recognized by the parents before or after the celebration of such marriage.

Uru. 204; Arg. 317; Guat. 260; Mex. 356.

122. Those legitimated by subsequent marriage shall enjoy the same rights as legitimate children.

Guat. 263; Arg. 319; Uru. 206; Mex. 359.

123. Legitimation shall produce its effects in any case from the date of the marriage.

Arg. 323; Uru. 207; Guat. 263.

---

* Codigo, book 3, tit. 27, law 5. Fuero Real, book 3, tit. 6, laws 1, 2, 12, 17. Part. 4, tit. 5, law 5; id. 4, tit. 13, law 1; id. 4, tit. 14, laws 1, 2; id. 4, tit. 15, laws 1, 4, 5, 7, 9; id. 4, tit. 15, laws 4, 5; id. 4, tit. 13, law 1. Royal Decree, July 6, 1803; id., January 11, 1837. Law of April 14, 1838, arts. 1, 2, 3, 4.

124. The legitimation of the children who have died before the celebration of the marriage shall benefit their descendants.

Uru. 205; Arg. 316; Guat. 264, 266.

125. For the legitimation by Royal Concession the following requirements are necessary:

1. That legitimation by subsequent marriage may not be possible.
2. That it may be asked by the parents or by one of them.
3. That the father or mother asking for it has no legitimate children, nor children legitimated by subsequent marriage, nor descendants of the same.
4. That if the party asking for it is married, he has to obtain the consent of the other consort.

126. Legitimation by Royal Concession may also be obtained by the child whose deceased father or mother has shown in his or her will or in a public instrument a desire to legitimate it, provided the condition stated in No. 3 of the preceding article is complied with.

127. Legitimation by Royal Concession entitles the legitimated child:

1. To bear the name of the father or mother who has asked for it.
2. To receive support from the same in the form expressed in article 143.
3. To the hereditary share prescribed in this Code.

128. The legitimation may be contested by those believing that their rights may be injured when it may be granted to persons not having the legal status of natural children, or when the requirements set forth in this chapter do not exist.

Arg. 321.

CHAPTER FOURTH.

*Illegitimate children.**

SECTION FIRST.

Recognition of natural children.

Article **129.** A natural child may be recognized by the father and mother conjointly or by only one of them.

Guat. 230, 236; Arg. 325; Mex. 364; Uru. 210.

130. In case the recognition is made by only one of the parents, it shall be presumed that the child is a natural one, if the party recogniz-

* Nov. Recop., book 10, tit. 5, law 1; id., book 10, tit. 20, law 5. Part. 4, tit. 5, laws 5, 6, 7; id. 4, tit. 19, law 5; id. 6, tit. 13, laws 8, 9, 11. Fuero Real, book 3, tit. 6, law 1, numbers 2, 3. Law of May 16, 1835, art. 2.

ing it had, at the time of the conception, legal capacity to contract marriage.

131. The recognition of a natural child shall be made in the record of birth, by will, or by any other public instrument.

Guat. 229; Arg. 318; Mex. 367; Uru. 108.

132. When the father or mother alone shall make the recognition, he or she shall not reveal the name of the person, the other parent of the child, nor express any circumstance by which it may be discovered. Public officials shall not authorize any document infringing such a prescription. If, notwithstanding this prohibition, they should make it, they will incur a fine of 125 to 500 *pesetas,* and besides the words containing such revelation shall be stricken out.

Arg. 334; Uru. 212; Mex. 368, 369.

133. A child of age cannot be recognized without his consent. When the recognition of the minor is not made in the record of birth or in a will, the judicial approval, after a hearing of the Public Attorney, shall be required.

The minor may, in any case, contest the recognition within four years next following its majority.

134. The recognized natural child has rights:

1. To bear the name of the person recognizing him.

2. To receive support from the same in accordance with article 143.

3. To receive, in the proper case, the hereditary share provided for in this Code.

Arg. 331, 337; Mex. 583.

135. The father is obliged to recognize the natural child in the following cases:

1. When an incontrovertible paper written by him, expressly recognizing his paternity, is in existence.

2. When the child is in continuous possession of the status of a natural child of the defendant father, justified by direct act of the same father or his family.

In cases of violation, ravishing or rape, the provisions prescribed in the Penal Code shall be followed in what refers to the recognition of the issue.

Arg. 325.

136. The mother shall be obliged to recognize the natural child:

1. When the child is, in relation to the mother, included in any of the cases set forth in the preceding article.

2. When the fact of the delivery and the identity of the child are fully proven.

Arg. 325.

137. The actions for the recognition of natural children can be instituted only during the life of the presumed parents, except in the following cases:

1. If the father or mother have died during the minority of the child, in which case, it may commence the action before the expiration of the first four years after its majority.

2. If, after the death of the father or mother, some document, before unknown, should be discovered in which the child is expressly recognized.

In this case the action should be commenced within six months next following the discovery of such document.

Arg. 325; Mex. 386, 387.

138. The recognition made in favor of a child which does not reunite the condition of the second paragraph of article 119, or in which the prescriptions of this section have not been complied with, may be contested by those to whom it may cause injury.

Arg. 335; Uru. 209.

SECTION SECOND.

*Other illegitimate children.**

Article **139.** Illegitimate children not having the legal status of natural children shall only have the right to claim support from their parents in accordance with article 143.

Mex. 384; Arg. 343.

140. The right to support, referred to in the preceding article, can only be claimed:

1. If the paternity or maternity is inferred from the final sentence rendered in a criminal or civil proceeding.

2. If the paternity or maternity is shown in an incontrovertible document, from the father or mother, in which the filiation is expressly recognized.

---

* Part. 4, tit. 15, laws 1, 2; id. 4, tit. 19, law 5; id. 6, tit. 13, laws 10, 11. Fuero Real, book 3, tit. 10, law 11; id. book 3, tit. 6, law 4. Nov. Recop., book 10, tit. 20, laws 4, 5.

3. In reference to the mother, whenever the fact of the delivery and the identity of the child are proven.

Uru. 222.

141. With exception of the cases expressed in Nos. 1 and 2 of the preceding article, no complaint shall be admitted in court the purpose of which may be to investigate either directly or indirectly the paternity of the illegitimate children who have not the legal status of natural children.

Mex. 376, 377; Arg. 341; Uru. 220.

TITLE VI.

*The support of relations.**

Article **142.** It is understood by support all that is indispensable for maintenance, residence, clothing and medical assistance, according to the social standing of the family.

Support includes also the education and instruction of the party receiving it when he is a minor.

Guat. 246; Arg. 372; Uru. 121; Mex. 222, 223.

143. The following are obliged to support each other reciprocally to the whole extent specified in the preceding article:

1. The consorts.
2. Legitimate ascendants and descendants.
3. Parents and children legitimated by Royal Concession and the legitimate descendants of the same.
4. Parents and the recognized natural children, and the legitimate descendants of such children.

Parents and illegitimate children not having the legal condition of natural children, owe each other, as support, all the help required for their subsistence. Parents, besides, are bound to bear the expenses of the elementary instruction of the children and of teaching them a profession, art, or office.

Brothers also owe to legitimate brothers, even when only on the mother's or father's side, the necessary help for living, when by a physical or moral defect or for any other cause not chargeable to the recipient, he may not be able to procure his maintenance. In this

---

* Part. 4, tit. 19, laws 1, 2, 3, 4, 5, 6, 12; id. 7, tit. 23, law 5; id. 4, tit. 2, law 7; id. 4, tit. 15, law 4. Fuero Real, book 3, tit. 8, laws 1, 3. Law of Civil Marriage, art. 44, 63, 73, 74, 75, 76, 77, 78. Law of Civil Procedure, art. 1604. Novela, 89, chap. 12, par. 6; id., 117, chap. 7. Digesto, laws 3, 32 of *amisis legatis.*

help is comprised, in proper cases, the indispensable expenses for paying the elementary instruction and for the learning of a profession, art, or office.

Mex. 217; Guat. 239; Uru. 118, 120; Arg. 367, 368, 369.

144. The claim for support, when proper, and two or more are obliged to give it, shall be made in the following order:

1. To the consort.
2. To the descendants in the nearest degree.
3. To the ascendants in the nearest degree also.
4. To the brothers.

Between descendants and ascendants, the graduation shall be regulated by the order in which they are called to the legitimate succession of the person entitled to support.

Arg. 367.

145. Whenever the obligation of giving support falls on two or more persons, the payment of the pension shall be divided among them at a rate in proportion to their respective capitals.

However, in case of urgent necessity and in special circumstances, the Judge may oblige only one of them to pay it provisionally, without prejudice to his right to claim from the other obligated parties the shares that correspond to them.

When two or more persons entitled to it claim support, at the same time, from the same persons legally bound to give it, and such person has not sufficient means to bear the expense of all, the order established in the preceding article shall be observed, unless the persons claiming the support are the consort and a child subject to the parental power, in which case, the latter shall be preferred to the former.

Arg. 375; Mex. 226.

146. The amount of support, in the cases included in the four classes of article 143, is to be proportioned to the capital or means of the person giving it and to the necessities of the recipient.

Uru. 122; Mex. 225; Guat. 246.

147. Support, in the cases to which the preceding article refers, shall be increased or reduced according to the increase or decrease suffered by the necessities of the recipient and the fortune of the person obliged to give it.

148. The obligation to give support shall be binding from the moment that the person having right to claim it may require it for his maintenance, but it shall be paid only from the date of the claim.

Payment shall be made monthly, in advance, and, when the recipient dies, his heirs shall not be obliged to refund whatever shall have been received in advance.

Arg. 370.

149. The person obliged to give support may, at his option, satisfy it, either by paying the pension that may be fixed or by receiving and maintaining in his own home the person having the right to the same.

Mex. 224.

150. The obligation to support ceases with the death of the person obliged to give it, even if he pays it in compliance with a final sentence.

Arg. 374.

151. The right to support cannot be renounced or transferred to a third party. Neither can it be set off against what the recipient owes to the party obliged to give it.

But pensions in arrears for support may be set off and renounced and the right to claim them may be transferred by a title with or without consideration.

Mex. 238; Guat. 245; Arg. 374; Uru. 124, 125, 126.

152. The obligation to give support shall cease:

1. By the death of the recipient.
2. When the fortune of the person obliged to pay it is reduced to the state where he cannot pay it without disregarding his own necessities and those of his family.
3. When the recipient is able to exercise an office, profession or industry or has obtained employment or improved his fortune in such a manner that the pension for support may not be necessary for his maintenance.
4. When the recipient, be he a forced heir or not, commits any offense which may cause disinheritance.
5. When the recipient is a descendant of the person obliged to give support, and such necessity is caused by bad conduct or by want of attention to work, while such cause exists.

Mex. 237, 236; Uru. 123; Guat. 250, 251, 253; Arg. 374, 373.

153. The preceding dispositions are applicable to all other cases in which, by this Code, by testament or by stipulation, a right to support may arise, with the exception of what is stipulated, ordered by the testator, or prescribed by law for the special case under consideration.

TITLE VII.

*The parental power (patria potestad).**

CHAPTER FIRST.

General provision.

Article **154.** The father, and, in his default, the mother has power over their legitimate children, not emancipated, and the children are bound to obey the parents while they remain under such power and always pay them respect and reverence.

Recognized natural children and adopted minors are under the power of the father or the mother who recognizes or adopts them, and are under the same obligations that are referred to in the preceding paragraph.

Uru. 232, 233; Arg. 265, 266; Guat. 285, 286; Mex. 389, 390.

CHAPTER SECOND.

Effects of parental power in respect to the persons of the children.†

Article **155.** The father, and, in his default, the mother has, in respect to their children, not emancipated:

1. The duty of maintaining them, to keep them in their company, educate and instruct them in proportion to their means, and represent them in the exercise of all actions that may contribute to their benefit.
2. The right to correct and punish them moderately.

Arg. 265, 274, 278; Guat. 287; Uru. 235, 238; Mex. 395.

156. The father, and, in his default, the mother may ask for the help of the gubernative authorities, which must be given to them in support of their own authority over children, not emancipated, either in the interior of the home or for the detention and even for the retention of the same in establishments for instruction, or in institutions legally authorized to receive them.

They can also claim the interference of the Municipal Judge for imposing on their children, up to one month of detention in an insti-

* Fuero Juzgo, book 3, tit. 1, law 8, par. 8. Fuero Real, book 3, tit. 7, law 3. Part. 4, tit. 17, laws 1, 2; id., 4, tit. 16, law 9, par. 2, law 10; id. 4, tit. 17, law 2. Law of Civil Marriage, 64, 70.

† Part. 4, tit. 17, laws 2, 11; id. 4, tit. 18, law 18; id. 7, tit. 8, law 9. Law of Civil Marriage, 63, 65. Law of Civil Procedure, art. 2.

tution for correctional purposes; the order of the father or mother with the *visé* of the Judge shall be sufficient for carrying into effect such detention.

The provisions of the two preceding paragraphs include children, either legitimate, legitimated, natural or recognized or adopted.

Arg. 278; Uru. 138.

157. When the father or mother have contracted a second marriage, and the child has been begotten in a former marriage, they shall be bound to state to the Judge the causes on which they base their decision to punish him and the Judge shall hear the child in a personal appearance and decree or deny the detention without any further remedy. The same thing shall be observed when the child, not emancipated, exercises any charge or office, even when the parents have not contracted a second marriage.

158. The father, and, in his default, the mother shall pay for the maintenance of the detained child, but they shall have no intervention in the conduct of the institution where he is detained; they can only have him released when they deem it proper.

CHAPTER THIRD.

*Effect of parental power in respect to the property of the children.**

Article **159.** The father, or, in his default, the mother is the legal administrator of the property of the children who are under their power.

Guat. 287; Arg. 293; Uru. 244; Mex. 400.

160. The property which the child, not emancipated, has acquired, or may acquire by his work or industry or by any lucrative title belongs to the child in ownership, and in usufruct to the father or mother who has him in his or her power and company, but if the child with the consent of the parents lives independently of them, he shall be considered as emancipated for all effects in respect to said property and shall hold the domain, usufruct, and administration of it.

Uru. 244; Arg. 287; Guat. 287.

161. The ownership and usufruct of what the child acquires with the capital of his parents belong to the latter. But should the parents

* Fuero Juzgo, book 4, tit. 2, law 13; id., book 4, tit. 5, law 5; id., book 4, tit. 17, laws 5, 6, 7; id., book 5, tit. 4, law 3; id., book 6, tit. 15, laws 3, 4, 5; id., book 5, tit. 23, law 24. Fuero Real, book 3, tit. 4, law 7. Nov. Recop., book 10, tit. 5, law 3. Law of Civil Marriage, 65, 66, 67, 68, 69. Royal Order, Aug. 28, 1876, art. 1. Law of Civil Procedure, 2011, 2030.

expressly assign to him the whole or a part of the benefits which he may obtain, such benefits shall not be chargeable to him as (a part of) the inheritance.

162. The property or rents donated or left by will to the child, not emancipated, for the expense of his education and instruction belong to him in ownership and usufruct, but the father or the mother shall have the administration thereof, if no other proviso has been made in the donation or bequest, in which case the will of the donors shall be strictly complied with.

Arg. 289, 290, 294.

163. The parents have, in respect to the property of the children, the usufruct or administration of which belongs to them, the obligations of every usufructuary or administrator, and the special obligations established by section third, title third of the Law of Mortgage.

An inventory shall be made with the intervention of the Public Attorney of all property of the children in which the parents have the administration only, and on petition of the same attorney, the Judge may decree the deposit of the stocks, bonds, etc. (*valores mobiliarios*) belonging to the child.

Arg. 291, 296; Mex. 406.

164. The father or the mother, in proper cases, shall not alienate the real property belonging to the child, the usufruct or administration of which belongs to the parents, nor incumber the same, unless for justified causes of utility or necessity and with previous authorization of the Judge of the domicile, upon consultation with the Public Attorney, without prejudice to the provisions which, in reference to the effects of transmission, are established by the Law of Mortgage.

Uru. 248; Guat. 297; Arg. 297; Mex. 409.

165. Whenever, in any matter, the father or mother may have an interest in opposition to that of the children, not emancipated, a next friend (*defensor*) shall be appointed for the children who is to represent them in or out of court.

The Judge, on petition of the father or the mother or the minor himself, or the Public Attorney, or of any other person capable of appearing in court, shall appoint, as the next friend, the relative of the minor to whom the legitimate guardianship should belong in such cases, and, in default of the above, to another relative or any other person.

Mex. 414.

166. The parents who recognize or adopt do not acquire the usufruct of the property of the children, recognized or adopted, neither shall they have the administration of such property unless they give bond for security of it to the satisfaction of the Judge of the domicile of the minor, or of such persons who must concur in the adoption.

CHAPTER FOURTH.

*Means of determining the parental power.**

Article **167.** Parental power is determined:

1. By the death of the parents or of the child.
2. By emancipation.
3. By the adoption of the child.

Uru. 257; Arg. 306; Guat. 292; Mex. 415.

168. The mother who contracts a second marriage, loses her parental power over her children, unless her deceased husband, father of them, should have in his will expressly anticipated that his widow could remarry and had ordered that, in such a case, she was to keep and exercise the parental power over his children.

Uru. 262; Arg. 308; Mex. 427.

169. The father, and, in similar cases, the mother loses the power over the children:

1. When, by a final sentence in criminal cases, the deprivement of said right is imposed on him as a penalty.

2. When, by a final sentence in a suit for divorce, such a declaration is made, and during the time that the effects of the same are in force.

Arg. 306; Guat. 295; Mex. 416.

170. The parental power is suspended by incapacity or absence of the father or, in similar cases, of the mother, when such causes are judicially declared, and also by civil interdiction.

Uru. 263; Arg. 310; Guat. 290; Mex. 918.

171. The court can deprive the parent of the parental power or suspend the exercise of the same, when they treat their children with excessive cruelty, or if they give them corrupting orders, advice, or examples. In these cases they can also deprive the parents, either totally or partially of the usufruct of the property of the child, or

* Part. 4, tit. 18, laws 1, 6, 7, 8, 9, 10, 11, 12, 13, 14, 18; id. 4, tit. 16, laws 10, 19; id. 4, tit. 17, law 15; id. 4, tit. 20, law 4; id. 6, tit. 16, laws 4, 5. Nov. Recop., book 10, tit. 5, law 3. Fuero Juzgo, book 4, tit. 2, law 14; id., book 4, tit. 3, law 3; id., book 4, tit. 4, law 3. Fuero Real, book 4, tit. 23, law 1. Law of Civil Marriage, 64, par. 2, 88. Digesto, book 37, tit. 12, law 5. Codigo, book 1, tit. 4, law 12; id., book 1, tit. 7, law 16.

adopt such measures as they may deem convenient for the interests of the same.

Uru. 261; Arg. 304, 309; Guat. 295; Mex. 417.

172. If the widowed mother, who has remarried, becomes once more a widow, she will recover from that moment her power over all the children, not emancipated.

Mex. 429.

CHAPTER FIFTH.

*Adoption.**

Article **173.** Persons who are in the full exercise of their civil rights and over forty-five years of age can adopt. The adopter must be at least fifteen years older than the adopted.

Uru. 223; Guat. 269.

174. Adoption is forbidden:

1. To clergymen.
2. To those having legitimate or legitimated descendants.
3. To the guardian respecting his ward, until his accounts have been finally approved.
4. To the consort without the consent of the other consort. Consorts may adopt conjointly, and, with the exception of this case, nobody can be adopted by more than one person.

Uru. 223, 224, 225; Guat. 269, 270, 271.

175. The adopted may bear together with the name of his family that of the adopter by so stating it in the deed of adoption.

Uru. 229; Guat. 273.

176. The adopter and the adopted owe support to each other. This obligation is understood without injury to the preference right of the recognized natural children and of the ascendants of the adopter to be supported by the same.

Uru. 230; Guat. 284.

177. The adopter acquires no right to inherit from the adopted. Neither does the adopted acquire any right to inherit from the adopter, unless by will, excepting when the adopter in the deed of

* Digesto, book 1, tit. 7, law 17. Fuero Real, book 4, tit. 22, laws 1, 2, 3, 5, 6. Part. 3, tit. 7, law 7; id. 3, tit. 18, law 91; id. 4, tit. 7, law 7; id. 4, tit. 16, laws 1, 2, 4, 6, 8, 9. Nov. Recop., book 10, tit. 20, law 1. Law of Civil Registry, art. 60.

adoption has obliged himself to institute him as an heir. This obligation shall produce no effect when the adopted dies before the adopter. The adopted retains all the rights belonging to him in his original (natural) family excepting those referring to the parental power.

Guat. 275, 276; Uru. 230, 229.

178. The adoption shall be made with judicial authorization and it must necessarily state the consent of the adopted, when of age; when a minor, that of the persons who must give consent to the minor's marriage, and, when an incapable, that of the guardian. The Public Attorney is to be heard about this matter and the Judge, after taking the steps he may consider necessary, shall approve the adoption, if according to law, and he believes it beneficial for the adopted.

Uru. 227; Guat. 267.

179. After the adoption is finally approved by the Judge, a deed is to be executed, and in it shall be stated the condition under which it has been done, and it shall be inscribed in the corresponding Civil Registry.

Uru. 228.

180. The minor or the incapable, who has been adopted, may contest the adoption within four years next following his majority or the date from which his incapacity has disappeared.

TITLE VIII.

*Absence.**

CHAPTER FIRST.

Provisional measures in case of absence.

Article **181.** When a person has disappeared from his domicile and his whereabouts is unknown and he has not left any attorney to manage his property, the Judge, on petition of a lawful party or the Public Attorney, may appoint some person to represent him in whatever may be necessary.

The same thing shall be done, when under similar circumstances, the power conferred by the absentee becomes void.

Chile, 473, 474; Col. 96; Uru. 56; Guat. 87, 88.

182. After the appointment referred to in the preceding chapter has been made, the Judge shall take the necessary measures to secure

---

* Part. 3, tit. 2, law 2.

the rights and interests of the absentee and shall determine the powers, duties and remuneration of the appointee, regulating them, according to circumstances, by the provisions established about guardians.

Guat. 90, 91.

183. The consort who absents himself shall be represented by the one present, whenever they are not legally separated.

If the consort is a minor, a guardian shall be appointed in the usual form.

In default of the consort, the absentee shall be represented by the parents, children or grandparents, in the order established in article 220.

Chile, 475, 462, 478, 448; Guat. 86.

CHAPTER SECOND.

*Declaration of absence.**

Article **184.** When two years have elapsed without any news having been received about the absentee, or from the receipt of the last news, and five years, in case the absentee has left a person in charge of the administration of his property, then the absence may be declared.

Uru. 59; Guat. 96.

185. The declaration of absence may be demanded by:

1. The consort who is present.
2. The heirs instituted in his testament and who present a trustworthy copy of the same.
3. The relations who are to inherit in case of intestacy.
4. Those having in the property of the absentee some right subordinate to the condition of his death.

Uru. 59; Guat. 96.

186. The judicial declaration of absence shall produce no effect until six months after its publication in the official papers.

Uru. 64.

CHAPTER THIRD.

Administration of property of the absentee.

Article **187.** The administration of the property of the absentee is to be granted, according to the order established in article 220, to the person specified therein.

Guat. 86.

---

* Nov. Recop., book 10, tit. 1, law 5.

188. The wife of the absentee, if of age, can freely dispose of any property belonging to her; but she cannot alienate, barter or mortgage the husband's own property, neither that of the conjugal society, unless under judicial authorization.

Guat. 156; Uru. 66.

189. When the administration belongs to the children of the absentee and they are minors, a guardian shall be provided for them who shall take charge of the property with legal formalities.

Guat. 105.

190. The administration shall cease in any of the following cases:

1. When the absentee may appear, either personally or through an attorney.

2. When the death of the absentee is proved and his testamentary heirs or the heirs of the intestate appear.

3. When a third party appears proving by proper instruments that he has acquired by purchase or by any other title the property of the absentee.

In these cases the administrator shall cease in the discharge of his duties and the property shall be placed at the disposal of those having a right to it.

Uru. 73, 74, 75; Guat. 93, 100.

CHAPTER FOURTH.

*Presumption of the death of the absentee.**

Article **191.** After thirty years have elapsed from the disappearance of the absentee or since the last news was received about him, or ninety years from his birth, the Judge, on petition of an interested party, shall declare the presumption of his death.

Chile, 80, 81, 83; Arg. 110; Col. 97, 98; Guat. 100.

192. The sentence declaring the presumption of death of an absentee shall not go into effect until after six months, to be counted from its publication in the official papers.

Arg. 118; Chile, 81, 83; Col. 97.

193. After the sentence of the presumption of death has been declared final, succession to the estate of the absentee shall be opened, and its distribution shall be made with the formalities of testamentary or intestate proceedings, according to the case.

Arg. 122; Guat. 100, 101; Chile, 91; Col. 99.

* Part. 3, tit. 14, law 14; id. 3, tit. 31, law 26.

194. Should the absentee appear, or, if without appearance, his existence be proven, then he shall recover his property in the condition in which it is found and the value of that sold or that acquired with such value, but he can claim neither the fruits nor the rents.

Col. 108, 109; Chile, 94; Arg. 124; Guat. 100.

CHAPTER FIFTH.

*Effects of absence upon the eventual rights of the absentee.**

Article **195.** The persons claiming a right belonging to another person, whose existence is not recognized, is bound to prove that such other person existed at the time in which his existence was necessary to acquire such right.

Chile, 92; Uru. 78; Col. 107; Arg. 125.

196. Notwithstanding what is prescribed in the preceding article, when a succession has been opened, and an absentee is called to it, the share of the absentee shall accrue to his co-heirs, unless there is some person having rights of his own to claim it. Both the former and the latter in such cases must make an inventory of said property with the intervention of the Public Attorney.

Uru. 79.

197. The prescription of the preceding article is to be understood as not impairing the actions of petition of inheritance or other rights belonging to the absentee, his representatives, and persons holding rights under him. Such rights shall not be extinguished, except by the lapse of time fixed for prescription. In the inscription to be made in the Registry of real property, which may accrue to the co-heirs, it shall be expressly stated that they are to remain subject to the provisions of this article.

Uru. 80; Arg. 125.

198. Those who have taken possession of the estate shall become owners of the fruits received by them in good faith, while the absentee does not appear and his rights are not claimed by his representatives or holders of rights under him.

Uru. 81; Arg. 124; Col. 104, 105.

---

* Fuero Viejo, book 5, tit. 3, law 5. Part. 3, tit. 23, laws 10, 11, 12; id. 3, tit. 29, law 18.

TITLE IX.

*Guardianship.**

CHAPTER FIRST.

General provisions.

Article **199.** The object of guardianship is the custody of the person and property or only the property of those who, not being under parental power, are incapable of governing themselves.

Guat. 305, 424; Col. 428; Arg. 377, 468; Chile, 338.

200. The following are subject to guardianship:

1. Minors not legally emancipated.
2. Insane and demented persons, though they may have lucid intervals, and the deaf and dumb who do not know how to read and write.
3. Those who have been declared prodigal by a final sentence.
4. Those who are suffering the penalty of civil interdiction.

Guat. 305, 424; Arg. 377, 469; Col. 431, 432; Chile, 341, 342.

201. Guardianship shall be exercised by a single guardian under the vigilance of a *protutor* (vigilant guardian) and the family council.

Guat. 305, 417; Arg. 386; Col. 437; Chile, 347.

202. The charges of guardian and *protutor* cannot be renounced unless for a lawful cause duly shown.

Chile, 520; Arg. 379.

203. Municipal Judges of the places in which persons subject to guardianship reside shall provide for their custody and for their personal property until a guardian shall be appointed, when there is no other person charged with these duties under the law.

Should they not comply herewith, they shall be liable for the damages accruing on this account, to minors or to incapable persons.

Arg. 491; Chile, 371.

204. Guardianship is conferred:

1. By testament.
2. By law.
3. By the family council.

Arg. 382; Col. 443; Guat. 306; Chile, 353, 360.

---

* Fuero Juzgo, book 4, tit. 3, law 4. Part. 5, tit. 11, law 5; id. 6, tit. 16, laws 1, 2, 12, 13.

205. The guardian shall not enter upon the discharge of his duties until his appointment has been inscribed in the Registry of guardianships.

Chile, 373.

CHAPTER SECOND.

*Testamentary guardianship.**

Article **206.** The father may appoint a guardian and a *protutor* for his minor children or for those of age who are incapable, be they legitimate or recognized as natural or for some of his illegitimate children who he is obliged to support, as provided in article 139.

The mother has similar rights, but if she has contracted a second marriage, the appointment made by her for the children of her first marriage shall not be effective without the approval of the family council.

In any case it shall be necessary that the person appointed guardian or *protutor* shall not be subject to the authority of any other person.

Guat. 317, 320, 456; Arg. 383, 479; Col. 444, 448; Chile, 354, 355, 358, 359, 500.

207. A guardian may also be appointed for minors or incapables by the person leaving them an inheritance or an important legacy. The appointment, however, shall produce no effect until the family council has decided to accept the inheritance or legacy.

Chile, 360.

208. The father as well as the mother may appoint a guardian for each of their children, and make different appointments in order that the appointees may be substituted one for another.

In case of doubt, it shall be understood that a single guardian has been appointed for all the children, and the charge shall be conferred upon the first of these named in the appointment.

Chile, 364, 362; Guat. 322, 323; Arg. 386; Col. 454.

209. If different persons should have appointed a guardian for the same minor, the charge shall devolve upon:

1. The one chosen by the father or mother.

2. The one appointed by the stranger who has instituted the minor or an incapable as his heir, if the amount of the inheritance is important.

---

* Part. 6, tit. 16, laws 3, 6, 8, 11. Law of Civil Procedure, arts. 1833, 1834.

3. The one who has been chosen by the person leaving an important legacy.

If there is more than one guardian in Nos. 2 and 3, specified in this article, the family council shall declare which one is to be preferred.

210. When the guardian is in the discharge of his duties and the one appointed by the father appears, the guardianship is to be immediately transferred to the latter. If the guardian who appears is the one appointed by a stranger, specified in Nos. 2 and 3 of the preceding article, he will limit himself to the administration of the property which belonged to the person who appointed him, until the incumbent guardian vacates.

CHAPTER THIRD.

Legitimate guardianship.

SECTION FIRST.

*Guardianship of minors.**

Article **211.** Legitimate guardianship of minors, not emancipated, belongs solely:

1. To the paternal grandfather.
2. To the maternal grandfather.
3. To the paternal and maternal grandmothers, in the same order, while they remain in widowhood.
4. To the eldest of the male brothers of full blood, and, in default of them, to the eldest of the brothers on the paternal or maternal side.

The guardianship, to which this article refers, does not apply to illegitimate children.

Chile, 367; Col. 456, 458; Guat. 326, 327; Arg. 390, 395.

212. Heads of foundling institutions are the guardians of those kept and educated therein. The representation in court of such officials as guardians shall be assumed by the Public Attorney.

Arg. 396.

SECTION SECOND.

Guardianship of the insane and the deaf and dumb.†

Article **213.** No guardians shall be appointed for insane, demented, and deaf and dumb persons, when of age, without a previous declara-

---

* Fuero Real, book 3, tit. 7, law 2. Part. 6, tit. 16, law 9.

† Digesto, book 27, tit. 10, laws 2, 4, 14, 6, 13. Codigo, book 5, tit. 34, law 2; id. book 5, tit. 7, laws 3, 5. Novela, chap. 13, par. 12. Part. 5, tit. 11, law 5; id. 6, tit. 16, law 13. Law of Civil Procedure, arts. 1849, 1850, 1851.

tion having been made that they are incapable of managing their property.

Arg. 470; Col. 546, 547; Chile, 456, 457, 458, 470.

214. This declaration may be asked by the consort and the relatives of the person presumed to be incapable who may have rights to succeed him, in case of intestacy.

Arg. 470; Chile, 443, 459; Col. 548.

215. The Public Attorney must demand it:

1. When the person is a raving maniac.

2. When none of the persons mentioned in the preceding article are in existence, or when they do not make any use of the rights granted to them by it.

3. When the consort and the heirs of the person presumed to be incapable are minors or have not the personality required to appear in court.

In all these cases, the court shall appoint a next friend for the person presumed to be incapable who does not wish or is not able to defend himself. In all other cases, the Public Attorney shall be their defender.

Chile, 443, 459; Col. 548; Arg. 470.

216. The courts, before declaring the incapacity, shall hear the family council and shall personally examine the persons denounced as incapable.

Col. 549; Chile, 460.

217. The relatives who have solicited the declaration of incapacity shall not be able to give information to the court as members of the family council, but they have the right to be heard by the council when they demand it.

218. The declaration of incapacity shall be made summarily. That which refers to the deaf and dumb shall fix the extent and limits of the guardianship, according to their degree of incapacity.

219. Against the decrees, determining the proceedings for incapacity, the interested parties may interpose a suit in the ordinary form. The next friend of the incapable shall, however, require for it special authorization from the family council.

220. Guardianship of the insane and the deaf and dumb belongs:

1. To the consort not legally separated.

2. To the father, and, in his default, to the mother.

3. To the children.

4. To the grandparents.

5. To the brothers and to the unmarried sisters with due preference to the double relationships stated in No. 4 of article 211.

If there are children, brothers and sisters, the male shall be preferred to the female, and the oldest to the youngest.

When there are paternal and maternal grandparents, the male shall also be preferred, and in case they are of the same sex, those of the paternal line.

Chile, 462; Col. 550; Guat. 428, 430; Arg. 390, 476, 477, 478.

SECTION THIRD.

*Guardianship of prodigals (spendthrifts).**

Article **221**. The declaration of prodigality must be made in a contradictory suit.

The sentence shall determine the acts which are forbidden to the incapable, the faculties which the guardian is to exercise in the name of the same, and the cases in which one or the other are bound to consult the family council.

222. The declaration, to which the preceding article refers, can be demanded only by the consort, and the forced heirs of the prodigal, and exceptionally by the Public Attorney, either by himself or on petition of some relative of the former, when they are minors or incapables.

Col. 214; Chile, 443.

223. When the defendant does not appear at the trial, he shall be represented by the Public Attorney, and, if the latter be a party thereto, by a next friend, appointed by the court, without impairing what the Law of Civil Procedure prescribes in proceedings in contempt.

Chile, 443.

224. The declaration of prodigality does not deprive the prodigal of the marital and parental power, nor does it give to the guardian any power over the person of the prodigal.

Chile, 442.

---

* Digesto, book 23, tit. 2, law 20. Codigo, book 5, tit. 4, law 8. Under the Institutes, book 1, tit. 2, chap. 3, guardians were appointed for persons under fifteen and curators for those over fourteen, and for prodigals.

225. The guardian shall administer the property of the children whom a prodigal may have had from a previous marriage.

The wife shall administer her dotal and paraphernal property, the property of the children in common, and that of the conjugal society. She will need a judicial authorization to sell them.

Col. 538, 539; Chile, 449, 450.

226. The acts of a prodigal, previous to the petition for interdiction, cannot be contested on account of prodigality.

Chile, book 1, tit. 24.

227. The guardianship of the prodigal belongs:

1. To the father, and, in his default, to the mother.
2. To the paternal and maternal grandparents.
3. To the eldest of the emancipated male children.

Col. 537; Chile, 448.

SECTION FOURTH.

Guardianship of persons suffering interdiction.

Article **228.** When the sentence in which the penalty of interdiction is interposed, has become final, the Public Attorney shall demand that articles 203 and 293 shall be complied with. If he fails to do it, he shall be liable for the damages and injuries caused thereby.

The consort and the intestate heirs of one so interdicted may also demand it.

229. Such guardianship shall be limited to the administration of the property and to the representation in court of the interdicted person.

The guardian of the interdicted person shall be obliged, furthermore, to care for the person and property of the minors or the incapables, who are under the power of the person subject to interdiction, until another guardian is provided for them.

The wife of the interdicted person shall have parental power over their common children while the interdiction lasts.

If she is a minor, she shall act under the direction of her father, and, in his default, that of her mother, and in default of both, that of her guardian.

230. The guardianship of those suffering interdiction is granted in accordance with the order established in article 220.

CHAPTER FOURTH.

*Guardianship by appointment.**

Article **231**. When there are neither testamentary guardian, nor persons called by law to the exercise of a vacant guardianship, it is the duty of the family council to elect the guardian in all the cases mentioned in article 200.

Chile, 370, 372, 460; Guat. 329.

232. A municipal judge, who may neglect calling a family council in any case in which a guardian ought to be provided for minors or incapables, shall be liable for the damage or injury caused by his negligence.

CHAPTER FIFTH.

Protutors (vigilant guardians).

Article **233**. The family council is entitled to appoint a *protutor* when he has not been appointed by those who have a right to elect a guardian for minors.

234. The guardian cannot begin to exercise guardianship until a *protutor* has been appointed. If he fails to apply for this appointment, he shall be removed from the guardianship and shall be liable for the damage suffered by the minor.

235. The appointment of a *protutor* shall not be given to a relative of the same line as the guardian.

236. The *protutor* is obliged:

1. To supervise the inventory of the property of the minor and the constitution of the bond of the guardian, when it must be given.

2. To maintain the rights of the minor in and out of court whenever they are opposed to the interests of the guardian.

3. To call the attention of the family council to the management of the guardian, whenever he may consider it injurious to the person or interests of the minor.

4. To promote the meeting of the family council for the appointment of a new guardian when the guardianship may become vacant or abandoned.

5. To discharge all further duties provided by law. The *protutor* shall be liable for the damages and injuries caused to the minor by his omission or neglect to comply with such duties.

The *protutor* may attend the deliberations of the family council and take part in them, but he has no right to vote.

*** Part. 6, tit. 16, laws 2, 12.**

CHAPTER SIXTH.

*Persons unable to be guardians and protutors, and the removal of the same.**

Article **237.** The following cannot be guardians or *protutors:*

1. Persons subject to guardianship.

2. Those who have been punished for the crimes of robbery, theft, fraud, forgery, corruption of minors, or public scandal.

3. Those condemned to any corporal punishment, until the sentence expires.

4. Those who have been legally removed from a former guardianship.

5. Persons of bad conduct, or having no visible means of support.

6. Bankrupts and insolvents, not discharged.

7. Women, with the exception of the cases in which they are expressly called by law.

8. Those who, at the time of taking charge of the guardianship, have a law suit pending with the minor in regard to his civil status.

9. Those in litigation with the minor in regard to the ownership of his property, unless the father, and, in his default, the mother, being aware of it, have disposed otherwise.

10. Those indebted to the minor in large sums, unless they have been appointed by the father, and, in his default, by the mother, with knowledge of the debt.

11. The relatives mentioned in the second paragraph of article 293, and the testamentary guardian when they have not complied with the duties imposed on them by said article.

12. Professed members of monastic orders.

13. Foreigners not residing in Spain.

Chile, 267, 497, 498, 499, 500, 502, 505, 506, 507; Col., book 1, tit. 38, chap. 7; Arg. 398; Guat. 340, 341, 342.

238. The following shall be removed from guardianship:

1. Those, who after having qualified, come under one of the classes of incapacity mentioned in Nos. 1, 2, 3, 4, 5, 6, 8, 12 and 13 of the preceding article.

---

* Digesto, book 26, tit. 10, law 3, pars. 8, 12; id., book 27, tit. 1, law 6, pars. 18, 21. Instituciones, book 1, tit. 12, par. 5; id., book 1, tit. 14, law 2; id., book 1, tit. 25, par. 13. Codigo, book 5, tit. 35, law 1; id., book 5, tit. 42, laws 1, 3; id., book 5, tit. 51, law 13. Novela, 72, chap. 1.

2. Those who have assumed the administration of the guardianship without having the family council convened nor having asked for the appointment of a *protutor* or without having given bonds, in cases in which they are required to give them, and having omitted to inscribe the mortgage bond.

3. Those who have not made the inventory within the term and in the manner prescribed by law or have not made it faithfully.

4. Those who have not behaved properly in the discharge of the guardianship.

Chile, 509, 174, 378, 395; Col. 627; Guat. and Arg. 457.

239. The family council shall not declare the incapacity of guardians and *protutors* or resolve upon their removal, without summoning and hearing them if they appear.

240. After the incapacity has been declared or the removal has been agreed on by the family council, such decision shall be considered final and the vacant guardianship shall be filled, if the guardian does not present his claims before the court within fifteen days next following the day on which the resolution has been communicated to him.

241. When the guardian institutes a judicial contention, the council shall litigate it, at the expense of the minor, but the members thereof may be personally condemned to pay the costs if they have acted with notorious malice.

Chile, 506, 507, 509.

242. When the resolution of the family council is favorable to the guardian, and has been unanimously adopted, there shall be no remedy against it.

243. If, by cause of incapacity, the guardian does not enter upon the discharge of his duties, the family council shall attend to the duties of the guardianship, until a final resolution is agreed upon about the impediment.

When the guardian has already entered upon the discharge of his duties and the family council has declared his incapacity and resolved to remove him, the decision which they may take to provide for the care of theg uardianship, in case a law suit should be instituted, shall not be executed without a previous judicial approval.

Chile, 371, 543.

CHAPTER SEVENTH.

*Excuses for not accepting guardianship and protutorship.**

Article **244.** The following may be excused from guardianship and *protutorship:*

1. Ministers of the Crown.
2. Presidents of the Co-legislative Houses, of the Council of State, of the Supreme Court, of the Supreme Council of War and Navy, and of the Court of Accounts of the Kingdom.
3. Archbishops and bishops.
4. Magistrates, Judges and officials of the Public Attorney's office.
5. Those who exercise authority immediately depending on the government.
6. Those in active military service.
7. Clergymen with curate charges.
8. Those having under their power five legitimate children.
9. Those that are so poor that they cannot attend to the guardianship without impairing their livelihood.
10. Those, who in consequence of continuous ill-health or because of inability to read or write, cannot well fulfill the duties of the charge.
11. Persons over sixty years of age.
12. Those who are already guardians or *protutors* of another person.

Arg. 386, 398; Col. 602; Chile, 514; Guat. 331 to 337.

245. Persons, not relatives of the minor or incapable, are not bound to accept the guardianship, if, within the territory of the court appointing the guardian, there are relatives within the sixth degree who may fulfill the charge.

246. The person, excused on petition of the guardian or *protutor*, may be compelled to accept the guardianship, as soon as the cause of the exemption has ceased.

247. An excuse, which has not been alleged before the family council in meeting held for the purpose of deciding upon the guardianship, shall not be acceptable.

If the guardian has not been present at the meeting of the council, nor has previously been made aware of his appointment, he must allege the excuse within the ten days next following the date on which he has been notified of it.

Chile, 519, 520; Guat. 339.

---

* Part. 6, tit. 16, law 12; id. 6, tit. 17, laws 1, 3, 4, 6. Nov. Recop., book 7, tit. 29, law 3; id., book 10, tit. 2, law 7.

248. If the causes of exemption are subsequent to the acceptance of the guardianship, the term for alleging them shall begin to be counted from the day on which the guardian may have become aware of the same.

Guat. 335; Chile, 522; Col. 610.

249. The resolution on which the family council rejects the excuse may be contested before the court within the term of fifteen days.

The resolutions of the family council shall be maintained by the same, at the expense of the minor; but if they should be affirmed, the person promoting the suit shall be condemned to the payment of the costs.

Chile, 525.

250. During the suit on account of excuses, the one presenting them shall be bound to exercise the guardianship. If he does not do so, the family council shall appoint some person to substitute him, and the substituted person shall be liable for the action of the former in case the excuses are not sustained.

251. The testamentary guardian who may excuse himself from the guardianship shall lose whatever may have been left to him by the person who voluntarily appointed him.

Chile, 531.

CHAPTER EIGHTH.

*Bonds of guardians.**

Article **252.** The guardian, before he assumes the guardianship, shall give bond as security for the performance of his duties.

Arg. 413, 399; Col. 464; Chile, 374; Guat. 349.

253. The bond must be secured either by mortgage or by pledge.

Personal bond shall be acccpted only when it is impossible to give bond, as above stated. The security given by the bondsmen shall not prevent the adoption of any decision proper for the good keeping of the property of the minor or incapable.

Chile, 374, 376; Col. 466; Guat. 344, 345.

254. The bond shall secure:

1. The value of any personal property which may come into the possession of the guardian.

2. The rents or profits which the property of the minor or incapable may produce during one year.

---

* Part. 3, tit. 18, law 94; id. 6, tit. 16, law 9. Law of Civil Procedure, art. 1867.

3. The profits which the minor may receive from mercantile or industrial undertakings during one year.

Guat. 346.

255. The guardian may have recourse to the courts against any resolution of the family council fixing the amount or qualifying the bond, but he shall not enter upon the discharge of his duties without having given the bond required.

256. Whilst the bond is being executed the *protutor* shall perform the acts of administration which the family council may consider indispensable for the safe-keping of the property and the collection of its proceeds.

257. The mortgage bond shall be inscribed in the Registry of Property. The pledge bond shall be made by the deposit of effects or values in one of the public institutions authorized for this purpose.

Chile, 1410.

258. The inscription or deposit shall be demanded:

1. By the guardian.
2. By the *protutor*.
3. By any of the members of the family council.

Those omitting to do it shall be liable for the damage and injury resulting therefrom.

259. The bond may be increased or reduced, durng the exercise of the guardianship, according to the changes which may occur in the capital of the minor or the incapable and in the values upon which the bond is based.

The bond shall not be totally cancelled until after the accounts of the guardianship are approved and the guardian has extinguished all the liabilities of his management.

Guat. 347.

260. The following are exempted from giving bond for guardianship:

1. The father, the mother, and the grandparents, when called upon to be the guardian of their descendants.

2. The testamentary guardian, released by the father or, in his default, by the mother, from such duty. This exception shall cease, when, subsequently to his appointment, causes unknown to the testator may arise which render the bond indispensable in the judgment of the family council.

3. The guardian, appointed without bonds, by strangers who may have instituted the minor or incapable as his heir, or left him a legacy

for a large amount. In this case, the exemption shall be limited to the property or rents of which the inheritance or legacy consists.

Chile, 374; Col. 465; **Guat. 350.**

CHAPTER NINTH.

*Exercise of the guardianship.**

Article **261.** The family council shall place the guardian and the *protutor* in possession.

262. The guardian represents the minor or incapable in all civil acts with the exception of those which the latter can execute by himself alone by express provision of law.

Guat. 361; Arg. 380, 411; Chile, 390.

263. Minors and incapables, subject to guardianship, owe respect and obedience to the guardian. He may punish them moderately.

Guat. 362; Arg. 415.

264. The guardian is obliged:

1. To maintain and educate the minor or incapable in accordance with his condition, and in strict subjection to the disposition of his parents, or, in default of these, with those adopted by the family council.
2. To endeavor that the insane, demented, or deaf or dumb may acquire or recover their capacity, by whatever means their capital may furnish.
3. To make an inventory of the property which the guardianship may cover within the terms fixed for this purpose by the family council.
4. To administer the estate of the minor or incapable with all the diligence of a good father of a family.
5. To ask in due time the authorization of the family council for everything that he may not do without such authorization.
6. To solicit the intervention of the *protutor* in all the cases which the law may deem it necessary.

Chile, 428, 431, 438, 467, 471, 378, 391, 393; Guat. 365, 368, 369, 353, 361; Col. 468, 481.

---

* Digesto, book 26, tit. 7, law 46, par. 7; id., book 5, tit. 37, law 16. Fuero Juzgo, book 2, tit. 5, law 10; id., book 4, tit. 3, laws 1, 3, 4; id., book 4, tit. 2, law 13. Fuero Viejo, book 5, tit. 4, laws 2, 3, 4. Fuero Real, book 1, tit. 2, law 7; id., book 3, tit. 7, law 2. Part. 3, tit. 2, law 11; id. 3, tit. 18, laws 60, 99; id. 3, tit. 7, law 2; id. 5, tit. 5, law 4; id. 5, tit. 11, laws 4, 5; id. 6, tit. 16, laws 12, 15, 16, 17, 18, 20, 21. Law of Civil Procedure, arts. 1041, 1049, 1862, 1864, 1868, 1870, 1872, 2011, 2012, 2015, 2022, 2025, 2027, 2030. Penal Code, art. 603, par. 8. Royal Decree, May 19, 1885, art. 8. Royal Order, Aug. 28, 1876, arts. 1, 2, 3. Nov. Recop., book 10, tit. 12, law 1.

265. The inventory shall be made with the intervention of the *protutor* and with the assistance of two witnesses chosen by the family council. The council shall decide, considering the importance of the capital, if the inventory is, in addition, to be authorized by a Notary.

Arg. 422; Col. 470, 471.

266. The jewelry, valuable furniture, public effects, and mercantile and industrial values, which in the judgment of the family council are not to remain in possession of the guardian, shall be deposited in an institution established for this purpose.

All other personal and self-moving (*semovientes*) property, if it is not appraised, shall be appraised by experts appointed by the family council.

Chile, 382, 384; Guat. 472.

267. The guardian, who having been summoned for this purpose through a Notary by the *protutor* or by the witnesses, should not enter in the inventory the credits he holds against the minor, shall be understood as renouncing them.

Arg. 419; Guat. 377; Chile, 382, 412.

268. When the will of the person who made the appointment of the guardian provides nothing about the alimentary pension to be allotted to the minor or incapable, the family council, after inspecting the inventory, shall decide the part of the rents or proceeds which shall be allotted for such purpose.

This resolution may be modified in proportion to the increase or decrease of the inheritance of the minors or incapables or the change their condition may suffer.

Chile, 431; Arg. 423.

269. The guardian requires to be authorized by the family council:

1. To impose on the minor the punishment referred to in No. 2, article 155 and article 156.

2. To give to the minor a profession or particular avocation when that has not been decided by the parents and to modify any disposition that they had made in this respect.

3. To place the incapable in a sanitarium, unless the guardianship is exercised by the father, mother or a son.

4. To follow the commercial or industrial calling to which the incapable, or his ascendants or the ascendants of the minor had pursued.

5. To alienate or incumber any property constituting the capital of the minor or incapable or to make contracts or act subject to inscription.

6. To invest any balance of money remaining each year, after meeting the obligations of the guardianship.

7. To cause the distribution of the inheritance or of any other thing which the minor or incapable may hold in common.

8. To withdraw from investment any sums producing interest.

9. To loan and borrow money.

10. To accept without the benefit inventory any inheritance or to repudiate such inheritance or donations.

11. To incur extraordinary expenses in connection with tenements, the administration of which is included under the guardianship.

12. To compromise and submit to arbitration the questions to which the minor or incapable may be interested.

13. To institute suits in the name of persons subject to guardianship, and to maintain the remedies of appeal and nullity (*casación*) against the sentences in which they may have been condemned. Demands or remedies in verbal suits are excepted.

Chile, 393, 396, 397, 398, 400, 401, 402, 404, 431; Col. 459, 485, 486, 489, 517; Arg. 424, 426, 434, 435, 443, 450.

270. The family council cannot empower the guardian to sell or incumber the property of the minor or incapable, unless it be for causes of necessity or utility which the guardian has to duly prove.

This power shall be exercised in regard to specified things.

Chile, 393; Guat. 373; Arg. 438.

271. The family council, before granting authorization to incumber real property or constitute real rights in favor of third persons, may previously hear the opinion of experts about the conditions of the incumbrances and possibilities of bettering them.

Guat. 274.

272. In respect to real property, rights to be inscribed, jewelry or furniture, the value of which is over 4,000 *pesetas*, any sale thereof is to be made at public auction with the intervention of the guardian or *protutor*.

Stock listed on exchanges, either public, commercial or industrial, shall be sold by a stock agent or a commercial broker.

Guat. 376; Arg. 441; Chile, 394.

273. The guardian is liable for the legal interest on the capital of the minor, when by his omission or negligence, it shall remain unproductive or without investment.

Arg. 413; Guat. 372; Col. 495; Chile, 406.

274. The authorization to settle or compromise through arbitrators shall be requested in writing, and therein the guardian shall explain all the condition and advantages of the settlement.

The family council may hear the opinion of one or more lawyers, according to the importance of the matter, and may grant or deny such authorization. In case of granting it, it shall be so stated in the minutes.

Arg. 443.

275. Guardians are forbidden:

1. To donate or renounce things or rights belonging to minors or incapables.

The donations made on account of marriage by minors, with the approval of the persons who are to give their consent to the marriage, shall be valid, provided they do not exceed the limits fixed by law.

2. To collect from the debtor of the minor or incapable, without the intervention of the *protutor*, sums over 5,000 *pesetas*, unless they are interests, rents or fruits.

Payments made without complying with this requirement shall be profitable to the debtors, only when they can prove that the money received has been invested for the benefit of the minor or incapable.

3. To pay themselves, without the intervention of the *protutor*, any sums due them.

4. To buy himself, or through another person, the property of the minor or incapable, unless he has been expressly authorized to do so by the family council.

Mex. 626, 618, 616; Chile, 402, 403, 407, 410, 412; Guat. 363, 382, 383, 385; Col. 491, 501.

276. The guardian is entitled to compensation from the property of the minor or incapable:

When it has not been fixed by those who appointed the testamentary guardian, or when the guardians are legitimate or appointed by court, the family council shall fix it, taking in consideration the importance of the estate and the work to be undertaken in its administration.

In no case shall the compensation be less than 4 per cent. nor more than 10 per cent. of the net rents or proceeds of the estate.

The guardian may ask a remedy from the courts against the resolution fixing his compensation.

Mex. 623, 624; Guat. 390; Col. 614; Chile, 526.

277. Should the family council maintain its resolution, the council shall then litigate at the expense of the minor or incapable.

278. The guardianship is determined:

1. By the minor attaining the age of twenty-three years, by habilitation as to age, and by adoption.

2. By the cessation of the causes originating the same in cases of persons incapable, subject to interdiction, or prodigals.

Mex. 637; Guat. 392, 431; Arg. 457, 484.

CHAPTER TENTH.

*Accounts of the guardianship.**

Article **279.** Collateral relatives of the minor or incapable, and strangers, who have not obtained the charge of guardian, with the assignment of proceeds for support, shall render to the family council yearly accounts of their administration.

The accounts, after being examined by the *protutor* and audited by the council, shall be deposited with the clerk of the court where the guardianship has been registered.

In case the guardian does not agree to the resolution of the council, he may apply to the courts before which the interests of the minor or incapable shall be defended by the *protutor*.

Chile, 416; Col. 504, 511; Mex. 646.

280. The guardian who may be replaced by another, as well as his heirs, shall be obliged to render a general account of his guardianship to the one taking his place; such account shall be examined and audited in the form prescribed in the preceding article. The new guardian shall be liable for the damages and injuries to the minor, if he does not claim and examine the accounts of his predecessor.

Mex. 648; Chile, 415; Arg. 421, 460; Guat. 401.

281. When the guardianship terminates, the guardian or his heirs are obliged to render account of his administration to the person who

---

* Fuero Juzgo, book 4, tit. 3, laws 3, 4. Fuero Real, book 3, tit. 7, law 2. Fuero Viejo, book 5, tit. 4, law 1. Part. 3, tit. 18, law 120; id. 5, tit. 13, law 23; id. 6, tit. 16, law 21; id. 6, tit. 19, laws 2, 8. Law of Civil Procedure, art. 1876.

has been under his guardianship or to his representatives or those holding rights under him.

Mex. 638, 640; Arg. 460; Guat. 393; Chile, 422.

282. The general accounts of the guardianship shall be audited and reported upon by the family council within a term not exceeding six months (after the receipt of the same).

Arg. 459, 460.

283. The accounts are to be accompanied by their vouchers. The only expenses which need not be vouched for are the petty expenses for which a diligent father of a family does not generally ask a receipt.

Chile, 415; Mex. 649; Guat. 402.

284. The expenses of rendering the accounts shall be borne by the minor or incapable.

Guat. 406; Chile, 414.

285. Until fifteen days after the rendering of the accounts with the vouchers, the persons holding rights under the minor or the minor himself, if of age, cannot enter into any agreement with the guardian which may have relation to the administration of the guardianship.

The family council, without detriment to the agreement which the interested parties may make between themselves, after the expiration of this term, shall denounce to the courts any wrongful act which may have been committed by the guardian in the exercise of the guardianship.

Arg. 465; Guat. 412.

286. The balance shown by the general account, either in favor of or against the guardian, shall bear legal interest. In the first case, from the time the minor is asked for the payment of the balance, after the delivery of his property.

In the second case, from the date of rendering the accounts, if they have been presented within the legal term, and, if not, from the expiration of such term.

Mex. 661; Chile, 424; Arg. 466; Guat. 413.

287. The actions, reciprocally belonging to the guardian and the minor on account of the exercise of the guardianship, are extinguished five years after the termination of the same.

Mex. 665; Chile, 425; Arg. 425; Col. 514; Guat. 414.

CHAPTER ELEVENTH.

*Registration of guardianships.**

Article **288.** There shall be in the courts of the First Instance one or several books in which entries shall be made of the guardianships, constituted within the year within their respective territories.

289. These books shall be in the custody of a judicial clerk who shall make the entries free of cost.

Mex. 107.

290. The registration of each guardianship shall contain:

1. The name, family name, age, and domicile of the minor or incapable, and the extent and limit of the guardianship, when the incapacity has been judicially declared.

2. The name, family name, profession, and domicile of the guardian, and the statement of whether he is a testamentary or legitimate guardian or is appointed by court.

3. The date on which the guardianship has been conferred, and the day on which the bond, required from the guardian, has been constituted, stating, in such cases, the kind of property on which it has been based.

4. The alimentary pension which has been assigned to the minor or incapable or the declaration of the compensation of proceeds for support.

291. At the foot of each inscription, at the beginning of the judicial year, it shall be recorded whether the guardian has rendered an account of his administration, if he is obliged to do so.

292. The judges shall examine every year such registries and shall take the necessary steps in each case to defend the interests of the person subject to guardianship.

TITLE X.

The family council.

SECTION FIRST.

Manner of constituting.

Article **293.** If the Public Attorney or Municipal Judge should become informed that in the territory within their jurisdiction are found any of the persons to which article 200 refers, the first shall ask

* Law of Civil Procedure, arts. 1875, 1876.

and the second shall order of his own motion, or upon the petition of the Public Attorney, as the case may be, the constitution of a family council.

The following persons are obliged to notify the Municipal Judge of any fact which gives cause for a guardianship, as soon as they have knowledge of it; the testamentary guardian, the relatives who are called to the legitimate guardianship and those that, according to law, are members of the council; and they are liable, should they not do so, to an indemnity for damages and injuries (caused thereby).

The Municipal Judge shall summon the persons who should compose the family council, stating to them the object of the meeting, and the day, hour, and place in which it shall be held.

294. The family council shall be composed of the persons whom the father, or, in proper cases, the mother may have appointed in the testament, and, in default of them, of the male ascendants and descendants, and the brothers and husbands of the living sisters of the minor or incapable, whatever their number may be. If they are less than five, this number shall be completed with the nearest male relatives of both the paternal and maternal lines, and, in the event that they do not exist or that they are not bound to form part of the council, the Municipal Judge shall appoint, instead, honest persons, preferring the friends of the parents of the minor or incapable.

If there be no ascendants, descendants, brothers or husbands of living sisters, the Municipal Judge shall constitute the council with the five nearest male relatives of the minor or incapable, and, when there are no relatives in part or at all, he will substitute them with honest persons, preferring always the friends of the parents.

295. In equal degrees, preference shall be given to the eldest relatives in forming the family council.

296. The courts may remedy the nullity which may be caused by the nonobservance of the preceding articles, if not due to fraud nor causing damage to the person or property of the person subject to guardianship, but taking care to amend the error committed in the formation of the council.

297. The relatives of the minor or incapable, called by law, who do not reside within 30 kilometres of the court having jurisdiction over the guardianship, shall not be obliged to form a part of the council, but they may be members of the council, if they willingly accept the charge, for which purpose they shall be summoned by the Municipal Judge.

298. The causes which excuse, disable, and give reason for the removal of guardians and *protutors* apply to the members of the family council. Neither can persons excluded from the charge by the father, or, in his default, by the mother in their wills, be members of it.

299. The guardian and *protutor* shall not be, at the same time, members of the family council.

300. The meeting for the formation of the family council shall be presided over by the Municipal Judge. The parties summoned are obliged to appear in person or by a special attorney who shall never represent more than one person. If they do not appear, the Judge may impose on them a fine not exceeding 50 *pesetas*.

301. After the family council has been constituted by the Municipal Judge, it shall proceed to prescribe all the measures required for the custody of the person and property of the minor or incapable and to constitute the guardianship.

302. The family council for natural children shall be constituted, under the same rules as that for legitimate children, but members thereof shall be appointed from the relatives of the father or mother who have recognized them.

The council for illegitimate children shall be constituted by the Municipal Attorney, who shall be the president, and four honest neighbors.

303. The administration of every Institute of Beneficence shall have over the orphans, under its care, all the faculties belonging to the guardian and to the family council.

SECTION SECOND.

Manner of proceeding of the family council.

Article **304.** The member elected by the other members shall be president of the council:

To the president belong:

1. To convoke the council, whenever he thinks it convenient or on petition of the members, of the guardian, or of the *protutor*, and to preside over its deliberations.

2. To draw up and to state the basis of the resolutions, giving therein the opinion of each of the members who shall authorize the minutes by signing the same.

3. To execute the resolutions:

305. The family council shall not adopt resolutions about matters submitted to it, unless, at least three members are present.

Resolutions shall always be adopted by a majority of the voters. The vote of the president shall decide in case of a tie.

306. The members of the family council are obliged to attend the meetings of the same for which they may be summoned. Should they not attend, nor present any lawful excuse, the president of the council shall give notice to the Municipal Judge, who may impose on them a fine not exceeding 50 *pesetas*.

307. No member of the family council shall attend its meetings nor vote when it has to deal with a matter in which he, his ascendants, descendants, or consort has any interest, but he may be heard, if the council deems it proper.

308. The guardian and the *protutor* are bound to attend the meetings of the family council, whenever convoked, but have no vote. They may also attend whenever the council meets on their petition.

The person subject to guardianship, who is over fourteen years of age, has a right to be present and to be heard.

309. The family council shall take cognizance of the affairs for which they are competent, in accordance with the provisions of this Code.

310. The members, who have dissented from the majority in voting on any resolution, may appeal to the Judge of the First Instance, as also may the guardian or *protutor* or any relative of the minor or other party interested in the decision, with the exception of the case in article 242.

311. On the determination of the guardianship, and the consequent dissolution of the family council, the latter shall deliver the minutes of its sessions to the person who has been subject to guardianship or to the person who represents his rights.

312. The members of the family council are liable for the damages which the person subject to guardianship may suffer on account of their malice or culpable neglect.

The members dissenting from the resolution, causing such injury, shall be exempted from this liability.

313. The family council shall be dissolved in the same cases in which the guardianship is extinguished.

TITLE XI.

Emancipation and majority.

CHAPTER FIRST.

*Emancipation.**

Article **314.** Emancipation takes place:

1. By marriage of the minor.

---

* Fuero Real, book 1, tit. 11, law 8. Toro, law 47. Nov. Recop., book 10, tit. 5, laws 3, 4. Part. 3, tit. 18, law 93; id. 4, tit. 17, law 4; id. 4, tit. 18, laws 15, 16, 17, 19; id. 6, tit. 16, law 12.

2. By majority.

3. By concession of the father or mother exercising the parental power.

Guat. 298; Arg. 131; Col. 312, 313, 314, 318.

315. Marriage produces lawful emancipation with the limitations contained in article 59 and in rule third of article 50.

Mex. 689; Chile, 266; Col. 314.

316. Emancipation, referred to in No. 3 of article 314, shall be granted by public deed or by appearance before the Municipal Judge, which appearance is to be inscribed in the Civil Registry, and, meanwhile, shall not produce any effect against third parties.

Chile, 265; Col. 313; Guat. 304; Mex. 691.

317. Emancipation enables the minor to control his person and property, as if of age, but, until he attains his majority, he cannot borrow money on loan, neither incumber nor sell real property without the consent of the father, and, in his default, of the mother, and, in default of both, without that of a guardian. Neither can he appear in court without the assistance of said persons.

318. In order that emancipation may take place by concession of the father or mother, it is required that the minor be over eighteen years of age and consent to it.

Chile, 265; Col. 313; Guat. 301; Arg. 131.

319. Emancipation once granted cannot be revoked.

Chile, 269; Arg. 183; Col. 317; Mex. 693.

CHAPTER SECOND.

*Majority.**

Article **320.** Majority commences after attaining twenty-three years of age. A person of age is qualified for all acts of civil life, with the exceptions established by this Code in special cases.

Mex. 694; Chile, 107, 266; Arg. 129; Col. 314; Guat. 28, 29.

321. Notwithstanding what is prescribed in the preceding article, unmarried daughters of age, but under twenty-five years, cannot leave the parental home with permission of the father or mother in whose

* Instituciones, book 1, tit. 23. Codigo, book 2, tit. 46, law 4. Fuero Juzgo, book 4, tit. 2, law 3; id., book 4, tit. 3, law 3. Fuero Real, book 3, tit. 7, law 1. Part. 6, tit. 19, law 2.

company they live, unless on account of marriage or when the father or mother have contracted another marriage.

Mex. 695; Col. 341.

322. The minor, orphan of both parents, may obtain the benefit of majority by the consent of the family council, approved by the President of the territorial Audiencia of the district, after the Public Attorney has been heard.

Col. 342, 340; Chile, 298, 300.

323. For (granting) the concession and approval stated in the preceding article, it is required:

1. That the minor be over eighteen years of age.
2. That he consents thereto.
3. That it is considered advantageous to the minor.

The authorization (*habilitación*) shall be inscribed in the Registry of guardianships and entered in the Civil Registry.

Col. 340, 341; Chile, 299.

324. The provisions of article 317 apply to the minor who has obtained authorization of majority.

Col. 339; Chile, 297.

TITLE XII.

*Registry of civil status.**

Article **325.** Acts, relating to the civil status of persons, shall be inscribed in the registry designated for such purpose.

Chile, 305; Arg. 104, 179; Col. 347; Guat. 434, 435.

326. The registry of civil status shall contain the inscriptions or entries of births, marriages, emancipations, recognitions, and legitimations, deaths, naturalizations, and residences (*vecindad*), and shall be under the charge of Municipal Judges or other officials of the civil order in Spain, and, in foreign countries, of consular or diplomatic agents.

Col. 349, 348; Guat. 439.

327. The minutes of the registry shall be evidence of the civil status and any other evidence can be admitted only when such minutes have never existed or the books of registry have disappeared or when a contention arises in court.

Mex. 55; Chile, 305, 309; Guat. 435; Col. 337.

---

* Law of Civil Register, arts. 1, 3, 4, 5, 35, 26, 43, 45, 46, 90. Regulation for the execution of law of Civil Register, arts. 1, 3.

328. It is not necessary that a newly-born child should be presented to the official in charge of the registry for inscription of birth; the declaration of the person obliged to make it shall be sufficient.

This declaration shall embrace all the requirements of law and shall be subscribed to by the deponent or two witnesses, at his request, if he cannot sign.

Mex. 75; Col. 350, 351, 352; Guat. 442, 443.

329. In canonical marriages, it shall be the duty of the contracting parties to furnish to the official representing the State, who attends the celebration, all the data required for its inscription in the Civil Registry.

Those referring to banns, impediments and their disposition, are excepted and not required to be entered in the Registry.

Guat. 358; Col. 364.

330. Naturalization shall have no legal effects, until it is inscribed in the Registry, whatever the evidence proving it and the date on which it has been granted may be.

331. Municipal Judges and those of the First Instance, in proper cases, may punish the infractions of the provisions about the Civil Registry with a fine of 20 to 100 *pesetas,* when they do not constitute a crime or a misdemeanor.

332. The law of June 17, 1870, shall continue in force in so far as it is not modified by the preceding articles.

BOOK SECOND.

PROPERTY, OWNERSHIP AND ITS MODIFICATIONS.

TITLE I.

Classification of property.

PRELIMINARY PROVISION.*

Article **333.** All things which are or may be an object of appropriation are considered either as personal or real property.

Col. 653, 654; Chile, 565, 566; Guat. 503, 504; Arg. 2311, 2312.

CHAPTER FIRST.

Real property.†

Article **334.** Real property consists of:

1. Lands, buildings, roads, and constructions of every kind adherent to the soil.

2. Trees, and plants, and ungathered fruits, while they are not separated from the land and form an integral part of the real property.

3. All that is attached to real property, in a fixed manner, in such a way that it cannot be separated from it without breaking the matter or causing injury to the object.

4. Statues, reliefs, paintings or other objects of use or ornament placed in a building and on lands or tenements by the owner of the same in such a manner as to reveal the intent of attaching them in a permanent way to the tenement.

5. Machinery, vessels, instruments, or implements, intended by the owner of the tenement for the industry or works that he may carry

* Part. 2, tit. 17, Int.

† Digesto, book 6, tit. 1, law 44; id., book 19, tit. 1, laws 15, 16, pars. 18 to 31; id., book 33, tit. 75; id., book 42, tit. 8, law 25, par. 6; id., book 50, tit. 16, law 86. Nov. Recop., book 10, tit. 16, law 3, number 4, and laws 3, 4. Part. 5, tit. 5, laws 16, 28, 29, 30, 31.

on in a building or tenement and which directly tend to meet the necessities of the same industry or works.

6. Vivaries for animals, pigeon-houses, beehives, fish-ponds or beds for similar purposes, when the owner has placed or kept them with the intent of maintaining the same attached to the tenement and forming a permanent part thereof.

7. Manures intended for the cultivation of lands when they are on the place where they are to be employed.

8. Mines, quarries, and slag lands, while the matter forms part of the beds, and waters, either running or stagnant.

9. Docks, and constructions, which, though floating, are intended by their purposes and conditions to remain at a fixed place in a river, lake or on a coast.

10. Administrative concessions for public works, and easements, and other real rights attached to real property.

Col. 656, 661, 665; Chile, 568, 573, 565, 576 to 581; Guat. 505; Arg. 2314, 2315, 2316; Mex. 782.

CHAPTER SECOND.

*Personal property.**

Article **335**. Personal property is considered anything susceptible of appropriation and not contained in the preceding chapter, and, in general, anything which can be carried from place to place without impairing the real property to which it may be attached.

Chile, 567; Guat. 504; Col. 655, 659; Uru. 414.

336. As personal property are also considered: Rents or pensions, either for life or hereditary, in favor of a person or family, provided they do not incumber real property with a real charge; also purchased public offices, contracts for public services, and bonds and certificates representing mortgage loans.

Col. 667, 668; Chile, 580, 581; Mex. 786.

337. Personal property is either consumable (*fungibles*) or non-consumable (*no fungibles*).

To the first class belong those which cannot be used, in a manner appropriate to their nature, without consuming them; all others belong to the second class.

Col. 663; Chile, 575; Uru. 422; Guat. 507.

---

* Digesto, book 12, tit. 1, law 2, par. 1. Instituciones, book 3, tit. 15. Part. 3, tit. 19, law 4; id. 5, tit. 1, laws 1, 2; id. 5, tit. 5, law 29.

CHAPTER THIRD.

*Property in respect to ownership.**

Article **338.** Things pertain to public domain or to private ownership.

Col. 674; Chile, 589; Uru. 428; Mex. 795.

339. To public domain belong:

1. Those intended for public use, as roads, canals, rivers, torrents, ports, and bridges, constructed by the State, and banks, shores, roadsteads, and others of a similar character.

2. Those belonging exclusively to the State, not for common use, and which are designed for some public service, or the development of the national wealth, as walls, fortresses, and other works for the defense of the territory, and mines, whilst their concession has not yet been granted.

Mex. 802; Chile, 595, 596, 598; Col. 677, 678.

340. All other property belonging to the State which has not the conditions, stated in the preceding article, is considered as private property.

Chile, 589; Col. 674.

341. Property of the public domain, when it is no longer dedicated to general uses or to the necessities of the defense of the territory, shall become a part of the property of the State.

342. Property of the Royal Patrimony is governed by its special law, and in all matters, not prescribed therein for it, by the general provisions established by this Code about private property.

343. The property of provinces and of towns is divided into property of public use and patrimonial property.

Mex. 796, 800, 804.

344. Property for public use in provinces, and towns, comprises the provincial and town roads, the squares, streets, fountains, and public waters, the walks, and public works for general service, paid for by the same towns or provinces.

All other property, possessed by either of them, are patrimonial, and shall be governed by the prescriptions of this Code, unless otherwise ordered by special laws.

---

* Digesto, book 1, tit. 8, law 4, par. 1; id., book 43, tit. 7, law 1; id., book 43, tit. 12, pars. 3, 4; id., book 33, tit. 7, law 27, par. 3; id., book 32, law 78, par. 1; id., book 33, tit. 3, law 18, par. 33. Part. 2, tit. 15, law 4; id. 2, tit. 17, law 1: id. 3, tit. 28, laws 2, 6, 9, 10; id. 3, tit. 32, law 23. Fuero Real, book 4, tit. 6, law 6. Fuero Juzgo, book 8, tit. 4, law 29. Nov. Recop., several laws of book 3, tit. 5; all the laws of same book, tit. X, laws 8, 9, 10 and 11, book 7, tit. 5; id., book 7, tit. 16, law 1.

345. Besides the patrimonial property of the State, of the provinces, and of the towns, that belonging to private parties, either individually or collectively, is property of private ownership.

PROVISIONS COMMON TO THE THREE PRECEDING CHAPTERS.

Article **346.** Whenever by provision of the laws or by an individual declaration, the expression "real things or real property" is used, or "personal things or personal property," it shall be understood as comprised in them, respectively, those enumerated in chapter first and in chapter second.

Whenever the word "personal" (*muebles*), alone, is used, then it shall not be understood as including: Money, credits, commercial effects, values, jewels, scientific or artistic collections, books, medals, arms, clothing, riding beasts, or carriages and their harnesses, breadstuffs, liquids (*caldos*) and merchandise or other things, the principal employment of which is to furnish or ornament rooms, with the exception of the cases in which, by the contexture of the law or of the individual disposition, the contrary clearly appears.

Col. 662; Chile, 574; Mex. 792 to 794; Guat. 506; Uru. 421.

347. Whenever, in a sale, legacy, or donation, or any other disposition in which reference is made to personal or real things, their possession or ownership is transferred with everything they may contain, there shall not be understood as comprised in the transfer, money values, credits, and actions, the titles to which are contained in the things transferred, unless the intention is clearly shown of including such values and rights in the transfer.

TITLE II.

Ownership.

CHAPTER FIRST.

*Ownership in general.**

Article **348.** Ownership is the right to enjoy and dispose of a thing, without further limitations than those established by the laws.

---

* Digesto, book 41, tit. 1, law 31, par. 1. Part. 2, tit. 1, law 2; id. 3, tit. 2, law 29; id. 3, tit. 18, law 31; id. 3, tit. 28, laws 1, 45; id. 7, tit. 23, law 10. Nov. Recop., book 10, tit. 23, law 3; id., book 11, tit. 3, law 4. Laws of May 9, 1835, art. 1, par. 4; of July 17, 1836. Constitution of 1869, art. 14; id. of 1876, art. 10. Codigo, book 4, tit. 35, law 21; id., book 10, law 15.

The owner has actions against the holder and the possessor of the thing to recover it.

Mex. 827; Guat. 510; Chile, 582.

349. No one shall be deprived of his property, unless it be by competent authority, and with justified cause for public utility, and never until he has previously been properly indemnified.

If this requirement has not been complied with, the judges shall protect, and, in proper cases, replace the condemned party in possession.

Arg. 2511; Mex. 828.

350. The owner of a parcel of ground is owner of its surface and everything under it, and he can make thereon any works, plantations, and excavations which may be convenient for him, without injury to the easements and subject to what is prescribed by the laws about mines and waters and by Police Regulations.

Arg. 2518.

351. Hidden treasures belong to the owner of the land on which they are found.

However, when the discovery is made on property belonging to a stranger or to the State and by chance, one-half of it shall be adjudged to the finder.

If the thing discovered is of interest to the sciences or arts, the State can acquire it at its just value, which shall be distributed in accordance with what has been prescribed.

Arg. 2550, 2559, 2561, 2562, 2563; Col. 701; Chile, 626; Guat. 563.

352. By treasure is understood, in its legal effects, hidden or unknown deposits of money, jewelry, or other precious objects, the lawful ownership of which is not proven.

CHAPTER SECOND.

Right of accession.

GENERAL PROVISION.

Article **353.** Ownership of property gives a right by accession to everything which is produced by it or which is either naturally or artificially united to or incorporated with it.

Chile, 643; Col. 713; Arg. 2571; Guat. 580; Mex. 869.

SECTION FIRST.

*Right of accession in respect to what is produced by property.**

Article **354.** To the owner belong:

1. Natural fruits.
2. Industrial fruits.
3. Civil fruits.

Mex. 870; Guat. 581; Arg. 2513, 2552; Chile, 646, 648.

355. Natural fruits are the spontaneous products of soil, and the brood, and all other produce of animals.

Industrial fruits are those produced by land of any kind through cultivation or labor.

Civil fruits are rents of buildings, receipts for leases of lands, and the amount of perpetual or life rents, and other similar returns.

Mex. 871, 873, 876; Guat. 582, 584, 587; Arg. 2424; Chile, 644, 645, 647; Col. 714, 715, 717.

356. The receiver of fruits is obliged to pay the expenses incurred by a third party in their production, gathering, and preservation.

Arg. 2426; Chile, 646.

357. Only those which are in sight or appearing are considered as natural or industrial fruits.

As to animals, it is sufficient if they are in the womb of the mother, though yet unborn.

Guat. 585, 586.

SECTION SECOND.

*Rights of accession in respect to real property.**

Article **358.** Whatever is built, planted or sown on another's land, and the improvements or repairs made on it, belong to the owner of the land, subject to what is prescribed in the following articles:

Mex. 878; Chile, 669; Col. 739; Guat. 589.

---

* Part. 3, tit. 28, laws 25, 39. Fuero Real, book 3, tit. 4, laws 1, 10.

† Digesto, book 5, tit. 3, law 29; id., book 6, tit. 1, law 62; id., book 7, tit. 1, laws 9, 51, par. 1; id., book 10, tit. 2, law 51; id., book 19, tit. 1, law 34; id., book 22, tit. 1, law 45; id., book 24, tit. 3, law 7. Instituciones, book 2, tit. 1, par. 37. Codigo, book 7, tit. 51, law 4. Part. 3, tit. 2, law 16; id. 3, tit. 28, laws 26, 27, 28, 29, 31, 32, 36, 38, 41, 42, 43. Fuero Juzgo, book 10, tit. 1, law 6; id., book 11, tit. 1, law 7. Fuero Real, book 3, tit. 4, laws 1, 14, number 5. Law of Waters, of 1879, arts. 40, 42, 44, 45, 46, 47, 49, 50.

13

359. All works, sown grounds, and plantings are presumed to be made by the owner, and, at his expense, unless the contrary is proven.

Arg. 2519; Mex. 879; Guat. 590.

360. The owner of the land who shall make on it, by himself or through another person, plantings, constructions or works, with material belonging to another person, is bound to pay for their value; and should he have acted in bad faith, he shall also be obliged to indemnify said person for damages and injuries caused thereby. The owner of the materials shall have a right to remove them, only in case he can do it without injury to the work constructed, and, when by doing it, the plantings, constructions, and work done, shall not be destroyed.

Chile, 668; Col. 738; Mex. 882; Guat. 593, 594; Arg. 2587.

361. The owner of the land on which somebody has built, sown, or planted, in good faith, is entitled to appropriate, as his own, the work, sowing or planting by previously paying the indemnity specified in articles 453 and 454 or to oblige the person who has built or planted the same to pay him the value of the land and to oblige him, who sowed, to pay the corresponding rents.

Chile, 669; Col. 739; Arg. 2588; Guat. 496; Mex. 886; Uru. 713.

362. He, who builds, plants, or sows, in bad faith, on another's land, loses what he has built, planted, or sown without right to any indemnity.

Guat. 597; Arg. 2589.

363. The owner of the land on which any one has built, planted, or sown, in bad faith, may exact the demolition of the work or the removal of the planting or sowing, and the replacing of everything in its former condition, at the expense of him who built, planted or sowed.

Guat. 598; Arg. 2589; Mex. 886.

364. When there has been bad faith, not only on the part of him who built, sowed or planted on another's land, but also on the part of the owner of such land, the right of both shall be the same as though both had acted in good faith.

Bad faith on the part of the owner is understood, whenever the act has been executed in his presence with his knowledge and forbearance and without opposition.

Guat. 599, 601; Arg. 2590; Chile, 669; Col. 739.

365. If the materials, plants or seed belong to a third party, who has not acted in bad faith, the owner of the land shall be liable subsidiarily for their value, but only in the event that the person who used them has no means to pay for the same.

This prescription shall have no force, if the owner make use of the rights given him by article 363.

Guat. 602; Arg. 2591; Mex. 891.

366. The augmentation which the banks of a river gradually receive from the effects of currents of waters, belongs to the owner of the land adjacent to such banks.

Mex. 893; Chile, 650; Col. 720; Guat. 604; Arg. 2572.

367. The owners of tenements, adjacent to ponds or lakes, do not acquire the land left dry by the natural decrease of waters, nor lose those inundated by them in extraordinary floods.

Arg. 2578; Chile, 650, par. 2; Col. 720, par. 2.

368. When the current of a river, rivulet or torrent cuts off from the tenement on its bank a known portion of land and transfers it to another tenement, the owner of the tenement to which the cut-off part belongs retains the ownership of the same.

Mex. 895; Chile, 652; Col. 722; Guat. 605; Arg. 2583 to 2585.

369. Trees, uprooted and carried away by currents of waters, belong to the owner of the land upon which they are carried, if the former owners do not claim them within the term of a month.

If such owner claims them, then they must pay all the expenses caused by the collecting and securing them in a safe place.

Guat. 606; Mex. 896.

370. The beds of rivers, which remain abandoned because the course of the water has naturally changed, belong to the owners of the riparian lands, throughout their respective extents. If the abandoned bed has divided tenements belonging to different owners, the new dividing line shall be run at equal distance therefrom.

Chile, 654; Col. 724; Mex. 897; Arg. 2573; Guat. 607.

371. Islands formed in the sea, adjacent to the coast of Spain, and in navigable or floatable rivers belong to the State.

Guat. 608, 609; Arg. 2340.

372. When in a navigable and floatable river, which changes its course by natural causes, a new bed is opened through a private tenement, this bed shall become public domain. The owner of the tenement shall recover it, in the event of the waters leaving it again dry, naturally or through work legally authorized for this purpose.

373. Islands which, through successive accumulations of descending alluviums, are slowly formed in rivers, belong to the owners of the banks or shores nearest to each of them or to those of both shores, if the island is in the middle of the river, and then shall be divided longitudinally in halves. If only one island thus formed be more distant from one bank than from the other, then the owner of the nearest bank shall be the sole owner of it.

Chile, 656; Col. 726; Guat. 610.

374. When the current of a river divides itself into branches, leaving a tenement or a part of it isolated, the owner of the same retains his property. He also retains it, if a portion of the land is rendered isolated by the current.

Mex. 901; Arg. 2576; Col. 726; Guat. 611.

SECTION THIRD.

*Rights of accession in respect to personal property.**

Article **375.** When two personal things, belonging to different owners, are united in such a way that they become a unit without bad faith on the part of either owner, the owner of the principal thing acquires the accessory upon indemnifying its former owner for its value.

Arg. 2594; Chile, 658; Col. 728; Guat. 512; Mex. 902; Uru. 699.

376. When two things are incorporated, the principal shall be considered the one to which the other had been united as an ornament or for its use and perfection.

Mex. 903; Guat. 613; Chile, 659; Col. 729; Arg. 2333.

377. When it is not possible by following the rules of the preceding article to determine which of the two incorporated things is the principal one, the thing of the greater value shall be considered as such, and between two things of equal value, that of the greater volume.

In paintings and sculptures, in writings, printed matter, prints, engravings, and lithographs, the board, metal, stone, canvas, paper or the parchment shall be considered as accessory things.

Col. 731, 732; Chile, 660, 661; Mex. 905; Guat. 615; Arg. 2334; Uru. 700, 701.

* Digesto, book 6, tit. 1, law 23, pars. 2, 5; id., book 34, tit. 2, law 19, par. 13; id., book 41, tit. 1, laws 26, par. 1, 27, 2. Instituciones, tit. 1, pars. 26, 33; id., book 2, tit. 1, par. 34, law 27. Part. 3, tit. 28, laws 33, 34, 35, 36, 37.

378. When things united can be separated without injury, their respective owners may claim their separation.

However, when the thing adjoined for the use, embellishment or perfection of another is much more precious than the principal thing, the owner of the first may demand their separation, though the thing to which it is joined may suffer some damage.

Arg. 2595, 2598; Chile, 663, 664; Col. 733; Guat. 616, 617; Mex. 906.

379. When the owner of the accessory thing has made the incorporation, in bad faith, he shall lose the thing incorporated and shall be obliged to indemnify the owner of the principal thing for the damages he may have suffered.

When the one acting in bad faith is the owner of the principal thing, the owner of the accessory shall have the right to choose between being paid by the first for the value of the thing or to have the thing, belonging to him, separated, though it may be necessary for such purpose to destroy the principal one, and besides, in both cases, an indemnity for damages and injury may be recovered.

If any of the owners have made the incorporation in the presence, with the knowledge and forbearance and without opposition from the other, their respective rights shall be determined in the manner provided for such cases where both had acted in good faith.

Arg. 2596; Chile, 664 to 667; Col. 734 to 737, and 618 to 620; Uru. 706 to 708; Mex. 908 to 912.

380. Whenever the owner of materials, used without his consent, has a right to an indemnity, he may exact that such indemnity consist in the delivery to him, either of a thing equal in quality and value and in all respects to the one employed or in its price, according to appraisement by experts.

Mex. 811; Guat. 621; Chile, 655; Col. 735.

381. When by the will of their owners, two things of equal or different kinds are mixed, or if the mixture is made by chance, and, in this last case, are not separable without injury, each owner shall acquire a right proportional to the part belonging to him with consideration as to the values of the things mixed or confounded.

Arg. 2600; Mex. 912; Guat. 622.

382. When by the will of only one of the owners, but, in good faith, two things of equal or different kinds are mixed or confounded, the rights of the owners shall be determined by the provisions of the preceding article.

When the one making the mixture or confusion acted, in bad faith, he will lose the thing belonging to him, mixed or confounded, besides being obliged to indemnify the owner of the thing with which he made the mixture for the damage caused thereby.

Guat. 623, 624; Chile, 663, 667; Col. 733, 737; Mex. 913, 914.

383. He who, in good faith, wholly or partially used material belonging to another party in making a work of a new kind, may make the work his own upon indemnifying the owner of the material for the value of the same.

When this (material) is more precious than the work on which it was used or superior in value, the owner of it may at his option become owner of the new thing by paying the price of the labor or claiming an indemnity for the material.

When in the making of the new work, there has been bad faith, the owner of the material has the right, either to keep the work without paying anything to the author or claiming from him an indemnity for the value of the material and the damages he may have suffered.

Mex. 915; Guat. 625 to 627; Chile, 662; Col. 732; Arg. 2567 to 2570.

CHAPTER THIRD.

*Fixing boundaries and placing land marks.**

Article **384.** Every owner has the right to fix the boundaries of his property by giving notice thereof to the owners of adjoining tenements.

The same right belongs to those having real rights.

Arg. 2746; Chile, 842; Col. 900; Guat. 1244, 1245.

385. The demarkation shall be made in accordance with the titles of each owner, and, when in default of sufficient title, from what may appear from the possession held by the contiguous owners.

386. When the titles do not specify the boundary or area belonging to each owner, and the question cannot be determined by the possession or by other means of proof, the demarkation shall be made by dividing the land in dispute in equal shares.

387. When the titles of the contiguous owners show an area, larger or smaller than that comprised in the total of said land, the increase or decrease shall be distributed in proportion.

---

* Part. 6, tit. 15, law 10. Law of Civil Procedure, art. 2061.

CHAPTER FOURTH.

*Right of inclosing agricultural lands.**

Article **388.** Every owner may close or fence his tenements with walls, ditches, live or dead hedges or in any other manner without injury to the easements existing thereon.

Arg. 2516; Chile, 841; Col. 902; Guat. 1200.

CHAPTER FIFTH.

Unstable buildings and trees about to fall.†

Article **389.** When a building, wall, column or any other construction is in danger of falling, the owner is obliged to demolish it or to do whatever is necessary to prevent its falling.

Should the owner of the ruinous work not do it, the authorities may have it demolished at the expense of the owner.

Chile, 932; Col. 988; Arg. 2616.

390. When a large tree threatens to fall in such a way as to cause damage to another person's tenement or to persons passing through a public or private way, the owner of the tree shall be obliged to pull it down and take it away; should he not do so, it shall be done at his expense by order of the authorities.

Chile, 935; Col. 992.

391. In the cases of the two preceding articles, should the tree or building fall, the provisions of articles 1907 and 1908 shall be enforced.

Chile, 934; Col. 909.

TITLE III.

Community of property.‡

Article **392.** There is community of property when the ownership of a thing or of a right belongs to different persons undividedly.

In default of contracts or of special provisions, communities shall be governed by the provisions of this title.

Chile, 2304; Col. 2322; Guat. 2266.

---

* Law of Cortes, 1813, art. 1. Decree, Sept. 6, 1836, and law of Hunting and Fishing, Jan. 10, 1879, art. 1.

† Part. 3, tit. 30, law 15; id. 3, tit. 32, laws 10, 12. Nov. Recop., book 7, tit. 32, law 2.

‡ Codigo, law 5, of *comuni dividundo;* id., book 3, tit. 37, law 3. Digesto, book 10, tit. 3, law 21; tit. 2, law 55. Part. 3, tit. 32, law 26; id. 5, tit. 5, laws 13, 55. Fuero Real, book 3, tit. 4, laws 2, 3.

393. The share of the participants in the benefits, as well as in the charges, shall be proportionate to their respective interests.

The interests belonging to the participants shall be presumed equal until the contrary is proven.

Chile, 2305, 2309; Col. 2323, 2327; Guat. 2271; Arg. 2707, 2708, 2689.

394. Every participant may use the things, held in common, provided he uses them in accordance with their office and in such a way as not to injure the interests of the community nor prevent the co-participants from utilizing them according to their rights.

Arg. 2684; Col. 2330.

395. Every participant shall have a right to oblige a co-participant to contribute to the expenses of keeping the thing or right held in common; only the party renouncing the share belonging to him in the ownership can exempt himself from this obligation.

Chile, 2309; Col. 2327; Arg. 2685; Guat. 2271.

396. When the different stories of a house belong to different owners, if the titles do not specify the conditions under which they must contribute the necessary expenses thereof, and there is no stipulation about it, the following provisions shall be observed:

1. The main and party walls, the roof, and other things of use in common shall be preserved at the expense of all the owners in proportion to the value of their stories.

2. Every owner shall pay the cost of maintaining the floor of his story. The floor of the porch, front door, common yard, and hygienic works, common to all, shall be paid *pro rata* by all the owners.

3. The stairs from the porch to the first story shall be paid for *pro rata* by all the owners, with the exception of the owner of the ground floor; the stairs from the first to the second story shall be paid for by all, excepting the owners of the ground floor and first story, and successively so on.

397. None of the owners shall, without consent of the others, make any change in the common property though benefits for all may accrue thereby.

Arg. 2681.

398. The resolution of the majority of the part-owners as to the management and better enjoyment of the thing held in common shall be binding (on all).

There shall be no majority, unless the resolution has been made by the part-owners representing a majority of the interests which constitutes the object of the community.

If there is no majority or the resolution of the same is seriously injurious to the parties interested in the thing held in common, the Judge, on petition of any part-owner, shall decree what may be proper, including the appointment of an administrator.

When a part of the things privately belong to one or to some of the part-owners and the remainder in common, the preceding prescription shall only apply to the latter.

Arg. 2703.

399. Each one of the part-owners shall have absolute ownership of his part and in the fruits and benefits belonging to it, and he, therefore, may sell, assign, or mortgage it, and even substitute another person in its enjoyment, unless personal rights are involved. But the effect of the sale or mortgage, in what refers to the part-owner, shall be limited to the share which may be allotted to him in the distribution on the determination of the community.

Arg. 2676; Guat. 2267.

400. No part-owner shall be obliged to remain a party to the community. Each of them may ask, at any time, the division of the thing held in common.

However, the stipulation of keeping the thing undivided for a stated period of time, not exceeding ten years, shall be valid. This term may be extended by a new agreement.

Arg. 2692; Chile, 2313; Col. 2334.

401. Notwithstanding what is provided in the preceding article, the part-owners cannot compel a division of the thing held in common to be made, when by so doing they may render it unserviceable for the use for which it was intended.

Arg. 2710.

402. The division of a thing held in common may be made by the parties in interest or by arbitrators or compromisers appointed at the will of the part-owners.

In case it is made by arbitrators or compromisers, they shall divide it into parts proportional to the rights of each part-owner, endeavoring to avoid payments of balances in cash as far as possible.

Arg. 2698.

403. The creditors or assignees of the part-owners may concur in the division of the property, held in common, and object to any division made without their concurrence. But they cannot object to the division already made, except in the cases of fraud or when they have made it, notwithstanding the opposition formally interposed in order to prevent it, but they shall always leave the rights of the debtor or assignee intact to maintain its validity.

404. When the thing is essentially indivisible and the part-owners cannot agree that it be adjudged to one of them, who shall indemnify the others, then it shall be sold and the proceeds be distributed.

Col. 2334; Chile, 2313.

405. The division of property held in common shall not cause injury to a third party who shall retain the rights of mortgage, easements, or any other real rights belonging to him before the division was made. The personal rights belonging to a third party against the community shall also remain in force notwithstanding the division.

406. The rules, relating to the division of estates, shall apply to the divisions among the part-owners.

Guat. 2275; Col. 2335; Chile, 2313.

TITLE IV.

Some special properties.

CHAPTER FIRST.

Waters.

SECTION FIRST.

*Ownership of waters.**

Article **407**. To the public domain belong:

1. Rivers and their natural beds.
2. Continuous or intermittent waters from sources or brooks running in their natural beds and the beds themselves.
3. Waters rising continuously or intermittently in lands on the same public domain.
4. Lakes and ponds formed by nature on public lands, and also their beds.
5. Rain water running through ravines or sandy beaches with their beds also belong to the public domain.
6. Subterranean waters existing on public lands.

---

* Digesto, book 1, tit. 8, law 4, par. 8; id., book 43, tit. 7, law 1. Part. 3, tit. 28, laws 6, 8. Royal Decree, April 29, 1860. Law of Aug. 3, 1866, arts. 30, 31, 33, 34, 38, 44, 67, 68, 71, 72, 79, 44 par. 2, 45, 138, 139, par. 2. Law of Waters, June 13, 1879, arts. 1, 4, 5, par. 1, 12, 13, 17, par. 2, 18, 28, 29, 30, 33, 34, 42, 98, 99, par. 2. Royal Decree, April 29, 1860, arts. 24, 25.

7. Waters found within the zone of operation of public works, even when they are made by a grantee.

8. Waters flowing continuously or intermittently from tenements belonging to private parties, to the State, to the provinces or to towns from the moment they leave such tenements.

9. The waste waters of fountains, sewers, and public institutions.

Guat. 509; Chile, 595; Col. 677.

408. To private dominion belong:

1. Waters, either continuous or intermittent, rising on private tenements as far as they run through them.

2. Lakes and ponds and their beds, when formed by nature on said tenements.

3. Subterranean waters found on the same.

4. Rain water falling on private tenements as long as they remain within boundaries of the same.

4. Rain water faling on private tenements as long as they remain within the boundaries of the same.

5. The beds of flowing waters, continuous or intermittent, formed by rain water, and those of brooks crossing tenements which do not belong to the public domain. In every drain or aqueduct the water, the bed, the sloping bank, and the sideways are considered as an integral part of the tenement or building for which the waters are intended. The owners of tenements, through which or along the boundaries of which the aqueduct passes, can allege no ownership over it, nor any right to profit by their beds or sideways, unless they base their claim on title deeds, specifying the right or the ownership claimed by them.

Chile, 305; Col. 677.

SECTION SECOND.

*Profitable use of public waters.**

Article **409.** The use of public waters is acquired:

1. By administrative concession.

2. By prescription of twenty years.

The limits of the rights and obligations of their uses shall be those shown, in the first case, by the terms of the concession; and, in the second, by the manner and form in which the waters have been used.

Chile, 598, 599, 603, 2517, 2519; Col. 678, 679, 683, 2519.

* Part. 3, tit. 32, law 18. Law of Aug. 3, 1886, arts. 192, 194, par. 1, 203. Law of June 13, 1879, arts. 11, 148, 149, 150, 158. Royal Decree, April 29, 1860, art. 2.

410. Every concession of use of waters is understood to be without injury to third parties.

Chile, 860; Col. 918.

411. The right to make use of public waters is extinguished by the forfeiture of the concession, and by the nonusage during twenty years.

SECTION THIRD.

*The use of waters of private ownership.**

Article **412.** The owner of a tenement which contains the source from which a brook rises, be it continuous or intermittent, may use its waters as far as they run through the tenement; after it leaves the tenement, it becomes public and its use is governed by the special law of waters.

Chile, 834; Col. 892; Guat. 1208.

413. Private ownership of the beds of rain waters does not give a right to make works and constructions which may divert the course of such waters with injury to a third party nor those, the destruction of which by the force of floods, may cause such injury.

Guat. 1216; Chile, 833, 838; Col. 896, 891.

414. No one may enter private property in search of waters or make use of them without permission from its owner.

415. The dominion which the proprietor of a tenement has over waters rising on his land cannot be exercised so as to interfere with the rights which the owner of an inferior tenement may have legally acquired to its use.

Chile, 835; Col. 669, 893.

416. Every owner of a tenement has a right to construct on his property receptacles for rain water, provided he does no damage thereby to the public or a third party.

SECTION FOURTH.

Subterranean waters.†

Article **417.** Only the owner of a tenement or another person, with his permission, may search for subterranean waters thereon.

---

* Law of Aug. 3, 1866, art. 30, par. 1, 34, 40, 42, 69, 167. Law of Waters of June 13, 1879, arts. 1, 5, 10, 14, 31, 127.

† Part. 3, tit. 32, law 19. Royal Decree, April 29, 1860. Law of Aug. 3, 1866, art. 47, par. 2, 48, 406. Law of June 13, 1879, arts. 19, 21, par. 2, 22.

The search for subterranean water on lands of the public domain can only be made with the permission of the administration.

Chile, 945; Col. 1002.

418. Artesian waters, according to the special law of waters, belong to the persons who discover the same.

419. When the owner of artesian wells abandons the same to their natural course, they become public domain.

SECTION FIFTH.

*General provisions.**

Article **420.** The owner of a tenement on which there are defensive works to check waters or on which, by the variation of their course, it may be necessary to reconstruct them, is bound, at his option, to make the necessary repairs or construction or to permit that, without damage to him, the owners of the tenements, who suffer or are clearly exposed to suffer damages, should make such works.

Guat. 1205.

421. The provisions of the preceding article apply to the cases in which it may be necessary to clear a tenement from the material, the accumulation or fall of which may obstruct the course of waters with injury or danger to a third party.

Guat. 1206; Chile, 939; Col. 996.

422. All the proprietors who participate in the benefits arising from the works, to which the preceding articles refer, shall be bound to contribute to the expenses of their construction in proportion to their interests. Those, who by their own fault may have caused the damages, shall be responsible for such expenses.

Guat. 1207; Chile, 939; Col. 996.

423. The ownership and use of waters belonging to corporations or private parties are subject to the law of expropriation for causes of public utility.

Chile, 835; Col. 893.

424. The provisions of this title shall not cause injury to rights previously acquired nor to the private ownership which the pro-

---

* Digesto, book 39, tit. 3, laws 1, 2, par. 1, 6; id., book 43, tit. 13, special law, par. 6, 7. Part. 3, tit. 32, laws 13, 14, 15, 16, 17. Law of Aug. 3, 1886, art. 116, par. 1, 299. Law of June 13, 1879, arts. 74, 257.

prietor of waters, drains, fountains or sources have to use, sell or to barter, as private property.

Guat. 1215; Chile, 835, 837; Col. 893, 895.

425. Anything not expressly determined by the provisions of this chapter shall be governed by the special law of waters.

CHAPTER SECOND.

*Mineral ores.**

Article **426.** Any Spaniard or foreigner may freely make prospect pits or excavations, not exceeding ten metres in length or depth, for the purpose of discovering ores on land belonging to the public domain; but they must previously give notice thereof to the local authorities. On land belonging to private parties no prospect pits can be sunk unless the permission of the owner or the party representing him has been previously obtained.

Chile, 591; Guat. 577, 578.

427. The limits of the rights mentioned in the preceding article, the previous formalities, and the conditions for their exercise, the designation of the matters which are to be considered as ores, and the determination of the rights belonging to the owner of the land and to the discoverer of the ores, in case of grants, shall be governed by the special law of mines.

Guat. 578; Chile, 591.

CHAPTER THIRD.

Intellectual property.†

Article **428.** The author of any literary, scientific or artistic work has the right to profit by it and dispose of it at his will.

429. The law of intellectual property determines the persons to whom such right belongs, the manner of exercising it, and the period of its duration. In cases not provided for nor determined by such special law, the general rules about ownership, established by this Code, shall govern.

---

* Nov. Recop., book 9, tit. 18, law 4.

† Nov. Recop., book 8, tit. 16, law 24.

TITLE V.

Possession.

CHAPTER FIRST.

*Possession and its kinds.**

Article **430.** Natural possession is the holding of a thing or the enjoyment of a right by some person. Civil possession is the same holding or enjoyment joined to the intent of having the thing or right as his own.

Arg. 2351; Chile, 700; Col. 762; Guat. 516.

431. Possession of things or rights is exercised, either by the same person who holds and enjoys them or by another in his behalf.

Guat. 516, 518, 532; Arg. 2351; Mex. 919.

432. Possession of things or rights may be held in one of two different ways, either as that of the owner or as that of the holder of the things or rights to keep and enjoy them when the ownership belongs to another person.

Arg. 2351; Chile, 714; Col. 775.

433. Any person who is not aware that there is in his title or in the manner of acquiring it any flaw, invalidating the same, shall be considered a possessor in good faith.

Possessors to the contrary are considered as possessors in bad faith.

Arg. 2356; Guat. 517; Chile, 702, 706, 768; Col. 764, 768.

434. Good faith is always presumed and any person averring bad faith on the part of the possessor is bound to prove it.

Arg. 2362; Chile, 707; Col. 769; Guat. 649.

435. Possession, when acquired in good faith, does not lose such character, except in the cases and from the moment in which some act exists proving that the possessor is aware that he possesses the thing unlawfully.

Mex. 932; Chile, 707; Col. 669.

---

* Digesto, book 5, tit. 3, law 25, par. 7; id., book 6, tit. 1, law 24; id., book 17, tit. 2, law 51; id., book 19, tit. 3, laws 2, 9, 19; id., book 41, tit. 2, laws 1, 3, par. 19; id., book 41, tit. 3, laws 9, 33; id., book 45, tit. 3, law 4, par. 18, 15, last par., 48, par. 1; id., book 50, tit. 16, law 109. Codigo, book 3, tit. 31, law 11; id., book 8, tit. 45, law 30. Part. 3, tit. 29, laws 6, 7, 9, 10, 11, 12, 14, 22; id. 3, tit. 30, laws 1, 2, 3, 4, 5, 10, 12; id. 7, tit. 33, law 9.

436. It is presumed that the enjoyment of the possession is continued under the same understanding with which it was acquired, until the contrary is proven.

Mex. 924; Chile, 700; Col. 762; Guat. 524.

437. Only things and rights susceptible of being appropriated can be the objects of possession.

CHAPTER SECOND.

*Acquisition of possession.**

Article **438.** Possession is acquired, either by the material occupation of the thing or right possessed, or by the fact that the same remains subject to the action of one's will, or by the proper act and legal formalities established for acquiring such a right.

Arg. 2373, 2377.

439. Possession may be acquired by the same person who is to enjoy it, by his legal representative, by his attorney or by a third person, without any power therefor, but, in this last case, possession shall not be considered as acquired, until the person, in whose name the act of possession has been executed, has ratified the same.

Arg. 2351, 2394, 2398; Guat. 518, 529; Chile, 720, 721.

440. He who repudiates an inheritance in a valid manner is understood as not having possessed it for a single moment.

The possession of hereditary property is understood as transferred to the heir without interruption and from the moment of the death of the testator, in case the inheritance be accepted.

Chile, 722; Col. 783; Guat. 534; Arg. 2475.

441. In no case can possession be forcibly acquired while there is a possessor contesting it. The person, believing that he has a right or action to deprive any other of the holding of a thing, should ask help of competent authority, whenever the holder refuses to deliver it up.

Chile, 710 to 712; Col. 772 to 774; Arg. 2364.

442. The successor, by an hereditary title, shall not suffer the consequences of a faulty possession of his testator, unless it is proven

---

* Digesto, book 4, tit. 3, laws 4, par. 1, 2; id., book 4, tit. 6, law 30; id., book 41, tit. 2, law 13, par. 4, 6, 41; id., book 41, tit. 3, law 4, par. 25; id., book 44, tit. 3, law 14, par. 4; id., book 47, tit. 8, law 6. Instituciones, book 2, tit. 6, pars. 2, 7. Part. 3, tit. 29, law 4; id. 3, tit. 30, laws 5, 6, 7, 8, 9, 10, 11, 13. Nov. Recop., book 11, tit. 8, laws 1, 2; id., book 11, tit. 34, law 3.

that he was informed of the flaws affecting it; however, the effects of the possession in good faith shall not benefit him, but from the death of the testator.

Chile, 717; Col. 778.

443. Minors and incapables can acquire the possession of things, but they shall require the assistance of their lawful representatives to make use of the rights in their favor arising from the possession.

Chile, 723; Col. 784; Guat. 528; Arg. 2393.

444. Acts merely tolerated and those clandestinely executed, and without knowledge of the possessor of a thing or with violence, do not affect the possession.

Guat. 520 to 523; Chile, 2499; Col. 2520; Uru. 1158.

445. Possession, as a fact, cannot be recognized in two different personalities, unless in cases of indivisibility. Should a question arise about the fact of the possession, the actual possessor shall be preferred, the oldest, when two appear; if the date of the possession is the same, the one presenting a title; and when all these conditions are equal, the thing shall be placed in deposit or judicial keeping, until a decision is rendered through proper proceedings about the possession or the ownership thereof.

Arg. 2401.

CHAPTER THIRD.

*Effect of possession.**

Article **446.** Every possessor has the right to be respected in his possession, and should he be disturbed in it, he shall be protected or possession be restored to him by the means established in the laws of procedure.

Mex. 955, 956; Chile, 921, 926, 928; Col. 977, 982, 984; Guat. 519.

* Digesto, book 6, tit. 1, law 45; id., book 8, tit. 6, laws 10, 16; id., book 5, tit. 3, law 31, par. 3; id., book 22, tit. 1, law 25, par. 1; id., book 23, tit. 3, law 10, pars. 1, 2; id., book 41, tit. 1, law 48; id., book 45, tit. 1, law 91, par. 3. Codigo, book 8, tit. 4, law 11; id., book 8, tit. 40, law 5; id., book 7, tit. 30, law 1; id., book 7, tit. 33, laws 1, 9. Fuero Juzgo, book 5, tit. 7, law 5; id., book 8, tit. 1, laws 2, 5. Fuero Real, book 2, tit. 11, law 1; id., book 3, tit. 4, laws 16, 17; id., book 4, tit. 4, law 4. Part. 3, tit. 2, law 30; id. 3, tit. 15, law 10; id. 3, tit. 28, laws 21, 22, 23, 24, 39, 40, 44; id. 3, tit. 29, laws 9, 12, 18, 29; id. 3, tit. 30, laws 10, 12, 13, 14, 17, 18; id. 7, tit. 10, law 10; id. 7, tit. 33, law 10. Nov. Recop., book 11, tit. 8, law 3; id., book 11, tit. 34, laws 11, 2. Fuerto Viejo of Castile, book 4, tit. 4, laws 2, 9. Estilo, law 242. Constitution of 1876, art. 10. Law of Expropriation, Jan. 10, 1879, art. 4. Law of Chase, Jan. 10, 1879, arts. 1, 2, 3, 4, 5, 6.

447. Only the possession acquired and enjoyed in the belief of being owner can serve as a title to acquire ownership.

Chile, 2498; Col. 2518; Guat. 630, 641.

448. The possessor who believes himself owner has in his favor the legal presumption that he possesses under a just title and he shall not be obliged to show it.

Chile, 700; Col. 762.

449. The possession of a real tenement is also a presumption of possession of the furniture and objects within it, as long as it is not shown or proven that they ought to be excluded.

450. Each one of the participants, in a thing held in common, is considered as having exclusively possessed the part which may be allotted to him on the distribution, during all the time prior to the division.

The interruption of the possession of the whole or of a part of the thing held in common shall injure all possessors equally.

Guat. 535; Chile, 718, 2504; Col. 779, 2525; Arg. 2409.

451. The fruits collected in good faith by the possessor become his own while the possession has not been lawfully interrupted.

Natural and industrial fruits are considered as collected from the moment they are gathered or separated.

Civil fruits are considered as daily proceeds and in this proportion belong to the possessor in good faith.

Chile, 646, 648; Col. 616, 718, 762; Mex. 931; Guat. 519; Arg. 2423, 2425.

452. If, at the date on which good faith ceases, some natural or industrial fruits are ungathered, the possessor shall have a right to recover the expenses incurred by him for their production and besides to a part of the net proceeds of the crop in proportion to the time of his possession.

The charges shall be distributed *pro rata,* in the same manner, between both the possessors.

The owner of a thing may, if he desires, grant to the possessor, in good faith, the right of finishing the cultivation and collecting the pending fruits as an indemnity for the parts of the expenses of cultivation and net proceeds belonging to him; the possessor in good faith, who, for any reason, may not desire to accept such a concession, shall lose the right to be indemnified in any other manner.

Uru. 611; Guat. 519, 526; Mex. 931; Chile, 700; Col. 762.

453. Necessary expenses are refunded to every possessor; but only those in good faith may retain the thing until they are repaid.

Useful expenses are refunded to the possessor in good faith under the same right of retention and he who has defeated him in his possession has the option, either of refunding the amount of the expenses, or paying him the increase of value which the thing has acquired in consequence of such expenses.

Guat. 526; Arg. 2427, 2428, 2440, 2441; Mex. 939.

454. The expenses purely for ostentation or mere pleasure are not to be refunded to the possessor in good faith, but he may carry away the ornaments with which he has embellished the principal thing, if it suffers no injury and if the successor in the possession does not prefer to refund the amount expended thereon.

Mex. 942.

455. A possessor in bad faith shall refund the fruits collected, and those which the lawful possessor could have received, and shall only have a right to be reimbursed for the necessary expenses made for the maintenance of the thing. The expenses incurred in improvements for ostentation and pleasure shall not be refunded to the possessor in bad faith, but he can take away the object for which such expenses have been incurred, provided the (principal) thing suffers no injury and the lawful possessor does not prefer to retain them, paying the value they have at the moment of his entering into possession.

Guat. 525; Arg. 2438; Mex. 939, 941.

456. The improvements caused by nature or time always pass to the benefit of the one who has won in the possession.

Mex. 948.

457. The possessor in good faith is not liable for the impairments or loss of the thing possessed, excepting the cases in which it may be proved that he has acted with deceit (*dolo*). The possessor in bad faith is liable for the impairment or loss in any case, even in those caused by *vis major*, when he maliciously has delayed the delivery of the thing to its lawful possessor.

Mex. 949, 950; Arg. 2431, 2435.

458. The person obtaining possession is not bound to pay for improvements which have ceased to exist, at the time of acquiring the thing.

459. The actual possessor who shows his possession, during a prior time, is presumed to have had possession also during the intermediate period, until the contrary is proven.

Guat. 524; Chile, 719, par. 3; Col. 780; Mex. 926; Uru. 616.

460. The possessor may lose his possession:

1. By the abandonment of the thing.

2. By assignment made to another party under an onerous or gratuitous title.

3. By the destruction or total loss of the thing or by the thing becoming not (lawfully) marketable.

4. By the possession of another, even against the will of a former possessor, if the new possession has lasted over a year.

Arg. 2451; Mex. 952; Uru. 617; Guat. 541, 539; Chile, 726, 728, 729; Col. 787, 789, 790.

461. The possession of personal property is not considered as lost while it is under the control of the possessor, though he may accidentally not know its whereabouts.

Guat. 538; Chile, 727; Col. 788; Arg. 2454.

462. The possession of real property and real rights is not considered as lost, nor transmitted for the effects of prescription to the injury of a third party, except with submission to the provisions of the Law of Mortgage.

Chile, 724; Col. 785; Guat. 539.

463. The acts relating to possession, either executed or consented to by the person possessing another person's thing as a mere holder for enjoying or retaining it for any cause, neither bind nor cause injury to the owner, unless he should have granted to the holder express powers to execute them or he ratifies them afterwards.

Col. 791; Chile, 730; Uru. 614; Guat. 540.

464. The possession of personal property, acquired in good faith, is equivalent to a title thereto. However, the person, who has lost the personal thing or has been unlawfully deprived of it, may recover it from whoever possesses it.

If the possessor of a personal thing, lost or stolen, has acquired it in good faith at a public auction, the owner cannot recover it, unless by reimbursing (the possessor) the price paid for it.

Neither can the owner of a thing pledged in the loan offices (*Montes de Piedad*), established under authority of the government, obtain the recovery thereof, whoever the person may be who has pledged them, without previously refunding to the institution the amount of the pledge and the interest due.

Things acquired on the exchange, at marts or markets or from a merchant lawfully established and habitually employed in a traffic of analogous objects, shall be governed by the provisions of the Code of Commerce.

Arg. 2412.

465. Wild animals are only possessed while they are under one's control; those domesticated or tamed are considered as tame or domestic as long as they retain the habit of returning to the home of their possessor.

Chile, 619, 700, par. 2; Col. 695, 762, par. 2; Guat. 554, par. 2, 555.

466. A person who lawfully recovers the possession, unduly lost, is considered as having enjoyed it without interruption for all the effects that may be beneficial to him.

Uru. 619; Mex. 960; Chile, 731; Col. 792.

TITLE VI.

Usufruct, use and habitation.

CHAPTER FIRST.

Usufruct.

SECTION FIRST.

*Usufruct in general.**

Article **467.** Usufruct gives a right to enjoy another's property under the obligation of maintaining its form and substance, unless the title constituting it or the law allows otherwise.

Guat. 1309; Arg. 2807; Chile, 764; Col. 823; Mex. 963; Uru. 456.

468. Usufruct is constituted by law, by wish of private persons specified in acts *inter vivos*, by last will, and by prescription.

Chile-Col. 825; Arg. 2812; Guat. 1312; Uru. 458; Mex. 964.

469. Usufruct can be constituted on the whole or on a part of the fruits of a thing, in favor of one or more persons, simultaneously or successively, and in any case from and up to a certain date, purely

---

* Digesto, book 7, tit. 1, laws 1, 4; id., book 7, tit. 6, law 4; id., book 10, tit. 2, law 16, par. 2; id., book 33, law 13. Instituciones, book 2, tit. 4. Law of *regulis juris*, 23. Codigo, book 3, tit. 32, law 13. Fuero Real, book 3, tit. 18, law 7. Part. 3, tit. 31, law 1, 20; id., 4, tit. 17, law 5. Nov. Recop., book 10, tit. 4, law 7. Law of October 11, 1820, art. 2. Law of Civil Marriage, 1870, art. 65.

or under conditions. It can also be constituted on a right, provided the same is not absolutely personal or unassignable.

Uru. 462; Guat. 1313; Mex. 965; Arg. 2821; Col. 839; Chile, 770.

470. The rights and duties of the usufructuaries shall be those specified in the title constituting the usufruct; in default of this or if it is not sufficient, the provisions contained in the two following sections shall be observed.

Guat. 1320.

SECTION SECOND.

*Rights of the usufructuary.**

Article **471.** The usufructuary is entitled to receive all the natural, industrial, and civil fruits of the property in usufruct. As to the treasures which may be found on the tenement, he shall be considered as a stranger.

Guat. 1322; Col. 840; Chile, 781; Arg. 2863, 2868; Mex. 974; Uru. 365.

472. Natural or industrial fruits, ungathered at the time of the beginning of the usufruct, belong to the usufructuary.

Those, pending at the time the usufruct expires, belong to the owner.

In the preceding cases, the usufructuary, at the beginning of the usufruct, is not bound to pay to the owner any of the expenses incurred; but, at the expiration of the usufruct, the owner is bound to pay from the proceeds of the pending fruits, the ordinary expenses of cultivation, for the seed, and other similar ones incurred by the usufructuary.

The provisions of this article shall not injure rights of a third party, acquired at the beginning or the determination of the usufruct.

Chile, 781; Col. 840; Guat. 1323; Mex. 975; Arg. 2864.

473. If the usufructuary has leased the lands or tenements given in usufruct, and this should be determined before the lease, he or his heirs shall only receive their proportional parts of the rent, which are to be paid by the lessee.

---

* Digesto, book 7, tit. 1, laws 9, 11, 12, 13, 15, 16, 17, 18, 19, 26, 27, 35, 38, 58; id., book 7, tit. 9, law 9; id., book 7, tit. 8, law 22; id., book 14, tit. 3, law 7; id., book 19, tit. 2, law 9; id., book 24, tit. 3, law 7; id., book 33, tit. 1, law 8. Instituciones, book 2, tit. 1, pars. 36, 38. Part. 3, tit. 28, law 30; id. 3, tit. 31, laws 20, 22, 24. Law of Mortgage, art. 107, par. 2. Law Decree of Dec. 29, 1868, art. 6.

474. The civil fruits are understood to be paid, day by day, and belong to the usufructuary in proportion to the time that the usufruct may last.

Chile, 790; Col. 849; Guat. 1326; Arg. 2846.

475. When a usufruct is constituted on the right to collect a rent or a periodical pension, consisting either of money or of fruits, or in interest on obligations, or certificates to the bearer, each payment due shall be considered as proceeds or fruits of said right.

When it consists in the enjoyments of the benefits, produced by an interest in any industrial or commercial enterprise, the distribution of which has not a fixed date, such benefits shall have the same consideration.

In either case, they shall be distributed as civil fruits and shall be applied in the manner provided in the preceding article.

476. The usufructuary of a tenement, on which mines are found, is not entitled to the proceeds of the mines denounced, granted, or on which there are workings, at the beginning of the usufruct, unless they are expressly granted to him by the title constituting the usufruct or in case such usufruct is universal.

The usufructuary, however, may remove stones, lime, and chalk from the quarries for repairs or works which he may be bound to make or which may be necessary.

Chile, 784; Col. 843; Arg. 2866; Guat. 1327; Uru. 473; Mex. 979.

477. Notwithstanding what is provided in the preceding article, the usufructuary, in the legal usufruct, may work the mines denounced, granted or being worked on the tenement, taking, as his own, one-half of the profits which may be obtained, after deducting the expenses which shall be equally shared by him and the owner.

478. The status of usufructuary does not deprive the person possessing it of the rights granted to every one, by the Law of Mines, to denounce and obtain the grant of mines existing on the tenement in usufruct, in the form and under the conditions established by said law.

Guat. 1327.

479. The usufructuary shall have a right to enjoy the increase, which the thing in usufruct may receive by accession, of the easements existing in its favor, and in general of all the benefits inherent in the same.

Mex. 981; Chile, 782, 785; Col. 841, 844; Guat. 1329; Arg. 2867.

480. The usufructuary may personally enjoy the thing in usufruct, may lease it to another person, or may alienate his rights to the usufruct, even under a gratuitous title; but all the contracts into which he may enter, as such usufructuary, shall terminate, at the expiration of the usufruct, except that of lease of rural tenements which shall be considered as subsisting during the agricultural year.

Chile, 793, 794; Col. 825; Guat. 1330; Uru. 474; Mex. 982.

481. When the usufruct embraces things, which without being destroyed, are slowly deteriorated by usage, the usufructuary shall have the right to make use of them in a proper way, and shall not be bound to return them at the determination of the usufruct, except in the condition in which they may be found; but he shall be obliged to indemnify the owner for the wear they may have received on account of his malice or neglect.

Arg. 2872; Mex. 985; Uru. 471; Guat. 1334; Chile, 787; Col. 846.

482. When the usufruct embraces things which cannot be used without being destroyed, the usufructuary shall have a right to use them, under the obligation of paying the appraised value on the determination of the usufruct, if they were appraised when given to him. When they have not been appraised, he shall have the right to return them by giving the same amount and quality or paying their market price at the time of the determination of the usufruct.

Chile, 789; Col. 848; Arg. 2871; Guat. 1309.

483. The usufructuary of vineyards, olive orchards and other trees or shrubs may use for his benefit the dead trunks and even those cut or torn off by accident, under the obligation of replacing them with others.

Arg. 2873; Chile, 783; Col. 842; Guat. 1351.

484. When, in consequence of an act of God (*vis major*), or by an extraordinary event, the vines, olive trees, or other trees or shrubs are destroyed, in such a considerable number that the replanting of them should not be practicable, or be too onerous, the usufructuary may leave the dead, fallen, or broken trunks at the disposal of the owner and oblige him to remove them and leave the land clear.

485. The usufructuary of wood land may enjoy all the profits which it may produce according to its nature.

If the wood land is a copse or of timber for building, the usufructuary may cut trees on it or make ordinary felling such as the owner was in the habit of doing, and, in default of this, he shall make them in accordance with the usage of the place as to manner, amount and season.

In any case, he shall make the cutting or felling of trees in such a manner that it will not damage the preservation of the tenement.

In the nurseries of trees, the usufructuary may make the thinnings required in order that the remaining trees may properly develop.

Besides what is provided in the preceding paragraphs, the usufructuary shall not cut the lower part of the trunk of any trees, unless it be for replacing or improving some of the things held in usufruct, and, in this case, he must give previous notice to the owner about the necessity of the work.

Mex. 986; Arg. 2813; Guat. 1335; Chile, 783.

486. The usufructuary of an action to recover a tenement or a real right, or personal property has a right to enforce it, and to oblige the owner of the action to assign him for this purpose, his proper power and to provide him with any elements of evidence which he may have. When, in consequence of the enforcement of such action, he acquires the thing claimed, the usufruct shall be limited to the fruits only and the ownership shall go to the proprietor.

Arg. 2876, 2877.

487. The usufructuary may make on the property held in usufruct any improvements, either useful or for recreation, which he may deem proper, provided he does not change the form or substance of the same; but he shall have no right to be indemnified for it. He may, however, remove said improvements, if it is possible to do so without damage to the property.

Arg. 874; Guat. 1338; Mex. 990; Uru. 475; Chile, 801; Col. 860.

488. The usufructuary can set off any damages to the property with the improvements he may have made thereon.

Uru. 475; Arg. 2874; Chile, 801; Col. 860.

489. The owner of property, the usufruct of which is held by another, may alienate it, but cannot change its form or substance nor do anything to the injury of the usufructuary.

Chile, 773, 779; Col. 832, 838; Guat. 1339; Mex. 991; Arg. 2916.

490. The usufructuary of a part of a thing, held in common, shall exercise all the rights belonging to the owner of it in respect to the administration and collection of fruits and interests. Should the community cease on account of the division of the thing held in common, the usufruct of the part allotted to the owner or part owner shall belong to the usufructuary.

SECTION THIRD.

*Obligation of the usufructuary.**

Article **491.** The usufructuary, before entering upon the enjoyment of the property, shall be obliged:

1. To make, after summoning the owner or his lawful representative, an inventory of all the property, to have the personal property appraised, and to make a description of the condition of the real property.

2. To give bond binding himself to comply with the duties imposed on him by this section.

Guat. 1340; Mex. 993; Chile, 775; Urù. 477; Col. 834; Arg. 2846.

492. The provision of paragraph 2, of the preceding article, is not to be applied to the vendor or donor, who has reserved to himself the usufruct of a thing sold or donated, neither to the parent who enjoyed the usufruct of the property of their children, nor to the surviving consort as to the hereditary share granted to him or her by articles 834, 836 and 837, except in the cases in which the parents or consort contract a second marriage.

Guat. 1349; Mex. 994, 995; Chile, 775; Col. 834; Arg. 2858.

493. The usufructuary, whatever the title for his usufruct be, may be excused from the obligation of making an inventory or of giving bond when no one will be injured thereby.

Col. 834; Chile, 775, par. 1.

494. When the usufructuary has not given bond, in the cases in which he ought to have given it, the owner may require that the real property be placed under administration, the personal property sold, that public effects, and bonds, notes, stocks, etc. (*valores*), either to order or to bearer, be converted into certificates or be deposited in a bank or public institution, and any capital or sums in cash and money received from sales of personal property, be invested in safe securities.

Interest on money received from the sale of personal property, interest on public effects and bonds, notes, stocks, shares, etc. (*valores*), and the proceeds of property, placed under administration, belong to the usufructuary.

---

* Digesto, book 7, tit. 1, law 13; id., book 7, tit. 4, law 30; id., book 7, tit. 9, laws 1, 7, 12, 52, 64, 65, 68, 69, 70; id., book 33, tit. 2, law 43; id., book 39, tit. 2, law 20. Codigo, book 6, tit. 61, law 8. Part. 3, tit. 31, laws 20, 22; id. 3, tit. 32, law 4; id. 7, tit. 14, law 12.

Furthermore, the owner may, if he so prefers, while the usufructuary gives no bond or is released from it, retain in his possession the property of the usufruct, as administrator under the obligation of delivering the net proceeds to the usufructuary, after deducting the sums which may be agreed upon or may be judicially fixed for his services during such administration.

Arg. 2856; Mex. 997; Col. 835, 836; Chile, 776; Guat. 1345.

495. When the usufructuary, who has not given bond, claims, under security given by oath (*caución juratoria*), the delivery of furniture required for his use, also a dwelling be given to him and his family in a house comprised in the usufruct, the Judge may assent to his petition, after due consideration of the facts in the case.

The same shall be understood about the instruments, implements, and other personal property, required for the industry in which it is employed.

When the owner should not wish that some pieces of furniture be sold, either on account of their artistic merit or because they have a special value in his eyes (*precio de afeccion*), he may require their delivery to him upon giving security for the payment of the legal interest on their appraised value.

Arg. 2857; Uru. 480; Chile, 477; Col. 836.

496. After the bonds are given by the usufructuary, he shall have a right to all the proceeds from the date on which he ought to have begun to receive them, in accordance with the title constituting the usufruct.

Guat. 1346; Mex. 998.

497. The usufructuary is bound to take care of the property given in usufruct as any good father of a family would do.

498. The usufructuary, who alienates or leases his right to the usufruct, shall be liable for the damages suffered by the property in usufruct by the fault or neglect of the person who substitutes him.

Chile, 793, par. 2; Col. 852; Mex. 999; Arg. 2870; Uru. 483; Guat. 1347.

499. Should the usufruct be constituted over a flock or herd of cattle, the usufructuary shall be bound to replace, with the young thereof, the animals dying annually or ordinarily and those carried away by the rapacity of preying animals.

Should the herd on which the usufruct is constituted wholly perish without fault of the usufructuary, in consequence of contagious diseases or any other uncommon event (*vis major*), the usufructuary shall fulfill his duty by delivering to the owner the remains saved from this misfortune.

Should the herd partially perish, also by accident and without the fault of the usufructuary, the usufruct shall continue in respect to the part saved.

Should the usufruct be of a sterile herd, it shall be considered for all its effects as constituted over things perishable (*fungibles*).

Chile, 788; Col. 847; Guat. 1350; Mex. 1002; Arg. 2902; Uru. 484.

500. The usufructuary is bound to make the ordinary repairs, required by the things given in usufruct. Ordinary repairs shall be considered those required by the wear and tear produced by the natural use of things, and which are indispensable for their preservation. Should he not make them after receiving an intimation from the owner, the latter may make them at the expense of the usufructuary.

Guat. 1532; Arg. 2881, 2884; Chile, 795; Col. 854.

501. Extraordinary repairs shall be made on the account of the owner. The usufructuary is bound to notify him, when the necessity of making them is urgent.

Arg. 2881, 2885; Chile, 797; Col. 856.

502. When the owner makes extraordinary repairs, he shall be entitled to reclaim from the usufructuary the legal interest on the sum invested in them, during the existence of the usufruct.

Should he not make repairs when they are indispensable for the preservation of the thing, the usufructuary may make them; but he shall have a right to claim from the owner, on the determination of the usufruct, the increase in value which the tenement may have acquired on that account.

Should the owner refuse to refund such amounts, the usufructuary is entitled to retain the thing, until he reimburses himself from the proceeds thereof.

Chile, 797, 900; Col. 856, 859.

503. The owner may make works and improvements which may be appropriate for the tenement in usufruct, and new plantations on it, if it is rural property, provided the value of the usufruct is not diminished by such acts, nor the rights of the usufructuary impaired.

Arg. 2914; Chile, 779; Cal. 838.

504. The payment of charges and annual taxes and of those considered as a lien on the fruits, shall be at the expense (*de cuenta*) of the usufructuary, during all the time that the usufruct lasts.

Chile, 796; Col. 855; Guat. 1359; Arg. 2894; Mex. 1011.

505. The taxes which may be imposed directly upon the capital, during the usufruct, shall be paid by the owner.

When the owner has paid them, the usufructuary is bound to pay him the legal interest upon any sums he may have disbursed for such causes, and when the usufructuary advances the amounts of such taxes, he shall recover such amounts, on the determination of the usufruct.

Guat. 1361; Chile, 796, pars. 2, 3; Col. 855.

506. Should the usufruct be constituted upon the whole of a patrimony, and if, at the time of its constitution, the owner has debts, the provisions of articles 642 and 643 about donations shall be applied to the maintenance of the usufruct as well as for the obligations of the usufructuary to pay such debts.

The same provisions are applicable in case the owner, at the time of the constitution of the usufruct, was obliged to pay periodical sums, even when there is no known principal (*aunque no tuvieran capital conocido*).

507. The usufructuary may personally claim the credits due which form a part of the usufruct, if he has given or gives the appropriate bond. If he has been released from giving bond or if he cannot give it, or if the one given is not sufficient, he shall require the authorization of the owner or, in his default, of the Judge to collect said credits.

The usufructuary under bond can invest the capital in any manner he may deem fit. The usufructuary without bond must invest said capital at interest, upon agreement with the owner, in default of such an agreement, under judicial authorization, and, in every case, with security sufficient to preserve the integrity of the capital in usufruct.

508. The universal usufructuary shall pay in full the legacy of life annuities or the pension for support.

The usufructuary of an aliquot part of the estate shall pay it in proportion to his share.

In neither of the two cases shall the owner be bound to make any reimbursements. The usufructuary of one or more specified things shall pay the legacy only when the rent or pension is expressly constituted upon them.

Chile, 796; Col. 855.

509. The usufructuary of a mortgaged tenement shall not be obliged to pay the debt for the security of which the mortgage was given.

When the tenement is seized or sold for the payment of the debt, the owner shall be liable to the usufructuary for what he may lose on that account.

Guat. 1363; Uru. 490; Arg. 2899; Mex. 1019.

510. When the usufruct is for the whole or for an aliquot part of an inheritance, the usufructuary may advance the sums which may belong to the property in usufruct for the payment of the debts of the estate and shall be entitled to claim from the owner its restoration, without interest, on the expiration of the usufruct.

When the usufructuary refuses to make this advance, the owner may ask for the sale of the part of the property in usufruct which may be necessary for the payment of such sums, or pay them with his own money with a right, in this last case, to claim from the usufructuary the corresponding interest.

Arg. 2900; Mex. 1019; Guat. 1366 to 1368.

511. The usufructuary is obliged to notify the owner of any act of a third party, coming to his knowledge, which may injure the rights of ownership, and shall be liable, should he not do so, for the damages and injuries as if they were caused by his own fault.

Chile, 802; Col. 861; Guat. 1369; Mex. 1022.

512. The expenses, costs, and condemnations of the suits, maintained about the usufruct, shall be charged to the usufructuary.

Guat. 1370, 1371; Mex. 1023.

SECTION FOURTH.

*Manner of extinguishing the usufruct.**

Article **513.** The usufruct is extinguished:

1. By the death of the usufructuary.
2. By the expiration of the term for which it was constituted or by the fulfillment of the resolutory condition stated in the constituting title.
3. By the merger of usufruct and ownership in the same person.
4. By renunciation of the usufructuary.
5. By total loss of the property in usufruct.

* Digesto, book 7, tit. 4, laws 3, 5, 8, 9, 10, 23; id., book 7, tit. 5, laws 23, 24; id., book 1, tit. 4, law 21; id., book 7, tit. 9, law 1; id., book 33, tit. 2, law 8; id., book 35, tit. 2, law 68. Instituciones, book 2, tit. 4 par. 3. Codigo, book 3, tit. 33, laws 5, 12. Part. 3, tit. 31, laws 20, 24, 25, 26.

6. By determination of the right of the constituent.
7. By prescription.

Col. 863 to 866; Chile, 804; Mex. 1026; Uru. 490.

514. If the thing given in usufruct should suffer a partial loss, the right shall continue as to the remaining part.

Arg. 2937; Guat. 1373; Chile, 807; Col. 866.

515. The usufruct cannot be constituted for over thirty years in favor of a town, a corporation or a society. Should it have been so constituted, and, before that time, the town becomes deserted or the corporation or society be dissolved, the usufruct shall be extinguished by such facts.

Guat. 1374; Chile, 770; Col. 829, par. 3.

516. The usufruct granted for such a time, until a third party becomes of certain age, shall subsist during the number of years specified, even if the third party dies before, unless the usufruct has been expressly granted only because of the existence of such person.

Arg. 2923; Chile, 804, par. 2; Col. 863.

517. When the usufruct is constituted on a tenement of which a building may form a part, and the building should be destroyed, in any manner whatever, the usufructuary shall have a right to enjoy the use of the land and materials.

The same thing shall happen when the usufruct is constituted only upon the building and it should be destroyed. But, in such a case, if the owner wants to construct another building, he shall have a right to the use of the ground and of the materials, under the obligation of paying to the usufructuary, during the time the usufruct lasts, the interest upon the sum equivalent to the value of the ground and of the materials.

Chile, 807, pars. 2, 3; Col. 866; Guat. 1375; Mex. 1029; Uru. 501.

518. When the owner joined with the usufructuary in the insurance of the tenement, given in usufruct, he shall continue, in the case of loss, in the enjoyment of the new building, if constructed, or shall receive the interest on the amount insured, if rebuilding is not convenient to the owner.

When the owner has refused to contribute towards the insurance of the tenement and the usufructuary alone is the insurer, the latter shall acquire the right, in case of loss, to collect in full the amount of the insurance, but under the obligation of investing it in rebuilding the tenement.

Should the usufructuary refuse to contribute to the insurance and the owner be the sole insurer, the latter shall receive, in case of loss, the full amount of insurance, but the usufructuary shall always have the right granted to him in the preceding article.

Arg. 2936.

519. When the thing in usufruct should be condemned for causes of public utility, the owner shall be obliged, either to replace it with another of the same value, and having similar conditions, or to pay to the usufructuary the legal interest on the amount of the indemnity, during all the time the usufruct is to last. If the owner chooses the second manner, he is bound to give security for the payment of the interest.

520. The usufruct is not extinguished by the bad use of the thing in usufruct; but if such abuse causes considerable damage to the owner, the latter may ask that the thing be delivered to him, binding himself to pay annually to the usufructuary the net proceeds of the same, after deducting the expenses and the compensation which may be allowed to him for the administration thereof.

Uru. 502; Guat. 1379; Mex. 1033; Chile, 809; Col. 868.

521. The usufruct constituted in favor of several persons in existence, at the time of its constitution, shall not be extinguished until the death of the last survivor of them.

Chile, 780; Col. 839.

522. Upon the determination thereof, the thing held in usufruct shall be delivered to the owner, unless the right of retention belonging to the usufructuary or to his heirs, for expenses which they should recover, is enforced. After the delivery is made, the bond or the mortgage shall be cancelled.

Arg. 2943; Mex. 1034; Chile, 794; Col. 853; Guat. 1380.

CHAPTER SECOND.

*Use and habitation.**

Article **523.** The rights and duties of the persons enjoying the use and of him who has the right of habitation shall be regulated by the title constituting such rights, and, in default thereof, by the following provisions.

Mex. 1035; Arg. 2952; Uru. 506; Chile, 814; Col. 873.

* Instituciones, book 2, tit. 5, pars. 1, 2, 4, 5. Digesto, book 7, tit. 1, law 7; id., book 7, tit. 8, laws 10, 11; id., book 7, tit. 9, law 5; id., book 7, tit. 18, law 15. Part. 3, tit. 31, laws 20, 21, 22, 27.

524. Use gives a right to receive, out of the fruits of another person's property, whatever may be needed to provide for the necessities of the person, enjoying the use, and his family, even when such family increases.

Habitation gives the person, having such a right, that of occupying in another person's house the apartments necessary for him and the members of his family.

Guat. 1381, 1390; Mex. 1037; Arg. 2948; Chile, 811, 874; Col. 870, 874.

525. The rights of use and habitation cannot be leased, nor transferred to another person by any title whatever.

Chile, 819; Col. 878; Guat. 1383, 1391; Mex. 1031; Uru. 511; Arg. 2959.

526. He, who has the use of a flock or a herd of cattle, may profit of the young, milk and wool thereof, in so far as it may be necessary for the consumption of himself and family, as well as of the dung required for manuring the land cultivated by him.

Arg. 2963; Mex. 1040.

527. When the person enjoying the use, consumes all the fruits of another person's property, or when he, who has the right of habitation, occupies the whole house, he will be bound to pay all the expenses of cultivation, of ordinary repairs for the preservation thereof, as well as the taxes, in the same manner as the usufructuary.

When he receives only a part of the fruits, or dwells only in a part of the house, he shall make no payments, provided that a part of the fruits or benefits, sufficient to cover the expenses and charges, remain to the owner. If they are not sufficient, the former shall pay the deficiency.

Guat. 1386, 1392, 1393; Arg. 2957; Chile, 818; Col. 877.

528. The provisions established for usufruct apply to the rights of use and habitation, in so far as they do not conflict with what is provided in this chapter.

Chile, 812; Col. 871; Guat. 1388, 1395.

529. The rights of use and habitation are extinguished by the same causes as that of usufruct, and besides by serious abuse of the thing or dwelling.

Arg. 2969.

TITLE VII.

Easements or servitudes.

CHAPTER FIRST.

Easements in general.

SECTION FIRST.

*Different classes of easements which may be established on tenements.**

Article **530**. An easement is a charge imposed upon real property or a tenement for the benefit of another tenement belonging to a different owner.

The tenement in favor of which the easement is constituted is called the dominant tenement, and the one suffering it, the servient tenement.

Guat. 1089; Chile, 820, 821; Col. 879, 880; Uru. 512; Mex. 1043; Arg. 1970, 2973.

531. Easements can also be established for the benefit of one or more persons or for a community to whom the incumbered tenement does not belong.

532. Easements may be continuous or discontinuous, apparent or not apparent.

Continuous are those the use of which is or may be incessant, without the intervention of any human act.

Discontinuous are those used at short or long intervals and which depend upon human acts.

Apparent are those which are well known and are continually in sight by external signs, revealing their use and benefit.

Not apparent are those which present no external show of their existence.

Guat. 1192 to 1196; Arg. 2975, 2976; Uru. 513, 514; Mex. 1046 to 1050; Chile, 821 to 824; Col. 880 to 883.

533. Easements are also either positive or negative.

A positive easement is one which imposes upon the owner of the servient tenement the obligation of allowing something to be done or doing it himself, and a negative easement is one which forbids the

* Digesto, book 8, tit. 1, laws 11, 17; id., book 8, tit. 4, law 12; id., book 8, tit. 6, law 12; id., book 47, tit. 1, law 72. Instituciones, book 2, tit. 3, par. 3. Part. 3, tit. 31, laws 1, 8, 9, 12, 13, 15.

owner of the servient tenement doing something which should be licit for him to do, if the easement did not exist.

534. Easements are inseparable from the tenement to which they actively or passively belong.

Mex. 1051; Chile, 825; Col. 883; Guat. 1197; Uru. 515; Arg. 3006.

535. Easements are indivisible. When the servient tenement is divided among two or more persons, the easement is not modified and each of them has to suffer the part corresponding to it.

If the dominant tenement is the one so divided, each part-holder may use the easement wholly, provided the place of its use is not changed, nor if it is not aggravated in any form.

Guat. 1199; Mex. 1053; Uru. 516; Chile, 826, 827; Col. 884, 890; Arg. 3007, 3008.

536. Easements are established either by law or by the will of the owners. The former are called legal and the latter voluntary easements.

Guat. 1200; Chile, 831; Col. 888.

SECTION SECOND.

*Manner of acquiring easements.**

Article **537.** Continuous and apparent easements are acquired, either by a title or by prescription of twenty years.

Arg. 3017; Guat. 1284; Mex. 1139; Chile, 882, par. 2; Col. 939.

538. In order to acquire by prescription, easements, referred to in the preceding article, the time of the possession shall be counted, in positive easements, from the day on which the owner of the dominant tenement or the one who has made use of the easement, has commenced to exert it over the servient tenement; and in negative easements, from the date on which the owner of the dominant tenement has, in a formal manner, forbidden the owner of the servient one, the execution of the act which might have been licit, had the easement not existed.

539. Continuous and not apparent easements and discontinuous ones, either apparent or not, can only be acquired under a title.

Guat. 1285; Chile, 882, par. 1; Mex. 1285; Col. 939, par. 1; Uru. 595; Arg. 3017.

---

* Digesto, book 8, tit. 2, law 30; id., book 8, tit. 2, law 20; tit. 4, law 11; tit. 3, law 3; id., book 2, tit. 1, law 2. Part. 3, tit. 31, law 14. Codigo, book 7, tit. 33, law 12.

540. The want of constitutive title of easements, which cannot be acquired by prescription, can only be remedied by deed of acknowledgment executed by the owner of the servient tenement or by a final sentence.

Col. 937, par. 2, 940; Chile, 880, par. 2, 883; Uru. 596; Mex. 1142; Guat. 1287.

541. The existence of apparent sign of an easement, between two tenements, established by the owner of both of them, shall be considered, should one be sold, as a title for the purpose that the easement should continue actively and passively, unless, at the time of the division of the ownership of both tenements, the contrary should be expressed in the deed of conveyance of either of them, or if such sign is taken away before the execution of such deed.

Chile, 881; Col. 938; Guat. 1288; Uru. 597; Mex. 1143; Arg. 2995.

542. Whenever an easement is established, all the rights required for its use are considered as granted.

Mex. 1144; Chile, 828; Col. 885; Guat. 1289; Uru. 549.

SECTION THIRD.

*Rights and obligations of owner of dominant and servient tenements.**

Article **543.** The owner of the dominant tenement may make, at his own expense on the servient tenement, all the works necessary for its use and maintenance of the easement but without changing it or rendering it more grievous.

He must choose for it the most convenient time and form for the purpose of causing the least possible trouble to the owner of the servient tenement.

Guat. 1292; Mex. 1147; Arg. 3022; Chile, 829; Col. 886.

544. When there are several dominant tenements, the owners of all of them are bound to contribute to the expenses, referred to in the preceding article, in proportion to the benefit, which each may obtain from the work. He, who does not wish to contribute, may exempt himself by renouncing his interest in the easement for the benefit of the others.

If the owner of the servient tenement should, in any manner, profit by the easement, he shall be obliged to contribute to the expenses in

* Digesto, book 8, tit. 5, law 5; 4, 10; id., book 11, tit. 7, law 2; id., book 8, tit. 5, law 9; id., book 8, tit. 2, law 11. Codigo, book 3, tit. 34, laws 1, 5. Part. 3, tit. 32, law 5.

the proportion already stated, unless there is a stipulation to the contrary.

Guat. 1301.

545. The owner of the servient tenement shall not impair, in any manner, the use of a constituted easement.

However, if by reason of the place originally assigned or by the form established for the use of the easement, this should become too troublesome to the owner of the servient tenement or should prevent him from making works, repairs, or important improvements, it may be changed, at his expense; provided, he offers another place or manner equally convenient, or a way that may not cause any injury to the owner of the dominant tenement or to those who have a right to the use of the easement.

Guat. 1295; Mex. 1251; Chile, 830; Col. 887; Uru. 603; Arg. 3037.

SECTION FOURTH.

*Manner in which easements are extinguished.**

Article **546.** Easements are extinguished:

1. By merger in the same person of the ownership of the servient and dominant tenements.

2. By non-use during twenty years.

In discontinuous easements, this term shall commence to be counted from the day on which it has ceased to be used, and, in respect to continuous ones, from the date on which an act in opposition to the easement may have taken place.

3. When the tenements become in such condition that the easement cannot be used, but this shall revive, if, later on, the condition of the tenements permits it to be used, unless, when the use becomes possible, sufficient time has elapsed for the prescription in accordance with the provisions of the preceding article.

4. When the day matures, or when the condition is complied with, in case the easement is temporal or conditional.

5. By the renunciation of the owner of the dominant tenement.

6. By redemption agreed to between the owners of the dominant and servient tenements.

Guat. 1302; Mex. 1157; Chile, 885, 887; Col. 942, 944; Uru. 605; Arg. 3045.

---

* Digesto, book 8, tit. 3, law 34; id., book 8, tit. 6, law 10; id., book 43, tit. 20, law 5; id., book 8, tit. 6, law 16. Part. 3, tit. 31, laws 16, 17, 18, 19.

547. The form of using the easement may be prescribed just in the same manner as the easement.

Mex. 1158; Col. 945; Chile, 888; Uru. 606; Guat. 1303; Arg. 3063.

548. When the dominant tenement belongs to several persons in common, the use of the easement, made by one of them, prevents the prescription in regard to the others.

Guat. 1304; Chile, 886; Col. 943; Mex. 1156; Arg. 3062; Uru. 607.

CHAPTER SECOND.

Legal easements.

SECTION FIRST.

General provisions.

Article **549.** The object of the easements, established by law, is either public utility or private interest.

Guat. 1201; Uru. 518; Chile, 839; Col. 897; Mex. 1066.

550. Anything concerning easements, established for public or for common utility, shall be governed by the special laws and regulations controlling them, and, in default thereof, by the provisions of the present title.

551. Easements, established by law for the interests of private persons or for causes of private utility, shall be controlled by the provisions of the present title without conflicting with what is established by the general laws, by-rules and ordinances or local ones about city or rural police.

These easements may be modified by agreement among the interested parties, whenever the law does not forbid it, or it causes no damage to a third party.

Chile, 841; Col. 889.

SECTION SECOND.

*Easements relating to waters.**

Article **552.** Inferior tenements are obliged to receive the waters, which naturally and without the intervention of man, come down from the superior tenements, as well as the stone or earth which they may drag along in their course.

* Part. 3, tit. 32, laws 13, 14; id. 3, tit. 28, law 6. Law of Waters of June 13, 1879, arts. 36, 69, 79, 80, 83, 96, 97, 102, 104, 105, 107, 109, 112, 116.

Neither can the owner of the inferior tenement make works which may prevent such an easement, nor can the owner of the superior one construct works aggravating it.

Chile, 833; Mex. 1058; Col. 891; Guat. 1203, 1204; Uru. 520.

553. The banks of the rivers, even when they are of private ownership, are subject in all their extent and margins, within a zone of three metres, to the easement of public use for the general interest of navigation, flotation, fishing, and salvage.

Tenements, adjacent to the banks of navigable or floatable rivers, are, besides, subject to the easement of a tow-path for the exclusive service of fluvial navigation and floatation.

Should it be necessary to occupy, for such purposes, lands of private ownership, the corresponding indemnity shall previously be paid.

Guat. 1212; Chile, 840; Col. 898.

554. Whenever for the diversion or taking of waters from a river or brook, or for the use of other continuous or discontinuous currents, it should be necessary to construct a dam, and the person who is to do it, is not the owner of the bank or of the land required as a support for it, he may establish the easement for abutment of the dam, by previously paying the proper indemnity (to the owner).

555. Forced easements for taking water and for drinking troughs for animals (*abrevadero*), can be imposed only for causes of public utility in favor of some town or village, indemnity having been previously paid.

Guat. 1214.

556. The easements for taking water and for watering animals carry with them the obligation on the servient tenements of giving passage for the persons and animals up to the place where they can be utilized, and the indemnity must embrace this service.

Chile, 828; Col. 885.

557. Whoever wishes to make use of waters, of which he can dispose for the use of a tenement belonging to him, has the right of causing it to pass through intermediate tenements, but he is obliged to indemnify the owners, and also those of the inferior tenements, upon which the waters may filter or fall.

Chile, 861, 865; Col. 919, 923; Guat. 1218; Mex. 1073.

558. A person desiring to make use of the rights granted in the preceding article is obliged:

1. To prove that he is entitled to dispose of the water, and that such water is sufficient for the use intended.

2. To show that the passage-way which he asks is the most convenient and less onerous to a third party.

3. To indemnify the owner of the servient tenement in the form provided by the laws and regulations.

Chile, 864, 865; Col. 922, 923; Guat. 1226; Mex. 1081.

559. The easement of an aqueduct for purposes of private interest cannot be imposed upon buildings nor their yards or dependencies, nor over gardens or orchards already in existence.

Chile, 826; Col. 920; Guat. 1219; Mex. 1074; Uru. 532.

560. The easement of an aqueduct does not prevent the owner of the servient tenement from closing and fencing it, nor from building over the aqueduct, in such a manner, that it may suffer no damage nor render impossible the necessary cleanings and repairs.

Chile, 923, 925; Col. 887.

561. The easement of aqueduct for its legal effects shall be considered as continuous and apparent, even when the passage of the water is not continuous or its use depends on the necessities of the dominant tenement, or, in turn, established by days or hours.

Chile, 822; Col. 881.

562. He, who for irrigating his tenement or improving it, has need to construct a stop-lock or a sluice-gate in a millrace, through which it is to receive water, may exact that the owners of the banks allow the construction of the same, upon his previously paying all damages and injuries, including those caused by the new easement to the said owners and to all other persons who irrigate.

563. The establishment, extent, form, and conditions of the easements of waters, to which this section refers, shall be governed by the special law on the matter in all that is not provided in this Code.

SECTION THIRD.

*Easement of ways.**

Article **564.** The owner of a tenement or property inclosed by others, belonging to several owners, and having no ingress or egress

---

* Digesto, book 11, tit. 7, law 12; id., book 8, tit. 1, law 9. Fuero Viejo of Castile, book 4, tit. 5, law 5. Part. 3, tit. 31, laws 3, 6; id. 3, tit. 32, law 7. Fuero Juzgo, book 8, tit. 4, laws 24, 26, 27. Nov. Recop., book 7, tit. 27, laws 5, 11.

to public roads, is entitled to exact a way or passage through the adjacent tenements, by previously paying the proper indemnity.

If this easement is constituted in such a manner that its use may be continuous for all the necessities of the dominant tenement, establishing a permanent way, then the indemnity shall comprise the value of the land occupied by it, and the amount of damage caused to the servient tenement.

When it is limited to the way required for the cultivation of the tenement, inclosed by others, and for the transportation of its crops through the servient tenement, without a permanent way, the indemnity shall consist in the payment of the injury caused by such burden.

Guat. 1236; Chile, 1847; Col. 905; Uru. 543.

565. The easement of way is to be located in the place where it shall cause the least damage to the servient tenement, in so far as consistent with this rule, through the place where the distance from the dominant tenement to the public road may be the shortest.

Guat. 1238.

566. The width of the easement of way shall be that which may be sufficient for the necessities of the dominant tenement.

Guat. 1242; Chile, 847; Col. 905; Uru. 545.

567. When a tenement, acquired by sale, barter or partition, remains inclosed by other tenements of the vendor, barterer or co-owner, he shall be obliged to grant to it the right of way, without indemnity, unless there is an agreement to the contrary.

Chile, 850; Col. 908; Uru. 549.

568. If the way granted to an inclosed tenement ceases to be necessary because the owner has joined it to another, adjacent to the public road, the owner of the servient tenement may demand the extinguishment of the easement, returning what he has received as an indemnity therefor.

The same thing is to be done in the event of the opening of a new road giving access to the inclosed tenement.

Chile, 849; Col. 907; Uru. 548.

569. When it is indispensable for the construction or repair of some building to carry the materials over another's tenement, or place scaffolding or other things on it for the work, the owner of such tenement is obliged to consent to it, receiving an indemnity in proportion to the injury it may have caused him.

570. Existing easements for the passage of animals, known under the name of sheepwalk (*cañada*), way, foot-path, or any others, and those of watering, and resting places, and sheep-cot shall be governed by the ordinances and regulations on the matter and, in default thereof, by the uses and customs of the place.

In any case a walk shall not exceed in width seventy-five metres, a way, thirty-seven metres, fifty centimetres, and a path twenty metres, except when they cause damages to rights lawfully acquired.

When it may be necessary to establish a forcible easement of way or that of a drinking trough for cattle, the provisions of this section and of articles 555 and 556 shall be followed. In this case the width shall not exceed ten metres.

SECTION FOURTH.

*Easements of party-walls and fences.**

Article **571.** The easements of party-walls and fences shall be governed by the provisions of this title, and by local ordinances and uses, in so far as they are not in conflict with them and no provisions exist in regard to the same.

Chile, 851; Col. 909.

572. The easement of party-walls and fences is presumed, whilst there is no title or exterior mark or proof to the contrary:

1. In dividing walls of contiguous buildings up to the point of elevation in common.

2. In dividing walls of gardens or yards, situated in cities or in the country.

3. In fences, inclosures and live hedges, dividing rural tenements.

Chile, 853; Col. 911; Guat. 1247; Mex. 1101; Uru. 560.

573. It is understood that there are exterior signs, contrary to the easement of party-wall, and fences:

1. When, in dividing walls of buildings, there are windows or openings.

2. When the dividing wall is, on one side, straight and vertical in all its facement and is also similar in the upper part of the other side, but in the lower part thereof it is tapering or has steps.

3. When the wall appears built entirely on the land of one of the tenements, and not half and half between the contiguous tenements.

---

* Digesto, book 8, tit. 2, laws 8, 13, 19. Instituciones, book 3, tit. 28, par. 3; Digesto, book 39, tit. 2, laws 35, 36, 37; id., book 10, tit. 3, law 28. Fuero Real, book 3, tit. 4, law 5. Part. 3, tit. 31, law 2. Fuero Viejo of Castile, book 4, tit. 5, law 3.

4. When it bears the burden of the binding beams, floors, and roof frame of one of the houses and not of the contiguous one.

5. When the dividing walls between yards, gardens and rural tenements is so constructed that the coping sheds the waters towards one of the tenements.

6. When the dividing wall, being constructed of stones, shows stepping stones, which, from distance to distance, jut out of the surface only on one side and not on the other.

7. When rural tenements, contiguous to others, included by fences or live hedges, are not closed. In all these cases, the ownership of the walls, inclosures, or hedges shall be understood to belong exclusively to the owner of the property or tenement who has in his favor the presumption based on any one of the above-mentioned signs.

Guat. 1248.

574. Ditches or drains, opened between tenements, are also considered, as common, when there is no title or sign showing the contrary.

There is a sign contrary to part ownership, when the earth or dirt excavated for opening the ditch or for its cleaning is only on one side thereof, in which case the ownership of the ditch shall belong exclusively to the owner of the tenement, having in its favor this exterior sign.

Guat. 1250, 1251.

575. The repairs and construction of party-walls and maintenance of inclosures, live-hedges, ditches, and drains, in common, shall be borne by all the owners of the tenements, who are interested in the same, in proportion to the rights of each one of them.

However, every owner may refuse to contribute to this charge by renouncing the part-ownership, except in the case when the party-wall supports his own building.

Chile, 858; Peru, 916; Mex. 1109; Uru. 561.

576. When the owner of a building, which is supported by a party-wall, desires to demolish it, he may also renounce the part-ownership, but he shall also pay for all repairs and work required for preventing, only on such occasion, damages which the demolition may cause to the party-wall.

Guat. 1256; Mex. 1111.

577. Every owner may construct a party-wall by raising it, at his own expense, and indemnifying (persons) against any damage which may be caused by the work, even when such damage is temporary.

He shall also have to pay for the expenses of maintaining the wall or the part newly raised or for the deepening of its foundations, compared with what they were before, and besides the indemnity for the further expenses which may be required to be incurred to maintain the party-wall by reason of the greater height or depth which has been added to it.

If the party-wall cannot bear the greater height, the owner desiring to raise it, shall be obliged to rebuild, at his own expense, and, if it is necessary to make it thicker, he shall give the extra space for it from his own land.

Guat. 1258 to 1260; Chile, 857; Col. 915; Mex. 1113; Uru. 564.

578. The other owners, who have not contributed in giving greater height, depth or thickness to the wall, may, however, acquire in it the right of party-ownership by paying proportionally for the amount of the work and one-half of the value of the land appropriated in giving it greater thickness.

Guat. 1262; Mex. 1117; Chile, 857; Col. 915.

579. Each owner of a party-wall may use it in proportion to the right he has in the part-ownership; he may, therefore, build, supporting his construction on the party-wall, or introduce joists up to one-half of the thickness thereof, but without impeding the common and respective uses of the other part-owners.

The part-owner, in order to use this right, must previously obtain the consent of the other parties interested in the part-ownership; and, if he cannot obtain it, the conditions required, in order that the new work may not injure the right of the part-owners, shall be fixed by experts.

Guat. 1263. 1264; Uru. 563; Chile, 855; Mex. 1118; Col. 913.

SECTION FIFTH.

*Easement of light and views.**

Article **580.** No part owner can, without the consent of the other, make in the party-wall a window or an opening of any kind.

Guat. 1273; Mex. 1128; Chile, 874; Col. 932; Uru. 578.

581. The owner of a wall which is not a party-wall, contiguous to the tenement of another person, may make in it windows or openings to receive light, at the height of the ceiling joists or near the ceiling,

* Digesto, book 8, tit. 2, laws 4, 40. Part. 3, tit. 31, law 2; id. 3, tit. 32, law 25.

of the dimensions of thirty centimetres square, and, in any event, with an iron grate imbedded in the wall and a wire netting.

However, the owner of the house or tenement, contiguous to the wall where the openings are made, may close them, if he acquires the part ownership of the wall and if the contrary has not been agreed upon.

He may also obstruct them by building on his land or raising a wall, adjacent to that having such opening or window.

582. It is forbidden to open windows with direct views or balconies or any similar openings jutting out over the property of the neighbor, if there is not a distance of, at least, two metres from the wall on which they are constructed to said property.

Neither can side or oblique views be opened over said property, unless there is (similarly) a distance of sixty centimetres.

Guat. 1276; Chile, 878; Col. 935; Uru. 580.

583. The distances, to which the preceding article refers, are to be measured where there are direct views, from the exterior line of the wall when the openings do not jut out, and from the line of these openings when they exist, and for slanting views from the dividing line of both tenements.

Mex. 1131; Chile, 878; Col. 935; Guat. 1276; Uru. 580.

584. The provisions of article 582 do not apply to buildings separated by a public way.

585. When, under any title, right has been acquired to have direct views, balconies, or belvederes over contiguous property, the owner of the servient tenement shall not build thereon, at a distance less than three metres, to be measured as stated in article 583.

SECTION SIXTH.

*Drainage of buildings.**

Article **586.** The owner of a building is obliged to construct his roofs or covers in such a manner that rain water may fall on his own land or on the street or a public place, and not on the land of his neighbor. Even if it falls on his own land, the owner is obliged to collect it, in such a way, that it will not cause damage to the neighboring tenement.

Guat. 1278; Mex. 1133; Uru. 581; Chile, 879; Col. 936.

---

* Digesto, book 8, tit. 2, laws 1, 2, 20; id., book 8, tit. 5, law 8. Fuero Viejo, book 4, tit. 5, law 1. Part. 3, tit. 31, law 2; id. 3, tit. 32, laws 7, 13, 14, 15. Instituciones, book 2, tit. 3, par. 1.

587. The owner of the tenement suffering the easement of receiving water, discharged from roofs, may so build as to receive the waters upon his own roof or give them another diversion, in accordance with local ordinances or customs, in such a manner as not to cause any burden or damage whatever to the dominant tenement.

588. When the yard or court of a house is inclosed between others, and it is not possible to give an outlet through the same house to the rain water collected in it, the establishment of an easement of outlet may be claimed to give passage to the waters through the place of the contiguous tenement, where the egress is the easiest, and to establish a conduit for the egress, in such a way, as to cause the least damage to the servient tenement, upon the payment of a proper indemnity.

Guat. 1279.

SECTION SEVENTH.

*Distances and intermediate works for certain constructions and plantations.**

Article **589.** It is forbidden to construct buildings or to make plantations near fortified cities or fortresses, without submitting to the prescriptions of the laws, ordinances, and regulations, peculiar to this matter.

Guat. 1266; Mex. 1121.

590. No one shall construct, near a wall belonging to a third party or a party-wall, wells, sewers, aqueducts, furnaces, forges, chimneys, stables, deposits of corrosive matters, factories driven by steam, or factories which by themselves or by their products are dangerous or noxious, without observing the distances prescribed by the regulations and uses of the place, and without making the necessary protective works, with subjection, as to form, to the conditions prescribed by said regulations.

In default of ordinances, precautions, considered necessary, shall be taken, after expert's inspection, for the purpose of avoiding all injuries to the neighboring tenements or buildings.

Guat. 1268; Uru. 574; Chile, 856; Col. 914.

---

* Digesto, book 8, tit. 2, law 13; id., book 8, tit. 2, law 19; id., book 8, tit. 5, law 17; id., book 39, tit. 2, law 24; id., book 10, tit. 1, law 13; id., book 43, tit. 27, law 1; id., book 8, tit. 1, law 1; id., book 41, tit. 2, laws 8, 9; id., book 10, tit. 3, law 19. Codigo, book 8, tit. 10, law 9; id., book 11, tit. 42, law 1. Part. 3, tit. 28, law 43; id. 3, tit. 32, law 12; id. 3, tit. 32, law 22. Supplement to Nov. Recop., book 7, tit. 1, law 1. Royal Order, issued by Charles the IV, Aug. 12, 1790. Fuero Real, book 4, tit. 4, law 19. Nov. Recop., book 7, tit. 40, law 5, par. 3; id., book 3, tit. 19, laws 8, 11, arts. 1, 6, 7, 13, 15, law 19; id., law 10; same title and book. Fuero Viejo of Castile, book 5, tit. 3, law 12. Part. 7, tit. 15, law 28; id., tit. 34, Rule 3.

591. No trees shall be planted near another man's tenement, unless it is at the distances authorized by the ordinances or customs of the place, and, in default of these, it shall be at a distance of two metres from the dividing line of the tenements, if the planting is made of tall trees, and at fifty centimetres, if the planting is made of shrubs or small trees.

Every owner has a right to ask that trees, which may be planted in the future at a shorter distance from his tenement, shall be uprooted.

Guat. 1269, 1270; Chile, 859; Col. 917; Mex. 1124.

592. Should the branches of any tree extend over a neighboring tenement, gardens or yards, the owner of the latter shall have a right to claim that they be cut, in so far as they extend over his property; and should the roots of the neighboring trees extend through the land of another person, the owner of the land which is penetrated may himself cut them, in so far as they are within his tenement.

Guat. 1271; Chile, 942; Col. 999; Mex. 1126; Uru. 573.

593. Trees existing in a party live-hedge shall also be considered as party trees, and any one of the owners has a right to exact that they be felled.

Trees serving as landmarks are excepted, and they may only be uprooted by mutual agreement amongst the adjoining owners.

Mex. 1127; Guat. 1272; Chile, 859; Col. 917.

CHAPTER THIRD.

*Voluntary easements.**

Article **594.** Every owner of a tenement has a right to burden it with all the easements he may deem fit, and in the manner and form that he may like best, provided he does not violate either the laws or the public order.

Guat. 1280; Mex. 1135; Uru. 583; Chile, 880; Col. 937.

595. The owner of a tenement, the usufruct of which belongs to another person, may impose upon it, without the consent of the usufructuary, any easements which may not damage the rights of the usufruct.

Guat. 1339, 1281; Mex. 1136.

596. When the direct dominion of a tenement belongs to one person and the beneficial dominion to another, no perpetual voluntary

* Part. 3, tit. 31, laws 10, 11, 14, 18; id. 5, tit. 8, law 29.

easement can be established upon it, without the consent of both owners.

597. The consent of every part-owner shall be required in order to impose an easement over an undivided tenement.

The concession, made by some of them, shall remain in suspension until everyone of the joint or common owners agrees to it.

But the concession, made by one of the part-owners severally, shall bind the grantors and his successors, even if they hold under a particular title, not to prevent the exercise of the right granted.

Mex. 1137; Uru. 590; Guat. 1282.

598. The title, and in some cases, the possession of an easement acquired by prescription, determines the right of the dominant tenement and the obligation of the servient tenement. In default of them, the easement shall be governed by the provisions of the present title which may apply to it.

Guat. 1284; Chile, 884; Mex. 1146; Uru. 600; Col. 941.

599. When the owner of the servient tenement has bound himself at the time of constituting the easement, to pay for the works required for the use and maintenance of the same, he may free himself from this charge, by abandoning his tenement to the owner of the dominant tenement.

Guat. 1294; Mex. 1149; Chile, 829; Uru. 601; Col. 886.

600. Pasturage in common shall only be established, in the future by express concession of the owners, to be proven by a contract or a last will, and shall not be made in favor of a universality of persons or a universality of property, but in favor of specified persons and over tenements also specified and determined.

The easement, established in accordance with this article, shall be governed by the title of its institution.

601. Pasturage in common in public land, whether it belongs to the municipalities or to the State, shall be governed by the administrative laws.

602. When pasturage in common exists amongst the residents of one or more villages, the owner, who incloses a tenement with a fence or a hedge, shall free the same from the pasturage in common. However, the other easements established over the same, shall remain subsistent.

The owner who closes his tenement shall keep his right to the pasturage in common in the other tenements not inclosed.

603. The owner of land, burdened with the easement of pasturage may redeem this charge by paying its value to the persons having the rights to the easement.

In default of an agreement, the capital for such redemption shall be fixed upon the basis of 4 per cent. of the annual value of the pasturage, regulated by appraisal by experts.

604. The provision of the preceding article applies to easements established for the use of fuel and other products of wood which belong to private property.

TITLE VIII.

*Registry of property.**

SOLE CHAPTER.

Article **605.** The registry of property has for its object the inscription or annotation of the acts and contracts relating to domain and other real rights pertaining to real property.

606. The titles of dominion or of other real rights, relating to real property which are not duly inscribed or annotated in the Registry of Property, work no injury to third parties.

607. The Registry of Property shall be public for those who have a known interest in investigating the condition of real property or real rights annotated or inscribed therein.

608. The provisions of the Law of Mortgage shall control the determination of titles, subject to inscription or annotation, the form, effect, and extinction of the same, and the manner of keeping the Registry and value of the entries in the books thereof.

---

* Nov. Recop., book 10, tit. 16, laws 1, 2, 3, 4. Law of Mortgage, arts. 2, 5, 23, 279, 280. Regulation of Law of Mortgage, arts. 154, 155.

BOOK THIRD.

DIFFERENT WAYS OF ACQUIRING OWNERSHIP.

PRELIMINARY PROVISION.

Article **609.** Ownership is acquired by occupancy.

Ownership and other rights over property are acquired and transmitted by law, by donation, by succession, either testate or intestate, and by tradition in consequence of certain contracts.

They may also be acquired by prescription.

TITLE I.

*Occupancy.**

Article **610.** By occupancy are acquired things appropriable, on account of their nature, which have no owners, as the animals which are objects of hunting and fishing, hidden treasures, and abandoned personal property.

Chile, 606; Col. 685; Guat. 562; Uru. 668.

611. The right to hunt and fish is governed by special laws.

612. The owner of a swarm of bees shall have a right to pursue the same on another person's tenement, indemnifying its possessor for the damage caused thereby. Should the tenement be inclosed, he shall need the consent of the owner to enter it.

If the owner has not pursued, or abandons the pursuit of the swarm for two successive days, the possessor of the tenement may occupy or retain the swarm.

The owner of tamed animals may also claim them during the twenty days following their occupation by another. After this term has elapsed, they shall belong to him who has caught and kept them.

Chile, 20; Col. 696; Guat. 956.

* Fuero Real, book 3, tit. 4, law 16. Part. 3, tit. 28, laws 5, 17, 19, 49, 50. Fuero Juzgo, book 8, tit. 6, law 1. Fuero Real, book 3, tit. 4, law 17. Part. 3, tit. 28, laws 19, 22, 23, 45. Nov. Recop., book 10, tit. 22, law 3. Law of May 9, 1835, art. 1. Fuero Juzgo, book 8, tit. 5, laws 4, 6, 7. Fuero Real, book 4, tit. 13, law 2. Nov. Recop., book 10, tit. 22, laws 4, 5, 6; id., book 6, tit. 7, law 10. Regulations of Marine, Aug. 12, 1802.

613. Pigeons, rabbits, and fish, which from their respective breeding places, should pass to another, belonging to a different owner, shall become the property of the latter, unless they have been enticed away through some trickery or fraud.

Col. 697; Chile, 621.

614. He who, by chance, finds a treasure, hidden on another man's property, shall have the right granted to him by article 351 of this Code.

Chile, 622; Col. 701.

615. He who finds any personal property, not a treasure, must return it to its former possessor. Should the possessor be not known, he must deliver it immediately to the mayor of the town where the finding has been made.

The mayor shall publish (notice of it) in the usual form, for two successive Sundays.

If the personal property found cannot be kept without injury or without causing expenses which may greatly reduce its value, it shall be sold at public auction, after eight days have elapsed from the second advertisement, without the owner having appeared, and the proceeds shall be deposited.

After two years have elapsed from the date of the second publication, without the owner having appeared, the thing found or its value shall be adjudged to the finder of it.

He, or the owner, as the case may be, shall be obliged to pay the expenses caused.

Col. 704; Chile, 629, 630; Guat. 566; Uru. 687; Mex. 808.

616. Should the owner appear, in due time, he shall be obliged to pay, as a reward to the person who found the thing, a tenth part of the sum or of the value of the article found. When the value of article exceeds 2,000 *pesetas*, the reward shall be reduced to one-twentieth part thereof in respect to any excess over that amount.

Chile, 632; Uru. 689.

617. Rights in respect to flotsam and jetsam, whatever their nature be, or in plants or herbs, grown on seashore, are regulated by special laws.

Mex. 826.

TITLE II.

Donations.

CHAPTER FIRST.

*Nature of donations.**

Article **618.** Donation is an act of liberality by which any person disposes gratuitously of a thing in favor of another who accepts it.

Col. 1443; Chile, 1386; Uru. 1574.

619. What is given to a person, on account of his merits or for services rendered to the donor, is also a donation, provided it does not constitute a recoverable debt, and a donation is also what imposes upon the donee a burden inferior to the amount donated.

Col. 1490; Chile, 1433; Guat. 721; Uru. 1576.

620. Donations which are to become effective upon the death of the donor partake of the nature of dispositions by last will and shall be governed by the laws on testamentary succession.

Guat. 744.

621. Donations which are to produce effects *inter vivos* shall be governed by the general provisions of contracts and obligations, in whatever is not prescribed in this title.

Chile, 1413; Col. 1473.

622. Donations having onerous causes, shall be regulated by the laws of contracts, and remunerative ones, by the provisions of the present title, in respect to the part exceeding the value of the burden imposed.

Col. 1443 to 1493; Chile, 1386 to 1436.

623. A donation is perfected upon the donor having knowledge of its acceptance by the donee.

Guat. 700; Col. 1469; Chile, 1412; Uru. 1581.

---

* Fuero Juzgo, book 5, tit. 2, law 1. Fuero Real, book 3, tit. 12, laws 1, 6, 10. Part. 3, tit. 18, law 105; id. 5, tit. 4, laws 1, 4, 5, 6, 7, 11. Nov. Recop., book 10, tit. 7, law 1; id., book 10, tit. 18, law 1.

CHAPTER SECOND.

*Persons who can make or receive donations.**

Article **624**. All persons who can contract and dispose of their property may make donations.

Guat. 709; Chile, 1387, 1388; Col. 1444.

625. All persons, who are not especially incapacitated from it by law, may accept donations.

Col. 1446; Chile, 1389; Guat. 718; Mex. 2747.

626. Persons, who cannot contract, cannot accept conditional or onerous donations, without the intervention of their lawful representative.

Col. 1468; Chile, 1411; Uru. 1584.

627. Donations made to persons, conceived but yet unborn, may be accepted by the persons who should lawfully represent them, were they already born.

Guat. 722; Mex. 2749; Col. 1447; Chile, 1390.

628. Donations made to incapable persons are null and void, though made in a concealed way, under the appearance of another contract, by intermediate persons.

Mex. 2750.

629. A donation does not bind the donor nor produce any effect until it is accepted.

Chile, 1412; Col. 1469; Mex. 2721; Uru. 1581; Guat. 700.

630. The donee shall accept the donation personally or by a person authorized by a special power for such purpose or having a general and sufficient power of attorney, otherwise it shall be null.

Chile, 1411; Col. 1468; Uru. 1582; Mex. 2730; Guat. 707.

631. Persons accepting a donation, in behalf of others who cannot accept it personally, are obliged to obtain the notification and annotation to which article 633 refers.

Guat. 720; Mex. 2730.

* Fuero Real, book 3, tit. 12, laws 2, 5, 10. Nov. Recop., book 10, tit. 1, laws 11, 12; id., book 10, tit. 7, law 1; id., book 10, tit. 16, law 4; id., book 10, tit. 20, law 10. Part. 5, Int.; id. 5, tit. 4, laws 1, 2, 3, 4, 6, 9; id. 3, tit. 18, law 67. Fuero Juzgo, book 5, tit. 2, law 6. Law of Civil Marriage, June 18, 1870, art. 49. Law of Mortgage, arts. 2, 3.

632. Donations of personal property may be made verbally or in writing. Verbal donations require the simultaneous delivery of the thing donated. In default of this requirement, the donation shall produce no effect, unless made in writing and the acceptance is shown in the same form.

Guat. 715; Mex. 2726.

633. In order that the donation of real property may be valid, it shall be made in a public deed and have expressed therein, severally, the property donated, and the amount of the incumbrances which the donee is obliged to satisfy.

The acceptance may be made in the same deed of donation or in a distinct one; but it shall produce no effects, unless made during the life of the donor.

When made in a distinct deed, notice of the acceptance shall be given to the donor, in an authentic manner, and this step shall be annotated in both deeds.

Chile, 1400; Col. 1457.

CHAPTER THIRD.

*Effects and limitations of donations.**

Article **634.** A donation may comprise all the actual property of the donor or a part of it, provided he reserves in fee-simple or in usufruct, what is required for his support in a condition corresponding to his circumstances.

Chile, 1408; Col. 1465; Uru. 1586; Mex. 2731.

635. A donation cannot embrace future property. As future property is considered that which the donor cannot dispose of at the time of the donation.

Guat. 708; Chile, 1409; Col. 1466.

636. Notwithstanding what is provided in article 634, no person can give or receive, by donation, more than what he can give or receive by testament.

A donation shall be considered inofficious in all that exceeds such limits.

Chile, 1185; Col. 1243; Guat. 708 to 711.

637. When a donation has been made to several persons conjointly, it shall be understood as in equal shares; and there shall be among them no right of accretion, unless the donor has otherwise ordered.

* Fuero Real, book 3, tit. 12, laws 3, 7. Part. 5, tit. 4, laws 4, 7, 8, 9. Toro, law 69. Nov. Recop., book 10, tit. 7, laws 2, 4.

From these provisions are excepted donations made to husband and wife conjointly, between whom such right shall obtain, unless the donor has disposed to the contrary.

Chile, 1416; Col. 1473.

638. The donee is subrogated to all the rights and actions which, in case of eviction, should belong to the donor. The latter on his part shall not be bound to warrant the things donated, unless the donation is onerous, in which case, the donor shall be liable for the eviction to the amount of the incumbrance.

Chile, 1418 to 1423; Col. 1475 to 1480.

639. The donor can reserve to himself the right to dispose of some of the property donated or of some amount as a lien over it; but should he die without making use of this right, the property or the sum, which the donor reserved, shall belong to the donee.

Uru. 1588; Mex. 2736.

640. The ownership of a thing can also be donated to a person, and its usufruct to another or others, under the limitations established by article 781 of this Code.

Uru. 1587; Chile, 1419; Col. 1476; Mex. 2738.

641. The reversion in favor of the donor only, in any case and under any circumstances, can also be validly established, but not in favor of other persons, except in the same cases and under equal limitations, as provided for in this Code for testamentary substitutions.

The reversion, stipulated by the donor in favor of a third party, against the provisions of the preceding paragraph, is null and void, but it shall not cause an annulment of the donation.

642. When the donation has been made, imposing on the donee the duty of paying the debts of the donor, if the clause contained no further declaration, it shall be understood that the donee is only bound to pay those contracted before the donation.

Chile, 1418, 1420; Col. 1475, 1477.

643. When there is no stipulation about the payment of debts, the donee shall be liable for them only in case that the donation has been made in fraud of the creditors.

The donation shall always be presumed to be made in fraud of the creditors, when, at the time of making it, the donor has not reserved for himself property sufficient to pay the debts contracted before the donation.

Mex. 2743.

CHAPTER FOURTH.

*Revocation and reduction of donations.**

Article **644.** Every donation *inter vivos,* made by a person having no legitimate children nor descendants nor legitimated by subsequent marriage, becomes revoked by the mere fact of the occurrence of any of the following cases:

1. When the donor, after the donation, has legitimate or legitimated or recognized natural children, even if they be posthumous.
2. When the child of the donor, whom he supposed dead when he made the donation, is found to be alive.

Chile, 1424; Col. 1481; Guat. 729, 730.

645. When the donation is rescinded by the supervention of children, the things donated shall be returned to the donor, or the value thereof, if the donee has sold them.

If they have been mortgaged, the donor may cancel the mortgage, paying the sum secured by it, and having a right to reclaim from the donee the sum paid.

When the things cannot be restored, they shall be appraised at the price they were worth when the donation was made.

Guat. 740.

646. The action of revocation by supervention of children shall be prescribed upon the lapse of five years, to be counted from the birth of the last child or from the legitimation or recognition, or from the time news was received of the existence of the child believed dead.

This action cannot be renounced and, on the death of the donor, passes to his children and to their legitimate issue.

Mex. 2759.

647. The donation shall be revoked on petition of the donor, when the donee has not complied with some of the conditions imposed upon him by the donor.

In this case, the things donated shall revert to the donor, and all the transfers made by the donee and the mortgages with which he may have burdened them, shall become null and void, with the limitations as to third parties, provided for in the Law of Mortgage.

Uru. 1593; Mex. 2763; Guat. 727; Chile, 1462; Col. 1483.

648. Donations may also be revoked, on petition of the donor, for causes of ingratitude in the following cases:

---

* Part. 5, tit. 4, laws 5, 6, 7, 8, 10. Fuero Real, book 3, tit. 12, laws 1, 11.

1. When the donee commits any crime against the person, the honor, or the property of the donor.

2. When the donee charges the donor with any of the crimes which give cause to official proceedings or public accusation, even if he proves it; unless the crime has been committed against the donee himself, his wife, or the children under his authority.

3. When the donee unduly refuses him support.

Guat. 732; Chile, 1428; Mex. 2764; Uru. 1595.

649. When a donation is revoked for causes of ingratitude, the transfers or mortgages, executed before the annotation of the complaint for revocation in the Registry of Property, shall, however, remain valid.

All those made, after this time, shall be null and void.

Uru. 1699; Guat. 740; Mex. 2765; Chile, 1429; Col. 1489, 1486.

650. In the cases, to which the first paragraph of the preceding article refers, the donor shall have a right to exact from the donee the value of the things sold, which he cannot recover from third parties, or the sum for which they have been mortgaged.

For the regulation of the value of such things, the time at which the donation was made will be considered.

Chile, 1432; Col. 1489.

651. When the donation is revoked by any of the causes, stated in article 644, or for ingratitude, or when it shall be reduced on account of being inofficious, the donee shall not return the fruits, except from the date of the presentation of the complaint.

When the revocation is based on the failure to comply with any one of the conditions imposed by the donation, the donee shall, besides the property, return the fruits he has collected after the noncompliance with such conditions.

Chile, 1483; Col. 1486; Guat. 742; Mex. 2784.

652. The action granted to the donor for causes of ingratitude cannot be renounced in advance. This action is prescribed, after the lapse of one year to be counted from the time the donor has knowledge of the fact and has been able to enforce the action.

653. This action shall not be transmitted to the heirs of the donor, if he did not enforce it when he could have done so.

Neither can it be enforced against the heirs of the donee, unless, at his death, the complaint had already been presented.

Chile, 1430; Col. 1487; Uru. 1597; Guat. 734.

654. Donations which, in accordance with the provisions of article 636, are found to be inofficious, after computing the net value of the property of the donor, at the time of his death, shall be reduced as to the excess, but this reduction shall not prevent them from being effectual during the life of the donor, nor the donee from appropriating fruits to his own use.

The reduction of donations shall be governed by the provisions of this chapter and by articles 820 and 821 of the present Code.

Chile, 1186; Col. 1244, 1245; Uru. 1600, 1601; Guat. 712.

655. The reduction of donations can be claimed only by the persons who are entitled to *legitime* or an aliquot part of the estate, and their heirs, or persons holding rights under them.

Persons comprised in the preceding article cannot renounce this right during the life of the donor, neither by express declaration nor by giving their consent to the donation.

The donees, the legatees who are not to receive an aliquot part, and the creditors of the decedent, cannot ask for this reduction or be benefited by it.

Chile, 1186; Col. 1244, 1245.

656. When there are two or more donations, and all cannot be covered by the free part of the estate, those of later date shall either be cancelled or reduced as to the excessive part.

Chile, 1187; Col. 1245.

TITLE III.

*Successions.**

GENERAL PROVISIONS.

Article **657.** The rights to the succession of a person are transmitted from the moment of his death.

Chile, 955, 956; Col. 1012, 1013.

658. Succession is bestowed, either by the will of a man as expressed in his testament or, in its default, by disposition of law.

The first is called testamentary, the second legitimate succession.

It may also be bestowed partly by will of man and partly by disposition of law.

Chile, 952; Col. 1009; Mex. 3365; Guat. 747.

* Fuero Juzgo, book 4, tit. 2, law 4. Fuero Real, book 3, tit. 5, law 3. Part. 6, tit. 3, laws 14, 21; id. 6, tit. 9, law 1; id. 7, tit. 9, law 13; id. 7, tit. 33, law 8. Nov. Recop., book 10, tit. 18, law 1.

659. Inheritance embraces all the property, rights, and obligations of a person, which are not extinguished by his death.

Col. 1008; Guat. 746; Uru. 793; Mex. 3364.

660. An heir is a person inheriting under an universal title; and a legatee, one inheriting under a special title.

Chile, 954; Col. 1011; Guat. 741.

661. Heirs succeed the decedent in all his rights and obligations by the mere fact of his death.

Guat. 746.

CHAPTER FIRST.

Testaments.

SECTION FIRST.

*Capacity to dispose by testaments.**

Article **662.** All persons who are not expressly forbidden by law may make a testament.

663. The following are incapable of making testaments:

1. Minors of both sexes under fourteen years of age.

2. Persons, who customarily or accidentally, are not of sound mind.

Guat. 795; Chile, 1005, 1061.

664. A testament made before mental alienation is valid.

Chile, 1006; Col. 1062.

665. Whenever a lunatic pretends to make a testament during a lucid interval, the Notary shall appoint two physicians who shall examine him previously, and he shall not execute the testament unless they assume the responsibility for the capacity of the testator, and they shall testify to their opinion in the testament, which shall be subscribed by the physicians besides the witnesses.

666. For the appreciation of the capacity of the testator, attention shall be exclusively given to his condition at the time of the execution of the testament.

Guat. 795.

---

* Fuero Real, book 3, tit. 5, law 5; id., book 3, tit. 6, law 11. Part. 6, tit. 1, laws 13, 16, 17. Nov. Recop., book 10, tit. 18, laws 3, 4. Fuero Juzgo, book 2, tit. 5, law 10. Fuero Viejo, book 5, tit. 2, laws 1, 6.

SECTION SECOND.

*Testaments in general.**

Article **667.** The act by which a person disposes of all his property or of a part of it, to take effect after his death, is called a testament (or will).

Guat. 766; Chile, 999; Col. 1055.

668. The testator can dispose of his property, either under title of inheritance or under that of legacy.

In case of doubt, even if the testator has not actually used the word "heir," if his will appears clearly on this point, his disposition shall be as valid as made under a title, either universal or of inheritance.

Uru. 742; Chile, 951; Col. 1008.

669. Two or more persons cannot make a testament conjointly or, in the same instrument, either for their reciprocal benefit or for the benefit of a third party.

Col. 1059; Chile, 1003; Uru. 743.

670. A testament is absolutely a personal act, the making of it, either wholly or partially, cannot be left to the discretion of a third party nor can it be made by a trustee or attorney.

Neither can there be left to the discretion of a third party, the permanency of the appointment of heirs or legatees, nor the designations of the portions they are to take, when they are nominally instituted.

Guat. 807; Chile, 1004; Col. 1060; Mex. 3376; Uru. 744.

671. The testator may commit to a third party the distribution of the sums which he may leave in general to specified classes, such as relatives, the poor, or beneficent institutions, and also the election of the persons or institutions to which such sums are applied.

Uru. 744; Mex. 3379.

672. Any disposition about the institution of heir, bequest, or legacy, made by the testator, referring to memoranda or private papers which after his death may appear in his domicile or out of it, shall

*Part. 5, tit. 11, law 33; id. 6, tit. 1, laws 26, 27, 29; id. 6, tit. 3, laws 6, 11, 13; id. 6, tit. 9, law 29; id. 6, tit. 10, law 3; id. 7, tit. 33, law 5. Ordenamiento of Alcalá, tit. 19, special law. Fuero Real, book 3, tit. 6, law 9; id., book 3, tit. 5, law 6; id., book 3, tit. 9, law 3.

be null and void, if such memoranda or papers do not contain all the requirements provided by law for holographic testaments.

Chile, 1002; Col. 1058.

673. A testament executed under duress, deceit or fraud shall be null and void.

Chile, 1007; Col. 1063; Uru. 751.

674. He, who by deceit, fraud, or violence prevents a person, of whom he is the intestate heir, from freely executing his last will, shall be deprived of his rights to the inheritance and shall besides be criminally liable for such acts.

Col. 1266; Chile, 1208; Mex. 3428; Uru. 804.

675. Every testamentary disposition shall be understood in the literal sense of its words, unless it clearly appears that the will of the testator was otherwise. In case of doubt, that which appears nearest in accordance with the intent of the testator, according to the tenor of the same testament, shall be observed.

The testator cannot forbid the contesting of his testament, in the cases in which there exists nullity specified by law.

Chile, 1069; Col. 1127; Mex. 3384.

SECTION THIRD.

*Form of testaments.**

Article **676.** Testaments are either ordinary or special. Ordinary testaments may be either holographic, open or secret.

Chile, 1008; Col. 1064; Guat. 767, 784; Uru. 752.

677. Military and maritime testaments and testaments executed in foreign countries are considered as special.

Chile, 1030; Col. 1087.

678. A testament is called holographic when the testator writes it in his own hand in the form and with the requisites specified in article 688.

679. A testament is called open whenever the testator expresses his last will in the presence of the persons who must authorize the act, and when they become informed of its dispositions.

Chile, 1008; Col. 1064; Guat. 777.

---

* Fuero Juzgo, book 2, tit. 4, law 12; id., book 2, tit. 5, laws 10, 11, 15. Fuero Real, book 2, tit. 8, law 9; id., book 3, tit. 5, law 8. Part. 3, tit. 16, law 18; id. 3, tit. 18, law 54; id. 6, tit. 1, laws 1, 7, 9, 10, 11. Notary law of May 28, 1862, arts. 21, 23, 27.

680. A testament is called secret (*cerrado*) when the testator, without revealing his last will, declares that it is contained in the writing which he presents to the persons who are to authorize the act.

Col. 1064; Chile, 1008; Guat. 768.

681. The following cannot be witnesses to testaments:

1. Women, with the exception of what is provided in article 701.
2. Males, under age, with the same exception.
3. Persons who are not residents or domiciled in the place of the execution thereof, unless in the cases excepted by law.
4. Blind persons and those totally deaf and dumb.
5. Persons who do not understand the language of the testator.
6. Persons of unsound mind.
7. Persons who have been condemned for the crimes of forgery of public or private documents, for perjury, and those suffering the penalty of civil interdiction.
8. Clerks, amanuenses, servants, or relatives within the fourth degree of consanguinity or within the second of affinity of the Notary who authorized the testament.

Chile, 1012; Guat. 793; Col. 1068; Mex. 3758; Uru. 771.

682. Neither can be witnesses to an open testament, the heirs and legatees instituted in it, nor the relatives of the same, within the fourth degree of consanguinity or second of affinity.

In this prohibition are not comprised the legatees and their relatives, when the legacy is of some pieces of personal property or of a sum of small importance compared with the amount of the estate.

Col. 1068.

683. In order that a witness may be declared disqualified, it is necessary that the cause of his incapacity should have existed at the time of the execution of the testament.

Col. 1069; Chile, 1013; Mex. 3759.

684. The presence of two interpreters, chosen by the testator to translate his disposition into Spanish, is required for making a testament in a foreign language. Such testament must be written in the two languages.

Chile, 1024; Col. 1081; Mex. 3760; Guat. 756.

685. The Notary and two of the witnesses who authorized the testament must personally know the testator, and should they not know him, such person shall be identified by two witnesses who know him and are known to the Notary and to the instrumental witnesses.

The Notary and the witnesses shall also assure themselves that in their opinion the testator has the legal capacity required to make a testament.

Witnesses authorizing a testament without the attendance of the Notary, in the cases of articles 700 and 701, are under the same obligation of personally knowing the testator.

686. When it is not possible to identify the person of the testator, in the manner provided by the preceding article, this circumstance shall be stated by the Notary or, in default thereof, by the witnesses who shall state any details about the documents which the testator may present for such purpose, and give a personal description of the testator.

If the testament is contested for such a cause, the burden of proof of the identity of the testator shall be borne by the person sustaining its validity.

687. Any testament, in the execution of which, the formalities, respectively established in this chapter, have not been observed, shall be null and void.

Chile, 1026; Guat. 1083.

SECTION FOURTH.

*Holographic testaments.**

Article **688.** Holographic testaments can only be executed by persons of lawful age.

In order that this testament should be valid, it shall be drawn on stamped paper, corresponding to the year of its execution, and be written all over and signed by the testator with specification of the year, month, and day of its execution.

When it contains words erased, corrected, or between lines, the testator must correct them under his own hand.

Foreigners may execute holographic testaments in their own language.

689. Holographic testaments shall be protocolled by presenting them for this purpose to the Judge of First Instance of the last domicile of the testator, or of the place where he died, within five years to be counted from the day of his death. They shall not be valid without this requisite.

690. The person, in whose hands such testament has been deposited, shall present it to the court, as soon as he receives notice of

* Fuero Juzgo, book 2, tit. 5, law 15. Part. 6, tit. 1, law 7. Notary law of May 28, 1862, art. 17.

the death of the testator, and should he not do it within ten days next following, he shall be liable for the damages and injury which may be caused by his delay.

It may also be presented by any person who may have interest in the testament, either as heir, legatee, executor, or in any other way.

691. After the holographic testament has been presented and the death of the testator has been proven, the Judge shall open it, if within a closed cover, and shall rubricate, together with the Notary, all the leaves and shall prove its identity by three witnesses who know the handwriting and subscription of the testator and who depose that they have no reasonable doubt whatever that the testament is written and subscribed by the testator's own hand.

In default of competent witnesses or if those examined have any doubts, and, whenever the Judge may consider it proper, he may employ experts in handwriting for the purpose of comparison.

692. For the carrying out of the proceedings, stated in the preceding article, and, as soon as possible, shall be summoned: The surviving consort, if any, the legitimate ascendants and descendants of the testator, and, in default of all of these, his brothers.

When these persons do not reside within the district, or their existence is unknown, or if they are minors or incapables, without legitimate representations, the Public Attorney shall be summoned.

Persons summoned may be present at the carrying out of such proceedings and verbally may make, at the time, the proper observations about the genuineness of the testament.

693. When the Judge considers that the identity of the testament has been proven, he shall order that it be protocolled, together with the proceedings taken, in the Registry of the corresponding Notary, who shall give to the interested parties the copies or authenticated copies which may be proper. In all other cases he shall refuse to protocol it.

Whatever the decision of the Judge may be, it shall be carried into effect, notwithstanding any opposition, and it shall not injure the rights of the interested parties to enforce it in any suit which may be proper.

SECTION FIFTH.

*Open testaments.**

Article **694.** Open testaments shall be executed before a Notary, qualified to act in the place of its execution, and three competent wit-

* Fuero Juzgo, book 2, tit. 5, laws 10, 11. Part. 6, tit. 2, law 4; id. 6, tit. 1, laws 1, 3, 13, 14. Nov. Recop., book 10, tit. 18, laws 1, 2. Toro, law 3.

nesses who can see and understand the testator and of whom one, at least, knows how and is able to write.

From this rule shall only be excepted the cases expressly determined in this same section.

Chile, 1014, 1015, 1012; Col. 1070, 1072, 1068; Mex. 3768; Uru. 755; Guat. 772, 775.

695. The testator shall state his last wishes to the Notary and to the witnesses. After the testament is drawn up in accordance with them, specifying the place, year, month, day, and hour of its execution, it shall be read aloud in order that the testator may declare, if it agrees with his will. If so, it shall be subscribed to immediately by the testator and the witnesses who are able to do so.

Should the testator declare that he does not know how or cannot subscribe it, one of the instrumental witnesses or any other person shall do it for him at his request, and the Notary shall certify to it. The same thing shall be done when any one of the witnesses is not able to sign.

The Notary shall always state that in his judgment the testator has the legal capacity required for executing the testament.

Guat. 772; Col. 1072 to 1075; Chile, 1015 to 1018; Uru. 756 to 758.

696. When the testator, who intends to make an open testament, presents his testamentary dispositions in writing, the Notary shall draw up the testament in accordance with them, and shall read it aloud in the presence of the witnesses, so that the testator may declare if its contents are the expression of his last will.

Col. 1074; Chile, 1017.

697. A person, who is absolutely deaf, shall read his testament himself; if he does not know how or cannot, he shall appoint two persons, who shall read it in his name always in the presence of the witnesses and of the Notary.

Uru. 759, 766; Mex. 3772.

698. When the testator is blind, the testament shall be read twice, once by the Notary, as provided by article 695, and the other time in the same manner by one of the witnesses or any other person appointed by the testator.

Col. 1076; Chile, 1019; Uru. 760; Guat. 774.

699. All the formalities, provided in this section, shall be made in a single act, and no interruption shall be allowed, except such a one as may be caused by a momentary incident.

The Notary shall certify, at the end of the testament, that all such formalities have been complied with and that he knows the testator or the witnesses of acquaintance, when they are required.

Col. 1072, 1075; Chile, 1015, 1018; Mex. 3773; Guat. 772.

700. When the testator is in imminent danger of death, the testament may be executed before five competent witnesses without the necessity of a Notary.

Chile, 1014, 1033, 1035; Col. 1071, 1092, 1090; Mex. 3807.

701. In case of epidemics, the testament shall also be executed, without intervention of a Notary, before three witnesses, over sixteen years of age, either male or female.

Guat. 786.

702. In the cases of the two preceding articles, the testament shall be written when possible; when not possible, the testament shall be valid, although the witnesses do not know how to write.

Chile, 1035; Col. 1092; Uru. 773; Guat. 786; Mex. 3806.

703. Testaments, executed in accordance with the provisions of the three preceding articles, shall become void, if two months have elapsed after the testator is out of danger of death or the epidemic has ceased.

When the testator dies within such term, the testament shall also become void, if, within three months after his demise, such testament is not taken to the competent tribunal, in order that it may be reduced to a public deed, whether it has been executed in writing or verbally.

Chile, 1036; Col. 1093.

704. Testaments, executed without the authorization of a Notary, shall be void, if they are not afterwards reduced to a public deed and protocolled in the form prescribed by the Law of Civil Procedure.

Chile, 1037, 1038; Col. 1094.

705. When an open testament is declared void for causes of non-compliance with the solemnities established for each case, the Notary authorizing it shall be responsible for the damages and injuries which may arise, if the fault is a result of his bad faith or by inexcusable negligence or ignorance.

Chile, 1023; Col. 1079, 1080.

SECTION SIXTH.

*Secret testaments.**

Article **706**. A secret testament may be written by the testator or by any other person, at his request, on common paper, stating the place, day, month, and year in which it has been written.

When the testator writes it in his own hand, he shall rubricate every sheet and set his signature at the end, after specifying all the words corrected, scratched or written between lines.

Should any other person write it, at his request, the testator shall put his full subscription on every sheet and at the end of the testament.

When the testator does not know how, or cannot subscribe his name, another person, at his request, shall do it for him, and shall also countersign every sheet, stating the cause of the testator's inability.

707. In the execution of the secret testament, the following solemnities shall be observed:

1. The paper on which the testament is drawn shall be placed within a closed and sealed cover in such a manner that the former cannot be taken out without tearing the latter.

2. The testator shall appear with the testament closed and sealed, or shall close and seal it at the time in the presence of the Notary, who is to authorize it, and of five competent witnesses, of whom three, at least, shall be able to sign.

3. The testator shall declare, in the presence of the Notary and the witnesses, that the cover which he presents contains his testament, stating if it is written, subscribed, and signed by him, or if written in another's hand, and subscribed by him at the end and on all of the leaves, or if, because he does not know how or cannot subscribe it, another person has done it for him, at his request.

4. On the cover of the testament, the Notary shall write the appropriate minutes of its execution, specifying the number and marks of the seals with which it is closed, and shall certify to the compliance with the above-mentioned solemnities, to his knowledge of the testator or of the identification of his person, in the manner provided by articles 685 and 686, and to the testator having, in his judgment, the legal capacity required for executing a testament.

* Part. 6, tit. 1, laws 1, 2, 13; id. 6, tit. 2, laws 1, 2, 3, 5, 6; id. 6, tit. 7, law 17. Nov. Recop., book 10, tit. 18, laws 2, 5. Notary law of May 28, 1862, art. 34. Royal Order, Oct. 16, 1853. Fuero Juzgo, book 2, tit. 5, laws 11, 13. Fuero Real, book 3, tit. 5, law 13. Law of Civil Procedure, art. 1956.

5. After the minutes have been drawn up and read, they shall be subscribed by the testator and the witnesses who know how to sign, and the Notary shall authorize them with his mark and subscription.

If the testator does not know how or cannot subscribe, one of the instrumental witnesses or any other person appointed by the testator, shall subscribe for him.

6. This circumstance shall also be expressed in the minutes, besides the place, hour, day, month, and year of its execution.

Chile, 1021, 1023; Col. 1078, 1080; Uru. 761; Mex. 3775; Guat. 777.

708. Blind persons, and those who do not know how or cannot read shall not make a secret testament.

Guat. 779; Chile, 1022; Col. 1079.

709. Deaf and dumb persons and those who cannot speak, but who are able to write, may execute a secret testament, if the following conditions are observed:

1. The testament shall be wholly written and subscribed by the testator, and the place, day, month, and year stated.

2. On presenting it, the testator shall write on the upper part of the cover, in the presence of the Notary and five witnesses, that such envelope contains his testament and that it is written and subscribed by him.

3. After what is written by the testator, the minutes of execution shall be noted and the Notary shall certify to the compliance with the provisions of the preceding number, and of all other provisions of article 707, in so far as they may apply to the case.

Guat. 782, 783; Chile, 1023; Col. 1080.

710. After the secret testament is certified to, the Notary shall deliver it to the testator, after filing in the secret protocol a certified copy of the execution.

Guat. 780; Mex. 3789.

711. The testator may keep the secret testament in his possession or intrust it to the custody of a person in whom he may have confidence or deposit it in the hands of the authorizing Notary for safekeeping in his archives.

In this last case, the Notary shall give a receipt to the testator, and shall note in his secret protocol, on the margin or at the foot of the minutes of the execution, that the testament remains in his hands. Should the testator afterwards receive it back, he shall sign a receipt at the foot of such a note.

Guat. 780; Mex. 3791.

712. The Notary or a person having in his possession a secret testament shall present it to a competent judge as soon as he learns of the death of the testator.

Should he not do so, within the term of ten days, he shall be responsible for the damages and injuries caused by his neglect.

Chile, 1025; Col. 1082; Uru. 767; Mex. 3796.

713. He, who, with malice, fails to present the secret testament, which is in his keeping, within the term fixed by the second paragraph of the preceding article, besides the responsibility stated in it, shall lose all right to the inheritance, should he have it as intestate heir, or as heir or legatee by the testament.

The same penalty shall be incurred by those who maliciously abstract the secret testament from the residence of the testator or from that of the person who keeps it in custody or deposit or by him who conceals, tears or renders it useless, in any other way, without being relieved from the proper criminal responsibility.

Mex. 3803.

714. For the opening and protocolling of a secret testament, the provisions of the Law of Civil Procedure shall be observed.

Chile, 1025; Col. 1082; Guat. 781; Uru. 767; Mex. 3796.

715. The secret testament, in the execution of which the formalities prescribed in this section have not been observed, shall be null and void, and the Notary who authorizes it shall be responsible for the damages and injuries which may be caused, if it is proven that the fault originated in malice, negligence or in inexcusable ignorance on his part. It shall be valid, however, as an holographic will, if it is written and subscribed all over by the testator and has the other conditions required in such testaments.

Mex. 3788.

SECTION SEVENTH.

*Military testaments.**

Article **716.** In times of war, soldiers in the field, volunteers, hostages, prisoners, and other persons, employed in the army or following the same, may execute their testaments before any officer, having, at least, the rank of captain.

* Fuero Juzgo, book 2, tit. 5, law 12. Part. 2, tit. 21, law 24; id. 6, tit. 1, law 4. Nov. Recop., book 10, tit. 18, laws 7, 8. Regulations of His Majesty for the regimen, discipline, subordination and service of his Armies, published in Oct. 22, 1768. Treaty 8, tit. 11, arts. 1, 2, 3, 4.

This provision applies to members of an army who are in a foreign country.

Should the testator be sick or wounded, he may execute it before the chaplain or physician attending him.

If he is with a detachment, before the person commanding, even if he be a noncommissioned officer.

In all the cases specified in this article, the presence of two competent witnesses shall always be necessary.

Chile, 1041, 1042; Col. 1098; Guat. 784; Uru. 775; Mex. 3817.

717. All the persons, mentioned in the preceding articles, may also execute a secret testament before (a staff officer), *comisario de guerra,* who shall exercise in such cases the functions of a Notary, and then the provisions of article 706 and the subsequent ones shall be observed.

Chile, 145; Col. 1102.

718. Testaments, executed in accordance with the two preceding articles, shall be forwarded, as soon as possible, to the general headquarters and by the latter to the Secretary of War.

If the testator has died, such Secretary shall forward the testament to the Judge of the last domicile of the decedent, and, if unknown to him, to the Senior Judge of Madrid, in order that he may officially summon the heirs and other persons interested in the succession.

These latter shall request that it be reduced to a public deed, and be protocolled in the form provided by the Code of Civil Procedure.

If the will is a secret one, the Judge shall officially proceed to open it, in the manner provided by said law, after summoning and with the intervention of the Public Attorney, and, after opening it, shall give notice of its contents to the heirs and other persons concerned.

719. Testaments, mentioned in article 716, shall become null and void four months after the testator has ceased to be in a campaign.

Chile, 1044; Col. 1101; Guat. 787.

720. During a battle, assault, engagement, and, generally, in every approximate danger of an action of war, a military testament can be made by word of mouth before two witnesses.

But this testament shall become void, if the testator is saved from the danger in view of which it was made.

Even if he does not escape, the testament shall become void, if not formalized by the witnesses before the Auditor of War or a judicial official following the army, and then it shall be acted upon in the from provided in article 718.

Chile, 1046; Col. 1103; Mex. 3819.

721. When a military testament is secret, the provisions of articles 706 and 707 shall be observed; but it shall be executed before the officer and two witnesses, required by article 716 for an open testament, and all of them shall subscribe the minutes of the execution, as well as the testator, if he is able to do so.

Chile, 1047; Col. 1104; Mex. 3819.

SECTION EIGHTH.

*Maritime testaments.**

Article **722.** Testaments, either open or secret, of persons on board a ship during a sea voyage, shall be executed, as follows:

When the vessel is a man-of-war, before the Paymaster or he who exercises his functions, in the presence of two competent witnesses, who can see and understand the testator. The Captain of the ship or the person occupying his place shall besides *visé* it.

On merchant vessels, the Captain or his representative shall authorize the testament with the assistance of two competent witnesses.

In both the first and second cases, the witnesses shall be selected from the passengers, if any; but one of them, at least, must be able to sign, and he shall sign it in his own name and in the name of the testator, if the latter does not know how or cannot do it.

When the testament is an open one, what is provided by article 695 shall besides be observed; and, if a secret one, what is ordered by section sixth of this chapter, excluding what refers to the number of witnesses, and the intervention of the Notary.

Chile, 1048, 1054, 1055; Col. 1105, 1111, 1112; Mex. 3825; Guat. 785, 788; Uru. 779.

723. The testament of the Paymaster of a man-of-war and of the Captain of a merchant vessel, shall be authorized by those who are to substitute them in their duties, and what is prescribed in the preceding article shall, furthermore, be observed.

Uru. 780; Mex. 3826.

724. Open testaments made on the high seas shall be kept in the custody of the Commander or the Captain and they shall be noted in the log-book.

The same entry shall be made of holographic and secret testaments.

Chile, 1049; Col. 1106.

725. Should a ship arrive at a foreign port, where there is a diplomatic or consular agent of Spain, the Commander of the man-of-war

* Regulations of the Navy, 1748. Treaty 6, tit. 6, arts. 1, 2, 3, 4, 15.

or the Captain of the merchant vessel, shall deliver to said agent a copy of the open testament or of the minutes of the execution of the secret one and of the notes entered in the log-book.

The copy of the testament or of the minutes must bear the same signatures as the original, if the persons who signed them are alive and on board; in other cases, they shall be authorized by the Paymaster or Captain who received the testament or the one acting in his place, and those remaining on board who took part in the testament shall also sign it.

The diplomatic or consular Agent shall have the proceedings of the delivery put in writing, and having closed and sealed the copy of the testament or of the minutes of its execution, if secret, he shall forward them with a copy of the entry in the log-book, in the proper way, to the Secretary of the Navy, who shall deposit them in the archives of his office.

The Commander or Captain, who shall deliver them, shall obtain from the diplomatic or consular Agent a certificate of having done so, and shall enter it in the log-book.

Chile, 1050; Col. 1107; Mex. 3828; Uru. 781.

726. When the vessel, either a merchantman or a man-of-war, arrives at the first port of the Kingdom, the Commander or Captain shall deliver the original testament, closed and sealed, to the local naval authority, with a copy of the entry made in the log-book, and, if the testator has died, in addition, a certificate proving it.

The delivery shall be proven in the form provided by the preceding article, and the naval authority shall forward all the papers, without delay, to the Secretary of the Navy.

Chile, 1050; Col. 1107.

727. When the testator has died and the testament is open, the Secretary of the Navy shall act, as provided by article 718.

Chile, 1050.

728. When the testament has been executed by a foreigner, on board of a Spanish vessel, the Secretary of the Navy shall forward the testament to the Secretary of State in order that it may be forwarded, in the proper way, through diplomatic channels.

729. When the testament is holographic and the testator dies during the voyage, the Commander or Captain shall take possession of the testament for the purpose of keeping it in custody, entering this fact in the log-book, and shall deliver the same to the local naval authority, in the form and for the effects provided in the preceding article, when the vessel arrives at the first port of the Kingdom.

The same thing shall be done when the testament is a secret one, if the testator has it in his possession at the time of his death.

730. Open and secret testaments, executed in accordance with the provisions of this section, shall be void after the lapse of four months from the day on which the testator landed at a place where he could make a testament in ordinary form.

Chile, 1052; Col. 1109; Mex. 3882.

731. When in danger of shipwreck, the provisions of article 720 shall apply to the crews and passengers of war or merchant vessels.

Chile, 1053; Col. 1110.

SECTION NINTH.

*Testaments made in foreign countries.**

Article **732.** Spaniards may make testaments out of the national territory, submitting themselves to the forms established by the laws of the country in which they may be.

They may also make testaments on the high seas, during their passage on a foreign vessel, in accordance with the laws of the country to which the ship belongs.

They may also make an holographic testament in accordance with article 688, omitting the requirement of stamped paper, even in countries where the laws do not recognize such testaments.

Chile, 1027; Col. 1084; Guat. 789; Uru. 790; Mex. 3834.

733. Joint testaments, forbidden by article 669, shall not be valid in Spain when executed by Spaniards in a foreign country, even when the laws of the country, where they have been executed, authorized them.

734. Spaniards who are in foreign countries may also execute their testaments, either open or secret, before the diplomatic or consular Agent of Spain, residing at the place of their execution.

In such cases, said agents shall act as notaries, and all the formalities, established by sections fifth and sixth of this chapter, shall be respectively observed; however, the condition of residence of the witnesses shall not be necessary.

Guat. 789; Chile, 1028; Col. 1083; Mex. 3835; Uru. 790.

735. The diplomatic or consular Agent shall forward a copy of the open testament, or of the act of execution of the secret testament,

* Nov. Recop., book 10, tit. 20, law 1, par. 1.

authorized under his hand and seal, to the Department of State to be deposited in its archives.

Chile, 1029; Col. 1085, 1086; Mex. 3833; Uru. 790; Guat. 789.

736. The diplomatic or consular Agent, in whose hands a Spaniard may have deposited his holographic or secret testament, shall forward it to the Department of State as soon as the testator dies, together with the certificate of the death.

The Department of State shall have the notice of the death published in the Gaceta of Madrid, in order that the parties concerned may obtain the testament and proceed to protocol it in the form prescribed.

SECTION TENTH.

*Revocation and inefficiency of testaments.**

Article **737.** All testamentary dispositions are essentially revocable, even when the testator states in the testament that his wish or resolution shall not be revoked.

All clauses, derogating future dispositions, shall be considered as not existing, as well as those in which the testator may order that the revocation of the testament should be void, unless marked with certain words and signs.

Chile, 1001; Col. 1057; Mex. 3665; Guat. 931; Uru. 960.

738. A testament cannot be revoked, wholly or in part, unless the same solemnities required for making it are observed in respect thereto.

Guat. 939.

739. A former testament becomes revoked by law by a later and perfect one, unless the testator states in the latter his wish of leaving the former subsisting in whole or in part.

However, a former testament recovers it force when the testator afterwards revokes the latter and expressly declares that it is his wish that the former should be valid.

Chile, 1213; Col. 1271; Guat. 932; Uru. 965.

740. The revocation shall be effective, even when the second testament becomes null by the incapacity of the heir or of the legatees appointed in it, or by the renunciation of the former or the latter.

Guat. 942; Uru. 965; Mex. 3671.

* Part. 6, tit. 1, laws 21, 22, 23, 24, 25. Fuero Real, book 3, tit. 5, law 2.

741. The recognition of an illegitimate child does not lose its force, even when the testament in which it was made is revoked.

Mex. 3667.

742. A secret testament, found in the domicile of the testator with the cover torn or the seals broken or the signature authorizing it effaced, erased or corrected is presumed revoked.

This testament, however, shall be valid when it may be proven that such damage has been caused without the wish or knowledge of the testator, or when he was in an insane condition; but, if the cover is found torn and the seals broken, it shall be necessary besides to prove the genuineness of the testament in order that it may be valid.

When the testament is found in the hands of another person, it shall be understood that any impairment was caused by such person, and the testament shall not be valid, unless its authenticity is proven, if the cover is torn or the seals broken; and if the former and latter are found intact, but the signatures effaced, erased or corrected, then the testament shall be valid, unless it is proven that it has been delivered in this condition by the testator himself.

Mex. 3802; Guat. 938.

743. Testaments shall become void or testamentary provisions ineffective, in whole or in part, only in the case expressly provided for in this Code.

CHAPTER SECOND.

Inheritances.

SECTION FIRST.

*Capacity for succession under or without a testament.**

Article **744.** All persons not incapacitated by law may succeed under or without a testament.

Chile, 961; Col. 1118; Guat. 810; Uru. 796.

---

* Law of October 11, 1820, art. 15. Concordat of 1851, art. 41. Law of May 1, 1853, art. 26. Agreement with the Holy See, Aug. 25, 1859, ordered to be published and observed by the law of April 4, 1860, arts. 3, 4. Part. 6, tit. 1, laws 26, 27, 28, 29, 30; id. 6, tit. 3, laws 2, 6, 10, 13, 20, 22, 45; id. 6, tit. 7, laws 13, 14, 17; id. 6, tit. 8, law 4; id. 6, tit. 9, law 34; id. 6, tit. 10, law 5. Council of Trent, session 25th, Dec. 3, 4, 1563. Decree on Purgatory, Royal Schedule May 30, 1830. Law of May 28, 1862, on constitution of the profession of Notary, art. 22. Nov. Recop., book 10, tit. 20, laws 11, 15, 16. Fuero Juzgo, book 3, tit. 2, laws 1, 8; id. book 4, tit. 3, law 4; id. book 5, tit. 2, law 5. Fuero Real, book 3, tit. 9, laws 3, 4, 5, 9.

745. The following are incapable of succeeding:

1. Abortive creatures, and as such are understood those who do not combine the conditions stated in article 30.
2. Associations or corporations not permitted by law.

Guat. 811; Col. 1019, 1020, 1021, 1022; Chile, 962, 963, 964, 965.

746. Church and church chapters, provincial deputations, provinces, city councils, municipalities, institutions for the sick, for beneficence or for public instruction, associations authorized or recognized by law, and all other judicial persons can acquire by testament in accordance with what is provided in article 38.

Col. 1021; Chile, 963.

747. When the testator disposes of the whole or part of his property for suffrages and pious works for the benefit of his soul and does it in an indeterminate manner and without specifying how it shall be applied, the executors shall sell the property and distribute the proceeds, giving one-half of it to the Diocesan to be employed for such suffrages and the care and necessities of the church, and the other half to the corresponding civil governor for the beneficent institutions of the domicile of the decedent, and, in default of such, for those of the province.

Chile, 1056; Col. 1113; Uru. 799; Mex. 345; Guat. 870.

748. A designation made in favor of a public institution, under condition or imposing a lien upon it, shall be valid only when approved by the government.

Mex. 3439.

749. Dispositions made in favor of the poor, in general, without designating persons or towns, shall be limited to those of the domicile of the testator at the time of his death, if it is not clearly shown that his will was otherwise.

The classification (*calificacion*) of the poor and distribution of the property shall be made by the person appointed by the testator, in default of such person, by the executors, and if there are none, by the curate, the Mayor, and the Municipal Judge, who shall decide by a majority of votes any doubts which may arise.

The same shall be done when the testator has disposed of his property in favor of the poor of a certain parish or town.

Col. 1113, 1115; Chile, 1056.

750. Every disposition in favor of an uncertain person shall be null and void, unless by some event the person may become certain.

Col. 1113; Chile, 1056; Uru. 747.

751. A disposition made generally in favor of the relatives of the testator is understood to be made in favor of those who stand in the nearest degree.

Chile, 1064; Col. 1122; Uru. 748.

752. Testamentary dispositions made by the testator, during his last illness in favor of the priest who confessed him during it, of the relatives of the latter within the fourth degree, or of his church, chapter, community or institute shall not be valid.

Guat. 811; Col. 1022; Chile, 965; Mex. 3434.

753. Neither shall be valid the testamentary dispositions of the ward in favor of his guardian, made before the final accounts of the guardian have been approved, even when the testator dies after such approval.

However, the dispositions made by the ward in favor of the guardian when the latter is his or her ascendant, descendant, brother, sister or consort, shall be valid.

754. The testator cannot dispose of the whole or a part of his estate in favor of the Notary who authorizes his testament, or of the latter's wife and relatives by consanguinity or affinity within the fourth degree, with the exception stated in article 682.

This prohibition applies to the witnesses of the open testament made with or without a Notary.

The provisions of this article apply also to the witnesses and persons before whom special testaments are executed.

Col. 1119; Chile, 1061; Guat. 811; Mex. 3436.

755. A testamentary disposition in favor of an incapable person, though concealed under the form of an onerous contract or made in favor of an intermediate person, shall be null and void.

Col. 1023; Chile, 966.

756. The following are incapable of succeeding on account of unworthiness:

1. Parents who have abandoned their children, or prostituted their daughters, or made attempts against their virtue.

2. Persons condemned in a trial for having made attempts against the life of the testator, his consort, and his descendants or ascendants.

When the offender is a forced heir, he shall lose his *legitime.*

3. He who has accused the testator of a crime for which the law imposes an afflictive penalty, when the accusation is declared as calumnious.

4. The heir of full age, who knowing of the violent death of the testator, has not denounced it to the courts within a month, unless proper judicial proceedings have already been taken *ex officio.*

This prohibition shall cease in cases in which, according to law, there is no obligation to make an accusation.

5. A person condemned at a trial for adultery with the wife of the testator.

6. He, who by menaces, fraud or violence forces the testator to make a testament or to alter it.

7. He, who by the same means, prevents another from making a testament or from revoking one already made, or who forges, conceals or alters a later one.

Col. 1025, 1026, 1027, 1028, 1029; Chile, 968, 969, 970, 971, 972.

757. The causes of unworthiness shall produce no effect, when the testator knew them at the time of making the testament or, if after having been informed of them, has pardoned the same by a public instrument.

Col. 1030; Chile, 973; Mex. 3430.

758. For determining the capacity of the heir or legatee, the time of the death of the person whose succession is questioned shall be taken into consideration.

In cases Nos. 2, 3 and 5 of article 756, it shall be necessary to wait until the final sentence is rendered, and in No. 4, until the month fixed for the accusation has elapsed.

When the institution or legacy is conditional, the time for the fulfilment of the condition shall, besides, be taken into consideration.

Chile, 974; Col. 1031; Mex. 3441.

759. The heir or legatee who dies before the condition is complied with, though he may survive the testator, transmits no rights whatever to his heirs.

Chile, 1078; Col. 1136.

760. Any person, incapable of succeeding, who, contrary to the prohibition of the preceding article, has entered into possession of the hereditary property, shall be obliged to return it, together with its accessions and with all the rents and fruits he may have collected.

Chile, 794; Col. 1031; Mex. 3452.

761. If the person, excluded from inheritance on account of incapacity, is a son or descendant of the testator and he has children or descendants, they shall acquire his rights to the *legitime.*

Persons so excluded shall have no rights to the usufruct and administration of the portion thus inherited by his children.

Chile, 976, 977; Col. 1033.

762. No action shall be instituted for the declaration of incapacity, after five years have elapsed from the time that the incapable took possession of the inheritance or legacy.

Chile, 975; Col. 1032; Mex. 3458.

SECTION SECOND.

*Institution of heir.**

Article **763.** A person who has no forced heirs may dispose by testament of all his property or part of it in favor of any person having capacity to acquire it.

A person who has forced heirs can dispose of his property only in the form and with the limitation provided by section fifth of this chapter.

Col. 1055; Chile, 999; Uru. 815; Guat. 799.

764. A testament shall be valid, even when it does not contain the institution of an heir, or it does not include the whole of the property, and although the person appointed does not accept the inheritance or is incapable of inheriting.

In such cases, the testamentary disposition, made in accordance with the laws, shall be complied with, and the remainder of the estate shall pass to the lawful heirs.

Guat. 825, 826; Chile, 999; Col. 1055.

765. The heirs appointed, without designation of shares, shall inherit share and share alike.

Guat. 827; Mex. 3801; Col. 1156; Chile, 1098; Uru. 817.

766. The voluntary heir, who dies before the testator, the incapable of inheriting, and he who renounces the inheritance, do not transmit any rights to their heirs, unless as provided in articles 761 and 857.

Col. 1014, 1019, 1034; Chile, 957, 962, 977; Guat. 813; Mex. 3450.

767. The statement of a false cause for the institution of an heir or of the appointment of legatee shall be considered as not written,

---

* Fuero Juzgo, book 4, tit. 5, law 1. Fuero Real, book 3, tit. 5, law 9. Part. 6, tit. 3, laws 6, 10, 13, 14, 17, 21; id. 6, tit. 9, laws 20, 35. Nov. Recop., book 10, tit. 20, law 28. Orden. of Alcala, tit. 19, special law.

unless it may appear from the testament that the testator would not have made such institution or legacy, had he known the falseness of such cause.

The statement of a cause contrary to law, even if true, shall also be considered as not written.

Chile, 1058; Col. 1117; Mex. 3380.

768. An heir to whom a certain and determined thing is left shall be considered as a legatee.

Chile, 1104; Col. 1162; Uru. 819.

769. When a testator appoints some heirs individually and others collectively, as when he says: "I institute as my heirs N. and N., and the children of N.," those collectively appointed shall be considered as individually appointed, unless it appears in a clear manner that the will of the testator was otherwise.

770. If the testator institutes his brothers, and he has some of full blood and others on the father's or mother's side only, the inheritance shall be divided as in cases of intestacy.

771. When the testator calls to the succession any person and his children, it shall be understood that all of them are instituted simultaneously and not successively.

Mex. 3506.

772. The testator shall designate the heir, by his name and family name; and when there are two having the same names, he must state some circumstances through which the instituted heir may be known.

Even when the testator has omitted the name of the heir, should he designate him in such a manner that no doubt may exist as to what person has been instituted, the institution shall be valid.

Chile, 1056, 1057; Col. 1113, 1116; Guat. 823; Mex. 3507.

773. An error in the name, family name, or qualities of the heir, shall not vitiate the institution when it may be possible, in any other manner, to know with certainty who is the person appointed.

If among persons of the same name and surname there is equality of circumstances, and these are such as do not permit the person who is instituted to be distinguished, none of them shall be an heir.

Guat. 824; Col. 1116, 1123; Chile, 1057, 1065; Mex. 3509.

SECTION THIRD.

*Substitution.**

Article **774.** The testator may substitute one or more persons in the place of the instituted heir or heirs in the cases where they may die before him or do not desire to or cannot accept the inheritance.

Simple substitution, without expressing which case, comprises the three stated in the preceding paragraph, unless the testator has ordered otherwise.

Mex. 3621; Guat. 832; Uru. 820; Col. 1215, 1216; Chile, 1156.

775. Parents and other ascendants may appoint substitutes in place of their descendants of both sexes, under fourteen years of age, for the cases where they may die before attaining such age.

Mex. 3625.

776. The ascendant may appoint a substitute for the descendant over fourteen years of age who has lawfully been declared incapable on account of unsound mind.

The substitution, to which the preceding article refers, shall be voided by the testament of the incapable made during a lucid interval or after he has recovered his reason.

777. The substitutions, to which the two preceding articles refer, in case the substitute has forced heirs, shall only be valid in so far as they do not injure the legitimate rights of such heirs.

Mex. 3627; Guat. 838.

778. Two or more persons can be substituted instead of a single one, contrariwise, a single person for two or more heirs.

Guat. 833; Col. 7218; Chile, 1159; Uru. 822; Mex. 3621.

779. When the heirs are instituted in unequal portions and are reciprocally substituted, they shall have in the substitution the same portions as in the institution, unless it may clearly appear that the will of the testator was otherwise.

Chile, 1160; Col. 1219; Uru. 824; Mex. 3630.

780. The substitute shall be subject to the same charges and conditions as imposed upon the instituted, unless the testator has

---

*Toro, law 31. Part. 6, tit. 5. Int. Part. 6, tit. 5, laws 1, 2, 3, 4, 5, 6, 7, 10, 11, 13, 14; id. 6, tit. 11, law 8. Law of Oct. 11, 1820, arts. 1, 4, 5, 14.

expressly disposed to the contrary or when the burdens or conditions may be merely personal, respecting the heir instituted.

Chile, 1161; Col. 1220; Mex. 3629.

781. Substitution in trust (*fideicomisarias*), by virtue of which the heir is charged with keeping and transmitting to a third party the whole or a part of the inheritance, shall be valid, and shall be effective, provided they do not go beyond the second degree or when made in favor of persons living at the time of the death of the testator.

Chile, 1164; Col. 1123; Mex. 3631.

782. Substitution in trust can never impair the *legitime*. Should they fall upon the third share intended for advantages (*mejora*), they can be made only in favor of the descendants.

Col. 1226.

783. To be valid, callings to the substitutions in trust, shall be expressly made.

A fiduciary is bound to deliver the inheritance to the fidei-commissary, without any deductions, excepting those falling upon him for lawful expenses, credits, and improvements, except when the testator has disposed otherwise.

Col. 804, 815; Chile, 744, 756.

784. The fidei-commissary shall acquire rights to the succession upon the death of the testator, even when he dies before the fiduciary. The rights of the former shall pass to his heirs.

Chile, 761; Col. 820.

785. No effects shall be produced by:

1. Fidei-commissary substitutions not made in an express manner, either by giving them such a name or by imposing upon the substitute the absolute obligation of delivering the property to a second heir.

2. Dispositions containing perpetual prohibitions of alienation and even a temporal one, when not within the limits provided by article 781.

3. Those imposing upon the heir the charge of paying a certain rent or pension to various persons in succession, beyond the second degree.

4. Those, the object of which is to leave to a person the whole or part of the estate, for the purpose of applying or investing the same, according to secret instructions communicated to him by the testator.

Uru. 827; Guat. 832.

786. The nullity of a fidei-commissary substitution shall not cause injury, either to the validity of the institution or to the heirs first called; the fidei-commissary clause shall simply be considered as not written (in such cases).

Mex. 3632.

787. The disposition by which the testator leaves the whole or a part of the inheritance to a person, and the usufruct to another, shall be valid. If various persons are called to the usufruct, not simultaneously, but in succession, the provisions of article 781 shall be followed.

Chile, 736; Col. 797; Uru. 830.

788. The disposition imposing upon the heir the duty of periodically investing certain sums for beneficent purposes, as dowers for poor maidens, pensions for students, or in favor of the poor or for any institution of beneficence, or of public instruction, shall be valid under the following conditions:

When the charge is imposed on real property and is temporal, the heir or heirs may dispose of the incumbered property, but the lien shall not cease until its inscription is cancelled.

When the charge is perpetual, the heir can capitalize it and invest the capital at interest, secured by a first and sufficient mortgage.

The capitalization and investment of the capital shall be made with the intervention of the civil governor of the province, and after a hearing of the Public Attorney.

In any event, when the testator has not established an order for the administration and application of the beneficent legacy, the administrative authority, who may be competent according to law, shall do it.

Mex. 3637.

789. All that is provided in this chapter in respect to heirs shall also apply to legatees.

Mex. 3644; Chile, 1164; Col. 1223.

SECTION FOURTH.

*Institution of heirs; and legacies conditional or for a term.**

Article **790.** Testamentary disposition, either by universal or special title, may be made conditionally.

Col. 1118; Chile, 1070; Guat. 816.

* Part. 6, tit. 4, Int.; id. 6, tit. 4, laws 1, 3, 4, 7, 8, 9; id. 6, tit. 11, law 21; id. 6, tit. 9, law 22.

791. Conditions imposed upon heirs and legatees shall be governed by the rules provided for conditional obligations in whatever is not prescribed in this section.

Col. 1128; Chile, 1070.

792. Impossible conditions and those contrary to law and good morals shall be considered as not existing and shall in no way injure the heir or legatee, even when the testator disposes otherwise.

Guat. 821.

793. The absolute condition of not contracting a first or subsequent marriage shall be considered as not existing, unless such condition has been imposed on the widower or widow by the deceased consort, or by the ascendants or descendants of the same.

However, the usufruct, use, or habitation or a pension or personal service may be bequeathed to anyone for the time during which such a person may remain unmarried or as a widow or widower.

Guat. 822; Col. 1132; Chile, 1074.

794. A disposition made under condition that the heir or legatee shall make in his testament some disposition in favor of the testator or of a third party shall be void.

Chile, 1059; Col. 1117.

795. A purely protestative condition imposed on the heir or legatee shall be complied with by them when, after the death of the testator, they are informed of it.

The case in which the condition has already been complied with and cannot be reiterated is excepted.

Col. 1125; Chile, 1067, 1072.

796. When the condition is casual or mixed, it shall be sufficient if it be realized or complied with at any time during the life or after the death of the testator, unless he has ordered otherwise.

If it had existed or had been complied with at the time the testament was executed and the testator did not know it, it shall be considered as complied with.

If he know it, it shall be considered as complied with only when of such a nature that it can no longer exist or be complied with again.

797. The statement of the object of the institution or of the legacy or the application to be given to what the testator has left of the lien imposed by the same shall not be considered as a condition, unless it may appear that such was his will.

What has been left in this manner may be immediately claimed and is transmissible to the heirs who may secure the compliance with the orders of the testator and the repayment of what they have received with fruits and interest, if they fail to comply with this obligation.

Col. 1147, 1153; Chile, 1089, 1095.

798. When, without the fault or a personal act of the heir or legatee, the institution or the legacy, to which the preceding article refers, cannot take place in the very terms ordered by the testator, it shall be complied with in terms as nearly analogous and in conformity with his will as possible.

When the party, having an interest in its compliance or noncompliance, should prevent it, without fault or a personal act of the heir or legatee, the condition shall be considered as complied with.

Col. 1151; Chile, 1093.

799. Suspensive conditions do not prevent the heir or legatee from acquiring his or her respective rights and transmitting them to their heirs, even before the fulfillment of such conditions.

Guat. 820; Col. 1136; Chile, 1078.

800. When the protestative condition, imposed on the heir or legatee, is a negative one, or of not giving or not doing (a certain thing), they shall comply with it by giving bonds that they will not do or will not give what was forbidden by the testator, and, in case of contravention, that they will refund what they have received with the fruits and interest thereon.

801. When the heir is instituted under a suspensive condition, the estate shall be placed in administration until the condition is complied with or until there is a certainty that it cannot be fulfiled.

The same shall be done when the heir or legatee shall not give the security, referred to in the preceding article.

802. The administration, to which the preceding article refers, shall be confided to the heir or heirs, unconditionally instituted, when among them and the conditional heir, the right of accretion exists. The same shall be understood in respect to legatees.

803. When the conditional heir has no co-heirs or when the right of accretion does not exist among them, he shall take charge of the administration upon giving bond.

If he does not give it, the administration shall be conferred upon the presumptive heir, also under bonds; and when neither of them can give bonds, the court shall appoint a third party who shall take charge of it, also under bonds, which shall be given with the intervention of the heir.

804. Administrators shall have the same rights and obligations as those who administer the property of an absentee.

805. The designation of the day or time on which the effect of the institution of heir or legatee shall begin or be determined shall be valid.

In both cases, the lawful successor shall be considered as called, until the time fixed arrives, or until such time expires. But in the first case, he shall not enter into possession of the property, until after having given sufficient bonds and with the intervention of the heir instituted.

Col. 1138; Chile, 1080; Guat. 816; Mex. 3382.

SECTION FIFTH.

*Legitimes.**

Article **806.** *Legitime* is that part of the property of which the testator cannot dispose because the law has reserved it for certain heirs, called, on that account, forced heirs.

Col. 1239; Chile, 1181; Uru. 846; Mex. 3460.

807. Forced heirs are:

1. Legitimate children and descendants in reference to their legitimate parents and ascendants.

2. In default of the preceding, the legitimate parents and ascendants in reference to their legitimate children and descendants.

3. The widower or widow, the natural children legally recognized, and the father or the mother of the same, in the form and proportion established by articles 834, 835, 836, 837, 840, 841, 842 and 846.

Col. 1230, 1240; Chile, 1172, 1182; Mex. 3477; Guat. 752 to 758.

808. The *legitime* of legitimate children and descendants is constituted by the two-third parts of the hereditary estate of the father and of the mother.

However, the parents may dispose of one of the two-third parts forming the *legitime* in order to apply it as an advantage to their legitimate children and descendants.

The remaining third part shall be at their free disposal.

Guat. 799; Col. 1242; Chile, 1184; Mex. 3463; Uru. 849.

* Fuero Juzgo, book 4, tit. 5, law 1. Fuero Real, book 3, tit. 5, law 9; id., book 3, tit. 12, law 7. Part. 5, tit. 5, law 13; id. 6, tit. 1, law 17; id. 6, tit. 3, law 21; id. 6, tit. 11, laws 1, 2, 3, 4; id. 6, tit. 13, laws 7, 8, 11; id. 6, tit. 4, law 11; id. 6, tit. 7, law 10; id. 6, tit. 8, laws 1, 5; id. 6, tit. 15, laws 4, 10; id. 7, tit. 33, law 8. Toro, laws 24, 26, 28, 29. Orden. Alcala, tit. 19, special law.

809. The *legitime* of the parents or ascendants is constituted by one-half of the hereditary estate of the children and descendants. The latter may freely dispose of the other half, with the exception of what is established in article 836.

Guat. 800; Col. 1242; Chile, 1184.

810. The *legitime,* reserved for the parents, shall be divided between both of them equally; when one of the parents is dead, the surviving shall take the whole of it.

When the testator leaves neither father nor mother, but ascendants in the same degree in the paternal or maternal line, the estate shall be divided share and share alike between both lines. When the ascendants are of a different degree, the *legitime* shall wholly belong to the nearest ones of either line.

811. The ascendant who inherits from his descendant property, acquired by the latter under gratuitous title from another ascendant or from a brother, shall be obliged to reserve such property, acquired by ministry of the law, in favor of the relatives within the third degree, belonging to the line from which such property came to him.

812. Ascendants succeed, to the exclusion of all other persons, to things given by them to their children or descendants, who died without issue, when the very objects donated are comprised in the estate. If they have been alienated, they shall succeed in all the actions which the donees have in respect to them, and in the value, if they have been sold, or in the property substituting them, if they were bartered or exchanged.

813. A testator cannot deprive the heirs of the *legitime,* except in the cases expressly determined by law.

Neither can he impose on it, any burden, condition, or substitution of any kind, with exception of what has been prescribed about the usufruct of the surviving consort.

Uru. 857; Guat. 803; Mex. 3461; Col. 1226, 1250; Chile, 1167, 1192.

814. The preterition of one or of all of the forced heirs in the direct line, either living, at the time of the execution of the testament, or born after the death of the testator, shall void the institution of heir. But the legacies and advantages shall be valid, in so far as they are not inofficious.

The preterition of the widower or widow does not annul the institution, but the person omitted shall keep all the rights granted to him by articles 834, 835, 836 and 837 of this Code.

If the omitted forced heirs die before the testator, the institution shall be valid.

Mex. 3844.

815. The forced heir to whom the testator has left, for any cause whatever, less than the *legitime* pertaining to him may claim the completion of the same.

Chile, 1189; Col. 1247; Mex. 3483.

816. All renunciations or compromises, about the future *legitime*, among the persons owing it and their forced heirs, are null and void, and the latter can claim it upon the death of the former, but they shall bring to collation whatever they have received on account of renunciations or compromises.

Uru. 850; Mex. 3496; Col. 1283; Chile, 1226.

817. Testamentary dispositions, diminishing the *legitime* of forced heirs, shall be reduced on petition of the same in so far as they are inofficious or excessive.

Uru. 952; Mex. 3489; Col. 1245, 1247; Chile, 1187, 1189.

818. To determine the *legitime,* consideration shall be given to the value of the property remaining at the death of the testator, after deducting all debts and charges, without comprising in them those imposed by the testament.

To the net value of the testamentary estate shall be added the value of all the collationable donations, made by the same testator at the time at which they were made.

Uru. 851; Mex. 3489; Chile, 1184, 1185; Col. 1252.

819. Donations made to children, not considered as advantages, shall be imputed to their *legitime.*

Donations made to strangers shall be imputed to the free part of which the testator may dispose by his last testament.

In so far as they be inofficious or may exceed the part disposable, they shall be reduced according to the rules of the following articles.

Col. 1244, 1256; Chile, 1186, 1198; Guat. 843; Uru. 851; Mex. 3517.

820. After the *legitime* is fixed, in accordance with the two preceding articles, the reduction shall be made as follows:

1. Donations shall be respected in so far as the *legitime* can be covered, reducing or voiding, if needs be, the legacies made in the testament.

2. Such reductions shall be made *pro rata,* without any distinction whatever.

When the testator has ordered that a certain legacy should be paid in preference to others, the former shall not suffer any reduction, until after the latter has been applied in full to the payment of the *legitime.*

3. When the legacy consists of an usufruct or annuity for life, the value of which may be considered greater than that of the disposable part, the forced heirs may choose between complying with the testamentary disposition or delivering to the legatee the part of the estate of which the testator could freely dispose.

Uru. 852; Mex. 3491.

821. When the legacy, subject to reduction, consists of a tenement, not convenient of division, it shall go to the legatee, if the reduction does not absorb one-half of its value, and, in the contrary case, to the forced heirs; but one or the other shall refund to the opposite party the respective balance in cash.

A legatee having a right to a *legitime* may retain all the tenement, provided its value does not exced the amount of the disposable portion and the quota belonging to him as *legitime.*

Uru. 853.

822. When the heirs or legatees do not wish to make use of the rights, granted to them by the preceding article, the one of them who has not such right may use it; if he does not wish to do so, the tenement shall be sold at public auction, on petition of any of the interested parties.

Uru. 854.

SECTION SIXTH.

Advantages (*mejoras*).*

Article **823.** The father or the mother may dispose of one of the two-third parts, intended as *legitime,* in favor of one or more of their children or descendants.

This portion is called advantage (*mejora*).

Col. 1242, 1253; Chile, 1184, 1195; Guat. 839.

824. No liens shall be imposed upon the advantage other than those in favor of the forced heirs or their descendants.

Col. 1253; Chile, 1195.

825. No donation by contract *inter vivos,* either simple or for onerous causes, in favor of children or descendants who are forced heirs shall be considered as an advantage, unless the donor has expressly declared his wish to give an advantage.

Mex. 3517; Guat. 841; Col. 1256; Chile, 1198.

---

* Fuero Juzgo, book 4, tit. 5, law 1. Fuero Real, book 3, tit. 5, law 9. Toro, laws 17, 18, 19, 20, 21, 22, 26, 27, 31. Part. 6, tit. 6, law 11.

826. The promise of giving or not giving an advantage, made in the public deed of a marriage contract (*capitulaciones matrimoniales*) shall be valid.

Any disposition of the testator, contrary to such promise, shall not be effectual.

Guat. 842; Mex. 3518; Chile, 1204; Col. 1263.

827. The advantage, even when made with delivery of the property, shall be revocable, unless made in a marriage contract or by an onerous contract entered into with a third party.

Chile, 1201; Col. 1259.

828. The bequest or legacy, made by the testator to one of the children or descendants, shall not be considered as an advantage, unless the testator has expressly declared that such is his will or when it cannot be included in the part at his free disposal.

Mex. 3520; Chile, 1198; Col. 1256; Guat. 843.

829. An advantage may be given in a specified thing. When the value of it exceeds both the third parts, designed for advantage and the share of the *legitime* belonging to him who receives the advantage, the latter shall pay the difference in cash to the other interested parties.

Col. 1264; Chile, 1206; Guat. 844; Mex. 3521.

830. The authority to give advantages cannot be delegated to a third party.

Chile, 1197; Col. 1255; Mex. 3523.

831. Notwithstanding the provisions of the preceding article in marriage contracts, it may be valid to agree that, when one of the consorts dies intestate, the widower or widow, who has not contracted a new marriage, may distribute, according to his or her prudent judgment, the estate of the decedent, and give advantages in it to the children in common, without damage to the *legitimes* and to the advantage given by the decedent while alive.

832. When the advantage has not been granted in specified things, it shall be paid out of the property of the inheritance, observing, in so far as it may be possible, the rules established by articles 1061 and 1062, in order to preserve the equality of the heirs in the distribution of the property.

Mex. 3522.

833. The legitimate son or descendant receiving an advantage may renounce the inheritance and accept the advantage.

SECTION SEVENTH.

Rights of the surviving consort.

Article **834.** The widower or widow, who at the death of his or her consort, is not divorced, or should be so by the fault of the decedent consort, shall have a right to a portion in the usufruct, equal to that which may belong as *legitime* to each of the legitimate children or descendants who have received no advantage.

When only one legitimate child or descendant remains, the widower or widow shall have the usufruct of the third part, designated for advantage, and the former shall keep the direct ownership, until by the death of the surviving consort the ownership is consolidated in him.

When the consorts are separated by a suit for divorce, the results of the suit are to be taken into account.

When there has been a pardon or a reconciliation between the divorced consorts, the surviving one shall retain his or her rights.

Col. 1230, 1231, 1236; Chile, 1172, 1173, 1178.

835. The hereditary portion, allotted in usufruct to the surviving consort, shall be taken from the third part of the estate which is designed for giving advantages to the children.

836. When the testator leaves no descendants, but only ascendants, the surviving consort shall have a right to the third part of the estate in usufruct.

This third part shall be taken out the free half part and the testator can dispose of the ownership of the same.

837. When the testator leaves no legitimate ascendants or descendants, the surviving consort shall be entitled to one-half of the estate also in usufruct.

838. The heirs may satisfy the surviving consort for such part of usufruct, assigning to him or her a life annuity or the proceeds of a certain property or a sum in cash, acting by mutual agreement or, in default of it, by virtue of a judicial decree.

Where this has not been done, all the property of inheritance shall be subject to the payment of the part of the usufruct belonging to the surviving consort.

839. In case of concurrence of the children of two or more marriages, the usufruct, belonging to the surviving consort of the second marriage, shall be taken from the one-third part at the free disposal of the parents.

SECTION EIGHTH.

*Rights of illegitimate children.**

Article **840.** When the testator leaves legitimate children or descendants, and natural children, legally recognized, each one of the latter shall be entitled to one-half of the portion which may belong to each of the legitimate children who have received no advantages, provided it may be comprised in the one-third part, at free disposal, from which it must be taken out, after deducting the expenses of the burial and funeral.

The legitimate children may satisfy the quota belonging to the natural ones in cash, or in other property belonging to the estate, according to just regulations.

Col. 1045; Chile, 988; Uru. 849; Guat. 969; Mex. 3463.

841. When the testator leaves no children or descendants but has legitimate ascendants, the recognized natural children shall be entitled to one-half of the part of the estate at the testator's free disposal.

This is understood without injury to the *legitime* of the surviving consort, in accordance with article 836; therefore, when the consort concurs with the natural recognized children, whatever may be wanting to complete their *legitime* shall be allotted to them only in naked property, while the consort survives.

Col. 1046; Chile, 989; Guat. 800.

842. When the testator leaves no legitimate descendants or ascendants, the recognized natural children shall be entitled to one-third part of the estate.

Col. 1048; Chile, 994; Uru. 849.

843. The rights recognized in natural children, by the preceding article, are transmitted, upon their death, to their legitimate descendants.

Guat. 970.

844. The hereditary portion of children, legitimated by Royal Concession, shall be equal to that established by law in favor of recognized natural children.

---

* Fuero Real, book 3, art. 6, laws 1, 4, 17; id., book 4, tit. 22, law 7; id., book 3, tit. 5, law 10; id., book 4, tit. 8, law 2. Toro, laws 9, 10, 12. Fuero Juzgo, book 3, tit. 5, law 2. Part. 4, tit. 15, laws 4, 9; id. 4, tit. 19, law 5; id. 6, tit. 3, law 4; id. 6, tit. 13, laws 8, 10, 11. Nov. Recop., book 10, tit. 20, law 4.

845. Illegitimate children, who have not the condition of natural children, shall only have a right to support.

The obligation of the person who has to support them shall be transmitted to his or her heir, and shall subsist until such children attain their majority, and in the event of being incapable, while the incapacity lasts.

Chile, 280, 332.

846. The right of succession which the laws grant to natural children, extends by reciprocity, in similar cases, to the natural father or mother.

Mex. 3479; Uru. 849; Chile, 993; Col. 1050.

847. The donations which the natural child may have received, during his life, from his father or mother, shall be charged to his *legitime*.

Should they exceed the third part at free disposal, they shall be reduced in the form provided by article 817 and those following it.

Chile, 1196; Mex. 3488; Uru. 851.

SECTION NINTH.

*Disinheritance.**

Article **848.** Disinheritance shall only take place for one of the causes expressly fixed by law.

Chile, 1207; Col. 1265; Uru. 858; Guat. 923.

849. Disinheritance can only be effected by a testament mentioning therein the legal cause on which it is based.

Col. 1265, 1267; Chile, 1207, 1209; Guat. 923; Mex. 3649; Uru. 859.

850. The proof of the truth of the cause of disinheritance shall be established by the heirs of the testator, should the disinherited deny it.

Chile, 1209; Col. 1267; Mex. 3650; Uru. 860.

851. Disinheritance, made without stating the cause, or for a cause, the truth of which, if contested, should not be proven or which is not one of those stated in the four following articles, shall void the institution of heir, in so far as it injures the disinherited,

* Nov. Recop., book 10, tit. 2, law 9. Part. 6, tit. 7, laws 1, 2, 3, 4, 5, 6, 7, 8, 10, 11; id. 6, tit. 8, laws 1, 4, 7. Fuero Juzgo, book 3, tit. 2, law 8; id., book 3, tit. 4, law 7; id., book 4, tit. 5, law 1. Fuero Real, book 3, tit. 9, laws 1, 2, 3. Fuero Viejo, book 3, tit. 5, laws 1, 2.

but the legacies, advantages and other testamentary dispositions, which cause no damage to said *legitime*, shall be valid.

Mex. 3651.

852. Just causes for disinheritance are, in their respective cases, those of incapacity for succeeding by unworthiness, specified in Nos. 1, 2, 3, 5 and 6 of article 756.

Mex. 3646; Uru. 866.

853. Besides the causes specified in Nos. 2, 3, 5, 6 of article 756 for disinheriting children and descendants, either legitimate or natural, the following shall be just causes therefor:

1. To have refused, without lawful cause, support to the father or ascendant who disinherits him.
2. Having used personal violence against or grievously offended the testator by words.
3. If the daughter or granddaughter has prostituted herself.
4. To have been condemned for a crime carrying with it the penalty of civil interdiction.

Col. 1266; Chile, 1208; Guat. 924.

854. Besides the causes mentioned in Nos. 1, 2, 3, 5 and 6 of article 756, the following are also just causes to disinherit the parents or ascendants, either legitimate or natural.

1. The loss of the parental power by the causes stated in article 169.
2. The refusal of support to the children or descendants without lawful cause.
3. An attempt of one of the parents against the life of the other, unless there has been a reconciliation between them.

Guat. 925.

855. Besides those specified in Nos. 2, 3 and 6 of article 756, the following shall also be just causes for disinheriting the consort:

1. Those which give cause for divorce under article 105.
2. Those which give cause for the loss of the parental power, as stated in article 169.
3. The refusal of support to the children or to the other consort.
4. An attempt against the life of the consort making the testament, unless they were reconciled.

In order that the causes which give reasons for divorce may also be causes for disinheritance, it is required that the consorts should not live under the same roof.

856. A succeeding reconciliation of the offender and the offended deprives the latter of the right to disinherit and render the disinheritance already made ineffective.

Guat. 829; Chile. 1211; Col. 1260.

857. The children of the disinherited shall take his or her place and shall retain the rights of forced heirs in respect to the *legitime*, but the disinherited parent shall have neither the usufruct nor the administration of the property of said *legitime.*

Chile, 243; Col. 291; Guat. 927.

SECTION TENTH.

*Legacies and bequests.**

Article **858.** A testator may burden with legacies and bequests, not only his heir, but also the legatees.

These shall be liable to the burden only to the extent of the value of the legacy.

Col. 1163; Chile. 1104; Mex. 3532; Uru. 857.

859. When the testator burdens one of the heirs with a legacy, he alone shall be obliged to comply with it. If he does not burden any one in particular, all shall be liable for it, in the same proportion in which they may be heirs of the estate.

Mex. 3532.

860. The person, bound to the delivery of the legacy, shall be responsible, in case of eviction, if the thing is undetermined and is designated only in kind or species.

Uru. 868.

861. The legacy of another person's property, when the testator knew, at the time of bequeathing it, that it was not his, is valid. The heir is bound to acquire the property for its delivery to the legatee, and, when not possible, to pay the latter its just value.

---

* Digesto, book 16, tit. 1, law 29; id., book 16, tit. 3, law 1; id., book 21, tit. 2, law 58; id., book 31, laws 4, 5, 12, 66; id., book 30, law 24, par. 2; 38, 44 par. 4; id., book 33, law 3; id., book 33, tit. 1, laws 5, 8, 22; id., book 34, tit. 1, law 23; id., book 34, tit. 8, 9; id., book 36, tit. 2, law 5; id., book 43, tit. 3, law 1, par. 2; id., book 47, tit. 2, law 64. De legatis, law 5, par. 2. Digesto, law 3, par. 1. Fuero Real, book 3, tit. 5, law 2. Nov. Recop., book 10, tit. 18, law 1. Project of 1882, arts. 858, 859, 862, par. 1, 872. Project of 1851, arts. 692, 696, 702. Instituciones, book 2, tit. 20, laws 4, 10; id., book 2, tit. 24, par. 1. Part. 6, tit. 9, laws 2, 3, 6, 10, 11, 13, 14, 15, 16, 17, 19, 20, 23, 24, 25, 34, 36, 37, 38, 40, 41, 42, 43, 44; id. 6, tit. 10, law 2; id. 6, tit. 11; id. 7, tit. 10, law 10.

The proof that the testator knew that the thing was not his own falls on the legatee.

Col. 1164, 1165; Chile, 1106, 1107; Guat. 870; Uru. 870; Mex. 3638.

862. When the testator did not know that the thing he bequeathed was not his, the bequest shall be null and void.

But it shall be valid, if he acquires the thing, after the execution of the testament.

Col. 1165; Chile, 1107.

863. A legacy to a third party of a thing belonging to the heir or to one of the legatees shall be valid, and they, on accepting the succession, shall deliver the thing bequeathed or the just value thereof, under the limitation established in the following article.

The provision of the preceding paragraph is understood without damage to the *legitime* of the forced heirs.

Mex. 3549.

864. When the testator, heir, or legatee have only a part or a right in the thing bequeathed, the legacy shall be understood as limited to such part or right, unless the testator expressly declares that he bequeathed the thing integrally.

Col. 1168; Chile, 1110; Mex. 3549.

865. A legacy of things, out of commerce, is null and void.

Col. 1163; Chile, 1105; Mex. 3540.

866. The legacy of a thing, which at the time of the execution of the testament, belonged already to the legatee, even when another person has some right to it, shall not be effectual.

When the testator expressly orders that such a thing should be liberated from such right or burden, the bequest shall be valid in that respect.

Col. 1164; Chile, 1106; Mex. 3570.

867. When the testator bequeaths something, pledged or mortgaged, for the security of an exigible (mature) debt, the payment of the same shall fall upon the heir.

If the legatee pays such debt because the heir has not done so, the legatee shall be subrogated in the place and right of the creditor to make claim against the heir therefor.

Any other lien, either perpetual or temporary, with which the thing bequeathed is burdened, passes together with it to the legatee, but, in both cases, the rents and interests or charges due, up to the death of the testator, are a charge upon the inheritance.

Mex. 3554; Uru. 871; Chile, 1135, 1193.

868. When the thing bequeathed is subject to the usufruct, use, or habitation, the legatee is obliged to respect such rights, until they are lawfully extinguished.

Mex. 3556.

869. The legacy shall not be effective:

1. When the testator makes such alterations in the thing bequeathed that it does not retain either the form or the denomination that it before had.

2. When the testator alienates, under any title or cause whatever, the thing bequeathed or a part of it, it being understood, in this last case, that the bequest becomes void only in relation to the alienated part. When, after the alienation, the thing reverts to the ownership of the testator, even by nullity of the contract, the bequest shall not be valid, after such fact; unless in the case in which the reacquisition is made under a contract of revertible sale.

3. When the thing bequeathed perishes in whole, during the life of the testator or after his death, without blame on the part of the heir. Nevertheless, the person obliged to pay the legacy shall be liable for the eviction, if the thing bequeathed has not been determined in species as provided in article 860.

Col. 1193; Chile, 1135; Uru. 903.

870. The legacy of a credit against a third party or of the remission or liberation of a debt of the legatee, shall be effectual only in that part of the credit or of the debt, yet existing at the time of the death of the testator.

In the first case, the heir shall fulfill his duty by assigning to the legatee all the actions he may have against the debtor.

In the second, by giving to the legatee the full release, if he asks for it.

In both cases, the legacy shall comprise the interests on the credits or the debts due to the testator, at the time of his death.

Col. 1185, 1187, 1188; Chile, 1127, 1129, 1130; Guat. 872; Uru. 876; Mex. 3559.

871. The legacy, to which the preceding article refers, is made void when the testator, after having made it, judicially demands from the debtor the payment of such debt, even when the payment has not been made at the time of the death.

By the legacy made to the debtor of a thing pledged, it is understood that only the right of pledge is remitted.

Col. 1186, 1187; Chile, 1128, 1129; Uru. 877; Mex. 3550.

872. The generic legacy of liberation or remission of debts comprises those existing at the time of the execution of the testament, and not subsequent ones.

Col. 1188; Chile, 1130; Uru. 878; Guat. 872; Mex. 3566.

873. A legacy made to a creditor shall not be imputed in payment of his credit, unless the testator so expressly declares.

In such case, the creditor shall have a right either to collect the excess of the credit or of the legacy.

Col. 1189; Chile, 1131; Guat. 874; Uru. 880; Mex. 3567.

874. In alternative legacies, the provisions made for obligations of the same kind shall be observed, excepting the modifications made by the express will of the testator.

Chile, 1117; Col. 1175; Uru. 889; Guat. 871.

875. A legacy of generic personal property shall be valid, although there may not be things of the same kind in the estate.

A legacy of an undetermined parcel of real property shall be valid, only if there are things of the same kind in the estate.

The heir shall have the option, and may fulfill his duty by giving a thing which may not be either of inferior or superior quality.

Guat. 871; Uru. 888; Mex. 3544; Col. 1173, 1174; Chile, 1115, 1116.

876. Whenever the testator expressly leaves an option to the heir or to the legatee, the former may give or the latter may select what he may consider best.

Col. 1175; Chile, 117; Uru. 889; Mex. 3546.

877. When the heir or legatee cannot make the election, in case of it having been granted to him, his right shall pass to the heir, but the choice once made shall be irrevocable.

Col. 1175; Chile, 1117.

878. When the thing bequeathed belonged to the legatee at the date of the will, the legacy is void, even when it has been alienated afterwards.

When the legatee has acquired it by lucrative title, after said date, he can claim nothing for it, but when the acquisition has been made by an onerous title, he can claim from the heir an indemnity for what he may have given for acquiring it.

Mex. 3590; Chili, 1106; Col. 1165.

879. A legacy for education subsists until the legatee is of age.

That for support lasts during the life of the legatee, unless the testator has otherwise disposed.

When the testator has not assigned any sum for said legacies, they shall be fixed in accordance with the position and condition of the legatee and the amount of the inheritance.

When the testator was, during his life, in the habit of giving to the legatee a certain sum of money or other things by way of support, the legacy shall be considered of an equal sum, unless it is greatly disproportionate with the amount of the estate.

Col. 1192; Chile, 1134; Mex. 358.

880. When a periodical pension or a certain sum, either annual, monthly, or weekly is bequeathed, the legatee may claim that of the first term, as soon as the testator dies, and those of the following at the beginning of each of them, without any right of reimbursement, even when the legatee dies before the expiration of the term begun.

Col. 1418; Chile, 1361; Mex. 3585; Uru., 876.

881. A legatee acquires a right to the pure and simple legacies from the death of the testator, and transmits it to his heirs.

Col. 1176; Chile, 118; Uru. 898; Guat. 877.

882. When the bequest is of a thing specific and determined belonging to the testator, the legatee acquires the property thereof upon the death of the testator, and makes the pending fruits or rents his own, but not those which were due and unpaid before said death.

The thing bequeathed shall, from the same moment (of said death), be at the risk of the legatee who, therefore, shall bear its loss or impairment, and he shall also be benefited by any increase or improvement thereof.

Guat. 877; Uru. 898; Mex. 363.

883. The thing bequeathed shall be delivered (to the legatee) with all its accessories and in the condition in which it is at the death of the testator.

Mex. 3611; Uru. 891.

884. When the bequest is not of a specific and determined thing, but generic or of quantity, its fruits and interests shall belong to the legatee from the death of the testator, if the testator expressly so ordered.

Col. 1395; Chile, 1338; Guat. 778.

885. The legatee cannot occupy the thing bequeathed of his own authority, but he shall ask the heir or the executor, when the latter is authorized to give it, for its delivery and possession.

Col. 1347; Chile, 1290; Mex. 3609; Guat. 877; Uru. 900.

886. The heir shall deliver the same thing bequeathed, if he is able to do so and he does not comply with this duty by paying for its value.

Legacies in cash shall be paid in cash, even if there is none in the estate.

The necessary expenses for the delivery of the thing bequeathed shall be at the charge of the estate, but without injury to the *legitime.*

Uru. 901; Mex. 3313; Col. 1432; Chile, 1375.

887. When the assets of the estate are not sufficient to cover all the legacies, payment shall be made in the following order:

1. Remuneratory legacies.
2. Legacies of things, certain and determined, forming a part of the estate.
3. Legacies declared by the testator as preferred.
4. Those for support.
5. Those for education.
6. All others *pro rata.*

Mex. 3617.

888. When the legatee cannot or does not wish to accept the bequest, or for any cause this may not be effectual, it shall be merged into the whole of the estate, excepting in cases of substitution, and rights of accretion.

Guat. 891; Uru. 905.

889. A legatee cannot accept a part of the legacy and repudiate the other part, when the latter is onerous to him.

If he dies before accepting the legacy, leaving several heirs, one of them can accept and another can repudiate the part belonging to him in the legacy.

Guat. 875; Mex. 3596; Uru. 906; Col. 1285; Chile, 1228.

890. A legatee of two legacies, one of which is onerous, cannot renounce this one and accept the former. When both are onerous or gratuitous, he is free to accept all of them or repudiate any one he wishes.

The heir, who is at the same time a legatee, may renounce the inheritance and accept the legacy or renounce the latter and accept the former.

Mex. 3598; Guat. 707.

891. When all the inheritance is distributed in legacies, the debts and burdens of the same shall be charged to the legatees *pro rata* according to their shares, unless the testator has provided otherwise.

Col. 1419; Chile, 1362; Uru. 902; Mex. 3616; Guat. 896.

SECTION ELEVENTH.

*Executors (albaceas ó testamentarios).**

Article **892**. A testator may appoint one or more executors.

Guat. 904; Uru. 926; Col. 1327; Chile, 1270; Mex. 3675.

893. A person, who has no capacity to obligate himself, cannot be executor.

A married woman may be an executrix with the permission of her husband; and such permission shall not be necessary when she is legally separated from him.

A minor cannot be executor, even with the authorization of the father or guardian.

Guat. 906; Mex. 3684; Uru. 928; Col. 1329; Chile, 1272.

894. Executors may be general or special. In any case, executors can be appointed, either severally, successively or conjointly.

Mex. 3690; Guat. 904.

895, When the executors are appointed severally, every act shall be made by all of them together in order that it may be valid, and shall be valid also when done by one of them, legally authorized by the others; and, in case of discord, when the act has been agreed to by the majority.

Col. 1338; Chile, 1289; Guat. 905; Mex. 3692; Uru. 934.

896. In case of extreme urgency, one of the several executors may do, upon his personal responsibility, such acts as may be necessary, giving notice thereof immediately to the others.

Mex. 3693.

897. When a testator does not clearly provide about the appointment of conjoint executors nor determine the order in which they are to discharge their function, it shall be understood that they have been appointed severally, and they shall discharge their duties in the form prescribed by the two preceding articles.

Col. 1338; Chile, 1281; Uru. 935; Guat. 995.

898. Executorship is a voluntary charge, and it shall be understood as accepted, if the person appointed does not excuse himself

---

* Digesto, book 17, tit. 1, law 57. Fuero Real, book 3, tit. 5, law 7. Project of 1882, arts. 895, 896, 897, 898, 899, 900, 901, 902, 904, 908, 909, 911, 914. Projecto of 1851, arts. 730, 737, 740. Part. 6, tit. 10, laws 1, 2, 3, 4, 6, 8.

within six days next following the one on which he has received notice of his appointment or if he was already aware of it during the six days next following that on which he knew of the death of testator.

Guat. 907; Uru. 931; Mex. 3675; Col. 1334; Chile, 1277, 971.

899. An executor who accepts this charge is bound to comply with its duties; but he may renounce it alleging a cause which may be just in the prudent judgment of the court.

Col. 1335; Chile, 1278; Guat. 907.

900. An executor who does not accept the charge or renounces it, without a just cause, shall lose what the testator has left him, but always without prejudice to the right which he has to the *legitime.*

Col. 1334; Chile, 1277; Uru. 931; Mex. 3696.

901. Executors shall have all the powers expressly granted to them by the testator and which are not contrary to law.

Col. 1358; Chile, 1301; Mex. 3605.

902. When the testator has not specially determined the powers of the executors, they shall have the following:

1. To dispose and pay the suffrages and funeral expenses of the testator in accordance with the dispositions made by the same in his testament, and, in default of them, according to the custom of the place.
2. To pay, with the knowledge and consent of the heir, the cash legacies.
3. To look carefully after the execution of whatever more has been ordered in the testament, and maintain, when just, its validity in and out of court.
4. To take the necessary precautions for the preservation and custody of the property, with the intervention of the heirs present.

Col. 1341, 1342, 1343, 1345, 1347, 1348; Chile, 1284, 1285, 1286, 1288, 1290, 1291; Mex. 3706; Uru. 936; Guat. 908.

903. When the estate has not cash enough for the payment of funeral (expenses) and legacies, and the heirs do not contribute their own money therefor, the executors shall endeavor to sell the personal property, and, if this is not enough, the real property with the intervention of the heirs.

When a minor, absentee, corporation or public institution has any interest in the estate, the sale of the property shall be made, under the formalities provided by the laws for such cases.

Col. 1350; Chile, 1293; Guat. 918; Mex. 3720.

904. An executor, for whom the testator has not fixed the term, shall comply with his charge within a year, to be counted from his acceptance, or from the determination of the law suit which may be instituted about the validity or the nullity of the testament or of any one of its provisions.

Guat. 914; Uru. 954; Col. 1360; Chile, 1303; Mex. 3727.

905. If the testator desires to extend the legal term, he shall expressly fix the time for the extension. When he has not done so, it shall be understood that the term is extended for one year.

When, after the expiration of this extension, the will of the testator has not yet been complied with, the Judge may grant another one for the time which may be necessary, in view of the circumstances of the case.

Mex. 3728; Uru. 954; Col. 1362; Chile, 1305; Guat. 915.

906. The heirs and legatees may, by common agreement, extend the term of the executorship for the time they deem necessary; but, if the agreement is only that of a majority, the extension shall not exceed one year.

Mex. 3729.

907. Executors shall render to the heirs an account of their charge.

When they have been appointed not to deliever the property to specified heirs, but to invest or distribute it in the form provided by the testator in the cases allowed by law, they shall render their accounts to the Judge.

Any disposition of the testator, contrary to this article, shall be null and void.

Uru. 958; Guat. 917; Mex. 3726; Col. 1366; Chile, 1309.

908. Executorship is a gratuitous charge. However, the testator may designate the executors, the compensation which he may consider convenient; all of this without injury to the rights which they may have to collect whatever may belong to them for their work in the distribution or for any other professional services.

When the testator bequeathes or designates conjointly any compensation for the executors, the shares of those, who do not accept the charge, shall accrue to those who shall discharge it.

Col. 1359; Chile, 1302; Guat. 919.

909. Executors cannot delegate their charge, unless they have express authority from the testator for so doing.

910. Executorship is determined by the death, impossibility, renunciation, or removal of the executor, and by the lapse of the term fixed by the testator, by law, and, in certain cases, by the parties concerned.

Uru. 933; Mex. 3699; Guat. 911; Col. 1337; Chile, 1280.

911. In the cases of the preceding article and when the executor has not accepted the charge, the execution of the will of the testator shall devolve upon the heirs.

Guat. 902; Col. 1328; Chile, 1271; Uru. 927; Mex. 3679.

CHAPTER THIRD.

*Intestate succession.**

SECTION FIRST.

General provisions.

Article **912.** Legitimate succession takes place:

1. When a person dies without a testament, or under a void testament or under one which afterwards has lost its validity.
2. When the testament does not contain the institution of heir in the whole estate or in a part of it or does not dispose of all that belongs to the testator. In this case the legitimate succession shall take place only in regard to the part of the estate of which the testator has not disposed.
3. When the condition imposed for the institution of heir is not complied with or when the heir dies before the testator repudiates the inheritance, without having a substitute, and there is no right of accretion.
4. When the heir instituted is incapable to succeed.

Uru. 973; Mex. 5840; Chile, 980; Col. 1037.

913. In default of testamentary heirs, the law gives the inheritance, according to the following rules, to the legitimate and natural relatives of the decedent, to the widower or widow, or to the State.

Guat. 950; Chile, 983; Col. 1040.

914. Provisions about incapacity to succeed by testament equally apply to intestate successions.

Uru. 974; Mex. 3841; Chile, 977; Col. 1034.

---

* Digesto, book 29, tit. 29, law 39. Part. 6, tit. 13, int. Part. 6, tit. 7, law 13; id. 6, tit. 13, law 1. Nov. Recop., book 10, tit. 6, law 8; id., book 10, tit. 18, law 1; id., book 10, tit. 20, law 1.

SECTION SECOND.

Relationship. *

Article **915.** The proximity of relationship is determined by the number of generations. Each generation forms a degree.

Uru. 977; Guat. 962; Chile, 27; Col. 37.

916. A series of degrees forms the line which may be either direct or collateral.

A direct line is one constituted by a series of degrees among persons descending one from the other.

A collateral line is that constituted by a series of degrees among persons not descending one from the other, but proceeding from a common trunk.

Guat. 3850; Mex. 193; Uru. 977; Col. 41; Chile, 27.

917. The right line is either descendant or ascendant.

The first joins the head of the family with those descending from him.

The second joins a person to those from whom he descends.

Mex. 195; Col. 43; Guat. 964; Uru. 978.

918. In the lines, as many degrees are counted as there are generations or persons, deducting the progenitor.

In the right line the ascent is made only to the trunk, thus the son is one degree distant from the father, two from the grandfather, and three from the great-grandfather.

In the collateral line, the ascent is made up to the common trunk, and then a descent is made down to the person with whom the computation is made. On account of this reason, the brother is two degrees distant from the brother, three from the uncle, brother of his father or mother; four from the first cousins, and so forth.

Guat. 976; Mex. 196; Uru. 978; Col. 3746; Chile, 27.

919. The computation, stated in the preceding article, governs in all matters, except in those which have relation to the impediments to canonical marriage.

Guat. 966; Chile, 34; Mex. 197, 3850; Uru. 978.

---

* Digesto, book 38, tit. 9; id., book 38, tit. 10, law 10, par. 10. Part. 4, tit. 6, laws 1, 2, 3; id. 6, tit. 13, laws 2, 3, 5, 6. Fuero Real, book 3, tit. 1, law 7; id., book 3, tit. 6, law 1. Novela, 127, 118, chap. 3, par. 1. Project of 1851, art. 759. Fuero Juzgo, book 4, tit. 1; id., book 4, tit. 2, laws 4, 10.

920. Double or whole blood relationship is the relation in the father's and mother's line at the same time.

Guat. 955; Chile, 990; Mex. 3877.

921. In every inheritance, the relative nearest in degree excludes the farther one, except in the cases in which the right of representation takes place.

The relatives, who are in the same degree, shall inherit in equal shares, with exception of what is provided in article 949 about relationships of whole blood.

Mex. 3846.

922. When there are several relatives in the same degree and one or some of them do not wish or cannot succeed, his portion shall accrue to the others of the same degree, without affecting the right of representation when it takes place.

Mex. 3846.

923. When the inheritance is repudiated by the nearest relative, if he is a single one, or by all the nearest relatives, called by law, if there are several, then those of the following degree shall inherit in their own right, without being able to represent those repudiating the inheritance.

Mex. 3849.

SECTION THIRD.

*Representation.**

Article **924.** The right which the relatives of a person have to succeed him in all the rights which he should have had, if alive, or if he had been able to inherit, is called right of representation.

Mex. 3852; Guat. 951; Chile, 984; Col. 1041.

925. The right of representation shall always take place in the direct descending line, but never in the ascending.

In the collateral line, it shall take place only in favor of the children of brothers, whether they are of the whole or half blood.

Uru. 983; Guat. 952; Chile, 986; Col. 1041.

926. Whenever the inheritance is taken by representation, the distribution of the estate shall be made *in stirpes:* Thus the representa-

* Part. 6, tit. 13, laws 3, 4, 5. Nov., 118, chaps. 1, 2. Fuero Juzgo, book 4, tit. 2, laws 2, 6. Fuero Real, book 3, tit. 6, laws 1, 13. Nov. Recop., book 10, tit. 20, law 2. Projects of 1851, of 1882, arts. 752, 938, 939.

tive or representatives shall inherit no more than that which the party represented would inherit, if alive.

Guat. 763; Col. 1042; Chile, 985; Uru. 985.

927. When children of one or more brothers of the decedent survive, they shall succeed the latter by representation, if their uncles also survive, but if they alone survive, they shall inherit in equal shares.

Uru. 989; Mex. 3784.

928. The right of representing a person is not lost by having renounced the inheritance.

Uru. 986; Guat. 765; Col. 1044; Chile, 987; Mex. 3858.

929. A living person cannot be represented, unless in cases of disinheritance or incapacity.

Col. 1044; Chile, 987; Uru. 986; Mex. 3851.

CHAPTER FOURTH.

Order of succession according to diversity of lines.

SECTION FIRST.

*Descending direct line.**

Article **930.** Succession goes, in the first place, to the descending direct line.

Uru. 987; Chile, 988; Guat. 951; Mex. 3860; Col. 1045.

931. Legitimate children and their descendants succeed the parents and other ascendants, without distinction of sex or age, and even if they come from different marriages.

Uru. 987; Guat. 951; Mex. 3680; Col. 1045; Chile, 988.

932. The children of the decedent shall always inherit from him in their own rights, dividing the inheritance in equal shares.

Uru. 981; Guat. 951; Mex. 3861.

933. The grandchildren and other descendants shall inherit by right of representation, and if one of them has died leaving several heirs, the portion belonging to him shall be distributed among such heirs in equal shares.

---

* Part. 6, tit. 13, law 3. Novela, 118, chap. 1. Fuero Juzgo, book 4, tit. 2, laws 1, 2. Fuero Real, book 3, tit. 6, laws 1, 7, 10.

934. If there are children and descendants of other deceased children, the former shall inherit in their own rights, and the latter by right of representation.

Uru. 985; Guat. 951; Mex. 3862.

SECTION SECOND.

*Ascending direct line.**

Article **935.** In default of legitimate children and descendants of the decedent, his ascendants shall inherit from him, excluding collaterals.

Guat. 952; Col. 1046; Chile. 989; Uru. 988; Mex. 3868.

936. The father and mother, if living, shall inherit share and share alike.

When only one of them survives, this one shall take all the son's inheritance.

937. In default of mother or father, the ascendants, nearest in degree, shall inherit.

If there are some of equal degree belonging to the same line, they shall share the inheritance *in capita;* if they are of different lines but of equal degree, one-half shall belong to the paternal, and the other half to the maternal ascendants. In each line the division shall be made *in capita.*

Mex. 3870.

938. The provisions of the two preceding articles are understood without prejudice to what is ordered by articles 811 and 812, which are applicable to intestate and testamentary successions.

SECTION THIRD.

Recognized natural children.†

Article **939.** In default of legitimate descendants and ascendants, natural children legally recognized, and those legitimated by Royal Concession shall succeed the decedent in the whole inheritance.

Guat. 969; Uru. 988; Chile, 889; Col. 1046.

940. When, together with the natural or legitimated children, concur descendants of another deceased natural or legitimated child, the

---

* Toro, law 6. Fuero Juzgo, book 4, tit. 2, laws 2, 3, 6. Fuero Real, book 3, tit. 6, law 1. Part. 6, tit. 13, law 4. Project of 1851, art. 765.

† Part. 6, tit. 13, laws 8, 11, 12. Toro, laws 9, 10, 12. Project of 1882, arts. 949, 950, 951, 952, 953. Project of 1851, arts. 748, 749.

former snall succeed by their own rights and the latter by right of representation.

Guat. 970; Mex. 3864.

941. The hereditary rights, granted by the two preceding articles to a natural or legitimated child, shall be transmitted upon its death to its descendants, who shall inherit from their deceased grandfather by right of representation.

942. In case that there are legitimate descendants and ascendants, the natural and legitimate children shall take from the inheritance only the portion granted to them by articles 840 and 841.

943. Natural and legitimated children have no rights to succeed intestate the legitimate children and relatives of the father or mother who have recognized them; nor shall such children or relatives inherit from the natural or legitimated child.

Chile, 993; Col. 1050; Guat. 980; Mex. 3880.

944. When the recognized natural or legitimated child dies without leaving issue, either lawful or recognized by it, the father or mother who recognized it shall inherit its whole estate, and if both recognized it and are alive, they shall inherit from it in equal shares.

Mex. 3479; Uru. 991; Guat. 973; Col. 1050; Chile, 993.

945. In default of natural ascendants, the natural and legitimated children shall be succeeded by their natural brothers, according to the rules established for legitimate brothers.

SECTION FOURTH.

*Successions of collaterals and of consorts.**

Article **946.** In default of the persons comprised in the three preceding sections, collateral relations and consorts shall inherit in the order established in the following article.

Uru. 989; Mex. 3875; Guat. 954; Chile, 550; Col. 1047.

947. When there are only brothers of the whole blood, they shall inherit in equal shares.

Mex. 3876; Guat. 954; Chile, 990, 985; Col. 1047; Uru. 889.

* Novela, 118, chap. 3, par. 1. Part. 6, tit. 13, laws 5, 6. Fuero Juzgo, book 4, tit. 2, laws 3, 5, 8, 10; id., book 4, tit. 2, 4, law 5; id., book 4, tit. 5, law 4. Fuero Real, book 3, tit. 6, laws 1, 11, 12, 13. Toro, law 8. Law of May 16, 1835.

948. When brothers survive with nephews, children of brothers of the whole blood, the former shall inherit *in capita,* and the latter *in stirpes.*

Guat. 954; Chile, 990, 985; Mex. 3876.

949. When brothers of the whole blood survive with brothers of the half blood, the former shall take a portion in the inheritance double that of the latter.

Uru. 989; Guat. 955; Mex. 3877.

950. When there are only brothers of the half blood, some on the father's and some on the mother's side, all shall inherit equal portions, whatever the property may be.

Mex. 3876; Col. 1047; Chile, 990.

951. Children of brothers of the half blood shall take *in capita* or *in stirpes,* according to the rules established for brothers of the whole blood.

Mex. 3881.

952. In default of brothers and of nephews, children of said brothers, be they or not of the whole blood, the surviving consort, not separated by a final sentence of divorce, shall take all the estate of the decedent.

Mex. 3884; Col. 1045; Chile, 988.

953. When there are brothers or children of brothers, the widow or widower shall have a right to take, in concurrence with the same, the portion of inheritance in usufruct provided in article 837.

954. When there are neither brothers or children of brothers, nor surviving consort, the other collateral relatives shall succeed in the inheritance of the decedent.

They shall take without difference of line, or preference among them on account of the whole blood.

Col. 1049; Chile, 992.

955. The right to inherit in the case of intestacy shall not extend beyond the sixth degree of relationship in the collateral line.

Col. 1049; Chile, 772; Guat. 957; Uru. 990; Mex. 3875.

SECTION FIFTH.

*Inheritance by the state.**

Article **956.** In default of persons having a right to succeed in accordance with the provisions of the preceding sections, the State

* Part. 16, tit. 13, law 6. Law of May 16, 1835, art. 2, Nos. 3, 9, 10. Project of 1851, art. 784.

shall inherit, and the property shall be destined for institutions of beneficence or of gratuitous instruction, in the following order:

1. Municipal institutions of beneficence and gratuitous schools of the domicile of the decedent.
2. Those of the same classes in the province of the decedent.
3. Those of beneficence and instruction of a general character.

Col. 1051; Guat. 957; Uru. 996; Mex. 3891.

957. The rights and obligations of institutions of beneficence and instruction, in the cases of the preceding articles, shall be the same that other heirs may have.

Mex. 3892.

958. In order that the State may take possession of the property of the inheritance, a previous judicial declaration has to be made by which the inheritance shall be adjudged to the State, in default of legitimate heirs.

Uru. 997.

CHAPTER FIFTH.

Provisions common to inheritance by testament or without it.

SECTION FIRST.

*Precautions to be adopted when the widow remains in a pregnant condition.**

Article **959.** When the widow believes that she has been left in a pregnant condition, she must give notice to those having in the inheritance, rights of such a kind that they shall disappear or be diminished by the birth of a posthumous child.

Chile, 198; Col. 232; Mex. 3893.

960. Interested persons, to which the preceding article refers, may ask the Municipal Judge or the Judge of the First Instance, when there is one, to take the proper measures in order to prevent the supposition of parturition or to accept the child born as viable, when, in truth, it is not so.

The Judge shall be careful that the measures which he orders to be taken shall not be offensive, either to the modesty or to the liberty of the widow.

Col. 226, 227; Chile, 198, 192, 193; Mex. 3894.

---

* Part. 3, tit. 14, law 9; id. 3, tit. 22, law 7; id. 4, tit. 23, law 3; id. 6, tit. 6, laws 1, 17. Fuero Juzgo, book 3, tit. 6, law 3. Fuero Real, book 3, tit. 6, law 3. Penal Code, arts. 483, 484. Project of 1882, art. 970. Digesto, book 25, tit. 4, laws 1, 2; id., book 37, tit. 9, law 1, pars. 14, 15.

961. Whether the notice stated in article 959 has been given or not, when the time of the parturition approaches, the widow shall give notice of this fact to the parties interested. They shall have a right to appoint a person in whom they have confidence in order that he may aver the reality of the delivery.

When the person appointed is rejected by the widow, one shall be appointed by the Judge, but said person must be a physician or a woman.

Col. 226; Chile, 192.

962. The omission of these formalities shall not injure the legitimacy of the parturition, which, when contested, may be proven by the mother or the child lawfully represented.

The action to contest, on the part of those having such right, is prescribed, after the terms specified in article 113.

Chile, 194, 195, 198; Col. 228, 229, 232; Mex. 3902.

963. When the husband has recognized by a document, either public or private, the certainty of the pregnancy of his wife, she shall be excused from giving the notice provided in article 959, but she shall be subject to comply with the provisions of article 961.

Mex. 3898.

964. A widow who remains pregnant, even when she is rich, shall receive support from the estate, taking into consideration the portion of it which may belong to the posthumous child, if he is born and is viable.

Col. 233; Chile, 199; Mex. 3899.

965. During the time intervening, until the parturition arrives, or until certainty is established that it cannot take place, either on account of a miscarriage, or because the maximum time for the gestation has been exceeded, the security and administration of the estate shall be attended to in the form provided in necessary testamentary proceedings.

Mex. 3905.

966. The distribution of the inheritance shall be suspended until the parturition or marriage takes place, or the lapse of time shows the widow was not pregnant.

An administrator, however, may pay the creditors under a judicial order.

Mex. 3907.

967. After the delivery or miscarriage has taken place or the time of gestation has elapsed, the administrator of the estate shall cease in his charge, and shall render account of his management to the heirs or their lawful representatives.

SECTION SECOND.

*Property subject to reservation.**

Article **968.** Besides the reservation imposed by article 811, the widower or widow contracting a second marriage shall be obliged to reserve for the children and descendants of the first, the ownership of all the property acquired from the deceased consort by will, by intestate succession, by donation, or by any other lucrative title; but not his or her half of the conjugal property.

969. The provision of the preceding article applies to property which has been acquired, under the titles already stated, by the widower or widow from any of the children of the first marriage, or that received from the relatives of the decedent on account of personal considerations for the same.

970. The obligation to reserve shall cease, when the children of a marriage, being of legal age and having a right to the estate, have expressly renounced it, or when the things in question have been given or left by the children to their father or mother, knowing that they had married a second time.

971. Reservation shall cease when, at the death of the father or mother who contracted a second marriage, there remains no legitimate children or descendants of the first marriage.

972. Notwithstanding the obligation to reserve, the father or mother, married a second time, may give advantages in the property, subject to reservation (*reservables*), to any of the children or descendants of the first marriage, as provided in article 823.

973. When the father or mother has not made use in whole or in part of the right granted to them in the preceding article, the legitimate children or descendants of the first marriage shall succeed to the property subject to reservation, in accordance with the rules prescribed for succession in the descending line, even when, by virtue of a testament, he or she should have unequally inherited from the first decedent consort, or should have renounced or repudiated his or her inheritance.

---

* Fuero Juzgo, book 4, tit. 5, law 2. Fuero Real, book 3, tit. 2, law 1. Part. 5, tit. 13, law 26. Toro, laws 14, 15. Project of 1851, art. 803. Project of 1882, art. 979. Law of Mortgage, arts. 168, 194, 201. Novela, 2, chap. 2, 22, chaps. 26, 29.

The son, justly disinherited by the father or by the mother, shall lose all right to the reservation, but, if he has legitimate children or descendants, the provisions of article 857 shall be followed.

974. Conveyances of reserved real property shall be valid when made by the surviving consort, before contracting a second marriage, under the obligation to secure, from the moment of the marriage, the value of such property in favor of the children and descendants of the first marriage.

975. Conveyances of real property, subject to reservation, made by the widower or widow, after contracting a second marriage, shall subsist only when, at his or her death, there remains no legitimate children or descendants of the former marriage; this without conflict with the provisions of the Law of Mortgage.

976. Conveyances of personal property, made before or after contracting a second marriage, shall be valid, but always under the obligation of paying an indemnity when proper.

977. A widower or widow, on contracting a new marriage, shall make an inventory of all the property subject to reservation, and annotate in the Registry of Property that such real property is subject to reservation in accordance with the provisions of the Law of Mortgage and shall have the personal property appraised.

978. A widower or widow, on marrying again, is also bound to secure by mortgage:

1. The restitution of the personal property, not alienated, in the condition in which it was at the time of the death of the decedent, when it was paraphernalia or the proceeds from an unestimated dowry; or of their value, if they arise from an estimated dowry.

2. The payment of the damages, caused or which may be caused by his or her fault or neglect.

3. The return of any sums received for the personal property already sold or the delivery of the value it had, at the time of the alienation, had it been made under a gratuitous title.

4. The value of the real property validly alienated.

979. The provisions of the preceding article for the second marriage shall equally control the third and subsequent marriages.

980. The obligation to reserve, imposed in the preceding article, shall apply to the widower or widow, who though not having contracted a new marriage, may afterwards have a recognized natural child or one judicially declared as such.

Said obligation shall be effective from the date of the birth of such child.

SECTION THIRD.

*Right of accretion.**

Article **981.** In legitimate succession, the part of him who repudiated the inheritance shall always accrue to the co-heirs.

Mex. 3914; Uru. 1006; Guat. 831.

982. In order that in testamentary succession the right of accretion may take place, it is required:

1. That two or more persons are called to the same inheritance or to the same portion of it, without a special designation of shares.

2. That one of the appointees dies before the testator or renounces the inheritance, or is incapable to receive it.

Uru. 1007; Mex. 3915; Col. 1206; Chile, 1147.

983. It shall be understood that a designation has been made by portion only in case that the testator may have expressly designated a quota to each heir.

The phrase " one-half to each," or " in equal parts " or any other, although specifying aliquot parts, which does not express this numerically or by such marks as may make each of them the owner of an estate severally, does not exclude the right of accretion.

Col. 1207; Chile, 1148; Uru. 1008; Mex. 3926.

984. The heirs, to whom the inheritance accrues, shall succeed in all the rights and obligations which would have belonged to the one who did not wish or could not receive it.

Col. 1211; Chile, 1152; Mex. 3920.

985. Among forced heirs, the right to accrue shall take place only when the part, at free disposal, is left to two or more of them or to any one of them and a stranger.

When the repudiated part is the *legitime,* the other co-heirs shall succeed to it in their own rights, and not by the right of accretion.

Mex. 3918.

986. In testamentary successions, when the right of accretion cannot take place, the vacant portion of the heir instituted, for whom no substitute has been appointed, passes to the lawful heirs of the testator who shall receive it under the same charges and obligations.

Mex. 3118.

*** Digesto, book 32, law 89. Instituciones, book 2, tit. 20, par. 8. Part. 6, tit. 6, law 18; id. 6, tit. 9, law 33. Nov. Recop., book 10, tit. 18, law 1. Project of 1882, art. 994.**

987. The right of accretion shall also take place between the legatees and the usufructuaries in the same terms established for heirs.

Col. 1213; Chile, 1154; Mex. 3922; Uru. 1009.

SECTION FOURTH.

*Acceptance and repudiation of the inheritance.**

Article **988.** Acceptance and repudiation of the inheritance are acts entirely voluntary and free.

Uru. 1013; Guat. 847; Mex. 3736; Col. 1282; Chile, 1225.

989. The effects of the acceptance and repudiation shall always relate back to the moment of the death of the person whose property is inherited.

Col. 1296; Chile, 1239.

990. Acceptance or repudiation of the inheritance cannot be made, either partially, up to a certain term, or conditionally.

Guat. 861; Col. 1296; Chile, 1239.

991. No person can accept or repudiate an inheritance, unless he is certain of the death of the person from whom he is to inherit and of his rights to the inheritance.

Col. 1283; Chile, 1226.

992. Any person having free disposal of his property may accept or repudiate an inheritance.

An inheritance left to minors or incapables may be accepted in the form provided by No. 10 of article 259. When the guardian accepts by himself, the acceptance shall be considered as made under benefit of inventory.

Acceptance of an inheritance, left to the poor, shall pertain to the persons appointed by the testator to classify them and distribute the property, and, in default of them, to those designated in article 749, and it shall also be understood as accepted under benefit of inventory.

Guat. 848.

---

* Digesto, book 2, tit. 4, law 2; id., book 29, laws 17, 79; id., book 29, tit. 2, laws 19, 20, 23, 29, 54, 93, 95; id., book 50, tit. 25, law 51, par. 2; id., book 50, tit. 15, law 28; id., book 50, tit. 16, laws 6, 70, 71, par. 41, 77, 134; id., book 50, tit. 17, law 138. Instituciones, book 2, tit. 19, par. 2. Nov. Recop., book 10, tit. 18, law 1. Novela, 60, chaps. 1, 115. Codigo, book 9, tit. 9, law 6. Part. 1, tit. 13, law 15; id. 3, tit. 18, law 101; id. 6, tit. 3, law 21; id. 6, tit. 6, laws 2, 5, 9, 10, 11, 12, 13, 15, 18, 19, 20; id. 6, tit. 14, law 7; id. 6, tit. 19, law 7; id. 7, tit. 9, law 13. Toro, law 54. Penal Code, art. 548, No. 5.

993. The lawful representatives of associations, corporations, and institutions having capacity to acquire can accept the inheritance left to the same; but for repudiating it they require judicial approval, after the Public Attorney has been heard.

Guat. 849.

994. Public official institutions can neither accept nor repudiate inheritances without the approval of the government.

995. A married woman can neither accept nor repudiate an inheritance, unless with permission of her husband, and, in his default, with the approval of the Judge.

In the last case, the property of the conjugal society, already existing, shall not be liable for the debts of the estate.

996. The deaf and dumb, knowing how to read and write, shall accept or repudiate the inheritance personally or through an attorney. If they cannot read or write, their guardian shall accept it under benefit of inventory, subject to what is provided in article 218 in relation to such disability.

997. Acceptance and repudiation of the inheritance, once made, are irrevocable, and can be contested only in case they suffer from any of the vices which annul the consent, or when an unknown testament appears.

Col. 1291, 1294; Chile, 1234, 1237.

998. Inheritances can be accepted purely and simply or under benefit of inventory.

Guat. 847.

999. Pure and simple inheritances may be either express or tacit. Express is one made in a public or private instrument. Tacit is one made by acts, which necessarily imply a will to accept, or acts which no one should have a right to execute unless in the capacity of an heir.

Acts of mere preservation, or provisional administration do not imply the acceptance of the inheritance, if, at the same time, the title and qualification of heir have not been assumed.

Col. 1298; Chile, 1241; Guat. 851.

1000. An inheritance is considered as accepted:

1. When the heir sells, donates or assigns a right to a stranger, to all his co-heirs or to one of them only.

2. When the heir renounces it, even gratuitously, for the benefit of one or more of his co-heirs.

3. When he renounces it for a consideration in favor of all his coheirs indiscriminately, but when this renunciation is gratuitous and

the co-heirs, in whose favor he makes it, are those to whom the share renounced must accrue, the inheritance shall not be considered as accepted.

Col. 1287; Chile, 1230.

1001. When the heir repudiates the inheritance to the damage of his own creditors, they may ask the Judge to authorize them to accept it on behalf of the latter.

The acceptance shall be of benefit to the creditors only in so far as it covers the amount of their credits. The excess, if any, shall not belong, in any case, to the renouncer but shall be allotted to the persons to whom, according to the rules of this Code, it may belong.

Guat. 864; Col. 1295; Chile, 1238.

1002. The heirs, who have subtracted or concealed any effects of the inheritance, lose the right to renounce it, and retain only the character of pure and simple heirs without being released from the penalties which they may have incurred.

Guat. 856; Col. 1288; Chile, 1231.

1003. By the acceptance, pure and simple, or without benefit of inventory, the heir shall be liable for all the charges of the estate, not only with the properties of the same, but also with his own.

Guat. 853; Chile, 1245; Col. 1302.

1004. Until nine days have elapsed from the death of the person whose inheritance is dealt with, no action can be instituted against the heir to compel him to accept or repudiate it.

1005. When a third party having an interest, urges in a suit that the heir should accept or repudiate the inheritance, the Judge shall give the latter a term, not exceeding thirty days, within which he shall declare his intention, warning him that, in case he does not do it, the inheritance shall be considered as accepted.

Guat. 857; Col. 1289; Chile, 1232.

1006. Upon the death of the heir, without having accepted or repudiated the inheritance, the same rights he had are transmitted to his heirs.

Col. 1285; Chile, 957, 1228.

1007. When there are several heirs called to an inheritance, some of them may accept and some repudiate it. Every one of the heirs shall enjoy the same liberty to accept it purely and simply, or under benefit of inventory.

Guat. 850.

1008. Repudiation of an inheritance shall be made by a public or authentic instrument or by a writ presented to the Judge, competent to take cognizance of testamentary or intestate proceedings.

Guat. 862.

1009. Any person called to an inheritance by a testament or by intestacy and who repudiates it under the former title, is considered as having repudiated under both titles.

If he repudiates it as intestate heir and has no knowledge of his testamentary title, he may yet accept it under the latter title.

SECTION FIFTH.

*Benefit of inventory and right to deliberate.**

Article **1010.** Every heir may accept an inheritance under benefit of inventory, even if the testator has forbidden it.

He may also ask for the making of the inventory, before accepting or repudiating the inheritance, in order to deliberate on this point.

Col. 1306; Chile, 1249; Guat. 487.

1011. Acceptance of the inheritance, under the benefit of inventory, may be made before a Notary, or in a writing before any of the Judges, competent for taking cognizance of the testamentary or intestate proceedings.

1012. When the heir, to whom the preceding article refers, is in a foreign land, he may make such declaration before a diplomatic or consular Agent of Spain, who may be authorized to exercise the duties of a Notary in the place of such execution.

1013. The declaration, to which the preceding articles refer, shall produce no effect, unless it be preceded or followed by a true and exact inventory of all the property of the estate, made with the formalities and within the term specified in the following articles.

1014. An heir, having in his hands the property of the estate or a part of it, and who wishes to make use of the benefit of inventory or of the right to deliberate shall so state to the Judge, competent to take cognizance of the testamentary or intestate proceedings, within ten days next following that on which he has become aware that he

---

* Digesto, book 26, tit. 7, law 57; id., book 42, tit. 6, law 1, pars. 5, 6. Instituciones, book 2, tit. 23, par. 7, 9. Codigo, book 5, tit. 51, law 13; id., book 13, tit. 72, laws 1, 2; id., book 6, tit. 30, law 22, pars. 4, 11. Regulation of July 23, 1883, for Consular Profession, art. 22. Part. 3, tit. 18, law 100; id. 6, tit. 6, laws 1, 2, 3, 5, 7, 9, 10. Law of Civil Procedure, art. 63, rules 5, 6, 7, 22, 1007, 1010, 1012, 1016, 1017, 1030, 1031, 1047, 1053, 1096, 1097, 1266. Royal Decree, Sept. 29, 1848, arts. 1, 6, 11.

is such an heir, if he resides in the place where the originator of his inheritance dies. If he resides out of the place, the term shall be thirty days.

In both cases, the heir shall ask, at the same time, for the making of an inventory, and that the creditors and legatees be summoned to be present at it, if convenient for them.

1015. When the heir has not in his possession the inheritance or a part of it, or has not executed any act as such heir, the terms, specified in the preceding article, shall be counted from the next day following the one on which shall expire the term fixed by the Judge for accepting or repudiating the inheritance, in accordance with article 1005, or from the day on which he has accepted it or has acted as heir.

1016. In the cases not provided for by the two preceding articles, if no complaint has been presented against the heir, he may accept, under the benefit of inventory, or with the right to deliberate while the action to claim an inheritance is not prescribed.

1017. An inventory shall be begun within thirty days next following the summoning of the creditors and legatees and shall be finished within sixty days more.

If, because the property is situated at a long distance, or is very valuable, or for any other just cause, said sixty days are considered insufficient, the Judge may extend this term to such a time as he may deem necessary, but it shall not exceed one year.

Guat. 859.

1018. If by the fault or neglect of the heir, the inventory is not begun or finished within the term, and with the solemnities prescribed in the preceding article, it shall be understood that he accepts the inheritance purely and simply.

Guat. 859.

1019. An heir, who has reserved to himself the right to deliberate, shall state to the court, within thirty days, counted from the day following that on which the inventory has been finished, whether he accepts or repudiates the inheritance.

After such thirty days have elapsed, if he has not made such a statement, it shall be understood that he accepts it purely and simply.

1020. In any case, the Judge may, on petition of any party interested, during the making of the inventory and until the acceptance of the inheritance, provide for the administration and custody of the hereditary estate, in accordance with the provisions of the Law of Civil Procedure about testamentary proceedings.

1021. A person who judicially claims an inheritance, which another has held in his possession for over a year and who wins the suit, shall not be obliged to make an inventory for enjoying such benefit, and he shall be liable for the burdens of the estate only with the property which has been delivered to him.

1022. The inventory made by the heir, who afterwards repudiates the inheritance, shall benefit the substitutes and the intestate heirs, in respect to whom, the thirty days for deliberation and in which to make the statement, provided by article 1019, shall be counted from the day next following that on which they were made aware of the repudiation.

1023. The benefit of inventory produces the following effects in favor of the heir:

1. The heir shall not be bound to pay the debts and other charges of the inheritance but up to the amount that the estate may be worth.
2. He retains against the estate all the rights and actions which he may have had against the decedent.
3. The private property of the heir shall not in anywise be confused, to his injury, with the property belonging to the estate.

Col. 1304, 1316; Chile, 1247, 1259; Guat. 854.

1024. The heir shall lose the benefit of inventory:

1. When, having knowledge of it, he fails to include in the inventory any of the property, rights or actions of the inheritance.
2. When, before completing the payment of the debts and legacies, he alienates any property of the estate without judicial authorization, or that of all the parties in interest, or, if he does not apply the value of what is sold to what has been ordered, when the authorization was granted to him.

Guat. 856; Col. 1313, 1317; Chile, 1256, 1260.

1025. During the making of the inventory and the term granted for deliberating, the legatees cannot claim the payment of their legacies.

Guat. 879.

1026. Until all known creditors and legatees have been paid, it shall be understood that the estate is under administration.

The administrator, whether it is the heir himself or any other person, shall have, as such, the representation of the estate to enforce all actions pertaining to it, and answer all complaints instituted against the same.

1027. The administrator shall not pay the legacies, until he has paid all the creditors.

1028. When there is a pending lawsuit among the creditors about the preference of their credits, they shall be paid in the order and according to the degree fixed by the final sentence of graduation.

When there is no pending lawsuit among the creditors, those presenting themselves first shall be paid first; but where it is well established that one of the known credits is preferred, payment shall not be made without previous security being given in favor of the creditor having a better right.

1029. If, after the legacies are paid, more creditors appear, they shall have a right to make claims against the legatees only in case that the estate may not have property enough to pay them.

1030. When for the payment of credits and legacies, the sale of the property of the estate may be necessary, it shall be made in the form established by the Code of Civil Procedure about intestate and testamentary proceedings, unless all the heirs, creditors, and legatees agree otherwise.

1031. When the hereditary estate is not sufficient for the payment of the debts and legacies, the administrator shall render an account of his administration to the creditors and legatees who have not been paid in full, and he shall be liable for the damages caused to the estate by his fault or negligence.

1032. After the creditors and legatees are paid, the heir shall have the full enjoyment of the remainder of the estate.

If the estate has been administered by another person, he shall render an account of his administration to the heir, under the responsibility imposed by the preceding article.

1033. The cost of the inventory and other expenses, caused by the administration of the inheritance, accepted under the benefit of inventory, and the defense of its rights, shall be paid by the same estate. The cost to which the heir may have been personally condemned, on account of his deceit or bad faith, shall be excepted.

The same thing shall be understood about the cost caused for making use of the right to deliberate, when the heir repudiates the inheritance.

1034. The private creditors of the heir cannot interfere with the operations of the estate, accepted by him under benefit of inventory, until the creditors and legatees of the same have been paid; but they may claim the retention or the seizure of the remainder which may be left in favor of the heirs.

CHAPTER SIXTH.

Collation and distribution.

SECTION FIRST.

*Collation.**

Article **1035**. A forced heir, concurring with others of the same character in a succession, shall bring to the estate the properties or values he may have received from the originator of the inheritance, during the life of the same, as dowry, donation, or under any other lucrative title for the purpose of computing it, the regulation of the *legitimes,* and in the account of the distribution.

Col. 1243; Chile, 1185; Guat. 993, 995, 1010.

1036. Collation shall not take place among forced heirs when the donor has so expressly ordered, or when the donee repudiates the inheritance, unless in the case in which the donation is to be reduced as inofficious.

Guat. 998.

1037. What is left by will is not subject to collation, unless the testator orders otherwise; but, in any case, the *legitime* shall remain free.

Col. 1243; Chile, 1185.

1038. When grandchildren inherit from their grandparents in representation of their parents, and concur with their uncles or cousins, they shall bring to collation all that their parents, if alive, would have been required to bring, though they may not have inherited it.

They shall also bring to collation whatever they may have received from the testator, during the life of the same, unless the testator has otherwise disposed, in which case, his will shall be respected, if it does no injury to the *legitime* of the co-heirs.

Guat. 996; Col. 1258; Chile, 1200.

1039. Parents are not obliged to bring to collation in the inheritance of their ascendants what may have been donated by the latter to their children.

---

* Digesto, book 24, law 7, par. 6; id., book 36, tit. 1, law 20; id., book 37, tit. 6, law 1, par. 9, law 2, par. 2; id., book 37, tit. 7, law 1, par. 7. Novela, 97, chap. 6. Fuero Viejo, book 5, tit. 3, law 6. Fuero Real, book 3, tit. 6, law 14. Part. 6, tit. 15, laws 3, 4, 5, 6; id. 7, tit. 33, law 5. Toro, law 29. Project of 1851, art. 880.

1040. Neither shall the donations made to the consort of the child be brought to collation; but if they have been made by the parent to both of them jointly, the child shall be obliged to bring to collation one-half of the thing donated.

1041. Expenses for support, education, for sickness, even if extraordinary, apprenticeship, ordinary equipment or the usual presents are not subject to collation.

Col. 1256, 1246; Chile, 1198, 1188; Guat. 994.

1042. Expenses, incurred by the parents in giving their children a professional or artistic career, shall not be brought to collation, unless the parent so disposes or they injure the *legitime*, but when it may be lawful to bring them to collation, the sum which the child should have spent, if living in the house and company of the parents, shall be deducted from them.

1043. The sums paid by the parents to redeem the children from the lot of soldiers, pay their debts, obtain for them a title of honor or other similar expenses, shall be brought to collation.

Col. 1261; Chile, 1203.

1044. Wedding presents, consisting of jewels, clothing and equipment, shall not be reduced as inofficious but in the amount exceeding one-tenth or more of the sum disposable by testament.

Col. 1256; Chile, 1198.

1045. The same things, donated or given in dowry, are not to be brought to collation and distribution, but only the value they had at the time of the donation or dowry, though they were not appraised at such time.

The subsequent increase or impairment and even their total loss, either casually or culpably, shall be to the account and risk for the benefit of the donee.

Col. 1243; Chile, 1185; Guat. 999.

1046. The dowry or donation, made jointly by both consorts, shall be brought to collation in equal parts in the inheritance of each one of them. That made by only one of them shall be brought to collation in his inheritance.

1047. The donee shall take from the funds of the succession a sum so much less than the sum already received by him, and the co-heirs shall receive the equivalent in property of the same nature, class and quality, in so far as possible.

1048. When what has been provided in the preceding article cannot be executed, if the property donated has consisted of real property, the co-heirs shall have a right to be equalized in cash, or in stocks and bonds, at the rate at which they are quoted; and when there are in the estate neither cash nor stocks and bonds, other property shall be sold at public auction up to the amount required.

When the property donated is a personal property, the co-heirs shall have only a right to be equalized in other personal property of the estate at its just value and at their free election.

1049. The fruits and interests of the property, subject to collation, are not due to the bulk of the estate, except from the day on which the succession is opened.

In order to regulate them, the rents and interests of the hereditary property of the same class as those brought to collation shall be taken into consideration.

Chile, 1205; Col. 1263; Guat. 1007, 1008.

1050. When a question arises among the heirs about the obligation to bring to collation or about the objects which are to be brought thereto, the distribution shall not be stopped for such a cause, but proper bond shall be given.

SECTION SECOND.

*Distribution.**

Article **1051.** No co-heir shall be obliged to continue in the estate in an undivided condition, unless the testator has expressly forbidden the distribution.

But even when it is so forbidden, the distribution shall always be made for any of the causes on account of which partnerships are extinguished.

Guat. 1014; Chile, 1317; Col. 1374.

1052. Every co-heir having the free administration and disposal of his property, may, at any time, ask for the distribution of the estate.

The lawful representatives of incapables and absentees may ask for the distribution on their behalf.

Guat. 1016; Col. 1374, 1379; Chile, 1317, 1322.

1053. The wife cannot ask for the distribution of the estate without authority of the husband, and, in certain cases, of the Judge. When

* Digesto, book 10, tit. 2, laws 4, 5, 25, par. 16, 40, 55; id., book 37, tit. 6, laws 1, 13. Codigo, book 3, tit. 36, laws 10, 19; id., book 3, tit. 37, law 3. Nov. Recop., book 10, tit. 21, law 10. Law of Civil Procedure, 1881, arts. 1037, 1041, 1043, 1048, 1095. Decisions of the Direction of Registers, April 27, 29, and June 15, 1885. Part. 6, tit. 1, law 7; id. 6, tit. 15, laws 2, 6, 7, 10. Fuero Viejo, book 5, tit. 3; id., book 5, tit. 3, law 2. Fuero Real, book 3, tit. 4.

the husband asks for it, in the name of his wife, he shall do it with her consent.

The co-heirs of the wife cannot ask for the distribution without the institution of a joint suit against her and her husband.

Guat. 1018; Chile, 1322; Col. 1379.

1054. The heirs, under condition, shall not ask for the distribution until the condition is fulfilled. But the other co-heirs may ask for it, by properly securing the rights of the former for the cases in which the condition may be fulfilled, and until it is known that it has failed or can no longer be complied with, the distribution shall be considered as provisional.

Col. 1306; Chile, 1319; Guat. 1019.

1055. When, before the distribution is made, one of the co-heirs dies leaving two or more heirs, a petition by one of them shall be sufficient; but all those who intervene in such capacity shall appear under a single representation.

Guat. 1025; Col. 1378; Chile, 1321.

1056. When the testator makes a distribution of his property by an act *inter vivos* or by a last will, it shall be accepted in so far as it does not injure the *legitime* of the forced heirs.

The father, who for the interest of his family, desires to keep undivided an agricultural, industrial or manufacturing enterprise, may make use of the powers, granted to him by this article, by disposing that the *legitimes* of the other children be paid in cash.

Col. 1375; Chile, 1318; Guat. 1027, 1030.

1057. The testator may, by an act *inter vivos* or *mortis causa*, confer the mere power of making the distribution, after his death, to any person who shall not be one of the co-heirs.

The provisions of this and the preceding articles shall be observed, even when there may be found a minor or a person subject to guardianship among the heirs; but the trustee shall, in this case, make an inventory of the property of the inheritance, after summoning the co-heirs, the creditors, and the legatees.

Col. 1381; Chile, 1324.

1058. When the testator has not made any distribution nor trusted this power to another person, if the heirs are of age and have the free administration of their property, they may distribute the estate in the manner they may deem fit.

Guat. 1034; Col. 1382; Chile, 1325.

1059. When the heirs of age cannot agree about the manner of making the distribution, they shall be free to enforce their rights in the manner prescribed by the Law of Civil Procedure.

1060. When the minors are subject to the parental power and are represented in the distribution by the father or, in his default, by the mother, neither the intervention nor the approval of the Judge shall be required.

1061. In the distribution of the estate, all possible fairness shall be observed by drawing lots or adjudging to each one of the heirs things of the same nature, quality, or kind.

Guat. 1035.

1062. When a thing is indivisible or loses considerable by being divided, it may be adjudged to one of the heirs, under condition of paying the excess in cash to the others.

But it shall be sufficient if a single one of the heirs ask for its sale at public auction and that strange bidders may take part in the auction in order that this may be so done.

Col. 1394; Chile, 1337; Guat. 1039.

1063. On making the distribution, the co-heirs shall reciprocally compensate one another for the rents and fruits which each of them may have collected from the estate for the useful and necessary expenses made on said property or for the injuries caused to it by malice or neglect.

Guat. 1060; Col. 1395; Chile, 1333.

1064 The expenses of the distribution, made for the common interests of all the co-heirs, shall be deducted from the estate, those made for the particular interest of one of them, shall be borne by the same.

Guat. 1072; Col. 1390; Chile, 1338.

1065. The title of acquisition or of ownership shall be delivered to the co-heir to whom the tenement or tenements, to which they refer, were adjudged.

Guat. 1056; Col. 1400; Chile, 1343.

1066. When the same title comprises several tenements adjudged to several co-heirs, or one only which may have been divided among two or more, the title shall remain in the possession of the person having a greater interest in the tenement or tenements, and authenticated copies of it shall be furnished to the other parties, at the expense of the estate. Should the interests be equal, the title shall be delivered to the male heir, and, where there are more than one, to the senior of them.

When the title is an original one, the person in whose possession it remains shall besides be obliged to exhibit it to the other interested parties, when they ask him to do so.

Guat. 1057, 1058; Col. 1400; Chile, 1343.

1067. When any of the heirs sell their hereditary rights to a stranger, before the distribution, all or any one of the heirs can subrogate himself in the place of the purchaser, reimbursing him for the value of the purchase, provided they do so within the term of a month, to be counted from the day on which they have been informed of it.

Guat. 1068, 1069; Col. 1377; Chile, 1320.

SECTION THIRD.

*Effects of the distribution.**

Article **1068.** A distribution lawfully made confers upon each heir the exclusive ownership of the property adjudged to him.

Guat. 1073; Col. 1401; Chile, 1344.

1069. After the distribution is made, the co-heirs are reciprocally bound to warrant and defend (*eviccion y saneamiento*) the property adjudged.

Guat. 1074; Col. 1402; Chile, 1345.

1070. The obligation, to which the preceding article refers, shall cease only in the following cases:

1. When the testator himself has made the distribution, unless it may appear or be reasonably presumed that he desired to do contrary, it always being understood not to conflict with the *legitime*.

2. When it has been expressly stipulated on making the distribution.

3. When the eviction originates from a cause subsequent to the distribution or has been caused by the fault of the person to whom it was adjudged.

Col. 1403; Chile, 1346; Guat. 1075.

1071. The reciprocal obligation of the co-heirs, in the case of eviction, is proportional to their respective hereditary shares; but if any

* Digesto, book 10, tit. 2, law 25, par. 2; id., book 31, law 77, par. 8. Codigo, book 8, tit. 32, law 2; id., book 3, tit. 36, law 14; id., book 3, tit. 38, law 1, Part. 6, tit. 15, laws 2, 9, 10.

one of them is insolvent, the other co-heirs shall be liable for his part, in the same proportion, deducting the part belonging to the one to be indemnified.

Those paying for the insolvent co-heir shall retain their action against him, until the time when his fortune may improve.

Col. 1404; Chile, 1347; Guat. 1076.

1072. When a credit is allotted as recoverable, the co-heirs shall not be liable for the subsequent insolvency of the debtor of the estate, and shall be responsible only for his insolvency, at the time the distribution is made.

No one shall be responsible for the credits, qualified as unrecoverable, but when collected, in whole or in part, the amount collected shall be proportionally distributed among the heirs.

Guat. 1080.

SECTION FOURTH.

*Rescission of distribution.**

Article **1073.** Distribution may be rescinded for the same causes as obligations.

Col. 1405; Chile, 1349; Guat. 1083.

1074. Distribution may also be rescinded on account of *lesion* exceeding the fourth part, taking into consideration the value of the things when they were adjudged.

Col. 1005; Chile, 1348.

1075. The distribution made by the testator, cannot be contested on account of *lesion*, excepting in the cases in which it may injure the *legitime* of the forced heirs, or when it may appear or it may be reasonably presumed that the will of the testator was otherwise.

1076. A rescissory action for *lesion* shall be brought within four years, to be counted from the time the distribution was made.

Col. 1409; Chile, 1352.

1077. A defendant heir shall have an option between paying an indemnity for the injury, or consent to a new distribution.

The indemnity may be paid in cash or in the same thing in which the damage took place.

* Codigo, book 3, art. 38, law 3. Part. 6, tit. 7, law 10; id. 6, tit. 8, law 1. Orden. Alcala, tit. 17, special law. Nov. Recop., book 10, tit. 1, law 2.

If a new distribution is made, it shall not be effectual as to those who were not injured nor to those who did not receive more than was justly due them.

Col. 1407; Chile, 1350.

1078. An heir, who has alienated the whole or a considerable part of the real property adjudged to him, cannot enforce the rescissory action for *lesion.*

Col. 1408; Chile, 1351.

1079. The omission of one or several objects or values of the estate shall not cause the rescission of the distribution for *lesion,* but only to complete or increase the estate with the objects or values omitted.

Guat. 1089; Col. 1406; Chile, 1349.

1080. A distribution, made with preterition of any of the heirs, shall not be rescinded, unless it is proven that there was bad faith or deceit on the part of the other parties concerned, but the latter shall be obliged to pay to the omitted person the proportionate share belonging to him.

Guat. 1085.

1081. When in a distribution, a person, who was believed to be an heir, without being so, has been included, it shall be null and void.

Guat. 1087.

SECTION FIFTH.

*Payment of hereditary debts.**

Article **1082.** Creditors, recognized as such, can object to the distribution of the estate being carried into effect, until they are paid or the amount of their credits is secured.

Guat. 1061; Col. 1411, 1343; Chile, 1354, 1286.

1083. Creditors of one or more of the co-heirs may intervene, at their own expense, in the distribution, in order to prevent it being made in fraud or to the injury of their rights.

1084. After the distribution is made, the creditors may exact the payment of the debts, in full, from any of the heirs who have not accepted the inheritance under benefit of inventory, or up to the amount of their hereditary share in case they have accepted it under such benefit.

---

* Digesto, book 32, tit. 23, law 11, par. 23. Law of Civil Procedure, 1881, arts. 973, 1038, 1040, 1093.

In both cases the defendant shall have a right to notify and summon his co-heirs, unless by disposition of the testator or in consequence of the distribution, he alone is bound to pay the debt.

1085. The co-heir, who has paid more than corresponds to his share in the estate, may claim from the others his proportionate part.

The same course shall be pursued, when because of the debt being secured by mortgage or consisting in a specified object, he has paid it in full. The person to whom it has been adjudged may, in such case, claim from his co-heirs only the proportional part, even when the creditor has assigned to him his actions and subrogated him in his place.

1086. When one of the tenements belonging to the estate is incumbered with a perpetual rent or real charge, it shall not be extinguished, even when redeemable, unless a majority of the heirs agree to do it.

When not agreed to or if the charge is not redeemable, its value or principal shall be deducted from the value or capital of the tenement, and this shall pass with the burden to the person to whom it is allotted or adjudged.

1087. The co-heir, who, at the same time, is a creditor of the decedent, may claim from the others the payment of his credit, deducting his proportional part, as such heir, and without prejudice to what is established in section fifth, chapter fifth of this title.

BOOK FOURTH.

OBLIGATIONS AND CONTRACTS.

TITLE I.

Obligations.

CHAPTER FIRST.

*General provisions.**

Article **1088**. Every obligation consists in giving, doing, or not doing a certain thing.

Chile, 1438; Col. 1495.

1089. Obligations are created by law, by contracts, by quasi-contracts, and by illicit acts and omissions or by those in which any kind of fault or neglect intervenes.

Col. 1494; Chile, 1437.

1090. Obligations emanating from law are not presumed. Those expressly determined by this Code or by special laws are the only exigible ones, and shall be governed by the provisions of the laws under which they have been established and by the provisions of this book in respect to what has not been provided by such law.

1091. Obligations arising from contracts have the force of law between the contracting parties, and must be complied with according to the tenor of the contracts.

Col. 1602; Chile, 1545.

1092. Civil obligations, arising from crimes or misdemeanors, shall be controlled by the provisions of the Penal Code.

1093. Those emanating from acts or omissions, in which faults or neglect, not punished by law, intervenes, shall be subject to the provisions of chapter second of title 16 of this book.

* Digesto, book 9, tit. 2; id., book 44, tit. 7, law 3. Part. 5, tit. 11, law 1; id. 5, tit. 12, law 5; id. 7, tit. 13, laws 14, 15; id. 7, tit. 15, law 6. Nov. Recop., book 10, tit. 1, law 1. Penal Code, 1870, arts. 18 to 21, 121 to 128.

CHAPTER SECOND.

*Nature and effect of obligations.**

Article **1094**. A person obliged to give something is also bound to preserve it with the proper diligence of a good father of a family.

Col. 1005; Chile, 1548; Uru. 1295.

1095. A creditor has a right to the fruits of a thing from the time the obligation of delivering it to him arises. However, he shall not acquire real rights therein, until it has been delivered to him.

1096. When the thing to be delivered is a specified one, the creditor, independently of the right granted to him by article 1001, may compel the debtor to make the delivery.

When the thing is undetermined or generic, he may ask that the obligation be complied with at the expense of the debtor.

When the person obliged is in default or has engaged himself to deliver the same thing to two or more different persons, until the delivery is made, the debtor shall be liable therefor in respect to unforeseen events (*vis major*).

Chile, 1549; Col. 1606.

1097. The obligation of giving a specified thing comprises that of delivering all its accessories, though they may not have been mentioned.

Arg. 575.

1098. When a person obliged to do a certain thing should not do it, it shall be ordered to be done at his expense.

The same shall be ordered, when he does it contrariwise to the tenor of the obligation.

Whatever has been badly done may be ordered to be undone.

Chile, 1555; Col. 1612.

1099. The provision of paragraph two of the preceding article shall also be observed when the obligation consists in not doing, and the debtor does what has been forbidden him.

Chile, 1555; Col. 1612.

---

*Digesto, book 13, tit. 6, law 18; id., book 22, tit. 1, law 43; id., book 43, tit. 1, law 127; id., book 46, tit. 8, law 15. Regulis juris, No. 23; id., law 155. Codigo, book 4, tit. 24, law 6. Law of March 14, 1856, art. 78. Project of 1851, arts. 1017, 1097. Commercial Code, arts. 316, 317, 318. Regulations of Monte de Piedad and Caja de Ahorros, of Madrid, Jan. 23, 1873, July 13, 1880. Roman Code, book 3, tit. 10, law 3. Part. 3, tit. 27, law 5; id. 5, tit. 2, law 3; id. 5, tit. 4, law 7; id. 5, tit. 5, laws 17, 23, 24, 25, 28, 50; id. 5, tit. 11, laws 12, 13, 18, 25, 29, 35; id. 5, tit. 8, law 8; id. 5, tit. 12, law 32; id. 5, tit. 13, law 34; id. 5, tit. 14, law 10; id. 5, tit. 15, law 7; id. 7, tit. 33, law 11.

1100. Persons obliged to deliver or to do something are in default from the moment on which the creditor exacts judicially or extrajudicially the compliance with their obligation.

However, the intimation of the creditor, in order that default may exist, shall not be necessary:

1. When the obligation or law declares it expressly.

2. When from its nature and circumstances, it may appear that the fixing of the time on which the thing was to be delivered or the service was to be done, was a determinate cause to constitute the obligation.

In reciprocal obligations, none of the obliged parties shall incur default, if the other does not comply with or does not submit to duly comply with what he is bound to do. From the moment on which one of the obligated parties complies with his obligation, the default begins for the other party.

Chile, 1557; Col. 1614.

1101. Those who, in compliance with their obligations, incur fraud, neglect or delay, and those who, in any way, act in opposition to the tenor of the same, become subject to pay indemnity for the damages and injuries caused thereby.

1102. Liability arising from fraud is exigible in all obligations. The renunciation of the action to enforce it is null and void.

1103. Liability arising from neglect is also exigible in the fulfillment of all kinds of obligations; but it may be mitigated by the court, according to the case.

1104. The fault or negligence of the debtor consists in the omission of such diligence, as may be required by the nature of the obligation, and may correspond to the circumstances of persons, time, and place.

When the obligation does not state what kind of diligence is to be exercised, that usually shown by a good father of a family shall be required.

1105. No one shall be held liable for events which could not be foreseen (*vis major*) or those, even when foreseen, were inevitable, aside from the cases expressly stated by law or those in which the obligation so declares.

Col. 1604; Chile, 1547.

1106. Indemnity for damages and injuries comprises not only the amount of the loss suffered, but also that of the benefit which the creditor has failed to obtain, with exception of the provisions contained in the following articles.

Col. 1613; Chile, 1556; Mex. 1306, 1581.

1107. The damages and injuries, for which the debtor in good faith is liable, are those foreseen or which may have been foreseen, at the time of constituting the obligation, and which are a necessary consequence of the failure to comply with it.

In case of fraud, the debtor shall be liable for all those which clearly may originate from the failure to fulfill the obligation.

Col. 1606; Chile, 1558; Guat. 1443.

1108. When the obligation consists in the payment of a sum of money, and the debtor is in default, the indemnity for damages and injuries, when there is no stipulation to the contrary, shall consist in the payment of the interest agreed upon, and, when there is no agreement, the legal interest shall be paid.

While another rate is not fixed by the government, interest, at the rate of six per cent. per year, shall be considered as legal.

Col. 1617; Chile, 1559; Uru. 1309; Guat. 1444.

1109. Interest due shall produce legal interest from the date on which it was judicially demanded, even if the obligation is silent on this point.

In commercial transactions, the provisions of the Code of Commerce shall govern.

Government pledging institutions (*Montes de Piedad*), and savings banks shall be governed by their special regulations.

Col. 1617; Chile, 1559; Guat. 1445.

1110. A receipt from the creditor for the principal, without making any reservation about interest, extinguishes the obligation of the debtor as to such interest.

The receipt for the last installment of a debt, when the creditor has made no reservation, shall also extinguish the obligation in respect to the preceding installment.

1111. Creditors, after having pursued the property, of which the debtor is in possession, for the purpose of collecting all that is due them, may enforce all the rights and actions of the debtor for the same purpose, excepting those inherent in his person; they may also contest the acts which the debtor may have done in fraud of their rights.

1112. All rights acquired by virtue of an obligation, are transmissible, subject to the laws, when there is no stipulation to the contrary.

Col. 1548; Chile, 1492.

CHAPTER THIRD.

Different kinds of obligations.

SECTION FIRST.

*Pure and conditional obligations.**

Article **1113.** Every obligation, the compliance with which does not depend upon a future or uncertain event or upon a past event, unknown to the parties concerned, shall be immediately exigible.

Every obligation, containing a resolutory condition, shall also be exigible without prejudice to the effects of the resolution.

Mex. 1444; Uru. 1367.

1114. In conditional obligations, the acquisition of rights, as well as the extinction or loss of those already acquired, shall depend upon the event constituting the condition.

Guat. 1454; Col. 1542; Chile, 1456; Uru. 1368; Mex. 1445.

1115. When the fulfillment of the condition depends upon the exclusive will of the debtor, the conditional obligation shall be null and void. If it depends upon chance or upon the will of a third person, the obligation shall produce all its effects in accordance with the provisions of this Code.

Uru. 1374; Col. 1534; Chile, 1477.

1116. Impossible conditions, those contrary to good morals, and those forbidden by law, shall void the obligation depending upon them. The condition of not doing a thing which is impossible is considered as non-existing.

Uru. 1369; Col. 1533, 1537; Chile, 1476, 1480.

1117. The condition, that a certain event shall happen within a certain time, shall extinguish the obligation as soon as the time has elapsed or it should be indubitable that the event cannot take place.

Col. 1539; Chile, 1482; Mex. 1451; Uru. 1379.

---

* Digesto, book 18, laws 2, 3; id., book 18, tit. 6, law 8; id., book 20, tit. 4, law 11, par. 1; id., book 35, tit. 1, laws 24, 81, par. 1; id., book 44, tit. 7, law 42; id., book 45, tit. 1, law 87, par. 1, law 27, par. 1, law 99, par. 1, 51; id., book 45, tit. 8, law 10; id., book 50, tit. 16, law 213. De regulis juris, laws 55, 151, 155. Instituciones, book 3, tit. 16, par. 4; id., book 3, tit. 20, par. 2, 24. Project of 1851, arts. 1040, 1041. Part. 4, tit. 4, law 1; id. 5, tit. 5, laws 14, 15, 16, 26, 38, 40, 58; id. 5, tit. 6, law 5; id. 5, tit. 11, laws 12, 13, 14, 15, 17, 21; id. 5, tit. 14, law 41; id. 5, tit. 28, law 46; id. 6, tit. 4, law 14; id. 6, tit. 9, law 22; id. 7, tit. 34, rule 29.

1118. The condition that a certain event shall not occur, at a certain time, shall render the obligation binding as soon as the time fixed has elapsed or when it becomes evident that such event cannot happen.

When there is no fixed time, the condition shall be considered as complied with, within the time which should probably have been fixed, considering the nature of the obligation.

Chile, 1482; Col. 1539; Uru. 1380.

1119. The condition shall be considered as complied with when the obligated party voluntarily prevents its compliance.

Guat. 1457; Uru. 1381; Chile, 1481; Col. 1538; Mex. 1452.

1120. The effects of the conditional obligation of giving, when the condition is complied with, will be retroactive from the day on which such obligation was constituted. Nevertheless, when the obligation imposes reciprocal prestations on the parties concerned, the fruits and interests for the time during which the condition has been pending, shall be understood as compensating each other. When the obligation is unilateral, the debtor shall become owner of the fruits and interests collected, unless by the nature and circumstances of the obligation, it must be inferred that the will of the person constituting it was otherwise.

In the obligation of doing or of not doing, the courts are to determine, in each case, the retroactive effect of the condition complied with.

Uru. 1282; Mex. 1451.

1121. The creditor may, before the fulfillment of the conditions, enforce the actions which may be proper for the preservation of his rights.

The debtor may recover what he has paid during the same period.

Uru. 1384.

1122. When the conditions were established with the intent of suspending the efficiency of the obligation of giving, the following rules shall be observed in the cases in which the thing improves, or is lost, or impaired, while the condition is pending:

1. When the thing is lost without fault of the debtor, the obligation shall become extinguished.

2. When the thing was lost by the fault of the debtor, he is obliged to make an indemnity for damages and injuries.

It is understood that the thing is lost whenever it perishes, remains out of market, or disappears in such a manner that its existence is unknown, or it is not possible to recover it.

3. When the thing is impaired without fault of the debtor, the impairment is to be borne by the creditor.

4. When the thing is impaired by fault of the debtor, the creditor may choose between the resolution of the obligation and its fulfillment, with indemnity for damages in both cases.

5. When the thing improves by its nature or by time, the improvements are for the benefit of the creditor.

6. When it improves at the expense of the debtor, the latter shall have no more right than those granted to the usufructuary.

Col. 1543; Mex. 1456; Chile, 1486.

1123. When the object of the conditions is to resolve the obligation of giving, after they are complied with, the parties in interest shall reciprocally return all that they have collected.

In cases of loss, impairment or improvement of the thing, the provisions in respect to the debtor, contained in the preceding article, shall be applied to the person bound to make restitution.

As to the obligation of doing or not doing, the provisions of the second paragraph of article 1120 shall be observed in regard to the effects of the resolution.

Col. 1544; Chile, 1489; Mex. 1462; Guat. 1456.

1124. The right to resolve the obligations is considered as implied in reciprocal ones, in the cases in which one of the obligated persons does not comply with his duties.

The injured party may choose between exacting the compliance with the obligation or its resolution with indemnity for damages and payments of interest in both cases. He may also ask for the resolution, even after having asked for the compliance, when the latter may appear impossible.

The court shall decree the resolution petitioned for, unless there are just causes authorizing it for a fixed term.

This is understood without prejudice to the rights of third acquirers, in accordance with articles 1295 and 1298, and with the provisions of the Law of Mortgage.

Col. 1546; Uru. 1392; Chile, 1489; Mex. 1466.

SECTION SECOND.

*Obligations depending on a term.**

Article **1125.** Obligations, the fulfillment of which has been fixed for a certain day, are exigible only when such day arrives.

---

* Digesto, book 45, law 41, par. 1. Part. 5, tit. 11, laws 12, 13. Law of Civil Procedure, arts. 203, 1155. Commercial Code, art. 60. Instituciones, book 3, tit. 16, par. 2.

By a certain day is understood one which shall necessarily arrive, even when the date of the arrival is unknown.

When the uncertainty consists in the arrival or nonarrival of the day, then the obligation is conditional and shall be controlled by the rules of the preceding section.

Col. 1551, 1553; Chile, 1494, 1496; Uru. 1394; Guat. 1458.

1126. In obligations depending on a certain term; what has been paid in advance cannot be recovered.

When he who paid was not aware, when he did it, of the existence of the term, he shall have a right to claim from the creditor the interests or fruits which the latter has received from the thing.

Col. 1552; Chile, 1495; Guat. 1459; Mex. 1475.

1127. Whenever there is a term fixed in obligations, it is presumed as established for the benefit of both the creditor and debtor, unless from its tenor or from other circumstances, it may appear that it has been established for the benefit of one or the other.

Mex. 1476; Uru. 1397.

1128. When the obligation does not fix a term, but it can be inferred from its nature and circumstances that there was an intention of granting it to the debtor, the courts shall fix the duration of such a term.

The courts shall also fix the duration of a term when it may have been left at the will of the debtor.

Chile, 1494; Col. 155.

1129. The debtor shall lose all right to profit by the term:

1. When, after the obligation has been contracted, it appears that he is insolvent, unless he gives security for the debt.

2. When he does not give to the creditor the security he is bound to give.

3. When by his own acts, he has reduced such security, after giving it, or when it disappears through an unforeseen event (*vis major*), unless it is immediately substituted by a new one equally safe.

Mex. 1477; Col. 1552; Chile, 1496; Uru. 1399.

1130. When the term of the obligation is fixed by days, to be counted from a specified one, such day shall be excluded from the computation which shall begin on the following day.

Chile, 1498; Col. 1555; Uru. 1400.

SECTION THIRD.

*Alternative obligations.**

Article **1131**. A person, who is alternatively obliged to make different prestations, shall fully comply with one of them.

A creditor cannot be compelled to receive a part of one and a part of another.

Mex. 1479; Col. 1557; Chile, 1500.

1132. The election belongs to the debtor, unless it has been expressly granted to the creditor.

A debtor shall not have the right to select prestations which are impossible, illicit or which could not have been the matter of such obligations.

Col. 1557; Chile, 1500.

1133. An election shall not be effectual, until due notice has been given of it.

1134. A debtor shall lose the right to elect when, of the prestations which he is alternatively obliged to fulfill, only one is feasible.

Col. 1560; Chile, 1503.

1135. A creditor shall have a right to be indemnified for damages and injuries when, by the fault of the debtor, all the things, which were alternatively the objects of the obligation, have disappeared, or it has become impossible to comply with the same.

The indemnity shall be fixed, taking as a base the price of the last thing which has disappeared or of the last service which has become impossible.

Col. 1561; Chile, 1504.

1136. When an election has been expressly given to the creditor, the obligation shall cease to be alternative, from the date on which notice of such election has been given to the debtor.

Until this date, the liability of such debtor shall be governed by the following rules:

1. When any of the things has been lost by an unforeseen event (*vis major*), he will comply by delivering the one which the creditor may select from among those remaining, or the one that remains, if only one exists.

2. When the loss of any of the things has been caused by the fault of the debtor, the creditor may claim any of those which still remain,

---

* Part. 5, tit. 11, laws 14, 23, 24.

or the value of the one which has disappeared by the fault of the debtor.

3. When all the things have been lost by the fault of the debtor, the creditor shall have a right to select the value of any one of them.

The same rules shall apply to the obligation of doing or not doing, in case that some or all of the prestations should be impossible.

Col. 1559 to 1561; Chile, 1502 to 1504.

SECTION FOURTH.

*Several and joint obligations.**

1137. The concurrence of two or more creditors or of two or more debtors, in a single obligation, does not imply that each one of the former has a right to ask, nor each one of the latter is bound to comply in full with the things which are the objects of such obligation. This shall only take place when the obligation determines it expressly, and is constituted as a joint obligation.

Guat. 1461; Col. 1568; Chile, 1511.

1138. If from the context of the obligation, referred to in the preceding article, any other thing does not appear, the credit or the debt shall be presumed as divided in as many equal parts as there are creditors or debtors, and shall be considered as credits or debts, each one different from the others.

Col. 1570; Chile, 1513.

1139. When the division is impossible, the right of the creditors shall only be impaired by the collective acts of the same, and the debts shall only be recoverable by proceedings against all of the debtors. If any one of them is found to be insolvent, the others shall not be obliged to pay his share.

1140. Solidarity may exist, even when the creditors and debtors are not bound in the same manner, and for the same periods and under the same conditions.

1141. Each one of the joint creditors can do whatever may be profitable, but not what may be injurious to the others.

Actions, enforced against any one of the joint debtors, shall be to the injury of all of them.

1142. A debtor may pay the debt to any one of the joint creditors,

* Digesto, book 16, tit. 3, law 43; id., book 45, tit. 2, laws 2, 7, 10; id., book 46, tit. 3, law 57. Instituciones, book 3, tit. 17, par. 1, 2; id., book 3, tit. 30, par. 1. Codigo, book 8, tit. 40, law 5. Nov. Recop., book 10, tit. 1, law 10. Part. 5, tit. 11, law 18; id. 5, tit. 12, law 8; id. 5, tit. 14, law 5.

but when it has been judicially demanded by any one of them, he must pay to this particular one.

1143. Novation, compensation, confusion or remission of the debt, made by one of the joint creditors, or with any of the debtors of the same class, extinguishes the obligation without prejudice to the provisions of article 1146.

A creditor who has executed any of these acts, and also the person who collects the debt, shall be responsible to the others for the part pertaining to them in the obligation.

Col. 1570; Chile, 1513, par. 2.

1144. A creditor may sue any of the joint debtors or all of them simultaneously. The claims instituted against one shall not be an obstacle for those that may be later presented against the others, as long as it does not appear that the debt has been collected in full.

Col. 1571; Chile, 1514.

1145. A payment made by one of the joint debtors extinguishes the obligation.

A person who has made the payment can only claim from his co-debtors shares pertaining to each one with the interest on the amounts advanced.

The failure to comply with the obligation, on account of the insolvency of a joint debtor, shall be made good by the co-debtors in proportion to the debt of each one of them.

Col. 1572; Chile, 1522.

1146. The liberation or remission, made by the creditor of the part affecting one of the joint debtors, does not release this one of his liability as to the co-debtors, in case the debt has been fully paid by any one of them.

1147. When the thing has perished, or the prestation has become impossible, without any fault of the joint debtors, the obligation shall be extinguished.

If there has been any fault on the part of any of them, all shall be liable, as to the creditor, for the value and the indemnity for damages and payments of interest, without injury to his action against the culpable or negligent.

Col. 1573; Chile, 1521.

1148. A joint debtor may utilize, against the claims of the creditor, all the exceptions derived from the nature of the obligation, and those which are personal to him. Those which personally pertain to the others may be employed by him only as to the share of the debt for which such co-debtors may be responsible.

Col. 1577; Chile, 1520.

SECTION FIFTH.

*Divisible and indivisible obligations.**

Article **1149.** The divisibility or indivisibility of things, objects of obligations, in which there is a single debtor and a single creditor, neither changes nor modifies the provisions of chapter second of this title.

1150. An indivisible several obligation is determined by paying the indemnity for damage and injury, from the moment that any of the debtors fails to comply with his duties. The debtors, who have been ready to comply with their duties, shall only contribute to the indemnity in a sum equivalent to the corresponding portion of the value of the thing or of the service in which the obligation consists.

1151. For the effects of the preceding articles, the obligation of giving specified things, and all those which are not susceptible of partial fulfillment, shall be considered as indivisible.

The obligations of doing shall be divisible when their object is the prestation of a number of days of work, the execution of work by units of measure, or any other similar things which by their nature are susceptible of partial fulfillment.

In the obligation of not doing, the divisibility or indivisibility shall be decided by characteristics of the prestation in each particular case.

SECTION SIXTH.

Obligations with penal clause.†

Article **1152.** In obligations with a penal clause, the penalty shall substitute the indemnity for damages and the payment of interest in case of a failure to comply therewith, if it has not been otherwise stipulated.

This penalty can only be made effective, when it is exigible in accordance with the provisions of this Code.

1153. The debtor cannot exempt himself from the fulfillment of the obligation by paying the penalty, unless in case that such right has been expressly reserved to him.

---

* Digesto, book 45, tit. 1, laws 3, 4, 85; id., book 45, tit. 35, laws 41, 45.

† Digesto, book 45, tit. 1, laws 35, 126. Part. 11, laws 38, 56. Commercial Code, art. 56.

Neither can the creditor jointly exact the fulfillment of the obligation and the payment of the penalty, unless such right has clearly been granted to him.

Col. 1594; Chile, 1537.

1154. The Judge shall equitably modify the penalty, when the principal obligation has been partly or irregularly complied with by the debtor.

Col. 1596; Chile, 1539.

1155. The nullity of the penal clause does not carry with it that of the principal obligation.

The nullity of the principal obligation carries with it that of the penal clause.

Col. 1593; Chile, 1536.

CHAPTER FOURTH.

Extinction of obligations.

GENERAL PROVISONS.

Article **1156**. Obligations are extinguished:

By their payment or compliance with them.

By the loss of the thing due.

By remission of the debt.

By the merging of the rights of the creditor and debtor.

By compensation.

By novation.

Chile, 1567; Col. 1625.

SECTION FIRST.

*Payment.**

Article **1157**. A debt shall not be considered as paid, until the total amount of the thing has been delivered, or the prestation of which the obligation consisted has been made.

Chile, 1568; Col. 1626.

---

* Digesto, book 5, tit. 8, law 8; id., book 14, tit. 3, law 14, par. 8; id., book 26, tit. 8, laws 1, 5, par. 1; id., book 21, tit. 1, law 18; id., book 46, tit. 3, laws 31, 41. Instituciones, book 3, tit. 8, par. 3. De regulis juris, laws 56, 160, 175, 177. Project of 1851, arts. 1089, 1092, 1096, 1099. Royal Decree, June 27, 1852. Royal Order, January 26, 1881. Law of Civil Procedure, tit. 62.

1158. Any person, whether he has interest or not in the compliance with the obligation, and whether the debtor knows it and approves it or is not aware of it, can make the payment.

He who pays the account of another may recover from the debtor what he has paid, unless he has done it against the latter's express will.

In this last case, he can only recover from the debtor in so far as the payment has been useful to him.

Chile, 1572; Col. 1630.

1159. He who pays in the name of the debtor, when the latter is not aware of it, cannot compel the creditor to subrogate him in the rights the creditor possesses.

Chile, 1573; Col. 1631.

1160. In obligations of giving, the payment made by the person who has not the free disposal of the thing due, and capacity for conveying it, shall not be valid.

However, when the payment has consisted in a sum of money or a thing perishable, no recovery shall be had against the creditor who has spent or consumed it in good faith.

1161. In obligations of doing, the creditor cannot be compelled to receive the prestation or the services from a third party, when the quality and circumstances of the person of the debtor has been taken into account in establishing the obligation.

Chile, 1572; Col. 1630.

1162. Payment shall be made to the person in whose favor the obligation is constituted, or to another authorized to receive it in his name.

Chile, 1576; Col. 1634.

1163. The payment, made to a person who is incapable to manage his property, shall be valid, in so far as it may be employed for his benefit.

A payment made to a third party shall also be valid in so far as it may have been beneficial to the creditor.

Chile, 1577; Col. 1635.

1164. A payment made, in good faith, to the person who is in possession of the credit shall release the debtor.

Chile, 1576; Col. 1634.

1165. A payment made by the debtor to the creditor, after he has been judicially ordered to retain the debt, shall not be valid.

Chile, 1678; Col. 1636.

1166. The debtor for a thing cannot oblige his creditor to receive a different one, even when it should be of equal or superior value to the thing due.

Neither in obligations of doing can a prestation be substituted by another against the will of the creditor.

Chile, 1569; Col. 1627.

1167. When the obligation consists in the delivery of a thing, not specified or generic, the quality and circumstances of which have not been expressed, the creditor cannot exact one of a superior quality nor can the debtor deliver an inferior one.

1168. Extrajudicial expenses, caused by the payment, shall be charged to the debtor. The court in accordance with the Code of Civil Procedure shall decide about the judicial expenses.

1169. Unless the contract expressly authorizes it, the creditor cannot be compelled to partially receive the prestations of which the obligation consists.

However, when the debt is in part liquid and in part illiquid, the creditor may exact, and the debtor can make payment of the former without awaiting for the liquidation of the latter.

1170. Payments of debts in money shall be made in the class of coins stipulated, and when it is not possible to deliver the same class, in legal silver or gold coin current in Spain.

The delivery of bills to order or drafts or other mercantile paper shall only produce the effects of payment, when collected or when, by the fault of the creditor, they have become dishonored.

Meanwhile, the action, derived from the original obligation, shall remain in suspense.

Chile, 1569; Col. 1627.

1171. Payments shall be made at the place designated in the obligation.

When it is not expressed and when a determined thing is to be delivered, the payment shall be made at the place where the thing existed, at the moment of constituting the obligation.

In any other case, the place of payment shall be that of the domicile of the debtor.

Col. 1645; Chile. 1587.

*Imputation of payments.**

Article **1172**. A person having several debts of the same class, in favor of a single creditor, can declare, at the time of making a payment, to which of them it must be applied.

When the debtor accepts a release from the creditor in which the application of the payment is made, he cannot make a claim against it, unless some cause has intervened which may invalidate the contract.

Col. 1654; Chile, 1576.

1173. If the debt bears interest, the payment cannot be considered as made on account of the principal, until the interest is covered.

Chile, 1595; Col. 1653.

1174. When the payment cannot be imputed, according to the preceding rules, the debt, which is most onerous for the debtor among those which have matured, shall be considered as the one paid.

When they have the same nature and liens, the payment shall be imputed to all *pro rata*.

Col. 1655; Chile, 1597.

Payment by assignment of property.†

Article **1175**. The debtor may assign his property to creditors in payment of his debts. This assignment liberates the former from liability to the net amount of the property assigned, unless there are stipulations to the contrary. Agreements in respect to the effects of an assignment, entered into between the debtor and his creditors, shall be made in accordance with the provisions of title seventeenth of this book, and with what is prescribed in the Code of Civil Procedure.

Chile, 1614, 1619; Col. 1672, 1678.

Tender of payment and consignation.‡

Article **1176**. When the creditor, to whom the tender of payment has been made, refuses to accept it, without reason, the debtor shall remain free from all liability by the consignation of the thing due.

---

* Digesto, book 5, tit. 7, law 85; id., book 46, tit. 3, laws 1, 2, 3. Codigo, book 8, tit. 43, law 1; id., book 11, tit. 39, law 1. Part. 5, tit. 14, law 10. Project of 1851, art. 1105.

† Digesto, book 42, tit. 3, law 9. Codigo, book 7, tit. 71, laws 7, 8. Part. 5, tit. 15, laws 1, 3. Project of 1851, arts. 1145 to 1155.

‡ Digesto, book 2, tit. 14, law 62; id., book 22, tit. 1, law 41, par. 1; id., book 46, tit. 3, law 72. Codigo, book 8, tit. 32, law 19; id., book 8, tit. 43, law 9. Part 5, tit. 14, law 8.

The same effect shall be produced by the consignation alone when made in the absence of the creditor, or when he is incapacitated from receiving the payment, at the time in which it is due, and when several persons pretend to have a right to collect it, or when the title of the obligation has been mislaid.

Col. 1658; Chile, 1599.

1177. In order that the consignation of the thing due may liberate the obligee, notice of it shall previously be given to the persons interested in the fulfillment of the obligation.

Consignation shall be ineffective when not strictly adjusted to the provision regulating payment.

Col. 1660; Chile, 1602.

1178. Consignation shall be made by depositing the things due, at the disposal of the judicial authority before whom it shall be proven that, in the proper case, the tender has been made and, in all other cases, that notice has been given of the consignation. After consignation is made, notice thereof shall also be given the parties concerned.

Chile, 1600, 1601; Col. 1658.

1179. The expenses of consignation, when proper, shall be charged to the creditor.

Chile, 1604; Col. 1662.

1180. After the consignation is duly made, the debtor can ask the Judge to order the cancellation of the obligation.

While the creditor has not accepted the consignation or no judicial decision has been rendered that it has been well done, the debtor may withdraw the thing or sum consigned, leaving the obligation subsisting.

Chile, 1605; Col. 1180.

1181. If, after the consignation is made, the creditor authorized the debtor to withdraw it, the former shall lose all the (right) of preference which he has in the thing.

The co-debtors and sureties shall become discharged.

Col. 1665; Chile, 1607.

SECTION SECOND.

*Loss of the thing due.**

Article **1182.** The obligation, which consists in the delivery of a specified thing, shall be extinguished when this thing is lost or destroyed without fault of the debtor and before he has become liable for delay.

Col. 1727; Chile. 1670.

1183. Whenever the thing is lost, when in the possession of the debtor, it shall be presumed that the loss has occurred by his fault and not by an unforeseen event (*vis major*), unless there is proof to the contrary and without prejudice to provision of article 1096.

Col. 1730; Chile, 1671.

1184. In obligations of doing, the debtor shall also be liberated when the prestation appears to be legally or physically impossible.

1185. When the debt for a certain and specified thing originates from a crime or fault, the debtor shall not be exempted from the payment of its value, whatever the cause of the loss may be, unless, when after he has offered the thing to the person, who should have received it, this person without reason had refused to accept it.

Chile, 1676; Col. 1735.

1186. Whenever the obligation is extinguished by the loss of the thing, all actions which the debtor should have against third persons, on account of it, pass to the creditor.

Col. 1736; Chile. 1677.

SECTION THIRD.

Remission of debts.†

Article **1187.** A remission may be made either expressly or tacitly. Both of them shall be governed by the provisions which rule inofficious donations.

---

* Digesto, book 13, tit. 1, law 20; id., book 19, tit. 2, law 9, par 4; id., book 43, tit. 16, law 19; id., book 45, tit. 1, laws 23, 49. Codigo, book 4, tit. 24, law 5. Part. 5, tit. 21, law 3; id. 5, tit. 3, law 4; id. 5, tit. 5, law 27; id. 5, tit. 8, law 15; id. 5, tit. 11, laws 20, 21; id. 5, tit. 13, law 20; id. 5, tit. 14, law 9; id. 5, tit. 23, law 29; id. 6, tit. 14, laws 6, 9, 44, 53, 54; id. 7, tit. 14, law 20. Penal Code, arts. 18, 121 to 128.

† Digesto, book 2, tit. 14, law 3; id., book 34, tit. 3, law 1. Codigo, book 8, tit. 26, law 9. Part. 3, tit. 19, law 11; id. 5, tit. 13, law 40; id. 5, tit. 14, laws 1, 9.

An express remission must, besides, be adjusted to the forms of a donation.

Col. 1712; Chile, 1653.

1188. A voluntary surrender, made by a creditor to his debtor, of a private document which bears evidence of a credit, implies the renunciation of the action which the former had against the latter.

When, for the purpose of invalidating this renunciation, it is claimed that it is inofficious, the debtor and his heirs may support it by proving that the delivery of the document was made on account of the payment of the debt.

Col. 1713; Chile, 1654.

1189. Whenever a private document from which the debt appears is in the possession of the debtor, it shall be presumed that the creditor delivered it by his own will, unless the contrary is proven.

Chile, 1654; Col. 1713.

1190. The remission of the principal debt shall extinguish the accessory obligations, but the remission of the latter shall leave the former existing.

1191. The accessory obligation of a pledge shall be considered remitted, when the pledge, after having been delivered to the creditor, is found in the possession of the debtor.

Col. 1713; Chile, 1654.

SECTION FOURTH.

*Confusion of rights.**

Article **1192.** Whenever the capacities of creditor and debtor are merged in the same person, the obligation becomes extinguished.

The case in which this confusion takes place by title of inheritance is excepted, when such inheritance has been accepted under benefit of inventory.

Col. 1724, 1728; Chile, 1665, 1669.

1193. The confusion which takes place in the person of the debtor or of the principal creditor is beneficial to the sureties. The one which takes place in the person of any of such sureties does not extinguish the obligation.

Chile, 1666; Col. 1725.

* Digesto, book 34, tit. 3, law 21; id., book 46, tit. 1, laws 21, 38, 50, 71, 21, par. 3; id., book 46, tit. 3, law 43; id., book 46, tit. 8, law 2. Project of 1851, art. 1158. Part. 6, tit. 6, law 8.

1194. Confusion does not extinguish debts in severalty, except as to the part which corresponds to the creditor or debtor in whom both capacities are merged.

Col. 1726; Chile, 1667.

SECTION FIFTH.

*Compensation (set-off).**

Article **1195.** Compensation shall take place when two persons, in their own rights, are reciprocally creditors and debtors of each other.

Col. 1714; Chile, 1653.

1196. In order that compensation may be effectual, it is required:

1. That each one of the persons bound may be principally so, and that he may be, at the same time, the principal creditor of the other.
2. That both debts consist in a sum of money or, when the things due are perishable, that they be of the same kind and also of the same quality, when the latter has been stipulated.
3. That both debts are due.
4. That they are liquid and exigible.
5. That no retention or suit, instituted by a third party and of which due notice has been given to the debtor, affects any of them.

Col. 1715; Chile, 1656.

1197. Notwithstanding the provisions of the preceding article, the sureties may oppose compensation in respect to what the creditor owes to his principal debtor.

1198. The debtor, who has consented to an assignment of rights, made by a creditor in favor of a third party, cannot oppose, against the assignee, the compensation which should pertain to him against the assignor.

When the creditor gave him notice of the assignment and the debtor did not consent to it, he may oppose compensation for the debts, prior to such assignment, but not for those contracted afterwards.

When the assignment is made without knowledge of the debtor, he can oppose compensation for the credits, prior to it, and for those contracted subsequently, until he has been informed of the assignment.

Chile, 1659; Col. 1718.

---

* Digesto, book 16, tit. 1, laws 4, 5; id., book 16, tit. 2, laws 1, 15, 23; id., book 20, tit. 4, law 4; id., book 40, tit. 12, law 19. Codigo, book 4, tit. 3, laws 4, 14, par. 2. Part. 5, tit. 3, law 5; id. 5, tit. 14, laws 20, 21, 22, 24, 27. Project of 1851, art. 1123.

1199. Debts payable in different places may be compensated by an indemnity for the expenses of transportation or for the exchange at the place of payment.

Col. 1723; Chile, 1664.

1200. Compensation shall not take place when any of the debts arises from a deposit or from the obligations of the depositary or borrower.

Neither can it be opposed to the creditor for support due under a gratuitous title.

1201. When a person has against himself different debts, which may be compensated, the provisions referring to imputation of payments shall be observed in the order of compensation.

Col. 1722; Chile, 1623.

1202. The effect of compensation is to extinguish both debts to the concurrent amount, even when the creditors and debtors have no knowledge of it.

Col. 1715; Chile, 1656.

SECTION SIXTH.

*Novation.**

Article **1203.** Obligations can be modified:

1. By change of object or their principal conditions.
2. By substituting the person of the debtor.
3. By subrogating a third party in the rights of the creditor.

Col. 1690; Chile, 1631.

1204. In order that an obligation may be extinguished by another which substitutes it, it is necessary that it should be so expressly declared, or that the old and new be absolutely incompatible.

Col. 1693; Chile, 1634.

1205. Novation, consisting in the substitution of any debtor in the place of the original one, can be made without the knowledge of the latter, but not without the consent of the creditor.

Col. 1694; Chile, 1635.

---

* Digesto, book 17, tit. 1, law 26, par. 2; id., book 18, tit. 4, law 4; id., book 42, tit. 3, law 2; id., book 42, tit. 6, law 1, par. 1; id., book 46, tit. 1, laws 17, 36; id., book 46, tit. 2, laws 2, 8; id., book 46, tit. 3, laws 43, 53, 76. Codigo, book 8, tit. 19, law 1; id., book 8, tit. 42, laws 1, 3, 6; id., book 8, tit. 48, law 8. De regulis juris, No. 129, 178. Part. 5, tit. 5, law 56; id. 5, tit. 12, law 11; id. 5, tit. 13, law 34; id. 5, tit. 14, law 15. Project of 1851, art. 1135, 1151.

1206. The insolvency of the new debtor, who has been accepted by the creditor, shall not revive the action of the latter against the original debtor, unless said solvency has been prior, public, and known to the debtor when he transfers his debt.

Chile, 1637; Col. 1696.

1207. When the principal obligation is extinguished by effect of the novation, the accessory obligations shall only subsist in so far as they benefit third parties who have not given their consent.

Col. 1700; Chile, 1641.

1208. Novation is null and void, if the original obligation is also so, unless the cause of nullity can be claimed by the debtor only or the ratification gives validity to acts which were null in their origin.

Col. 1689; Chile, 1630.

1209. The subrogation of a third party in the rights of a creditor cannot be presumed, except in the cases expressly mentioned in this Code.

In other cases, it shall be necessary to prove it clearly in order that it may be effectual.

1210. Subrogation is presumed:

1. When a creditor pays another preferred creditor.
2. When a third party, who is not interested in the obligation, pays with the express or tacit approval of the debtor.
3. When the person, who has interest in the fulfillment of the obligation, pays, without injury to the effect of the confusion in respect to the share belonging to him.

1211. A debtor may make the subrogation, without the consent of the creditor, when for paying the debt, he has borrowed money by a public deed, stating therein his intent and setting forth, in the release, the origin of the sum paid.

1212. Subrogation transfers to the subrogated the credit with the rights annexed to it, either against the debtor or against third parties, be they sureties or holders of mortgages.

1213. A creditor, to whom a partial payment has been made, may enforce his right for the balance, with preference to the person subrogated in his stead by virtue of the partial payment of the same credit.

CHAPTER FIFTH.

Proof of obligations.

GENERAL PROVISIONS.

Article **1214.** Proof of obligations devolves upon the persons claiming their fulfillment, and that of their extinguishment falls upon those who oppose the same.

Chile, 1698; Col. 1757.

1215. Proofs can be made by instruments, by confession, by the personal inspection of a Judge, by experts, by witnesses, and by presumptions.

Col. 1757; Chile, 1698.

SECTION FIRST.

*Public documents.**

Article **1216.** Public documents are those authorized by a Notary or by a competent public official, with the solemnities required by law.

Col. 1758; Chile, 1699.

1217. Documents in which a Notary Public intervenes shall be governed by the Notarial Law.

1218. Public instruments are evidence, even against a third party, of the fact which gave cause for their execution and of the date of the same.

They shall also be evidence against the contracting parties and those holding rights under them, as to the declarations made in them by the former.

Col. 1759; Chile, 1701.

1219. Public instruments, made for the purpose of weakening a former deed, between the same parties, shall be effectual against third parties only when their contents have been annotated in the proper public registry or on the margin of the original deed, and on the transcription or copy by virtue of which the third parties have acted.

Chile, 1707; Col. 1766.

---

* Digesto, book 22, tit. 3, law 2. Novela, 23, chap. 2. Nov. Recop., book 10, tit. 23, laws 1, 5, 6. Part. 3, tit. 18, law 114; id. 3, tit. 19, laws 8, 10, 11. Law of Civil Procedure, arts. 596, 597, 598, 600. Project of 1851, art. 1216. Notary Law, May 28, 1862, art. 1, and regulation Nov. 9, 1874, art. 9. Law of Mortgage, art. 396.

1220. Copies of public instruments of which there is an original or protocol, when contested by those to whom they cause damage, shall have probatory force only when they have been duly collated.

If there is any difference between the original and the copy, the contents of the former shall govern.

1221. When the original deed, the protocol, and the original file have disappeared, the following shall constitute evidence:

1. The first copies taken by the public officer who had authorized them.

2. The subsequent copies, issued by order of a court, after summoning the interested parties.

3. Those which may have been taken in the presence of the interested parties and with their assent, but without judicial order.

In default of the above-mentioned copies, any other copies, thirty or more years old, shall be evidence, provided they have been taken from the original by the officer who authorized them or by any other in charge of their custody.

Copies less than thirty years old, or which are authorized by a public official, in which the circumstances, specified in the preceding paragraph do not concur, shall serve only as a beginning of written evidence.

The probatory force of copies of a copy shall be valued by the courts according to circumstances.

1222. The inscription in any public registry of a document which has disappeared shall be valued, according to the rules established in the last two paragraphs of the preceding articles.

1223. An instrument, defective by the incompetency of the Notary, or by any other fault in its form, shall be considered as a private document when signed by the parties who executed the same.

1224. An instrument of recognition of an act or contract proves nothing against the instrument by which the same was executed, when, by excess or omission, they disagree with it, unless the novation of the former is expressly proven.

*Private documents.**

Article **1225.** A private document legally recognized shall have, as to those who executed it and those holding rights under them, the same force as a public instrument.

Col. 1761; Chile, 1702.

* Digesto, book 13, tit. 5, laws 24, 26; id., book 16, tit. 3, law 26; id., book 22, tit. 3, law 25; id., book 26, tit. 7, law 16. Codigo, book 4, tit. 19, law 6; id., book 4, tit. 30, law 4; id., book 8, tit. 18, law 11. Part. 3, tit. 18, laws 119, 121. Nov. Recop., book 11, tit. 9, laws 1, 2. Project of 1851, arts. 1204, 1209. Law of Civil Procedure, arts. 579, 593, 604, 1429, 1430, 1431. Commercial Code, art. 48.

1226. A person against whom a written obligation, which appears subscribed by him, is set up in court is bound to declare whether the subscription is or is not his own.

The heirs and those holding rights under the person bound may limit themselves to state if they know whether the subscription of the obligation is, or is not that of their principal.

Refusal, without a just cause, to make the declaration mentioned in the preceding paragraph, may be considered by the court as a confession of the genuineness of the document.

Col. 1761; Chile, 1702.

1227. The date of a private document shall be considered, in respect to third parties, only from the date on which it has been filed or inscribed in a public registry, from the death of any of the persons who subscribe it, or from the date on which it is delivered to a public official by virtue of his office.

Col. 1762; Chile, 1703.

1228. Entries, registries, and private papers shall be evidence only against the person who has written them in all that may appear clearly stated, but the person who wants to be benefited by such is bound to accept them also in the part which is injurious to him.

Col. 1763; Chile, 1704.

1229. A note written or signed by a creditor, at the end, in the margin, or on the back of a document held by him, constitutes evidence in all that is favorable to the debtor.

The same thing shall be understood of the notes written or signed by the creditor, on the back, in the margin, or at the foot of the duplicate of a document or receipt which the debtor holds.

In both cases, the debtor, who wishes to avail himself of what is favorable to him, shall have to abide by what is injurious as well.

Col. 1764; Chile, 1715.

1230. Private documents made for the purpose of changing the stipulations made in a public instrument produce no effect against a third party.

Col. 1766; Chile, 1707.

SECTION SECOND.

*Confession.**

Article **1231.** Confession may be made either judicially or extrajudicially.

In both cases, it shall be an indispensable condition for the validity of the confession that it should relate to personal acts of the confessor and that he may have legal capacity for making it.

1232. Confession is evidence against the author.

Exception is made of the cases in which compliance with the laws may be evaded by such confession.

Col. 1769; Chile, 1713.

1233. The confession cannot be partially used against him who makes it, unless it refers to different facts or when a part of the confession is proven by other means, or when, in any particular, it may be contrary to nature or law.

1234. Confession loses its effectiveness only when it is proven that on the making of it an error of fact was committed.

1235. A judicial confession must be made under oath before a competent Judge, and when he who may be benefited by it has actual representation in the proceedings.

1236. When judicial confession under decisory oath is demanded, the party from whom it is requested may ask the oath to be referred to the adversary, and if the latter refuses to give it, it shall be considered that the person has confessed.

1237. Decisory oath cannot be demanded about incriminating facts nor on questions about which the parties cannot compromise.

1238. Confession made under decisory oath, whether deferred or referred, constitutes a proof only in favor or against the parties who submitted to it or their heirs, and persons holding rights under them.

No proof shall be admitted about the falseness of such oath.

1239. Extrajudicial confession shall be considered as an act subject to the appreciation of the courts, according to the rules established about evidence.

---

* Digesto, book 2, tit. 1, law 15; id., book 11, tit. 1, law 9, par. 3, 19; id., book 12, tit. 2, laws 1, 2. Part. 3, tit. 11, laws 1, 5; id. 3, tit. 13, laws 1, 2, 4, 7; id. 7, tit. 33, law 11. Nov. Recop., book 11, tit. 28, law 4. Law of Civil Procedure, arts. 380, 387, 637, 1430, 1431.

SECTION THIRD.

*Personal inspection by the judge.**

Article **1240.** Evidence by personal inspection of the Judge shall only be effective in so far as it clearly permits the court to estimate, by the external appearance of the thing inspected, the fact which he tries to ascertain.

Col. 177; Chile, 1314.

1241. The inspection made by a Judge may be estimated in the sentence rendered by another Judge, provided the former has set forth with perfect clearness, in the proceedings, the details and circumstances of the things inspected.

SECTION FOURTH.

Evidence by experts.†

Article **1242.** This class of evidence can only be used, when, in order to estimate the facts, scientific, artistic or practical knowledge is necessary or convenient.

1243. The value of this evidence and the form in which it must be given are the subjects of the provisions of the Code of Civil Procedure.

SECTION FIFTH.

Evidence by witnesses.‡

Article **1244.** Evidence by witnesses shall be admissible in all cases in which it has not been expressly forbidden.

1245. All persons, of either sex, who are not unable by natural incapacity or by the provisions of law, can be witnesses.

1246. The following cannot be witnesses by natural incapacity:

1. Lunatics or insane persons.
2. The blind and deaf, in those things, knowledge of which depends upon sight and hearing.
3. Minors under fourteen years of age.

---

* Part. 3, tit. 15, laws 8, 13. Law of Civil Procedure, arts. 633, 636.

† Law of Civil Procedure, arts. 610, 632.

‡ Part. 3, tit. 16, laws 1, 8, 9, 10, 11, 14, 15, 16, 18, 32. Law of Civil Procedure, art. 659.

1247. The following persons are incapable by provisions of law:

1. Those who are directly interested in the suit.

2. The ascendants in the suits of their descendants and the latter in those of the former.

3. The father-in-law or mother-in-law in the suits of the son-in-law or daughter-in-law, and *vice-versa.*

4. The husband in the suits of his wife and the wife in those of the husband.

5. Those who, on account of their condition or profession, are bound to keep secrecy in matters relating to their profession or condition.

6. Those who are especially disqualified to be witnesses in certain acts.

The provisions of Nos. 2, 3, and 4 shall not be applied in suits in which it is intended to prove the birth or death of children or any other private family act, which it may not be possible to verify by any other means.

1248. The probatory force of the depositions of the witnesses shall be valued by the courts in accordance with the provisions of the Law of Civil Procedure, taking care to avoid that, by the simple coincidences of some depositions, unless their truthfulness be evident, the affairs may be finally decided in which are usually employed public deeds, private documents, or any commencement of written evidence.

SECTION SIXTH.

*Presumptions.**

Article **1249.** Presumptions are only admissible when the facts from which they are to be deduced are completely proven.

1250. Presumptions established by law exempt those favored by them from producing any further evidence.

1251. Presumptions established by law can be destroyed by evidence to the contrary, except in those cases in which it is expressly prohibited.

Only a sentence obtained in a suit for revision shall be effective against the presumption that a final judgment is true.

1252. In order that the presumption of a final sentence may be effective in another suit, it is necessary that between the case determined by the sentence and that in which the same is invoked, there

* Digesto, book 44, tit. 2, laws 12, 13, 14. Part. 3, tit. 2, law 25; id. 3, tit. 14, laws 8, 10, 11, 14; id. 3, tit. 22, law 19, 20, 21; id. 3, tit. 26, laws 1, 2. Law of Civil Procedure, art. 1692, No. 5.

shall be the most perfect identity, between the things, the causes, and the persons of the litigants, and the capacity, under which they litigated.

In questions relating to the civil condition of persons and in those about the validity or nullity of testamentary provisions, the presumption of a final sentence shall be effective against third parties, even if they have not litigated.

It is understood that there is identity of persons whenever the litigants of the second suit hold rights under those who litigated in the preceding suit, or when they are united to them by liens of solidarity, or by those which are established by the indivisibility of prestations among those who have the right to exact them, or those who are bound to satisfy the same.

1253. In order that presumptions, not established by law, may be considered as means of evidence, it is indispensable that between the facts demonstrated and the one that is to be deduced, should exist a precise and direct connection according to the rules of human criterion.

TITLE II.

Contracts.

CHAPTER FIRST.

*General provisions.**

Article **1254.** A contract exists from the moment when one or several persons consent to bind himself or themselves, in respect to another or others, to give something or to render some service.

Col. 1495; Chile, 1438.

1255. The contracting parties may establish any pacts, clauses, and conditions which they deem convenient, provided they do not conflict with the laws, morals, or public order.

1256. The validity and fulfillment of contracts cannot be left to the will of one of the contracting parties.

1257. Contracts shall only be effectual between the parties by whom they are executed and their heirs, except, with respect to the latter, in the cases where the rights and obligations originating from

* Digesto, book 2, tit. 14, law 27; id., book 21, tit. 1, law 31, par. 2; id., book 28, tit. 7, law 28; id., book 44, tit. 7, law 2. Codigo, book 7, tit. 60. Institutes, book 3, tit. 20, par. 18. Part. 5, tit. 11, laws 1, 7, 8, 9, 10, 11; id. 6, tit. 4, law 6; id. 7, tit. 34, rule 10. Recopilada, book 10, tit. 1, law 1; id., book 12, tit. 6, law 2. Nov. Recop., book 10, tit. 1, law 6. Project of 1882, arts. 1267, 1268, 1269. Project of 1851, arts. 973, 977.

the contract are not transmissible, either by their nature, or by pact, or by provision of law.

When the contract contains any stipulation in favor of a third party, he can exact its fulfillment, whenever he has given notice of his acceptance to the person bound, before the said stipulation has been revoked.

1258. Contracts are perfected by mere consent and from that time they are binding, not only in respect to the fulfillment of what has been expressly stipulated, but also in all the consequences which, according to their nature, are in accordance with good faith, use, and law.

1259. No one can contract in the name of another without being authorized by him, or without lawfully having his legal representation.

A contract entered into in the name of another by one who has not either his authorization or legal representation, shall be null and void, unless it is ratified by the person in whose name it was executed, before it is revoked by the other contracting party.

Col. 1505; Chile, 1448.

1260. Oaths shall not be admitted in contracts. If admitted, they shall be considered as not existing.

CHAPTER SECOND.

Essential requirements for the validity of contracts.

Article **1261.** There is no contract unless the following requirements are present:

1. The consent of the contracting parties.
2. A definite object which may be a matter of contract.
3. A cause for the obligation which is established therein.

SECTION FIRST.

*Consent.**

Article **1262.** Consent is shown by the concurrence of the offer and of the acceptance of the thing and the cause which shall constitute the contract.

* Digesto, book 4, tit. 2, law 1, rule 116; 1, par. 1; 9, par. 3; id., book 4, tit. 3, laws 1, 7, 9, 18; id., book 4, tit. 2; id., book 12, tit. 1, laws 4, 5, 6; id., book 18, tit. 1, law 9; id., book 44, tit. 7, law 6, 1, par. 12, 13; id., book 50, tit. 14, law 2. Codigo, book 2, tit. 53; id., book 1, tit. 20, law 5. Part. 4, tit. 2, law 15; id. 4, tit. 5, law 56; id. 5, tit. 5, law 21, 57; id. 5, tit. 11, laws 4, 5, 21, 28; id. 5, tit. 14, law 49; id. 7, tit. 16, law 3; id. 7, tit. 33, law 7. Nov. Recop., book 10, tit. 1, laws 11, 15. Project of 1851, art. 992. Commercial Code, art. 54.

Acceptance made by letter only binds the person who made the offer when it came to his notice. The contract, in this case, is presumed as entered into at the place where the offer was made.

1263. The following persons cannot give their consent:

1. Minors who are not emancipated.
2. Lunatics or the insane, and the deaf and dumb who cannot write.
3. Married women, in the cases specified by law.

1264. The incapacity, set forth in the preceding article, is subject to the modifications which are determined by law and is to be understood without prejudice to the special incapacities established by such law.

1265. Consent given by error, under violence, intimidation or by deceit shall be void.

Col. 1508; Chile, 1451.

1266. In order that the error may invalidate the consent, it must refer to the substance of the thing, object of the contract, or to those conditions of the same, which should have been principally the cause of its celebration.

An error as to the person shall invalidate a contract only when the consideration of the person should have been the principal cause of the contract.

A mere error of accounts shall only give cause for its correction.

Col. 1510; Chile, 1453.

1267. Violence exists when, to exact the consent, an irresistible force is used.

Intimidation exists when one of the contracting parties is inspired with a reasonable and well-grounded fear of suffering an imminent and serious injury to his person or property, or to the person or property of his consort, descendants or ascendants.

To qualify the intimidation, the age, sex, and status of the person must be considered.

Fear of displeasing the persons to whom obedience and respect is due shall not annul the contract.

Col. 1513; Chile, 1456.

1268. Violence or intimidation shall annul the obligation, even if they have been employed by a third person who did not intervene in the contract.

Col. 1514; Chile, 1457.

1269. There is deceit, when by words or insidious contrivances on the part of one of the contracting parties, the other is induced to enter into a contract which he would not have done without the use of them.

Col. 1515; Chile, 1458.

1270. In order that deceit may cause the nullity of a contract, it should be grievous and must not have been employed by both of the contracting parties.

Incidental deceit renders only the party who employed it liable to indemnity for damages and injuries.

SECTION SECOND.

*Objects of contracts.**

Article **1271.** All things, even future ones, which are not out of the commerce of men, can be objects of contracts.

Notwithstanding, no contract can be entered into in respect to future inheritances, other than those whose object is to make a distribution *inter vivos* of the estate, according to article 1056.

All services not contrary to law or to good morals may also be the object of a contract.

Col. 1518; Chile, 1461.

1272. Things or services which are impossible cannot be the object of a contract.

Col. 1518; Chile, 1461.

1273. The object of every contract must be a thing determined as to its kind. The indetermination of the sum cannot be an obstacle to the existence of the contract, provided it may be possible to determine it without necessity of a new agreement between the contracting parties.

Col. 1518; Chile, 1461.

SECTION THIRD.

Consideration (causa) for contracts.†

Article **1274.** In onerous contracts, the prestation or promise of a thing or services by the other party is understood as a consideration

---

* Digesto, book 18, tit. 1, laws 8, 34, par. 1; id., book 45, tit. 1, laws 74, 75, 94, 115. Codigo, book 2, tit. 3, laws 6, 30. Roman Law, rule 31, 185. Instituta, book 3, tit. 16, par. 7. Part. 5, tit. 5, laws 11, 13; id. 5, tit. 11, laws 1, 2, 20, 21, 38.

† Digesto, book 12, tit. 6, laws 32, par. 2, 52; id., book 12, tit. 7, laws 1, 3, 5; id., book 22, tit. 3, law 25, par. 4. Part. 5, tit. 14, law 35; id. 6, tit. 13, law 7.

for each contracting party; in remuneratory ones, the services or benefits remunerated, and in those of pure beneficence, the mere liberality of the benefactor.

Col. 1524; Chile, 1467.

1275. Contracts without consideration or with an illicit one are not effectual. A consideration is illicit, when it is contrary to law and good morals.

Col. 1524; Chile, 1467.

1276. The statement of a false consideration in contracts shall render them void, unless it is proven that they were based on another real and licit one.

1277. Although the consideration is not expressed in the contract, it is presumed as existing and that it is licit, unless the debtor proves the contrary.

Col. 1524; Chile, 1467.

CHAPTER THIRD.

*Effectiveness of contracts.**

Article **1278.** Contracts shall be binding, whatever the form may be in which they have been entered into, provided the essential conditions required for their validity are present.

1279. When the law exacts the execution of a deed or other special form for making effectual suitable obligations of a contract, the contracting parties may compel each other to comply with such forms, from the moment in which consent and the other requirements, necessary for their validity, have taken place.

1280. The following must be executed by a public instrument:

1. Acts and contracts the object of which is the creation, transmission, modification or extinction of real rights on real property.

2. The leases of the same property for six or more years, whenever they shall cause damage to third parties.

3. Marriage contracts, and the constitution and increase of dowries, whenever it is intended to enforce them against third parties.

4. The assignment, repudiation, and renunciation of hereditary rights or of those of the conjugal society.

5. The power for contracting marriage, the general one for lawsuits, and the special ones which are to be presented in a lawsuit; the

* Codigo, book 5, tit. 4. Novelas, 117, 118. Recopilada, book 10, tit. 1, law 1. Part. 3, tit. 18, law 114. Law of Mortgage, art. 2. Regulation for Law of Mortgage, art. 1. Instruction of Nov. 9, 1874. Law of March 14, 1856, art. 2. Project of 1882, art. 1292. Commercial Code, art. 51.

power for administering property and any other, the object of which is an act drawn or which is to be drawn in a public instrument, or which may do injury to a third party.

6. The assignment of actions or rights proceeding from an act specified in a public instrument.

All other contracts, on which the amount of the prestations of one or both of the contracting parties exceed 1,500 *pesetas,* must be drawn in writing, even when a private document.

CHAPTER FOURTH.

*Interpretation of contracts.**

Article **1281.** When the terms of a contract are clear and leave no doubt about the intentions of the contracting parties, the literal sense of its clauses shall rule.

When the words appear contrary to the evident intention of the contracting parties, the intention is to prevail.

Col. 1618, 1621; Chile, 1560, 1563.

1282. To form a judgment about the intention of the contracting parties, attention must principally be paid to their acts, contemporaneous and subsequent to the contract.

1283. However general the terms of a contract may be, there should not be understood as comprised in it, things and cases different from those about which the parties interested intended to contract.

Col. 1619; Chile, 1561.

1284. When any of the clauses of a contract admits of different meanings, it should be understood in the sense most suitable to be effective.

1285. The clauses of a contract should be interpreted in relation to one another giving to those that are doubtful the meaning which may result from the consideration of all of them together.

Col. 1622; Chile, 1564.

1286. Words which may have different meanings shall be taken in the meaning which may be nearest in accordance with the nature and object of the contract.

1287. The uses or customs of the country shall be taken in consideration in interpreting the ambiguity in contracts, and shall supply in them the omissions or clauses which are usually established therein.

* Digesto, book 2, tit. 14, law 39; id., book 18, tit. 1, laws 6, 21; id., book 21, tit. 1, law 31; id., book 21, tit. 2, law 6; id., book 30, tit. 3, law 50; id., book 32, law 75; id., book 33, tit. 10, law 7; id., book 34, tit. 5, law 12; id., book 45, tit. 1, laws 12, 38, par. 18; 53, 80, 99, 219. Codigo, book 4, tit. 22, law 1. Roman Law, rule 67 — De regulis juris, No. 34, 114. Part. 5, tit. 11, law 25; id. 7, tit. 23, laws 2, 5. Commercial Code, art. 57.

1288. The interpretation of the obscure clauses of a contract shall not favor the party who caused such obscurity.

Col. 1624; Chile, 1566.

1289. When it is absolutely impossible to resolve the doubts by the rules set forth in the preceding articles, if these deal with incidental circumstances of the contract, and this contract be gratuitous, they shall be resolved in favor of the smallest transmission of rights and interests. If the contract be onerous, the doubt shall be decided in favor of the greatest reciprocity of interests.

When the doubts, a decision about which is referred to in this article, deal about the principal object of the contract, in such a way that the intention or will of the contracting parties cannot be ascertained, the contract shall be null and void.

CHAPTER FIFTH.

*Rescission of contracts.**

Article **1290.** Contracts validly entered into may be rescinded in the cases provided by law.

1291. The following contracts are rescindable:

1. Those which may be entered into by guardians without the authorization of the family council, whenever the person represented by them has suffered *lesion* of more than one-fourth part of the value of the things which have been the object of such contracts.

2. Those entered into in representation of absentees, provided they have suffered the *lesion*, referred to in the preceding paragraph.

3. Those entered into in fraud of the creditors, when they cannot recover, in any other way, what is due them.

4. Contracts which refer to litigious things, when they have been entered into by the defendant without the knowledge and approval of the parties in litigation or of competent judicial authority.

5. Any others specially determined by law.

1292. Payments made, while in the condition of insolvency, by a debtor on account of obligations, the compliance with which at the

* Digesto, book 4, tit. 4, laws 11, par. 4, 5, 24, par. 4; id., book 4, tit. 6, law 28, par. 6; id., book 21, tit. 1, law 25, par. 10; id., book 42, tit. 8, law 10, par. 1; id., book 43, tit. 8, law 6. Codigo, book 2, tit. 25, laws 3, 5; id., book 2, tit. 48, special law; id., book 2, tit. 53, law 7; id., book 4, tit. 44, law 2. Fuero Real, book 3, tit. 10, law 5. Fuero Juzgo, book 5, tit. 4, law 6. Part. 3, tit. 25, law 2; id. 5, tit. 5, law 56; id. 5, tit. 15, laws 7, 9; id. 6, tit. 13, law 1; id. 6, tit. 14, law 4; id. 6, tit. 19, laws 2, 5, 8. Commercial Code, arts. 879, 880, 888. Penal Code, art. 536. Law of Mortgage, arts. 37, 39.

time of making them the debtor could not be compelled to do, are also rescindable.

1293. No contract shall be rescinded for *lesion*, except those specified in Nos. 1 and 2 of article 1291.

1294. The action for rescission is a subsidiary one and can be enforced only when the injured party has no other legal remedy to obtain the reparation for the injury.

1295. Rescission obliges the return of the things which were the objects of the contract, together with their fruits and the value with interest, therefore, it can only be carried into effect when the person who claims it can return that which, on his part, he is bound to do.

Neither can rescission take place when the things, objects of the contract, are lawfully in the possession of third parties who have not acted in bad faith.

In this case the indemnity for damages may be claimed from the person who caused the *lesion.*

1296. The rescission, to which No. 2 of article 1291 refers, shall not be allowed in contracts made with judicial authorization.

1297. All contracts by virtue of which the debtor conveys property, under gratuitous title, are presumed to be made in fraud of creditors.

Conveyances, under onerous titles, made by persons against whom a condemnatory sentence, in any instance, has been previously rendered, or a writ of seizure of property has been issued, shall also be presumed fraudulent.

1298. Any person, who has in bad faith acquired things, alienated in fraud of creditors, shall indemnify the latter for the damages and injuries caused to them by the conveyance, whenever, by any reason, it may be impossible for him to return them.

1299. The action asking rescission must be brought within four years.

For persons subject to guardianship and for absentees, the four years shall not commence to run until the incapacity of the former has ceased to exist or the domicile of the latter is known.

CHAPTER SIXTH.

*Nullity of contracts.**

Article **1300.** Contracts, in which the requirements stated in article 1261 concur, can be annulled, even when there is no *lesion* to the

* Digesto, book 18, tit. 1, law 13, par. 29; id., book 12, tit. 1, law 31; id., book 12, tit. 5, laws 3, 4, par. 2; id., book 21, tit. 1, laws 13, 25, 57; id., book 26, tit. 8, laws 1, 5, par. 1. Codigo, book 1, tit. 14, law 6; id., book 2, tit. 38, laws 1, 2; id., book 4, tit. 7; id., book 5, tit. 74, law 3. Instituta, book 1, tit. 21. Part. 5, tit. 11, law 28; id. 5, tit. 14, laws 47 to 54; id. 6, tit. 16, law 7; id. 7, tit. 34, rule 17. Project of 1851, arts. 1190, 1192. Project of 1882, arts. 1320, 1323, 1325 to 1327.

contracting parties, whenever they are effected by one of the vices which invalidate them according to law.

1301. The action for nullity shall last only four years.

This term shall commence to run in cases of intimidation or violence from the day on which it has ceased.

In those of error or deceit or falseness of consideration, from the date of the consummation of the contract.

When the object of the action is to invalidate contracts, made by a married woman, without consent or by competent authority, from the date of the dissolution of the marriage.

And when it refers to contracts, entered into by minors or incapables, from the date when they were freed from guardianship.

Col. 1750; Chile, 1691.

1302. The action for nullity of contracts can be exercised by those who are principally or subsidiarily obligated by virtue of them. Capable persons cannot, however, allege the incapacity of those who contracted with them; neither those who caused the intimidation or violence, or employed deceit, or caused the error, can base their action on such vices of the contract.

Col. 1742; Chile, 1683, 1684.

1303. When the nullity of an obligation has been declared, the contracting parties shall restore to each other the things which have been the matter of the contract with their fruits, and the value with its interest, except what is provided by the following articles.

Col. 1746; Chile, 1687.

1304. When the nullity is caused by the incapacity of one of the contracting parties, the incapable is not obliged to make restitution, except to the extent he has profited by the thing or by the value received by him.

Col. 1747; Chile, 1688.

1305. When the nullity arises from the illegality of the consideration or the object of the contract, if the fact constitutes a crime or fault, common to both contracting parties, they shall have no action against each other and proceedings shall be instituted against them, and the things or value which may have been the matter of the contract shall be applied, as provided in the Penal Code in respect to the goods or instruments of the crime or fault.

This provision is applicable to the cases in which there is a crime or fault on the part of only one of the contracting parties, but the one who is not culpable shall be entitled to recover what he has given, and shall not be bound to comply with what he has promised.

Col. 1747 to 1756; Chile, 1687 to 1696.

1306. If the fact of which the illicit consideration consists does not constitute either a crime or fault, the following rules shall be observed:

1. When both parties are culpable, neither of them can recover what he has given by virtue of the contract, nor claim the fulfillment of what the other party has offered.

2. When only one of the contracting parties is culpable, this one shall not recover what he has given by virtue of the contract, nor ask for the fulfillment of what has been offered to him. The other party, who has had nothing to do with the illicit consideration, may claim what he has given, without being obliged to comply with what he has offered.

1307. Whenever a person, who is obliged by a declaration of nullity to return a thing, cannot return it because it has been lost, he shall return the fruits collected and the value which the thing had when lost, together with the interest from the same date.

1308. While one of the contracting parties does not return that which he is obliged to deliver by virtue of the declaration of nullity, the other cannot be compelled to comply with what is incumbent on him.

1309. The action of nullity becomes extinguished from the moment in which the validity of the contract has been confirmed.

1310. Only contracts which have all the requirements stated in article 1261, can be confirmed.

1311. The confirmation can be made either expressly or tacitly. It shall be understood that there is a tacit confirmation, when being aware of the cause of the nullity and such cause having ceased to exist, the person, who has the right to invoke it, executes an act which necessarily implies his will to renounce such a right.

1312. Confirmation does not require the consent of the contracting parties who are not entitled to exercise the action of nullity.

1313. Confirmation cures the contract of all vices which affected it from the moment of its execution.

1314. The action for nullity of a contract shall also be extinguished when the thing, object of the contract, is lost by deceit or blame of the person entitled to enforce the action.

When the cause of the action is the incapacity of one of the contracting parties, the loss of the things shall be no obstacle for the action to prevail, unless it has occurred by deceit or blame on the part of the plaintiff, after having acquired capacity.

TITLE III.

Contracts about property on account of marriage.

CHAPTER FIRST.

*General provisions.**

Article **1315.** Persons who are to be united in marriage may, before entering into it, execute contracts, stipulating the conditions for the conjugal society in reference to present and future property without any other limitations than those stated in this Code.

In default of contracts about property, it shall be understood that the marriage has been contracted under the system of legal conjugal community.

Col. 1771, 1774; Chile, 1715, 1718.

1316. In the contracts, to which the preceding article refers, the contracting parties shall not stipulate anything contrary to law or to good morals, nor humiliating to the authority belonging respectively to the future consorts within the family.

All stipulations not conformable to the provisions of this article shall be considered null and void.

Col. 1773; Chile, 1717.

1317. Shall also be considered as null and void and as not written in the contracts, mentioned in the two preceding articles, the clauses by which the contracting parties, in a general manner, stipulate that the property of the consorts shall be submitted to the local laws and customs of regions governed by such laws, and not by the general provisions of this Code.

Chile, 1721.

1318. A minor, who can marry in accordance with law, may also execute his marriage contract, but it shall be valid only when in its execution there take part the persons designated by the same law for giving consent to the minor for the purpose of contracting marriage.

In case the marriage contract is null and void, because the concurrence and subscription of the aforesaid persons are wanting and

* Digesto, book 2, tit. 14, laws 1, 4, par. 2, 28, 38; id., book 23, tit. 3, laws 9, par. 1, 21, 68, 73; id., book 23, tit. 4, law 8; id., book 24, tit. 1, law 31, par. 3. Codigo, book 5, tit. 3, law 16; id., book 5, tit. 4, art. 1319; id., book 5, tit. 4, law 23, par. 1; id., book 5, tit. 13, special law; id., book 5, tit. 11, law 6; id., book 5, tit. 12, laws 25, 28. Novela, 78, 117, chap. 4. Instituciones, book 2, tit. 7, par. 3. Fuero Juzgo, book 3, tit. 1, law 5; id., book 4, tit. 2, law 17. Recopilada, book 10, tit. 3, law 3. Part. 4, tit. 11, laws 13, 14, 18, 19. Estilo, law 223. Toro, law 60.

yet the marriage is valid according to law, it shall be understood that the minor has contracted it, under the system of conjugal community.

1319. In order that any change in the marriage contract be valid, this change should be made before the celebration of the marriage and in the presence and with the concurrence of the persons who took part in the contract as executors. The attendance of the same witnesses shall not be necessary.

Any of the persons, who attended the execution of the original contract, can only be substituted by another, or his attendance may not be required when, by cause of death or any other legal cause, at the time of the execution of the new stipulation or the modification of the preceding one, the attendance is impossible or might not be required according to law.

Col. 1778; Chile, 1722.

1320. After the marriage has been celebrated, the marriage contract, executed before the marriage, cannot be changed, whether present or future property is involved.

1321. Marriage contracts and modifications made in them shall be executed in a public instrument before the celebration of the marriage.

Property in the conditions referred to in article 1324, is an exception to the preceding rule.

Col. 1772; Chile, 1716.

1322. Any modification made in the marriage contract shall be legally ineffectual in respect to third persons, if it does not comprise the following conditions:

1. That in the respective protocol and by marginal note, reference be made to the notarial act or instrument which contains the modification of the previous contract.

2. That in case the original contract is inscribable in the Registry of property, the document by which the former has been modified must also be inscribed.

The Notary shall set forth these modifications in the authenticated copies of the stipulations or original contract which he may issue, under the penalty of indemnifying the parties for any damages and injuries, if he fails to do so.

1323. For the validity of the marriage contract, made by a person against whom a judgment of civil interdiction or incapacity has been rendered or against whom a suit for the same cause has been instituted, the attendance and consent of the guardian shall be indispensable and said guardian shall be appointed, to his end, by the persons who are entitled to do so according to the provisions of this Code, and of the Code of Civil Procedure.

Col. 1777.

1324. When the property brought by the consorts is not real, and that of the husband and wife together amount to a total sum not exceeding 2,500 *pesetas,* and no Notary exists in the town of their residence, the marriage contract may be executed in the presence of the Secretary of the Municipal Board and two witnesses, who shall state, on their responsibility, that they know said property has been delivered or that it has been brought to the marriage, as the case may be.

The original contract or contracts shall be kept in custody, under registry, in the archives of the corresponding municipality.

When amongst the property brought to the marriage, whatever its value may be, there are one or more tenements, or the contracts refer to real property, they shall always be executed in a public instrument, before a Notary, as provided in article 1321.

Col. 1772; Chile, 1716.

1325. When the marriage is contracted in a foreign country, between a Spaniard and a foreign woman or between a foreigner and a Spanish woman, and the contracting parties do not state or stipulate anything about their property, it shall be understood, when the husband is a Spaniard, that he marries under the system of the legal conjugal community, and when the wife is a Spaniard that she marries under the system of laws which are in force in the husband's country, all without prejudice to what is established in this Code in respect to real property.

1326. All that is agreed to in the stipulations or contracts about which the preceding articles refer, in contemplation of a future marriage, shall be null and ineffectual in case the marriage is not celebrated.

CHAPTER SECOND.

*Donations on account of marriage.**

Article **1327**, Donations on account of marriage are those made, before its celebration, in consideration of the same, and in favor of one or of both intented consorts.

Col. 1842; Chile, 1786.

* Digesto, book 23, tit. 3, law 73; id., book 23, tit. 4, law 8; id., book 24, tit. 1, laws 7, par. 6, 16, 31, par. 8, 32, par. 2, 49. Codigo, book 4, tit. 22, laws 2, 3; id., book 5, tit. 12, law 28. Part. 41, tit. 11, laws 4, 5, 6, 14. Fuero Juzgo, book 3, tit. 1, law 6. Recopilada, book 10, tit. 3, laws 5, 67. Fuero Real, book 3, tit. 12, law 10; id., book 3, tit. 6, law 9; id., book 5, tit. 2, law 7.

1328. These donations shall be governed by the rules established in title second, book third, in so far as they are not modified by the following articles.

Col. 1845; Chile, 1789.

1329. Persons under age may grant and receive donations in their antenuptial contracts, provided they are authorized by persons who must give their consent for contracting marriage.

1330. Acceptance is not required for the validity of such donations.

1331. Affianced persons may give each other in their marriage contract as much as the tenth part of their actual property, and, in regard to future property, they can give to each other, only in case of death, a portion within the limit set forth in the provisions of this Code which refer to succession by testament.

Col. 1844; Chile, 1788.

1332. The donor, on account of marriage, must liberate the property donated from mortgages and any other charges burdening them, except ground-rents and easements, unless in the marriage stipulations or contract the contrary has been specified.

1333. A donation made on account of marriage can only be revoked in the following cases:

1. When it is conditional and the condition is not fulfilled.
2. When the marriage does not take place.
3. When the persons marry without having obtained the consent according to the provisions of rule 2, article 50, or when the marriage is annulled and there exists bad faith on the part of one of the consorts, in conformity with No. 3, article 73 of this Code.

1334. All donations between consorts, made during the marriage, shall be null and void.

Moderate gifts which the consorts make to each other on days of rejoicing of the family are not included in this rule.

1335. All donations made during marriage by one of the consorts to the children, whom the other consort had by a former marriage, or to the persons of whom he or she is a presumptive heir, when the donation is made, shall be null and void.

CHAPTER THIRD.

Dowry.

SECTION FIRST.

*The constitution of and guarantee for dowry.**

Article **1336.** Dowry is composed of the property and rights brought, as such, by the wife to the marriage, at the time of contracting it, and of those which she acquires during the marriage by donation, inheritance or legacy, as dotal property.

1337. Real property, acquired during the marriage, shall also be considered as dotal in the following cases:

1. When they are exchanged for other dotal property.
2. By right of redemption belonging to the wife.
3. By delivery in payment of the dowry.
4. By purchase with money pertaining to the dowry.

1338. The parents and relatives of the consorts and persons not belonging to the family may constitute the dowry in behalf of the wife, either before or after the celebration of the marriage.

The husband may also constitute it before the marriage but not after it.

1339. The dowry, constituted before, or at the time of the celebration of the marriage, shall be governed, in all that is not provided in this chapter, by the rules of donations made in contemplation of marriage.

Dowry constituted after the marriage shall be governed by the rules of common donations.

1340. The father or the mother or whichever one of them is alive is bound to give a dowry to his or her legitimate daughters, except in the cases in which they need their consent, according to law, to contract marriage and yet marry without obtaining said consent.

1341. The obligatory dowry, to which the preceding article refers, shall consist in a moiety of the presumptive rigorous *legitime*. When the daughter has property equivalent to the moiety of her *legitime*, this obligation shall cease, and if the value of the property does not

---

* Digesto, book 23, tit. 3, laws 2, 7, 27, 28, 56, par. 1, 76; id., book 24, tit. 3, laws 14, 28, par. 13. Instituciones, book 2, tit. 7, law 3. Codigo, book 5, tit. 11, laws 7, 14. Part. 4, tit. 11, laws 1, 8, 9, 11, 16, 18, 19; id. 5, tit. 5, law 49; id. 5, tit. 13, law 24. Law of Mortgage, arts. 170, 171, 175, 176, 177, 182, 186. Fuero Real, book 3, tit. 4, law 11. Toro, law 35. Nov. Recop., book 10, tit. 1, law 2. Penal Code, arts. 489, 494.

cover the moiety of the *legitime*, the donor shall supply the balance required to complete it.

In any event, it is prohibited to make investigations about the fortune of the parents, in order to determine the amount of the dowry, and the courts, in an act of voluntary jurisdiction, shall regulate it without any further investigations than the statement of the same parents who are to give the dowry and of the two nearest relatives of the daughter, male and of full age, one of the paternal line and the other of the maternal, residing in the same place or within the judicial district.

In default of relatives of full age, the courts shall decide, in their prudent judgment, only by the statements of the parents.

1342. The parents may comply with the obligation of giving dowries to their daughters, either by delivering to them the capital of the dowry, or by paying them an annual rent, as fruits or interest of the same.

1343. When the husband alone or both consorts jointly constitute a dowry for their daughters, it shall be paid out of the property of the conjugal community; if there is no property, said dowry shall be paid by halves or in the proportion in which the parents may have respectively bound themselves with the property belonging to each consort. When the wife alone grants the dowry, what she has given or promised should be charged to her own property.

1344. The dowry confessed by the husband, the delivery of which is not proven, or is shown only in a private document, shall produce no other effect than that of a personal obligation.

1345. Notwithstanding the provisions of the preceding article, the wife in whose behalf a confessed dowry has been constituted by the husband before the celebration of the marriage, or within the first year of such marriage, may require, at any time, that the said husband secure it with a mortgage, provided she judicially proves the existence of the dotal property or of other similar or equivalent property, at the time she instituted her claims.

1346. Dowry may be either estimated or not estimated.

It shall be estimated, if the property of which it consists was appraised, at the time of the constitution of the dowry, and when the ownership was transferred to the husband who became obliged to return its value.

It shall not be estimated, if the wife retains the ownership of the property, whether appraised or not, and the husband remains bound to return the same property.

When the marriage contract does not state the kind of dowry, it shall be considered as not estimated.

1347. The increase or the impairment of the estimated dowry shall be on the account of the husband, who shall remain bound only to return the value at which he received it and to guarantee the rights of the wife, in the manner provided in the following articles.

1348. When the husband who has received the estimated dowry believes himself injured by its appraisal, he may ask that the error or injury be remedied.

1349. The husband is bound:

1. To inscribe in his name and to mortgage in behalf of his wife the real property and real rights which he received as estimated dowry, or other sufficient ones to secure the value of the same.

2. To secure with a sufficient special mortgage all other property which has been delivered to him as estimated dowry.

1350. The sum which must be secured by reason of the estimated dowry shall not exceed the amount of the valuation, and if that of said dowry be reduced, the mortgage shall be reduced in the same proportion.

1351. The mortgage, constituted by the husband in behalf of the wife, shall be security for the restitution of the property or of the valuation of the same, in case it should be effected according to the laws and with the limitations therein provided, and it shall become ineffectual and may be cancelled when, for any lawful cause, the husband may be exempted from the obligation of making the restitution.

1352. A married woman of full age may herself exact the constitution of the mortgage and the inscription of the property referred to in article 1349.

When she has not yet celebrated the marriage, or if having contracted it, she is a minor, said right should be enforced in her name and the qualification of the sufficiency of the mortgage, which is constituted, shall be passed upon by the father, the mother, or the person who has given the dowry or the properties which must be secured.

In default of these persons, and when the woman is a minor, whether she be married or not, the guardian, the *protutor*, family council or any of its members, shall require that the same rights be enforced.

1353. When the guardian, *protutor* or the family council do not ask for the constitution of the mortgage, the Public Attorney shall officially, or upon the request of any other party, demand that the husband be compelled to execute the same.

The Municipal Judge shall also be obliged to interest and to urge the Public Attorney to comply with the provisions of the preceding paragraph.

1354. When the husband has no property of his own upon which to constitute the mortgage, stated in article 1349, he shall remain bound to constitute the same on the first real estate or real rights which he may acquire.

1355. Whenever whole or a part of the property which constitutes the estimated dowry consists in government securities or stocks listed on the exchange (*efectos publicos ó valores cotizables*), and as long as the value is not secured by the mortgage which the husband is bound to constitute, the titles, inscriptions or documents representing that value, shall be deposited, in the name of the wife and with the knowledge of the husband, in any of the public institutions designated for that purpose.

1356. When the husband is bound so secure, with a mortgage, personal property belonging to not estimated dowry, the provisions of articles 1349 to 1355, with regard to estimated dowries, shall apply.

SECTION SECOND.

*Administration and usufruct of the dowry.**

Article **1357.** The husband is the administrator and usufructuary of the properties which constitute the not estimated dowry with the rights and obligations annexed to the administration and the usufruct, but with the modifications set forth in the following articles.

1358. The husband is not bound to give the bonds required from common usufructuaries, but is obliged to inscribe in the Registry, when they are not registered, in the name of the wife and as not estimated dowry, all the real property and real rights which he may receive as such, and to constitute a sufficient mortgage as security for his administration, usufruct, and restitution of the personal property.

1359. Notwithstanding the provisions of the two preceding articles, the husband who receives bonds, stocks, or values listed on the exchange, or perishable property, as estimated or not estimated dowry, and has not secured them with a mortgage, may, nevertheless, substitute them with others, equivalent to the same, with the consent of the wife, if she is of age or of the persons referred to in article 1352, if she is a minor.

Said property may also be alienated by the husband with the consent of the wife, and, when proper, with that of the aforesaid persons,

---

* Digesto, book 23, tit. 3, laws 7, 10, par. 3. Codigo, book 5, tit. 12, laws 20, 30. Part. 4, tit. 11, laws 1, 7, 15, 18. Law of Mortgage, arts. 168, 169, 177, 188. Project of 1851, art. 1280.

under the condition that the amount of its value shall be invested in other property, bonds or rights equally safe.

1360. The wife preserves her dominion over the property which constitutes the not estimated dowry, and, consequently, to her belongs also any increase or decrease the same may have.

The husband is only liable for the impairment which such property may suffer by his fault or neglect.

1361. The wife may alienate, incumber or mortgage the property of the not estimated dowry, when she is of full age, with the license of the husband, and, when she is a minor, with judicial license and with the intervention of the persons stated in article 1352.

When she alienates said property, the husband shall be bound to constitute a mortgage, in the same manner and under the same conditions as in respect to the property of the estimated dowry.

1362. The property of the not estimated dowry shall be security for the usual daily expenses of the family, incurred by the wife or by her order, under the tacit assent of the husband, but in this case levy (*excusion*) shall first be made on the properties belonging to the conjugal society, and then on that belonging to the husband.

1363. The husband shall not, without the consent of the wife, lease for longer than six years the real property of the not estimated dowry.

In any case, the advancement of the rents or leases, made to the husband for more than three years, shall be considered void.

1364. When the consorts, by virtue of the provisions of article 1315, have stipulated that the legal conjugal community shall not exist between them, without stating the rules by which their property is to be governed, or if the wife or her heirs renounce said community, the provisions of this chapter shall be observed and the husband in compliance with the obligations stated in the same chapter, shall receive all the fruits which should be considered as earnings of the community, in case it should exist.

SECTION THIRD.

*Restitution of dowry.**

Article **1365.** Dowry shall be restored to the wife or to her heirs in the following cases:

1. When the marriage is dissolved or declared null.

---

* Digesto, book 25, tit. 1, law 5. Codigo, book 8, tit. 18, law 12. Part. 4, tit. 11, laws 15, 18, 23, 26, 31, 32; id. 5, tit. 14, law 50; id. 5, tit. 13, law 23. Recopilada, book 12, tit. 28. Fuero Real, book 3, tit. 6, law 6; id., book 3, tit. 4, law 10. Law of Mortgage, arts. 172, 173, 175, 177.

2. When the administration of the dowry is transferred to the wife in the case provided by the second paragraph of article 225.

3. When the courts order it, in accordance with the provisions of this Code.

1366. The restitution of the estimated dowry shall be effected by the husband or his heirs delivering to the wife or her heirs the value at which it was estimated when the husband received the same.

From the value shall be deducted:

1. The dowry constituted in favor of the daughters, in so far as it can be imputed to the sole property of the wife, in accordance with article 1343.

2. The debts contracted by the wife before the marriage and which the husband may have paid.

1367. The real property of the not estimated dowry shall be restored in the condition in which it may be found; and when it has been alienated, the proceeds of the sale shall be delivered, deducting what may have been applied to the payment of the exclusive obligations of the wife.

1368. The payments of the expenses and the improvements, made by the husband in the not estimated dotal property, shall be governed by what is provided with regard to the possessor in good faith.

1369. After the marriage is dissolved or has been declared null, the husband or his heirs may be compelled to the immediate restitution of the real and personal property of the not estimated dowry.

1370. Until one year, to be counted from the dissolution of the marriage, has elapsed, neither the husband nor his heirs can be required to return the money, the perishable property and public effects which do not exist totally or in part upon the dissolution of the conjugal society.

1371. The husband or his heirs shall pay to the wife or to her heirs, from the date of the dissolution of the marriage until the restitution of the dowry, the legal interest on what they are bound to return in money, also that on the amount of the perishable property and what may be produced by public values or credits, in the meantime, according to their condition or nature, without conflict with the provision of article 1379.

1372. In default of an agreement between the persons interested, or of an express stipulation in the marriage contract, the credit of not estimated dowry or the part of the same which is not restored in the same property which had constituted the dowry or in those which substituted the same, shall be restored and paid in money.

From this rule is excepted the restitution of the value of personal dotal property which does not exist, and said value may be paid with other personal property of the same kind, if there is any such remaining to the conjugal society.

The restitution of the perishable property, not appraised, shall be made with an equal amount of property of the same kind.

1373. In the same manner, as designated in the preceding article, shall be restored the part of the dotal credit consisting:

1. Of marriage donations, legally made by the husband to his wife to be effectual after his death, excepting the provisions in respect to the consort who has acted in bad faith, in the case of the nullity of the marriage, and in that of article 1440.

2. Of indemnities which the husband may owe to the wife in accordance with this Code.

1374. The daily bed, with whatever constitutes it, and the clothing and dresses for ordinary use of the widow shall be delivered to her without charging them to her dowry.

1375. The credits or rights brought to the marriage as not estimated dowry, or assigned with this character, shall be delivered in the condition in which they are, at the time of the dissolution of the marriage, unless through negligence of the husband, said credits have not been collected or have become unrecoverable, in which cases, the wife and her heirs shall have the right of exacting their value.

1376. When two or more dowries are to be restored, at the same time, each of them shall be paid with the property which may exist and originally belonged to them respectively, and, in default of the same, if the estate inventoried is not sufficient to cover both of them, their payment shall be effected according to priority of time.

1377. For the liquidation and restitution of the not estimated dowry, the following items shall be deducted in case they have been paid by the husband:

1. The amount of the judicial costs and expenses incurred for the collection and defense of the dowry.

2. The debts and obligations inherent to or affected by the dowry, which in accordance with the marriage contract or with the provisions of this Code are not chargeable to the conjugal community.

3. The sums for which the wife may be peculiarly liable, in accordance with the provisions of this Code.

1378. At the time of the restitution of the dowry, the marriage donations legally made to the husband by his wife shall be paid to him without conflict with the provisions of this Code for the cases of separation of property, or that of nullity of the marriage in which bad faith has existed on the part of one of the consorts.

1379. When the marriage is dissolved by the death of the wife, the interests or fruits of the dowry which are to be restored shall commence to run in favor of the heirs from the day of the dissolution of the marriage.

When the marriage is dissolved by the death of the husband, the wife may, either demand the interests and fruits of one year of the dowry, or that support be given her from the estate of the inheritance of the husband. In any case, the widow shall receive from the estate the value of the mourning apparel.

1380. After the dissolution of the marriage, the pending fruits or rents shall be divided *pro rata* among the surviving consort and the heirs of the deceased, in accordance with the rules established for the cases in which the usufruct ceases.

CHAPTER FOURTH.

*Parapherna.**

Article **1381.** Parapherna is the property which the wife brings to the marriage, not included in the dowry, and what she acquires after the constitution of the same and which is not added to such dowry.

1382. The wife retains dominion over the parapherna.

1383. The husband shall not institute actions of any kind whatever, in regard to the parapherna, without the intervention of the wife or her consent.

1384. The wife shall have the management of the parapherna, unless she has delivered the same to her husband, before a Notary, with the intent that he may administer said property.

In this case, the husband is bound to constitute a mortgage for the value of the personal property which he receives, or to secure said property, in the manner provided for dotal property.

1385. The fruits of the parapherna form a part of the capital of the conjugal community, and are liable for the payment of the expenses of the marriage state.

The property itself also shall be liable, in the case of article 1362, whenever that of the husband and the dotals are insufficient to pay the liabilities set forth in the same.

1386. The personal obligations of the husband shall not be paid out of the fruits of the parapherna, unless it is proven that they were incurred for the benefit of the family.

1387. The wife shall not alienate, incumber or mortgage the parapherna without the permission of the husband, nor appear in

* Part. 4, tit. 11, law 17. Code Repetitie Prelectiones, book 50, tit. 14, law 8. Law of Mortgage, art. 169; No. 3, arts. 180 to 188. Law of Civil Marriage, art. 49.

court to litigate about the same, unless she has been judicially authorized for that purpose.

1388. When the parapherna, the administration of which has been reserved by the wife, consists in money or public stocks or valuable personal property, the husband shall have a right to require that said property be deposited or invested in such a way that the alienation or pignoration of the same should be impossible without his consent.

1389. The husband, to whom the parapherna has been delivered, shall be governed, with regard to the management of the same, by the provisions in respect to the property of the not estimated dowry.

1390. The alienation of the parapherna entitles the wife to demand the constitution of a mortgage for the amount of the value which the husband may have received. Both the husband and the wife may, in their respective cases, exercise, with regard to the value of the sale, the right granted by articles 1384 and 1388.

1391. The return of the parapherna, the management of which has been granted to the husband, shall take place in the same cases and in the same manner as that of property belonging to the not estimated dowry.

CHAPTER FIFTH.

Conjugal community.

SECTION FIRST.

*General provisions.**

Article **1392.** By virtue of the conjugal community, the earnings or profits indiscriminately obtained by either of the consorts, during the marriage, shall belong to the husband and the wife, share and share alike, when the marriage is dissolved.

1393. The conjugal community shall always begin on the same day that the marriage is celebrated.

Any stipulation to the contrary shall be void.

1394. This community cannot be renounced during the marriage, except in case of judicial separation.

When the renunciation takes place on account of a separation, or after the marriage has been dissolved or declared null, said renuncia-

---

* Estilo, laws 203, 205. Fuero Juzgo, book 4, tit. 2, law 17. Fuero Real, tit. 3, laws 1, 3. Nov. Recop., book 3, tit. 4. Toro, law 60. Part. 4, tit. 11, law 24.

tion shall be set forth in a public instrument, and the creditors shall have the right granted them in article 1001.

1395. The conjugal community shall be governed by the rules of the contract of partnership in all that does not conflict with the express provisions of this chapter.

SECTION SECOND.

Property belonging to each one of the consorts. *

Article **1396.** The following is the separate property of each of the consorts:

1. That brought to the marriage as his or her own.

2. That acquired under a lucrative title by either of them, during the marriage.

3. That acquired by right of redemption or by exchange for other property belonging to only one of the consorts.

4. That bought with money belonging exclusively to the wife or to the husband.

Col. 1782, 1783, 1788; Chile, 1726, 1727, 1732.

1397. A person giving or promising capital to the husband shall not be subject to eviction, except in case of fraud.

1398. Property, donated or left by will conjointly to the consorts and with designation of specified shares, shall belong as dowry to the wife and as capital to the husband, in the proportion directed by the donor or testator; and, in default of such designation, share and share alike, without conflict with provisions of article 637.

1399. When donations are onerous, the amount of the burdens shall be deducted from the dowry, or from the capital of the consort who makes them, provided they have been borne by the conjugal community.

1400. In case that any credit, payable within a certain number of years, or a pension for life belongs to either of the consorts, the provisions of article 1402 and 1403 shall be observed for determining what constitutes the dowry, and what forms the capital of the husband.

Col. 1792; Chile, 1736.

---

* Recopiladas, book 10, tit. 4, laws 1, 2, 5. Part. 4, tit. 11, law 22, sec. 33.

SECTION THIRD.

*Property of the conjugal community.**

Article **1401.** To the conjugal community belong:

1. Property acquired by onerous title, during the marriage, at the expense of the community property, whether the acquisition is made for the community or for only one of the consorts.

2. That obtained by the industry, salaries or work of the consorts or of either of them.

3. The fruits, rents, or interests collected or accrued during the marriage, and which come from the community property, or from that which belongs to either one of the consorts.

Col. 1781; Chile, 1725.

1402. Whenever a sum or credit, payable in a certain number of years, belongs to one of the consorts, the sums collected for installments due during the marriage shall not be community property, but shall be considered as capital of the husband or of the wife, according to whom the credit belongs.

1403. The right to an usufruct or pension, belonging to one of the consorts, either in perpetuity or for life, shall form part of his or her own property; but the fruits, pensions, and interests due, during the marriage, shall be community property.

In this provision is comprised the usufruct which the consorts have in the property of their children, even when they are of another marriage.

1404. The useful expenses, made on behalf of the private property of either one of the consorts, through advancements made by the community, or by the industry of husband or wife, are community property.

Buildings constructed, during the marriage, on land belonging to one of the consorts, shall also belong to the community, but the value of the land shall be paid to the consort owning the same.

1405. Whenever the dowry or the capital belonging to the husband consists, in whole or in part, of cattle existing at the time of the dissolution of the community, the heads of cattle, exceeding the number which were brought to the marriage, shall be considered as common property.

1406. The earnings obtained by the husband or wife by gambling or proceeding from other causes, exempted from restitution, shall

* Digesto, book 17, tit. 2, law 7; id., book 23, tit. 3, laws 66, 78; id., book 24, tit. 3, law 57. Fuero Real, book 3, tit. 4, laws 3, 9. Recopiladas, book 10, tit. 4, laws 1, 3, 5. Estilo, law 203.

belong to the conjugal community, without conflicting, in certain cases, with the provisions of the Penal Code.

1407. All the property of the marriage shall be considered as community property, until it is proven that it belongs exclusively to the husband or to the wife.

SECTION FOURTH.

*Charges and obligations of the conjugal community.**

Article **1408.** The conjugal community shall be responsible for:

1. All the debts and obligations contracted during the marriage by the husband, and also those contracted by the wife in the cases in which she can legally bind the community.

2. The arrears or interests, matured during the marriage, of obligations which affect the private property of the consorts as well as the community property.

3. The minor repairs or of mere preservation, made during the marriage, on the private property of the husband or the wife. Extensive repairs shall not be chargeable to the community.

4. Extensive or minor repairs of the property of the community.

5. The maintenance of the family and the education of the children in common, and of the legitimate children of only one of the consorts.

1409. The conjugal community shall also bear the amount of what has been donated or promised to the children in common by the husband, only for their establishment or for a professional career, or by both consorts by common consent, when it may not have been stipulated that it should be paid in whole or in part out of the private property of one of them.

Col. 1796, 1800; Chile, 1740, 1744.

1410. The payment of debts contracted by the husband or by the wife, before the marriage, shall not be borne by the community.

Neither shall it bear the payment of fines or pecuniary condemnations imposed on either of them.

However, the payment of debts contracted by the husband or the wife, prior to the marriage, and that of fines and condemnations imposed on either of them may be claimed against the community property, after covering the erogations, enumerated in article 1408, when the debtor consort has no private capital, or it be insufficient; but at the time of the liquidation of the community, the payments, made for the specified causes, shall be charged to said consort.

Col. 1806; Chile, 1750.

---

* Digesto, book 17, tit. 2, law 59, par. 1. Recopilada, book 10, tit. 3, law 4; id., book 10, tit. 4, law 9. Part. 5, tit. 10, laws 7, 13.

1411. What has been lost and paid for, during the marriage, by either of the consorts, in any kind of game whatever, shall not diminish his or her respective share in the community.

Whatever has been lost and not paid for by either of the consorts, in licit games, shall be charged to the conjugal community.

SECTION FIFTH.

*Administration of the conjugal community.**

Article **1412.** The husband is the administrator of the conjugal community, with the exception of what is prescribed in article 59.

Col. 1805; Chile, 1749.

1413. Besides the faculties which the husband has as administrator, he may alienate and burden by onerous title the property of the conjugal community without the consent of the wife.

Notwithstanding, every alienation or agreement which the husband may make, respecting said property in opposition to this Code or in fraud of the wife, shall not cause injury to her or to her heirs.

Col. 1807; Chile, 1751.

1414. The husband can dispose of his half of the property of the conjugal community only by testament.

1415. The husband may dispose of the property of the conjugal community for the purposes stated in article 1409.

He may also make moderate donations for objects of piety or beneficence, but without reserving to himself the usufruct.

1416. The wife cannot bind the property of the conjugal community without the consent of the husband.

The cases provided in articles 1362, 1441, and 1442 are excepted from this rule.

Col. 1808; Chile, 1752.

SECTION SIXTH.

Dissolution of the conjugal community.†

Article **1417.** The conjugal community expires on the dissolution of the marriage or when it is declared null.

The consort who, on account of his or her bad faith, caused the nullity, shall not share any part of the property of the community.

The conjugal society shall also terminate in the cases specified in article 1433.

Col. 1820; Chile, 1764.

* Part. 4, tit. 11, laws 7, 25. Recopilada, book 10, tit. 4, law 5. Nov. Recop., book 10, tit. 4, law 6. Law of Civil Marriage, art. 49.

†See legal foundations of restitution of dowry.

SECTION SEVENTH.

*Liquidation of the property of the conjugal community.**

Article **1418.** Upon the dissolution of the community, an inventory shall immediately be made, but the same shall not be required for the liquidation:

1. When, after the community is dissolved, one of the consorts or the persons holding rights under him have, in due time, renounced its effects and consequences.
2. When the separation of property has preceded the dissolution of the community.
3. In the case to which paragraph second of the preceding article refers.

In case of renunciation, the rights granted to the creditors by article 1101 shall always continue in force.

Col. 1821; Chile, 1765.

1419. The inventory shall comprise numerically (*numéricamente*) for the purpose of collating them, the sums, which having been paid by the conjugal society, are to be deducted from the dowry or from the capital of the husband, in accordance with articles 1366, 1377, and 1427.

The amount of the donations and alienations which may be considered illegal or fraudulent, as provided in article 1413, shall also be brought to collation.

1420. In the inventory shall not be included things constituting the bed and bedding (*lecho*) ordinarily used by the consorts. These things, as well as the clothing and dresses ordinarily used by the deceased consort, shall be delivered to the surviving one.

1421. When the inventory is completed, the dowry of the wife shall first be liquidated and paid, according to the rules, which for its restitution are determined in section third, chapter third of this title, and subject to the provisions of the following articles.

Col. 1832; Chile, 1776.

1422. After the dowry and the paripherna of the wife have been paid, the debts, charges, and obligations of the community shall be paid.

When the inventoried estate is not sufficient to satisfy all the provisions of this and the preceding article, the prescriptions of title seventeen of this book shall be observed.

---

* Recopilada, book 10, tit. 4, law 1. Fuero Real, book 3, tit. 3, laws 1, 3.

1423. After the debts, charges, and obligations of the community are paid, the capital of the husband shall be liquidated and paid, in so far as the inventoried estate may reach, making the corresponding deductions according to the same rules which are prescribed in article 1366, in reference to dowry.

1424. After the deductions from the inventoried estate, specified in the three preceding articles, have been made, the remainder of the same estate shall constitute the assets of the conjugal community.

1425. The losses or impairments which any personal property, belonging to either of the consorts, may have suffered even by unforeseen events (*vis major*) shall be paid out of the conjugal property, when any remains.

Those suffered by the real property shall not be payable, in any case, except those falling upon the dotal property, and which have been caused by the fault of the husband, when an indemnity shall be paid for them as provided in articles 1360 and 1373.

1426. The net remainder of the community property shall be divided, share and share alike, between the husband and the wife or their respective heirs.

1427. The mourning apparel of the widow shall be paid out of the estate of the inheritance of the husband, as provided in article 1379. The heirs of the husband shall pay it according to the standing and means of the decedent.

1428. In regard to making the inventory, rules for the appraisal and sales of the property belonging to the conjugal community, security and bonds for the respective dowries, and all other particulars, not expressly determined in the present chapter, the prescriptions of section fifth, chapter fifth, title third, book third, and sections second and third, chapter third of this title shall be observed.

1429. When the conjugal community is dissolved by the nullity of the marriage, the provisions of articles 1373, 1378, 1417 and 1440 shall be observed, and if it is dissolved by reason of the separation of the property of the consorts, what is prescribed in chapter sixth of this title shall be complied with.

1430. Support shall be given out of the property belonging to the community to the surviving consort and his or her children, pending the liquidation of the inventoried estate and until they have received their share; but it shall be deducted from their portion in so far as it exceeds what should have belonged to them as fruits or rents.

1431. Whenever the liquidation of the community properties of two or more marriages, contracted by the same person, has to be simultaneously effected in order to determine the estate of each community, every kind of evidence shall be admitted, in default of inventories;

and, in case of doubt, the community property shall be distributed between the different communities in proportion to the time of the duration of the same and to the property belonging to the respective consorts.

CHAPTER SIXTH.

*Separation of the property of the consorts and its administration by the wife during the marriage.**

Article **1432.** In default of express declarations in the marriage contract, the separation of the property of the consorts, during the marriage, shall only take place by virtue of a judicial decree, except in the case provided by article 50.

1433. The husband and the wife may demand the separation of the property, and it shall be decreed, whenever the consort of the plaintiff has been condemned to a penalty to which civil interdiction is annexed, or has been declared an absentee or has given cause for the divorce.

In order that the separation may be decreed, it shall be sufficient to present the final sentence rendered against the culpable or absent consort in each one of the three cases, above stated.

1434. After the separation of property is ordered, the legal conjugal community becomes dissolved, and its liquidation shall be made according to the provisions of this Code.

Husband and wife, however, shall reciprocally attend to their maintenance during the separation, and to the maintenance of the children, as well as the education of the same; each one in proportion to his or her respective means.

1435. The power to administer the property of the marriage, granted to the husband by this Code, shall subsist when the separation has been granted on his petition; but, in such case, the wife shall not have any right to the future profits of the community, and the rights and obligations of the husband shall be governed by the provisions of sections second and third, chapter third of this title.

1436. When the separation has been granted on the petition of the wife by the civil interdiction of the husband, the administration of all the property belonging to the marriage, and the rights to all the future community property, shall be transferred to the wife to the exclusion of the husband.

When the separation is granted because the husband has been declared an absentee, or because he has given cause for divorce, the wife

---

* Codigo, book 5, tit. 12, law 29. Penal Code, arts. 43, 54, 57. Law of Civil Procedure, art. 2031. Law of Mortgage, arts. 2, No. 4, 25, 27, 42. Project of 1851, art. 1364.

shall enter upon the administration of her dowry, and of all further property which may have been apportioned to her, as a result of the liquidation.

In every case, to which this article refers, the wife shall remain obliged to comply with all that is prescribed in paragraph second of article 1434.

1437. The demand for separation and the final sentence in which it is declared, when rendered about real property, must be noted and inscribed respectively in the corresponding Registries of Property.

1438. Separation of the property shall not injure the rights previously acquired by creditors.

1439. Whenever the separation ceases by reconciliation, in cases of divorce, or, because, in the other cases the causes have disappeared, the property belonging to the marriage shall be governed by the same rules as before the separation, without injury to what may have been lawfully done during the same.

The consorts, at the time of their reuniting, shall specify in a public instrument the property which they bring anew, and such property shall be that forming the private estate of each one of them respectively.

In the case provided in this article, all said property shall always be considered as new property brought to the marriage, even when it is the same, either partially or wholly, as existed before the liquidation made on account of the separation.

1440. Separation shall not entitle the consorts to exercise the rights provided under the presumption of death of one of them, nor those granted to them by articles 1374 and 1420, neither shall it injure them in the exercise of the same, when such case occurs, except as provided in article 73.

1441. The administration of the property belonging to the marriage shall be transferred to the wife:

1. Whenever she is the guardian of the husband in accordance with article 220.

2. When she asks for the declaration of absence of her husband, in accordance with articles 183 and 185.

3. In the case stated in paragraph first of article 1436.

The courts shall also confer the administration upon the wife, with such limitations as they may consider convenient, when the husband is a fugitive or has been declared contumacious in a criminal prosecution, or if, when he is absolutely incapacitated for the administration, he has taken no steps in respect thereto.

Col. 1814; Chile, 1758.

1442. The wife, upon whom the administration of all the property of the marriage may devolve, shall have, in respect thereto, the identical powers and liabilities as the husband when he exercises it, but always subject to what is provided in the last paragraph of the preceding article, and in article 1444.

Col. 204; Chile, 159.

1443. The administration of her dowry shall be transferred to the wife, in the case provided by article 225, and when the court orders it by virtue of the provisions of article 441; but she shall remain subject to what is prescribed in paragraph second of article 1434.

GENERAL PROVISION.

Article **1444.** During the marriage, the wife can neither alienate nor incumber, without judicial permission, the real property which may have been allotted to her, in case of separation, nor that, the administration of which, has been transferred to her.

Such permission shall be granted whenever the convenience or necessity of the alienation be justified.

When it refers to public bonds or stocks of mercantile enterprises, and companies and cannot be delayed without serious or imminent injury to the estate in administration, the wife, with the intervention of an agent or broker, may sell them placing the proceeds in judicial deposit, until the approval of a competent Judge or tribunal is obtained.

The agent or broker shall always be personally responsible for the making of the consignation or deposit to which the preceding paragraph refers.

TITLE IV.

Contract of purchase and sale.

CHAPTER FIRST.

*Nature and form of this contract.**

Article **1445.** By the contract of purchase and sale, one of the contracting parties binds himself to deliver a specified thing and the

* Digesto, book 18, tit. 1, law 7, par. 1; 34, par. 5; id., book 18, tit. 6, laws 4, par. 1, 8; id., book 19, tit. 1, law 6, par. 1; id., book 19, tit. 5, law 5, par. 1. Codigo, tit. 54, law 6; id., tit. 64, law 1; id., book 4, tit. 38, law 15. Instituciones, book 3, tit. 14; id., book 3, tit. 24, par. 1. Part. 5, tit. 5, laws 1, 7, 9, 10, 23, 24, 25. Nov. Recop., book 10, tit. 1, law 1; id., book 10, tit. 12, law 11. Fuero Real, book 3, tit. 10, law 2. Law of January 10, and Regulation of June 13, 1879.

other (binds himself) to pay a certain price for it, either in money or in something (*signo*) representing the same.

Chile, 1793; Col. 1849.

1446. When the price of the sale consists partly in money and partly in something else, the contract shall be qualified by the manifest intention of the contracting parties. When this intention does not appear, the contract shall be considered as a barter, if the value of the thing given as a part of the price exceeds that of the money or its equivalent; and, otherwise, it shall be considered as a sale.

Col. 1850; Chile, 1794.

1447. In order that the price may be held as certain, it shall be sufficient that it be certain with reference to another thing also certain, or that the determination of the same be left to the will of a specified person.

When such person cannot or will not fix the price, the contract shall be inoperative.

Col. 1864; Chile, 1808.

1448. The price of bonds, grain, liquids, and of other perishable things shall also be held as certain, when the prices fixed are the same as the things, if sold, would have on a certain day on the exchange or market, or when a certain amount is fixed above or below the price of such day, exchange or market, provided said price be certain.

Col. 1864; Chile, 1808.

1449. The determination of the price shall never be left to the judgment of one of the contracting parties.

Col. 1865; Chile, 1809.

1450. The sale shall be perfected between vendor and vendee and shall be binding on both of them, if they have agreed upon the thing, object of the contract, and as to the price, even when neither one nor the other has been delivered.

Col. 1857; Chile, 1805.

1451. A promise to sell or to buy, when there has been an agreement about the thing and the price, gives a right to both the parties reciprocally to claim the compliance with the contract.

Whenever a promise of purchase and sale cannot be complied with, the provisions about obligations and contracts, set forth in this present book, shall govern the vendor and the vendee, according to the case.

1452. The injury to or the profit of the thing sold shall, after the contract is perfected, be governed by the provisions of articles 1096 and 1182.

This rule shall be applied to the sale of perishable things, made independently and for a single price, or without consideration as to weight, number, or measure.

If the perishable things are sold for a price fixed with relation to weight, number, or measure, the risk shall not be imputed to the vendee, until they have been weighed, counted, or measured, unless the vendee is in default.

Col. 1876; Chile, 1820.

1453. A sale, made subject to approval or trial of the things sold, and the sales of things which are customarily tested or tried before being received, shall always be considered as made under suspensive conditions.

Col. 1879; Chile, 1823.

1454. When earnest or binding money has been given in the contract of purchase and sale, the contract may be rescinded, when the vendee agrees to forfeit the money, or the vendor to return double the amount of it.

Col. 1859; Chile, 1803.

1455. The expenses of the execution of a public deed shall be on account of the vendor, and those of the first copy and subsequent ones, after the sale, shall be charged to the vendee, unless the contrary is stipulated.

Col. 1862; Chile, 1806.

1456. Forcible expropriation on account of public utility shall be governed by the provisions of special laws.

CHAPTER SECOND.

*Capacity to purchase or sell.**

Article **1457.** The contract of purchase and sale may be entered into by all persons who, according to this Code, are authorized to bind themselves, with the modifications, however, contained in the following articles.

Col. 1851; Chile, 1795.

* Digesto, book 18, tit. 1, law 34, par. 7; id., book 19, tit. 1, law 13, par. 25; id., book 24, tit. 1, law 5, 35, 52; id., book 26, tit. 8, law 5, par. 5. Part. 4, tit. 11, law 4; id. 5, tit. 5, laws 2, 4. Codigo, book 4, tit. 38, law 5. Toro, law 55. Recopilada, book 10, tit. 12, law 1. Penal Code, arts. 411, 412.

1458. The husband and the wife cannot reciprocally sell any property to each other, except in the cases in which they have stipulated about the separation of their property or when a judicial separation of the same property exists, authorized, under the provisions of chapter sixth, title third, of this book.

Chile, 1796; Col. 1852.

1459. The following persons cannot acquire by purchase, even at public or judicial auction, neither in person nor by an intermediate representative:

1. The guardian or *protutor* as to the property of the person or persons who are under their guardianship.
2. The attorneys as to the property of which they have been given charge to administer or sell.
3. Executors as to the property intrusted to their care.
4. Public officials as to the property of the State, municipalities, towns, and also of public institutions, the administration of which has been intrusted to them.

This provision shall apply to Judges and experts who, in any way whatever, intervene in the sale.

5. Magistrates, Judges, Public Attorney, and their assistants, clerks of tribunals and courts, and officials of justice as to the property and rights about which litigation is pending before the tribunal in the jurisdiction or territory over which they exercise their respective functions; this prohibition includes the act of acquiring by assignment.

From this rule shall be excepted the cases in which hereditary action among co-heirs are dealt with, or of assignments in payment of debts, or of warranty of the goods they may possess.

The prohibition contained in this number shall comprise the lawyers and attorneys as to the property and rights, matters of the suit, in which they intervene by virtue of their profession or office.

Col. 1853; Chile, 1797.

CHAPTER THIRD.

*Effects of the contract of purchase and sale when the thing sold has been lost.**

Article **1460.** When, at the time of making the sale, the thing, object of the contract, has been wholly lost, the contract shall be ineffectual.

*** Digesto, book 18, tit. 1, law 15. Part. 5, tit. 5, law 14. Commercial Code, art. 330.**

But if the thing is lost only in part, the vendee shall choose either to withdraw from the contract or to claim the existing part, paying its price, in proportion to the total sum agreed upon.

CHAPTER FOURTH.

Obligations of the vendor.

SECTION FIRST.

General provisions. *

Article **1461**. A vendor is bound to deliver and warrant the thing, object of the sale.

Chile, 1824; Col. 1880.

SECTION SECOND.

Delivery of the thing sold.†

Article **1462**. A thing sold shall be considered as delivered, when it is placed in the hands and possession of the vendee.

When the sale is effected by a public instrument, the execution of the same shall be equivalent to the delivery of the thing, object of the contract, provided that in the same instrument the contrary does not appear or may be clearly inferred.

Chile, 1824; Col. 1880.

1463. Except in the cases stated in the preceding article, the delivery of personal property shall be made by the delivery of the keys of the place or depository where it is stored or kept, and by the mere consent and agreement of the contracting parties, if the thing sold cannot be transferred to the possession of the vendee, at the time of the sale, or if the latter already held it in his possession for any other cause.

Col. 754; Chile, 684.

---

* Part. 5, tit. 5, law 32.

† Digesto, book 8, tit. 1, law 20; id., book 18, tit. 1, law 40, par. 20; id., book 18, tit. 6, law 7; id., book 19, tit. 1, law 1, 1, par. 1, 2, 13, par. 8, 14; id., book 35, tit. 1, law 17; id., book 21, tit. 2, laws 69, par. 6, 45. Instituciones, par. 41. Codigo, book 4, tit. 49, laws 13, 16; id., book 8, tit. 45, law 5; id., book 8, tit. 54, law 1. De regulis juris, par. 19. Part. 3, tit. 28, laws 46, 47; id. 3, tit. 30, law 1, 7, 8; id. 5, tit. 5, laws 23, 32, 50. Nov. Recop., book 16, tit. 12, law 11. Recopilada, book 10, tit. 1, law 3. Orden. de Alcala, tit. 17, special law. Law of Mortgage, arts. 17, 23, 25, 33.

1464. With regard to incorporeal things, the provision of paragraph second of article 1462 shall govern. In any other case in which this paragraph cannot be applied, the fact of placing the titles of ownership in the possession of the vendee or the use which the vendee may make of his right with the consent of the vendor shall be considered as a delivery.

Col. 756, 761; Chile, 686, 699.

1465. The expenses of the delivery of the thing sold shall be borne by the vendor, and those of the removal or transportation of the same by the vendee, except in case of special stipulation.

Chile, 1825; Col. 1881.

1466. A vendor shall not be bound to deliver the thing sold, when the vendee has not paid the price, or when a term for such payment has not been designated in the contract.

Col. 1882; Chile, 1826.

1467. Neither shall the vendor be bound to deliver the thing sold, when a delay or time for payment has been agreed upon, and it is discovered after the sale that the vendee is insolvent to such a degree that the vendor is in imminent danger of losing the price.

From this rule is excepted the case in which the vendee gives security for the payment within the time agreed upon.

Col. 1882; Chile, 1826.

1468. A vendor is bound to deliver the thing sold in the condition in which it existed on the completion of the contract.

All the fruits shall belong to the vendee from the day on which the contract was perfected.

1469. The obligation to deliver the thing sold includes that of placing in possession of the vendee all that is set forth in the contract, according to the following rules:

When the sale of real property has been made and its dimensions stated at the rate of a certain price for an unit of measure or number, the vendor shall be bound to deliver to the vendee, if the latter requires it, all that has been mentioned in the contract; but when this is not possible, the vendee may choose between proportional reduction of the price or the rescission of the contract, provided that, in this last case, the decrease of the tenement, is not inferior to the tenth part of the dimensions attributed to it.

The same thing shall be observed, even when the dimensions appear to be the same, if any part of the tenement is not of the quality stated in the contract.

The rescission, in this case, shall only take place, at the will of the vendee, when the inferior value of the thing sold exceeds the tenth part of the price agreed upon.

Col. 1884, 1888; Chile, 1828, 1832.

1470. When, in the case of the preceding article, there are greater dimensions or number in real property, than those stated in the contract, the vendee shall be bound to pay the price of the excess, if the greater dimensions or number does not exceed the one-twentieth part of those set forth in the contract; but when it surpasses such one-twentieth part, the vendee may choose between paying the greater value of the estate or withdrawing from the contract.

Col. 1888; Chile, 1832.

1471. In the sale of a parcel of real estate made for a fixed price and not at the rate of a specified sum for an unity of measure or number, the increase or decrease of the same shall not be considered, even when greater or less dimensions or amount than that stated in the contract may be found.

The same provision shall apply when two or more tenements are sold for a single price, but, if besides mentioning the boundaries, indispensable in every conveyance of real property, their dimensions and number are designated in the contract, the vendor shall be bound to deliver all that is included within such boundaries, even when they exceed the dimensions or number specified in the contract; and, if he is not able to do it, he shall suffer a reduction in the price, in proportion to what is wanting in the dimensions or number, unless the contract be annulled because the vendee does not accept the default of delivery of what had been stipulated.

Col. 1887; Chile, 1831.

1472. Actions, arising from the three preceding articles, shall be prescribed after six months, counted from the day of the delivery.

Col. 1890; Chile, 1834.

1473. When the same thing has been sold to different vendees, the ownership shall be transferred to the person who first took possession of it in good faith, if the thing is personal.

When the thing is a piece of real property, it shall belong to the person acquiring it who first inscribed it in the Registry.

When there is no inscription, the property shall belong to the person who first took possession of it in good faith, and, in default of said possession, to the person who presents the oldest title, provided there is good faith.

Col. 1873; Chile, 1817.

SECTION THIRD.

*Warranty.**

Article **1474.** By virtue of the warranty to which article 1461 refers, the vendor shall warrant to the vendee:

1. The lawful and peaceful possession of the thing sold.
2. That there are no hidden vices or defects in said thing.

Col. 1893; Chile, 1837.

§ 1°.

Warranty in case of eviction.†

Article **1475.** Eviction shall take place, when by a final sentence and by virtue of a right prior to the sale, the vendee is deprived of the whole or of a part of the thing purchased.

The vendor shall be liable for the eviction even when nothing has been stipulated about it in the contract.

The contracting parties may, however, increase, decrease, or suppress this legal obligation of the vendor.

Col. 1874; Chile, 1838.

1476. Any stipulation exempting the vendor from the obligation of answering for the eviction shall be void, whenever there is bad faith on his part.

Col. 1898; Chile, 1842.

1477. When a vendee has renounced the right of warranty in the case of eviction and it occurs, the vendor shall only be bound to deliver the price which the thing had, at the time of the eviction, unless the vendee has made the renunciation, knowing the risk of eviction and submitting himself to the consequences thereof.

Chile, 1852; Col. 1909.

1478. When a warranty has been stipulated or when nothing has been agreed upon about this point, if the eviction has been effected, the vendee shall have the right to claim from the vendor:

---

* Fuero Viejo, tit. 1, law 9; id., tit. 2, laws 1, 2, 3. Part. 5, tit. 5, laws 32, 64.

†Digesto, book 19, tit. 1, law 6, par. 9 and 11, par. 18, 41, 45, par. 1, id., book 21, tit. 1, laws 38, par. 14, 49, 61; id., book 21, tit. 2, laws 57, par. 1; 66, par. 3, 70, 74, par. 1. Codigo, book 4, tit. 58, law 4. Part. 5, tit. 5, laws 32, 33, 34, 35, 36, 63. Fuero Real, book 3, tit. 10, law 7. Com. Code, art. 345.

1. The restitution of the price which the thing sold had at the time of the eviction, whether it be greater or less than that of the sale.

2. The fruits or proceeds, when he has been condemned to deliver them to the person who won the suit instituted against such vendee.

3. The costs incurred in the suits which caused the eviction, and, in proper cases, the costs of the suit instituted against the vendor for the warranty.

4. The expenses of the contract, when the vendee has paid them.

5. The damages and interests and the voluntary expenses or of mere recreation or ornamentation, when the sale was made in bad faith.

Chile, 1847; Col. 1904.

1479. When the vendee loses, on account of the eviction, a part of the thing sold of such importance, in relation to the whole, that he would not have purchased it without such part, he may claim the rescission of the contract; but under the obligation of returning the thing without other incumbrances than those it had when he acquired it.

The same provision shall be observed when two or more things are conjointly sold for a total price, or a partial price for each one of them, when it clearly appears that the vendee would not have purchased one without the other.

1480. A warranty cannot be claimed until a final sentence has been rendered by which the vendee is condemned to lose the thing acquired or a part of it.

Col. 1894; Chile, 1838.

1481. A vendor shall be bound to the corresponding warranty, whenever it is proved that he was given notice of the demand for eviction on petition of the vendee. In default of this notice, the vendor shall not be bound to the warranty.

Col. 1899; Chile, 1843.

1482. A defendant vendee shall ask, within the term fixed by the Code of Civil Procedure for answering the demand, that notice thereof be given to the vendor or vendors with the least possible delay.

This notification shall be made in the manner provided by the same law for the summoning of defendants.

The term for answering the complaint granted to the vendee shall be suspended until the expiration of that granted to the vendor or vendors for appearing and answering the complaint; said terms shall be the same granted to all defendants by the aforesaid law of Civil

Procedure, and shall be counted from the notification provided by the first paragraph of this article.

When the persons summoned for eviction do not appear, in time and form, the term in which to answer the complaint shall continue with regard to the vendee.

1483. When the tenement sold is incumbered by any nonapparent burden or easement which is not stated in the deed, but is of such a nature that it must be presumed that the vendee would not have acquired it if he was aware of the same, he may ask for the rescission of the contract, unless he prefers the corresponding indemnity.

During a year, to be counted from the date of the execution of the deed, the vendee may either exercise the rescissory action or claim an indemnity.

After the lapse of one year, he can only claim such indemnity within an equal period, to be counted from the date on which the lien or easement was discovered by him.

§ 2°.

*Warranty against hidden defects or burdens of the thing sold.**

Article **1484.** A vendor is bound to give a warranty against hidden defects in the thing sold, when these defects render it unfit for the use for which it was intended, or when they diminish said use in such a way that had the vendee known them, he would not have acquired it, or would have given a lower price for it; but said vendor shall not be liable for the patent defects or those which may be visible, neither for those which are not in sight, when the vendee is an expert and by reason of his office or profession ought easily to perceive them.

Col. 1914; Chile, 1857.

1485. The vendor is responsible to the vendee for the warranty against vices or hidden defects in the thing sold, even when the same were unknown to him.

This provision shall not rule when the contrary has been stipulated and the vendor was not aware of such vices or hidden defects.

Col. 1916; Chile, 1859.

1486. In the cases of the two preceding articles, the vendee may elect, either to withdraw from the contract, the expenses which he

* Digesto, book 18, tit. 1, laws 13, 43, par. 2, 45; id. 19, tit. 1, law 13; id., book 21, tit. 1, laws 1, par. 8; 1, par. 3, 18, 19, par. 28, 25, 27; 11, par. 6, 14, last par., 31, par. 11, 34, 36, 38, 48, par. 3, 52. Part. 5, tit. 5, laws 63, 64, 65, 66.

incurred being returned to him, or to demand a proportional reduction of the price, according to the judgment of experts.

When the vendor knew the vices or hidden defects in the thing sold, and did not give notice of them to the vendee, the latter shall have the same option, and, furthermore, he shall be indemnified for the damages and injuries, should he choose the rescission.

Col. 1917; Chile, 1860.

1487. When the thing sold is lost on account of hidden vices, and the vendor was aware of them, he shall bear the loss, and return the price and pay the expenses of the contract, with damages and injuries. When he was not aware of them, he shall only return the price and pay the expenses of the contract, which may have been paid by the vendee.

Col. 1918; Chile, 1861.

1488. When the thing sold has any hidden vice, at the time of the sale, and is lost afterwards by an unforeseen event (*vis major*), or by fault of the vendee, the latter may claim from the vendor the price he paid, deducting the value which the thing had when lost.

When the vendor acted in bad faith, he shall pay damages and interests to the vendee.

Col. 1919; Chile, 1862.

1489. The liability for damages and injuries shall never take place in judicial sales, but all the other provisions of the preceding articles shall be applied.

Col. 1922; Chile, 1865.

1490. Actions growing out of the provisions of the five preceding articles shall be extinguished after six months, to be counted from the delivery of the thing sold.

Chile, 1866; Col. 1923.

1491. When two or more animals are sold together, whether it be for a lump sum or by fixing a separate price for each one of them, the redhibitory vice of each one shall only cause the redhibition of the same and not that of the others, unless it appears that the vendee would not have bought the sound one or ones without defective ones.

The latter is presumed when a team, yoke, pair or set is bought, even when a separate price has been fixed for each one of the animals composing the same.

Col. 1921; Chile, 1864.

1492. The provision of the preceding article, with regard to the sale of animals, shall be understood applicable also to the sale of any other things.

1493. Warranty for the hidden vices of animals and cattle shall not take place in the sales made at fairs or public auctions, nor that of riding beasts, sold as condemned, except in the case determined in the following article.

1494. Animals and cattle suffering from contagious diseases shall not be objects of a contract of sale. Any contracts made with respect to the same shall be null and void.

A contract of sale of animals and cattle shall also be null and void, when the use or service for which they were acquired is stated, and they are found useless therefor.

1495. When the hidden vice of animals, even if they have been subject to a professional inspection, is of such a nature that the knowledge of experts is not sufficient to discover it, it shall be considered as redhibitory.

But when the veterinarian (*professor*), through ignorance or bad faith, shall fail to discover or to give notice of it, he shall be liable for damages and injuries.

1496. The redhibitory action, based on the vices or defects of animals, shall be instituted within forty days, to be counted from the delivery of the same to the vendee, unless owing to the usages in each locality, longer or shorter terms are established.

This action, in the sale of animals, shall only be enforced in reference to the vices and defects of the same, determined by law or by local usages.

1497. When the animal dies, within three days after it has been bought, the vendor shall be responsible, provided that the disease that caused the death, according to the judgment of veterinarians (*professors*), existed before the contract.

1498. When the sale is rescinded, the animal shall be returned in the condition in which it was sold and delivered, and the vendee shall be liable for any injury caused by his negligence and which does not arise from the redhibitory vice or defect.

1499. In the sale of animals and cattle with redhibitory vices, the vendee shall also have the power set forth in article 1486; but he shall make use of the same within the same term which has been respectively determined for the exercise of the redhibitory action.

CHAPTER FIFTH.

*Obligations of the vendee.**

Article **1500.** A vendee is bound to pay the price of the thing sold at the time and place stipulated in the contract.

When the time and place have not been fixed, the payment shall be made at the time and place where the thing sold is delivered.

Col. 1928; Chile, 1872.

1501. In the three following cases the vendee shall owe interest from the time the thing is delivered, until the payment of the price:

1. When it has been so stipulated.
2. When the thing sold and delivered produces fruits and rents.
3. When he is in default in accordance with article 1100.

Col. 1930; Chile, 1873.

1502. When the vendee is disturbed in the possession or dominion of the thing acquired, or may have reasonable grounds to fear being disturbed by a revindicatory or hypothecary action, he may suspend the payment of the price until the vendor has caused the disturbance or danger to cease, unless the latter gives security for the restitution of the price, if needs be, or when it has been stipulated that, notwithstanding such contingency, the vendee shall be bound to make the payment.

Col. 1929; Chile, 1872.

1503. When the vendor has reasonable grounds to fear the loss of the real property sold and the price of the same, he may immediately ask for the resolution of the sale.

When such reasonable grounds do not exist, the provisions of article 1124 shall be observed.

1504. In the sale of real property, even when it is stipulated that in default of the payment of the price, within the time agreed upon, the resolution of the contract shall take place by full right, the vendee may pay, even after the expiration of the term, as long as he has not been summoned either judicially or by a notarial act.

After such summons have been made the Judge shall not grant him a further term.

Col. 1937; Chile, 1879.

* Digesto, book 18, tit. 1, law 19; id., book 18, tit. 3; id., book 18, tit. 6, law 18, par .1; id., book 19, tit. 1, laws 13, par. 8, 20, 21. De regulis juris, law 14. Codigo, book 4, tit. 38, law 8; id., book 4, tit. 44, law 14; id., book 4, tit. 49, law 6; id., book 4, tit. 54, law 5. Part., tit. 5, laws 28, 38. Commercial Code, art. 341.

1505. With regard to personal property, the resolution of the sale shall take place by full right for the benefit of the vendor when the vendee, before the maturity of the term fixed for the delivery of the thing, has not presented himself, to receive it, or when having presented himself, he has not offered the price, at the same time, unless a longer term has been stipulated for the payment of said price.

CHAPTER SIXTH.

Resolution of the sale.

Article **1506.** The sale shall be resolved by the same causes as all other obligations, and furthermore those set forth in the preceding chapters and by conventional or legal redemption (*retracto*).

SECTION FIRST.

*Conventional redemption (retracto convencional).**

Article **1507.** Conventional redemption shall exist when the vendor reserves to himself the right to recover the thing sold, binding himself to fulfill that which is stated in article 1518, and whatever more may have been stipulated.

Col. 1939; Chile, 1881.

1508. The right stated in the preceding article, in default of an express stipulation, shall last four years to be counted from the date of the contract.

When a stipulation exists, the term shall not exceed ten years.

1509. When the vendor does not comply with the provisions of article 1518, the vendee shall irrevocably acquire the ownership of the thing sold.

1510. A vendor may exercise his action against every possessor whose right originates from that of the vendee, even when in the second contract mention has not been made of the conventional redemption; without conflict with the provisions of the Law of Mortgage in respect to third parties.

Col. 1940; Chile, 1882.

---

* Digesto, book 4, tit. 4, law 47, par. 1. De regulis juris, 10, 156, 160, 175, 177. Codigo, book 4, tit. 16, law 2; id., book 4, tit. 56, laws 2, 7; id., book 6, tit. 2, law 22, par. 3. Part. 5, tit. 5, law 42; id. 7, tit. 34, law 29.

1511. A vendee substitutes the vendor in all his rights and actions.

1512. The creditors of the vendor shall only be able to make use of the conventional redemption against the vendee, after having levied upon the property of the vendor.

1513. A vendee who has a stipulation for redemption of a part of an undivided estate and who acquires the whole estate, in the case of article 404, may oblige the vendor to redeem the whole estate, if said vendor pretends to make use of the redemption.

1514. When several persons, conjointly and in one and the same contract, sell an undivided estate under condition of redemption, neither of them shall exercise this right for more than his respective share.

The same rule shall be observed, when the person alone who has sold an estate has left several heirs, in which case each one of them may only redeem the part which he may have acquired.

1515. In the cases of the preceding article, the vendee may require all the vendors and co-heirs to agree about the redemption of the whole of the thing sold; and when they do not do so, the vendee shall not be bound to the partial redemption.

1516. Each one of the owners in common of an undivided estate, who has separately sold his share, may independently exercise the right of redemption for his respective share and the vendee cannot oblige him to redeem the whole of the estate.

1517. When the vendee leaves several heirs, the action of redemption cannot be exercised against each of them, except for his respective share, whether it be undivided, or whether it has been distributed among them.

But when the inheritance has been divided, and the thing sold has been adjudicated to one of the heirs, the action of redemption may be exercised against him for the whole.

1518. A vendor cannot exercise the right of redemption without returning to the vendee the price of the sale, and furthermore:

1. The expenses of the contract and any other legitimate payments made on account of the sale.

2. The useful and necessary expenses incurred by the thing sold.

Col. 1939; Chile, 1885.

1519. When on the execution of the sale, there are on the tenement visible and grown fruits, no indemnity or payment *pro rata* shall be made for those existing at the time of the redemption.

When there were no fruits, at the time of the sale, but some exist at the time of the redemption, they shall be divided *pro rata*, between the redemptor and the vendee, giving to the latter the share corresponding to the time he possessed the estate during the last year, counted from the date of the sale.

1520. A vendor, who recovers the thing sold, shall receive it free of all burdens and mortgages, imposed by the vendee, but he shall remain bound to respect the contracts of lease, executed by the latter in good faith and according to the usage of the place, where it is located.

SECTION SECOND.

Legal redemption (*retracto legal*).*

Article **1521.** Legal redemption is the right to be subrogated, under the same conditions, stipulated in the contract, in the place of the person who acquires a thing by purchase or in payment of a debt.

1522. An owner in common of a thing held in common may exercise the redemption when the shares of all the other owners in common or of any of them are sold to a third party.

When two or more owners in common wish to exercise the right of redemption, they shall only do so *pro rata* as to the shares they have in the thing held in common.

1523. Proprietors of adjacent lands shall also have the right of redemption, when the rural tenement is sold, the extent of which does not exceed one hectare.

The right, to which the preceding paragraph refers, shall not apply to adjacent lands which are divided by brooks, drains, ravines, roads and other apparent easements for the benefit of other tenements.

When two or more adjacent owners make use of the redemption, at the same time, the one who is owner of the adjacent land of lesser area shall be preferred; and if both are equal in area, the person who first asks for it.

1524. The right of legal redemption cannot be exercised except within nine days to be counted from the inscription in the Registry, and, in default of it, from the time the redemptor has been informed of the same.

The redemption of an owner in common excludes that of adjacent owners.

1525. In legal redemptions, the provisions of articles 1511 and 1518 shall be observed.

---

* Fuero Viejo, book 4, tit. 1, laws 2, 3, 4. Fuero Real, book 3, tit. 10, laws 13, 16. Estilo, laws 220, 230. Toro, laws 70, 75. Nov. Recop., book 10, tit. 13, law 11. Part. 5, tit. 5, law 55. Law of Civil Procedure, arts. 1, 6, 18, 1620. Recopilada, book 10, tit. 13, laws 2, 9.

CHAPTER SEVENTH.

*Assignments of credits and other incorporeal rights.**

Article **1526**. The assignment of a credit, right or action, shall produce no effect against a third party but from the time when the date is considered certain, in accordance with articles 1218 and 1227.

When said assignment refers to real property, from the date of its inscription in the Registry.

1527. A debtor, who before having been informed of the assignment pays the creditor, shall be free from the obligation.

1528. The sale or assignment of a credit includes that of all the accessory rights, as the security, mortgage, pledge or privilege.

1529. A vendor in good faith shall be responsible for the existence and legitimacy of the credit, at the time of the sale, unless said credit has been sold as doubtful, but said vendor is not responsible for the solvency of the debtor, unless it has been expressly stipulated, or when the insolvency is prior and public.

Even in these cases, he shall only be liable for the price received and for the expenses stated in No. 1 of article 1518.

The vendor in bad faith shall always be liable for the payment of all the expenses and for the damages and injuries.

1530. When the assignor in good faith has made himself responsible for the solvency of the debtor, and the contracting parties have not stipulated anything about the duration of such responsibility, it shall only last one year, to be counted from the assignment of the credit, if the term had already matured.

When the credit is payable within a term or period not yet expired, the responsibility shall cease one year after its maturity.

When the credit consists of a perpetual rent, the responsibility shall be extinguished after ten years, to be counted from the date of the assignment.

1531. A person who sells an inheritance, without enumerating the things of which it is composed, shall only be obliged to prove that he is an heir.

1532. A person who sells for a total or lump sum certain rights, rents, or products as a whole, shall comply by answering for the legitimacy of the whole in general, but he shall not be bound to war-

---

*Digesto, book 18, tit. 4, laws 2, par. 1, 9, 11, 14, 15, 23; id., book 26, tit. 7, law 42. Codigo, book 4, tit. 35, laws 22, 23, 24; id., book 8, tit. 45, law 1. De regulis juris, laws 68, 96. Part. 5, tit. 5, laws 34, 54. Law of Mortgage, arts. 23, 25.

rant each of the parts of which it is composed, unless in the case of eviction of the whole or of the greater part.

1533. When the vendor has profited by some of the fruits, or has received anything from the inheritance which he sells, he must pay the vendee therefor, if the contrary has not been stipulated.

1534. The vendee shall, on his part, pay to the vendor all that the latter has paid for debts or charges on the estate and for the credits which he may have against the same, unless the contrary has been stipulated.

1535. When the litigious credit is sold, the debtor shall have the right to extinguish the same by reimbursing the assignee for the price the latter paid for it, the judicial expenses incurred by him, and the interest on the price, from the day on which the same was paid.

A credit shall be held as litigious from the day on which the demand relating to the same, has been answered.

The debtor may make use of his right within nine days, counted from the day the assignee claimed the payment from him.

1536. From the provisions of the preceding article are excepted the assignments or sales made:

1. To a co-heir or co-owner of the right assigned.
2. To a creditor in payment of his credit.
3. To the possessor of a tenement, subject to the litigious right which has been assigned.

CHAPTER EIGHTH.

General provision.

Article **1537.** All that is prescribed in this title is understood subject to the provisions of the Law of Mortgage in regard to real property.

TITLE V.

*Barter or exchange.**

Article **1538.** Barter or exchange is a contract by which each of the contracting parties binds himself to give a thing in order to receive another.

Col. 1955; Chile. 1897.

---

* **Digesto, book 19, tit. 5, law 5, par. 1; id., book 19, tit. 4, laws 1, par. 3, 2, 4. Codigo, book 4, tit. 64, law 1. Part. 6, tit. 6, law 1.**

1539. When one of the contracting parties has received the thing promised to him in exchange, and he proves that it did not belong to the person who gave it, he shall not be bound to deliver the one which he offered in exchange, and he shall comply with his duty by returning the one that he received.

1540. A person, who loses by eviction the thing received in exchange, may choose between recovering the one which he gave in exchange or claiming an indemnity for damages and injuries; but he shall only be able to enforce the right of recovering the thing which he delivered in so far as said thing remains in the hands of the other party, and without damage to any rights acquired to such thing, in good faith in the meantime, by a third party.

1541. Exchange shall be governed by the provisions relating to purchase and sale in all that is not specially determined in this title.

TITLE VI.

Contract of lease.

CHAPTER FIRST.

General provisions. *

Article **1542.** Leases may be made in respect to things, works (*obras*), or services.

1543. In a lease of things, one of the parties thereto binds himself to give to the other the enjoyment or use of a thing for a specified time and at a determined price.

Col. 1971; Chile, 1915.

1544. In a lease for works or services, one of the parties binds himself to execute a work or to render a service to the other for a determined price.

1545. Perishable things, which are consumed by use, cannot be a matter of this contract.

Chile, 1916; Col. 1974.

---

* Digesto, book 19, tit. 2, laws 25, 31; id., book 19, tit. 5, law 5, par. 2. Novela, 122. Instituciones, book 3, tit. 25, par. 1, 2. Part. 5, tit. 8, law 1; id. 6, tit. 8, law 1.

CHAPTER SECOND.

Leases of rural and city tenements.

SECTION FIRST.

*General provisions.**

Article **1546.** A person who binds himself to grant the use of a thing, execute a work, or render a service is called the lessor; and the person, who acquires the use of a thing or a right to the work or service, for which he binds himself to pay, is the lessee.

Col. 1977; Chile, 1919.

1547. When the performance of a contract of verbal lease has begun and the evidence of the price is wanting, the lessee shall return to the lessor the thing leased, paying him such price as may be adjudged for the time he has enjoyed such thing.

1548. The husband cannot give, in lease, the property of the wife, the father and guardian, that of the son or minor, and the administrator of property, that for which he has not a special power, for a term exceeding six years.

Chile, 1969; Col. 2027.

1549. In regard to third parties, leases of real property, which are not duly recorded in the Registry of property, shall not be effectual.

1550. When it is not expressly forbidden in the contract of lease of things, the lessee may sublet the whole or a part of the things leased, without lessening his responsibility for the fulfillment of the contract entered into with the lessor.

Col. 2004; Chile, 1946.

1551. A sub-lessee, notwithstanding his obligation with regard to the sub-lessor, shall remain bound to the lessor with all the acts which refer to the use and preservation of the thing leased, in the manner agreed upon between the lessor and the lessee.

1552. The sub-lessee shall also remain bound with respect to the lessor for the amount of the price agreed upon in the contract of sub-lease, which said sub-lessee owes, at the time of the summons, considering the payments made in advance as not made, unless he has paid them according to usage.

---

* Law of Mortgage, arts. 2, Nos. 5, 24, 25, 27. Instruction of Nov. 9, 1874. Codigo, book 4, tit. 65, law 6. Recopilada, 8a, book 10, tit. 10, art. 4. Decree of Cortes, June 8, 1813.

1553. The provisions respecting warranty, contained under the title of purchase and sale, shall apply to the contract of lease.

In the cases in which restitution of the price is required, a deduction of the price should be made proportional to the time for which the lessee has enjoyed the thing.

SECTION SECOND.

*Rights and obligations of the lessor and lessee.**

Article **1554.** The lessor is bound:

1. To deliver to the lessee the thing which is the object of the contract.

2. To make thereon, during the lease, all the necessary repairs with a view of preserving it in condition to serve for the purpose for which it was intended.

3. To maintain the lessee in the peaceful enjoyment of the lease during all the time of the contract.

Col. 1982; Chile, 1924.

1555. The lessee is bound:

1. To pay the price of the lease in the terms stipulated.

2. To use the thing leased as a diligent father of a family would do, applying the same to the use agreed upon: and, in default of a stipulation, to the use which may be inferred from the nature of the thing leased according to the custom of the land.

3. To pay the expenses incurred for the deed of contract.

Col. 1996; Chile, 1938.

1556. When the lessor or lessee does not comply with the obligations, set forth in the preceding articles, they may ask for the rescission of the contract and the indemnity for damages and injuries, or only for the latter, leaving the contract in force.

1557. The lessor shall not change the form of the thing leased.

Col. 1986; Chile, 1928.

1558. When, during the lease, it becomes necessary to make any urgent repairs in the thing leased, which cannot be delayed until the expiration thereof, the lessee shall be obliged to suffer the execution

*Digesto, book 19, tit. 2, laws 1, 13, par. 1, 14, 19, par. 4, 25, par. 3, 4, 30, 41, 55, par. 1. Codigo, book 3, tit. 19, law 2; id., book 4, tit. 49, law 17; id., book 4, tit. 65, laws 1, 7, 3, 12, 29. Part. 5, tit. 8, laws 4, 6, 7, 8, 19, 20, 21, 24. Law of Mortgage, arts. 24, 27. Law of April 9, 1842, art. 2. Remarks No. 8, to the Recopilada, book 10, tit. 10, law 8. Decree of Cortes, June 8, 1813, art. 5. Law of Civil Procedure, arts. 1562, 1590, 1593.

of the work, even when it is very annoying to him, and even when, during such repairs, he may be deprived of a part of the tenement.

When the repairs last more than forty days, the price of the lease shall be reduced in proportion to the time and the part of the tenement of which the lessee is deprived.

When the work is of such a nature that the part which the lessee and his family require for a dwelling becomes inhabitable, the lessee may rescind the contract.

Col. 1986; Chile, 1928.

1559. The lessee is bound to give notice to the owner, with the least possible delay, of any usurpation or injurious alterations (*novedad*) which any other person may have done or openly is preparing to do to the thing leased.

He is also bound to give notice with the same promptness to the owner of the necessity of all repairs, stated in No. 2 of article 1554.

In both cases the lessee shall be liable for the damages and injuries, which, through his negligence, may be caused to the lessor.

Col. 1989, 1993; Chile, 1931, 1935.

1560. The lessor shall not be obliged to answer for the mere fact of a trespass (*perturbacion de mero hecho*), made by a third party in the use of the tenement leased, but the lessee shall have a direct action against the trespasser.

The fact of trespass does not exist, when the third person, whether it be the administration or a private party, has acted by virtue of a right belonging to the same.

Col. 1988; Chile, 1930.

1561. The lessee shall return the tenement at the expiration of the lease, in the same condition in which he received it, except what may have been destroyed or impaired by time or by inevitable causes (*vis major*).

Col. 2005; Chile, 1947.

1562. When, at the time of the lease of the tenement, the condition of the same was not stated, the law presumes that the lessee received it in good condition, unless there be proof to the contrary.

1563. The lessee is liable for the impairment or loss of the thing leased, unless he proves that the same was caused without his fault.

1564. A lessee is liable for the impairment caused by the members of his household.

1565. When the lease has been entered into for a specified time, it shall expire on the day previously fixed without the necessity of any notice.

Col. 1208, 1212; Chile, 1950, 1954.

1566. When, at the expiration of the contract, the lessee continues enjoying the thing leased for fifteen days (longer) with the acquiescence of the lessor, it shall be understood that there is a tacit new lease for the time set forth in articles 1577 and 1581, unless a notice has previously been given.

Col. 2014; Chile, 1956.

1567. In the case of a tacit renewal, the obligations contracted by a third party for the security of the principal contract shall cease in regard thereto.

Col. 2015; Chile, 1957.

1568. When the thing leased is lost, or any of the contracting parties do not comply with what has been stipulated, the provisions of articles 1182, 1183, 1101, and 1124 shall be respectively observed.

1569. The lessor may judicially eject the lessee for any of the following causes:

1. Upon the expiration of the conventional term or the one fixed for the duration of leases by articles 1577 and 1581.
2. Default in payment of the rent agreed upon.
3. Breach of any of the conditions stipulated in the contract.
4. When the lessee employs the thing leased in uses or services not stipulated and which cause the same to be impaired, or when he does not comply, in respect to its use, with what is prescribed in No. 2 of article 1555.

1570. Besides the cases mentioned in the preceding article, the lessee shall have the right to avail himself of the terms fixed in articles 1577 and 1581.

1571. The purchaser of a leased tenement has the right to determine the lease in force at the time of the consummation of the sale, unless there is a stipulation to the contrary, and the provisions of the Law of Mortgage are considered.

When the purchaser exercises this right, the lessee may require to be allowed to gather the fruits of the crop corresponding to the current agricultural year and to be indemnified by the vendor for the damages and injuries which he may have suffered.

1572. A purchaser with a stipulation of redemption cannot use the power of ejecting the lessee, until the term for the use of the right of redemption has expired.

1573. A lessee shall have, in respect to the useful and voluntary improvements, the same rights granted to the usufructuary.

1574. When no stipulation exists about the place and time of the payment of rent, the provision of article 1171 shall govern as to place, and the custom of the land in respect to time.

SECTION THIRD.

*Special provisions for leases of rural property.**

Article **1575.** A lessee shall not have the right to a reduction of the rent on account of the sterility of the land leased or on account of the loss of the fruits, through usual unforeseen events (*vis major*), but he shall have said right in case of loss of more than half of the fruits through extraordinary unforeseen events, unless there are special stipulations to the contrary.

By extraordinary unforeseen events shall be understood fire, war, pestilence, extraordinary inundations, locusts, earthquakes or any other equally unfrequent events, and which the contracting parties could not have reasonably foreseen.

Col. 2041; Chile, 1983.

1576. A lessee shall neither have the right to a reduction of the rent, when the fruits have been lost, after having been separated from their roots or trunks.

1577. The lease of a rural tenement, when its duration has not been fixed, shall be understood as executed for all the time which is necessary for the gathering of the fruits which the whole tenement leased might produce in one year, or all it could produce, at one time, even when two or more years must be required for obtaining such fruits.

That of arable lands, divided into two or more terms (*hojas*), shall be considered as executed for as many years as there are terms.

1578. The outgoing lessee shall permit the incoming one the use of the place and of all other necessary means for the preparatory labor for the following year, and, reciprocally, the latter is bound to permit the outgoing one all that may be necessary for the gathering and enjoyment of the fruits, all according to the custom of the place.

1579. Leases for partnerships of arable lands, breeding cattle, and for industrial or manufacturing establishments, shall be governed by the provisions, relating to the contract of partnership and by the stipulations of the contracting parties, and, in default of the same, by the customs of the land.

---

* Digesto, book 18, tit. 1, law 78, par. 3; id., book 19, tit. 2, law 15, pars. 2 to 6, 25, par. 6. Codigo, book 4, tit. 65, law 18. Part. 5, tit. 8, laws 22, 23. Decree of Cortes, June 8, 1813, art. 6.

SECTION FOURTH.

*Special provisions for the lease of urban tenements.**

Article **1580.** In default of a special stipulation for the repairs of urban tenements, which should be borne by the owner, the customs of the place shall rule. In case of doubt, said repairs shall be understood as chargeable to the owner.

Col. 2028; Chile, 1970.

1581. When a term has not been fixed for the lease; it is understood for years, when an annual rent has been fixed, for months, when the rent is monthly, and for days, when it is daily.

In every case, the lease ceases without the necessity of a special notice upon the expiration of the term.

1582. When the lessor of a house, or of a part of the same, intended as a dwelling for a family, or for a store or storehouse or industrial establishment, leases also the furniture, the lease of the latter shall be understood as executed for a time equal to that of the house leased.

CHAPTER THIRD.

Leases of works and services.

SECTION FIRST.

Services of hired servants and laborers.†

Article **1583.** This class of services may be contracted, either without a time being specified, for a fixed time, or for a specified work. A lease made for the whole life is null.

Col. 2046; Chile, 1988.

1584. A domestic servant, hired for a fixed time and to be employed in the personal service of his master or of the family of the latter, may leave the service or be dismissed before the expiration of the term; but when the master dismisses such servant, without a just cause, he shall indemnify him by paying him the salary due and that for fifteen additional days.

---

* Digesto, book 19, tit. 2, law 15, par. 1, 25, pars. 2 and 3. Law of April 9, 1842, art. 2.

† Part. 4, tit. 22, law 8; id. 7, tit. 34, law 1. Recopilada, 1, book 6, tit. 16, law 4. Fuero Viejo, book 4, tit. 3, law 5.

The master's (statement) shall be believed, unless there is proof to the contrary:

1. About the amount of the salary of the domestic servant.

2. About the payment of the salaries earned during the current year.

1585. Besides what is prescribed in the preceding articles, with regard to masters and servants, what is determined in the special laws and ordinances shall be observed.

1586. Fieldhands, mechanics, artisans, and other hired laborers, for a certain time and for a certain work, shall not leave nor be dismissed, without just cause, before the fulfillment of the contract.

1587. The dismissal of servants, mechanics, artisans and other hired laborers, to which the preceding articles refer, gives the right to dispossess them of the working tools and of the buildings which they occupy by reason of their duties.

SECTION SECOND.

*Works at a price agreed upon or for a lump sum.**

Article **1588.** The execution of a work may be contracted by agreeing that the person, who is to execute the same, shall employ only his labor or industry, or that he shall furnish the materials in addition.

Col. 2053; Chile, 1966.

1589. When the person, who contracted for the work, bound himself to furnish the materials, he shall bear the loss, in case of the destruction of the work before it is delivered, unless delay has been incurred in receiving the work.

Col. 2053; Chile, 1996.

1590. A person, who has bound himself to provide only his labor or industry, shall not claim any payment, when the work is destroyed before it is delivered, unless delay has been incurred in receiving the same, or when the destruction has been due to the bad quality of the materials, provided that he may have given due notice of this circumstance to the owner.

Col. 2057; Chile, 2000.

---

*Digesto, book 18, tit. 1, law 2; id., book 19, tit. 2, laws 6, 13, par. 5, 24, 25, par. 7, 30, par. 3, 37, 38, 59, 62; id., book 46, tit. 3, law 31. Codigo, book 8, tit. 2, law 8. Part 3, tit. 32, law 21; id. 5, tit. 8, laws 9, 10, 12, 15, 16, 17; id. 5, tit. 11, law 12; id. 5, tit. 13, laws 15, 21. Nov. Recop., book 8, tit. 23, law 2; id., book 10, tit. 1, law 4. Penal Code, art. 21.

1591. The contractor of a building, which has been destroyed on account of vices of construction, shall be liable for any damages and injuries, when said building falls down within ten years, to be counted from the completion of the construction; and, during the same time, the same liability shall be incurred by the architect, who directed the work, when the ruin is on account of vices of the ground or of his directions.

When the cause is the noncompliance of the contractor with the conditions of the contract, the action for indemnity can be enforced within fifteen years.

Col. 2060; Chile, 2003.

1592. A person who binds himself to do a work, by piece or by measure, may require from the owner to receive it by parts and to pay for it in proportion. The part paid for shall be presumed approved and received.

Col. 2058; Chile, 2001.

1593. An architect or contractor, who for a lump sum, takes charge of the construction of a building, or of any other work by inspection of plans agreed upon, with the owner of the ground, cannot ask for an increase in the price, even when that of the materials or wages have increased, but he may do so when any change which increases the work is made in the plans, provided the owner has given his authorization.

Col. 2060; Chile, 2003.

1594. The owner may desist, by his own will, from the construction of the work, even when it has been begun, indemnifying the contractor for all the expenses, labor, and profits which he may have obtained from the same.

Col. 2056; Chile, 1999.

1595. When a certain work has been intrusted to a person by reason of his personal qualities, the contract shall be rescinded upon the death of said person.

In this case, the owner shall pay to the heirs of the constructor, in proportion to the price agreed upon, the value of the part of the work which has been executed, and for the prepared materials, provided he may obtain any benefit from such materials.

The same provision shall apply, when the person who contracted the work cannot finish it on account of any cause independent of his will.

Col. 2062; Chile, 2005.

1596. A contractor is responsible for the labor done by the persons he employs on the work.

1597. Those, who furnish their labor and materials in a work agreed upon for a lump sum by a contractor, shall have no action against the owner, except for the sum which the latter may owe to the former when the claim is made.

Col. 2060; Chile, 2003.

1598. When it is agreed that the work is to be made to the satisfaction of the owner, in default of his acceptance, such approval shall be understood as reserved for the proper judgment of experts.

When the person who has to approve the work is a third party, his decision shall govern.

1599. When there is no stipulation or custom to the contrary, the price for the work shall be paid upon delivery.

1600. A person, who has performed a work on personal things, has the right to retain the same as a pledge until he is paid therefor.

SECTION THIRD.

*Transportation by water and land, either of persons or of things.**

Article **1601.** Carriers of goods by land or by water shall be subjected, as to the keeping and preservation of the things intrusted to them, to the same obligations as prescribed for inn-keepers by articles 1783 and 1784.

The provision of this article shall be understood without prejudice to what is prescribed by the Code of Commerce, with regard to transportation by sea and land.

Col. 2072; Chile, 2015.

1602. Carriers are also responsible for the losses and damages of the things which they receive, unless they prove that the loss or damage has happened on account of an unforeseen event (*vis major*).

Col. 2072; Chile, 2015.

1603. The provisions of the foregoing articles are understood without conflict with what is prescribed by special laws and regulations.

---

* Digesto, book 4, tit. 9, laws 1, 3; id., book 19, tit. 2, law 25, par. 7. Commercial Code, art. 349 to 379, 652 to 718. Part. 5, tit. 18, laws 13, 26; id. 5, tit. 8, law 26. Law of June 3, 1855, and regulation of Sept. 8, 1878, on Railroads.

TITLE VII.

*Rents of land or ground-rents (censos).**

CHAPTER FIRST.

General provisions.†

Article **1604.** A ground-rent (*censo*) is constituted when any real property is subjected to the payment of a pension or annual rent in compensation, either for a capital which is received in cash, or for the full or partial ownership of the property which is conveyed.

Chile, 2022.

1605. A ground-rent is called emphyteusis (*enfitéutico*) when a person transfers to another the useful ownership of a tenement, reserving to himself the direct ownership and a right to receive from the *emphyteuta* an annual pension in recognition of such dominion.

1606. A ground-rent is consignative (*consignativo*) when the owner of land imposes upon a tenement belonging to him the burden of a rent or pension which he binds himself to pay to the lender for a sum in cash which he has received from the latter.

1607. A ground-rent is reservative (*reservativo*) when a person transfers to another the complete ownership of a tenement, reserving to himself the right to receive from said tenement an annual pension which is to be paid by the holder of the land.

1608. The nature of a ground-rent requires that the transfer of the capital or of the tenement should be perpetual or for an unlimited time; however, the *censatario* (‡) may redeem the ground-rent, at his will, though the contrary is stipulated, and this provision is applicable to ground-rents actually existing.

It may, however, be stipulated, that the redemption of the ground-rent cannot be made during the life of the *censualista* (§) or of a

---

* Designated as ground-rents, instead of annuities (personalty), as they partake of the nature of purchase and sale and also resemble rent or lease. La. Civil Code, arts. 2779 (2750) to 2800 (2771); Schmidt's Civil Law in Spain and Mexico, p. 149; Molina de Just. et Jure, Tract. 2; Covarubias, 3 var.; Res. Febrero, Reform., chap. 20, sec. 1, vol. 2, which coincides with Palacio; decisions of Pa. and Md. courts; Rawles' Bouvier, White's Recop., and Tapia, Febr. Novis, b. 2, t. 4, chaps. 8, 9, 10, and 11.

† Part. 1, tit. 14, law 3; id. 1, tit. 22, law 8; id. 3, tit. 18, law 69; id. 5, tit. 8, law 28. Nov. Recop., book 10, tit. 15; id., book 10, tit. 15, laws 3, 4, 9, 12, 22, 24. Royal Schedule, January 17, 1805. Decree of Cortes, June 6, 1837. Law of May 3, 1823. Law of Mortgage, arts. 149, 150, 151, 152, 183, 384, 385, 386.

‡ *Censatario*, the person who pays the ground-rent.

§ *Censualista*, the person to whom the ground-rent is owed.

specified person, or that it may not be redeemed within a certain number of years, which cannot exceed twenty years, in consignative ground-rents, nor sixty years in reservative ground-rents and in emphyteusis.

Chile, 2029.

1609. To carry into effect such redemption, the *censatario* must give notice thereof one year in advance to the *censualista*, or must pay to him, in advance, the amount of one year's pension.

Chile, 2037.

1610. Ground-rents cannot be partially redeemed, unless by virtue of an express stipulation.

Neither can they be redeemed against the will of the *censualista*, unless the payment of all the pensions due have been made.

Chile, 2040.

1611. For the redemption of all ground-rents, constituted before the promulgation of this Code, when the capital is unknown, it shall be regulated by the principal which may result, by computing the pension on the basis of three per centum.

When the pension is payable in fruits, for the determination of the capital, they shall be appraised, at the average price which such fruits may have had during the last five years.

The provisions of this title shall not apply to local ground-rents (*foros* and *sub foros*), rights of surface, or any other similar burdens, in which the principles of redemption of dominion shall be regulated by a special law.

1612. The expenses, caused for the redemption and liberation of ground-rents, shall be borne by the *censatario*, except those caused by temerarious opposition which are subject to the discretion of the courts.

1613. The pension or rent of ground-rents shall be agreed to by the parties upon the execution of the contract.

It may consist in money or of fruits.

Chile, 2027.

1614. The pensions shall be paid at the times agreed upon, and, in default of a contract, if they consist in money, by the years, as due, to be counted from the date of the contract; and, if in fruits, at the end of the respective crops.

Chile, 2032.

1615. When the place, at which the pensions are to be paid, has not been designated in the contract, this obligation shall be complied with at the place in which the tenements, incumbered with the ground-rent, are located, provided the *censualista* or his attorney have their domicile in the Municipal district of the same town. When such person has not his domicile in said town, but the *censatario* resides there, the payment shall be made at the domicile of the latter.

1616. The *censualista,* at the time of the delivery of the receipt of any pension, can oblige the *censatario* to give him a written notice in which it may appear that the payment has been made.

1617. Tenements, incumbered with ground-rents, may be conveyed by virtue of an onerous or lucrative title, and the same can be done with the right to receive the pensions.

Chile, 2031, 2043.

1618. Tenements, incumbered with ground-rents, shall not be divided among two or more persons without the express consent of the *censualista,* even when acquired by a title of inheritance.

When the *censualista* consents to the division, the part of the ground-rent, with which each portion remains incumbered, shall be designated with his consent, and as many different ground-rents shall be constituted as there are portions in which the tenement is divided.

Chile, 2036.

1619. When the tenement incumbered with a ground-rent is to be adjudged to several heirs, and the *censualista* does not give his consent to the division, it shall be placed at auction among said heirs.

In default of agreement or when none of the parties in interest offers the price of the appraisement, the tenement shall be sold with the incumbrances and the proceeds shall be distributed among the heirs.

1620. The principal as well as the pension of ground-rents may be prescribed, in accordance with the provisions of title 18 of this book.

Chile, 2044.

1621. Notwithstanding the provisions of article 1110, the payment of two consecutive pensions shall be necessary to presume that all the preceding ones have been paid.

1622. The *censatario* shall be bound to pay the taxes and all other imposts which affect the tenement burdened with the ground-rent.

At the time the *censatario* pays the pension, he may deduct from the same the part of the imposts which pertains to the *censualista.*

1623. Ground-rents give cause for a real action against the tenement incumbered. Besides the real action, the *censualista* may enforce a personal action for the payment of the pensions in arrears, and when proper for damages and interests.

1624. A *censatario* shall not ask for the remission or reduction of the pension on account of an accidental sterility of the tenement nor on account of the loss of its fruits.

1625. When a tenement incumbered with a ground-rent is totally destroyed or rendered useless by an act of God or by an unforeseen event (*vis major*), the ground-rent shall be extinguished and the payment of the pension shall also cease.

When it is partially destroyed, the *censatario* shall not be exempt from the payment of the pension, unless he prefers to abandon the tenement to the *censualista.*

When there is fault on the part of the *censatario,* he shall be bound, in both cases, to an indemnity for damages and injuries.

Chile, 2035, 2041.

1626. In the case of the first paragraph of the preceding article, when the tenement is insured, the amount of the insurance shall be subject to the payment of the principal of the ground-rent and of the pensions due, unless the *censatario* prefers to invest it in rebuilding the tenement, in which case the ground-rent shall survive with all its effects, including the payment of the unpaid pensions. The *censualista* may exact from the *censatario* that he secure the investment of the amount of the insurance in the rebuilding of the tenement.

1627. When a tenement, incumbered with a ground-rent, is expropriated on account of public utility, the price of the same shall remain liable for the payment of the principal of the ground-rent and of the pensions due, and said ground-rent shall be extinguished.

The preceding provision is also applicable in the case in which the forced expropriation is only of a part of the tenement when its price is sufficient to cover the principal of the ground-rent.

When this price is not sufficient, the ground-rent shall continue to incumber the remainder of the tenement, provided its price be sufficient to cover the principal of the ground-rent and an additional twenty-five per centum over and above it.

In any other case the *censatario* shall be bound, either to substitute the part expropriated with another security, or to redeem the ground-rent, at his option, without prejudice to what is provided in article 1631, in respect to emphyteusis.

CHAPTER SECOND.

Emphyteusis (censo enfitéutico).

SECTION FIRST.

*Provisions referring to emphyteusis.**

Article **1628.** Emphyteusis can only be constituted on real property and by a public deed.

Chile, 2024, 2027.

1629. At the time of the constitution of the emphyteusis, the value of the tenement and the annual pension to be paid shall be fixed in the contract, under the penalty of nullity.

1630. When the pension consists of a fixed amount of fruits, the kind and quality of the same shall be stated in the contract.

When it consists in an aliquot part of what the tenement may produce, in default of an express stipulation, as to the intervention which the direct owner may exercise, the *emphyteuta* shall give to said owner or his representative previous notice of the day on which he intends to commence the gathering of each kind of fruit, in order that he may be able, either personally or by his representative, to inspect all the operations, until he receives the share belonging to him.

After the notice is given, the *emphyteuta* may gather the crops, even when neither the direct owner nor his representative or intervenor is present.

1631. In case of forcible expropriation, the provisions of the first paragraph of article 1627 shall be applied when the whole tenement is expropriated.

When it is expropriated only in part, the price of what has been expropriated shall be distributed between the direct owner and the *emphyteuta*, the former receiving the part of the principal of the ground-rent, which proportionally belongs to the expropriated part, according to the value given to the whole tenement when the ground-rent was constituted, or to that which has served as a basis for the redemption, and the remainder shall belong to the *emphyteuta*.

In this case the ground-rent shall continue on the rest of the tenement, with the proper reduction of the principal and the pension,

* Part. 5, tit. 8, laws 28, par. 1, 29; id. 1, tit. 14, law 3. Recopilada, book 10, tit. 13, law 8; id., book 10, tit. 15, law 12, par. 11; id., book 10, tit. 5, law 12. Law of Mortgage, art. 38. Law of Civil Procedure, arts. 1618, 1620.

unless the *emphyteuta* elects between the total redemption or the abandonment in behalf of the direct owner.

When, in accordance with what has been stipulated, *laudemium* is to be paid, the direct owner shall receive that, which for this reason belongs to him, only from the part of the price belonging to the *emphyteuta.*

1632. To the *emphyteuta* belongs the products of the tenement and of its accessions.

He has the same rights which the owner would have in the treasures and mines which may be discovered on the tenement held in emphyteusis.

1633. The *emphyteuta* may dispose of the tenement held in emphyteusis and of its accessions, by acts *inter vivos,* as well as by last will, leaving intact the rights of the direct owner, and subject to the provisions of the following articles.

1634. When the pension consists of an aliquot part of the fruits of the tenement held in emphyteusis, neither an easement nor any other burden which may diminish the proceeds of the same, shall be imposed upon it, without the express consent of the direct owner.

1635. The *emphyteuta* may freely donate or exchange the tenement, giving notice of it to the direct owner.

1636. To the direct owner and to the *emphyteuta* reciprocally belong the right of pre-emption and of redemption, whenever they sell or give in payment their respective ownerships of the tenement held in emphyteusis.

These provisions shall not apply to forcible sales for causes of public utility.

1637. For the effects of the preceding article, the persons who intend to alienate the ownership of a tenement, held in emphyteusis, shill give notice of it to the other owner stating the final price which is offered to him or the one for which he intends to alienate his ownership.

Within twenty days after the notice is given, the other owner may make use of the right of pre-emption by paying the price indicated. When he does not do this, he shall lose such right and the alienation may be carried into effect.

1638. When the direct owner or the *emphyteuta,* in certain cases, has not made use of the right of pre-emption, to which the preceding article refers, he may make use of that of redemption to acquire the tenement for the price at which it has been sold.

In this case, the redemption shall be made use of within nine working days next following the execution of the deed of sale. If this sale is concealed, said term shall be counted from the inscription of the same in the Registry of property.

Concealment is presumed when the deed is not filed in the Registry within the nine days next following its execution.

Besides this presumption, the concealment may be proven by any other lawful means.

1639. When the alienation has been affected without the previous notice, which article 1637 prescribes, the direct owner, and, in certain cases, the *emphyteuta* may exercise the action of redemption, at any time, until the lapse of a year to be counted from the day the alienation is inscribed in the Registry of property.

1640. In judicial sales of tenements held in emphyteusis, the direct owner and the *emphyteuta,* in their respective cases, may make use of the right of pre-emption, within the term fixed in the notices of the sale at auction, paying the price which served as a basis for the auction, and that of the redemption within the nine working days next following that of the execution of the deed.

In this case, the previous notice, required by article 1637, shall not be necessary.

1641. When there are several tenements alienated, subject to the same ground-rent, the right of pre-emption or that of redemption cannot be exercised with regard to some of them and to the exclusion of others.

1642. When the direct or useful ownership undividedly belongs to several persons, each one of them may make use of the right of redemption subject to the rules set forth for that of owners in common and preference shall be given to the direct owner, if a part of the useful ownership has been alienated; or to the *emphyteuta,* when the alienation has been of the direct ownership.

1643. When the *emphyteuta* is disturbed in his right by a third party who disputes the direct ownership or the validity of the emphyteusis, he shall not have the right to claim the corresponding indemnity from the direct owner, if he does not summon him for the eviction, in accordance with the provisions of article 1481.

1644. In alienations under an onerous title of tenements held in emphyteusis, *laudemium* shall be paid to the direct owner only, when it has been expressly stipulated in the contract of emphyteusis.

If when it has been stipulated, a fixed sum has not been determined, this sum shall consist of two per centum of the price of the alienation.

In emphyteusis, prior to the promulgation of this Code, subject to the payment *laudemium,* even when it has not been stipulated, this prestation shall continue in the usual manner, but it shall not exceed two per cent. of the price of the alienation, unless a higher one has been expressly contracted.

1645. The obligation to pay *laudemium* corresponds to the person who acquires the tenement, unless there is a stipulation to the contrary.

1646. When the *emphyteuta* has obtained permission from the direct owner for the alienation or has given him the previous notice, prescribed in article 1637, the direct owner shall not have the right to claim the payment of the *laudemium,* except within a year following the day on which the public deed is inscribed in the Registry of property. Besides said cases, this action shall be subject to ordinary prescription.

1647. The direct owner may, every twenty-nine years, exact the recognition of his right by the person who is in possession of the tenement held in emphyteusis.

The expenses of the recognition shall be borne by the *emphyteuta* and no other prestation, whatever, for this reason, shall be required from him.

1648. The tenement shall be forfeited and the direct owner may claim its restitution:

1. By default in the payment of the pension during three consecutive years.

2. When the *emphyteuta* does not comply with the conditions stipulated in the contract or seriously impairs the tenement.

1649. In order that the direct owner may claim the confiscation in the first case of the preceding article, he shall demand payment from the *emphyteuta,* either judicially or through a Notary, and when said *emphyteuta* does not pay within thirty days next following the demand, the right of the owner may be freely exercised.

1650. The *emphyteuta* may free himself from the forfeiture, in every case, by redeeming the ground-rent and paying the pension due, within thirty days next following the formal demand for the payment or the summons for the suit.

Creditors of the *emphyteuta* may make use of the same right, within thirty days after the one upon which the direct owner has recovered the full domain.

1651. The redemption of the emphyteusis shall consist in a payment of cash in full to the direct owner for the capital which may have been fixed as the value of the tenement, at the time of the constitution of the ground-rent, and no other prestation can be exacted, unless it has been stipulated.

1652. In case of forfeiture, or in that of rescission of the contract of emphyteusis on account of any cause whatever, the direct owner shall pay for the improvements which may have increased the value of the tenement, provided such increase exists at the time of the restitution.

When the tenement has been damaged, through fault or negligence on the part of the *emphyteuta*, the same shall be set off against the improvements, and as to those which these do not cover, the *emphyteuta* shall remain personally bound to pay for them, as well as for the pensions due and not prescribed.

1653. In default of testamentary heirs, descendants, ascendants, the surviving consort and relatives within the sixth degree of the last *emphyteuta*, the tenement shall revert to the direct owner in the condition in which it may exist, unless the *emphyteuta* did not otherwise dispose of it.

1654. The contract of sub-emphyteusis shall not be valid in the future.

SECTION SECOND.

*Local ground-rents (foros), and other contracts analogous to that of emphyteusis.**

Article **1655.** Local ground-rents (*foros*), and any other burdens of analogous nature which may be established after the promulgation of this Code, when they are for an unlimited time, shall be governed by the provisions of emphyteusis, set forth in the preceding section.

When they are temporal or for limited times, they shall be considered as leases and shall be governed by the provisions relating to such contracts.

1656. The contract by virtue of which the owner of land grants its use for the plantation of vines, during the time that the first root-stocks may live, the grantee paying him an annual pension or rent in fruits or in money, shall be governed by the following rules:

1. It shall be considered extinguished fifty years after the grant, when no other time has been expressly fixed in the same grant.

2. It shall also be extinguished by the death of the first root-stocks, or when two-thirds of those planted have become barren.

3. The grantee or parcenary may make sprigs or shoots from new vines during the time of the contract.

---

* Fuero Juzgo, book 10, laws 11, 12, 19. Nov. Recop., book 10, tit. 15, law 24. Royal Pragmatica, May 10, 1763. Law of Mortgage, arts. 387, 410. Regulation, October 29, 1870, art. 317. Royal Decree, Nov. 8, 1875. Royal Order, May 20, 1878. Law of Civil Procedure, arts. 2071 to 2108. Project of 1851, art. 1563, rule 9.

4. This contract does not lose its character by the power of making other plantations on the lands granted, provided its main object is the plantation of vines.

5. The grantee may freely transmit his right under an onerous or gratuitous title, but the use of the tenement shall not be divided, unless the owner expressly consents to it.

6. In the alienations under an onerous title, the grantor and grantee shall reciprocally have the rights of pre-emption and redemption in accordance with the provisions set forth for emphyteusis, and with the obligation of giving previous notice, as prescribed in article 1637.

7. A parcenary or grantee may relinquish or return the tenement to the grantor, when convenient, upon paying for the impairments caused by his fault.

8. The grantee shall have no right to the improvements existing on the tenement at the time of the expiration of the contract, provided they are necessary or have been made in fulfillment of what has been stipulated.

In respect to the useful and voluntary improvements, said grantee shall not have a right to be paid for the same, unless he made them with the written consent of the owner of the land, who bound himself to pay for them. In this case, said improvements shall be paid for according to the value which they may have when the tenement is returned.

9. A grantor may make use of the action of ejectment upon the expiration of the term of the contract.

10. When, after the expiration of the term of fifty years or the one expressly fixed by the persons interested, the grantee continues in the use and enjoyment of the tenement by the implied consent of the grantor, the former cannot be ejected without previous notice which the latter should give him a year in advance to determine the contract.

CHAPTER THIRD.

Consignative ground-rents (*censo consignativo*).*

Article **1657.** When the payment of the pension for the consignative ground-rent is stipulated in fruits, the species, quantity and quality of the same shall be fixed, and it cannot consist of an aliquot part of those which the tenement, held in ground-rent, produces.

1658. The redemption of the consignative ground-rent shall consist in the restitution to the *censualista* in cash and in full of the capital paid for the constitution of the ground-rent.

---

* Nov. Recop., book 10, tit. 15, laws 8, 23, rule 2; id., book 10, law 24, chap. 24.

1659. When a real action is instituted against a tenement, held under a ground-rent, for the payment of pensions, if what remains of the value of the same is not sufficient to cover the capital of the ground-rent and twenty-five per cent. over and above the same, the *censualista* may oblige the *censatario,* at the latter's option, either to redeem the ground-rent or to complete the guarantee or to abandon the remainder of the tenement in behalf of the former.

1660. The *censualista* may also exercise the right, set forth in the preceding article, in all the other cases in which the value of the tenement is not sufficient to cover the capital of the ground-rent and twenty-five per cent. more, when any of the following circumstances exist:

1. When the value of the tenement has decreased by the fault or negligence of the *censatario.*

In this case the latter shall also be liable for such damages and injuries.

2. When the *censatario* has failed to pay the pensions during two consecutive years.

3. When the *censatario* may have been declared in bankruptcy, in failure (*en concurso*), or in insolvency.

CHAPTER FOURTH.

*Reservative ground-rent (censo reservativo).**

Article **1661.** Reservative ground-rent cannot be validly constituted, unless preceded by an avaluation of the tenement for a sum agreed to by the parties or upon a just appraisement by experts.

1662. The redemption of this ground-rent shall be effected by the *censatario* delivering to the *censualista,* in cash and in full, the principal which may have been fixed in accordance with the preceding article.

1663. The provisions of article 1657 are applicable to reservative ground-rent.

1664. In the cases provided in articles 1659 and 1660, the debtor of the reservative ground-rent can only be bound, either to redeem the ground-rent, or to relinquish the tenement in favor of the *censualista.*

---

* Nov. Recop., book 10, tit. 15, laws 6, 7, 8.

TITLE VIII.

Partnership.

CHAPTER FIRST.

*General provisions.**

Article **1665.** Partnership is a contract by which two or more persons bind themselves to place money, property, or industry, in common, with the intention of dividing the profits among themselves.

Col. 2079; Chile, 2053.

1666. Partnerships must have licit objects, and be established for the common interests of the partners.

When the dissolution of an illicit partnership is declared, the profits shall be destined for the institutions of beneficence of the domicile of the partnership, and, in default of the same, to those of the province.

1667. Civil partnerships may be constituted in any form whatever, unless when real property or real rights are brought to the same, in which case a public deed is necessary.

1668. A contract of partnership is null and void, when real property is brought to the same, if an inventory of said property is not made and signed by the partners and annexed to the deed.

1669. Partnerships, the stipulations of which are kept secret among the partners, and in which each one of the partners may contract in his own name with third parties, shall have no juridical personality.

This kind of partnership shall be governed by the provisions referring to property held in common.

1670. Civil partnerships, on account of the objects for which they are destined, may adopt all the forms accepted by the Code of Commerce. In this case, the provisions of the same shall be applicable, in so far as they are not in conflict with those of the present Code.

1671. Partnerships are either general or particular.

1672. General partnerships may consist of all the present property or of all the profits.

Col. 2082; Chile, 2056.

---

* Digesto, book 17, tit. 2, laws 1, 5, 73, 5, par. 2. Part. 3, tit. 28, law 47; id. 3, tit. 18, laws 78, 79, 114; id. 5, tit. 10, laws 1, 2, 3, 4, 5, 6, 7. Commercial Code, arts. 116, 119, 240. Penal Code, art. 198. Constitution, art. 13. Law of July 30, 1887.

1673. Partnerships which comprise all the present property are those in which the parties place all the property which actually belong to them, in common, with the intention of dividing the same among themselves, as well as all the profits which they may acquire through said property.

1674. In general partnerships of all the present property, what belongs to each of the partners becomes common property of all the partners, as well as all the profits which they may acquire through the same.

A general partnership of any other property may also be agreed upon, but the property which the partners acquire, thereafter, by inheritance, legacy or donations shall not be comprised in the same, though the fruits of said property shall be included therein.

1675. General partnerships for profits comprise all that the partners may acquire by their industry or work, as long as the partnership lasts.

Personal or real property which each of the partners possess, at the time of the celebration of the contract, shall continue to be their private property, and the usufruct only passes to the partnership.

1676. A contract of general partnership, entered into without specifying its nature, only constitutes a general partnership of profits.

1677. Persons who are forbidden to reciprocally grant to each other donations or advantages cannot contract a general partnership.

1678. A particular partnership has for its object only specified things, their uses or profits, or a specified undertaking, or the exercise of a profession or art.

CHAPTER SECOND.

Obligations of partners.

SECTION FIRST.

*Obligations of the partners among themselves.**

Article **1679.** A partnership begins from the moment of the celebration of the contract, when not otherwise stipulated.

Col. 2091; Chile, 2065.

* Digesto, book 10, tit. 3, law 6, pars. 12, 19, 20, 28; id., book 17, tit. 2, laws 1, 4, 6, 12, 15, 52, par. 3, 58, par. 1, 63, par. 2, 79; id., book 22, tit. 1, law 1, par. 1; id., book 24, tit. 1, law 1, pars. 13, 14. Part. 5, tit. 10, laws 1, 3, 4, 5, 7, 13, 15. Commercial Code, art. 171.

1680. A partnership lasts, during the time agreed upon; in default of an agreement, for such time as the business which has been the exclusive object of the partnership may last, if by its nature, it has a limited duration; and, in any other case, during the lives of the partners, without prejudice to the rights reserved to them in article 1700, and to the provisions of article 1704.

Col. 2091; Chile, 2065.

1681. Each partner is a debtor of the partnership for whatever he has promised to bring to it.

He is also bound to eviction in regard to the specified and determined things brought by him to the partnership, in the same cases and in the same manner as a vendor is bound in respect to the vendee.

1682. A partner who has bound himself to bring to the partnership a sum of money, and fails to do so, is, at law, a debtor for the interest thereon from the day on which he should have brought it, and may also be bound to pay an indemnity for the damages which he may have caused thereby.

The same thing shall be observed with regard to sums which he may have taken from partnership funds, and interest shall be counted from the day on which he took them for his private benefit.

1683. An industrial partner owes to the partnership the profits which, during its existence, he has earned in a branch of the industry which is the object of the partnership.

1684. When a partner who is authorized as a manager collects an exigible sum, which was owed to him in his own name, from a person who owed to the partnership another sum, also exigible, the sum collected shall be imputed to the two credits in proportion to their amounts, even when he has given a receipt for his own account only; but when he has given it on account of the partnership, it shall all be imputed to the credit of the latter.

It shall be understood that the provisions of this article shall not prevent the debtor using the power granted to him in article 1172, but only in the case where the personal credit of the partner is more onerous to him.

Chile, 2092; Col. 2118.

1685. A partner who has received in full his share of a partnership credit, when the other partners had not collected theirs, remains bound, when the debtor afterwards becomes insolvent, to bring to the partnership capital what he received, even when he gave the receipt for his part only.

Chile, 2090; Col. 2116.

1686. Every partner shall be liable to the partnership for the damages and injuries caused to the same by his fault, and he cannot set off against them the benefits which he may have given to the partnership by his industry.

Chile, 2093; Col. 2119.

1687. The risk of things, certain and specified, which are not perishable, brought to the partnership, in order that only their use and fruits be common, shall be borne by the partner owning them.

When the things brought are perishable, or when they cannot be kept without being impaired, or when they were brought to be sold, the risk shall be assumed by the partnership. It shall also be assumed by the same, in default of a special stipulation in respect to the things brought and appraised in the inventory, and, in this case, the claim shall be limited to the value at which they were appraised.

Chile, 2084; Col. 2110.

1688. The partnership is liable to each partner for the sums which he may have disbursed on account of the same and for the corresponding interest; it shall also be liable to each partner for the obligations which he may have contracted in good faith on account of the partnership business, and for risks inseparable from its management.

Col. 2115; Chile, 2089.

1689. The losses and profits shall be distributed in conformity with what has been stipulated. When a stipulation exists only in respect to the share of each one in the profits, his share in the losses shall be in the same proportion.

In default of a stipulation, the share of each partner in the profits and losses shall be in proportion to what he brought. The partner who contributes only his industry shall have a share equal to the one who has brought less. When besides his industry, he has brought a capital, he shall also receive the proportional share which may belong to him for this capital.

Col. 2094; Chile, 2068.

1690. When the partners have agreed to intrust to a third person the designation of the share of each one in the profits and losses, such designation shall be contested only when it has evidently been made contrary to equity. In no case shall the partner, who has commenced to execute the decision of the third party or who has not contested the same within three months, to be counted from when it was known to him, make a claim against it.

The designation of the profits and losses shall not be intrusted to one of the partners.

Col. 2093; Chile, 2067.

1691. A stipulation in which one or more of the partners are excluded from any share in the profits or in the losses is void.

Only the industrial partner may be exempted from any liability in the losses.

1692. A partner, who has been appointed manager in a contract of partnership, may execute all administrative acts, notwithstanding the opposition of his partners, unless he acts in bad faith, and his power is irrevocable, unless it be for a legitimate cause.

A power, executed after the contract, without having it stipulated therein that it should be conferred, may be revoked at any time.

Col. 2100; Chile, 2074.

1693. When two or more partners have been charged with the management of a partnership without their functions being specified, or when it has not been expressed that one of them shall not act without the consent of the others, each one may severally exercise all acts of administration; but any of them may oppose the acts of the others before the same has produced any legal effect.

Col. 2102; Chile, 2076.

1694. When it has been stipulated that some of the managing partners cannot act without the consent of the others, the consent of all shall be necessary for the validity of the acts; and the absence or impossibility of any one of them to act shall not be alleged, unless there is imminent danger of a serious or irreparable damage to the partnership.

Col. 2102; Chile, 2076.

1695. When no stipulation has been made about the form of management, the following rules shall be observed:

1. All the partners shall be considered agents, and whatever any one of them does by himself alone shall bind the partnership; but each one may oppose the operations of the others before the same has produced any legal effect.

2. Each partner may make use of the things which compose the partnership capital, according to the customs of the land, provided he does not use them against the interest of the partnership or in such a way as to prevent the use of them to which his co-partners are entitled.

3. Every partner can bind the others to bear together with him the expenses necessary for the preservation of the things held in common.

4. None of the partners shall, without the consent of the others, make any alteration in the partnership real property, even when he alleges that it is useful to the partnership.

Chile, 2081; Col. 2107.

1696. Each partner may associate another person in his share; but said person shall not enter the partnership without the unanimous consent of the other partners, even when the former is the manager.

Col. 2114; Chile, 2088.

SECTION SECOND.

*Obligations of partners in respect to third persons.**

Article **1697.** In order that the partnership may remain liable to a third person for the acts of one of the partners, it is necessary:

1. That the partner may have acted as such and on account of the partnership.

2. That he may have had the power to bind the partnership by virtue of an express or implied power of attorney.

3. That he may have acted within the limits of the power granted to him.

1698. Partners do not remain jointly bound in respect to the debts of the partnerships, and none of them can bind the others by a personal act, if a power has not been conferred on him therefor.

A partnership does not remain liable in respect to a third person for the acts which one of the partners has done in his own name and without a power from the partnership therefor, but it remains liable to the partner in so far as said acts have benefited said partnership.

The provision of this article shall be understood without prejudice to what is set forth in rule first of article 1695.

Col. 2121; Chile, 2095.

1699. Creditors of the partnership shall be preferred to the creditors of each partner as to the partnership property. Notwithstanding this right, the private creditors of each partner may ask for the seizure and sale at auction of the latter's share in the partnership capital.

* Part. 7, tit. 34, law 27.

CHAPTER THIRD.

*Manners of extinguishing partnership.**

Article **1700.** Partnership is extinguished:

1. When the term for which it was constituted expires.

2. When the thing is lost, or the business for which it was constituted ends.

3. By the natural death, civil interdiction, or insolvency of any of the partners, and in the case provided for in article 1699.

4. By the will of any of the partners, subject to the provisions of articles 1705 and 1707.

Partnerships, to which article 1670 refers, are excepted from provisions of Nos. 3 and 4 of this article, in the cases in which they should exist, according to the Code of Commerce.

Col. 2124; Chile, 2098.

1701. When a specific thing, which a partner has promised to bring to the partnership, perishes before the delivery has been effected, its loss produces the dissolution of the partnership.

A partnership shall also be dissolved, in every case, by the loss of the thing, when the partner who brings it reserves to himself the ownership thereof and transfers to the partnership only the use or enjoyment of the same.

But the partnership shall not be dissolved by the loss of the thing, when this loss happens after the property thereof has been acquired by the partnership.

Col. 2128; Chile, 2102.

1702. A partnership constituted for a specified time may be extended by the consent of all the partners.

Such consent may be express or implied and it may be shown by any ordinary means.

1703. When the partnership is extended, after the expiration of its term, it shall be understood that a new partnership is constituted. When it is extended before the expiration of such term, the original partnership continues.

1704. A stipulation is valid which provides that, on the death of one of the partners, the partnership shall continue among the survivors. In this case, the heir of the decedent shall have only the

---

* Digesto, book 17, tit. 2, laws 58, 63, 63, par. 10, 50. Part. 5, tit. 10, laws 1, 10, 11, 12, 14. Instituciones, book 3, tit. 26, par. 4.

right to have a distribution made, fixing it on the day of the death of his constituent; and he shall not participate in the successive rights and obligations only in so far as they are a necessary result of what has been done before said day.

When the stipulation is that the partnership shall continue with the heir, it shall be enforced, without prejudice to the provisions of No. 4 of article 1700.

Col. 2131; Chile, 2105.

1705. The dissolution of the partnership by the will or renunciation of one of the partners shall only take place when a term for its duration has not been fixed, or this term does not appear from the nature of the business.

In order that the renunciation may be effectual, it shall be made in good faith and timely; notice thereof shall also be given to the other partners.

1706. A renunciation shall be considered in bad faith when the person who makes it proposes to appropriate to himself alone the benefits which should be common for all. In this case the person who renounces it does not free himself from responsibility to his partners, and they shall have the power to exclude him from the partnership.

A renunciation shall be presumed as not made in time when, the things not being integral, the partnership is interested in delaying its dissolution. In this case the partnership shall continue until the termination of the pending business.

Col. 2137; Chile, 2111.

1707. No partner can demand the dissolution of a partnership, which either by a provision of the contract, or by the nature of the business, has been constituted for a specified time, unless there exists a just cause, such as when one of the co-partners fails to comply with his obligations, or when he becomes incapacitated for the partnership business, or any other similar cause, according to the judgment of the courts.

Chile, 2108.

1708. Distribution among the partners shall be governed by the rules of inheritances, both with regard to its form and to the obligations resulting from the same. To the industrial partner shall not be given any part of the property brought to it, but only its fruits and profits, according to the provisions of article 1689, unless the contrary has been expressly stipulated.

TITLE IX.

Agency.

CHAPTER FIRST.

*Nature, form and kind of agency.**

Article **1709.** By the contract of agency, a person binds himself to render some service, or to do something in behalf of or at the request of another person.

Chile, 2116; Col. 2142.

1710. Agency may be express or tacit.

Express agency may be given by a public or private instrument and even by parol.

The acceptance may also be express or tacit, and the latter may be inferred from the acts of the agent.

Col. 2149.

1711. In default of a stipulation to the contrary, the agency is presumed to be gratuitous.

Nevertheless, when the agent has for an occupation the performance of services of the kind to which the agency refers, the obligation of giving him a compensation is presumed.

Col. 2143; Chile, 2117.

1712. Agency is general or special.

The former embraces all the business of the principal.

The latter, one or more specified businesses.

Col. 2156 to 2177; Chile, 2130 to 2151.

1713. Agency stated in general terms only comprises acts of administration.

To compromise, alienate, mortgage or to execute any other act of rigorous ownership express authority is required.

The power to compromise does not give authority to place the matter in the hands of arbitrators or compromisers.

1714. An agent shall not exceed the limits of the authority granted to him.

---

* Digesto, book 3, tit. 3, law 1, par. 1, 60, 63; id., book 17, tit. 1, laws 1, 5, 5, par. 5, 22, 41. Codigo, book 2, tit. 13, law 16; id., book 4, tit. 35, law 6. Instituciones, book 3, tit. 27, pars. 8, 13. Part. 3, tit. 5, laws 19, 29; id. 5, tit. 12, laws 20, 21, 22, 24. Commercial Code, arts. 244, 249, 281, 283, 284. Law of Judicial Power, arts. 873, 881.

1715. The limits of the authority shall not be presumed exceeded, when the business is complied with in a manner more advantageous for the principal than that specified.

1716. An emancipated minor can be an agent; but the principal shall only have an action against him in conformity with the provisions concerning the obligations of minors.

Married women can only accept an agency with authorization of their husbands.

1717. When an agent acts in his own name, the principal shall have no action against the persons with whom the agent has contracted, nor the said persons against the principal.

In this case, the agent remains directly bound to the person with whom he has contracted, as if it were his own personal business. The case in which the contract refers to things belonging to the principal is excepted.

The provision of this article shall be understood without prejudice to actions between the principal and the agent.

CHAPTER SECOND.

*Obligations of the agent.**

Article **1718.** An agent by his acceptance remains bound to comply with the agency and shall be liable for the damages and injuries caused to the principal for his noncompliance.

Business, which has already been begun at the death of the principal, must be completed by him, when there is any peril in delay.

1719. In compliance with the agency, the agent shall observe the instructions received from the principal.

In default of the same, he shall do all that, which according to the nature of the business, a good father of a family would do.

1720. Every agent is bound to render an account of his operations and to pay to the principal all that he has received by virtue of the agency, even when what he has received is not owed to the principal.

1721. An agent may appoint a substitute, when the principal has not forbidden him to do so, but he shall be liable for the acts of the substitute:

1. When the power to appoint such substitute was not given to him.

*** Digesto, book 3, tit. 5, laws 21, par. 13, 31; id., book 10, tit. 1, laws 1, par. 11, 10, par. 3; id., book 17, tit. 1, laws 10, par. 3, 8, par. 3, 20, 21, 27, par. 2, 60, par. 20. Part. 3, tit. 5, law 26; id. 5, tit. 12, laws 21, 24. Commercial Code, arts. 243, 248, 263, 286.**

2. When such power was granted to him, but without designating the person, and the person appointed by said agent was notoriously incapable or insolvent.

Whatever is done by the substitute, who has been appointed against the prohibition of the principal, shall be null and void.

1722. In the cases stated in the two numbers of the preceding article, the principal shall also have the right to enforce his action against the substitute.

1723. The liability of two or more agents, even when they have been so simultaneously appointed, shall not be joint, unless it has been so stated.

1724. An agent shall owe interest for the sums which he has applied to his own use, from the day on which he did so, and of those which he still owes, after the expiration of the agency and from the time of his default.

1725. An agent who acts as such shall not be personally liable towards the persons with whom he contracted, except when he expressly binds himself therefor, or when he exceeds the limits of his authority without giving a sufficient notice of his powers to said person.

1726. An agent shall be liable not only for deceit, but also for his negligence, which shall be judged with more or less severity by the courts, taking into consideration whether the agent has been paid for his services or not.

CHAPTER THIRD.

*Obligations of the principal.**

Article **1727.** A principal shall comply with all the obligations which the agent has contracted, within the limits of his power.

A principal remains liable, in so far as the agent has exceeded his power, only when he expressly or tacitly ratifies the same.

1728. A principal shall advance to the agent, if the latter asks it, such sums as may be necessary for the execution of the agency.

When the agent has advanced them, the principal shall reimburse him for the same, even when the business has not succeeded, provided the agent be exempt from blame.

The reimbursement shall comprise the interests on the sums advanced, counted from the day on which the advance was made.

---

* Digesto, book 15, tit. 4, law 5, par. 1; id., book 17, laws 12, 26, par. 6, 7, 27, 39, par. 3, 45; id., book 46, tit. 3, law 56. Codigo, book 2, tit. 39, law 18; id., book 4, tit. 35, law 1. Part. 5, tit. 12, laws 20, 21, 22, 28; id. 7, tit. 34, law 10. Commercial Code, arts. 278, 298.

1729. A principal shall also indemnify the agent for all damages and injuries caused to him in complying with the agency, when there is no fault or imprudence on the part of said agent.

1730. An agent may retain the things, which are the objects of the agency, in pledge, until the principal pays the indemnity and reimbursement referred to in the two preceding articles.

1731. When two or more persons have appointed an agent for a business in common, they shall remain jointly bound to the latter for all the effects of the agency.

CHAPTER FOURTH.

*Manner of determining the agency.**

Article **1732.** Agency is determined:

1. By revocation.
2. By renunciation of the agent.
3. By death, interdiction, bankruptcy or insolvency of either the principal or the agent.

Chile, 2163; Col. 2189.

1733. A principal may, at his will, revoke the power and compel the agent to return the document in which the authority was given.

Col. 2191.

1734. When an agency has been granted to contract with determined persons, the revocation of the agency shall not be to the injury of said persons, unless notice was given to them.

1735. The appointment of a new agent for the same business produces a revocation of the preceding power of attorney from the day on which notice was given to the former agent, without prejudice to the provisions of the preceding article.

Col. 2190; Chile, 2164.

1736. An agent may renounce the agency by giving notice to the principal. When the latter suffers any injuries by the renunciation, he should be indemnified for the same by the agent, unless the latter bases his renunciation on the impossibility of continuing to act as such without serious detriment to himself.

1737. Even when the agent has renounced the power for a just cause, he should continue acting as such until the principal shall be able to take the necessary steps to provide therefor.

* Digesto, book 3, tit. 3, law 31, par. 2; id., book 17, tit. 1, law 12, par. 6, 12, par. 16, 22 to 27, par. 3, 26, 58; id., book 17, tit. 2, law 40. Instituciones, book 3, tit. 27, pars. 3, 9, 10, 11. Commercial Code, arts. 279, 280, 290.

1738. What has been done by the agent, when he was not aware that the principal was dead, or of any other of the causes which terminate the agency, shall be valid and effectual with regard to third persons who have contracted with the agent in good faith.

Col. 2199; Chile, 2173.

1739. When the agent dies, his heirs shall give notice of his death to the principal, and, meanwhile, adopt the measures which circumstances may require for the interests of the latter.

Col. 2196; Chile, 2170.

TITLE X.

Loans.

*General provision.**

Article **1740.** By the contract of loan, one of the parties delivers to the other, either anything not perishable, in order that the latter may use it during a certain time and return it to the former, in which case it is named *commodatum*, or money or any other perishable thing, under the condition to return an equal amount of the same kind and quality, in which case it is merely called a loan.

Commodatum is essentially gratuitous.

A simple loan may be gratuitous, or made under a stipulation to pay interest.

Col. 2200; Chile, 2174.

CHAPTER FIRST.

Commodatum.

SECTION FIRST.

Nature of commodatum.†

Article **1741.** A lender (*comodante*) retains the ownership of the thing loaned. The borrower (*comodatario*) acquires the use of the same, but not its fruits; when the person who acquires the use has to pay any compensation, the agreement shall cease to be a *commodatum.*

1742. The obligations and rights which grow out of the *commo-*

---

* Instituciones, book 3, tit. 15, par. 2. Part. 5, tit. 1, law 1; id. 5, tit. 2, law 1. Commercial Code, art. 312.

† Digesto, book 13, tit. 6, laws 8, 9. Recopilada, book 11, tit. 8, law 1. Part. 3, tit. 14, law 11; id. 5, tit. 2, law 5; id. 5, tit. 11, law 14.

datum shall pass to the heirs of both contracting parties, unless the loan has been made in consideration for the person of the borrower, in which case his heirs shall not have the right to continue using the thing loaned.

SECTION SECOND.

*Obligations of the borrower (comodatario).**

Article **1743.** The borrower shall be bound to pay the ordinary expenses which are necessary for the use and preservation of the thing loaned.

1744. When the borrower puts the thing to a different use than that for which it was loaned, or keeps the same in his possession for a longer time than that agreed upon, he shall be liable for its loss, even when said loss occurs by an unforeseen event (*vis major*).

1745. When the thing loaned was delivered under appraisal and is lost, even if it be by an unforeseen event (*vis major*), the borrower shall be liable for its value, unless there is a stipulation in which he is expressly exempted from said liability.

1746. The borrower shall not be liable for the wear and tear caused to the thing loaned only on account of its use and without fault on his part.

1747. A borrower shall not retain the thing loaned under the pretext that the lender owes him something, even if it is on account of expenses.

Col. 2207.

1748. All the borrowers to whom the thing is jointly loaned shall be jointly liable for the same, according to the provisions of this section.

SECTION THIRD.

Obligations of the lender (comodante).†

Article **1749.** A lender cannot claim the thing loaned, except after the termination of the use for which it was loaned. Nevertheless, when, previous to such term, the lender has an urgent necessity for the same, he may claim its restitution.

Col. 2205; Chile, 2180.

---

* Digesto, book 13, tit. 6, laws 5, par. 3, 4, 7, 18, par. 2. Part. 5, tit. 2, laws 3, 5, 7, 9. Codigo, book 4, tit. 23, law 4.

† Part. 5, tit. 2, law 9.

1750. When the duration of the *commodatum* has not been stipulated, nor the use to which the thing loaned was to be destined, and the latter does not appear determined by the customs of the land, the lender may claim it at his will.

In case of doubt, the burden of proof falls upon the borrower.

1751. The lender shall pay the extraordinary expenses, caused during the contract for the preservation of the thing loaned, provided that the borrower gives notice of the same before making them, unless when they are so urgent that the answer to the notice cannot be waited for without risk.

Col. 2216; Chile, 2191.

1752. A lender, who, knowing the vices of the thing loaned, has not given notice thereof to the borrower, shall be liable to the same for the damages which he may have suffered on that account.

CHAPTER SECOND.

*Simple loan.**

Article **1753.** A person who receives money or any other perishable thing on loan acquires its ownership, and is bound to return to the creditor an equal amount of the same kind and quality.

1754. The obligations of a person who takes money on loan shall be governed by the provisions of article 1170 of this Code.

When what has been loaned is some other perishable thing, or a quantity of metal, not in coin, the debtor owes a quantity, equal to the one received, and of the same kind and quality, although it may have suffered a change in its value.

1755. Interests shall only be owed when they have been expressly stipulated.

1756. A borrower, who has paid interests without it being stipulated, cannot claim them nor impute them to the capital.

1757. Pawn shops shall besides be subject to the ordinances relating to them.

---

* Digesto, book 12, tit. 1, law 12. Part. 5, tit. 1, law 2. Penal Code, arts. 559, 560.

TITLE XI.

Deposit.

CHAPTER FIRST.

*Deposits in general and different kinds thereof.**

Article **1758.** A deposit is constituted when a person receives a thing belonging to another under the obligation of keeping and returning the same.

Col. 2236; Chile, 2211.

1759. A deposit may be judicially or extrajudicially constituted.

CHAPTER SECOND.

Deposits properly speaking.

SECTION FIRST.

Nature and essence of the contract of deposit.†

Article **1760.** Deposit is a gratuitous contract, unless the contrary is stipulated.

Col. 2244; Chile, 2219.

1761. Personal property only shall be an object of deposit.

1762. Extrajudicial deposit is either necessary or voluntary.

SECTION SECOND.

Voluntary deposit.‡

Article **1763.** Voluntary deposit is that in which the delivery is made by the will of the depositor. The deposit may be effected by two or more persons who believe themselves to have a right to the thing deposited in the hands of a third person who shall, in proper cases, deliver said thing to the party to whom it belongs.

---

* Digesto, book 16, tit. 3, law 1. Part. 3, tit. 9. Commercial Code, arts. 305, 506.

† Digesto, book 16, tit. 3, law 1, par. 1, 8. Fuero Real, book 3, tit. 15. Fuero Juzgo, book 5, tit. 5. Part. 5, tit. 3, laws 1, 2.

‡ Digesto, book 12, tit. 6, law 14; id., book 16, law 1, par. 15. Instituciones, book 1, tit. 21. Part. 6, tit. 16, law 17; id. 7, tit. 34, law 17.

1764. When a person able to contract accepts the deposit made by another who is incapable, the former remains bound to all the obligations of a depositary, and may be compelled to return it by the guardian, curator or administrator of the person who made the deposit or by the same person, if he becomes capable.

1765. When the deposit has been made by a capable person, in the hands of another who is incapable, the depositor shall only have the action to revindicate the thing deposited as long as it remains in the hands of the depositary, or to oblige the latter to pay him the sum by which he may have profited on account of the thing or its price.

SECTION THIRD.

*Obligations of the depositary.**

Article **1766.** A depositary is bound to keep the thing, and, when required, to return it to the depositor or person holding rights under the same, or to the person who has been designated in the contract. His liability, with regard to the keeping and loss of the thing, shall be governed by the provisions of title first of this book.

1767. A depositary shall not make use of the thing deposited without the express permission of the depositor.

Otherwise he shall be liable for damages and injuries.

1768. When the depositary has permission to serve himself or make use of the thing deposited, the contract loses the character of deposit and becomes a loan or a *commodatum.*

Such permission shall not be presumed, and its existence must be proven.

1769. When the deposit is delivered closed and sealed, the depositary shall return it in the same condition and he shall be liable for damages and injuries when the seal or lock has been broken by his fault.

Such depositary is presumed to be culpable, unless the contrary is proven.

With regard to the value of the thing deposited, the statement of the depositor shall be admitted, when the forcible opening is chargeable to the depositary, unless there is proof to the contrary.

1770. The thing deposited shall be returned with all its proceeds and accretions.

---

* Digesto, book 12, tit. 1, law 10; id., book 16, tit. 3, laws 1, pars. 5, 36, 39, 2, par. 45, 5, pars. 2, 12, 24, 29, par. 1, 31, pars. 1, 44, 46; id., book 19, tit. 2, law 31; id., book 47, tit. 2, law 61, par. 5. Instituciones, book 3, tit. 14, par. 3. Part. 5, tit. 3, laws 2, 3, 5, 68. Fuero Real, book 3, tit. 5, law 5. Commercial Code, arts. 306, 307.

When the deposit consists of money, the provisions in regard to agents, set forth in article 1724, shall be applied to the depositary.

1771. The depositary cannot force the depositor to prove that he is the owner of the thing deposited.

Nevertheless, if he discovers that the thing has been stolen and who is the true owner, he shall give notice of its deposit to the latter.

When the owner, notwithstanding said notice, does not claim it within the term of one month the depositary shall be free from any liability by returning the thing deposited to the person from whom he received it.

1772. When there are two or more depositors and they are not joint and the thing can be divided, each one of them can ask for his part only.

When they are joint depositors or the thing does not admit of division, the provisions of articles 1141 and 1142 of this Code shall rule.

1773. When the depositor loses his capacity to contract after having made the deposit, the latter cannot be returned, except to the persons who have the management of the property and rights of the depositor.

1774. When, on making the deposit, a place is designated for the return of the thing deposited, the depositary should take it to such place, but the expense caused by the conveyance shall be chargeable to the depositor.

When a place has not been designated for the return thereof, it shall be made at the place where the thing deposited is, even when it is not the same place where the deposit was made, provided that malice on the part of the depositary has not intervened.

1775. The deposit shall be restored to the depositor, when he claims it, even though a term or specified time for such return has been fixed in the contract.

This disposition shall not be observed when the deposit has been judicially seized or attached in the hands of the depositary, or when the latter has been notified of the opposition of a third party to the return or to the transfer of the thing deposited.

1776. The depositary, who has just motives for not keeping the deposit, may, even before the term designated, return it to the depositor, and if the latter refuses it, he may obtain its consignation from the Judge.

1777. The depositary, who has lost the thing deposited through an act of God (*vis major*) and received another in its place, shall be bound to deliver the latter thing to the depositor.

1778. An heir of the depositor who, in good faith, has sold the thing, which he did not know was deposited, shall only be bound to return the price which he may have received or to assign his actions against the purchaser in case the price has not been paid to him.

SECTION FOURTH.

*Obligations of the depositor.**

Article **1779.** A depositor is bound to reimburse the depositary for the expenses incurred by the latter in the preservation of the thing deposited, and to indemnify him for all the injuries which may have been caused to him on account of the deposit.

1780. The depositary may retain the thing deposited in pledge until the total payment of what is due him on account of the deposit.

SECTION FIFTH.

Necessary deposit.†

Article **1781.** A deposit shall be necessary:

1. When made in compliance with a legal obligation.

2. When made on account of any calamity, such as fire, ruin, pillage, shipwreck or any other similar cases.

1782. A deposit, comprised in the first number of the preceding article, shall be governed by the provisions of the law which establishes it, and, default of the same, by those of voluntary deposit.

Those comprised in the second number shall be governed by the rules of voluntary deposit.

1783. The deposit of effects, made by travellers, in inns or hostelries, shall also be considered a necessary one.

The keepers of inns and hostelries shall be liable for them as such depositaries, provided that notice thereof has been given to them or to their clerks, and that the travellers on their part observe the precautions which said innkeepers or their substitutes may have about the care and watchfulness over such effects.

1784. The liability to which the preceding article refers shall comprise damages to the goods of travellers, caused by servants or clerks of the keepers of inns or hostelries as well as by strangers, but not for those arising from robbery or which may be caused by any other case of *vis major*.

---

* Digesto, book 16, tit. 3, laws 5, 8, 23. Part. 5, tit. 3, law 10.

† Digesto, book 4, tit. 9, law 1, pars. 1, 5, 7. Part. 5, tit. 3, laws 1, 8; id. 5, tit. 8, law 26. Penal Code, arts. 20, 546, 548.

CHAPTER THIRD.

Sequestration. *

Article **1785.** A judicial deposit or sequestration takes place when a seizure or placing in security of property in litigation is decreed.

1786. Personal as well as real property may be subject to sequestration.

1787. A depositary of the property or things sequestrated shall not be released from his charge, until the controversy which caused it is ended, unless the Judge orders it on account of the consent of all the persons interested, or for any other lawful cause.

1788. A depositary of property sequestrated is bound in respect to the same to comply with all the obligations of a good father of a family.

1789. Judicial sequestration shall be governed by the provisions of the Law of Civil Procedure in whatever is not provided for in this Code.

TITLE XII.

Aleatory or hazardous (contingent) contracts.

CHAPTER FIRST.

General provision.

Article **1790.** By an aleatory contract, one of the parties binds himself, or both reciprocally bind themselves to give or do something as an equivalent for what the other party has to give or to do, in case of the happening of an event which is uncertain or is to happen at an undetermined time.

CHAPTER SECOND.

Contract of insurance.†

Article **1791.** A contract of insurance is one by which the insurer is liable for the fortuitous damages which may occur to the personal or real property insured, in consideration of a certain price, which may be freely fixed by the parties.

1792. Two or more proprietors may mutually insure against fortuitous damages which may happen to their respective properties. This contract is called mutual insurance, and, when it has not been otherwise stipulated, it is understood that the indemnity for such

---

* Part. 3, tit. 9; id. 3, tit. 9, law 2.

† Digesto, book 22, tit. 2. Codigo, book 4, tit. 33. Commercial Code, arts. 380 to 438, 783 to 805.

damages shall be paid by all the contracting parties in proportion to the value of the property which each one has insured.

1793. A contract of insurance shall be made in a public or private instrument signed by the contracting parties.

1794. Said instrument shall specify:

1. The designation and situation of the things insured and their value.

2. The classes of risks for which indemnification is stipulated.

3. The day and hour on which the effects of the contract commence and end.

4. All the other conditions to which the contracting parties have agreed.

1795. The contract shall not be effectual as to the part in which the sum of the insurance exceeds the value of the thing insured, and only one insurance can be collected for the whole value of the same.

When two or more contracts of insurance exist in respect to the same object, each insurer shall be liable for the damage, in proportion to the capital which he has insured, until the total value of the thing insured has been paid in full by them.

1796. When the damage occurs, the insured must give notice of the same to the insurer and all the other persons concerned, within the term agreed to; and, in default of the same, within twenty-four hours to be counted from the time the insured had knowledge of the loss. When he fails to do so, he shall have no action against them.

1797. A contract shall be null when, at the time it was made, the insured knew that the damage, which was the object of the same, had occurred, or when the insurer knew that the property insured was already free from said danger.

CHAPTER THIRD.

*Gaming and betting.**

Article **1798.** The law does not give any action to claim what is won in a game of chance, luck or hazard, but the person who loses cannot recover what he has voluntarily paid, unless fraud has intervened, or he is a minor or incapacitated to administer his property.

1799. The provisions of the preceding article in regard to gambling are also applicable to betting.

Bets which have analogy with prohibited games are considered as prohibited.

---

* Digesto, book 11, tit. 5, laws 1, 2, 3, 4; id., book 19, tit. 5, law 17, par. 5; id., book 44, tit. 5, law 2. Codigo, book 3, tit. 43, laws 1, 3. Nov. Recop., book 12, tit. 23, law 15, art. 6. Recopilada, book 12, tit. 33, law 15. Penal Code, arts. 358 to 360.

1800. Games which contribute to the exercise of the body, as those whose object is to acquire skill in the management of arms, and races on foot or horseback, by vehicles, ball games, and others of an analogous nature are not considered prohibited.

1801. A person who loses in a game or a bet which is not prohibited shall be civilly liable therefor.

Nevertheless, judicial authority may, either not consider the claim when the sum which was wagered in the game or bet is excessive, or such authority may reduce the obligation to the extent it exceeds the customs of a good father of a family.

CHAPTER FOURTH.

Annuities for life.

Article **1802.** An aleatory contract of annuity binds the debtor to pay a pension or annual sum to one or more specified persons, during their lives, for a capital in personal or real property, the ownership of which is at once transferred to such debtor with the liability of paying such pension.

1803. An annuity may be constituted on the life of the person who gives the capital, on that of a third person, or on that of several persons.

It may also be constituted in behalf of the person or persons for whose life it is agreed, or in behalf of another or other different persons.

1804. An annuity constituted on the life of persons dead, at the time of making the contract, or who, at the same time, is suffering from disease which may cause his death, within twenty days next following that date, is null and void.

1805. Default in payment of pensions due does not authorize the receiver of the life annuity to exact the reimbursement of the capital, nor to re-enter the possession of the tenement alienated; he shall only have the right to judicially claim the payment of the pensions in arrears, and security for future ones.

1806. Annuity, corresponding to the year in which the person who enjoys it dies, shall be paid in proportion to the days which he has lived; when it must be paid in installments in advance, the total amount for such a term, which began to run during his life, shall be paid.

1807. A person, who by gratuitous title constitutes an annuity on his property, may dispose, at the time of the execution of the contract, that said annuity shall not be subject to attachments for debts of the annuitant.

1808. Annuity cannot be claimed without proving the existence of the person on whose life it was constituted.

TITLE XIII.

Compromises and arbitrations.

CHAPTER FIRST.

*Compromises.**

Article **1809.** Compromise is a contract by which each one of the parties by giving, promising, or retaining something avoids the provocation of a suit, or puts an end to the one that has already been instituted.

1810. A guardian cannot compromise the right of a person who is under guardianship, except in the manner prescribed in No. 12 of article 269, and in article 274 of the present Code.

The father, and, in certain cases, the mother, may compromise in regard to the property and rights of the child who is under their power, but if the value of the object about which the compromise is made exceeds two thousand *pesetas,* it shall not be effective without judicial approval.

1811. Neither the husband nor the wife can compromise in regard to dotal property and rights, except in the cases and with the formalities provided for alienating or incumbering the same.

1812. Corporations which have a juridical personality can only make compromises in the manner and with the requisites necessary for alienating their property.

1813. A civil action arising from a crime may be compromised; but the public action for the imposition of the legal penalty shall not be extinguished thereby.

1814. No compromises can be made in regard to the civil status of persons, neither in regard to matrimonial questions, nor about future support.

1815. A compromise shall only embrace the objects specifically set forth in the same, or those which by a necessary induction from its words must be considered embraced therein.

A general renunciation of rights shall be understood as including only those which have relation with the question about which the compromise has been made.

---

* Digesto, book 2, tit. 14, law 35; id., book 2, tit. 15, laws 1, 6, 7, 8, 9, par. 1; id. book 12, tit. 6, law 2, par. 1. Codigo, book 2, tit. 4, laws 12, 13, 19, 20, 38, 42; id., book 7, tit. 52, law 4. Part. 3, tit. 4, law 24; id. 3, tit. 22, law 19; id. 5, tit. 14, law 34; id. 6, tit. 1, law 22; id. 6, tit. 2, law 1. Law of Civil Procedure, arts. 476, 487, 1306, 1313, 1389, 2025. Penal Code, art. 24.

1816. A compromise has, as among the parties, the same authority as a final judgment, but summary proceedings shall not be taken, except when they are in compliance with a judicial compromise.

1817. A compromise, in which error, deceit, violence, or forgery of documents intervenes, shall be subject to the provisions of article 1265 of this Code.

Nevertheless, one of the parties shall not oppose an error of fact against the other, when, on account of a compromise, the latter has withdrawn from a suit already begun.

1818. The discovery of new documents is not a cause for annulling or rescinding a compromise, unless bad faith has been shown.

1819. When a suit has been decided by a final sentence and a compromise about the same has been made, because one of the parties interested did not know about the existence of such a final sentence, said party may ask that the compromise be rescinded.

Ignorance of a revocable sentence is not a cause for contesting a compromise.

CHAPTER SECOND.

*Arbitration.**

Article **1820.** The same persons who can compromise may also submit their contentions to a third party for decision.

1821. The provisions of the preceding chapter about compromises are applicable to arbitrations. With regard to the form of procedure in arbitrations and as to the extent and effects of the same, the provisions of the Law of Civil Procedure shall be observed.

TITLE XIV.

Security.

CHAPTER FIRST.

Nature and extent of security.†

Article **1822.** By security a person binds himself to pay or to comply with some obligation for a third party in case the latter fails to do so.

---

* Digesto, book 4, tit. 8, law 27, par. 5. Part. 3, tit. 4, law 25. Recopilada, book 11, tit. 17, law 4. Law of Civil Procedure, book 2, tit. 5.

† Digesto, book 2, tit. 8, laws 2, 8, pars. 1, 2; id., book 9, tit. 2, law 13; id., book 36, tit. 4, law 4; id., book 17, tit. 1, law 6, pars. 1, 2, 18, 20, pars. 1, 40; id., book 46, tit. 1, laws 1, 2, 3, 4, 6, 8, par. 5, 6, 12, 27, pars. 3, 4, 56, last par., 57. Instituciones, book 3, tit. 21, par. 1, 5; id., book 4, tit. 7, par. 7. Codigo, book 8, tit. 42, law 2. Part. 5, tit. 1, laws 4, 5, 6; id. 5, tit. 12, laws 1, 5, 6, 7, 12, 13. Commercial Code, art. 440. Fuero Real, book 3. tit. 18, law 1.

When the surety binds himself jointly with the principal debtor, the provisions of section fourth, chapter third, title first of this book shall be observed.

1823. Security may be conventional, legal or judicial, gratuitous, or under an onerous title.

It may also be constituted, not only in behalf of the principal debtor, but in behalf of another surety, either with the consent, ignorance, and even against the opposition of the latter.

1824. Security cannot exist without a valid obligation.

Nevertheless, an obligation, the nullity of which may be claimed by virtue of an exception purely personal on the part of the obligee, as that of minority, may be the subject of security.

From the provisions of the preceding paragraph is excepted the case in which a loan is made to a minor, not emancipated.

1825. Security may also be given as a guaranty for future debts, the amount of which is not yet known, but no claim shall be instituted against the surety until the debt is liquid.

1826. A surety may bind himself to less, but not more than the principal debtor, as to quantity as well as to the oppressiveness of the conditions.

When he binds himself for more, his obligation shall be reduced to the same limits as that of the debtor.

1827. Security shall not be presumed, it must be express and shall not be extended farther than that specified therein.

When it is simple and indefinite, it shall comprise not only the principal obligation, but all its accessories, including the expenses of the suit, it being understood in regard to the latter that the surety shall only be liable for those incurred, after he has been asked to pay.

1828. A party who is bound to give security shall present a person having capacity to bind himself and with sufficient property to answer for the obligation which he guarantees. The surety shall be understood as submitting himself to the jurisdiction of the judge of the place where this obligation is to be fulfilled.

1829. When the surety becomes insolvent, the creditor may require another who may have all the qualifications set forth in the preceding article.

The case is excepted where the creditor has required and stipulated that a specified person should be the surety.

CHAPTER SECOND.

Effects of security.

SECTION FIRST.

*Effects of security between surety and creditor.**

Article **1830.** A surety cannot be compelled to pay a creditor, until a levy has been previously made upon all the property of the debtor.

1831. A levy shall not be made:

1. When the surety has expressly renounced it.
2. When he has jointly bound himself with the debtor.
3. In case of bankruptcy or general assignment of the debtor.
4. When the debtor cannot be judicially sued within the Kingdom.

1832. In order that the surety may avail himself of the benefit of a levy, he must set it up against the creditor, as soon as the latter summons the former for payment, and points out the property of the debtor to him, which can be sold within Spanish territory and which is sufficient to cover the amount of the debt.

1833. When the surety has fulfilled all the conditions of the preceding article, the creditor who is negligent in making a levy upon the property, pointed out to him, shall be liable, to the extent of the value of said property, for the insolvency of the debtor, resulting from said negligence.

1834. A creditor may summon the surety, when he institutes the claim against the principal debtor, but the benefit of a levy shall always be effective, even when a sentence is rendered against both of them.

1835. A compromise made by a surety with a creditor shall have no effect in respect to the principal debtor.

That made by the latter shall neither be of any effect in respect to a surety against his will.

1836. A surety of a surety enjoys the benefit of a levy both with respect to the surety and to the principal debtor.

1837. When there are several sureties but only one debtor for the same debt, the obligation to answer for it shall be divided among them all. The creditor can only claim from each surety the corresponding portion which he has to pay, unless the solidarity has been expressly stipulated.

---

* Digesto, book 46, tit. 1, law 27, pars. 1 to 4. Instituciones, book 3, tit. 21, par. 4. Codigo, book 2, tit. 3, last law, No. 1. Novela, 4, chap. 1. Part. 5, tit. 12, laws 3, 8, 9, Nos. 4, 10.

The benefit of division against the co-sureties ceases in the same cases and for the same causes as that for levy against the principal debtor.

SECTION SECOND.

*Effects of security between the debtor and the surety.**

Article **1838.** A surety who pays for a debtor shall be indemnified by the latter.

Such indemnity comprises:

1. The total amount of the debt.

2. Legal interest on the same from the day on which the payment was made known to the debtor, even when it did not produce interest for the creditor.

3. The expenses caused to the surety after the latter has given notice to the debtor that he has been required to pay.

4. Damages and injuries, when proper.

The provision of this article shall be effective, even when the security has been given without knowledge of the debtor.

1839. By virtue of such payment the surety is subrogated in all the rights which the creditor had against the debtor.

When the surety has compromised with the creditor, he shall not ask from the debtor more than that which he has really paid.

1840. When the surety pays without giving notice to the debtor, the latter may make use against the former of all the exceptions which he could have set up against the creditor, at the time of making the payment.

1841. When the debt is for a term and the surety pays before the expiration, he cannot require the debtor to reimburse him until such term has expired.

1842. When the surety has paid without giving notice to the debtor, and the latter, not having knowledge of the payment, also pays it, the former has no remedy against the debtor.

1843. The surety, even before paying, may proceed against the principal debtor:

1. When he is judicially sued for the payment.

2. In case of bankruptcy, general assignment of property, or insolvency.

3. When the debtor has bound himself to relieve him from the security within a specified term, and this term has expired.

---

* Digesto, book 17, tit. 1, laws 22, par. 1, 29, par. 3, 38, 56; id., book 45, tit. 1, law 4. Instituciones, book 3, tit. 21, par. 6. Codigo, book 4, tit. 35, law 10. Part. 5, tit. 12, laws 11, 12, 14, 15, 16.

4. When the debt has become exigible because the term in which it should have been paid has elapsed.

5. At the end of ten years, when the principal obligation has not a fixed term for its expiration, unless it be of such a nature that it cannot be extinguished except in a term longer than ten years.

In all these cases, the action of the surety tends to obtain his release from the security or a guaranty to defend him against any proceedings of the creditor and from the danger of insolvency of the debtor.

SECTION THIRD.

*Effects of security amongst the co-sureties.**

Article **1844.** When there are two or more sureties for the same debtor and for the same debt, the one who has paid it may claim from each of the others the portion which he or they should proportionally have paid.

If any one of them is insolvent, his portion shall be paid by all in the same proportion.

In order that the provision of this article be applicable, the payment must have been made by virtue of a judicial demand, or when the principal debtor has made a general assignment, or is a bankrupt.

1845. In the case of the preceding article, the co-sureties may set up against the one who paid, the same exceptions which would have corresponded to the principal debtor against the creditor, and which are not purely personal on the part of the same debtor.

1846. A surety for a surety (*subfiador*), in case of the insolvency of the surety for whom he bound himself, remains liable to the co-sureties in the same terms as the surety was bound.

CHAPTER THIRD.

Extinguishment of security.†

Article **1847.** The obligations of a surety shall expire at the same time as that of the debtor, and for the same causes as all other obligations.

---

* Digesto, book 49, tit. 1, laws 17, 36, 39. Codigo, book 8, tit. 42, laws 2, 11, 15. Part. 5, tit. 12, law 11.

† Digesto, book 5, tit. 1, law 24; id., book 17, tit. 2, law 63, par. 1; id., book 46, tit. 1, law 32; id., book 46, tit. 2, laws 15, 18; id., book 46, tit. 3, laws 2, 3, pars. 2, 3, 43. Fuero Real, book 3, tit. 18, law 10. Instituciones, book 3, tit. 30. Part. 5, tit. 12, laws 14, 15.

1848. A merger which takes place in the person of the debtor and of the surety, when one of them becomes the heir of the other, does not extinguish the obligation of the surety for the surety.

1849. A surety shall be released when the creditor voluntarily accepts a tenement, or any other things in payment of a debt, even when he afterwards loses them on account of eviction.

1850. Liberation, made by a creditor to one of the sureties, without the consent of the others, shall avail all the others to the extent of the portion of the surety to whom it has been granted.

1851. An extension granted to a debtor by a creditor, without the consent of the surety, extinguishes the security.

1852. Sureties, even when they are joint, shall be released from their obligation, whenever by any act of the creditor, they cannot remain subrogated in the rights, mortgages, and privileges of the same.

1853. A surety may set up against the creditor all the exceptions which pertain to the principal debtor and which may be inherent in the debt, but not those which are purely personal in respect to the debtor.

CHAPTER FOURTH.

*Legal and judicial security.**

Article **1854.** Sureties, who must give bail by provision of law or by a judicial decree, shall possess the qualifications prescribed in article 1828.

1855. When a person who is bound to give security, in the cases of the preceding articles, does not obtain it, a pledge or mortgage which may be considered sufficient to cover his obligation shall be accepted in place of it.

1856. A judicial surety cannot ask for a levy on the property of the principal debtor.

A person who offers security for a surety, in the same case, shall not ask for either a levy on the property of the debtor nor on that of the surety.

---

* Digesto, book 45, tit. 1, law 52; id., book 46, tit. 5, law 1. Part. 3, tit. 2, law 41.

TITLE XV.

Contracts of pledge, mortgage, and antichresis.

CHAPTER FIRST.

*Provisions common to (contracts of) pledge and of mortgage.**

Article **1857.** The following are essential requisites of the contracts of pledge and of mortgage:

1. That they be constituted to secure the fulfillment of a principal obligation.

2. That the ownership of the thing pledged or mortgaged belongs to the person who pledges or mortgages the same.

3. That the persons, who constitute the pledge or mortgage, may have the free disposition of their property, and, in case they do not have the same, it may be lawfully authorized for such purpose.

Third persons, strangers to the principal obligation, may secure the latter by pledging or mortgaging their own property.

1858. It is also essential in these contracts that when the principal obligation is due, the things of which the pledge or mortgage consists may be sold to pay the creditor.

1859. A creditor cannot appropriate to himself the things given in pledge or mortgage, nor dispose of the same.

1860. The pledge and the mortgage are indivisible, even when the debt is divided among persons holding rights under the debtor or the creditor.

An heir of the debtor who has paid a part of the debt shall not therefore ask that the pledge or mortgage be proportionally extinguished, as long as the debt has not been paid in full.

Neither can an heir of the creditor, who received his part of the debt, return the pledge nor cancel the mortgage to the prejudice of other heirs who have not been paid.

From these provisions is excepted the case in which there are several things given in mortgage or pledge and each of them secures only a specified portion of the credit.

The debtor, in this case, shall be entitled to have the pledge or mortgage extinguished in proportion as the part of the debt for which each thing is particularly held liable is paid.

---

* Digesto, book 20, tit. 1, law 20. Part. 5, tit. 13; id. 5, tit. 13, laws 7, 20, 41, 42, 44. Law of Mortgage, arts. 105, 131. Penal Code, art. 550.

1861. A contract of pledge and of mortgage can secure all kinds of obligations, either pure or subject to suspensive or resolutory conditions.

1862. A promise to constitute a pledge or mortgage gives rise only to a personal action among the contracting parties, without prejudice to the criminal responsibility which a person incurs who defrauds another in offering in pledge or mortgage, as not incumbered, things which he knew were incumbered, or pretending to be the owner of things which do not belong to him.

CHAPTER SECOND.

*Pledge.**

Article **1863.** Besides the requisites, specified in article 1857, it is necessary, to constitute the contract of pledge, that the thing pledged should be placed in possession of the creditor or of a third person by common agreement.

1864. All personal things which are in commerce may be given in a pledge, provided they be susceptible of possession.

1865. A pledge shall not be effective against a third person, when evidence of its date does not appear in a public instrument.

1866. A contract of pledge gives a right to the creditor to retain the thing in his possession or in that of the third person to whom it was delivered, until his credit is paid.

If, while the creditor retains the pledge, the debtor contract with him another debt to be paid before the first one has been paid, the creditor may extend the retention until both credits are paid to him, even when it has not been stipulated that the pledge should be subject to the security for the second debt.

1867. A creditor shall take care of the thing given in pledge with the diligence of a good father of a family; he has the right to recover the expenses incurred for the preservation of the same, and is liable for its loss or impairment, in accordance with the provisions of this Code.

1868. When the pledge produces interest, the creditor shall set off that collected by him against that due him; and if none is due to him, or to the extent that it exceeds that legally due, he shall impute it to the principal.

---

* Digesto, book 13, tit. 7, law 9, pars. 2, 3; id., book 46, tit. 3, law 5, par. 3. Instituciones, book 3, tit. 15, par. 4. Codigo, book 4, tit. 24, law 1. Commercial Code, arts. 320, 323, 324. Part. 5, tit. 13, laws 1, 20, 21, 41, 42, 43, 44. Laws and Regulations on Constitucion and Management of Cajas de Ahorro, and Monte de Piedad Regulations, January 23, 1873, and July 13, 1880.

1869. As long as the case of expropriation of the thing given in pledge does not happen, the debtor shall continue as owner of the same.

Nevertheless, the creditor may exercise the actions which belong to the owner of the thing pledged in order to reclaim or defend it against a third person.

1870. A creditor shall not make use of a thing given in pledge without the authorization of the owner, and when he does so or misuses said thing, in any other manner, the latter may ask it to be placed in deposit.

1871. The debtor cannot ask for the restitution of the thing pledged, against the will of the creditor, until he has paid the debt and its interest with the expenses, when proper.

1872. A creditor, to whom the debt has not been paid in due time, may proceed, before a Notary, to sell the pledge. This sale shall in every case be made at public auction and with due notice, in proper cases, to the debtor and to the owner of the thing pledged. When the pledge has not been sold, at the first sale, a second auction with the same formalities may be held, and when no sale is made, the creditor may become owner of the pledge. In this case he shall be bound to give a discharge for the full amount of his credit.

When the pledge consists of stocks, listed on exchange, they shall be sold in the manner provided for in the Code of Commerce.

1873. Government pawnshops (*Montes de Piedad*), and other public institutions, which by their character or special purpose loan money on pledge, shall be governed by the special laws and regulations in respect thereto, and subsidiarily by the provisions of this title.

CHAPTER THIRD.

*Mortgage.**

Article **1874.** Only the following property may be the object of the contract or mortgage:

1. Real property.

2. Real rights which may be alienated according to law, when imposed on real property.

1875. Besides the requisites, specified in article 1857, it is indispensable, in order that the mortgage be validly constituted, that the instrument in which it is constituted be inscribed in the Registry of property.

*** Law of Mortgage, arts. 12, 23, 24, 25, 26, 106, 107, 105, 110, 111, 127, 153, 217.**

The persons, in behalf of whom the law establishes a mortgage, shall have no other right than to exact the execution and inscription of the instrument in which the mortgage is formally drawn, without prejudice to what the Law of Mortgage provides in favor of the State, provinces, and towns for the amount of the last year's taxes, and in favor of the insurers for the premium of the insurance.

1876. A mortgage directly and immediately binds the property on which it is imposed, whoever its possessor may be, for the fulfillment of the obligation for the security of which it was given.

1877. A mortgage is extensive to the natural accessions, to the improvements, to the fruits pending and rents uncollected, when the obligation is due, and to the amount of the indemnities granted or owed to the owner by the insurers of the property mortgaged, or by virtue of expropriation or on account of public utility, with the declarations, amplifications and limitations established by law, whether in the case in which the tenement continues in the power of the person who mortgaged it, or when it passes to the hands of a third party.

1878. A hypothecary credit may be alienated or assigned to a third party, wholly or partially, under the formalities required by law.

1879. A creditor may claim from a third possessor of the property mortgaged the payment of the portion of the credit secured with what the latter possesses, according to the terms and with the formalities established by law.

1880. The form, extension and effects of the mortgage, and also whatever relates to its constitution, modification, and extinction, and all that has not been comprised in this chapter, shall remain subject to the provisions of the Law of Mortgage which continues in force.

CHAPTER FOURTH.

*Antichresis.**

Article **1881.** By antichresis a creditor acquires a right to receive the fruits of certain real property of his debtor, with the obligation to apply them to the payment of interest, when due, and then to the principal of his credit.

1882. A creditor is bound to pay the taxes and charges which burden the tenement, unless there is a stipulation to the contrary.

He shall also be bound to meet the expenses necessary for its preservation and repair.

From the fruits shall be deducted the sums which may be employed for both purposes.

---

* Law of Civil Procedure, art. 1447.

1883. A debtor cannot recover the enjoyment of the real property, unless he has previously paid in full what he owes to his creditor.

But in order to free himself from the obligations imposed on him by the preceding article, the creditor may always oblige the debtor to re-enter upon the enjoymnt of the tenement, unless there be a stipulation to the contrary.

1884. A creditor does not acquire ownership of the real property by default in payment of the debt within the term agreed upon.

Any stipulation to the contrary shall be void. But in this case, the creditor may ask, in the manner provided for in the Code of Civil Procedure, either for the payment of the debt, or for the sale of the real property.

1885. The contracting parties may stipulate that the interest of the debt be set off against the fruits of the tenement given in antichresis.

1886. The last paragraph of article 1857, paragraph second of article 1866, and articles 1860 and 1861 shall be applicable to this contract.

TITLE XVI.

Obligations contracted without agreement.

CHAPTER FIRST.

*Quasi-contracts.**

Article **1887.** Quasi-contracts are those lawful and purely voluntary acts by which the author thereof becomes obligated in regard to a third person, and, sometimes, by which there results a reciprocal obligation amongst the parties concerned.

SECTION FIRST.

Management of a stranger's business.†

Article **1888.** A person who voluntarily takes charge of the agency or administration of the business of another, without authorization, is bound to continue managing the same until the end of the business and its incidents, or to notify the interested person in order that the latter may come to substitute him in his management, if such a one is in condition to personally do it.

1889. An officious manager must discharge his duties with all the diligence of a good father of a family and make an indemnity for

---

* Instituciones, book 3, tit. 28.

† Digesto, book 3, tit. 5, laws 2, 3, par. 9, 10, par. 1; id., book 44, tit. 7, law 5. Instituciones, book 3, tit. 28, par. 1. Part. 1, tit. 13, law 3; id. 4, tit. 20, laws 3, 4; id. 5, tit. 12, laws 26, 28, 30, 34. Law of Civil Procedure, art. 961.

injuries which, through his fault or negligence, may be caused to the owner of the property or business which he is managing.

Notwithstanding, the courts may moderate the amount of the indemnity, according to the circumstances of the case.

1890. When the manager delegates all or some of the duties of his charge to another person, he shall answer for the acts of the delegate, without prejudice to the direct obligation of the latter towards the proprietor of the business.

The responsibility of the managers, when they are two or more, shall be joint.

1891. A manager of a business shall be liable for unforeseen events (*vis major*), when he undertakes venturesome operations, which the proprietor was not in the habit of doing, or when he has postponed the interests of the latter in favor of his own business.

1892. Ratification of such management by the proprietor of the business produces the effect of an express authorization.

1893. The owner of property or a business who avails himself of the advantages of the administration of another, even when he has not expressly ratified the same, shall be liable for the obligations contracted for his benefit, and he shall indemnify the administrator for the necessary and useful expenses which he may have incurred and for the injuries which he may have suffered in the discharge of his duties.

The same obligations shall be incumbent on said owner, when the object of said administration was to avoid any imminent or manifest damage, even when no profit results therefrom.

1894. When, without knowledge of the person who is bound to give support, a stranger supplies it, the latter shall have the right to claim the same from the former, unless it appears that he gave it out of charity, and without the intention of recovering it.

Funeral expenses, suitable to the status of the person and to the customs of the locality, shall be paid by those who during their life would have had the obligation to support him, even when the deceased has left no property.

SECTION SECOND.

*Collection of what is not due.**

Article **1895.** When there was no right to claim a thing which was received and which, through an error, has been unduly delivered, there arises an obligation to restore the same.

* Digesto, book 12, tit. 6, laws 7, 15, 26, par. 12; id., book 13, tit. 1, law 8; id., book 46, tit. 3, law 38, par. 1. Instituciones, book 3, tit. 28, par. 6. Part. 5, tit. 14, laws 28, 29, 37.

1896. A person who accepts an undue payment, when he has acted in bad faith, shall pay the legal interest, when a sum of money has been received, or shall pay for the fruits collected or which ought to have been collected, if the thing received produces them.

He shall also be liable for the impairments which the thing may have suffered on account of any cause whatever and for the damages caused to the person who delivered it, until the latter recovers it. He shall not be liable for unforeseen events (*vis major*), when such events may have affected the things, in the same manner, had they been in the possession of the person who delivered them.

1897. A person, who in good faith has accepted an undue payment of a certain and specified thing, shall only be liable for the impairment or loss of the same and its accessories, in so far as he may have enriched himself from it. When he has alienated it, he shall return the price or assign the action to make the same effective.

1898. With regard to the payment for improvements and expenses, made by the person who unduly received the thing, the provision of title fifth of book second shall rule.

1899. A person shall be exempted from the obligation of restitution, who, believing in good faith that the payment was made on the account of a legitimate and subsistent credit, destroys the title or has allowed the action to be prescribed, or has abandoned the pledge or cancelled the warranties of his right. A person who has unduly made a payment can only address himself to the true debtor or to the sureties with regard to whom the action may yet be enforced.

1900. The proof of payment is incumbent upon the person who pretends to have made the same. He shall also be obliged to prove the error under which he made it, unless the defendant denies having received the thing claimed from him. In this case, when the plaintiff has proven the delivery, he shall be released from any further proof.

This does not limit the right of the defendant to justify that (the thing) which he is supposed to have received was due him.

1901. It is presumed that there has been an error in the payment, when a thing which was never owed or which was already paid for has been delivered, but the person from whom the return is asked may prove that the delivery was made through liberality or for any other just cause.

CHAPTER SECOND.

*Obligations which arise from fault or negligence.**

Article **1902.** A person who by an act or omission causes damage to another, when blame or negligence intervenes, shall be bound to make an indemnity for the damage so done.

1903. The obligation imposed by the preceding article is exigible, not only for personal acts and omissions, but also for those of the persons for whom they should be responsible.

The father, and when he is dead or has been incapacitated, the mother is liable for the injuries caused by the minors who live with them.

Guardians are liable for the injuries caused by minors or incapacitated persons who are under their authority and live with them.

Owners or directors of an establishment or enterprise are equally liable for the damages, caused by their clerks in the service of the branches in which the latter are employed, or on account of their duties.

The State is liable, in this sense, when it acts through a special agent, but not when the damage has been caused by the official to whom properly it pertains to do the act already done, in which case the provision of the preceding article shall apply.

Finally, masters or directors of arts and trades are liable for the damages caused by their pupils or apprentices, while they are under their custody.

The responsibility, to which this article refers, shall cease, when the persons mentioned in the same prove that they employed all the diligence of a good father of a family to avoid the danger.

1904. A person who pays the damage caused by his subordinates may recover from the latter what he has paid.

1905. The possessor of an animal, or a person who uses the same, shall be liable for the damages which it may cause, even when said animal escaped or becomes strayed.

This liability shall only cease in case that the damage proceeds from main force or from the blame of the person who has suffered the damage.

1906. The proprietor of a game-preserve shall be liable for the damage caused by the game to the neighboring tenements, when what is

---

* Digesto, book 39, tit. 2. Instituciones, book 4, tit. 5, par. 1. Part. 7, tit. 15, laws 5, 6, 21, 22, 23, 25, 56; id. 3, tit. 32, laws 10, 11. Penal Code, arts. 18, 121, 599, No. 3. Project of 1851, art. 1904.

necessary to avoid the increase of the same has not been done, or when the efforts of the owners of said tenements to preserve the game has been hindered.

1907. The proprietor of a building is liable for the damages which may result from the ruin of the whole or a part thereof, when this happens through default of the necessary repairs.

1908. The owners shall also be liable for the damages caused:

1. By the explosion of machines of which care has not been taken with due diligence, and for inflammation of explosive substances which were not placed in a safe and proper place.

2. By excessive smoke, which may be injurious to persons or properties.

3. Through the fall of trees, located in places of transit, when it has not been caused by main force.

4. By the emanation of sewers or deposits of infectious matters, when constructed without precautions proper for the place where they are located.

1909. When the damages considered in the two preceding articles occur by defects in the construction, a third person who suffers it may claim damages against the architect, or, in proper cases, against the constructor, only within the term prescribed by law.

1910. The head of a family who dwells in a house or in a part of the same is liable for the damages caused by the things which may be thrown or may fall from the same.

TITLE XVII.

Concurrence and preference of credits.

CHAPTER FIRST.

*General provisions.**

Article **1911.** A debtor is liable for the fulfillment of his obligations to the extent of all his present and future property.

1912. A debtor may judicially ask from his creditors a reduction in the amount and an extension of time in the payment of his debts, or either of the two things, but the exercise of this right shall not produce juridical effects, except in the cases and in the manner set forth in the Code of Civil Procedure.

* Part. 7, tit. 33, law 8. Com. Code, arts. 870, 878, 879, 883, 884, 904, 906, 907. Penal Code, art. 542, No. 5. Law of Civil Procedure, arts. 1130, 1140, 1141, 1144, 1146, 1155, 1161, 1172.

1913. A debtor, whose liabilities are greater than his assets, and who has failed to meet his current obligations, shall file a petition of bankruptcy (*concurso*) in a competent court, as soon as he is aware of being in such condition.

1914. A declaration in bankruptcy, incapacitates the bankrupt (*concursado*) from administering his property and any other, which by law pertains to him.

He shall be reinstated in his rights, upon the termination of the bankruptcy when no cause preventing it appears in the qualification of bankruptcy.

1915. By the declaration in bankruptcy, all the immature debts of the bankrupt become due.

Should they be paid before the time fixed in the obligation, they shall suffer the discount corresponding to the amount of the legal interest of the money.

1916. From the date of the declaration in bankruptcy, all the debts of the bankrupt shall no longer bear interest, with the exception of mortgage and pledge credits to the amount of their respective guarantees.

When, after the principal of the debt is paid, any sum remains, interest, reduced to the legal rate, unless the one stipulated is less, shall be paid.

1917. Agreements, which the debtor and his creditors judicially enter into, under the formalities of law about reduction of the amount and extension of time, or in bankruptcy, shall be binding on all the concurrent parties and on those who, having been summoned and notified in due form, did not protest in time. Those creditors who, having the right to abstain, have duly made use of such right, shall be excepted.

Creditors comprised in articles 1922, 1923, and 1924 have the right to so abstain.

1918. When an agreement for reduction of amount and extension of time is entered into with creditors of the same class, the lawful agreement of the majority shall be binding on all, without prejudice to the respective preference of creditors.

1919. When the debtor complies with the agreement, his obligations shall be extinguished in accordance with the conditions stipulated in the same; but, when he fails to comply with the whole or a part of said agreement, the right of the creditors shall revive for the sums of their original credits which they have not received, and any of said creditors may ask for a declaration in or continuance of bankruptcy.

1920. When there is no express stipulation to the contrary, between the debtor and the creditors, the latter shall preserve their rights, after the termination of the bankruptcy, to collect from the property, which the debtor may afterwards acquire, that portion of their credits, which they have not received.

CHAPTER SECOND.

*Classification of credits.**

Article **1921.** Credits shall be classified for their graduation and payment according to the order and terms set forth in this chapter.

1922. In respect to the specified personal property of the debtor, the following are preferred:

1. Credits for the construction, repair, preservation or for the amount of the sale of personal property which may be in the possession of the debtor to the extent of the value of such property.

2. Those secured by a pledge which is in the possession of the creditor, in respect to the thing pledged and to the extent of its value.

3. Those guaranteed by a security of goods or negotiable paper, constituted in a public or mercantile establishment in respect to security and for the value of the same.

4. Credits for transportation, in respect to the goods transported, for the amount of said transportation, expenses and rates of carriage and preservation, until the time of the delivery and for a period of thirty days afterwards.

5. Expenses of boarding in respect to the personal property of the debtor remaining in inns.

6. Credits for seeds and expenses of cultivation and harvesting, advanced to the debtor in respect to fruits of the crops for which they were applied.

7. Credits for rents and leases for one year in respect to the personal property of the lessee existing on the tenement leased and on the fruits thereof.

When the personal property, in respect to which the preference is allowed, has been surreptitiously removed, the creditor may claim it from the person who has the same, within the term of thirty days to be counted from the time it was so removed.

1923. In respect to determined real property and real rights of the debtor, the following are preferred:

1. The credits in favor of the State, in respect to property of taxpayers for the amounts of the last annual assessments, due and not paid, of the taxes which burden the same.

---

* Law of Civil Procedure, art. 1268. Com. Code, arts. 320, 375, 908, 912, 914, 918, 919. Law of Mortgage, arts. 59, 92, 105, 168, 218.

2. The credit of insurers, in respect to the property insured, for the premiums of insurance for two years, and when the insurance is mutual, for the last two assessments declared.

3. Mortgage, and statutory and agricultural (*refaccionarios*) credits, noted and inscribed in the Registry of property, in respect to property mortgaged, or which has been the object of the advance (*refacción*).

4. Credits, preventively noted in the Registry of property by virtue of a judicial order, for attachments, seizures, or execution of sentences, in respect to the property noted therein and only in regard to subsequent credits.

5. Statutory agricultural credits, neither annotated nor inscribed, in respect to the real estate to which the advance (*refacción*) refers, and only with regard to other credits different from those stated in the four preceding numbers.

1924. In respect to the other personal and real property of the debtor, the following credits are preferred:

1. Credits in favor of the province or municipality for the taxes of the last year, due and unpaid, not comprised in number one of article 1923.

2. Those incurred:

A. For judicial expenses and those of administration of the bankruptcy for the common interest of the creditors, made with due authorization or approval.

B. For the funeral expenses of the debtor, according to the customs of the place, and also those for his wife and for his children, under parental power, when they have no property of their own.

C. For expenses of the last illness of the same persons, caused during the last year, counted up to the day of their death.

D. For daily wages and salaries of the clerks and domestic servants, corresponding to the last year.

E. For advances made to the debtor for himself and his family, constituted under his authority, in provisions, clothing or shoes, during the same period of time.

F. For pensions for support during the proceedings in bankruptcy, unless they are based on a title of liberality only.

3. Credits which without a special privilege appear:

A. In a public instrument.

B. In a final judgment, when they have been the object of litigation.

These credits shall have preference among themselves, according to the priority of dates of the instruments and of the judgments.

1925. Credits of any other kind or by any other title, not comprised in the preceding article, shall have no preference.

CHAPTER THIRD.

*Priority of payment of credits.**

Article **1926.** Credits, which enjoy preference in respect to certain personal property, exclude all others to the extent of the value of the personal property to which the preference refers.

When two or more creditors claim preference in respect to certain personal property, the following rules shall be observed, as to priority of payment:

1. Credits secured by a pledge exclude all others, to the extent of the value of the thing given in pledge.

2. In case there is a security, and if it is lawfully constituted in behalf of more than one creditor, the priority amongst them shall be determined by the order of the dates of the execution of the guarantee.

3. Credits for advances for seeds, expenses of cultivation and gathering, shall be preferred over those for rents and leases, in regard to the fruits of the crop for which they were incurred.

4. In all other cases, the value of the personal property shall be distributed *pro rata* among the credits which enjoy special preference in regard to the same property.

1927. Credits, which enjoy preference in regard to certain real property or real rights, exclude all others for their full amounts to the extent of the value of the real estate or real rights to which the preference refers.

When two or more credits affecting certain real property or real rights concur, the following rules shall be observed in respect to their priority:

1. Those set forth in Nos. 1 and 2 of article 1923 shall be preferred, according to the order, to those comprised in the other numbers of the same article.

2. Mortgages and statutory agricultural credits, annotated or inscribed and specified in No. 3 of said article, and those comprised in No. 4 of the same, shall enjoy priority among themselves, according to the order of the dates of the respective inscriptions or annotations in the Registry of property.

3. Statutory agricultural credits not annotated or inscribed in the Registry, to which No. 5 of article 1923 refers, shall enjoy preference among themselves in the inverse order of their dates.

---

* Recopilada, law book 10, tit. 11, law 6. Com. Code, arts. 917, 918, 919. Law of Mortgage, arts. 25 to 29. Law of Civil Procedure, arts. 1286, 1290.

1928. The residue of the estate of a debtor, after the credits which enjoy preference in regard to certain property, personal or real, have been paid, shall become part of the free property which the latter may possess for the payment of the other credits.

Those which enjoy preference in regard to certain property, personal or real, and which have not been totally paid in full with the amount of such property, shall be paid as to the deficit in the order and place pertaining to the same, according to their respective natures.

1929. Credits which have no preference in regard to certain property; those which have preference for the amount not collected; and those which, by prescription, have lost the right of preference, shall be paid according to the following rules:

1. In the order established in article 1924.

2. Those by priority of dates, according to the order of the same, and those which have a common date, *pro rata*.

3. Common credits, to which article 1925 refers, without consideration of their dates.

TITLE XVIII.

Prescription.

CHAPTER FIRST.

*General provisions.**

Article **1930.** Ownership and other real rights are acquired by prescription in the manner and under the conditions specified by law. Rights and actions, of whatever kind, also become extinguished by prescription in the same manner.

1931. Persons able to acquire property or rights by other lawful means can also acquire the same by prescription.

1932. Rights and actions shall be extinguished by prescription to the prejudice of all classes of persons, including juridical ones, according to the terms provided by law.

Persons incapacitated to administer their property shall always retain the right to make claim against their lawful representatives whose negligence may have been the cause of the prescription.

* Digesto, book 4, tit. 3, law 4, pars. 1, 2; id., book 29, tit. 2, law 1; id., book 41, tit. 3, laws 1, 3, 9, 45; id., book 42, tit. 8, law 10, par. 1, 1, par. 2. Codigo, book 8, tit. 40, law 5. Estilo, laws 192, 221, 242. Fuero Juzgo, book 10, tit. 2. Fuero Viejo, book 4, tit. 4. Fuero Real, book 2, tit. 11, law 3. Nov. Recop., book 10, tit. 11; id., book 11, law 8. Recopilada, book 11, tit. 8, laws 4, 7, 8, 9. Orden. of Alcala, tit. 9, 27. Part. 3, tit. 29, laws 1, 6, 7; id. 5, tit. 15, law 7.

1933. Prescription gained by a co-proprietor or owner in common shall be for the benefit of all the others.

1934. Prescription produces its juridical effects in behalf and against the estate of inheritance, before the latter has been accepted, and during the time granted to make an inventory and for deliberation.

1935. Persons with the capacity to alienate may renounce the prescription gained, but not the right to prescription in the future.

Prescription shall be understood as tacitly renounced when the renunciation results from facts which lead to the supposition that the right acquired has been abandoned.

1936. All things which are in commerce are susceptible of prescription.

1937. Creditors and all other persons, interested in making a prescription valid may profit by the same, notwithstanding the express or tacit renunciation of the debtor or owner.

1938. The provisions of the present title shall be understood without prejudice to what may be established in this Code or in special laws in respect to specified cases of prescription.

1939. Prescription, which began to run before the publication of this Code, shall be governed by the laws then prevailing; but if, after this Code is in force, all the time required in the same for prescription has elapsed, such prescription shall be effectual, even when according to the former laws a longer period of time was required.

CHAPTER SECOND.

*Prescription of ownership and other real rights.**

Article **1940.** For ordinary prescription of ownership and other real rights, it is necessary to possess things in good faith and under a just title, during the time specified by law.

1941. Possession must be held under belief of ownership, and be public, peaceful, and uninterrupted.

1942. Acts of a possessory character, executed by virtue of permission, or by mere tolerance of the owner, are of no effect for establishing possession.

1943. For the effects of prescription, possession is interrupted either naturally or civilly.

* Digesto, book 41, tit. 13, laws 3, 5, 31, par. 1, 41; id., book 44, tit. 3, law 13, par. 4; id., tit. 3, law 27; id., book 50, tit. 16, law 109. Codigo, book 7, tit. 33, laws 1, 9, 12; id., book 7, tit. 35, law 7; id., book 7, tit. 39, laws 3, 7, par. 5, 6, 8, par. 1; id., book 8, tit. 4, law 11. Instituciones, book 2, tit. 6. Toro, law 5. Part. 3, tit. 29, laws 4, 7, 9, 14, 16, 18, 19, 21, 26, 29. Recopilada, book 11, tit. 8, law 3. Fuero Real, book 2, tit. 11, law 1. Law of Mortgage, arts. 25, 27, 35. Law of Civil Procedure, art. 479.

1944. Possession is interrupted naturally, when, for any cause, it ceases for more than one year.

1945. Civil interruption is caused by a judicial summons on the possessor, even when made by order of an incompetent judge.

1946. A judicial summons shall be considered not made and shall fail to cause interruption:

1. When it is null and void by lack of legal solemnities.

2. When the plaintiff withdraws his complaint or fails to prosecute it in due time.

3. When the possessor is discharged from the suit.

1947. Civil interruption shall also be caused by a judgment of peace (*acto de conciliación*), provided that within two months from its celebration, the complaint as to possession or ownership of the thing contested be presented in court.

1948. An express or tacit acknowledgment which the possessor may make in respect to the right of the owner also interrupts possession.

1949. Against the title recorded in the Registry of property, the ordinary prescription of ownership or of real rights shall not obtain against a third person, except by virtue of another title similarly recorded, and the time shall begin to run from the date of the inscription of the second.

1950. Good faith of the possessor consists in his belief that the person from whom he received the thing was the owner of the same, and could convey the ownership thereof.

1951. The conditions of good faith, required for possession in articles 433, 434, 435, and 436 of this Code, are equally necessary for the determination of said requirement in the prescription of ownership and of other real rights.

1952. By a just title is understood that which legally suffices to transfer the ownership or real rights, the prescription of which is in question.

1953. Title for prescription must be true and valid.

1954. A just title must be proven; it never can be presumed.

1955. Ownership of personal property is prescribed by an uninterrupted possession in good faith for a period of three years. Ownership of personal property is also prescribed by an uninterrupted possession of six years, without the necessity of any other condition.

The provisions of article 464 of this Code shall be observed in respect to the rights of the owner to revindicate the personal thing lost or of which he has been unlawfully deprived, and also in regard to those acquired at an auction, on exchanges, at fairs or markets, or from a merchant lawfully established or habitually engaged in the traffic of similar objects.

1956. Personal property stolen or robbed cannot be prescribed by the persons who stole or robbed the same, nor by their accomplices, or harborers, unless the crime or misdemeanor or their penalties and the actions to exact the civil responsibility, arising from the crime or misdemeanor, have been prescribed.

1957. Ownership and other real rights in respect to real property shall be prescribed by possession for ten years as to persons present, and by twenty years in respect to those absent, when held in good faith and under a just title.

1958. For the effects of prescription, a person, who resides in a foreign country or beyond the seas, shall be considered as absent.

When said person has been present during part of the time, and absent during another part, every two years of absence shall be considered as one year to complete the ten years of the time required to be present.

Absence which is not for a whole and continuous year shall not be considered in the computation.

1959. Ownership and other real rights in respect to real property shall also be prescribed by the uninterrupted possession of the same for thirty years, without the necessity of title or good faith, and without distinction of persons, absent or present, save the exception set forth in article 539.

1960. In the computation of the time necessary for prescription, the following rules shall be observed:

1. The actual possessor may complete the time necessary for prescription by adding to his time that of the person under whom he holds rights.

2. It is presumed that the actual possessor, who has been a possessor in a former time, has continued to be such possessor during the time intervening, unless there is proof to the contrary.

3. The day on which the time begins to run is considered as a whole day but the last day should be wholly completed.

CHAPTER THIRD.

*Prescription of actions.**

Article **1961.** Actions are prescribed by the mere lapse of the time specified by law.

---

* Digesto, book 17, tit. 10, law 17, par. 6; id., book 45, tit. 1, law 91, par. 4. Codigo, book 7, tit. 33, law 7; id., book 7, tit. 39, laws 3, 4, 7; id., book 8, tit. 40, law 5; id., book 9, tit. 35, law 5. Recopilada, book 11, tit. 8, law 5. Orden. of Alcala, book 9, tit. 9, laws 2, 11. Fuero Juzgo, book 10, tit. 2, laws 3, 4. Fuero Real, book 2, tit. 11, law 4. Nov. Recop., book 10, tit. 11, laws 9, 10; id., book 11, tit. 8, law 3. Part. 3, tit. 29, law 21; id. 7, tit. 29, laws 22, 29, Law of Mortgage, arts. 35, 134. Project of 1851, art. 1970.

1962. Real actions in respect to personal property are prescribed by the lapse of six years after the loss of possession, unless the possessor has, during a shorter term, gained the ownership in accordance with article 1955, and with the exception of the cases of loss and public sale, and those of theft and robbery, in which cases the provision of paragraph third of said article shall rule.

1963. Real actions in respect to real property are prescribed after thirty years.

This provision is understood without prejudice to what is provided in respect to the acquisition of ownership or of real rights by prescription.

1964. Hypothecary actions are prescribed after twenty years, and those which are personal and which have no special term of prescription fixed, after fifteen years.

1965. Among co-heirs, co-owners or proprietors of adjacent tenements, the action to ask partition of the inheritance, the division of the thing held in common or of the demarkation of the adjacent properties shall not be prescribed.

1966. Actions to exact the fulfillment of the following obligations are prescribed by the lapse of five years:

1. For the payment of pensions for support.

2. For the payment of rents, whether they are derived either from rural or city tenements.

3. That of any other payments which should have been made annually or in shorter periods.

1967. Actions for the fulfillment of the following obligations shall be prescribed after the lapse of three years:

1. For the payment of judges, lawyers, registrars, notaries, with and without records (*notarios excribanos*), experts, agents and clerks for their honoraries and fees and the charges and disbursements made by them in the discharge of their duties or offices in the matters to which the obligations refer.

2. For payments to apothecaries for medicines which they have supplied; to professors and teachers for their salaries and stipends for the instruction which they have given, or for the exercise of their profession, art or avocation.

3. For the payment of mechanics, servants, and laborers the amounts due for their services, and for the supplies or disbursements which they may have made concerning the same.

4. For the payment of board and habitation to innkeepers and to traders for the value of goods, sold to others who are not traders, or who being traders are engaged in a different trade.

The time for the prescription of actions, to which the three preceding paragraphs refer, shall be counted from the time the respective services have ceased to be rendered.

1968. By the lapse of one year, are prescribed:

1. Actions to recover or retain possession.

2. Actions to exact civil responsibility for contumely, or calumny, and for obligations derived from blame or negligence, set forth in article 1902 from the time the aggrieved person knew it.

1969. The time for the prescription of all kinds of actions, when there is no special disposition providing otherwise, shall be counted from the day on which they could have been exercised.

1970. The time for the prescription of actions, the object of which is to claim the fulfillment of obligations in respect to principal with interest or rent shall run from the last payment of rent or interest.

The same shall be understood in regard to the principal of the consignative ground rent.

In the emphyteusis, and reservative ground rent, the time for the running of the prescription shall be counted from the last payment of the pension or rent.

1971. The period for the prescription of actions to exact the fulfillment of obligations, declared in a final judgment, shall begin from the day the judgment became final.

1972. The term for the prescription of actions to exact the rendering of accounts shall run from the day on which those who should have rendered them ceased in the discharge of their duties.

That pertaining to the action for the balance of accounts, from the date on which the latter was acknowledged by agreement of the parties interested.

1973. Prescription of actions is interrupted by the exercise of the same before the courts, by extrajudicial claim of the creditor, and by any other act of acknowledgment of the debt by the debtor.

1974. Interruption of prescription of actions in joint obligations shall equally benefit or injure all the creditors or debtors.

This provision shall equally rule with regard to the heirs of the debtor in all kinds of obligations.

In obligations in severalty, when the creditor does not claim from one of the debtors more than the portion corresponding to him, the prescription shall not be interrupted for that reason, in respect to the other co-debtors.

1975. Interruption of the prescription, against the principal debtor by judicial claim of the debt, shall also be effective against his surety; but that produced by extrajudicial claims of the creditor, or private acknowledgements of the debtor, shall not injure said surety.

Final provision.

Article **1976.** All the legal compilations, uses, and customs which constitute the common civil law in all matters which are the object of this Code are hereby abrogated and they shall remain without force or effect, either as direct obligatory laws, or as supplementary law. This provision shall not apply to the laws which have been declared in force by this Code.

Transient provisions.

Changes introduced in this Code to the injury of rights, acquired under preceding civil legislation, shall have no retroactive effect.

To apply the corresponding legislation in cases not expressly specified in this Code, the following rules shall be observed:

1. Rights arising under the legislation preceding this Code, from acts realized under its rules, shall be governed by said preceding legislation, even when this Code regulates them in another manner, or does not recognize the same. But when such rights appear declared for the first time in this Code, they shall at once be effective, even when the facts which originated them have been accomplished under the preceding legislation, provided that they do not injure other acquired rights having the same origin.

2. Acts and contracts entered into under the *regime* of the preceding legislation, and which are valid according to the same, shall produce all their effects according to the same legislation, with the limitations set forth in these rules. Therefore, last wills, even when jointly executed; powers of attorney to execute wills and testamentary notes, executed or written before this Code was in force, shall be valid; and the clause *ad cautelam*, the trusts (*fideicomisos*) for applying the estate in accordance with the secret instructions of the testator, and any other acts, prescribed by the preceding legislation, shall be effective; but the revocation or modification of these acts or of any of the clauses contained in the same, shall not be effective, after this Code has been enforced, except by making the testament according to the same.

The provisions of this Code which sanction, with a civil penalty or deprivation of rights, acts or omissions which had no sanction in the preceding legislation, shall not be applicable to the person who, when the latter was in force, had incurred the omission or committed the act forbidden by this Code.

When the fault is also punished by the preceding legislation, the mildest provision shall be applied.

4. Actions and rights arising before this Code was in force, and not exercised, shall subsist with the extension and according to the terms acknowledged by the preceding legislation, but shall be subject, in regard to the exercise, duration, and proceedings for enforcing them, to the provisions of this Code.

When the exercise of the right or of the actions is dependent upon official proceedings, begun under the preceding legislation, and these are different from those established in this Code, the persons interested may choose either one or the other.

5. Children who have attained the age of twenty-three years, when this Code becomes effective, are emancipated and not subject to the parental power, but when they continue living in the house and at the expense of their parents, the latter may retain the usufruct, the administration, and other rights which they are enjoying in respect to the private property of their children, up to the time when the children should be freed from the parental power according to the preceding legislation.

6. A father who may have voluntarily emancipated a child, reserving to himself some rights out of his adventitious property, may continue enjoying the same up to the time when the son should be freed from the parental power according to the preceding legislation.

7. Fathers, mothers, and grandparents, who are exercising guardianship of their descendants, shall not withdraw the securities which they have constituted, nor be obliged to constitute them, when said securities have not been given, nor to complete the same, when those given appear to be insufficient.

8. Guardians and curators, named under the provisions of the preceding legislation, and with subjection to the same, shall preserve their charges, subject as to the exercise of the same to the provisions of this Code.

This rule is also applicable to the possessors, and temporary administrators of the property of other persons, in those cases in which the law establishes the same.

9. Guardianships and curatorships, the definite constitution of which is pending the decision of the courts, at the time this Code becomes effective, shall be constituted according to the preceding legislation, without prejudice to the preceding rule.

10. Judges and municipal attorneys shall not of their own accord proceed to name family councils, except in regard to minors whose guardianship may not be definitely constituted, when this Code becomes effective. When the guardian or curator has already begun to exercise his charge, the family council shall not be named until one of the persons who has to form a part of the same, or the same

guardian or curator existing petitions for the constitution of said council, and meanwhile the appointment of a *protutor* shall remain in suspense.

11. Proceedings for adoption, those for voluntary emancipation, those for dispensation of law, pending before the Government or the courts, shall be continued in accordance with preceding legislation, unless the fathers or petitioners for such grace desist from these proceedings and prefer those established in this Code.

12. Rights to the inheritance of persons who have died, with or without a will, before this Code is in force, shall be ruled by the preceding legislation. The inheritances of those who die after that time, with or without a testament, shall be adjudicated and distributed according to this Code, but complying, in so far as the latter permits it, with the testamentary provisions. Therefore, the *legitimes*, advantages, and legacies shall be respected; but their amounts shall be reduced, when it is not possible, in any other manner, to give to each participant in the inheritance, the portion corresponding to him, according to this Code.

13. Cases, not directly comprised in the preceding provisions, shall be determined by applying the principles on which they are founded.

Additional provisions.

1. The President of the Supreme Court and those of the Territorial Audiencias shall transmit to the Secretary of Grace and Justice, at the end of each year, a report in which, referring to the affairs of which the civil branches have taken cognizance during the same year, they may point out the deficiencies and doubts which they have met in applying this Code. They shall state, in detail in the same, the questions and points of law controverted, and the articles or omissions of the Code which have given cause for doubts to the Court.

2. The Secretary of Grace and Justice shall transmit these reports and a copy of the civil statistics of the same year to the General Commission on Codification.

3. In view of this data, of the progress made in other countries, which may be utilized in our country, and of the jurisprudence of the Supreme Court, the Commission on Codification shall formulate and transmit to the Government, every ten years, such reforms as it may be convenient to introduce.

AMENDMENTS AND FORMS.

FIRST.

Requisites or formalities necessary before consent by the family council to contract marriage may be given.

The following requisites shall be necessary when, according to the provisions of article 46 of the Civil Code, the family council has to give its consent to a minor to contract marriage:

1. The person wishing to contract marriage must prove, by documents or by means of testimony of witnesses to the judge of his domicile: That he has neither a father nor a mother, paternal nor maternal grandparents, or that they are legally or physically incapacitated to give their consent; that the residence of said parents or grandparents is unknown; or, finally, that they are in countries so remote that it would take several months to communicate with them.
2. The proceedings shall then be forwarded to the public attorney in order that within the period of three days the latter may state if it considers them complete or suggest the proceedings which, in its opinion, should be had.
3. After the proceedings have been returned by the public attorney and completed, if proper, the judge shall issue an order calling the family council, which shall proceed in the manner prescribed in articles 304, *et seq.*, of the Civil Code.

SECOND.

Record of canonical marriages in the civil registry.

INSTRUCTIONS.

For the execution of articles 77, 78, 79, and 82 of the Civil Code, with regard to the recording of canonical marriages in the civil registry, and of the decrees of annullment or of divorce of the same.

ARTICLE 1. The record of canonical marriages shall be made in the office of the civil registry under the jurisdiction of which is situated the parish whose rector has himself, or through a delegate, celebrated the marriage.

ART. 2. A marriage *in articula mortis* contracted by military men in the field far from the Spanish territory, or those contracted on the high seas, shall be recorded in the office of the registry in the jurisdiction of which the husband is known to have his domicile, or in default thereof, that of the wife. Should neither of them have any known domicile, the marriage shall be recorded in the office of the general direction.

ART. 3. The officials in charge of this office shall draft these entries in accordance with the formalities established by the law of the civil registry and these instructions, without being permitted to postpone or refuse the recording of canonical marriages or the transcription of the marriage certificate, in a proper case.

ART. 4. Those in charge of the registry shall keep in packages, and in the manner prescribed in articles 28 and 29 of the regulations of the civil registry, all the instruments, communications, and documents relating to canonical marriages, the celebration of which may have been communicated to them in due form, or the certificates of which may have been copied.

ART. 5. In order to comply with the provisions of article 77 of the Civil Code, the contracting parties shall advise the municipal judge, at least twenty-four hours in advance, of the day, hour, and place where the canonical marriage is to be celebrated. This notification shall be written on common paper, signed by the contracting parties, and should they or one of them not be able to do so by a neighbor at his or their request, and it shall be drafted in the terms specified in Form A. The written notification may be presented by the contracting parties, by either of them or by their respective agents, even though the authorization be verbal.

ART. 6. The municipal judge or he who performs the duties of the same, shall deliver the proper receipt to the person presenting the notification, and should he not do so he shall incur a fine of not more than 100 pesetas nor less than 20. (See Form B.) He shall at the same time designate the official who, as his delegate, is to be present at the celebration of the marriage, should he for any reason whatsoever not be able to perform this duty, and shall communicate it in due time to the person designated so that he may attend.

ART. 7. The municipal judge may delegate the following persons to discharge his duty of attending the celebration of a marriage: Those who, by reason of their office, legally substitute him in case of vacancy, absence, or incapacity; the municipal fiscal; the secretary of the court and his substitute; a notary of the judicial district; the mayor of the ward within the limits of which the marriage is to take place, or any other person who merits the confidence of the municipal judge.

ART. 8. After the notification to the municipal judge has been acknowledged by the presentation of the receipt, his nonattendance nor that of his delegate shall be no obstacle to the celebration of the canonical marriage and to the transcription of the marriage certificate according to the provisions of article 77 of the Civil Code.

ART. 9. After the celebration of the marriage has been concluded, the municipal judge shall make the proper memorandum in the respective book of the registry, should he have the same with him, and otherwise, on a piece of white paper, on which he shall state the following circumstances, in view of the data which the contracting parties must previously submit to him:

1. The place, day, hour, month, and year on which the marriage has taken place.

2. The name, surname, and ecclestiastical rank of the priest celebrating the marriage.

3. The names, paternal and maternal surnames, nativity, profession or trade, and domicile of the contracting parties.

4. The names, paternal and maternal surnames, and nativity of the parents, stating if the contracting parties are legitimate or natural children.

5. The names, surnames, and residence of the witnesses.

Mention shall also be made, if known, first, of the name and surnames, status, nativity, and profession of the proxy, if the marriage is to be thus contracted, and the date, place, and notary before whom the power was executed; second, the date of the permission or request for advice required by the Civil Code when proper; and, third, if one of the contracting parties is widowed, the name and surname of the deceased spouse, as well as the date and place of death.

The memorandum shall be signed by the contracting parties and by the witnesses, and for a person who can not do so, by another at his request, and by the municipal judge. (See Form C.)

ART. 10. In addition to the circumstances enumerated in the preceding article there may be included in the memorandum, should the contracting parties request it, those mentioned in Nos. 1, 9, and 10, of article 67, of the Law of the Civil Registry, the declaration of the contracting parties being sufficient, with the exception of what is expressed in No. 9, which must be proved by the instruments required by the law of the registry and its regulations. The municipal judges shall apply to this kind of records the provisions of No. 4, of article 20, of the law of the registry.

ART. 11. If a delegate of the municipal judge should have attended the celebration of the marriage, said official must draft, after the ceremony, the proper memorandum on a sheet of common paper which may be printed, and state in the same all the circumstances mentioned in the two preceding articles. (See Form D.)

ART. 12. The official who may have attended the celebration of the marriage as a delegate shall forward the memorandum referred to in the preceding article, within the next twenty-four hours, to the office of the civil registry.

ART. 13. The memorandum drafted on common paper by the municipal judge, should he have attended the celebration of the marriage, as well as the one drawn up by the delegate, if the latter should have represented the former in this ceremony, shall be literally copied into the proper book, stating in the entry the date of the same, the number of the bundle in which the original has been filed, and the name of the municipal judge and that of the secretary, who shall authenticate the entry referred to, with their signatures and the seal of the court. (See Form E.)

At the time of copying the memorandum the municipal judge may add the circumstances mentioned in article 10, in the terms therein stated.

ART. 14. At the foot of the memoranda, when recorded the following note shall be stamped: This memorandum is recorded in liber ———, folio ———, number ———, of the section of marriages of this civil registry. (Date and signature of the judge, and of the secretary, and seal of the court.)

ART. 15. The certificates of canonical marriages, celebrated without the attendance of the municipal judge or his delegate, shall be literally copied in the civil registry. The record may be requested by the contracting parties, their parents, or any other person interested, in person or through an agent, even though the mandate be verbal. The municipal judge shall order that the record of the certificate of marriage take place immediately, stating if the contracting parties have given or not the proper notification to the court in order to exact the proper liability, and for the purposes of the third and fourth paragraphs of article 77 of the civil code.

In this record there shall be stated: 1, the place, hour, day, month, and year it takes place; and 2, the name and surname of the official in charge of the registry, as well as those of the secretary. In this record there may also be stated, even though not appearing in the marriage certificate, should the interested parties request it, the circumstances mentioned in Nos. 1, 9, and 10 of article 67 of the law on the civil registry, in the manner prescribed in article 8 of these instructions. (See form F.)

ART. 16. At the foot of the marriage certificate which is to be filed there shall be placed a note in the following form: "This certificate is recorded in the civil registry under my charge, liber ———, folio ———, number ———, of the section of marriages." (Date and signatures of the judge and of the secretary, and seal.)

ART. 17. The record of a marriage *in articulo mortis* may be requested when the competent official of the State did not attend its celebration, by either of the spouses, their parents, or persons interested in them, or the proxy even though the mandate may have been verbal, presenting the proper certificate of marriage. The record shall contain, in addition to all the circumstances referred to in article 15, the date of the presentation of the certificate in the registry.

ART. 18. The official in charge of the civil registry shall enter, at the instance of any legitimate party, the final judgments by which the ecclesiastical courts may have declared the annulment or divorce in canonical marriages, also making the marginal notes of reference in the proper records.

ART. 19. The doubts arising from the fulfillment of articles 77, 78, 79, and 82 of the Civil Code, in so far as they refer to the entry of canonical marriages and of the provisions included in these instructions, shall be submitted by the municipal judges in a clear and precise communication to the proper judges of first instance. Should the latter in their turn be in doubt, they shall forward the proper consultation to the general direction of civil property and notarial registries.

In no case can the record or transcription of a marriage be suspended by reason of the doubts with regard to which the judges should think it necessary to consult.

The decisions which the general direction may render on the doubts submitted by the judges of first instance shall be published in the *Gaceta de Madrid*, always omitting the name of the interested party.

MADRID, *April* 26, 1889.

Approved.

CANALEJAS Y MENDEZ.

FORM A.

(Written declaration of those about to contract a canonical marriage.)

(Article 5.)

To his honor, the municipal judge of ——— ———:

Mr. ——— ———, a native of ——— ———, municipal district of ———, province of ———, ——— years of age, single (professon or trade), domiciled in this city, street of ———, number ———, son of Mr. ——— ———, and Mrs. ——— ———.

And Miss (or Mrs.) ——— ———, a native of ———, municipal district of ———, province of ———, ——— years of age, single (profession or trade), domiciled in ——— street, of ———, number ———, daughter of Mr. ——— ——— and Mrs. ——— ———, have agreed to celebrate a canonical marriage before the parochial priest of the church of ———, of this district, at 8 o'clock in the morning, the ——— instant, at the chapel altar, of ———, of the same church (or at the domicile of ——— street, number ———), and in compliance with the provisions of article 77 of the civil code, inform your honor thereof, for the purposes mentioned therein.

Madrid,———, the ———, 189—.

FORM B.

(Receipt of the notification or written statement.)

I, the undersigned, municipal judge of ——— ———, hereby certify that to-day, at ——— o'clock in the morning, Mr. ——— presented a written statement in which he notifies this court that on ———, at ——— o'clock, the celebration of his marriage with Miss (or Mrs.) ——— ———, at the parochial church of ———, will take place.

In witness whereof I issue these presents, which I sign on the ——— ———.

FORM C.

(Memorandum of entry of a canonical marriage which the municipal judge attends.)

[Article 9.]

In the city of ———, on ———, 189—, I, the undersigned ——— ———, municipal judge for the district of ———, being in the church of San Juan of this city, where I came in order to attend the celebration of the canonical marriage agreed upon between Mr. ——— ———, and Miss (or Mrs.) ——— ———, in virtue of the previous notification received by me in due form from the same, declare: That in my presence ———, parochial priest of the said church, proceeded to unite in canonical marriage the above-mentioned Mr. ——— ———, ——— years of age, single, a native of ———, resident of ———, legitimate son of Mr. ——— ——— and Mrs. ——— ———; and Miss (or Mrs.) ———, ——— years of age, a native of ———, and resident of ———, legitimate daughter of Mr. ——— ——— and Mrs. ——— ———, there having also attended this ceremony the father and mother of the groom and bride, and the witnesses, Mr. ——— ———, ——— of age, citizen of ———, and Mr. ——— ———.

In witness whereof I draft this memorandum of record of the above-mentioned marriage for the purposes of article 77 of the civil code, which is signed with me by the contracting parties and by the witnesses after being informed of its contents.

Remarks for drafting the memorandum.

1. In case either of the contracting parties should not be a legitimate child it shall be stated in the special place indicated in the memorandum that he or she is illegitimate, stating whether natural or a foundling, without stating in other cases any other kind of illegitimacy.

2. When either of the contracting parties is represented by a proxy, mention shall be made of the power of attorney in which the representation has been granted as well as the name and surname, age, nativity, domicile, profession, or trade of the proxy.

3. Should the contracting parties state that they have natural children which are to be legitimized by the marriage, this statement and the names of the children shall be entered.

4. When one of the contracting parties is widowed, the name and surname of the deceased spouse shall be entered in the memorandum, as well as the date and place of death, and the civil or parochial registry in which it may have been recorded.

5. In the memorandum there shall be stated the date of the permission or request for advice required by the civil code, when proper.

6. Should those who are to give their consent or advice for the marriage attend the same, and should state their consent in the memorandum, they shall sign the same in person or request another to do so in their stead, should they not be able or not know how to sign.

7. Should special cases occur, unforeseen in these remarks, the municipal judges shall observe, in order to decide and record them in the memorandum, when proper, the legal provisions referring thereto.

FORM D.

Memorandum of record of a canonical marriage which the delegate of the municipal judge attends.

(Article 11.)

In the village of ———, municipal district of ——— ———, on ———, 189—, I, the undersigned, petty mayor of the said ward, being in the parochial church of San Pedro, where I came as a delegate designated by the municipal judge of the said subdistrict, in order to attend, in compliance with the provisions of article 77 of the Civil Code, the celebration of the marriage agreed upon between Mr. ——— ——— and Miss (or Mrs.) ——— ———; and in virtue of the order of the said judge I declare that in my presence ——— ———, parochial priest of the above-mentioned church, proceeded to unite in canonical marriage the said Mr. ——— ———, ——— years of age, single, a native of ———, resident of ———, legitimate son of Mr. ——— ——— and Mrs. ——— ———, and Miss (or Mrs.) ——— ———, ——— years of age, a native of ——— and resident of ———, legitimate daughter of Mr. ——— ——— and Mrs. ——— ———, the father and mother of the groom and bride also attending said ceremony, as well as the witnesses, Mr. ——— ———, ——— of age, a resident of ———, and Mr. ——— ———.

In witness whereof I draft this memorandum of record of the said marriage, which shall be immediately entered in the section of marriages of the civil registry of the municipal court for the purposes of article 77 of the Civil Code, being signed by myself, the contracting parties, the parents, and the witnesses present at this ceremony after its contents have been made known to them, to which I certify.

FORM E.

Copy of the memorandum drafted on common paper regarding a canonical marriage which the municipal judge or his delegate attended.

(Article 13.)

In the city, village, or locality of ———, on this date, is being entered the canonical marriage to which the memorandum refers and which is literally as follows:

[Copy in full.]

The copied memorandum is deposited in this civil registry in package No. ——— of the section of marriages.

[Date and signature.]

FORM F.

Transcription of the certificate of a canonical marriage which neither the judge nor his delegate attended.

(Article 15.)

In the city of ———, before ———, municipal judge, and ——— ———, secretary, appeared Mr. ——— ———, and stated that in the name of ——— he presented the certificate of the canonical marriage that was celebrated on ——— of the month of ———, 18—, between Mr. ——— ——— and Miss (or Mrs.) ——— ———, before the parochial priest of the church of ———, which neither the municipal judge nor his delegate attended, in order that the said certificate be entered in this registry in compliance with the provisions of article 77 of the Civil Code. In view thereof, and it appearing that the contracting parties gave (or did not give) timely notice of the celebration of the canonical marriage, the judge ordered that the record of the canonical certificate of the above-mentioned marriage be made. In consequence thereof the above certificate is copied literally, as follows:

[Here the certificate.]

The foregoing certificate is deposited in this registry in package No.——— of the section of marriages.

THIRD.

Before whom and how opposition to marriage shall be made.

From the context of the provisions of the Code in article 97, *et seq.*, and in connection with the existing additional laws, may be deduced the rules relating to the proceedings and competency of the matter referred to in the title of this appendix and which may be summed up as follows:

1. The judge competent to take cognizance of the opposition to the marriage is the judge of first instance under whose jurisdiction is the municipal district within which it is to be celebrated.

2. In the objection made to the municipal judge, in addition to the ordinary requisites, there shall be clearly stated the reasons for the opposition and the qualification given the objecting party the right to make it.

3. The judge receiving it shall deliver the ratification to the objecting party and communicate the same to the public attorney within the term of three days.

4. Should the latter find a legal foundation he shall request that, with the suspension of the celebration of the proposed marriage, the objection be transmitted to the judge of first instance, in order that he may draft the opposition in the form provided by article 524 of the Law of Civil Procedure.

5. The party interested in the noncelebration of the marriage, instead of the objection, may make the opposition in person within the fifteen following days to the judge of first instance, who, if the objection has the legal requisites, shall have immediately a written order issued to the municipal judge in order that he suspend the celebration of the marriage until the certification of the judgment or final decision terminating the proceedings be delivered to him.

6. The municipal judge shall give notice of the mandate suspending the celebration of the marriage to those intending to contract it and to their parents or guardians, if they be under twenty-three years of age.

7. At the time of the notice or within the following twenty-four hours the interested parties or any of them may state that they desist from celebrating the marriage, in which case the proceedings shall be transmitted to the judge of first instance, who shall decree their termination and officially award the costs.

8. The public attorney shall be heard in these proceedings when it has not itself instituted the opposition by virtue of the provisions of article 98 of the Civil Code.

9. From the decision of the judge of first instance appeal can only be made to the territorial audiencia.

10. Should the objection be dismissed and the interested parties demand indemnity for losses and damages, the proceedings shall follow the provisions of articles 928, *et seq.*, of the Law of Civil Procedure.

11. Should the judge or court consider the objection malicious, he shall reserve to those injured the right to bring the proper civil or criminal action, transmitting the decrees to the public attorney in order that the criminal action may be instituted, if proper.

12. All the time fixed for the prosecution of these proceedings cannot be extended and cannot be suspended for any reason whatsoever. Moreover, there shall be applied thereto the rules governing urgent business.

FOURTH.

HAVANA, *May* 31, 1899.

The Military Governor of Cuba directs the publication of the following order:

I. Hereafter civil marriages only shall be legally valid. The contracting parties may conform to the precepts of whatever religion they may profess, in addition to the formalities necessary to contract the civil marriage.

II. The officials in charge of the execution of the laws respecting marriage shall not accept as legal the written license or consent of the parent, when the same shall have been taken before an Ecclesiastical Notary, nor shall any such certificate be accepted which is not attested by the civil functionaries.

III. Clergymen of the different religious denominations represented in this island, in performing the ceremony of marriage, shall not be required to take other action than that imposed upon them by their respective religious beliefs; but the performance of this ceremony shall have no civil effect.

IV. All marriages, heretofore solemnized in the Island of Cuba, shall be deemed and adjudged to be valid and the validity thereof shall in no wise be affected by any want of authority in the person solemnizing the same, if consummated with a full belief on the part of the persons so married, or either of them, that they were lawfully joined in wedlock. *Provided;* That such marriage shall be duly recorded within a period of one year from the date of this order.

Record of such marriages shall be made upon presentation of satisfactory proof thereof.

V. The said marriages shall be proved by the presentation of documentary evidence of the same. If no such proof can be furnished, the fact of the marriage may be established in the form prescribed in articles 2001 to 2008, both inclusive, of the Law of Civil Procedure; by the declaration of the functionary performing the ceremony, and of the witnesses thereto; or by such other proofs as the law allows.

VI. The regulations to be observed in recording marriages, under this order will be issued by the secretary of justice and public instruction.

VII. The fee for performing the ceremony of marriage shall be one dollar in United States money, or its equivalent.

VIII. All decrees, orders, laws, or parts thereof, in conflict with the provisions of this order, are hereby revoked.

ADNA R. CHAFFEE,

Brigadier General, Chief of Staff.

[Similar provisions made for Puerto Rico and the Philippines.]

FIFTH

Preliminary proceedings in trials for divorce or annulment of civil marriages.

(Article 107.)

There being no special precept in our law of procedure in force that may be applied to the subject in question, it seems opportune to give a few suggestions in order that the reader may know the thought and point of view of the illustrious jurists and the most honorable officials of the judicial department, and which may serve as a guide in the cases in which nothing has been provided for in the substantive law.

These suggestions are the following:

1. The spouse who intends to institute the proper action shall present to the competent court of first instance a document containing a summary statement of the facts and claims he proposes to sustain, accompanied by documents in support thereof; should he have none, a preliminary investigation shall take place with the participation of the public attorney, in order to corroborate the same.

2. The judge shall render a decision granting the ratification, which shall be done immediately; and should the plaintiff not be able to appear in person, the judge shall go to his domicile or address the proper letters rogatory when the latter resides in another judicial district.

3. Before delivering the writ of ratification, the judge shall make the proper observations to the plaintiff, informing him of the importance of the suit he is beginning and of the consequences it may produce in the family.

If, notwithstanding this, the plaintiff should persist, a decision shall issue citing the two spouses to appear on the day and hour appointed.

4. Should the plaintiff, without alleging a legal excuse, not appear before the court, he shall be considered as having abandoned the suit and the costs shall be charged to him; should the defendant not appear, he shall incur a fine of 10 to 100 pesetas and the payment of the costs caused thereby, and a second citation shall be sent him, with the warning that proper procedure will be taken against him, should he persist in his contempt.

5. The appearance shall take place without the presence of next friends or defenders, and should reconciliation be impossible the judge shall issue an order authorizing the party instituting the proceedings to make his complaint in accordance with law within the term of thirty days, otherwise being barred.

6. In the same decree he shall order the steps taken indicated in article 68 of the Civil Code, and if the reasons for divorce are based on one or more of causes 1, 2, 3, and 6 of article 105 of the Civil Code the parents shall provide by mutual agreement for the care and education of the children.

7. At the instance of any of the parties, and at their expense, reconciliation may be attempted during the course of this kind of actions.

8. Notwithstanding the provisions of the preceding rules, when in compliance with the provisions of article 102 of the Civil Code, the action for annulment of marriage may be instituted not only by the spouses, but by the public attorney or by any of the persons interested therein, the complaint shall be presented immediately, together with the necessary documents, and an

attempt at reconciliation shall not take place; but in the order admitting it there shall be adopted the measures indicated in said article 68.

9. It is likewise not necessary to attempt reconciliation when the residence of the defendant is unknown, or when the latter is in a foreign country, or there be any other obstacle difficult to overcome and for which the plaintiff is not responsible.

10. The public attorney shall always be a party to suits of this kind, and if it should not have begun the suit it shall be heard last. At its instance, should it appear that the plaintiff is also culpable or is guilty of any of the causes which give rise to a divorce, in case a countercharge is made by the defendant, it may be declared, without further proceedings, that neither has the right to continue the suit.

11. Nevertheless, in one of the cases mentioned in the second paragraph of article 74 of the Civil Code the suit instituted by the public attorney shall be continued.

12. The spouses, whether minors or of age, shall appear in person and without the attendance of their parents or legal representatives unless they are otherwise incapacitated.

SIXTH.

Rules containing the modifications which may be considered indispensable in proceeding relating to guardianship in accordance with the provisions of the Code. (Articles 203, 206, 214, et seq., 222 and 228.)

The following are the general indications that may be made:

1. The municipal judge of the place, in the case forseen in article 203 of the Civil Code, shall officially make an order which shall head the papers in the proceedings, naming, on his responsibility, a defender having all the conditions required for the duties of a judicial manager, taking care of the person and property of the minor, informing the public attorney and the person designated of the decree.

2. Should the said attorney make opposition to the memorandum of notification, what may be proper shall be clearly decided.

3. The charge once accepted by the person designated, he shall immediately enter upon his duties, and shall bear all the obligations of the guardian.

4. As soon as the guardian is appointed the defender shall cease to be such and shall render account to the former.

5. These provisions are applicable in all cases where the minor or incapacitated person has no legal representative according to law.

The followng rules may be applied to testamentary guardians:

That the appointments made by the mother or a stranger, in the conditions determined in paragraph second of articles 206 and 207 of the Civil Code, shall not be ratified without a certification of the agreement of the family council, expressing the necessary approval and acceptance.

In regard to legal guardians the following rules may be established:

1. Should no guardian have been named by the father, mother, or any other person, designating a minor as an heir, or has left him an important legacy, the judge shall designate for this charge the relative upon whom this is incumbent, according to the provisions of article 211 of the Civil Code.

2. When the relative upon whom the guardianship is incumbent is not well known, the judge shall make investigations concerning him through the civil and ecclesiastical authorities, and the appointment shall be made according to the same.

3. Should any one of these have any known incapacity, this shall be stated, and the appointment of his successor shall then be made.

4. Should there be objection to the appointment, it shall be discussed and decided by judicial procedure between him who institutes the same and the appointed guardian, the interests of the minor being represented by the public attorney.

5. During the prosecution of the suit the guardian elect, who shall act as the defendant, shall have the custody of the minor and the management of his property, giving a guaranty that may appear sufficient to the judge.

6. Should the guardian elect refuse to accept the charge, the public attorney shall be heard, and should the latter consent the judge shall appoint another guardian.

7. Should the public attorney not consent, the opposition shall be discussed and decided in interlocutory procedure, observing the provisions of rule 5.

8. After the acceptance of the person designated, and his giving security in a proper case, he shall be appointed to the office.

The following rules may be established for the appointment of guardians of incapacitated persons:

1. When a judicial authority or a police agent has knowledge of the existence of an insane or deaf and dumb orphan, having no person appointed by law to take care of and defend him, he shall notify the competent judge and the latter shall officially proceed to institute proceedings of provisional incapacity.

2. In this procedure there shall be observed the provisions of articles 214 and 220, both inclusive, of the Civil Code.

3. The rules established in the law of civil procedure for the adoption of urgent measures, in so far as not modified by the Civil Code, shall be observed in the proof.

The two following rules shall be observed for the appointment of a guardian for prodigals:

1. The declaration of prodigality shall be instituted by means of a complaint with the requisites mentioned in article 524 of the law of civil procedure, presented by one of the persons authorized therefor, according to article 222 of the Civil Code.

2. The declaration requested, having been obtained by final judgment after proceedings as in declaratory suits involving a large amount, in which the necessary urgent measures may be adopted, subject to summary proceedings, the literal certificate of the same shall be taken to head the papers in the case, and a guardian for the property shall be immediately appointed.

Lastly, in regard to the appointment of guardians for those under civil interdiction the following shall be observed:

1. That in the case provided for in article 228 of the Civil Code the department of public prosecution shall request that the certificate of the paper heading the proceedings, and that part of the final judgment decreeing the penalty of interdiction that may have been imposed, shall serve as the heading to the papers of the proceedings demanding the appointment of the guardian.

2. That should the appointment of a guardian be requested by any of the persons having such a right, at the end of the document a mandate shall be made annexing the aforesaid certificate, which mandate shall be requested of the judge, or court before whom the execution of the judgment rendered in the criminal cause may be pending.

3. That although the case has not been instituted by the public attorney, the latter should be a party to the same.

4. That the proceedings shall in other matters be governed by the modifications established by the Civil Code.

SEVENTH.

Alienation, encumbrance, etc., of property of minors. (Articles 269 and 903.)

Although in the note to article 903 of the Code some indications and references are made as to the proceedings for the alienation, encumbrances, and compromises involving property of minors, etc., they must be completed by others, which we consider useful, for the resolution of the difficulties that may arise necessarily on this point, in the application of the new provisions of our civil law, to cases occurring in practice. These indications are the following:

1. In cases mentioned in No. 5 of article 269 of the Civil Code, the guardian shall solicit of the the president of the family council, or in his absence of the municipal judge, to convoke said council in order that it may give the necessary authorization.

2. The council, in view of the documents presented by the soliciting party or of the report given, shall concede or refuse the authorization without further appeal, and may establish the rules to which the alienation or encumbrance shall be subject.

3. In all cases the guardian shall be assisted by the secretary, acting as such in the family council, and the price for the sale shall be that of the appraisement made when the inventory was drawn up.

4. When the sale, by resolution of the family council or in compliance with the law, has to take place by public auction the secretary shall issue a notice in which shall be given the place, day, and hour of the sale, the name of the officer before whom it shall be held, as well as the names of the guardian and the minor, the description of the property about to be sold, with the data required in summary proceedings, if it consists of real property, and should it be personal the indication of its kind and quality shall be sufficient. Copies of the notice shall be affixed in proper places, in order that the sale may have greater publicity, advertising it in the local paper that has the largest circulation, and, should it be necessary, in the "Boletin Official" of the province.

5. In the public sale the guardian and officer shall observe the provisions of section second, title XV of book second of the law of civil procedure.

6. A bid that does not cover the amount of value fixed for the property shall not be admitted.

7. No admissible bid having been made, the guardian may make before the family council one of the following propositions:

a. That he may be considered as relieved from duty and be substituted in the case.

b. That a second public sale be announced with a reduction of 20 per cent of the price.

8. The second public sale shall take place with the same formalities as the first.

9. When the sale is made for the payment of debts or any other necessity, at the request of the guardian, a third auction may take place with a reduction of another 20 per cent. from the price set for the second.

10. Should, even then, no admissible bid be made, the representative of the minor may be authorized to privately sell for the price fixed for the third auction.

11. The sale once made, the family council shall see that the price obtained is applied as indicated in the request for authorization.

12. The price shall be delivered, while the proper application is made to the guardian, if he is exempted from giving security, or if the one given by him is sufficient to insure the same. Otherwise, it will be deposited in a public institution in which the judicial deposits may be made.

13. The authorization for compromises of the rights of the minors and incapacitated persons shall be solicited by the same persons as may request the sale of property. In the document in which the authorization is solicited must be expressed the reason and object of the compromise, the doubts and difficulties of the business, and the reasons for considering the same as useful and convenient, and the document shall be accompanied by the one in which the basis of the compromise is stated. With the document shall also be delivered those necessary to form an exact judgment on the subject, together with the necessary data.

14. The family council, in view of the opinion of the guardian and hearing one or more lawyers strangers to the suit or business in question, should it be deemed necessary, shall concede or refuse the authorization requested.

15. When it is conceded it shall be expressed in the memorandum, and with the certification thereof the guardian shall apply to the judge or court, should the suit be pending, in order that it may be given effect.

16. The same formalities as those established for the sale, without necessity of public bids, shall be observed for the mortgaging or encumbering of real property, or for the extinction of real rights pertaining to minors or incapacitated persons.

EIGHTH.

Method of procedure of the family council. (Article 304, *et seq.*)

From the character of the institution, as well as from the provisions of the Civil Code, the following method of procedure may be established for family councils:

1. The council shall meet by virtue of a summons issued in a decision, which heads the papers of the proceeding and which shall be issued ex officio by the municipal judge or at the request of the public attorney, in cases in which the latter must participate according to the code or the Law on Civil Procedure, and in which shall be designated the persons that are to take part.

2. The summons shall be made by the secretary or a subaltern officer of the court in the form provided for oral trials; but should any of the members reside outside the seat of the municipal district, or in another municipal district, he shall be notified directly by means of a registered letter, or through the respective petty mayor.

3. The questions arising from the constitution of the family council, the excuses or better right to form part of the same, shall follow the proceedings for urgent measures, and shall be decided by the municipal judge according to the documents accompanying the claim.

4. The decision of the municipal judge may be appealed from for review only, to the judge of first instance, who shall decide the same, without any further appeal, by the same proceedings as those established for oral trials.

5. Should the family council not find any urgent measures to deliberate upon, its meeting shall be postponed until the appeal has been decided.

6. The family council having been constituted for the first time, for the next sessions it shall be convoked by the president, who may make use therefor of the subaltern officers of the municipal court or of the petty mayors; the municipal judge shall cure the defects of the summons, and shall do it whenever for some cause or other the personnel of the family council is renewed.

7. Each deliberation and decision of the family council shall be contained in a memorandum drawn up by the secretary of the municipal court, the secretary of the municipal council, their substitutes, or a notary to be selected by the family council, and shall state:

(*a*) The date and place of the meeting and the authority that has ordered the same.

(*b*) The names and surnames of those summoned, stating those who were present.

(*c*) The subject of the meeting and the summary statement of the deliberations.

(*d*) The other statements required by law, and especially the vote given by each member when the decision has not been adopted unanimously.

In order that a decision be adopted, there must be at least two favorable votes.

8. The memorandum shall be signed by all those present, and shall be filed, at the disposition of the family council, in the municipal court or some other public depositary, until it is delivered to the minor after his having reached ma-

jority; those referring to the same, shall be affixed one to the other, and shall have the same validity as the other judicial documents.

9. Should the guardian, or in his absence, the protutor, not be present at the deliberations of the family council, he shall be notified of the decision, together with a copy of the proceedings, to enable him to fully execute the same.

10. When the decision of the family council is not final without the approbation of the judicial authority, the guardian or protutor shall fully present it to the same within the fifteen days of its adoption, should there be no other term established in the same.

11. Should the guardian not fulfill this obligation any of those forming part of the council or the public attorney shall take his place; the expenses, however, shall be imposed personally upon the negligent party.

12. The appeal presented before the judge of first instance, referred to in article 310 of the Civil Code, and the approval of the decision necessary in a proper case, shall follow the same procedure of oral trials; the same to be confirmed before the municipal judge within the fifteen following days.

13. When the decision that has been appealed from is not final without judicial approval, the same shall be given or refused in the same decision which is rendered on the appeal.

14. When, in the judicial guardianship proceedings, the absence of a relative in the required degree for conferring upon him the legitimate guardianship has been proved, the family council shall meet and appoint for this duty a person worthy of its confidence.

15. The appointment shall be communicated by means of a certificate signed by the secretary and countersigned by the president, to the court of the first instance, which, after the acceptance of the person designated and his giving security, shall appoint him as guardian.

CHAPTER III.

Law of Civil Procedure or Enjuiciamiento Civil.

Until the publication of the Law of Civil Procedure of October 5, 1855, the Partidas and Novisima Recopilacion, together with the reforms of Article 12 of the Constitution of 1812, governed matters of civil procedure, except in minor cases. These laws were supplemented by the Provisional Regulation of September 26, 1835, for the administration of justice, the law in regard to courts of first instance of May 1, 1844, and numerous other laws.

In 1853 the *Instruccíon del procedimiento civil con respecto a la Real jurisdiccíon ordinaria* was issued to facilitate suits, render them less expensive and to correct numerous evils of the existing system; notwithstanding its good features, it was abrogated August 18, 1854.

October 5, 1855, a new law of civil procedure was adopted, went into effect January 1, 1856, was extended to Cuba and Puerto Rico, December 9, 1865, and, with some modifications, continued in force until the issuance of the revised edition of February 3, 1881, which edition was amended, as to articles 483, 484 and 710, May 11, 1888. The law of 1881, altered in some respects, was extended to Cuba* and Puerto Rico, September 25, 1885, and a law, almost identical with the Cuban law, was extended to the Philippines February 3, 1888.

The present Civil Code of Practice of Spain, or the Law of Civil Procedure, took effect on April 1, 1881. It is an extensive and complicated work, somewhat longer than the Civil Code of Law, and contains two thousand one hundred and eighty-two articles divided into three books and fifty-nine titles. The first book contains provisions concerning the jurisdiction and procedure of courts in all cases. The second book is devoted to *jurisdiccíon*

* For recent amendments, see *Ley de Casacion*, of June 26, 1899, and orders Nos. 124 and 205, of July 29, and October 28, 1899.

contenciosa, or contentious jurisdiction, that is, where parties are suing each other contradictorily. The third book is devoted to what is known as *jurisdiccíon voluntaria* or voluntary jurisdiction, or, in French, *jurisdiction gracieuse,* where persons go into court, generally in an ex parte way, for the purpose of conducting proceedings for adoption, for the appointment of tutors or guardians, and curators, for the probate of wills, and opening and administration of successions. This book also includes rules in regard to the voluntary jurisdiction as applied in commercial cases.*

Criminal Laws and Codes.

Provisions of criminal law of the ancient codes of Spain have been referred to in previous chapters, and of these the Partidas contained the most complete laws on penal legislation.† The latter, although long observed, were found to be too harsh and not in harmony with modern institutions.‡ Reforms were initiated in the constitutional Cortes of Cadiz in 1812, and in that of 1820, and a penal code, containing some wise provisions and numerous defects, was published July 9, 1822.

This Code contained a preliminary title and is divided into two parts: The title treats of crimes and misdemeanors, persons responsible for them, and of those who are answerable for the acts of others, of penalties, their effects and mode of execution, of the gradation of crimes, according to aggravating and extenuating circumstances, of the obligations of giving notice of crimes and delivering up guilty persons, of absent and contumacious offenders, of the reduction of penalties, of prescription of crimes, and of indemnification. The first book treats of crimes against society, and the second, of those against persons.

Attempts were made in 1826 and in 1829 to publish a new Code, without results, but in 1843, a commission was appointed and completed a Code which became approved July 1, 1848. This Code was revised and in an amended form republished in 1850, but the work is considered inferior to the Code of 1848. It embraces three books, divided into five hundred and six articles.

---

* Transferred to the law of civil procedure in 1868; see com. codes.

† For the penal laws of Spanish-America, see chapter on the Laws of the Indies.

‡ The work of Cesar Becaria, at the end of the eighteenth century, produced a revolution in European penal legislation.

Book 1. Defines crimes and offenders, prescribes penalties, their effects and manner of fulfillment, defines civil responsibility, and the relation between crime and and penalty and prescribes the responsibility which principals, accomplices and harborers incur.

Book 2. Distinguishes crimes as grave, less grave and as misdemeanors, and treats of the penalties in respect to the first two.

Book 3. Considers misdemeanors and determines the punishments to be applied.

This Code was in force until the promulgation of the Constitution of 1869, when, in order to harmonize the two, new reforms, especially those relating to individual rights, the free exercise of religious worship, punishments for various crimes committed by one person, limiting perpetual punishments to a fixed period, suppressing *argolla,* etc., were inaugurated which led to the Penal Code which was authorized June 17 to go into effect August 30, 1870. Up to this time certain crimes, like those of libel, etc., incurred by printing and publishing, were under special laws.

The progress of civilization and the adoption of the Constitution of 1876, necessitated some further modifications of the existing Penal Code which are being discussed, but which have not yet been adopted.

The Penal Code of 1870, subsequently revised and finally completed in its present form by the law of July 17, 1876, was extended to Cuba and Puerto Rico, in a modified form, May 23, 1879, and to the Philippines September 4, 1884, to go into effect December 17, 1886.*

The present Penal Code consists of six hundred and twenty-six laws divided into three books and twenty-six titles.

Book 1. Treats of crimes and misdemeanors, persons responsible, and the penalties therefor and their application.

Book 2. Considers crimes against the State and Constitution, of *Lèse Majesté,* also crimes against various public officials, rebellion, sedition, public disorders, counterfeiting, forgery, usurpation of office, rank and title, infraction of laws of interments and against public health, violation of sepulchres, gambling, faithlessness of public officials, offenses against chastity, bribery,

---

* See Royal Orders of promulgation of above dates, as to differences between the Peninsular and Ultramar editions.

malversation of public funds, frauds and exactions, parricide, assassination, homicide, infanticide, abortions, lesion, duelling, adultery, rape, public scandal, seduction, abduction, calumny, contumely, crimes against the civil status of persons, crimes against personal liberty and security, crimes against property, robbery,* etc., frauds, pawnbroking establishments, arson and negligence.

Book 3. Treats of misdemeanors against public order, public interest and government of cities and against persons and property.†

Under the Spanish penal laws not only the consummated crime is punishable but also the frustrated attempt, and in certain cases the conspiracy or proposition to do wrong. Misdemeanors frustrated against persons and property are likewise included in certain cases.

Elaborate provisions are made for extenuating and aggravating circumstances, and persons criminally responsible are considered, either as principals, accomplices and accessories, the latter class being omitted in respect to misdemeanors. Bail is accepted in cases similar to those in common-law countries. The classification and scale of punishments is too extensive and complicated and should be simplified and certain penalties moderated. Many of the provisions of book 2 are inapplicable to free institutions in the former Spanish colonies and can be eliminated or modified, especially those in relation to treason, Lèse Majesté, and crimes against the state, a multitude of monarchical officers, religious worship, public order, and usurpation of rank, title and office.

The laws of calumny or contumely need overhauling and direct responsibility fixed for offenses so committed, inasmuch as offenders now shelter themselves behind irresponsible persons or criminals and so escape the consequences of their acts.

The laws of bribery, especially in respect to the judiciary, need amendment and more effective enforcement to break up and to prevent certain corrupting practices which by usage have become open and notorious.

A new pardon law is required in place of that of June 18, 1870, which power was exercised by the King.‡

---

* Burglary is included under this head.

† Under this head, see also Ordenanzas Municipales de Policía Urbana y Rural; Policía de Gobierno, and Poderes y Obigaciones del Jefe de Policía.

‡ See Autonomical Constitution, art. 41, sec. 3.

Law of Criminal Procedure or Enjuiciamiento Criminal.

The modern Spanish laws of criminal procedure are founded on the Constitution of 1812, prior to which time and until the Royal Cedula of January 30, 1855, for the Ultramar,* the laws of the Indies were observed in Spanish-America. In Spain the Fuero Juzgo, Fuero Real, Partidas and Novisima Recopilacion were in force† until the Reformed Provisional Law of March 19, 1850, which latter continued until the adoption of the Law of 1872.

The Royal Cedula, promulgated to correct existing abuses and illegal practices, and continued in force until the decree of May, 1879, comprises twelve chapters, the first of which treats of inferior judges, known as *jueces locales*, the second of judges of the first instance, the third of royal audiencias, the fourth of the Supreme Court, the fifth of special courts and tribunals, the sixth of the authority of courts in administrative affairs, seventh of auxiliary offices and officers of tribunals, and judges, eighth of the Public Prosecuting Attorney, ninth of rights of challenge, tenth of sentences, eleventh of appeals, and twelfth of responsibility and punishments. The Law of March 19, 1850, embraces fifty-seven rules, the first twenty-three of which treat of misdemeanor proceedings, the following to thirty-seven of imprisonment and its effects, and the remainder consider general provisions about various steps and formalities of procedure.

Trial by jury was discussed in connection with the liberty of the press as early as 1814, and the jury system for offenses committed by printing and publication was approved by the Law of October 22, 1820, and again recognized in 1836, 1854 and 1864, but up to this time, the law did not have the power and support that its adherents expected; however, the matter continued being agitated with the result that the subject was given a broader scope by the Law of Jury of December 22, 1872, which law marks the first general and public trial of crimes by jury in Spain similar to that which exists in criminal cases in common-law countries. This law comprises a preliminary title and three books.

---

* Also applied to the Philippines.

† Books 2 of F. J. and F. R. Part. 3, tit. 14, and 7, tit. 30; Nov. Recop., book 12, tits. 32 to 42; Rule 45 of Prov. Law, applied to Penal Code, of 1850.

Book 1. Consider the *sumario* or preliminary investigation, corresponding to that of the grand jury under the common law and similar to provisions of book 2 of the present law.

Book 2. Treats of public trials and trials by jury, similarly to book 3 of the law of 1882.

Book 3. Takes up special proceedings.

Book 4. Considers the prosecution of misdemeanors, corresponding to book 6 of the existing law, concluding with extradition provisions, similar to articles 824 to 833 of the present law.

The principal innovation, made in this law, was the provision for trial by jury, part of which was superseded by the decree of January 3, 1875, and the remainder included in the Law of October 16, 1879, for which, in time, the laws of September 14, 1882, and April 20, 1888, have been substituted. The compilation of October 16, 1879, which contained many errors and provoked considerable criticism, was reformed by the Law of May 6, 1880, and continued in force until the adoption of the present law of February 11, 1881, based on that of 1879, and promulgated September 14, 1882. This law, in a modified form, was extended to Cuba* and Puerto Rico, October 19, 1888, to be effective January 1, 1889, and to the Philippines, September 4, 1884, to go in force in 1888. The law of 1882 embraces forty titles, nine hundred and ninety-eight laws and a final provision, classed under seven books, as follows:

Book 1. Treats of general provisions, jurisdiction of courts as to districts and crimes, rights of challenge, prosecution and defense, procedure, exceptions, decisions as to matters of form, jurisdiction, etc., sentences, summons, communications between courts, appeals and costs.

Book 2. Considers the *sumario,* or preliminary investigation corresponding to that of a grand jury.

Book 3. Embraces public trials and trials by jury.

Book 4. Treats of special proceedings and extradition.

Book 5. Considers appeals and reviews.

Book 6. Relates to the prosecution of misdemeanors.

Book 7. Deals with the execution of sentences.

* For recent amendments, see *Ley de Casacion,* of June 26, 1899.

Differences Between Common and Civil Law Criminal Procedures.

One of the principal differences between the common and civil law criminal procedures lies in the jury system,* which, in a modified form, exists to-day in Spain and in the Federal District of Mexico, but which has never been extended to Cuba, Puerto Rico or the Philippines and does not now exist in most of the Mexican states and Spanish-American countries.

The assertions often made by ignorant people that under the old Spanish or Roman system the proceedings are secret and that the accused does not know who are his accusers or what the witnesses have testified against him is incorrect, misleading and one which has caused Spanish-American countries much trouble when United States citizens have been concerned.

Little difficulty is caused by the minor offenses or misdemeanors which are tried before the lowest courts held by municipal judges and from which appeals lie to the higher courts, in a manner similar to the common-law system, hence such cases may be eliminated.

In the more serious criminal offenses, every criminal trial is divided into two stages; the summary or preliminary investigation (*sumario*) carried on under the old Spanish system, usually by a judge of the first instance, a *fiscal* or public attorney and an *escribano* or clerk, who immediately repair to the spot of the crime and beging a thorough *ex parte* investigation. The testimony of the accused is often taken down without his knowing with what crime he is charged or who the witnesses against him are, and during this stage, the accused is kept in solitary confinement so that he cannot connive any scheme which might defeat the ends of justice, and while in such confinement, he is called in *incomunicado.*

Under the Spanish Constitution (see articles 4 and 5) a person cannot be detained but for just cause, and solitary confinement is limited. These provisions can be exercised similarly to a writ of *habeas corpus.*†

---

* The jury system is not indigenous to England, as popularly believed, but was based on the Frankish kings' *inquisito,* which recent researches show was copied from the jury system of the Romans who, after trial, had discharged it. Brunner's Schwurgerichte, p. 87 et seq.

† A writ of *habeas corpus* was known to the Aragonese, under the name of *manifestacion,* in the thirteenth century. Hallam's History of the Middle Ages, and Prescott's Ferdinand and Isabella.

Persons who have resided in Spanish-American countries appreciate how necessary the *incomunicado* system is to prevent the defeat of justice; the great evil of the system, which is not vicious, if properly enforced, is its lack of supervision and administration.

The summary or preliminary proceedings correspond to the secret investigation of a grand jury in the United States who listen to such testimony as is offered or is deemed sufficient without permitting the accused to be present or to know what transpires, and, if, in their judgment, there is sufficient ground, an indictment is found, and, thereafter, a trial begins in public court.

This is not unlike the civil law system in which the judge of the first instance, the public attorney and clerk constitute a grand jury, and, if there is no case made out, the prisoner is given his liberty; should a *prima facie* showing be made against the accused, he is released from solitary and committed to ordinary confinement.

The trial does not take place before the judge who has conducted the investigation (as is often erroneously stated), but this judge refers the whole record of proceedings to the criminal branch of the next higher court or *audiencia* for a public trial where the prisoner is faced with his accuser and witnesses, and is provided with a competent attorney to defend him.

In the Spanish-American countries testimony is taken down in writing, and, after being read to the witness, is signed by him and by the judge, in order to prove that his statements have been correctly recorded.

This gives a degree of certainty to the correctness of the testimony which cannot be obtained by a stenographic report; and it renders it impossible for the judge or opposing counsel to record language different from that actually used.

When the summary is ended, all the testimony is presented to the accused for his examination; and the right is then given him to cross-examine the witnesses who have appeared against him.

The cross-examination is an old Spanish proceeding, called *careo,* which means that the accused is personally confronted with the witnesses in presence of the judge, for the purpose of cross-examining them. It is, therefore, quite incorrect to assert that, because the *sumario,* or first stage under the Latin system, is kept secret, the accused does not know anything regarding the evidence against him; the fact being that during the second or plenary stage of the proceeding he is fully informed of all that has been done and is given an opportunity to refute it, either by presenting his own witnesses or by cross-examining such as have been presented by the other side or have been called by the judge.

It should not be difficult to see which system of criminal jurisprudence is best calculated to do justice by ascertaining the real facts of the case, whether by a judge of long experience and proficiency in his profession and with no personal interest in the case tried before him, or by a jury composed of men who have had no experience in criminal jurisprudence. If the judge may sometimes be derelict in his duties so may the jury sometimes be controlled by their emotions or prejudices. If the judge fails to do justice, his failure may be corrected by an appellate court, as all cases must be reviewed upon appeal.

The common-law criminal jurisprudence is founded upon the principle that it is better to let one hundred criminals go unpunished than to inflict punishment upon one innocent person. While the Spanish system accepts that humanitarian principle, it is nevertheless better calculated to prevent the escape of a criminal unpunished.

American citizens who are tried in Spanish-American countries often expect and insist that the proceedings be conducted in accordance with the laws of their own country, and when they find it otherwise they complain that the Spanish system is inquisitorial, outrageous, and even barbarous.*

The Law of Mortgage or Ley Hipotecari.

A commission was appointed in Spain in 1855 to frame a general mortgage law to take the place of the special legislation on the subject which, on account of the conflicting laws and decisions, was causing much confusion and rendering values unstable. The Law of February 8, 1861, was the result of the com-

* Observations of the author as Major and Counsel on the Staff of Major-General John R. Brooke, during the Puerto Rico campaign, and in his official investigations of the prisons of Havana, during the winter and spring of 1899, while holding a similar position on the staff of Major-General Ludlow.

mission's work, and this law, revised and amended and embracing three hundred and thirty-three articles, became the Law of December 21, 1869, and with its rules of application of October 29, 1870, went into effect January 1, 1871.

This law was extended to Puerto Rico, December 6, 1878, with its rules of application of February 28, 1879, to Cuba, May 16, 1879, with special rules of June 27, 1879, and to the Philippines May 10, 1889, in connection with its rules of application of August 16, 1889.

On account of the uncertainty produced by different legislation for Spain and its ultramarine possessions, a uniform law applicable to all alike was finally prepared and on July 14, 1893, became approved for Spain, Cuba, Puerto Rico and the Philippines.

This law comprises four hundred and thirteen articles, arranged under fifteen titles, followed by nine additional articles, schedule of fees, general rules and provisional articles.

Title 1 treats of instruments requiring record; title 2 considers record, its method and its effects; title 3 embraces cautionary notices; title 4 treats of cancellation of the record and of the entry of cautionary notices; title 5 considers mortgages; title 6 of the manner of keeping the registries; title 7 of the corrections of entries in registries; title 8 of the administration and inspection of registries; title 9 of the publicity of registries; title 10 of appointment, qualifications, and duties of registers; title 11 of the responsibility of registers; title 12 of the fees of registers; title 13 of redemption from existing incumbrances; title 14 of unrecorded documents and records of possession; and title 15 of the effects of entries contained in the old books and of the restoration of those rendered useless by fire or other accidents.

The exposition of the Mortgage Law to the Cortes by the Spanish Colonial Minister Maura is herewith appended for general information on the subject.

"The Mortgage Law, which has been in force in the Peninsula for the past thirty years, was applied to the Antilles, with such changes as were indispensable for its adaptation to those islands, on May 1, 1880, and to the Philippines on December 1, 1889, reforming the laws regarding real property in those countries, and consequently giving a new impetus to land securities. Although this work is not without its imperfections, being human, the Mortgage Law must be looked upon as one of our most important legal works, and all that is fundamental therein, and even that which appears of less value, should be religiously respected as long as the results of experience and the necessity of reconciling it with the other legal measures in force permit its observance. This has been the rule adhered to by the Government in the preparation of the revision herewith submitted to the Cortes.

The Civil Code for the Colonies as well as for the Peninsula, among other special laws, left the Mortgage Law expressly in force, without eliminating from it, or diverting from itself entirely, provisions which by their nature would have corresponded to the Code had both originated at the same period. It was an inevitable necessity, therefore, to overcome the differences, and in the revision which took place with this object in view, it was concluded that the Code should prevail whenever a question arose, and not only support the structure of the Mortgage Law, but that said law should be the only one for all ultramarine provinces; and, further, that it should coincide, as far as possible, with the text of the Peninsular law, thus avoiding the confusion and practical difficulties which were noted in the quotations and references by reason of four different sets of numbers for the articles.

The necessity of harmonizing these differences between the law mentioned and the Code is not the only motive which animates the Government in presenting this plan. Experience and the especial conditions of real property in some of the ultramarine provinces also urgently suggest, and even demand, important amendments, which naturally, however, should retain the cardinal principles of the system.

The law having been enacted so that all real property should be recorded in authentic official books, it was at once observed that a considerable portion was not subjected to this beneficent rule, by which it could be freed from usury and its possession guaranteed. The taxes, the schedule of notarial and register's fees, and the complications as well as the requirements of form, made this object of the legislator unattainable. It was necessary to remove these obstacles, so that small properties could enjoy the advantages of credit. Furthermore, the omission of the record of deeds keeps from the registry a considerable portion of land,

and as this evil can only be remedied by notices of possession, it is advisable to still further facilitate them, notwithstanding the undesirable features thereof, by permitting their conversion into absolute titles twenty years after their date. These two reforms have already been fully discussed by the Senate, and were approved in 1890, in order to incorporate them in the Peninsular law.

At that time another reform was also considered which had been urgently demanded. The old books of property, which were to be replaced by those created by the Mortgage Law, contained a multitude of liens and claims which had absolutely expired, but had not been cancelled in a definite manner, thus depreciating the value of property without reason.

It was an urgent requisite of credit to declare those books without force as to third persons after a certain period, and it was, therefore, proposed that all persons who had any interest recorded in the same should transfer them to the new books if they desired the State to force third persons to respect them. By re-enforcing this provision in giving greater scope to proceedings for clearing the title, the certificate of a register will indicate the legal status of the realty, thus giving contracts the security which they should enjoy.

But where the voice of experience has been heard with the greatest clamor against the law, demanding immediate relief, is where it refers to the procedure for making mortgage debts effective. Its crushing confusion, the uncertainty of results, and its incalculable cost restrain capital or suggest usurious conditions; sales and resales take the place of loans, with the object of avoiding all proceedings to the prejudice of the landowner; interest is stipulated which triplicates the capital loaned, and perhaps by the employment of other means the debtor is exposed to penal responsibility, converting the sanctity of laws enacted for the punishment of crimes into a vile instrument of avarice against the unfortunate. Distrust causes these means to be employed because the legal procedure does not satisfy the reasonable requisites of contracts, and to uproot these evils, to furnish land with the capital it needs, and to give the lender assurances of speedy and easy recovery of his loans, is the object of the most important reform proposed by the Government, suppressing proceedings which, without positively guaranteeing one's rights, destroy those most sacred. Previous appraisement, uniformity of judicial action in all necessary investigations, suppression of all litigation, only one summons and the immediate sale by auction, are the basis of the new law. We have abolished suits, exemptions, letters requisitorial (*exhortos*), writs of attachment on the mortgaged property, proceedings in the nature of a demurrer, simultaneous auctions, and a great many other barriers in the path of the credit of realty, which had been placed with the best of intentions, but from which those in good faith were the only victims.

The special conditions existing in the ultramarine provinces have suggested other amendments, especially for the Island of Cuba. The reforms mentioned, equally useful for Puerto Rico and the Philippines, have been proposed in accordance with the crisis which is complained of with regard to the development of their credit on real property, but all of them would be worthless without the enactment of a measure which has been unanimously and most justly demanded, and which will in itself promote credit and prevent the repetition of the statement that in Cuba there as yet exist no mortgage regulations. This measure consists in abolishing the time, which has been indefinitely extended by royal decree of May 6, 1882, during which mortgages as well as other implied liens remain in force; these secret incumbrances, which do not appear in the registry, rendering all contracts involving realty hazardous, although they appear completely unincumbered according to the record. The time which was just and reasonable during a period of transition, and which was allowed in the Peninsula, Puerto Rico, and the Philippines, has already lapsed, while it is still running in Cuba, and has been for the past thirteen years, placing all parties to contracts in a state of uncertainty and causing them to be suspicious. The new law will fix a time for its termination, which will not be extended.

Credit of land requires more. On account of the provisions of articles 73 to 78 of the Cuban Mortgage Law loans are now reduced to 50 per cent. of the value of estates, said articles reserving the other half for the security of subsequent lenders, who may wish to aid the cultivation and production of the soil. These articles place such obstacles and difficulties in the way of such loans, incorrectly called "agricultural loans" (*refaccionarios*), that, according to all information, the privilege is not made use of in practice, and in point of fact this compensation for the evil suffered by mortgage contract is lacking. To re-establish credit of lands to its fullest extent by the abolition of these articles is to comply with a legitimate demand of Cuban landowners whom it is intended to protect.

The law fills another requisite. To facilitate the acquisition on time payments of machines and other agricultural implements it is necessary that the simple attachment to the soil of an article sold, when the vendor has not yet been fully paid, should not turn it over to the mercy of prior mortgage creditors, inasmuch as subsequent acquisitions of the debtor are not security for the fulfillment of their contracts. The provisions of paragraph 2 of article 112 of the new law correct this fault, which was a great impediment in the way of a perfect and strong re-establishment of Cuban industries.

Two other reforms which are demanded by that island have no appropriate place in the Mortgage Law, and will, therefore, have to be otherwise disposed of, viz., loans which are secured only by the products and the survey of estates owned by tenants in common. This law, embracing real property only, cannot be applied to products when considered apart from the soil itself; agricultural credit cannot be considered as embraced by a credit of the land. The survey of estates of tenants in common is in that island a question of as great difficulty in its social aspect as the question of emphyteusis in Galicia, and pertains to the Civil Code and the Code of Procedure, and not to a law which presupposes and requires that the property already is surveyed to give publicity and permanent stability to its legal situation.

An attempt was made some time ago to apply the registry system known by the name of "Acta Torrens" to the Philippines, but the confusion which would attend a radical change of system within four years of the establishment of the present one, and when the last quarterly statistics show that it is becoming customary and generalized, and together with an examination of the former system with regard to the condition of property in the Philiippines, the Government has desisted from that intention which, furthermore, could not be effected without making considable changes in civil law and without involving the public treasury in hazardous and indefinite responsibilities. Our Mortgage Law, which already had a large number of precedents in the Archipelago, can be reformed by slight amendments, which, together with the reforms of the provisions regarding the readjustment of royal patrimonies, will pave the way for the advent of the institutions of credit for lands, which is based on a sound Mortgage Law, and legally recorded deeds, which define and secure all interests in the land.

It would be superfluous to repeat here the benefits which may be expected in Puerto Rico through these reforms. The institution of the registry is running smoothly there, without causing complaints, and now, in giving greater power and clearness to the same system, it is logical to expect that its salutary effects will increase.

To undertake the reforms mentioned, the Government depended on various legal authorizations, but the vote of the Cortes is necessary to put an end to implied mortgages, according to the text of article 3 of the royal decree of May 6, 1882. It appears desirable, therefore, to go beyond the limit which those authorizations seemed to fix; and, even if such reasons did not exist, the gravity of the question and the special respect which provisions regulated by private civil legislation deserve would have induced the Government to submit the reform to the Cortes, notwithstanding its urgent need for the Island of Cuba. The plan which is herewith presented has been compiled, with the full approval of the Committee on Codes for the Colonies, in its essential points as well as in the method adopted to facilitate parliamentary deliberations, and to reconcile formalities of law with the necessity so urgently impressed by Cuba. If the Cortes will condescend to pass this new law, containing all that has been approved by the Senate, for the Peninsula, as well as the changes derived from the Civil Code, and if His Majesty will sanction the same, the Colonies will enjoy in advance remedies which are for the most part desired by the whole national territory.

In accordance with these remarks, with the authority of His Majesty and with the approval of the Council of Ministers, the undersigned has the honor to submit for the approval of the Cortes the following

Proposed Law.

Article first and last. The Government is hereby authorized to put into effect the law submitted by the Colonial Minister, with the approval of the Committee on Codes, amending the Mortgage Law for Cuba, Puerto Rico, and the Philippines.

Madrid, May 26, 1893.

The Colonial Minister, ANTONIO MAURA Y MONTANER.

Recent Modifications.

HEADQUARTERS DIVISION OF CUBA,
HAVANA, *February* 10, 1899.

The Military Governor of Cuba directs that all taxes due, under Spanish laws in force on this island, and unpaid on January 1, 1899, be remitted. Taxes collected on railway passengers, and freight prior to that date and not heretofore deposited with the government will be paid at once into the treasury of the island.

ADNA R. CHAFFEE,
Major-General of Volunteers, Chief of Staff.

HEADQUARTERS DIVISION OF CUBA,
HAVANA, *March* 29, 1899.

The Military Governor of Cuba directs the publication of the following order:

The operation of the Decree of March 5, 1898, of Captain-General D. Ramon Blanco, extending the provisions of previous decrees with regard to the collection of debts upon city and country properties, is hereby further extended until the 30th day of April, 1899. Before that date the Military Government will publish a final decree, which shall govern in these matters.

L. W. V. KENNON,
Assistant Adjutant-General.

No. 44.

HEADQUARTERS DIVISION OF CUBA,
HAVANA, *April* 19, 1899.

The Military Governor of Cuba directs the publication of the following order:

I. Hereafter and until further orders, the regulations governing the administration and collection of taxes on real estate securities and conveyance of property in the Island of Cuba, published in the *Gaceta de la Habana*, on the 17th, 18th, 19th and 20th days of August, 1892, are hereby modified as follows:

II. The rates of taxation specified in articles 4, 5, 6, 7, and 8, are reduced to one third of the figures therein stated.

III. The rates fixed in articles 9, 14, and 18, are reduced to one half of the figures therein specified.

IV. The existing article 22, from which are henceforth exempted conveyances *mortis causa*, in legitimate line of descent, shall read as follows: Inheritances, substitutions, bequests *mortis causa*, and legacies of all kinds of property and securities on real estate shall pay according to the degree of relationship between the deceased and his heirs, donees and legatees, in strict compliance with the following schedule:

	Per cent.
Between natural parents and descendants, children legitimatized by royal concession, and husband and wife	1
Collateral relations of the 2d degree	2
Collateral relations of the 3d degree	3
Collateral relations of the 4th degree	4
Collateral relations of the 5th degree	5
Collateral relations of the 6th degree	6
No consanguinity	7
Bequests for repose of soul	8

V. Article 23 shall be replaced by the following: That portion of an inheritance in which a surviving consort holds a life interest under articles 834, *et seq.*, of the existing Civil Code, shall pay no tax whatever.

VI. Uncollected taxes, namely, those remaining unpaid upon acts or contracts that have been entered into or made since January 1st, shall be settled and collected in accordance with regulations now in force, but shall be exempt from the payment of the interest prescribed in article 185.

VII. All war taxes are hereby abolished.

VIII. Taxes shall be paid in United States money, whatever be the kind of money stipulated in the contract, but the payment may be made in its equivalent as specified in the order of the President of the United States of January 4, 1899, published in the *Gaceta de la Habana*, on March 4, 1899.

IX. The tax on the consolidation, recognition or modification or mortgage securities, shall be computed on the secured capital, as the *Reglamento* prescribes without any accumulation of interest nor fixed charge for costs of judicial proceedings.

ADNA R. CHAFFEE,
Brigadier-General, Chief of Staff.

No. 46.

HEADQUARTERS DIVISION OF CUBA,
HAVANA, *April* 24, 1899.

The Military Governor of Cuba directs the publication of the following order:

An extension of two years, terminating on the 1st day of May, 1901, is hereby granted for the collection of all obligations, whether or not secured by mortgage on real property, where it may be necessary to sell said property or its products to make collection. This extension shall not apply to obligations contracted since the 31st day of December, 1898.

O. H. ERNST,
Brigadier-General of Volunteers, Acting Chief of Staff.

No. 69.

HEADQUARTERS DIVISION OF CUBA,
HAVANA, *June* 3, 1899.

The Military Governor of Cuba directs the publication of the following order:

I. The order of April 24, 1899, whereby an extension of two years, terminating on the 1st day of May, 1901, was granted for the collection and enforcement of the obligations therein stated, and contracted before the 31st day of December, 1898, is hereby modified as specified in the following articles:

II. Except as otherwise prescribed in this order an extension of two years, terminating on the 1st day of May, 1901, is granted for the collection and enforcement on real estate, or its products, of all obligations, whether or not secured by mortgage, or any other security on real property; provided, that this extension shall not apply to liabilities contracted since the 31st day of December, 1898.

III. The said extension shall be for one year only, terminating on the 1st day of May, 1900, on all obligations, whether or not secured by mortgage, where it may be necessary to enforce collection through levy and sale of city real property, or of rural property in a condition of normal production; but creditors may institute suit at law to collect interests due on all obligations, whether or not secured by mortgage, and on censos or ground rents, provided that said interests shall have accrued since the 31st day of December, 1898, and that in case of default of payment, collection shall be made on the rents only of said city property, or on the rents or products of rural property in a condition of normal production.

IV. At the expiration of the said year of extension, creditors shall be at liberty to institute suit to recover principal, interest and costs due and unpaid on said date, or that may thereafter become due, without restriction or limitation of any kind, so far only as city property, or the rural property mentioned in the preceding article is concerned.

V. Property, either urban or rural, belonging to debtors, who may have been declared bankrupt, or who may have made assignment for the benefit of creditors, shall not be protected from the action of creditors, nor included in the benefits of the extension hereby ordered when the proceedings of bankruptcy or assignment for the benefit of creditors shall have been initiated prior to the 16th day of May, 1896.

VI. In like manner city or rural property in regard to which final judgment of judicial sale shall have been rendered prior to the 16th day of May, 1896, either in an ordinary action or in a special executive proceeding, shall not be exempt from the legal action of creditors who, as regards such property, may freely institute suit without restriction or limitation of any kind.

VII. In like manner, the provisions of the extension granted shall not apply to rural property abandoned by its owners, nor to property left uncultivated during the remainder of the present year. Property will be concondsidered thus abandoned in cases wherein the owner shall be absent from the country, without having provided, through the appointment of an attorney, manager or any other similar agency, for the management and control of his property.

VIII. It shall be lawful in all cases for creditors to take such judicial action as the law may entitle them to, so far only as may be necessary to secure their right of priority in regard to other creditors, through the attachment of the property and the record of such action in the registry books.

Said judicial action, however, and the attachment of the property, shall not confer on the creditor any right to prosecute his suit otherwise than as prescribed in this order.

IX. The provisions of this order shall not apply to those debts, for the collection of which the creditor may have obtained the control and administration of the property of the debtor, in conformity with the provisions of article 1503 of the Law of Civil Procedure.

X. All liabilities for costs, either incurred, or which may hereafter be incurred, in suits against debtors, shall be collected and enforced under the restrictions and limitations prescribed in this order, for the liabilities in which said costs may accrue.

XI. In all proceedings against the products or rents of rural property, the creditor shall, at the time of filing his claim, present a statement from the Alcalde of the municipality in which the property may be situated, certifying that said property is in a condition of normal production. The Alcalde issuing such certificate shall state therein the facts and grounds on which he bases his conclusions. If the Alcalde should not think that the property is in the condition claimed by the creditors, he shall so state in writing.

XII. Rural property shall be deemed in a condition of normal production, when, besides the fact that its plant and machinery are in good condition, it shall have produced either in rent or products during the agricultural year of 1898 to 1899 more than 50 per cent. of the amount of rents or products obtained from the said property in the agricultural year of 1894 to 1895.

XIII. The certificate, issued by the Alcalde under article XI. of this order, shall not be conclusive evidence of the fact therein stated, and it shall be lawful, therefore, for the debtor to submit his denial of said statements. The issue thus raised shall be tried according to the provisions for special or incidental proceedings, in articles 740, *et seq.*, of the law of Civil Procedure, and the action of the creditor will be stayed until final decision shall be rendered. The burden of proof as to the fact that the production of the property has exceeded the 50 per cent. mentioned in article XII. of this order, shall be on the creditor. The debtor shall submit his denial within ten days after the notice of the order of the Judge issing execution against the rent and products of the property in question.

XIV. In the proceedings mentioned in article XIII. of this order, no recourse may be had from the decision of the Audiencia, which decision shall be final.

XV. When city property, on the rents of which the creditor may have a right to enforce the collection of interest as prescribed in article III of this order, is occupied by the debtor, or by some other person not paying rent, or which may be attached by another creditor without a preferent right, the creditor shall have the right to take such judicial action as the laws may entitle him to, in order so to administer the said property that it may produce adequate rents.

ADNA R. CHAFFEE,
Brigadier-General, Chief of Staff.

No. 77.

HEADQUARTERS DIVISION OF CUBA,
HAVANA, *June* 14, 1899.

The Military Governor of Cuba directs the publication of the following order:

I. The order of the 10th of February, 1899, remitting all taxes due before the 1st day of January of the present year, and unpaid at the date of said order, is hereby extended to cover all taxes, for the collection of which the State or a municipality may hold property.

II. In pursuance of this order, all property, either urban or rural, which may, at this date, be held by the State or by a municipality, as a result of proceedings for the collection of said taxes, shall be returned to the owners or heirs, provided that the title to said property has not been finally vested in the State or a municipality, and that the property be such as may at present be held by the State for the objects and purposes specified in article 49 of the Instructions of the 15th of May, 1885, approved by the Royal Order of the 24th of December, 1888, prescribing the rules to be followed against delinquent taxpayers.

III. Such property as may already have been sold by the State, and the title to which is therefore vested in the purchaser thereof, shall not be understood to be covered by the provisions of this order.

IV. The only persons entitled to recover their property under this order shall be the owners of the same, or their heirs, and not those who may have acquired the rights and equities of said owners or heirs.

V. All expenses of release and restoration of the property herein referred to shall be borne by the owners or heirs of the same.

VI. The property shall be returned to its owners in the condition in which it may be found at the time of its release.

VII. The Department of Finance is charged with the execution of the provisions of this order.

ADNA R. CHAFFEE,
Brigadier-General, Chief of Staff.

No. 106.

HEADQUARTERS DIVISION OF CUBA,
HAVANA, *July* 11, 1899.

The Military Governor of Cuba directs the publication of the following order:

I. From the date of publication of this order, the tax known as Industrial Tax shall be paid to the State, and not to the municipalities, by all such companies and corporations as are enumerated in sections 5, 6, 7 and 8 of Tariff Second, which is amended to read as follows:

1. Banks of issue and discount, transacting business either on real estate or on personal property, shall pay taxes at the rate of 9.4 per cent. of their net profits.

2. Stock companies shall pay taxes at the rate of 7.5 per cent. of their net profits, except mining companies, savings banks, and such government loan and pledge companies as may be officially recognized and included accordingly in the list of tax exemptions.

3. Railroad and shipping companies shall pay 4.7 per cent. of their net profits. The amounts paid to stockholders from the reserve fund, or from funds which may be otherwise taxed, shall not be construed as net profits for the purpose of taxation.

4. Insurance companies shall pay 2 per cent. of the premiums annually collected from the insured, with the exception of mutual insurance corporations where no profits are distributed, and whose operations may consist only in assessing the stockholders for the proportional amount of the damages that any of them may have suffered.

5. Foreign corporations and companies, or branches thereof, duly authorized to transact business in this island, shall pay taxes, according to the head under which they are classified.

II. The said tax quotas shall be paid to the Department of Finance, according to the rules and regulations now in force.

III. Municipalities are authorized to collect, independently of the State, the land tax on such real property, either rural or urban, owned by said corporations or companies, as may appear on the assessment rolls of the municipal district in which such property is situated.

ADNA R. CHAFFEE,
Brigadier-General, Chief of Staff.

No. 181.

HEADQUARTERS DIVISION OF CUBA,

HAVANA, *September* 27, 1899.

The Military Governor of Cuba directs the publication of the following order:

1st. For the purpose of the security which, according to the existing law, insurance companies, either foreign or domestic, have to give, they will be classified as follows:

Fire Insurance Companies.
Life Insurance Companies.
Surety Companies.
Casualty Companies.
Marine Insurance Companies.
Title Guaranty Companies.

2d. The security which they shall have to give according to the provisions of the law now in force, in order to be authorized to transact business in the Island of Cuba, is modified and shall be given as hereinafter provided.

3d. The said security shall be given either by depositing its amount in cash in the general treasury of the island or by investing the same in mortgage bonds of corporations or companies doing business in the Island of Cuba, or in real estate mortgage on the terms and conditions prescribed by the law now in force. United States government bonds will also be accepted as security.

4th. The security offered shall be submitted to the approval of the Secretary of Finance and after acceptance by him, will be deposited for safe keeping in the treasury of the island.

5th. The amount of the security shall be:

Fire Insurance Companies	$75,000
Life Insurance Companies	25,000
Surety Companies	25,000
Casualty Companies	25,000
Marine Insurance Companies	25,000
Title Guaranty Companies	25,000

6th. Insurance companies now doing business in the island shall have to comply with the provisions of this order within the period of forty-five days from the date of its publication in the *Official Gazette*. Those that may hereafter commence business in the island shall first comply with the provisions of this order.

7th. Insurance companies whose main office is not Havana, may apply to the Chief Administrator of Finance of the province where their main office may be situated, for the purpose of giving the security and acceptance by said Chief Administrator of Hacienda who, in such cases, shall act as the delegate of the Secretary of Finance.

ADNA R. CHAFFEE,

Brigadier-General, Chief of Staff.

NOTARIAL LAWS.

The Spanish Notarial Law of May 28, 1862, comprising forty-eight articles, afterwards amended by the addition of one hundred and twenty-four articles, November 9, 1874, was promulgated, in a modified form, in Cuba and in Puerto Rico, October 29, 1873. The law of February 15, 1889, and the regulations of April 11, 1890, are in force in the Philippines.

Organic Laws of Tribunals.

The present Organic Law of Tribunals, comprising nine hundred and thirty-two articles, was adopted September 15, 1870, and amended October 14, 1882. The law is principally based on the Constitution of 1812, the laws of 1835, and 1844, and various amendments have been added from time to time. This law, in a modified form, was extended to Cuba,* Puerto Rico, and the Philippines, January 5, 1891.

---

* The judiciary of Havana comprises the following courts in the order of their importance:

1. The Supreme Court of The Island of Cuba.
2. The Audiencia of Havana, divided into three sections; one for civil, and two for criminal cases.
3. Six Courts of First Instance, one judge for each of the six judicial districts.
4. Six Courts of Municipal Judges, one judge for each of the judicial districts.

(a) Alcades and teniente Alcades have jurisdiction of infractions of municipal ordinances up to the amount of ten dollars, but in case of default in payment, have to refer such cases to corresponding municipal judges for enforcement.

The Courts of Havana.

The Supreme Court of the Island of Cuba, created April 14, 1899, consists of a Chief Justice and six associate justices, and as a court of last resort, supersedes the Supreme Court of Madrid, besides other duties and functions set out in the order of its creation.

The Audiencia of Havana.

Consists of a chairman and eight associate judges. In civil matters three judges form a quorum for hearing and determining cases, and in criminal matters, the same number of judges is sufficient, except when the death

Military and Naval Laws and Courts.

This matter is treated under one head in view of the fact that the Supreme Council of War and Navy has jurisdiction over both branches of the service.

Military Laws.

The Law of December 6, 1868, abrogated the existing special laws relating to the Army, and said law was later supplemented by the decrees of December 1, 1868, February 8, 1869, November 30, 1872, June 4, 1873, July 19, 1876, and others, and on March 10, 1884, the Organic Law, known as the *Ley de organizacion y atribuciones de los Tribunales de Guerra* was published. The Military Penal Code or *Codigo penal para el ejercito* was promulgated November 17, 1884; the laws of practice for the Army or *Ley de Enjuiciamiento militar*, embracing three hundred and forty-three articles, became effective September 29, 1886, and on September 27, 1890, the Code of Military Justice or *Codigo de Justicia militar* was authorized and still continues in force. This work comprises three books and seven hundred and fifty articles. Book 1. Treats of the organization and powers of military tribunals, their competency and jurisdiction in both civil and military matters. Book 2. Considers penal laws. Book 3. Takes up the law of military procedure. The Penal Code, known as

---

sentence is passed, when five judges must be present, of which a majority may pass the death sentence. Appeal lies from the Audiencia to the Supreme Court.

Judges of First Instance.

A judge of First Instance is provided for each of the six Judicial Districts into which the City of Havana is divided and has original jurisdiction of civil contentions involving more than one thousand *pesetas*, comprising usually what are known as *contenciosa y voluntaria* cases, as provided in the law of Civil Procedure, and of civil cases on appeal from the Municipal Judges, where less than the above amount is involved.

In criminal cases of a serious nature, such as included in book two of the Criminal Code, they have original jurisdiction,— see Criminal Procedure.

Municipal Judges.

There are six Municipal Judges in Havana, one for each of the six judicial districts, who have original jurisdiction to try and give decisions in civil cases where the amount involved is less than one thousand pesetas, and in criminal cases for minor offenses — misdemeanors — covered by book third of the Criminal Code. Appeals from decisions of such judges lie to courts of first instance.

the *Codigo penal de la marina de guerra,* embracing three hundred and forty-three articles, went into effect August 24, 1888, and the Organic Law of the Supreme Council of the Army and Navy or the *Reglamento Organico y del regimen interior del Consejo Supremo de Guerra y Marina,* consisting of two hundred and fifteen articles, was promulgated December 17, 1890, and considers the organization, powers and duties of the officials composing the same, the manner of procedure and records.

Naval Laws.

Naval jurisdiction exists, at present, as a part of the military establishment, the special laws on the Navy having been superseded by the Law of 1868, and, although the law of bases of July 14, 1882, was extended to this branch of the service, it has not yet been granted an independent code but the penal code, known as *Codigo penal de la marina de guerra* of August 24, 1888, is in force, and matters of procedure are governed by the decree of November 30, 1872, and the instructions for the observance of the same of June 4, 1873, comprising two hundred and thirty-nine articles.

Military and naval courts in Spain have a much broader jurisdiction than similar courts in the United States and cannot only try persons in service but can also acquire jurisdiction over civilians in certain cases, as for example in case of minor crimes involving property belonging to either branch of the service.*

---

* See *Cuerpos juridicos de Guerra y de la Armada,* which became effective, as to the Navy, Nov. 17, 1886, and as to the Army, Jan. 14, 1893, for the latest reforms and laws on this general subject.

THE COMMERCIAL CODES OF SPAIN AND SPANISH-AMERICA.

The Aragonese were considered the most accomplished sailors of the thirteenth century, as well as the earliest and most progressive of European merchants. Their celebrated code of maritime laws, called the *Codigo de las Costumbres Maritimas de Barcelona,* better known as the *Libro del Consulado,* according to Capmany, appears to have been compiled from existing laws and customs during the reign of King Jayme of Aragon, about the middle of the thirteenth century, although Pardessus sets a later date. It was first published in Catalan at Barcelona in 1494,* under the above title, to which were added the *Ordenanzas de las Antiguas forma judiciaria del Consulado del Mar* from the *tribunales consulares de la Corona de Aragon* which work embraces some ordinances in Latin of the *Prohombres* of Barcelona on nautical laws of earlier date:— part of these laws was confirmed to Valencia by Peter III of Aragon in 1283, the first Spanish city to possess a regular organized maritime court. The maritime laws *Formas de los Juicios* were adopted in Mallorca in 1343 and in Barcelona in 1347.

The edition of the *Libro del Consulado,* published in 1494, is composed of two hundred and fifty-two chapters, without any plan of organization, and was translated into Castilian in 1791 by Capmany and methodized and distributed under fourteen titles embracing two hundred and ninety-two laws. Other ancient and notable codes of Catalonia which deserve mention are:— the *Costumbres de Tortosa,* published about 1279, which includes political, civil and penal, as well as maritime laws, comprising nine books, subdivided into titles and the latter into *rubricas ó costumbres;* also the *Privilegio Recognoverunt Proceres* which con-

* Barcelona has statutes on maritime laws of record as far back as 1436.

tains rules about bankers and banking from the years 1258 to 1484; and the renowned *Ordenanzas de Bilbao,* published in 1737 by order of Philip V for the determination of suits and differences which arose before the commercial tribunal of Bilbao as to transactions both on land and sea.

They were officially entitled *Ordenanzas de la ilustre Universidad y casa de contratacion de la M. N. y M. L. villa de Bilbao,* and were revised in 1819. These ordinances comprise twenty-eight chapters, the first eight of which treat of the jurisdiction of the commercial tribunal; the ninth of traders and their books; the tenth of commercial companies; the eleventh of commercial contracts; the twelfth of commission agents; the thirteenth of bills of exchange; the fourteenth of promissory notes, bonds, drafts and marine contracts; the fifteenth of brokers; the sixteenth of auxiliary ship-broking interpreters; the seventeenth of bankrupts; and from the eighteenth to the twenty-eighth inclusive of maritime commerce.

These important and later ordinances formed the commercial law of the greater part of Spain, and were observed throughout the kingdoms from the time of publication until the adoption of the Code of Commerce of 1829.

The Modern Codes.

On account of the uncertainty and confusion arising from the different ordinances in force and the conflicting opinions of the various tribunals of commerce, a commission was appointed in 1828 to formulate a new and general commercial code, based on the *Consulado del Mare* and the *Ordenanzas de Bilbao,* which was completed and sanctioned May 30, 1829, to go into effect January 1, 1830, and this Code superseded all former laws on the subject throughout the Spanish possessions, until the adoption of the Code of 1885.

It contained twelve hundred and nineteen articles divided into five books. The first book relates to commerce, commercial people and commercial business; the second book treats of commercial contracts, such as partnership, sale, exchange, loan, deposit, suretyship, insurance, bills of exchange, and letters of credit; the third book considers maritime commerce; the fourth book treats of bankruptcy and the various proceedings in bankrupt cases; while the fifth book treats of the administration of justice in commercial matters, including commercial courts, their jurisdiction and their practice.

This work proved to be such an excellent one that it and its amendments, made from time to time, have been taken largely as the basis of the commercial codes of the Spanish-American countries.*

On July 24, 1830, the Law of Mercantile Procedure was approved and continued in effect until December 6, 1868, when, except as to bankrupt cases, it became part of the civil procedure. The Law of Exchanges followed in 1831, also laws on banks and credit societies in 1848, 1869, and 1878.† Provisional regulations for the organization and government of the Commercial Registry and Commercial Exchanges went into effect January 1, 1886, and were extended to Cuba and Puerto Rico, June 12 and April 16, 1886, respectively, and the law in regard to Suspension of Payments of June 10, 1897 (arts. 870 to 874) was extended to Ultramar June 25, 1897.

The present Code of Commerce, adopted by Royal Decree of August 22, 1885, went into effect in Spain and the adjacent islands January 1, 1886, and was extended to Cuba and Puerto Rico, January 28, 1886, and to the Philippines on August 6, 1888.

This Code contains four books, embracing twenty-seven titles and nine hundred and fifty-five articles. Book 1. Treats of commerce and commercial people in general and registry. Book 2. Treats of contracts which are especially commercial in their character, including mercantile corporations and companies, their expiration and liquidation, banks, railways, exchanges, insurance, pledges, commercial paper, etc. Book 3. Is devoted to maritime commerce, and contains elaborate provisions in regard to the law of shipping. Book 4. Contains provisions in regard to suspension of payments, and bankruptcies of merchants and mercantile corporations, and also treats of prescription in commercial matters.

---

* The prize codes have been based on both those of France and Spain.

† In Cuba and Puerto Rico, see amendments of Feb. 17, 1832, Nov. 1, 1878, Aug. 12, 1881, and March 12, 1885, extended later to the Philippines; also R. O. of Sept. 20, 1891, as to Spanish commerce in foreign countries.

PART THIRD.

CHAPTER I.

*The Government of the Indies or of the Spanish-American Colonies.**

Soon after the discovery of the Americas, it became necessary for Spain to devise means for the control and government of her new and vast colonial possessions acquired by her brave and hardy explorers.

The establishment of the *Casa de la Contratacion* or India House at Seville by an ordinance of 1503 was the first step in this direction; it had authority to grant licenses, to dispatch fleets, and to dispose of the results of trade and exploration, and, upon the establishment of the Council of the Indies by the Emperor Charles and Queen Joanna in the year 1524,† it became subordinate to the latter, and transacted commercial business, maintaining a strict and exclusive monopoly of all the trade for Span-

* Those who judge the merits of the Recopilacion de Indias, solely from the results of the civilization which it was intended to direct, will do but poor justice to the most complete and comprehensive scheme of colonial government which the world has ever known. Although, no doubt, greatly defective in many particulars, and tinctured most prejudicially with the errors in political economy which were peculiar to the times, the Recopilacion bears all about it evidences of the most far-seeing wisdom, the most laborious and comprehensive investigation and management of details, and a spirit of enlightened humanity not easily exceeded.—Wallis, Spain, her Institutions, etc.

† ORDINANCE ESTABLISHING THE COUNCIL OF THE INDIES.

That the royal council of the Indies may reside in the court, and have the servants and officers which this ordinance declares:

Considering the great benefits and advantages which, by the grace of God, we have received, and every day do receive, from the increase and growth of the kingdom and dominions of our Indies: and being well advised of the obligation and duty towards them which this imposes upon us, we are solicitous, on our part (with God's assistance), to devise suitable means by which such great kingdoms and dominions may be governed and ruled in a proper manner. And in order that we may provide with the greater judgment, deliberation, and prudence, in matters relating to religion and the good of these states, we establish and ordain, that our council of the Indies may always reside in our court, near our person, and in it a president thereof, a grand chancellor of the Indies, who must also be a counsellor; and the counsellor's learned men, which the business to come before them will necessarily require,

ish merchants.* Spanish-America was governed from Spain by the Council of the Indies, under authority and direction of the King; it was devised by Ferdinand V, and the powers of the Council were much enlarged under Charles V and his successors.

The Council of the Indies had supreme jurisdiction over all the colonies, all the laws and ordinances of viceroys and governors were subject to its approval, and it had power to frame laws: one of its principal objects was the conversion of the Indians.

When a vacancy occurred in any government office, it had to submit three names to the King for a selection, and it was afterwards charged with the equipment and dispatch of the royal fleets. The Council consisted of a president, a grand chancellor and a deputy, eight counsellors, a fiscal whose duty it was to watch over the interests of the royal revenues, and two secretaries with a staff of attorneys, solicitors, accountants, clerks, etc.

There was also a chronicler or historiographer, and a cosmographer whose duties were not only to construct maps and charts, but also to deliver lectures and to examine officers of the fleets.

The Spanish possessions in America† before the revolution formed nine distinct governments, all constructed on the same plan and independent of one another. Four of these, of the first rank were vice-royalties, viz.: Mexico, Peru, La Plata, and New Granada; and five were captain-general ships, viz.: Yucatan,

---

of whom, for the present, there may be eight: a chancellor of the exchequer, and two secretaries; a deputy grand chancellor; all of whom must be men of approved morals, of noble and pure lineage, fearing God, and eminent for their learning and prudence; three reporters, and a clerk of the chamber of justice, skillful and diligent in the discharge of their offices, and of approved fidelity; four auditors of accounts, able and competent persons, and a receiver of the fines imposed by the chamber, and confiscations and deposits; two fiscal solicitors; a chief chronicler and cosmographer, and a professor of mathematics; an assessor of suits, an advocate and a proctor of poor persons; a chaplain, who may say Mass to the council on the days of it; four porters, and a constable, who must all be men of the requisite ability and qualifications; and before being admitted to their offices, they shall take an oath that they will discharge them well and faithfully, and that they will keep the ordinances of the council, those already made and those which shall be made, and the secret of it.

* In 1717, the Casa de la Contratacion was transferred to Cadiz for convenience in superintending the shipping to America.

† Spain held her American colonies as the fiefs or personal property of the monarch, not so much by reason of her discovery and possession of them, as by reason of the Bull of Pope Alexander VI, which divided the ownership of the American continent between the Kings of Spain and Portugal, in virtue of the jurisdiction which the Pope had over the world as the head of all mankind (Solorzano, in his Politica Indiana, vol. 1, chapters 10 and 11).

Guatamala, Chili, Venezuela, and the Island of Cuba. The government was vested in the viceroy or captain-general, who was held to represent the King, and to enjoy all his prerogatives within the colony. But in these countries, as in others where the supreme power is apparently unlimited, it was indirectly restrained by the influence of the courts of justice, corporations, and other public bodies. The Royal Audiencias or Supreme Courts, composed of Spaniards nominated by the Crown, had extensive judicial powers, and were independent of the viceroys. The cabildos or municipalities, and the fueros or corporations, also possessed considerable privileges, which derived security and importance from long prescription.*

The viceroy of Peru was undoubtedly the most important official in Spanish-America. He resided at Lima and received a salary of 30,000 ducats, 10,000 more than that of the viceroy of Mexico.

He not only had charge of the civil and military government of Peru, but also the supervision of Chili, Quito, Caracas, and even of New Granada, and Buenos Ayres, whose captains-general were under his jurisdiction, so that Lima was practically the capital of all of Spanish South America.

The viceroys lived in considerable state, with body guards and numerous attendants, and they presided over the Royal Audiencias or chief courts of justice, and over the financial and revenue departments, besides being commanders-in-chief of the land and naval forces.

It was the custom for viceroys to write detailed memoirs of their administration, and many of these valuable state papers have been preserved and some printed. The corregidors, who governed the districts under the viceroys, held their offices for six years.

The Church exercised great power and influence with its bishops and dignataries, its convents and fraternities, its parish priests in every village, its missionaries, its complete control over education, and its all powerful inquisition methods.

The clergy, who were numerous and rich, necessarily possessed great influence among a superstitious people. The vices naturally

* The two great authorities on the history and laws of the Indies are: Bartolomé de las Casas, philosopher and missionary, who spent most of his life in the Indies, and Pereira Solorzano, jurisconsult, who was a public attorney and judge in the Indies, and a member of the Council of the Indies.

inherent to the colonial system existed in full force in the Spanish-American dominions. There was tolerable security for all classes except the Indians, who were regarded and treated as beasts of burden, out of whose toil and suffering a provision as ample as possible was to be extracted, first to supply the wants of the royal treasury, and next to provide for and satisfy the cupidity of a shoal of do-nothing public officers and priests. In justice to Spain, it must be said that edicts were indeed issued for the protection of the Indians, and persons appointed to enforce them;* but in their administration there was failure to correct the evils rooted in the system, and not infrequently it increased their weight. The Indians, after the conquest, were at first slaves; they paid a capitation tax to the crown, and their labor was entirely at the disposal of their lord. This system was modified from time to time; but all the changes carried into effect down to the revolution, did not release them from their state of vassalage. They still continued liable, in a greater or less degree, to the performance of compulsory labor, under the orders of persons against whom they had no protection. This was an enormous grievance; but, what was equally bad, being held incompetent, in law, to buy or sell, or enter into any pecuniary engagement beyond the value of a few dollars, without the agency of white men, the swarm of public functionaries had an unlimited power of interfering in their concerns, of vexing, harassing, and plundering them, under forms of law. The Memoirs of Ulloa, long buried in the Spanish archives, and Las Casas' Destruction of the Indies, and various other documents published since the revolution, depict acts of extortion, perfidy, cruelty, and oppression practiced upon the Indians that have rarely been paralleled.

The original aim of the Spaniards in the colonies was to enrich themselves, and the government at home framed its acts and regulations subordinate to the grand object of raising a revenue; however, later on many restrictions in favor of the Indians were made.

Spain retained in her control the whole trade of the colonies, and guarded her monopoly with most severe penalties.

To create a race of servants devoted to its purposes, the Crown bestowed all offices, from the highest to the lowest, on natives of the Peninsula exclusively. The wisdom of the plan seems

* Recop., lib. 3, tit. 3, l. 2; lib. 4, tit. 12, laws 9, 12, 17; lib. 6, tit. 3, l. 9.

questionable, but was natural and adhered to with wonderful pertinacity.

The Spanish were of a class distinct from the natives in feelings, habits and interests, considering themselves as a privileged caste, and regarding their own existence as intimately connected with that of the system of which they were the principal support. With all such means and appliances, it is not extraordinary that Spain should have been able to uphold for three centuries a system in which the interests of so many millions of human beings were so habitually and unrelentingly sacrificed.

It was the course of events, more than mal-administration, which ultimately caused its overthrow.

COMPILATION OF THE LAWS OF THE KINGDOMS OF THE INDIES.

(*Recopilacion de Leyes de los Reynos de las Indias.*)

The various laws enacted in Spain for the government of the Indies, which had been promulgated, at different periods, in the form of *cédulas, decretos, resoluciones, ordenamientos, reglamentos, pragmáticas,* etc.* were collected and digested or compiled by order of Philip IV and published in 1661 in the same form as the Recopilacion of Castile† in order to make the government of such provinces better known, and to secure by general and permanent laws the obedience and welfare of the natives who inhabited them. A subsequent and better digested edition was ordered published by Charles II in 1681, and editions were printed in 1756, 1774, 1791 and 1841.

The Recopilacion de Indias is regarded as the only authentic collection of the ordinances and decrees governing Spanish-America prior to the year 1680.

For a knowledge of the laws and regulations subsequent to this period, we are indebted to the labors of a Mexican judge, Don Eusebio Ventura Beleña. The title of his work, published at

---

* *Cédulas* were orders emanating from some superior tribunal, promulgated in the name, and by the authority of the sovereign.

Decretos were similar orders in ecclesiastical matters.

Ordenamientos and *Pragmaticas* were also orders emanating from the King, and differing from cédulas only in form, and in the mode of promulgation.

Reglamentos were written instructions given by a competent authority without the observance of any peculiar form.

Resoluciones were opinions formed by some superior authority on matters referred to it for its decision, and forwarded to the inferior authorities for their instruction and government.

† 1st. Moreau and Carleton.— Partidas, p. xv.

Mexico in two volumes folio in 1787, is *Recopilacion Sumaria de todos los Autos Acordados de la Real Audiencia y Sala del Crimen de esta Nueva España,* etc.

Beleña did not confine himself to giving mere extracts of the laws published since the appearance of the Recopilacion de Indies, but published these laws at length. He also republished all the cédulas and decrees promulgated from 1528 to 1677, which had been previously collected by Montemayor, by order of the viceroys of Mexico, to which he added all such further orders and decrees as had appeared from 1677 to 1680.

This work is not official, however, but the collection has often been verified, and throughout the Spanish colonies, it is constantly quoted, and relied on as unquestionable authority.

The revolution of Spain, which followed the French invasion, gave rise to a new form of government under the direction of the Cortes, whose decrees were held obligatory in the colonies, whenever they had been either expressly declared to apply to those countries, or had been promulgated therein.

After the re-establishment of the absolute monarchy in Spain in 1814, the sovereigns of that country continued to enact laws for the government of America, until 1821.

The method adopted in the Recopilacion de Indies is the same as that pursued in the Nueva Recopilacion of the laws of Spain. It is divided into nine books, comprising two hundred and eighteen titles, which contain six thousand four hundred and forty-seven different legal enactments, all of which, derived from the orders, decrees and regulations of different sovereigns.

Book 1 treats principally of ecclesiastical laws and matters, church officials, and educational institutions.

Book 2 considers the laws in general, prescribes the order of government for the council of the Indies, the superior and inferior tribunals thereof and their officials.

Book 3 treats of the royal domain and jurisdiction, officials and their fees, war, fortifications and munitions, officers and soldiers, pirates, prizes, ceremonies, and the post.

Book 4 considers discoveries by land and sea, peacemakers, founders of towns, population of cities and towns, corporations and councils and officials thereof, the sale, union and division of lands and water, granaries, assessments and contributions, public works, the discovery and development of mines, assaying, etc., fisheries, and shipment of pearls and valuable stones.

Book 5 includes the boundaries and divisions of the governments, civil officials, doctors, clerks, fees, lawsuits and sentences, exceptions, appeals, executions, and the residences of judges.

Book 6 treats of the Indians, their liberties, conversion, tributes and taxes, protectors of the Indians, good treatment and services thereof.

Book 7 embraces criminal laws and their application, and jails.

Book 8 treats principally of the royal treasury and its officials, taxes, *repartimientos,* privileges, duties, monopolies, assignments and consignments, bills of exchange and remittances.

Book 9 considers the Royal Audencias, and House of Contracts or India House (*Casa de Contratacion*), their officials, judges, taxes, claims, estates in the Indies, vessels, fleets and their officials, passengers, foreigners, ship builders, equipment and fitting out of ships, navigation laws, underwriters, navigation and commerce in other parts of the world, and the consuls and judges of Lima and Mexico.

There is found united in this compilation many laws, on the same subject, in which the preceding law is only repeated, others in which it is modified, and still others in which it is abrogated, either in whole or in part.

The Recopilacion de Indies, notwithstanding its dimensions, is a mere digest of the royal orders, etc., issued from time to time for the better government of the American colonies. It appears exclusively intended to regulate the political, military, ecclesiastical and fiscal administration of the Spanish possessions in the New World. Hence, this code was not by itself a complete code for the government of Spanish-America, but it was necessary to supplement it by the general and common law of Spain. One does not find among its numerous enactments provisions treating of the civil law, or indeed of any laws which have not exclusive reference to the mode of administering the various departments of the government of the colonies. It is on this account that laws 1 and 2, title 1 of book 2, provide, that in cases where the Recopilacion de Indias has no provision on the subject, the laws of Castile must be observed.*

* Law 1, after declaring the effect of the Recopilacion de Indias, says "y en lo que no estuviere decidido por las leyes de esta Recopilacion para las decisiones de las causas y su determinacion, se guarden las leyes de la Recopilacion y Partidas de estos Reynos de Castilla, conforme a la sey siguiente." Law 2 provides, "Ordenamos y mandamos que en todos los casos, negocios y pleytos en que no estuviere decidido, ni declarado lo que se debe proveer

Thus the civil law of Spain became the fundamental law of America; but inasmuch as the condition and wants of the colonies varied in many respects from that of the mother country, Philip IV, by a law, found in the Recopilacion de Indias (l. 40, t. 1, b. 2), decreed that no law enacted in Spain, should be obligatory in America unless accompanied by a cédula to that effect emanating from the Council of the Indies.

As a consequence many legal enactments in force in Spain were never extended to the American colonies, while several others of no efficacy at home, were promulgated exclusively for Spanish-America. Besides this source of legislation, the Audiencias or supreme tribunals of Mexico and Peru, etc., published from time to time rules and regulations, which, although their authority was questionable, were, as well as orders emanating from the viceroy, held to be obligatory.

The different changes made from time to time, finally rendered a revision of the Recopilacion de Indias indispensable, and it was accordingly ordered about the year 1777. This undertaking was, however, never completed, and it was abandoned after one book had been finished. This portion of the new colonial code was published and sanctioned by an order dated at Aranjuez, 25th of March, 1792, and it has reference exclusively to the Council of the Indies.

APPLICATION OF SPANISH LAWS IN THE INDIES.

Murillo, an able Spanish writer, in his treatise, entitled *Cursus Juris Canonici Hispani et Indici,* speaks of the manner in which the Spanish laws ought to be received in the Indies, stating that in such dominions courts of justice should first have recourse to the royal and special edicts which may have been directed to the chancery of the place where the cause is pending; and, if there are none, they should then decide according to the common law, which is to be found in the laws of the Recopilacion of the Indies; and when these last are silent, recourse must be had to the Recopilacion of Castile (Nueva Recopilacion), and to the Partidas.

He also observes that the rescripts or royal ordinances are of no authority in the Indies, unless they have been directed to the Supreme Council of those countries.*

por las leyes de esta Recopilacion, ó por Cédulas, Provisiones ú Ordonanzas dadas, y no revocadas para las Indias, y las que por nuestra orden se despacharon, se guarden las leyes de nuestro Reyno de Castilla, conforme á la de Toro, asi en cuanto á la substancia, resolucion y decision de los casos, negocios y pleytos, como a la forma y orden de substanciar."

*See book 2, tit. 1, law 2.— Recop.

CHAPTER II.

Laws and Codes of Mexico.

The laws of Mexico subsequent to the Laws of the Indies to 1787 may be found in the excellent private compilation of a Mexican judge, Beleña, in two volumes, entitled "*Recopilacion Sumaria de todos los Autos Acordados de la Real Audiencia y Sala del Crimen de esta Nueva España, y providencias de su Superior Gobierno,*" etc., and to 1821 in the Mexican official compilation, "*Colleccion de los Decretos y Ordenes de las Cortes de España, que se reputan vigentes en la Republica de los Estados Mexicanos.*" Mexico, 1829.

Mexican legislation from the date of independence to the present time (1821–1900) is embraced in the compilation of Dublan and Lozano — the *Recopilacion de Leyes Mexicanas.*

The Mexican Mining Code, which was approved November 22, 1884, abrogated the former laws on the subject.

The Commercial Code, of September 15, 1889, has superseded the Code of 1884. It is divided into five books, embracing one thousand five hundred articles. It is based largely on Spanish commercial law.

The Mexican Civil Code of March 31, 1884, repealed the Code of 1870,— is in force in the federal district of Mexico, and the territories; and most of the States, which formerly had civil codes of their own, have adopted the Federal Code with slight amendments. It embraces four books, and three thousand eight hundred and twenty-three articles, arranged similarly to the Spanish Civil Code.

Mexican Constitutions.

The independence of Mexico was first proclaimed by the Mexican patriot Hidalgo, and instead of being a covert and popular movement as in the other American colonies, it was spontaneous and open amongst a limited class — the lower clergy.

The struggle, which began in 1810, lasted, with some interruptions, until 1824. Soon after the defeat of Hidalgo's forces and the capture of the leader, an assembly, composed largely of officers of the patriot army, was convened to formulate a constituted government, and accordingly it established a council consisting at first of three members and later of five, designated as the "Supreme Governmental Council of America," which cited the military officers, the governors, and alcaldes of the Indian pueblos of the vicinity to take the oath of obedience and fidelity to the council, which governed in the name of King Ferdinand VII, whose name was used as an act of policy to gain the support of all those who desired independence. The council, in fact, was an illegal body, deriving authority neither from a popular election nor from any existing legitimate source. It was feared, however, by the Spanish party that it might gain recognition and exercise the functions of a legitimate government. A price was, therefore, set on the head of each member, but it subsequently became dissolved by internal dissension.

On the 1st of September, 1813, a Congress constituted by popular election was assembled in Chilpancingo, proclaimed anew the independence of Mexico, and agreed upon a republican Constitution, which was published in Apanzingan in October, 1814. This Constitution was short-lived, being set aside by the adoption of the Spanish Constitution of 1812, in so far as it was applicable to Mexico.

Upon the failure of an independent imperial government and the exile of Iturbide, a new Congress was installed on the 7th of November, 1823, and on the 3d of December it began the discussion of a project for a fundamental law, which was approved January 31, 1824, and "in thirty-six articles contained the basis of the future political constitution." Through the adoption of this Constitution the nation acquired a popular representative, federal, republican government, which was only a provisional government. This was set aside on the adoption of the Constitution of 1824, which in many particulars was a copy of the Constitution of the United States.

The Constitution of 1824 remained in force eleven years, but during these years Mexico was not without its internal disturbances, and in 1833, by a revolution, Santana was made President. After a temporary retirement a reactionary movement restored him to power in 1834. Having allied himself with the Clericals and Centralists, he dissolved the Congress on the 31st of May, set aside the liberal decrees which that body had passed, and broke openly with the Federalists.

The new Congress, which was installed in January, 1835, undertook to reform the Constitution of 1824, and in 1836 a new fundamental law was issued, which rejected the federal principle and established a centralized government, the whole territory of the Republic being divided into departments instead of the pre-existing States, the departments into districts, and these again into *partidos*. Adherents of federalism became opponents of the new order of things, and in the next decade Mexico was without an effective Constitution, the power being with the most successful military leader. In 1847, however, the Congress passed an act which brought into force again the Constitution of 1824, with certain amendments.

Upon the retirement of Santana, Alvarez was elected *ad interim* President, and in February, 1856, the Constituent Congress, or Constitutional Convention, was assembled. Comonfort, who had become President on the Resignation of Alvarez, now issued, in accordance with authority conferred upon him, the "*Estatuto orgânico provisional de la Republica Mejicana.*" The *estatuto* was a quasi-constitution, in one hundred and twenty-five articles, which organized completely the executive and judicial powers in accordance with the principles of centralism, and which detailed with such method and in a liberal sense the civil and political rights of the Mexicans; but which contained a sovereignty saving clause, peculiar to early Spanish Constitutions, in article 82, which provided that: "The President of the Republic shall be able to act discretionally, when, in the judgment of the council of ministers, this shall be necessary in order to defend the independence or the integrity of the territory, or to maintain the established order, or to preserve the public tranquillity; but in no case shall he be able to impose the penalty of death, nor those penalties prohibited by article 55."

The new Constitution, which was formulated in the meantime by the Constituent Congress, was finally adopted on the 5th of February, 1857, but by abolishing the ecclesiastical and military privileges, excited vigorous opposition, which, in 1858, led to a civil war, with Juarez as leader of the Constitutional party, while Zuloaga, and later Miramon, led the Revolutionary party. In 1861 Juarez overcame the Revolutionary forces and took possession of the capital. During the same year (1861) the Revolutionary party entered into certain foreign alliances against the Constitutional party, led by Juarez, and from these alliances proceeded the series of well-known events which led to the downfall of imperialism and the death of Maximilian. The Constitution of 1857 was revived as the fundamental law of the land,

and, with subsequent amendments, has continued in force to the present time.

CONSTITUTION OF THE UNITED STATES OF MEXICO.

PREAMBLE.

In the name of God and with the authority of the Mexican people.

The representatives of the different States, of the District and Territories which compose the Republic of Mexico, called by the Plan proclaimed in Ayutla the 1st of March, 1854, amended in Acapulco the 11th day of the same month and year, and by the summons issued the 17th of October, 1855, to constitute the nation under the form of a popular, representative, democratic republic, exercising the powers with which they are invested, comply with the requirements of their high office, decreeing the following political Constitution of the Mexican Republic, on the indestructible basis of its legitimate independence, proclaimed the 16th of September, 1810, and completed the 27th of September, 1821.

TITLE I.

SECTION I.— OF THE RIGHTS OF MAN.

Article 1. The Mexican people recognize that the rights of man are the basis and the object of social institutions. Consequently they declare that all the laws and all the authorities of the country must respect and maintain the guarantees which the present Constitution establishes.

Art. 2. In the Republic all are born free. Slaves who set foot upon the national territory recover, by that act alone, their liberty, and have a right to the protection of the laws.

Art. 3. Instruction is free. The law shall determine what professions require a diploma for their exercise, and with what requisites they must be issued.

Art. 4. Every man is free to adopt the profession, industrial pursuit, or occupation which suits him, the same being useful and honorable, and to avail himself of its products. Nor shall any one be hindered in the exercise of such profession, industrial pursuit, or occupation, unless by judicial sentence when such exercise attacks the rights of a third party, or by governmental resolution, dictated in terms which the law marks out, when it offends the rights of society.

Art. 5. No one shall be obliged to give personal services without just compensation, and without his full consent. The state shall not permit any contract, pact, or agreement to be carried into effect which has for its object the diminution, loss, or irrevocable sacrifice of the liberty of man, whether it be for the sake of labor, education, or a religious vow. The law, consequently, may not recognize monastic orders, nor may it permit their establishment, whatever may be the denomination or object with which they claim to be formed.* Neither may an agreement be permitted in which any one stipulates for his proscription or banishment.

Art. 6. The expression of ideas shall not be the object of any judicial or administrative inquisitions, except in case it attacks morality, the rights of a third party, provokes some crime or misdemeanor, or disturbs public order.

Art. 7. The liberty to write and to publish writings on any subject whatsoever is inviolable. No law or authority shall establish previous censure, nor require security from authors or printers, nor restrict the liberty of the press, which has no other limits than respect of private life, morality, and the public peace. The crimes which are committed by means of the press shall be judged by the competent tribunals of the Federation, or by those of the States, those of the Federal District and the Territory of Lower California, in accordance with their penal laws.†

Art. 8. The right of petition, exercised in writing in a peaceful and respectful manner, is inviolable; but in political matters only citizens of the Republic may exercise it. To every petition must be returned a written opinion by the authority to whom it may have been addressed, and the latter is obliged to make the result known to the petitioner.

Art. 9. No one may be deprived of the right peacefully to assemble or unite with others for any lawful object whatsoever, but only citizens of the Republic may do this in order to take part in the political affairs of the country. No armed assembly has a right to deliberate.

Art. 10. Every man has a right to possess and carry arms for his security and legitimate defense. The law shall designate what arms are prohibited and the punishment which those shall incur who carry them.

---

* This sentence was introduced into the original article September 25, 1873, with other less important amendments.

† This article was amended May 15, 1883, by introducing the last sentence as a substitute for the following: "The crimes of the press shall be judged by one jury, which attests the fact, and by another, which applies the law and designates the punishment."

Art. 11. Every man has a right to enter and to go out of the Republic, to travel through its territory and change his residence, without the necessity of a letter of security, passport, safe-conduct, or other similar requisite. The exercise of this right shall not prejudice the legitimate faculties of the judicial or administrative authority in cases of criminal or civil responsibility.

Art. 12. There are not, nor shall there be recognized in the Republic, titles of nobility, or prerogatives, or hereditary honors. Only the people, legitimately represented, may decree recompenses in honor of those who may have rendered or may render eminent services to the country or to humanity.

Art. 13. In the Mexican Republic no one may be judged by special law nor by special tribunals. No person or corporation may have privileges, or enjoy emoluments, which are not compensation for a public service and are established by law. Martial law may exist only for crimes and offences which have a definite connection with military discipline. The law shall determine with all clearness the cases included in this exception.

Art. 14. No retroactive law shall be enacted. No one may be judged or sentenced except by laws made prior to the act, and exactly applicable to it, and by a tribunal which shall have been previously established by law.

Art. 15. Treaties shall never be made for the extradition of political offenders, nor for the extradition of those violators of the public order who may have held in the country where they committed the offence the position of slaves; nor agreements or treaties in virtue of which may be altered the guarantees and rights which this Constitution grants to the man and to the citizen.

Art. 16. No one may be molested in his person, family, domicile, papers and possessions, except in virtue of an order written by the competent authority, which shall establish and assign the legal cause for the proceedings. In the case of *in flagrante delicto* any person may apprehend the offender and his accomplices, placing them without delay at the disposal of the nearest authorities.

Art. 17. No one may be arrested for debts of a purely civil character. No one may exercise violence in order to reclaim his rights. The tribunals shall always be prompt to administer justice. This shall be gratuitous, judicial costs being consequently abolished.

Art. 18. Imprisonment shall take place only for crimes which deserve corporal punishment. In any state of the process in which it shall appear that such a punishment might not be imposed upon the accused, he shall be set at liberty under bail. In no case shall the imprisonment or detention be prolonged for default of payment of fees, or of any furnishing of money whatever.

Art. 19. No detention shall exceed the term of three days, unless justified by a writ showing cause of imprisonment and other requisites which the law establishes. The mere lapse of this term shall render responsible the authority that orders or consents to it, and the agents, ministers, wardens, or jailers who execute it. Any maltreatment in the apprehension or in the confinement of the prisoners, any injury which may be inflicted without legal ground, any tax or contribution in the prisons, is an abuse which the laws must correct and the authorities severally punish.

Art. 20. In every criminal trial the accused shall have the following guarantees:

I. That the grounds of the proceedings and the name of the accuser, if there shall be one, shall be made known to him.

II. That his preparatory declaration shall be taken within forty-eight hours, counting from the time he may be placed at the disposal of the judge.

III. That he shall be confronted with the witnesses who testify against him.

IV. That he shall be furnished with the *data* which he requires and which appear in the process, in order to prepare for his defence.

V. That he shall be heard in defence by himself or by counsel, or by both, as he may desire. In case he should have no one to defend him, a list of official defenders shall be presented to him, in order that he may choose one or more who may suit him.

Art. 21. The application of penalties properly so called belongs exclusively to the judicial authority. The political or administrative authorities may only impose fines, as correction, to the extent of five hundred dollars, or imprisonment to the extent of one month, in the cases and manner which the law shall expressly determine.

Art. 22. Punishments by mutilation and infamy, by branding, flogging, the bastinado, torture of whatever kind, excessive fines, confiscation of property, or any other unusual or extraordinary penalties, shall be forever prohibited.

Art. 23. In order to abolish the penalty of death, the administrative power is charged to establish, as soon as possible, a penitentiary system. In the meantime the penalty of death shall be abolished for political offences, and shall not be extended to other cases than treason during foreign war, highway robbery, arson, parricide, homicide with treachery, premeditation or advantage, to grave offences of the military order, and piracy, which the law shall define.

Art. 24. No criminal proceeding may have more than three instances. No one shall be tried twice for the same offence, whether by the judgment he be absolved or condemned. The practice of absolving from the instance is abolished.

Art. 25. Sealed correspondence which circulates by the mails is free from all registry. The violation of this guarantee is an offence which the law shall punish severely.

Art. 26. In time of peace no soldier may demand quarters, supplies, or other real or personal service without the consent of the proprietor. In time of war he shall do this only in the manner prescribed by the law.

Art. 27. Private property shall not be appropriated without the consent of the owner, except for the sake of public use, and with previous indemnification. The law shall determine the authority which may make the appropriation and the conditions under which it may be carried out.

No corporation, civil or ecclesiastical, whatever may be its character, denomination, or object, shall have legal capacity to acquire in proprietorship or administer for its self real estate, with the single exception of edifices destined immediately and directly to the service and object of the institution.*

Art. 28. There shall be no monopolies, nor places of any kind for the sale of privileged goods, nor prohibitions under titles of protection to industry. There shall be excepted only those relative to the coining of money, to the mails, and to the privileges which, for a limited time, the law may concede to inventors or perfectors of some improvement.

Art. 29. In cases of invasion, grave disturbance of the public peace, or any other cases whatsoever which may place society in great danger or conflict, only the President of the Republic in concurrence with the Council of Ministers and with the approbation of the Congress of the Union, and, in the recess thereof, of the permanent deputation, may suspend the guarantees established by this Constitution, with the exception of those which assure the life of man; but such suspension shall be made only for a limited time, by means of general provisions, and without being limited to a determined person. If the suspension should take place during the session of Congress, this body shall concede the authorizations which it may esteem necessary in order that the Executive may meet properly the situation. If the suspension should take place during the recess, the permanent deputation shall convoke the Congress without delay in order that it may make the authorizations.

---

* See article 3 of Additions to the Constitution, and law of September 25, 1873.

SECTION II.— OF MEXICANS.

Article 30. Mexicans are:

I. All those born, within or without the Republic, of Mexican parents.

II. Foreigners who are naturalized in conformity with the laws of the Federation.

III. Foreigners who acquire real estate in the Republic or have Mexican children; provided they do not manifest their resolution to preserve their nationality.

Art. 31. It is an obligation of every Mexican:

I. To defend the independence, the territory, the honor, the rights and interests of his country.

II. To contribute for the public expenses, as well of the Federation as of the State and municipality in which he resides, in the proportional and equitable manner which the laws may provide.

Art. 32. Mexicans shall be preferred to foreigners in equal circumstances, for all employments, charges, or commissions of appointment by the authorities, in which the condition of citizenship may not be indispensable. Laws shall be issued to improve the condition of Mexican laborers, rewarding those who distinguish themselves in any science or art, stimulating labor, and founding practical colleges and schools of arts and trades.

SECTION III.— OF FOREIGNERS.

Article 33. Foreigners are those who do not possess the qualifications determined in Article 30. They have a right to the guarantees established by Section I, Title I, of the present Constitution, except that in all cases the Government has the right to expel pernicious foreigners. They are under obligation to contribute to the public expenses in the manner which the laws may provide, and to obey and respect the institutions, laws, and authorities of the country, subjecting themselves to the judgments and sentences of the tribunals, without power to seek other protection than that which the laws concede to Mexican citizens.

SECTION IV.— OF MEXICAN CITIZENS.

Article 34. Citizens of the Republic are all those who, having the quality of Mexicans, have also the following qualifications:

I. Eighteen years of age if married, or twenty-one if not married.

II. An honest means of livelihood.

Art. 35. The prerogatives of the citizen are:

I. To vote at popular elections.

II. The privilege of being voted for *for* any office subject to popular election, and of being selected for any other employment or commission, having the qualifications established by law.

III. To associate to discuss the political affairs of the country.

IV. To take up arms in the army or in the national guard for the defence of the Republic and its institutions.

V. To exercise in all cases the right of petition.

Art. 36. Every citizen of the Republic is under the following obligations:

I. To be inscribed on the municipal roll, stating the property which he has, or the industry, profession, or labor by which he subsists.

II. To enlist in the national guard.

III. To vote at popular elections in the district to which he belongs.

IV. To discharge the duties of the offices of popular election of the Federation, which in no case shall be gratuitous.

Art. 37. The character of citizen is lost:

I. By naturalization in a foreign country.

II. By serving officially the government of another country or accepting its decorations, titles, or employments without previous permission from the Federal Congress; excepting literary, scientific, and humanitarian titles, which may be accepted freely.

Art. 38. The law shall prescribe the cases and the form in which may be lost or suspended the rights of citizenship and the manner in which they may be regained.

TITLE II.

SECTION I.—OF THE NATIONAL SOVEREIGNTY AND OF THE FORM OF GOVERNMENT.

Article 39. The national sovereignty resides essentially and originally in the people. All public power emanates from the people, and is instituted for their benefit. The people have at all times the inalienable right to alter or modify the form of their government.

Art. 40. The Mexican people voluntarily constitute themselves a democratic, federal, representative republic, composed of States free and sovereign in all that concerns their internal government, but united in a federation established according to the principles of this fundamental law.

Art. 41. The people exercise their sovereignty by means of Federal officers in cases belonging to the Federation, and through those of the States in all that relates to the internal affairs of the States within the limits respectively established by this Federal Constitution, and by the special Constitutions of the States, which latter shall in no case contravene the stipulations of the Federal Compact.

SECTION II.—OF THE INTEGRAL PARTS OF THE FEDERATION AND OF THE NATIONAL TERRITORY.

Article 42. The National Territory comprises that of the integral parts of the Federation and that of the adjacent islands in both oceans.

Art. 43. The integral parts of the Federation are: The States of Aguascalientes, Colima, Chiapas, Chihuahua, Durango, Guanajuato, Guerrero, Jalisco, Mexico, Mihoacan, Nuevo Leon and Coahuila, Oajaca, Puebla, Querétaro, San Luis Potosi, Sinaloa, Sonora, Tabasco, Tamaulipas, Tlascala, Valle de Mexico, Veracruz, Yucatan, Zacatecas, and the Territory of Lower California.*

Art. 44. The States of Aguascalientes, Chiapas, Chihuahua, Durango, Guerrero, Mexico, Puebla, Querétaro, Sinaloa, Sonora, Tamaulipas, and the Territory of Lower California shall preserve the limits which they now have.

Art. 45. The States of Colima and Tlascala shall preserve in their new character of States the limits which they have had as Territories of the Federation.

Art. 46. The State of the Valley of Mexico shall be formed of the territory actually composing the Federal District, but the erection into a State shall only have effect when the supreme Federal authorities are removed to another place.

Art. 47. The State of Nuevo Leon and Coahuila shall comprise the territory which has belonged to the two distinct States of which it is now formed, except the part of the hacienda of Bonanza, which shall be reincorporated in Zacatecas, on the same terms in which it was before its incorporation in Coahuila.

Art. 48. The States of Guanajuato, Jalisco, Michoacan, Oajaca, San Luis Potosi, Tabasco, Veracruz, Yucatan, and Zacatecas shall recover the extension and limits which they had on the 31st of December, 1852, with the alterations the following Article establishes.

Art. 49. The town of Contepec, which has belonged to Guanajuato, shall be incorporated in Michoacan. The municipality of Ahualulco, which has belonged to Zacatecas, shall be incorporated in San Luis Potosi. The municipalities of Ojo-Caliente and San Francisco de los Adames, which have belonged to San Luis, as well as the towns of Nueva Tlascala and San Andres del Teul, which have belonged to Jalisco, shall be incorporated in Zacatecas. The department of Tux-

* Decree of Dec. 12, 1884.

pan shall continue to form a part of Veracruz. The canton of Huimanguillo, which has belonged to Veracruz, shall be incorporated in Tabasco.*

TITLE III.

OF THE DIVISION OF POWERS.

Article 50. The supreme power of the Federation is divided for its exercise into legislative, executive, and judicial. Two or more of these powers shall never be united in one person or corporation, nor the legislative power be deposited in one individual.

SECTION I.— OF THE LEGISLATIVE POWER.

Article 51. The legislative power of the nation is deposited in a general Congress, which shall be divided into two houses, one of Deputies and the other of Senators.†

Paragraph I.— Of the Election and Installation of Congress.

Article 52. The House of Deputies shall be composed of representatives of the nation, elected in their entire number every two years by Mexican citizens.‡

Art. 53. One deputy shall be elected for each forty thousand inhabitants, or for a fraction which exceeds twenty thousand. The territory in which the population is less than that determined in this article shall, nevertheless, elect one deputy.

Art. 54. For each deputy there shall be elected one alternate.

Art. 55. The election for deputies shall be indirect in the first degree, and by secret ballot, in the manner which the law shall prescribe.

Art. 56. In order to be eligible to the position of a deputy it is required that the candidate be a Mexican citizen in the enjoyment

---

* Besides the twenty-four States which are mentioned in this section there have been created subsequently, according to executive decrees issued in accordance with the Constitution, the four following:

XXV. That of Campeche, separated from Yucatan, April 29, 1863.

XXVI. That of Coahuila, separated from Nuevo Leon, Nov. 20, 1868.

XXVII. That of Hidalgo, in territory of the ancient State of Mexico, which formed the second military district, Jan. 16, 1869.

XXVIII. That of Morelos, in territory also of the ancient State of Mexico, which formed the third military district, April 17, 1869.

† The original form of this article was as follows: "The exercise of the supreme legislative power is vested in one assembly, which shall be denominated Congress of the Union."

‡ Law of Nov. 17, 1874.

of his rights; that he be fully twenty-five years of age on the day of the opening of the session; that he be a resident of the State or Territory which makes the election, and that he be not an ecclesiastic. Residence is not lost by absence in the discharge of any public trust bestowed by popular election.

Art. 57. The positions of Deputy and of Senator are incompatible with any Federal commission or office whatsoever for which a salary is received.

Art. 58. The Deputies and the Senators, from the day of their election to the day on which their trust is concluded, may not accept any commission or office offered by the Federal Executive, for which a salary is received, except with the previous license of the respective house. The same requisites are necessary for the alternates of Deputies and Senators when in the exercise of their functions.

A. The Senate is composed of two Senators for each State and two for the Federal District. The election of Senators shall be indirect in the first degree. The Legislature of each State shall declare elected the person who shall have obtained the absolute majority of the votes cast, or shall elect from among those who shall have obtained the relative majority in the manner which the electoral law shall prescribe. For each Senator there shall be elected an alternate.

B. The Senate shall be renewed one-half every two years. The Senators named in the second place shall go out at the end of the first two years, and thereafter the half who have held longer.

C. The same qualifications are required for a Senator as for a Deputy, except that of age, which must be at least thirty years on the day of the opening of the session.

Art. 59. The Deputies and Senators are privileged from arrest for their opinions manifested in the performance of their duties, and shall never be liable to be called to account for them.

Art. 60. Each house shall judge of the election of its members, and shall solve the doubts which may arise regarding them.

Art. 61. The houses may not open their sessions nor perform their functions without the presence in the Senate of at least two-thirds, and in the House of Deputies of more than one-half of the whole number of their members, but those present of one or the other body must meet on the day indicated by the law and compel the attendance of absent members under penalties which the law shall designate.

Art. 62. The Congress shall have each year two periods of ordinary sessions: The first, which may be prorogued for thirty days, shall begin on the 16th of September and end on the 15th of December, and the second, which may be prorogued for fifteen days, shall begin the 1st of April and end the last day of May.

Art. 63. At the opening of the sessions of the Congress the President of the Union shall be present and shall pronounce a discourse in which he shall set forth the state of the country. The President of the Congress shall reply in general terms.

Art. 64. Every resolution of the Congress shall have the character of a law or decree. The laws and decrees shall be communicated to the Executive, signed by the Presidents of both houses and by a Secretary of each of them, and shall be promulgated in this form: "The Congress of the United States of Mexico decrees:" (*Text of the law or decree.*)

Paragraph II.— Of the Initiative and Formation of the Laws.

Article 65. The right to initiate laws or decrees belongs:

I. To the President of the Union.

II. To the Deputies and Senators of the general Congress.

III. To the Legislatures of the States.

Art. 66. Bills presented by the President of the Republic, by the Legislatures of the States, or by deputations from the same, shall pass immediately to a committee. Those which the Deputies or the Senators may present shall be subjected to the procedure which the rules of debate may prescribe.

Art. 67. Every bill which shall be rejected in the house where it originated, before passing to the other house, shall not again be presented during the sessions of that year.*

Art. 68. The second period of sessions shall be destined, in all preference, to the examination of and action upon the estimates of the following fiscal year, to passing the necessary appropriations to cover the same, and to the examination of the accounts of the past year, which the Executive shall present.

Art. 69. The last day but one of the first period of sessions the Executive shall present to the House of Deputies the bill of appropriations for the next year following and the accounts of the preceding year. Both shall pass to a committee of five Representatives appointed on the same day, which shall be under obligation to examine said documents, and present a report on them at the second session of the second period.

Art. 70. The formation of the laws and of the decrees may begin indiscriminately in either of the two houses, with the exception of bills which treat of loans, taxes, or imposts, or of the recruiting of troops, all of which must be discussed first in the House of Deputies.

---

* Law of Nov. 13, 1874.

Art. 71. Every bill, the consideration of which does not belong exclusively to one of the houses, shall be discussed successively in both, the rules of debate being observed with reference to the form, the intervals, and manner of proceeding in discussions and voting.

A. A bill having been approved in the house where it originated, shall pass for its discussion to the other house. If the latter body should approve it, it will be remitted to the Executive, who, if he shall have no observations to make, shall publish it immediately.

B. Every bill shall be considered as approved by the Executive if not returned with observations to the house where it originated within ten working days, unless during this term Congress shall have closed or suspended its sessions, in which case the return must be made the first working day on which it shall meet.

C. A bill rejected wholly or in part by the Executive must be returned with his observations to the house where it originated. It shall be discussed again by this body, and if it should be confirmed by an absolute majority of votes, it shall pass again to the other house. If by this house it should be sanctioned with the same majority, the bill shall be a law or decree, and shall be returned to the Executive for promulgation. The voting on the law or decree shall be by name.

D. If any bill should be rejected wholly in the house in which it did not originate, it shall be returned to that in which it originated with the observations which the former shall have made upon it. If having been examined anew it should be approved by the absolute majority of the members present, it shall be returned to the house which rejected it, which shall again take it into consideration, and if it should approve it by the same majority it shall pass to the Executive, to be treated in accordance with division A; but, if it should reject it, it shall not be presented again until the following sessions.

E. If a bill should be rejected only in part, or modified, or receive additions by the house of revision, the new discussion in the house where it originated shall treat only of the rejected party, or of the amendments or additions, without being able to alter in any manner the articles approved. If the additions or amendments made by the house of revision should be approved by the absolute majority of the votes present in the house where it originated, the whole bill shall be passed to the Executive, to be treated in accordance with division A. But if the additions or amendments made by the house of revision should be rejected by the majority of the votes in the house where it originated, they shall be returned to the former, in order that the reasons of the latter may be taken into consideration;

and if by the absolute majority of the votes present said additions or amendments shall be rejected in this second revision, the bill, in so far as it has been approved by both houses, shall be passed to the Executive, to be treated in accordance with division A; but if the house of revision should insist, by the absolute majority of the votes present, on said additions or amendments, the whole bill shall not be again presented until the following sessions, unless both houses agree by the absolute majority of their members present that the law or decree shall be issued solely with the articles approved, and that the parts added or amended shall be reserved to be examined and voted in the following sessions.

F. In the interpretation, amendment, or repeal of the laws or decrees, the rules established for their formation shall be observed.

G. Both houses shall reside in the same place, and they shall not remove to another without first agreeing to the removal and on the time and manner of making it, designating the same point for the meeting of both. But if both houses, agreeing to the removal, should differ as to time, manner, or place, the Executive shall terminate the difference by choosing one of the places in question. Neither house shall suspend its sessions for more than three days without the consent of the other.

H. When the general Congress meets in extra sessions, it shall occupy itself exclusively with the object or objects designated in the summons; and if the special business shall not have been completed on the day on which the regular session should open, the extra sessions shall be closed nevertheless, leaving the points pending to be treated of in the regular sessions.

The Executive of the Union shall not make observations on the resolutions of the Congress when this body prorogues its sessions or exercises functions of an electoral body or a jury.

Paragraph III.— Of the Powers of the General Congress.

Article 72. The Congress has power:*

I. To admit new States or Territories into the Federal Union, incorporating them in the nation.

II. To erect Territories into States when they shall have a population of eighty thousand inhabitants and the necessary elements to provide for their political existence.

III. To form new States within the limits of those existing, it being necessary to this end:

---

* See amendment of Dec. 19, 1885.

1. That the fraction or fractions which ask to be erected into a State shall number a population of at least one hundred and twenty thousand inhabitants.

2. That it shall be proved before Congress that they have elements sufficient to provide for their political existence.

3. That the Legislatures of the States, the territories of which are in question, shall have been heard on the expediency or inexpediency of the establishment of the new State, and they shall be obliged to make their reports within six months, counted from the day on which the communication relating to it shall have been remitted to them.

4. That the Executive of the Federation shall likewise be heard, who shall send his report within seven days, counted from the date on which he shall have been asked for it.

5. That the establishment of the new State shall have been voted for by two-thirds of the Deputies and Senators present in their respective houses.

6. That the resolution of Congress shall have been ratified by the majority of the Legislatures of the States, after examining a copy of the proceedings; provided that the Legislatures of the States whose territory is in question shall have given their consent.

7. If the Legislatures of the States whose territory is in question shall not have given their consent, the ratification mentioned in the preceding clause must be made by two-thirds of the Legislatures of the other States.

A. The exclusive powers of the House of Deputies are:

I. To constitute itself an Electoral College in order to exercise the powers which the law may assign to it, in respect to the election of the Constitutional President of the Republic, Magistrates of the Supreme Court, and Senators for the Federal District.

II. To judge and decide upon the resignations which the President of the Republic or the Magistrates of the Supreme Court of Justice may make. The same power belongs to it in treating of licenses solicited by the first.

III. To watch over, by means of an inspecting committee from its own body, the exact performance of the business of the chief auditorship.

IV. To appoint the principal officers and other employés of the same.

V. To constitute itself a jury of accusation, for the high functionaries of whom Article 103 of this Constitution treats.

VI. To examine the accounts which the Executive must present annually, to approve the annual estimate of expenses, and to initiate the taxes which in its judgment ought to be decreed to cover these expenses.

B. The exclusive powers of the Senate are:

I. To approve the treaties and diplomatic conventions which the Executive may make with foreign powers.

II. To ratify the appointments which the President of the Republic may make of ministers, diplomatic agents, consuls-general, superior employés of the Treasury, colonels and other superior officers of the national army and navy, on the terms which the law shall provide.

III. To authorize the Executive to permit the departure of national troops beyond the limits of the Republic, the passage of foreign troops through the national territory, the station of squadrons of other powers for more than a month in the waters of the Republic.

IV. To give its consent in order that the Executive may dispose of the national guard outside of their respective States or Territories, determining the necessary force.

V. To declare, when the Constitutional legislative and executive powers of a State shall have disappeared, that the case has arrived for appointing to it a provisional Governor, who shall call elections in conformity with the Constitutional laws of the said State. The appointment of Governor shall be made by the Federal Executive with the approval of the Senate, and in its recesses with the approval of the Permanent Commission. Said functionary shall not be elected Constitutional Governor at the elections which are had in virtue of the summons which he shall issue.

VI. To decide political questions which may arise between the powers of a State, when any of them may appear with this purpose in the Senate, or when on account of said questions Constitutional order shall have been interrupted during a conflict of arms. In this case the Senate shall dictate its resolution, being subject to the general Constitution of the Republic and to that of the State.

The law shall regulate the exercise of this power and that of the preceding.

VII. To constitute itself a jury of judgment in accordance with Article 105 of this Constitution.

C. Each of the houses may, without the intervention of the other:

I. Dictate economic resolutions relative to its internal regimen.

II. Communicate within itself, and with the Executive of the Union, by means of committees from its own body.

III. Appoint the employés of its secretaryship, and make the internal regulations for the same.

IV. Issue summons for extraordinary elections, with the object of filling the vacancies of their respective members.

IV. To regulate definitely the limits of the States, terminating the differences which may arise between them relative to the demarcation of their respective territories, except when these difficulties have a contentious character.

V. To change the residence of the supreme powers of the Federation.

VI. To establish the internal order of the Federal District and Territories, taking as a basis that the citizens shall choose by popular election the political, municipal, and judicial authorities, and designating the taxes necessary to cover their local expenditure.

VII. To approve the estimates of the Federal expenditure, which the Executive must annually present to it, and to impose the necessary taxes to cover them.

VIII. To give rules under which the Executive may make loans on the credit of the nation; to approve said loans, and to recognize and order the payment of the national debt.

IX. To establish tariffs on foreign commerce, and to prevent, by means of general laws, onerous restrictions from being established with reference to the commerce between the States.

X. To issue codes, obligatory throughout the Republic, of mines and commerce, comprehending in this last banking institutions.

XI. To create and suppress public Federal employments and to establish, augment, or diminish their salaries.

XII. To ratify the appointments which the Executive may make of ministers, diplomatic agents, and consuls, of the higher employés of the Treasury, of the colonels and other superior officers of the national army and navy.

XIII. To approve the treaties, contracts, or diplomatic conventions which the Executive may make.

XIV. To declare war in view of the data which the Executive may present to it.

XV. To regulate the manner in which letters of marque may be issued; to dictate laws according to which must be declared good or bad the prizes on sea and land, and to issue laws relating to maritime rights in peace and war.

XVI. To permit or deny the entrance of foreign troops into the territory of the Republic, and to consent to the station of squadrons of other powers for more than a month in the waters of the Republic.

XVII. To permit the departure of national troops beyond the limits of the Republic.*

*** Amended by Section B, Clause III, Article 72, of the law of the 13th of November, 1874. See p. 189.**

XVIII. To raise and maintain the army and navy of the Union, and to regulate their organization and service.

XIX. To establish regulations with the purpose of organizing, arming, and disciplining the national guard, reserving respectively to the citizens who compose it the appointment of the commanders and officers, and to the States the power of instructing it in conformity with the discipline prescribed by said regulations.

XX. To give its consent in order that the Executive may control the national guard outside of its respective States and Territories, determining the necessary force.

XXI. To dictate laws on naturalization, colonization, and citizenship.

XXII. To dictate laws on the general means of communication and on the post-office and mails.

XXIII. To establish mints, fixing the conditions of their operation, to determine the value of foreign money, and adopt a general system of weights and measures.

XXIV. To fix rules to which must be subject the occupation and sale of public lands and the price of these lands.

XXV. To grant pardons for crimes cognizable by the tribunals of the Federation.

XXVI. To grant rewards or recompense for eminent services rendered to the country or humanity.*

XXVII. To prorogue for thirty working days the first period of its ordinary sessions.

XXVIII. To form rules for its internal regulation, to take the necessary measures to compel the attendance of absent members, and to correct the faults or omissions of those present.

XXIX. To appoint and remove freely the employés of its secretaryship and those of the chief auditorship, which shall be organized in accordance with the provisions of the law.

XXX. To make all laws which may be necessary and proper to render effective the foregoing powers and all others granted by this Constitution and the authorities of the Union.†

Paragraph IV.— Of the Permanent Deputation.

Article 73. During the recess of Congress there shall be a Permanent Deputation composed of twenty-nine members, of whom fifteen

* Decree of June 2, 1882.

† See respecting this article the additions A, B, and C to article 72 of the law of the 13th of November, already cited.

shall be Deputies and fourteen Senators, appointed by their respective houses the evening before the close of the sessions.

Art. 74. The attributes of the Permanent Deputation are:

I. To give its consent to the use of the national guard in the cases mentioned in Article 72, Clause XX.

II. To determine by itself, or on the proposal of the Executive, after hearing him in the first place, the summons of Congress, or of one house alone, for extra sessions, the vote of two-thirds of the members present being necessary in both cases. The summons shall designate the object or objects of the extra sessions.

III. To approve the appointments which are referred to in Article 85, Clause III.

IV. To administer the oath of office to the President of the Republic, and to the Justices of the Supreme Court, in the cases provided by this Constitution.*

V. To report upon all the business not disposed of, in order that the Legislature which follows may immediately take up such unfinished business.

SECTION II.— OF THE EXECUTIVE POWER.

Article 75. The exercise of the supreme executive power of the Union is vested in a single individual, who shall be called "President of the United States of Mexico."

Art. 76. The election of President shall be indirect in the first degree, and by secret ballot, in such manner as may be prescribed by the electoral law.

Art. 77. To be eligible to the position of President, the candidate must be a Mexican citizen by birth, in the exercise of his rights, be fully thirty-five years old at the time of the election, not belong to the ecclesiastical order, and reside in the country at the time the election is held.

Art. 78. The President shall enter upon the performance of the duties of his office on the first of December, and shall continue in office four years, being eligible for the Constitutional period immediately following; but he shall remain incapable thereafter to occupy the presidency by a new election until four years shall have passed, counting from the day on which he ceased to perform his functions.†

Art. 79. In the temporary default of the President of the Republic, and in the vacancy before the installation of the newly-elected President, the citizen who may have performed the duties of President or

---

* See the amendment of September 25, 1873, art. 4.

† Limitation removed, December 20, 1890.

Vice-President of the Senate, or of the Permanent Commission in the periods of recess, during the month prior to that in which said default may have occurred, shall enter upon the exercise of the executive power of the Union.*

A. The President and Vice-President of the Senate and of the Permanent Commission shall not be reëlected to those offices until a year after having held them.

B. If the period of sessions of the Senate or of the Permanent Commission shall begin in the second half of a month, the default of the President of the Republic shall be covered by the President or Vice-President who may have acted in the Senate or in the Permanent Commission during the first half of the said month.

C. The Senate and the Permanent Commission shall renew, the last day of each month, their Presidents and Vice-Presidents. For these offices the Permanent Commission shall elect, alternatively, in one month two Deputies and in the following month two Senators.

D. When the office of President of the Republic is vacant, the functionary who shall take it constitutionally as his substitute must issue, within the definite term of fifteen days, the summons to proceed to a new election, which shall be held within the term of three months, and in accordance with the provisions of Article 76 of this Constitution. The provisional President shall not be eligible to the presidency at the elections which are held to put an end to his provisional term.

E. If, on account of death or any other reason, the functionaries who, according to this law, should take the place of the President of the Republic might not be able in any absolute manner to do so, it shall be taken, under predetermined conditions, by the citizen who may have been President or Vice-President of the Senate or the Permanent Commission in the month prior to that in which they discharged those offices.

F. When the office of President of the Republic shall become vacant within the last six months of the constitutional period, the functionary who shall take the place of the President shall terminate this period.

G. To be eligible to the position of President or Vice-President of the Senate or of the Permanent Commission, one must be a Mexican citizen by birth.

H. If the vacancy in the office of President of the Republic should occur when the Senate and Permanent Commission are performing their functions in extra sessions, the President of the Commission shall fill the vacancy, under conditions indicated in this article.

---

* See amendment of December 19, 1895.

I. The Vice-President of the Senate or of the Permanent Commission shall enter upon the performance of the functions which this Article confers upon them, in the vacancies of the office of President of the Senate or of the Permanent Commission, and in the periods only while the impediment lasts.

J. The newly-elected President shall enter upon the discharge of his duties, at the latest, sixty days after that of the election. In case the House of Deputies shall not be in session, it shall be convened in extra session, in order to make the computation of votes within the term mentioned.

Art. 80. In the vacancy of the office of President, the period of the newly-elected President shall be computed from the first of December of the year prior to that of his election, provided he may not have taken possession of his office on the date which Article 78 determines.*

Art. 81. The office of President of the Union may not be resigned, except for grave cause, approved by Congress, before whom the resignation shall be presented.

Art. 82. If for any reason the election of President shall not have been made and published by the first of December, on which the transfer of the office should be made, or the President-elect shall not have been ready to enter upon the discharge of his duties, the term of the former President shall end nevertheless, and the supreme executive power shall be deposited provisionally in the functionary to whom it belongs according to the provisions of the reformed Article 79 of this Constitution.*

Art. 83. The President, on taking possession of his office, shall take an oath before Congress, and in its recess before the Permanent Commission, under the following formula: "I swear to perform loyally and patriotically the duties of President of the United States of Mexico, according to the Constitution, and seek in everything for the welfare and prosperity of the Union."

Art. 84. The President may not remove from the place of the residence of the Federal powers, nor lay aside the exercise of his functions, without grave cause, approved by the Congress, and in its recesses by the Permanent Commission.

Art. 85. The powers and obligations of the President are the following:

I. To promulgate and execute the laws passed by the congress of the Union, providing, in the administrative sphere, for their exact observance.

---

* See amendments of arts. 79, 80, 82, 83, December 19, 1895.

II. To appoint and remove freely the Secretaries of the Cabinet, to remove the diplomatic agents and superior employés of the Treasury, and to appoint and remove freely the other employés of the Union whose appointment and removal are not otherwise provided for in the Constitution or in the laws.

III. To appoint ministers, diplomatic agents, consuls-general, with the approval of Congress, and, in its recess, of the Permanent Commission.

IV. To appoint, with the approval of Congress, the colonels and other superior officers of the national army and navy, and the superior employés of the treasury.

V. To appoint the other officers of the national army and navy, according to the laws.

VI. To control the permanent armed force by sea and land for the internal security and external defence of the Federation.

VII. To control the national guard for the same objects within the limits established by Article 72, Clause XX.

VIII. To declare war in the name of the United States of Mexico, after the passage of the necessary law by the Congress of the Union.

IX. To grant letters of marque, subject to bases fixed by the Congress.

X. To direct diplomatic negotiations and make treaties with foreign powers, submitting them for the ratification of the Federal Congress.

XI. To receive ministers and other envoys from foreign powers.

XII. To convoke Congress in extra sessions when the Permanent Commission shall consent to it.

XIII. To furnish the judicial power with that assistance which may be necessary for the prompt exercise of its functions.

XIV. To open all classes of ports, to establish maritime and frontier custom houses and designate their situation.

XV. To grant, in accordance with the laws, pardons to criminals sentenced for crimes within the jurisdiction of the Federal tribunals.

XVI. To grant exclusive privileges, for a limited time and according to the proper law, to discoverers, inventors, or perfecters of any branch of industry.*

Art. 86. For the dispatch of the business of the administrative department of the Federation there shall be the number of Secretaries which the Congress may establish by a law, which shall provide for the distribution of business and prescribe what shall be in charge of each Secretary.

* Decree of June 2, 1882.

Art. 87. To be a Secretary of the Cabinet it is required that one shall be a Mexican citizen by birth, in the exercise of his rights, and fully twenty-five years old.

Art. 88. All the regulations, decrees, and orders of the President must be signed by the Secretary of the Cabinet who is in charge of the department to which the subject belongs. Without this requisite they shall not be obeyed.

Art. 89. The Secretaries of the Cabinet, as soon as the sessions of the first period shall be opened, shall render an account to the Congress of the state of their respective departments.

SECTION II.—OF THE JUDICIAL POWER.

Article 90. The exercise of the judicial power of the Federation is vested in a Supreme Court of Justice, and in the district and circuit courts.

Art. 91. The Supreme Court of Justice shall be composed of eleven judges, four supernumeraries, one fiscal, and one attorney-general.

Art. 92. Each of the members of the Supreme Court of Justice shall remain in office six years, and his election shall be indirect in the first degree, under conditions established by the electoral law.

Art. 93. In order to be elected a member of the Supreme Court of Justice it is necessary that one be learned in the science of the law in the judgment of the electors, more than thirty-five years old, and a Mexican citizen by birth, in the exercise of his rights.

Art. 94. The members of the Supreme Court of Justice, on entering upon the exercise of their charge, shall take an oath before Congress, and, in its recesses, before the Permanent Commission, in the following form: "Do you swear to perform loyally and patriotically the charge of Magistrate of the Supreme Court of Justice, which the people have conferred upon you in conformity with the Constitution, seeking in everything the welfare and prosperity of the Union?" *

Art. 95. A member of the Supreme Court of Justice may resign his office only for grave cause, approved by the Congress, to whom the resignation shall be presented. In the recesses of the Congress the judgment shall be rendered by the Permanent Commission.

Art. 96. The law shall establish and organize the circuit and district courts.

Art. 97. It belongs to the Federal tribunals to take cognizance of: †

I. All controversies which may arise in regard to the fulfillment and application of the Federal laws, except in the case in which the application affects only private interests; such a case falls within the competence of the local judges and tribunals of the common order of the

* See Additions to the Constitution, September 25, 1873.

† Decree of May 29, 1884.

States, of the Federal District, and of the Territory of Lower California.

II. All cases pertaining to maritime law.

III. Those in which the Federation may be a party.

IV. Those that may arise between two or more States.

V. Those that may arise between a State and one or more citizens of another State.

VI. Civil or criminal cases that may arise under treaties with foreign powers.

VII. Cases concerning diplomatic agents and consuls.

Art. 98. It belongs to the Supreme Court of Justice, in the first instance, to take cognizance of controversies which may arise between one State and another, and of those in which the Union may be a party.

Art. 99. It belongs also to the Supreme Court of Justice to determine the questions of jurisdiction which may arise between the Federal tribunals, between these and those of the States, or between the courts of one State and those of another.

Art. 100. In the other cases comprehended in Article 97, the Supreme Court of Justice shall be a court of appeal or, rather, of last resort, according to the graduation which the law may make in the jurisdiction of the circuit and district courts.

Art. 101. The tribunals of the Federation shall decide all questions which arise:

I. Under laws or acts of whatever authority which violate individual guarantees.

II. Under laws or acts of the State authority which violate or restrain the sovereignty of the States.

III. Under laws or acts of the State authority which invade the sphere of the Federal authority.

Art. 102. All the judgments which the preceding article mentions shall be had on petition of the aggrieved party, by means of judicial proceedings and forms which shall be prescribed by law. The sentence shall be always such as to affect private individuals only, limiting itself to defend and protect them in the special case to which the process refers, without making any general declaration respecting the law or act which gave rise to it.

TITLE IV.

OF THE RESPONSIBILITY OF THE PUBLIC FUNCTIONARIES.

Article 103. The Senators, the Deputies, the members of the Supreme Court of Justice, and the Secretaries of the Cabinet are responsible for the common crimes which they may commit during their terms of office, and for the crimes, misdemeanors, and negligence into which they may fall in the performance of the duties of said office. The overnors of the States are likewise responsible for the infraction of the Constitution and Federal laws. The President of the Republic is also responsible; but during the term of his office he may be accused only for the crimes of treason against the country, express violation of the Constitution, attack on the freedom of election, and grave crimes of the common order. The high functionaries of the Fedration shall not enjoy any Constitutional privilege for the official crimes, misdemeanors, or negligence into which they may fall in the performance of any employment, office, or public commission which they may have accepted during the period for which, in conformity with the law, they shall have been elected. The same shall happen with respect to those common crimes which they may commit during the performance of said employment, office, or commission. In order that the cause may be initiated when the high functionary shall have returned to the exercise of his proper functions, proceeding should be undertaken in accordance with the provision of Article 104 of this Constitution.

Art. 104. If the crime should be a common one, the House of Representatives, formed into a grand jury, shall declare, by an absolute majority of votes, whether there is or is not ground to proceed against the accused. In the negative case, there shall be no ground for further proceedings; in the affirmative, the accused shall be, by the said act, deprived of his office, and subjected to the action of the ordinary tribunals.

Art. 105. The houses shall take cognizance of official crimes, the House of Deputies as a jury of accusation, the Senators as a jury of judgment.

The jury of accusation shall have for its object to declare, by an absolute majority of votes, whether the accused is or is not culpable. If the declaration should be absolutory, the functionary shall continue in the exercise of his office; if it should be condemnatory, he shall be immediately deprived of his office, and shall be placed at the disposal of the Senate. The latter, formed into a jury or judgment, and, with the presence of the criminal and of the accuser, if there should be one, shall proceed to apply, by an absolute majority of votes, the punishment which the law designates.

Art. 106. A judgment of responsibility for official crimes having been pronounced, no favor of pardon may be extended to the offender.

Art. 107. The responsibility for official crimes and misdemeanors may be required only during the period in which the functionary remains in office, and one year thereafter.

Art. 108. With respect to demands of the civil order, there shall be no privilege or immunity for any public functionary.

TITLE V.

OF THE STATES OF THE FEDERATION.

Article 109. The States shall adopt for their internal regimen the popular, representative, republican form of government,* and may provide in their respective Constitutions for the reëlection of the Governors in accordance with what Article 78 provides for the President of the Republic.

Art. 110. The States may regulate among themselves, by friendly agreements, their respective boundaries; but those regulations shall not be carried into effect without the approval of the Congress of the Union.

Art. 111. The States may not in any case:†

I. Form alliances, treaties, or coalitions with another State, or with foreign powers, excepting the coalition which the frontier States may make for offensive or defensive war against the Indians.

II. Grant letters of marque or reprisal.

III. Coin money, or emit paper money or stamped paper.

Art. 112. Neither may any State, without the consent of the Congress of the Union:

I. Establish tonnage duties, or any port duty, or impose taxes or duties upon importations or exportations.

II. Have at any time permanent troops or vessels of war.

III. Make war by itself on any foreign power except in cases of invasion or of such imminent peril as to admit of no delay. In these cases the State shall give notice immediately to the President of the Republic.

Art. 113. Each State is under obligation to deliver without delay the criminals of other States to the authority that claims them.

Art. 114. The Governors of the States are obliged to publish and cause to be obeyed the Federal laws.

Art. 115. In each State of the Federation entire faith and credit shall be given to the public acts, records, and judicial proceedings of all the other States. The Congress may, by means of general laws, prescribe the manner of proving said acts, records, and proceedings, and the effect thereof.

Art. 116. The powers of the Union are bound to protect the States against all invasion or external violence. In case of insurrection or internal disturbance they shall give them like protection, provided the

---

* See Decree of Oct. 21, 1887, and Sept. 20, 1890.

† See amendment of April 23, 1896.

Legislature of the State, or the Executive, if the Legislature is not in session, shall request it.

TITLE VI.

GENERAL PROVISIONS.

Article 117. The powers which are not expressly granted by this Constitution to the Federal authorities are understood to be reserved to the States.

Art. 118. No person may at the same time hold two Federal elective offices; but if elected to two, he may choose which of them he will fill.

Art. 119. No payment shall be made which is not comprehended in the budget or determined by a subsequent law.

Art. 120. The President of the Republic, the members of the Supreme Court of Justice, the Deputies, and other public officers of the Federation, who are chosen by popular election, shall receive a compensation for their services, which shall be determined by law and paid by the Federal Treasury. This compensation may not be renounced, and any law which augments or diminishes it shall not have effect during the period for which a functionary holds the office.

Art. 121. Every public officer, without any exception, before taking possession of his office, shall take an oath to maintain this Constitution and the laws which emanate from it.*

Art. 122. In time of peace no military authority may exercise more functions than those which have close connection with military discipline. There shall be fixed and permanent military commands only in the castles, fortresses, and magazines which are immediately under the government of the Union; or in encampments, barracks, or depots which may be established outside of towns for stationing troops.

Art. 123. It belongs exclusively to the Federal authorities to exercise, in matters of religious worship and external discipline, the intervention which the laws may designate.

Art. 124. The States shall not impose any duty for the simple passage of goods in the internal commerce. The Government of the Union alone may decree transit duties, but only with respect to foreign goods which cross the country by international or interoceanic lines, without being on the national territory more time than is necessary to traverse it and depart to the foreign country. †

They shall not prohibit, either directly or indirectly, the entrance to their territory, or the departure from it, of any merchandise, except

---

* See the Additions of September 25, 1873.

† See Decrees of November 22, 1886, and April 23, 1896.

on police grounds; nor burden the articles of national production on their departure for a foreign country or for another State.

The exemptions from duties which they concede shall be general; they may not be decreed in favor of the products of specified origin.

The quota of the import for a given amount of merchandise shall be the same, whatever may have been its origin, and no heavier burden may be assigned to it than that which the similar products of the political entity in which the import is decreed bear.

The national merchandise shall not be submitted to definite route nor to inspection or registry on the ways, nor any fiscal document be demanded for its internal circulation.

Nor shall they burden foreign merchandise with a greater quota than that which may have been permitted them by the Federal law to receive.

Art. 125. The forts, military quarters, magazines, and other edifices necessary to the government of the Union shall be under the immediate inspection of the Federal authorities.

Art. 126. This Constitution, the laws of the Congress of the Union which emanate from it, and all the treaties made or which shall be made by the President of the Republic, with the approval of Congress, shall be the supreme law of the whole Union. The judges of each State shall be guided by said Constitution, law, and treaties in spite of provisions to the contrary which may appear in the Constitutions or laws of the States.

TITLE VII.

OF THE REFORM OF THE CONSTITUTION.

Article 127. The present Constitution may be added to or reformed. In order that additions or alterations may become part of the Constitution, it is required that the Congress of the Union, by a vote of two-thirds of the members present, shall agree to the alterations or additions, and that these shall be approved by the majority of the Legislatures of the States. The Congress of the Union shall count the votes of the Legislatures and make the declaration that the reforms or additions have been approved.

TITLE VIII.

OF THE INVIOLABILITY OF THE CONSTITUTION.

Article 128. This Constitution shall not lose its force and vigor even if its observance be interrupted by a rebellion. In case that by any public disturbance a government contrary to the principles which it sanctions shall be established, as soon as the people recover their liberty its observance shall be reëstablished, and in accordance with it and the laws which shall have been issued in virtue of it, shall be judged not only those who shall have figured in the government emanating from the rebellion, but also those who shall have coöperated with it.

ADDITIONS TO THE CONSTITUTION.

Article 1. The State and the Church are independent of one another. The Congress may not pass laws establishing or prohibiting any religion.

Art. 2. Marriage is a civil contract. This and the other acts relating to the civil state of persons belong to the exclusive jurisdiction of the functionaries and authorities of the civil order, within limits provided by the laws, and they shall have the force and validity which the same attribute to them.

Art. 3. No religious institution may acquire real estate or capital fixed upon it, with the single exception established in Article 27 of this Constitution.

Art. 4. The simple promise to speak the truth and to comply with the obligations which have been incurred, shall be substituted for the religious oath, with its effects and penalties.

CHAPTER III.

GOVERNMENT OF CUBA PRIOR TO AUTONOMY.

Prior to November 25, 1897, the Island of Cuba was governed by Spain through a Captain-General, usually a Lieutenant-General in the Spanish Army, and a *Junta de Autoridades* (somewhat similar to a cabinet of officers in the United States, but of less influence), as follows:

(1.) *Segundo Cabo,* usually a Major-General in the Spanish Army, to act in the place of the Captain-General.

(2.) *Intendente-General de Hacienda* (Treasurer of the Island).

(3.) *Secretario del Gobierno-General* (Secretary of the General Government of the Island).

(4.) *General de Marina* (Naval Affairs).

(5.) *Fiscal de Su Majestad* (Attorney-General).

(6.) *Obispo de la Habana*(Clerical Affairs and Ecclesiastical Laws).

(7) *Gobernador Civil de la Habana* (Civil Governor of Havana),

which held conferences with the Captain-General when important matters were considered.

Under the Autonomical Decree of November 25, 1897, the first Cuban cabinet of officers,* similar to the Madrid Cabinet, was authorized to include the following (see article 45), to-wit:

1. Secretary of Grace and Justice.*
2. Secretary of Finance.
3. Secretary of Public Instruction.
4. Department of Public Works and Means of Communications.
5. Department of Agriculture, Industry and Commerce.

* The judiciary in Spain and in other civil law and European countries is not a co-ordinate branch of the government, as it is in the United States. Its highest court cannot declare a law unconstitutional, and its head has the dual character of a political-judicial officer.

It also provided for a secretary, appointed by the Governor-General, who should be president, and the Governor-General had authority to appoint a president without a determinate department.

The Insular Parliament had power to increase or diminish the number of secretaries of the government, and also to determine what matters belonged to the department of each.

Additional articles 1 and 2 provide that until colonial statutes shall be published in due form, the laws of the Kingdom shall be applicable, and also that the colonial constitution shall be ratified by the Cortes, which was never done.

Shortly after its promulgation, cabinet officers were named in Cuba and an attempt made to carry autonomy into effect.

The Governor-General, under section 3, Article 42 (within the limits specially marked out), had power to use undefined pardoning power in place of the King, and in pursuance thereof, pardons in certain cases were issued and published in the Official Gazette, prior to December 31, 1898, proceedings being conducted through the Office of the Minister of Grace and Justice, etc., following in part the law of the Royal Decree of June 18, 1870.

How far the Decree of Autonomy was a political measure, and whether it was promulgated in good faith or not are contested questions; the fact remains, however, that it was never fully tested and is defective and incomprehensible. It would be manifestly unjust to criticise Spanish institutions and reforms from an Anglo-Saxon standpoint without carefully considering the principles and usages which differentiate the two systems.

SOME CUBAN OBSERVATIONS REGARDING THE DECREE WHICH ESTABLISHES ON THE ISLAND OF CUBA THE AUTONOMIC REGIME.

1. Article 3 grants to the insular chambers, together with the Governor-General, the power to legislate regarding colonial affairs "in the form and terms designated by law." What law? Those decreed by the Cortes of Madrid? It appears so, because the provisions of a general character emanating from the said Cortes shall receive the name of laws, while the colonial legislative provisions shall be called statutes. And if the Cortes of the Kingdom is the one to fix the form and terms of the colonial

resolutions, it has a powerful arm in its hands and can annul the action of the insular chambers.

2. The insular representation is composed of two bodies, with the same authority — the chamber of representatives and the council of administration. Article 4 provides that the chamber is formed by popular election; but that concession, which at first seems extensive, when examined in its relations with the other powers given to the insular representation, is practically deficient. No colonial resolution can be in force unless it has been approved by the chamber and the council. The council, as we shall see later, from the nature of its composition, will be controlled by the Government in such a manner that the representatives of the people to the chamber will always find themselves in the power of the Government in some way. They will not be able to do anything, because if the council does not approve, or should modify the decision of the other house — the chamber — the latter's decisions will have no effect. The veto granted by article 43 will not be required.

3. The council of administration is composed of twenty-five members; seventeen are appointed directly by the Government; the remaining eighteen are elected by popular vote. To be elected a member of said council it is necessary to be a Spaniard (Spanish subject), thirty-five years of age, and possessing an income of $4,000 for two years previous to election. The formation of the council will be, therefore, controlled by the Government, because the Government will appoint unconditionally the seventeen members, and it will be very easy for the Government to find one or more votes among those owing their election to the people, the more so as the conditions required to be a councillor are favorable to those near the Government. In order to pass any measure the presence of a majority of those composing this legislative body is required. It will be very difficult to have all the eighteen members elected by the people vote as a unit, and the absence of one or two will be sufficient to give the governmental members control of the body, or the vote be a tie.

If the members elected should stand together on any measure objectionable to the Government, they could be sent to their homes by the Governor-General, and he can instruct or direct the election of others more accommodating. On the other hand, the members by governmental appointment cannot be removed — their offices or positions cease with their lives. The Governor-General cannot remove them. And to this end they will be carefully selected as faithful instruments of the Government, in whose hands the whole autonomistic machine will be placed. It is known that in Canada all senators are appointed by the Government; but it should be remembered that the Governor-General appoints them, with the advice and consent of its counselors or ministers, and that these counselors are elected by the parliament, and the parliament by the people, the result is, that in Canada the senators are representatives of the people, while here in Cuba the Government can control them.

4. As if the authority to veto was not sufficient (article 43), and the power did not exist to suspend, close the sessions, and adjourn both bodies, or either of them, by the decree of the Governor-General, article 30 grants more authority or power to present [prevent?] or annul the freedom or liberty of the discussions of the colonial parliament, when, in the opinion of the Governor-General, the national interests will be affected by a colonial statute. The bill in question cannot even be discussed unless previously authorized by the central government, and it is a limitation or restriction which has no precedent in any known autonomistic legislation. It is improper because the restriction arises before the debates show the character of the measure to be discussed. It reveals, besides, a mistrust or want of confidence of the mere discussion of the subject.

A Governor-General may decree that all bills or colonial statutes may be, in his opinion, contrary to the national interest, and that nothing should be discussed in the local legislative bodies without the previous consent of the Madrid Government. All guaranties are for the Madrid power; there are none for the colony, except the one named in article 43, which fixes the limit within which the Madrid Government has to decide regarding the right of a veto which a colonial statute may have received from the Governor-General.

5. Article 36 grants exclusive power to the Cortes of the Kingdom to determine the expenses of sovereignty which the colony has to pay and the necessary receipts to cover them, for the

Cortes' can alter them at pleasure. Therefore, the colony has no direct vote in a matter of so great importance. It may be said that she is allowed to appoint her deputies to the Cortes of the Kingdom, and that through them the colony can be heard. But the colony's voice will be lost, because their number would be insignificant before the remaining deputies of the nation. And it may happen that the expenses of sovereignty, put by the Cortes on the colony, absorb all of its receipts, because neither of the two houses (chambers) can deliberate regarding the colonial budget without having first voted to pay the expenses of sovereignty.

6. Article 37 speaks of treaties of commerce which may affect Cuba, and states that the Madrid Government shall make them, aided by the delegates of the colonial government. And, further, that when the treaties are approved by the Cortes of the Kingdom they will be published as general laws, and as such will be respected in the insular territory, but it is left doubtful whether they would be laws in Cuba if the colonial delegates should reject them. If the Madrid Government is not to rule in such a case it should be so stated. And if it is a law notwithstanding the colonial opposition, why is the concurrence of the colony asked? The case referred to in article 38 does not decide it, because it only refers to those treaties in the negotiation of which the insular government has had nothing to do.

7. Article 40 gives in a very ingenious manner a method of deciding the differences arising from privileged articles of commerce, in comparison to similar foreign articles, and in reference to the extension of such a privilege, within the maximum limit of 35 per cent. differential duty. When the two governments making the treaty do not agree, a committee is formed of the same number of Cuban and peninsular deputies. These deputies appoint their president; if they do not agree, the eldest in age presides. And the president has the casting vote. Let us suppose the Cuban deputies to be very patriotic, which is, by the way, supposing a great deal, but as they will never be more patriotic than the peninsular delegates, it will result that they will not agree, and then the eldest will decide. As there are a large number of peninsular deputies and a very small number of insular deputies to select from, care will be taken that some aged peninsular deputy

be appointed on said committee, and he would be the one to decide. The matter would have been simplified by stating that the eldest peninsular deputy would be the one to make the lists, as such will be the result.

8. Article 40 also refers to the schedules of the merchandise, which will appear in the privileged lists. The decree only says that they shall be made by mutual consent (meaning Cuban and Peninsular deputies). It does not make any reference to the case when there is no mutual consent, which makes us suppose that the same procedure recommended in the other lists will be observed. The eldest peninsular deputy will, therefore, make the said schedules.

9. The Governor-General has the power to suspend the constitutional guarantees, apply legislation of public order (*ley de órden público*), and adopt any measures he may deem fit to maintain peace, etc. This power the Governor-General can exercise at will, without any limitation, because he is not obliged to hear the opinion of the council of secretaries (ministry), and thus the whole political system of the country lies with the Governor-General. The latter can, therefore, find any pretext for courts-martial, the application of the code of military justice, and all that series of proclamations and orders which have caused so much harm, and which rob the citizen of all guaranties and protection.

10. The distribution of the public debt of Cuba remains completely in the hands and subject to the decision of the Cortes of the Kingdom, which will try to assign to Cuba as much of it as it can, so that Spain will pay the smallest part.

Beyond all this, even, the fact remains and makes useless, while it exists, all orderly and pacific development of the autonomistic régime, and this fact is the existence of the volunteers in arms. the political party in power is unarmed, has no force of its own, while the Spanish radical (intransigente) party, which is in the opposition, is armed, having on its side the armed volunteers. Under such conditions there can be no genuine autonomistic government, because the opposition can ride over, whenever it pleases, the authority of the local government, and of which we had a very recent example, and it can have it repeated whenever the radical Spanish (intransigente) party so desire.

[From the Gaceta de Madrid, Saturday, November 27, 1897.]

OFFICIAL.—PRESIDENT OF THE COUNCIL OF MINISTERS.

STATEMENT.

Madam.—In endeavoring to solve the problem of introducing colonial autonomy into the islands of Cuba and Puerto Rico, which task, together with that of the pacification of the territory of Cuba, constitutes the engagements which the Government has contracted with the nation, the ministers think that detailed explanations and comments on the complex matters embraced in the plan should give way to a temperate but full statement of its fundamental character, or of the spheres of action to which it extends and of the consequences which, in their opinion, must be the result of the régime which they propose to Your Majesty for the government of the Spanish Antilles.

Criticism and analysis will speedily elucidate all that relates to the details; the essential ideas and the inspiration of the decree have their appropriate place here and at this time only.

This is the more necessary, since the first and most essential condition of success in reforms of this kind is absolute sincerity of purpose. With this sincerity the Government has examined the best form of an autonomic constitution for the islands of Cuba and Puerto Rico, and it hopes clearly to demonstrate, in these observations, that the intention and the results have gone hand in hand.

It was proposed, in the first place, clearly to establish the principle, to develop it in its entirety, and to surround it with every guaranty of success, because, when it is sought to intrust the direction of affairs to peoples that have reached the age of virility, either no mention of autonomy should be made to them or it should be given to them complete, with the conviction that they are started on the right road with the restrictions or shackles which are born of distrust and suspicion. Either the defense of nationality is confided to repression and force or it is turned over to a reconciliation of affection and tradition with interest, and this reconciliation is strengthened according as it is developed by the advantages of a system of government that teaches and gives evidence to the colonies that under no other will it be possible for them to attain a higher degree of welfare, security, and greatness.

This being the case, it was a condition essential to the attainment of the purpose had in view to seek for that principle a practical form and one that was intelligible to the people that had to be governed by it, and the Government found this in the program of that insular party, considerable in numbers, but still more important by reason of its intelligence and perseverance, the predictions of which party have, for twenty years past, made the people of Cuba familiar with the spirit, the procedure and the great importance of the serious innovation which they are called upon to introduce into their political and social life.

It is asserted by the foregoing that the project is in nowise theoretical, and that it is not an imitation or copy of other colonial constitutions which have been justly regarded as models in the matter, for although the Government has carefully considered what those instruments teach it realizes that the institutions of peoples which, in their history and their race, differ so much from that of Cuba, cannot take root where they have neither precedent nor atmosphere, nor that preparation which is the outgrowth of education and belief.

The problem having been thus defined, inasmuch as the question was to give an autonomic constitution to a Spanish territory peopled by a Spanish race and civilized by Europe, there was no longer any doubt as to the decision to be reached; autonomy had to be developed according to the ideas and the program which bears that name in the Antilles, without eliminating anything of its contents, and especially without altering its spirit, but rather by completing and harmonizing it and giving it greater guaranties of stability, as should be done by the government of a mother country which feels itself called to establish such a program, from a conviction of its advantages, from a desire to carry peace and tranquillity to those highly-prized territories, and from a consciousness of its own responsibility, not only to the colonies, but also to its own vast interests which time has connected and woven together in the impenetrable net of years.

Being thus aware of the form which best fitted its design, the Government found it easy to distinguish the three aspects offered by the establishment of an autonomic constitution. In the first place, the sacred interests of the mother country, which, being alarmed and distrustful on account of the course pursued by many of her sons, and wounded by the ingratitude of those who put more trust in the selfishness of the speculator than they do in brotherly affection, desires above all things that the change for which she is prepared should draw closer and strengthen the bond of sovereignty, and that in the midst of a blessed peace the interests of all her sons, which are not at variance with each other, although they may be at times different, should be harmonized and developed by the free consent of all.

Next are to be considered the aspirations, the needs, and the desires of our colonial population, which is anxious to be treated like an unfortunate daughter instead of being crushed like an enemy, which is obedient to the call of affection, and ready to rebel like Spaniards against the brutal imposition of exterminating force. These people expect from the mother country a form in which their initiative may be molded and a mode of procedure that may authorize them to manage their own interests.

And finally, this vast and interesting mass of relations created of interests developed in that long past which nobody, still less a Government, is at liberty to disregard or forget, and whose preservation and development involve the fulfillment of the destiny of our race in America, and the glory of the Spanish flag in lands that were discovered and civilized by our ancestors.

These three orders of ideas find their answer in the fundamental provisions of the draft submitted to Your Majesty for approval. To the first, that is, to the point of view of the mother country, belong the questions of sovereignty which have been confided to the highest authorities of the Spanish nation. The representation and authority of the King, who is the nation itself, the command of the army and navy, the administration of justice, diplomatic understanding with America, the constant and beneficent relations between the colony and the mother country, the pardoning power and the upholding and defense of the constitution are intrusted to the Governor-General as the King's representative, and under the direction of the council of ministers. Nothing that is essential has been forgotten; the authority of the central power is in nowise diminished or abated.

The insular aspect is, in its turn, developed in a manner as full and complete as could be desired by those who are most exacting, in central, provincial, and municipal autonomy; in the application without reserve or equivocation of the parliamentary system; in the powers of the insular chambers and in the creation of a responsible government, at the head of which, and forming the supreme bond of nationality as regards the executive power, again appears the Governor-General who, on the one hand, presides through responsible ministers over the development of colonial life, and, on the other, associates and connects it with the general life of the nation.

And that third aspect, in which is recapitulated the history of the relations between the Antilles and the mother country, and within which their commerce, their credit, and their wealth, must also be developed, is defined in a series of provisions of a permanent character, which connects the two executive powers — the insular and the national, and at times, their chambers — in such a manner that at every moment they lend each other mutual aid, and assist each other in developing the common interests.

And all this manifold and complex, though not complicated, system is sanctioned and rendered practical by a series of guaranties of associations of constant understandings and public discussions which will absolutely prevent, so far as it is allowable for man to predict that which is to come, unyielding dilemmas, insurmountable difficulties, and collisions between the colonies and the mother country.

This is a point of so great importance that the Government would certainly have subordinated all other questions to it if such subordination had been necessary, which it cannot be nor is there any reason to fear it, since the bases of the new régime are established upon harmony of interests, scrupulous respect for the rights of others, and the desire in the mother country unremittingly to aid the development, prosperity, and peaceful aggrandizement of her beautiful Antilles, which desire the Government does not doubt will be fully shared there.

This does not mean that no questions will arise in which the two spheres of action will be confounded, and that there will be no legitimate doubts as to which is the predominant interest in them, or that there will not be, after the doubts, more or less of passionate discussion. In no colony enjoying autonomy has this failed to happen; in none has the case arisen in which the central Government was always and systematically in accord with the acts of the colonial government. Long is the list of the legislative enactments of Canada which have been vetoed by the British Government, and curious and exceedingly interesting is the list of judicial decisions which have defined the diverse jurisdictions of their local assemblies, either among themselves or with their Governors. This has been the case notwithstanding the fact that the great decentralization, the antecedents of Canadian history, and freedom of trade greatly simplify the relations between the two countries.

The excellence of the system, however, lies in the fact that when such cases arise, and especially when they are frequent, the balance of power both within the colonial constitution and in the relations of the colony to the mother country is such that a remedy is always to be had, that a basis of understanding is never lacking, and that a common ground is always to be found on which interests are either harmonized or their antagonism is settled or the will of the people bows to the decision of the courts.

If, therefore, the rights which are recognized by the constitution as belonging to the citizens are violated or their interests are disregarded by the town boards and deputations which are, in their turn, within the system, entirely autonomous, the courts of justice will defend and uphold them; if corporations go beyond their powers, or if, on the other hand, the executive power undertakes to impair what the constitution of the kingdom or the provisions of this decree declare to be powers belonging to the town boards or the provincial corporations, the accused party has the right to appeal to the courts of the island, and as a last resort to the Supreme Court, whose duty it will be to settle disputes of jurisdiction between the Governor-General and the colonial parliament, whoever may have given rise to such disputes; both will have the same rights to complain and to seek legal redress for their wrongs.

Thus, whatever difficulties may arise from the establishment of a system, or be the outgrowth of its exercise, will be decided by the courts, which have been, since ancient Rome down to modern England, the most progressive source of right, and which have afforded the most flexible procedure for the harmonization of the growing demands of real life and the slow process of legislation.

Thus the autonomic constitution which the Government proposes for the islands of Cuba and Puerto Rico is not exotic or copied, nor is it an imitation. It is an organization *sui generis*, conceived and upheld by the natives of the Spanish Antilles, gladly inscribed by the liberal party in their program in order that the nation might know what it had to expect from that party when it should come into power, and characterized by a feature which no colonial régime has thus far presented, viz.: that the Antilles can be wholly autonomous, in the fullest sense of the word, and at the same time have their representatives and form a part of the national parliament.

So that, while the representatives of the insular people direct from their local chambers the special interests of their country, others elected by the same people aid and co-operate in the Cortes in the making of those laws in whose mould are formed and unified the different elements of Spanish nationality. And this is not a small or paltry advantage; still less does it furnish ground for surprise, as some might, perhaps, think, because this present of the deputies from the Antilles in the Cortes is a close bond of the nationality which is raised above all the unities which live in its bosom, now sought as one of the greatest political steps in advance of our day by the autonomous English colonies, which are anxious to take part in an imperial parliament in the supreme function of legislators and directors of the great British Empire.

This form, therefore, which is characteristic of the system now adopted by Spain, while it gives it its own meaning, signifies, if not a step in advance, such as those engendered by the present time, an advantage which circumstances offer us as a just compensation for the immense disasters which our colonial history recounts.

The Government frankly acknowledges that for the success of its work public discussion in Parliament would have been better, together with the analysis of public opinion in the press, on the lecture platform, and in books; but it is not its fault, as it was not that of the previous Government, if the pressure of circumstances compels it to do without this precious guaranty. Yet if the party which now serves the interests of the Crown and the country in the Government did not hesitate a moment to approve, in its day, the initiative taken by the conservative party, or in voting for the appropriation which it asked from the Cortes, it has a right, now that the weight of circumstances is still heavier than it was then, to hope that public opinion will approve to-day the course pursued by it, and that the Cortes will do so to-morrow.

For this reason it does not hesitate to face the responsibility, and it intends to put into immediate action and practice the solutions which are implied in the present decree with the same sincerity with which it has prepared it, thus removing the suspicion of any indecision in its course or of reservations in its promises. If the régime shall be found wanting in practice for lack of good faith in anybody it will never be — and we are proud to proclaim this — the fault of the men who are actuated above all things by the noble desire to pacify their country.

The Government thinks that it has thus said everything necessary to make known the genesis, the inspiration, and the character of the plan which, establishing in Cuba and Puerto Rico an autonomic régime, it now submits to Your Majesty.

To those who are familiar with the constitution of the Monarchy, the plan will certainly not present any great difficulties, for the Government has, as far as possible, taken for its guide the organic system of that instrument, the division of its titles, and even its wording. The modifications of the constitutional articles are accessory and circumstantial; the additions respond to its specialty and seek to secure the efficiency of its provisions and the facility of their execution.

Doubtless something will remain to be done, and some reforms will be needed; this will be shown simultaneously by the defense of its provisions and the criticisms made thereon, and gradually the good grounds upon which both are based will be ascertained; this will render it possible to incorporate what is good in the plan and to reject what does not harmonize with its fundamental ideas when the time comes for it to receive the sanction of the Cortes.

Let it be understood, nevertheless, that the Government will not eliminate from it, nor will it consent that anything be eliminated that goes to form colonial liberties, guaranties, and privileges, because being prepared to complete its work or to throw light upon doubts, it does not intend that when it presents its plan for parliamentary sanction the concessions made shall suffer any impairment, nor can it consent to do so if it has a majority in the chambers.

But though all that the Government considers necessary to explain in the general lines of the decree has been set forth in the foregoing, it still deems it indispensable, for reasons which will readily be understood, to fix the sense of the articles which refer to autonomy with regard to the tariff, and which refer to the debt which burdens the Cuban treasury.

The export trade from the Peninsula to Cuba, which amounts to about $30,000,000 per annum, and which, moreover, furnishes ground for important combinations for navigation on the high seas, has hitherto been subjected to an exceptional régime which is absolutely incompatible with the principle of colonial autonomy.

This implies the power to regulate the conditions of its import and export trade and to have free control of its custom-houses. To refuse these privileges to Cuba or Puerto Rico would be tantamount to nullifying the value of the principles laid down; to endeavor to defeat their object would be incompatible with the dignity of the nation. What it behooves the Government to do, after recognizing the principle in its entirety, is to endeavor to cause the transition to take place without violence or injury to the interests which have been developed under the old system, and for this purpose to pave the way to an understanding with the governments of the Antilles.

The most earnest advocates of autonomy have never denied the willingness of those countries to recognize, in behalf of genuinely national industry and commerce, a margin that should secure that market to them.

This assurance has always been given by their representatives in the Cortes, and is still given by their representatives in the Cortes, and is still given by all parties in the island of Cuba, according to statements which the Government considers irrecusable. Complaints arose, not from the existence of discriminating duties, but from the fact that those duties were too high, and that this prevented the Antilles from securing the markets which they needed for their rich and abundant productions, and from the lack of reciprocity. Thus, as no insurmountable difficulties exist, there is ground for saying that an understanding is more than possible; that it is certain, especially when it is considered that the exports from the peninsula to Cuba consist of about fifty articles of the four hundred that are specified in the tariff, and that of these fifty many, owing to their special character, and owing to the customs and tastes of the Cubans, will never have reason to fear the competition of foreign articles.

The manufacturers and shipowners of the Peninsula have no cause for alarm owing to the establishment of a system of autonomy, which, while it modifies the conditions on which the tariff is based, does not alter the essential bases of the economic relations between Spain and the Antilles. There will doubtless be some difficulties to be harmonized, or it will be necessary to settle the inevitable differences accompanying any change of the mercantile régime; it will be necessary to combine both tariffs in some way; but neither are the interests of Cuba opposed to those of the Peninsula, nor is it to anyone's interest to diminish the commercial relations existing between the two countries.

If, then, the insular government were already established, and if with it it had been possible to agree upon a system of mercantile relations, this question would not have assumed proportions which it does not possess; nor would there be any cause for predicting ruin and disaster; the facts would put suppositions to silence. Notwithstanding this, the Government has thought that, in order to quiet alarm, it was proper for it to anticipate events, and that instead of leaving the settlement of the question to the natural working of the new constitution, it was proper to fix without further delay the bases of our future mercantile relations. In doing this and with a view to removing all cause of distrust, it has gone so far as to fix a maximum for the differential duties that are to be obtained by peninsular goods, offering, as was right and just, the same rates to insular productions.

The basis of the understanding having been fixed and determined, the principle of autonomy having been guaranteed, the equality of powers having been established in an unquestionable manner in the procedure that is to be observed, and the spirit which actuates those islanders being known, the negotiation will be easy and its results will be advantageous to both parties.

As to the debt which burdens the Cuban treasury, either directly or owing to the guarantee which it has given to that of the Peninsula, and which the latter bears analogously, the justice of dividing it in an equitable manner when the termination of the war shall render it possible to fix its definitive amount is not to be doubted for a moment.

This debt, let us hope, will not be so enormous as to amount to an insupportable burden upon the energy of the nation, nor is the nation so lacking in resources that it needs to feel alarm at the prospect before it. A country which during the past few months has given such strong evidence of virility and social discipline; a territory like that of Cuba, which, even in the midst of its political convulsions and of war scarcely interrupted for thirty years, has produced so great wealth by cultivating only a small part of its fertile soil, and which has done this by its own strength alone, with few institutions of credit, struggling against sugar on which a bounty is paid, the American market being closed to its manufactured tobacco, and at the same time changing slave labor into free labor, may calmly contemplate the payment of its obligations and inspire its creditors with confidence.

Consequently, in the opinion of the Government, it is important to think from this time forward of the manner in which the debt is to be paid, rather than of its division, applying the economic methods of our day to the great wealth which the soil of Cuba secures to agriculturists and which the bowels of the earth secure to miners, and taking advantage of the extraordinary facilities offered to the commerce of the world by the insular form and the geographical situation of what has rightly been called the "Pearl of the Antilles."

If no legislation can yet be enacted concerning these things, it is proper to bear them in mind very carefully and to pay much attention to them, since it has occurred to others who certainly cannot be charged with being visionary or forming illusions — it has occurred to them, I say, to take advantage of this great germ of wealth, not, indeed, for the benefit of Spain or to uphold her sovereignty; when they do this, it would be fooling not to follow their example and not to convert into a redemption of the past and a guaranty of the future what has perhaps been an incentive to war and the origin in a great measure of the evils which we are now so eagerly seeking to remedy.

Basing its action on these considerations, the Government has the honor to submit the inclosed draft of a decree to Your Majesty for approval.

Madrid, November 25, 1897.

PRAXEDES MATEO SAGASTA.

ROYAL DECREE.

Upon the proposition of my Prime Minister, and with the concurrence of the Council of Ministers in the name of my august son, King Alfonso XIII, and as Queen Regent of the Kingdom, I hereby decree as follows:

TITLE I.*

GOVERNMENT AND ADMINISTRATION OF THE ISLANDS OF CUBA AND PUERTO RICO.

Article 1. The islands of Cuba and Puerto Rico shall hereafter be governed and administered in conformity with the following provisions:

Art. 2. Each island shall be governed by an insular parliament, consisting of two chambers, and by the Governor-General, representing the mother country, who shall exercise supreme authority.

TITLE II.

THE INSULAR CHAMBERS.

Article 3. The insular chambers, together with the Governor-General, shall have power to legislate concerning colonial affairs in the manner and on the terms provided by law.

Art. 4. Insular representation shall consist of two bodies of equal powers, which shall be known as chamber of representatives and council of administration.

---

* EXPLANATORY NOTE.— To facilitate the understanding of this decree, and to avoid confusion as to the legal value of the terms employed therein, the following definitions are to be observed:

Central Executive Power	The King with his Council of Ministers.
The Spanish Parliament	The Cortes with the King.
The Spanish Chambers	The Congress and the Senate.
The Central Government	The Council of Ministers of the Kingdom.
The Colonial Parliament	The two Chambers with the Governor-General.
The Colonial Chambers	The Council of Administration and the Chamber of Representatives.
Colonial Legislative Assemblies	The Council of Administration and the Chamber of Representatives.
Governor-General in Council	The Governor-General with the Secretaries of his Cabinet.
Instructions of the Governor-General...	Those which he may have received when named for his office.
Statute	Colonial measure of a legislative character.
Colonial Statutes	Colonial Legislation.
Legislation or General Laws	Legislation or laws of the Kingdom

TITLE III.

COUNCIL OF ADMINISTRATION.

Article 5. The council shall be composed of thirty-five members, of whom eighteen shall be elected in the manner directed by the electoral law and seventeen shall be designated by the Governor-General acting for the Crown, from among such persons as have the qualifications specified in the following articles:

Art. 6. To be entitled to sit in the council of administration it is necessary to be a Spanish subject; to have attained the age of thirty-five years; to have been born in the island, or to have had four years' constant residence therein; not to be subject to any pending criminal prosecution; to be in the full enjoyment of his political rights; to have his property free from attachment; to have had for two or more years previous an annual income of four thousand dollars; to have no interest in any contract with either the insular or the home Government.

The shareholders of a stock company shall not be considered as Government contractors, even if the company has a contract with the Government.

Art. 7. Persons are also qualified to serve as councilors who, besides the above-stated requirements, have any of the following qualifications:

1. To be or to have been a senator of the Kingdom, or to possess the requirements for being a senator, in conformity with Article III of the Constitution.

2. To have held for a period of two years any of the following offices: President, or prosecuting attorney of the pretorian court of Havana; rector of the University of Havana; councilor of administration in the council formerly thus designated; president of the Havana Chamber of Commerce; president of the Economic Society of Friends of the Country; president of the Sugar Planters' Association; president of the Tobacco Manufacturers' Union; president of the Merchants, Tradesmens, and Agriculturists' League; dean of the bar of Havana; mayor of Havana; president of the provincial assembly of Havana during two terms or of any provincial assembly during three terms; dean of either of the chapters of the two cathedrals.

3. Likewise may be elected or appointed as council or any property-owner from among the fifty taxpayers paying the highest taxes, either on real estate or on industries, commerce, arts, and the professions.

Art. 8. The councilors appointed by the Crown shall be appointed by special decrees, stating the qualification entitling the appointee to serve as councilor.

Councilors thus appointed shall hold office for life.

One-half the number of elective councilors shall be elected every five years, and the whole number shall be elected whenever the council of administration shall be dissolved by the Governor-General.

Art. 9. The qualifications required in order to be appointed or elected councilor of administration may be changed by a national law, at the request or upon the proposition of the insular chambers.

Art. 10. No councilor shall, during the session of the council, accept any civil office, promotion (unless it be strictly by seniority), title, or decoration; but any councilor may be appointed by either the local or the home government to any commission within his own profession or category, whenever the public service shall require it.

The secretaries of the insular government shall be excepted from the foregoing rule.

TITLE IV.

THE CHAMBER OF REPRESENTATIVES.

Article 11. The chamber of representatives shall be composed of members named by the electoral boards in the manner prescribed by law and in the proportion of one for every twenty-five thousand inhabitants.

Art. 12. To be elected as representative the candidate must have the following requirements: To be a Spanish citizen, to be a layman, to have attained his majority, to be in full enjoyment of civil rights, to have been born in the island or to have had four years' constant residence therein, and not to be subject to any pending criminal prosecution.

Art. 13. Representatives shall be elected every five years, and any representative may be re-elected any number of times.

The insular chamber shall determine what classes of offices are incompatible with the office of representative, as well as the cases governing re-election.

Art. 14. Any representative upon whom either the local or home government shall confer a pension, or any employment, promotion (unless it be by strict seniority), paid commission, title, or decoration, shall cease to be such without necessity of any declaration to that effect, unless he shall within fifteen days of his appointment notify the chamber of his having declined the favor.

The provisions of the preceding paragraph shall not include the representatives who shall be appointed members of the cabinet.

TITLE V.

PROCEEDINGS OF THE INSULAR CHAMBERS AND THEIR RELATIONS TO EACH OTHER.

Article 15. The chambers will meet every year. The King, the Governor-General acting in his name, shall convene, suspend, and adjourn the sessions and dissolve the chamber of representatives and the council of administration, either separately or simultaneously, under the obligation to call them together again or renew them within three months.

Art. 16. Each of the two legislative bodies shall determine the rules of their proceedings and shall be the judges of the qualifications of their respective members and the legality of their election.

Until the chamber and the council shall pass their own rules, they shall be governed by the rules of the national house of representatives and of the senate, respectively.

Art. 17. Each chamber shall choose its president, vice-president, and secretaries.

Art. 18. Neither chamber shall sit unless the other be sitting also, except when the council exercises judicial functions.

Art. 19. The two insular chambers shall not deliberate together nor in the presence of the Governor-General.

The sessions shall be public, but either chamber may hold secret sessions whenever business of a private nature shall require it.

Art. 20. To the Governor-General, through his secretaries, as well as to either of the two chambers, belongs the power to initiate and propose colonial statutes.

Art. 21. All colonial statutes in regard to taxes and the public credit shall originate in the chamber of representatives.

Art. 22. Resolutions may be passed by either chamber by a plurality of votes; but in order to pass a measure of a legislative character a majority of all the members constituting the body must be present. Nevertheless, one-third of the members shall constitute a quorum for deliberation.

Art. 23. No resolution or law shall be considered passed by the insular parliament unless it has had the concurrence of the chamber of representatives and the council of administration.

Art. 24. Every colonial statute, as soon as it has been approved in the form prescribed in the preceding article, shall be presented to the Governor-General by the officers of both chambers for his sanction and proclamation of the same.

Art. 25. Members of the council and the chamber of representatives shall have immunity for any speech or vote in either chamber.

Art. 26. No councilor of administration shall be indicted or arrested without a previous resolution of the council, unless he shall be found *in flaganti* or the council shall not be in session, but in every case notice shall be given to that body as soon as possible, that it may determine what should be done. Nor shall the representatives be indicted or arrested during the sessions without the permission of the chamber unless they are found *in flaganti,* but in this last case, or in case of indictment or arrest when the chamber is not sitting, notice shall be given as soon as possible to the chamber of representatives for its information and action. All proceedings against councilors and representatives shall be brought before the pretorian court at Havana in the cases and manner that shall be prescribed by colonial statutes.

Art. 27. The guarantees established in the foregoging section shall not apply to a councilor or representative who shall himself admit that he is the author of any article, book, pamphlet, or printed matter wherein military sedition is incited or invoked, or the Governor-General is insulted and maligned, or national sovereignty is assailed.

Art. 28. The relations between the two chambers shall be governed, until otherwise provided, by the act of July 19, 1837, regulating the relations between the two legislative houses of the Cortes.

Art. 29. Besides the power of enacting laws for the colony the insular chambers shall have power:

1. To receive the oath of the Governor-General to preserve the constitution and the laws which guarantee the autonomy of the colony.

2. To enforce the responsibility of the secretaries of the executive, who shall be tried by the council, whenever impeached by the chamber of representatives.

3. To address the home Government through the Governor-General, proposing the abrogation or modification of existing laws of the Kingdom; to invite the home Government to present bills as to particular matters, or to ask a decision of an executive character on matters which interest the colony.

Art. 30. The Governor-General shall communicate to the home Government before presenting to the insular parliament any bill originating in the executive government of the island whenever, in his judgment, said bill may affect national interests. Should any such bill originate in the insular parliament, the government of the island shall ask for a postponement of the debate until the home Government shall have given its opinion.

In either case the correspondence passing between the two governments shall be laid before the chambers and published in the Official Gazette.

Art. 31. All differences of jurisdiction between the several municipal, provincial, and insular assemblies, or between any of them and the executive, which by their nature may not be referred to the home Government, shall be submitted to the courts of justice in accordance with the rules herein prescribed.

TITLE VI.

Powers Vested in the Insular Parliament.

Article 32. The insular chambers shall have power to pass upon all matters not specially and expressly reserved to the Cortes of the Kingdom or to the central Government as herein provided, or as may be provided hereafter, in accordance with the prescription set forth in additional article 2.

In this manner, and without implying that the following enumeration presupposes any limitation of their power to legislate on other subjects, they shall have power to legislate on all matters and subjects concerning the departments of justice, interior, treasury, public works, education, and agriculture.

They shall likewise have exclusive cognizance of all matters of a purely local nature which may principally affect the colonial territory; and to this end they shall have power to legislate on civil administration; on provincial, municipal, or judicial apportionment; on public health, by land or sea, and on public credit, banks, and the monetary system.

This power, however, shall not impair the powers vested in the colonial executive according to the laws in connection with the matters above mentioned.

Art. 33. It shall be incumbent upon the colonial parliament to make regulations under such national laws as may be passed by the Cortes and expressly intrusted to it. Especially among such measures, parliament shall legislate, and may do so at the first sitting, for the purpose of regulating the elections, the taking of the electoral census, qualifying electors, and exercising the right of suffrage; but in no event shall these dispositions affect the rights of the citizens, as established by the electoral laws.

Art. 34. Notwithstanding that the laws governing the judiciary and the administration of justice are of a national character, and therefore obligatory for the colony, the insular parliament may, within the provisions of said laws, make rules or propose to the home Government such measures as shall render easier the admission, continuance, or promotion in the local courts of lawyers, natives of the island, or practicing therein.

The Governor-General in council shall have, as far as the island of Cuba is concerned, the same power that has been vested heretofore in the minister for the colonies for the appointment of the functionaries and subordinate and auxiliary officers of the judicial order and as to the other matters connected with the administration of justice.

Art. 35. The insular parliament shall have exclusive power to frame the local budget of expenditures and revenues, including the revenue corresponding to the island as her quota of the national budget.

To this end the Governor-General shall present to the chambers every year before the month of January the budget for the next fiscal year, divided in two parts, as follows: The first part shall state the revenues needed to defray the expenses of sovereignty, and the second part shall state the revenues and expenditures estimated for the maintenance of the colonial administration.

Neither chamber shall take up the budget of the colonial government without having finally voted the part for the maintenance of sovereignty.

Art. 36. The Cortes of the Kingdom shall determine what expenditures are to be considered by reason of their nature as obligatory expenses inherent to sovereignty, and shall fix the amount every three years and the revenue needed to defray the same, the Cortes reserving the right to alter this rule.

Art. 37. All treaties of commerce affecting the island of Cuba, be they suggested by the insular or by the home Government, shall be made by the latter with the co-operation of special delegates duly authorized by the colonial government, whose concurrence shall be acknowledged upon submitting the treaties to the Cortes.

Said treaties, when approved by the Cortes, shall be proclaimed as laws of the Kingdom and as such shall obtain in the colony.

Art. 38. Notice shall be given to the insular government of any commercial treaties made without its participation as soon as said treaties shall become laws, to the end that, within a period of three months, it may declare its acceptance or nonacceptance of their stipulations. In case of acceptance the Governor-General shall cause the treaty to be published in the Gazette as a colonial statute.

Art. 39. The insular parliament shall also have power to frame the tariff and fix the duties to be paid on merchandise as well for its importation into the territory of the island as for the exportation thereof.

Art. 40. As a transition from the old régime to the new constitution, and until the home and insular governments may otherwise conjointly determine hereafter, the commercial relations between the island and the metropolis shall be governed by the following rules:

1. No differential duty, whether fiscal or otherwise, either on imports or exports, shall be imposed to the detriment of either insular or peninsular production.

2. The two governments shall make a schedule of articles of direct national origin to which shall be allowed by common consent preferential duty over similar foreign products.

In another schedule made in like manner shall be determined such articles of direct insular production as shall be entitled to privileged treatment on their importation into the peninsula and the amount of preferential duties thereon.

In neither case shall the preferential duty exceed 35 per cent.

Should the home and the colonial government agree upon the schedules and the preferential duties, they shall be considered final and shall be enforced at once. In cases of disagreement the point in dispute shall be submitted to a committee of representatives of the Cortes, consisting of an equal number of Cubans and Peninsulars. The committee shall appoint its chairman, and in case of disagreement the eldest member shall preside. The chairman shall have the casting vote.

3. The valuation tables concerning the articles in the schedules above mentioned shall be fixed by mutual agreement, and shall be revised after discussion every two years. The modifications which may thereupon become necessary in the tariff duties shall be carried out at once by the respective governments.

TITLE VII.

THE GOVERNOR-GENERAL.

Article 41. The supreme authority of the colony shall be vested in a Governor-General, appointed by the King on the nomination of the council of ministers. In his capacity he shall have as viceroyal patron the power inherent in the patronate of the Indies; he shall have command of all military and naval forces in the island; he shall act as delegate of the departments of state, war, navy, and the colonies; all other authorities in the island shall be subordinate to his, and he shall be responsible for the preservation of order and the safety of the colony.

The Governor-General shall, before taking possession of his office, take an oath in the presence of the King to discharge his duties faithfully and loyally.

Art. 42. The Governor-General, representing the nation, will discharge by himself and with the aid of his secretaries all the functions indicated in the preceding articles and such others as may devolve upon him as direct delegate of the King in matters of a national character.

It shall be incumbent upon the Governor-General as representing the home Government:

1. To appoint without restriction the secretaries of his cabinet.

2. To proclaim, execute, and cause to be executed in the island all laws, decrees, treaties, international covenants, and all other acts emanating from the legislative branch of the Government, as well as all decrees, royal commands, and other measures emanating from the executive which shall be communicated to him by the departments of which he acts as delegate.

Whenever in his judgment and in that of his secretaries he considers the resolutions of the home Government as liable to injure the general interests of the nation or the special interests of the island, he shall have power to suspend the publication and execution thereof, and shall so notify the respective department, stating the reasons for his action.

3. To grant pardons in the name of the King, within the limitations specially prescribed to him in his instructions from the Government, and to stay the execution of a death sentence whenever the gravity of the circumstances shall so demand or the urgency of the case shall allow of no time to solicit and obtain His Majesty's pardon; but in either case he shall hear the counsel of his secretaries.

4. To suspend the guarantees set forth in articles 3, 5, 6, and 9, and in the first, second, and third paragraphs of article 13 of the constitution; to enforce legislation in regard to public order, and to take all measures which he may deem necessary to preserve the peace within and the safety without for the territory intrusted to him after hearing the counsel of his cabinet.

5. To take care that in the colony justice be promptly and fully administered, and that it shall always be administered in the name of the King.

6. To hold direct communication on foreign affairs with the ministers, diplomatic agents, and consuls of Spain throughout America.

A full copy of such correspondence shall be simultaneously forwarded to the home Department of State.

Art. 43. It behooves the Governor-General, as the superior authority in the colony and head of its administration:

1. To take care that the rights, powers, and privileges now vested or that may henceforth be vested in the colonial administration be respected and protected.

2. To sanction and proclaim the acts of the insular parliament, which shall be submitted to him by the president and secretaries of the respective chambers.

Whenever, in the judgment of the Governor-General, an act of the insular parliament goes beyond its powers or impairs the rights of the citizens as set forth in Article I of the Constitution, or curtails the guarantees prescribed by law for the exercise of said rights, or jeopards the interest of the colony or of the nation, he shall forward the act to the council of ministers of the Kingdom, which, within a period that shall not exceed two months, shall either assent to it or return it to the Governor-General with the objections to its sanction and proclamation. The insular parliament may, in view of the objections, reconsider or modify the act, if it deems fit, without a special proposition.

If two months shall elapse without the central government giving any opinion as to a measure agreed upon by the chambers which has been transmitted to it by the Governor-General, the latter shall sanction and proclaim the same.

3. To appoint, suspend, and discharge the employees of the colonial administration, upon the suggestion of the secretaries of the departments and in accordance with the laws.

4. To appoint and remove, without restriction, the secretaries of his cabinet.

Art. 44. No executive order of the Governor-General, acting as representative and chief of the colony, shall take effect unless countersigned by a secretary of the cabinet, who by this act alone shall make himself responsible for the same.

Art. 45. There shall be five secretaries of department, to-wit:

Grace and justice and interior; finance; public education, public works and posts and telegraphs; agriculture, industry, and commerce.

The Governor-General shall appoint the president of the cabinet from among the secretaries, and shall also have power to appoint a president without a secretaryship.

The power to increase or diminish the number of secretaries composing the colonial cabinet, and to determine the scope of each department, is vested in the insular parliament.

Art. 46. The secretaries of the cabinet may be members of either the chamber of representatives or the council of administration and take part in the debates of either chamber, but a secretary shall only vote in the chamber of which he is a member.

Art. 47. The secretaries of the cabinet shall be responsible to the insular parliament.

Art. 48. The Governor-General shall not modify or abrogate his own orders after they are assented to by the home Government, or when they shall declare some rights, or when a sentence by a judicial court or administrative tribunal shall have been based upon said orders, or when they shall deal with his own competency.

Art. 49. The Governor-General shall not turn over his office when leaving the island except by special command from the home Government. In case of absence from the seat of government which prevents his discharging the duties of his office or of disability to perform such duties, he can appoint one or more persons to take his place, provided the home Government has not previously done so or the method of substitution shall not be stated in his instructions.

Art. 50. The supreme court shall have the sole power to try the Governor-General when impeached for his responsibilities as defined by the Penal Code.

The council of ministers shall take cognizance of his other responsibilities.

Art. 51. The Governor-General shall have the power, in spite of the provisions of the different articles of this decree, to act upon his own responsibility, without consulting his secretaries, in the following cases:

1. When forwarding to the home Government a bill passed by the insular parliament, especially when, in his opinion, it shall abridge the rights set forth in Article 1 of the constitution of the monarchy or the guarantees for the exercise thereof vouchsafed by the laws.

2. When it shall be necessary to enforce the law or public order, especially if there be no time or possibility to consult the home Government.

3. When enforcing the national laws that shall have been approved by the Crown and made applicable to all of the Spanish or to the colony under his government.

The proceedings and means of action which the Governor-General shall employ in the above cases shall be determined by a special law.

TITLE VIII.

Municipal and Provincial Government.

Article 52. Municipal organization shall be compulsory for every group of population of more than one thousand inhabitants.

Groups of less number of inhabitants may organize the service of their community by special covenants.

Every legally constituted municipality shall have power to frame its own laws regarding public education; highways by land, river, and sea; public health; municipal finances, as well as to freely appoint and remove its own employees.

Art. 53. At the head of each province there shall be an assembly, which shall be elected in the manner provided for by the colonial statutes, and shall be composed of a number of members in proportion to the population.

Art. 54. The provincial assembly shall be autonomous as regards the creation and maintenance of public schools and colleges; charitable institutions and provincial roads and ways by land, river, or sea; also as regards their own budgets and the appointment and removal of their respective employees.

Art. 55. The municipalities, as well as the provincial assemblies, shall have power to freely raise the necessary revenue to cover their expenditures, with no other limitation than to make the means adopted compatible with the general system of taxation which shall obtain in the island.

The resources for provincial appropriations shall be independent of municipal resources.

Art. 56. The mayors and presidents of boards of aldermen shall be chosen by their respective boards from among their members.

Art. 57. The mayors shall discharge without limitation the active duties of the municipal administration, as executors of the resolutions of the board of aldermen or their representatives.

Art. 58. The aldermen and the provincial assemblymen shall be civilly responsible for the damages caused by their acts.

Their responsibility shall be exacted before the ordinary courts of justice.

Art. 59. The provincial assemblies shall freely choose their respective presidents.

Art. 60. The elections of aldermen and assemblymen shall be conducted in such manner as to allow for a legitimate representation of the minorities.

Art. 61. The provincial and municipal laws now obtaining in the island shall continue in vogue, wherever not in conflict with the provisions of this decree, until the insular parliament shall legislate upon the matter.

Art. 62. No colonial statute shall abridge the powers vested by the preceding articles in the municipalities and the provincial assemblies.

TITLE IX.

AS TO THE GUARANTIES FOR THE FULFILLMENT OF THE COLONIAL CONSTITUTION.

Article 63. Whenever a citizen shall consider that his rights have been violated or his interests injured by the action of a municipality or a provincial assembly he shall have the right to apply to the courts of justice for redress.

The department of justice shall, if so required by the agents of the executive government of the colony, prosecute before the courts the boards of aldermen or provincial assemblies charged with breaking the laws or abusing their power.

Art. 64. In the cases referred to in the preceding article, the following courts shall have jurisdiction: The territorial audiencia shall try all claims against municipalities; and the pretorian court of Havana shall try all claims against provincial assemblies.

Said courts, when the charges against any of the above-mentioned corporations shall be for abuse of power, shall render their decisions by a full bench. From the decision of the territorial audiencia an appeal shall be allowed to the pretorian court of Havana, and from the decisions of the latter an appeal shall be allowed to the supreme court of the Kingdom.

Art. 65. The redress of grievances which Article 62 grants to any citizen can also be had collectively by means of public action, by appointing an attorney or representative claimant.

Art. 66. Without in any way impairing the powers vested in the Governor-General by Title V of the present decree, he may, whenever he deems fit, appear before the pretorian court of Havana in his capacity as chief of the executive government of the colony, to the end that said court shall finally decide any conflict of jurisdiction between the executive power and the legislative chambers of the colony.

Art. 67. Should any question of jurisdiction be raised between the insular parliament and the Governor-General in his capacity as representative of the home Government, which shall not have been submitted to the council of ministers of the Kingdom by petition of the insular parliament, either party shall have power to bring the matter before the supreme court of the Kingdom, which shall render its decision by a full bench and in the first instance.

Art. 68. The decisions rendered in all cases provided for in the preceding articles shall be published in the collection of colonial statutes and shall form part of the insular legislation.

Art. 69. Every municipal measure for the purpose of contracting a loan or a municipal debt shall be without effect, unless it be assented to by a majority of the townspeople whenever one-third of the number of aldermen shall so demand.

The amount of the loan or debt which, according to the number of inhabitants of a township, shall make the referendum proceeding necessary, shall be determined by special statute.

Art. 70. All legislative acts originating in the insular parliament or the Cortes shall be compiled under the title of colonial statutes in a legislative collection, the formation and publication of which shall be intrusted to the Governor-General as chief of the colonial executive.

Additional Articles.

Article 1. Until the colonial statutes shall be published in due form, the laws of the Kingdom shall be deemed applicable to all matters reserved to the jurisdiction of the insular government.

Art. 2. When the present constitution shall be once approved by the Cortes of the Kingdom for the islands of Cuba and Porto Rico, it shall not be amended except by virtue of a special law and upon the petition of 'the insular parliament.

Art. 3. The provisions of the present decree shall obtain in their entirety in the island of Puerto Rico; they shall, however, be ordained by special decree in order to conform them to the population and nomenclature of said island.

Art. 4. Pending contracts for public services affecting in common the Antilles and the Peninsula shall continue in their present shape until termination, and shall be entirely governed by the conditions and stipulations therein made.

As regards other contracts already entered into, but not yet in operation, the Governor-General shall consult the home Government, or the colonial chambers, as the case may be, and the two governments shall by mutual accord decide as between themselves the final form of such contract.

TRANSITORY PROVISIONS.

Article 1. With a view to carry out the transition from the present régime to the system hereby established with the greatest possible dispatch and the least interruption of the public business, the Governor-General shall, whenever he deems it timely and after consulting the home Government, appoint the secretaries of the executive office as per Article 45 of this decree, and with their aid he shall conduct the local government of the island until the insular chambers shall have been constituted. The secretaries thus appointed shall vacate their offices as soon as the Governor-General shall take his oath of office before the insular chambers, and the Governor-General shall immediately appoint as their successors the members of parliament who, in his judgment, most fully represent the majorities in the chamber of representatives and the council of administration.

Art. 2. The manner of meeting the expenditures occasioned by the debt now weighing upon the Spanish and Cuban treasuries, and the debt that may be contracted until the termination of the war, shall be determined by a law fixing the share that shall be borne by each treasury, and the special ways and means for the payment of the interest, and the sinking fund, and for refunding the principal in due time.

Until the Cortes of the Kingdom shall decide this point no changes shall be made in the conditions under which said debts were contracted, nor in the payment of the interest, nor provisions for a sinking fund, nor in the guarantees which they enjoy, nor in the actual terms of payment.

When the apportionment shall have been made by the Cortes, it shall be for each one of the treasuries to make payment of the part assigned to it.

Obligations contracted with creditors under a pledge of the good faith of the Spanish nation, shall in all cases be scrupulously respected.

Given at the Palace, this 25th day of November, 1897.

MARIA CRISTINA.

Práxedes Mateo Sagasta,

President of the Council of Ministers.

CHAPTER IV.

Attitude of the United States Administration in Respect to Cuba, Puerto Rico and the Philippine Islands.

General Orders, No. 101.	WAR DEPARTMENT, Adjutant-General's Office, *Washington, July* 18, 1898.

The following, received from the President of the United States, is published for the information and guidance of all concerned:

Executive Mansion,
Washington, July 13, 1898.

To the Secretary of War:

Sir.— The capitulation of the Spanish forces in Santiago de Cuba and in the eastern part of the Province of Santiago, and the occupation of the territory by the forces of the United States, render it necessary to instruct the military commander of the United States as to the conduct which he is to observe during the military occupation.

The first effect of the military occupation of the enemy's territory is the severance of the former political relations of the inhabitants and the establishment of a new political power. Under this changed condition of things the inhabitants, so long as they perform their duties, are entitled to security in their persons and property and in all their private rights and relations. It is my desire that the inhabitants of Cuba should be acquainted with the purpose of the United States to discharge to the fullest extent its obligations in this regard. It will therefore be the duty of the commander of the army of occupation to announce and proclaim in the most public manner that we come not to make war upon the inhabitants of Cuba, nor upon any party or faction among them, but to protect them in their homes, in their employments, and in their personal and religious rights. All persons who, either by active aid or by honest submission, co-operate with the United States in its efforts to give effect to this beneficent purpose will receive the reward of its support and protection. Our occupation should be as free from severity as possible.

Though the powers of the military occupant are absolute and supreme and immediately operate upon the political condition of the inhabitants, the municipal laws of the conquered territory, such as affect private rights of person and property and provide for the punishment of crime, are considered as continuing in force, so far as they are compatible with the new order of things, until they are suspended or superseded by the occupying belligerent and in practice they are not usually abrogated, but are allowed to remain in force and to be administered by the ordinary tribunals, substantially as they were before the occupation. This enlightened practice is, so far as possible, to be adhered to on the present occasion. The judges and the other officials connected with the administration of justice may, if they accept the supremacy of the United States, continue to administer the ordinary law of the land, as between man and man, under the supervision of the American Commander-in-Chief. The native constabulary will, so far as may be practicable, be preserved. The freedom of the people to pursue their accustomed occupations will be abridged only when it may be necessary to do so.

While the rule of conduct of the American Commander-in-Chief will be such as has just been defined, it will be his duty to adopt measures of a different kind, if, unfortunately, the course of the people should render such measures indispensable to the maintenance of law and order. He will then possess the power to replace or expel the native officials in part or altogether, to substitute new courts of his own constitution for those that now exist, or to create such new or supplementary tribunals as may be necessary. In the exercise of these high powers the commander must be guided by his judgment and his experience and a high sense of justice.

One of the most important and most practical problems with which it will be necessary to deal is that of the treatment of property and the collection and administration of the revenues. It is conceded that all public funds and securities belonging to the government of the country in its own right, and all arms and supplies and other movable property of such government, may be seized by the military occupant and converted to his own use. The real property of the State he may hold and administer, at the same time enjoying the revenues thereof, but he is not to destroy it save in the case of military necessity. All public means of transportation, such as telegraph lines, cables, railways and boats belonging to the State may be appropriated to his use, but unless in case of military necessity they are not to be destroyed. All churches and buildings devoted to religious worship and to the arts and sciences, all schoolhouses, are, so far as possible, to be protected, and all destruction or intentional defacement of such places, of historical monuments or archives, or of works of science or art, is prohibited, save when required by urgent military necessity.

Private property, whether belonging to individuals or corporations, is to be respected, and can be confiscated only for cause. Means of transportation, such as telegraph lines and cables, railways and boats, may, although they belong to private individuals or corporations be seized by the military occupant, but unless destroyed under military necessity are not to be retained.

While it is held to be the right of the conqueror to levy contributions upon the enemy in their seaports, towns, or provinces which may be in his military possession by conquest and to apply the proceeds to defray the expenses of the war, this right is to be exercised within such limitations that it may not savor of confiscation. As the result of military occupation the taxes and duties payable by the inhabitants to the former government become payable to the military occupant, unless he sees fit to substitute for them other rates or modes of contribution to the expenses of the government. The moneys so collected are to be used for the purpose of paying the expenses of government under the military occupation, such as the salaries of the judges and the police, and for the payment of the expenses of the Army.

Private property taken for the use of the Army is to be paid for when possible in cash at a fair valuation, and when payment in cash is not possible, receipts are to be given.

All ports and places in Cuba which may be in the actual possession of our land and naval forces will be opened to the commerce of all neutral nations, as well as our own, in articles not contraband of war, upon payment of the prescribed rates of duty which may be in force at the time of the importation.

WILLIAM McKINLEY.

By order of the Secretary of War:

H. C. CORBIN,
Adjutant-General.

HEADQUARTERS, DIVISION OF CUBA,
Havana, January 1, 1899.

PROCLAMATION.

To the People of Cuba: Coming among you as the representative of the President, in furtherance and in continuation of the humane purpose with which my country interfered to put an end to the distressing condition in this Island, I deem it proper to say that the object of the present government is to give protection to the people, security to person and property, to restore confidence, to encourage the people to resume the pursuits of peace, to build up waste plantations, to resume commercial traffic; and to afford full protection in the exercise of all civil and religious rights.

To this end, the protection of the United States government will be directed, and every possible provision made to carry out these objects through the channels of civil administration, although under military control, in the interest and for the benefit of all the people of Cuba, and those possessed of rights and property in the Island.

The civil and criminal code which prevailed prior to the relinquishment of Spanish sovereignty will remain in force, with such modifications and changes as may from time to time be found necessary in the interest of good government.

The people of Cuba, without regard to previous affiliations, are invited and urged to co-operate in these objects by the exercise of moderation, conciliation, and good will one toward another; and a hearty accord in our humanitarian purposes will insure kind and beneficent government.

The Military Governor of the Island will always be pleased to confer with those who may desire to consult him on matters of public interest.

JOHN R. BROOKE,*

Major-General, Commanding Division of Cuba, and Military Governor.

[From President McKinley's Message of December 5, 1899.]

CUBA.

My Annual Message of last year was necessarily devoted in great part to a consideration of the Spanish war and of the results it wrought and the conditions it imposed for the future. I am gratified to announce that the treaty of peace has restored friendly relations between the two powers. Effect has been given to its most important provisions. The evacuation of Puerto Rico having already been accomplished on the 18th of October, 1898, nothing remained necessary there but to continue the provisional military control of the island until Congress should enact a suitable government for the ceded territory. Of the character and scope of the measures to that end I shall treat in another part of this message.

The withdrawal of the authority of Spain from the island of Cuba was effected by the 1st of January, so that the full re-establishment of peace found the relinquished territory held by us in trust for the inhabitants, maintaining, under the direction of the Executive, such government and control therein as should conserve public order, restore the productive conditions of peace so long disturbed by the instability and disorder which prevailed for the greater part of the preceding three decades, and build up that tranquil development of the domestic state whereby alone can be realized the high purpose,

*** In December, 1899, Major-General Leonard Wood, having succeeded General Brooke, continued to carry out the Administration's Policy in Cuba.**

as proclaimed in the joint resolution adopted by Congress on the 19th of April, 1898, by which the United States disclaimed any disposition or intention to exercise sovereignty, jurisdiction, or control over Cuba, except for the pacification thereof, and asserted its determination when that was accomplished to leave the government and control of the island to its people. The pledge contained in this resolution is of the highest honorable obligation and must be sacredly kept.

I believe that substantial progress has been made in this direction. All the administrative measures adopted in Cuba have aimed to fit it for a regenerated existence by enforcing the supremacy of law and justice; by placing wherever practicable the machinery of administration in the hands of the inhabitants; by instituting needed sanitary reforms; by spreading education; by fostering industry and trade; by inculcating public morality, and, in short, by taking every rational step to aid the Cuban people to attain to that plane of self-conscious respect and self-reliant unity which fits an enlightened community for self-government within its own sphere, while enabling it to fulfill all outward obligations.

This nation has assumed before the world a grave responsibility for the future good government of Cuba. We have accepted a trust the fulfillment of which calls for the sternest integrity of purpose and the exercise of the highest wisdom. The new Cuba yet to arise from the ashes of the past must needs be bound to us by ties of singular intimacy and strength if its enduring welfare is to be assured. Whether those ties shall be organic or conventional, the destinies of Cuba are in some rightful form and manner irrevocably linked with our own, but how and how far is for the future to determine in the ripeness of events. Whatever be the outcome, we must see to it that free Cuba be a reality, not a name, a perfect entity, not a hasty experiment bearing within itself the elements of failure. Our mission, to accomplish which we took up the wages of battle, is not to be fulfilled by turning adrift any loosely framed commonwealth to face the vicissitudes which too often attend weaker states whose natural wealth and abundant resources are offset by the incongruities of their political organization and the recurring occasions for internal rivalries to sap their strength and dissipate their energies. The greatest blessing which can come to Cuba is the restoration of her agricultural and industrial prosperity, which will give employment to idle men and re-establish the pursuits of peace. This is her chief and immediate need.

On the 19th of August last an order was made for the taking of the census in the island, to be completed on the 30th of November. By the treaty of peace the Spanish people on the island have until April 11, 1900, to elect whether they will remain citizens of Spain or become citizens of Cuba. Until then it cannot be definitely ascertained who shall be entitled to participate in the formation of the government of Cuba. By that time the results of the census will have been tabulated and we shall proceed to provide for elections which will commit the municipal governments of the island to the officers elected by the people. The experience thus acquired will prove of great value in the formation of a representative convention of the people to draft a constitution and establish a general system of independent government for the island. In the meantime and so long as we exercise control over the island the products of Cuba should have a market in the United States on as good terms and with as favorable rates of duty as are given to the West India Islands under treaties of reciprocity which shall be made.

For the relief of the distressed in the island of Cuba the War Department has issued supplies to destitute persons through the officers of the Army, which have amounted to 5,493,000 rations, at a cost of $1,417,554.07.

To promote the disarmament of the Cuban volunteer army, and in the interest of public peace and the welfare of the people, the sum of $75 was paid to each Cuban soldier borne upon the authentic rolls, on condition that he should deposit his arms with the authorities designated by the United States. The sum thus disbursed aggregated $2,547,750, which was paid from the emergency fund provided by the act of January 5, 1899, for that purpose.

Out of the Cuban island revenues during the six months ending June 30, 1899, $1,712,014.20 was expended for sanitation, $293,881.70 for charities and hospitals, and $88,944.03 for aid to the destitute.

Following the exchange of ratifications of the treaty of peace the two governments accredited ministers to each other, Spain sending to Washington the Duke of Arcos, an eminent diplomatist, previously stationed in Mexico, while the United States transferred to Madrid Hon. Bellamy Storer, its minister at Brussels. This was followed by the respective appointment of consuls, thereby fully resuming the relations interrupted by the war. In addition to its consular representation in the United States, the Spanish government has appointed consuls for Cuba, who have been provisionally recognized during the military administration of the affairs of that island.

Judicial intercourse between the courts of Cuba and Puerto Rico and of Spain has been established, as provided by the treaty of peace. The Cuban political prisoners in Spanish penal stations have been and are being released and returned to their homes, in accordance with Article VI of the treaty. Negotiations are about to be had for defining the conventional relations between the two countries, which fell into abeyance by reason of the war. I trust that these will include a favorable arrangement for commercial reciprocity under the terms of sections 3 and 4 of the current tariff act. In these, as in all matters of international concern, no effort will be spared to respond to the good disposition of Spain, and to cultivate in all practicable ways the intimacy which should prevail between two nations whose past history has so often and in so many ways been marked by sincere friendship and by community of interests.

I would recommend appropriate legislation in order to carry into execution Article VII of the Treaty of Peace with Spain, by which the United States assured the payment of certain claims for indemnity of its citizens against Spain.

PUERTO RICO.

I recommend that legislation to the same end be had with reference to the government of Puerto Rico. The time is ripe for the adoption of a temporary form of government for this island; and many suggestions made with reference to Alaska are applicable also to Puerto Rico.

The system of civil jurisprudence now adopted by the people of this island is described by competent lawyers who are familiar with it, as thoroughly modern and scientific, so far as it relates to matters of internal business, trade, production, and social and private right in general. The cities of the island are governed under charters which probably require very little or no change. So that with relation to matters of local concern and private right, it is not probable that much, if any, legislation is desirable; but with reference to public administration and the relations of the island to the Federal Government, there are many matters which are of pressing urgency. The same necessity exists for legislation on the part of Congress to establish Federal courts and Federal jurisdiction in the island as has been previously pointed out by me with reference to Hawaii. Besides the administration of justice, there are the subjects of the public lands; the control and improvement of rivers and harbors; the control of the waters or streams not navigable, which, under the Spanish law, belonged to the Crown of Spain, and have by the treaty of cession passed to the United States; the immigration of people from foreign countries; the importation of contract labor; the imposition and collection of internal revenue; the application of the navigation laws; the regulation of the current money; the establishment of post-offices and post-roads; the regulation of tariff rates on merchandise imported from the island into the United States; the establishment of ports of entry and delivery; the regulation of patents and copyrights; these, with various other subjects which rest entirely within the power of the Congress, call for careful consideration and immediate action.

It must be borne in mind that since the cession Puerto Rico has been denied the principal markets she had long enjoyed and our tariffs have been continued against her products as when she was under Spanish sovereignty. The markets of Spain are closed to her products except upon terms to which the commerce of all nations is subjected. The island of Cuba, which used to buy her cattle and tobacco without customs duties, now imposes the same duties upon these products as from any other country entering her ports. She has therefore lost her free intercourse with Spain and Cuba without any compensating benefits in this market. Her coffee was little known and not in use by our people, and therefore there was no demand here for this, one of her chief products. The markets of the United States should be opened up to her products. Our plain duty is to abolish all customs tariffs between the United States and Puerto Rico and give her products free access to our markets.

As a result of the hurricane which swept over Puerto Rico on the 8th of August, 1899, over 100,000 people were reduced to absolute destitution, without homes, and deprived of the necessaries of life. To the appeal of the War Department the people of the United States made prompt and generous response. In addition to the private charity of our people, the War Department has expended for the relief of the distressed $392,342.63, which does not include the cost of transportation.

It is desirable that the government of the island under the law of belligerent right, now maintained through the Executive Department, should be superseded by an administration entirely civil in its nature. For present purposes I recommend that Congress pass a law for the organization of a temporary government, which shall provide for the appointment by the President, subject to confirmation by the Senate, of a governor and such other officers as the general administration of the island may require, and that for legislative purposes upon subjects of a local nature not partaking of a Federal character a legislative council, composed partly of Puerto Ricans and partly of citizens of the United States, shall be nominated and appointed by the President, subject to confirmation by the Senate, their acts to be subject to the approval of the Congress or the President prior to going into effect. In the municipalities and other local subdivisions I recommend that the principle of local self-government be applied at once, so as to enable the intelligent citizens of the island to participate in their own government and to learn by practical experience the duties and requirements of a self-contained and self-governed people. I have not thought it wise to commit the entire government of the island to officers selected by the people, because I doubt whether in habits, training, and experience they are such as to fit them to exercise at once so large a degree of self-government; but it is my judgment and expectation that they will soon arrive at an attainment of experience and wisdom and self-control that will justify conferring upon them a much larger participation in the choice of their insular officers.

The fundamental requirement for these people, as for all people, is education. The free schoolhouse is the best preceptor for citizenship. In the introduction of modern educational methods care, however, must be exercised that changes be not made too abruptly and that the history and racial peculiarities of the inhabitants shall be given due weight. Systems of education in these new possessions founded upon common-sense methods, adapted to existing conditions and looking to the future moral and industrial advancement of the people, will commend to them in a pecuniary effective manner the blessings of free government.

The love of law and the sense of obedience and submission to the lawfully constituted judicial tribunals are embodied in the hearts of our people, and any violation of these sentiments and disregard of their obligations justly arouses public condemnation. The guaranties of life, liberty, and of civil rights should be faithfully upheld; the right of trial by jury respected and defended. The rule of the courts should assure the public of the prompt trial of those charged with criminal offenses, and upon conviction the punishment should be commensurate with the enormity of the crime.

Those who, in disregard of law and the public peace, unwilling to await the judgment of court and jury, constitute themselves judges and executioners should not escape the severest penalties for their crimes.

What I said in my Inaugural Address of March 4, 1897, I now repeat:

"The constituted authorities must be cheerfully and vigorously upheld. Lynchings must not be tolerated in a great and civilized country like the United States. Courts, not mobs, must execute the penalties of the laws. The preservation of public order, the right of discussion, the integrity of courts, and the orderly administration of justice must continue forever the rock of safety upon which our government securely rests."

THE PHILIPPINES.

On the 10th of December, 1898, the treaty of peace between the United States and Spain was signed. It provided, among other things, that Spain should cede to the United States the archipelago known as the Philippine Islands, that the United States should pay to Spain the sum of twenty million of dollars, and that the civil rights and political status of the native inhabitants of the territories thus ceded to the United States should be determined by the Congress. The treaty was ratified by the Senate on the 6th of February, 1899, and by the Government of Spain on the 19th of March following. The ratifications were exchanged on the 11th of April and the treaty publicly proclaimed. On the 2d of March the Congress voted the sum contemplated by the treaty, and the amount was paid over to the Spanish Government on the 1st of May.

In this manner the Philippines came to the United States. The islands were ceded by the Government of Spain, which had been in undisputed possession of them for centuries. They were accepted not merely by our authorized commissioners in Paris, under the direction of the Executive, but by the constitutional and well-considered action of the representatives of the people of the United States in both Houses of Congress. I had every reason to believe, and I still believe, that this transfer of sovereignty was in accordance with the wishes and the aspirations of the great mass of the Filipino people.

From the earliest moment no opportunity was lost of assuring the people of the islands of our ardent desire for their welfare and of the intention of this Government to do everything possible to advance their interests. In my order of the 19th of May, 1898, the commander of the military expedition dispatched to the Philippines was instructed to declare that we came not to make war upon the people of that country, "nor upon any party or faction among them, but to protect them in their homes, in their employments, and in their personal and religious rights." That there should be no doubt as to the paramount authority there, on the 17th of August it was directed that "there must be no joint occupation with the insurgents;" that the United States must preserve the peace and protect persons and property within the territory occupied by their military and naval forces; that the insurgents and all others must recognize the military occupation and authority of the United States. As early as December 4, before the cession, and in anticipation of that event, the commander in Manila was urged to restore peace and tranquillity and to undertake the establishment of a beneficent government, which should afford the fullest security for life and property.

On the 21st of December, after the treaty was signed, the commander of the forces of occupation was instructed "to announce and proclaim in the most public manner that we come, not as invaders and conquerors, but as friends to protect the natives in their homes, in their employments, and in their personal and religious rights." On the same day, while ordering General Otis to see that the peace should be preserved in Iloilo, he was admonished that: "It is most important that there should be no conflict with the insurgents." On the 1st day of January, 1899, urgent orders were reiterated that the kindly intentions of this Government should be in every possible way communicated to the insurgents.

* * * * * * *

RESPONSIBILITY OF CONGRESS.

The future government of the Philippines rests with the Congress of the United States. Few graver responsibilities have ever been confided to us. If we accept them in a spirit worthy of our race and our traditions, a great opportunity comes with them. The islands lie under the shelter of our flag. They are ours by every title of law and equity. They cannot be abandoned. If we desert them we leave them at once to anarchy and finally to barbarism. We fling them, a golden apple of discord, among the rival powers, no one of which could permit another to seize them unquestioned. Their rich plains and valleys would be the scene of endless strife and bloodshed. The advent of Dewey's fleet in Manila Bay instead of being, as we hope, the dawn of a new day of freedom and progress, will have been the beginning of an era of misery and violence worse than any which has darkened their unhappy past. The suggestion has been made that we could renounce our authority over the islands and, giving them independence, could retain a protectorate over them. This proposition will not be found, I am sure, worthy of your serious attention. Such an arrangement would involve at the outset a cruel breach of faith. It would place the peaceable and loyal majority, who ask nothing better than to accept our authority, at the mercy of the minority of armed insurgents. It would make us responsible for the acts of the insurgent leaders and give us no power to control them. It would charge us with the task of protecting them against each other and defending them against any foreign power with which they chose to quarrel. In short, it would take from the Congress of the United States the power of declaring war and vest that tremendous prerogative in the Tagal leader of the hour.

It does not seem desirable that I should recommend at this time a specific and final form of government for these islands. When peace shall be restored it will be the duty of Congress to construct a plan of government which shall establish and maintain freedom and order and peace in the Philippines. The insurrection is still existing, and when it terminates further information will be required as to the actual condition of affairs before inaugurating a permanent scheme of civil government. The full report of the Commission, now in preparation, will contain information and suggestions which will be of value to Congress, and which I will transmit as soon as it is completed. As long as the insurrection continues the military arm must necessarily be supreme. But there is no reason why steps should not be taken from time to time to inaugurate governments essentially popular in their form as fast as territory is held and controlled by our troops. To this end I am considering the advisability of the return of the Commission, or such of the members thereof as can be secured, to aid the existing authorities and facilitate this work throughout the islands. I have believed that reconstruction should not begin by the establishment of one central civil government for all the islands, with its seat at Manila, but rather that the work should be commenced by building up from the bottom, first establishing municipal governments and then provincial governments, a central government at last to follow.

Until Congress shall have made known the formal expression of its will I shall use the authority vested in me by the Constitution and the statutes to uphold the sovereignty of the United States in those distant islands as in all other places where our flag rightfully floats. I shall put at the disposal of the Army and Navy all the means which the liberality of Congress and the people have provided to cause this unprovoked and wasteful insurrection to cease. If any orders of mine were required to insure the merciful conduct of military and naval operations, they would not be lacking; but every step of the progress of our troops has been marked by a humanity which has surpassed even the misguided insurgents. The truest kindness to them will be a swift and effective defeat of their present leader. The hour of victory will be the hour of clemency and reconstruction.

No effort will be spared to build up the waste places desolated by war and by long years of misgovernment. We shall not wait for the end of the strife to begin the beneficent work. We shall continue, as we have begun, to open the schools and the churches, to set the courts in operation, to foster industry and trade and agriculture, and in every way in our power to make these people whom Providence has brought within our jurisdiction feel that it is their liberty and not our power, their welfare and not our gain, we are seeking to enhance. Our flag has never waived over any community but in blessing. I believe the Filipinos will soon recognize the fact that it has not lost its gift of benediction in its world-wide journey to their shores.

* * * * * * *

TABLE OF CASES.

[Continued from page 81.]

Codes at present in force in Spain, Cuba, Puerto Rico and the Philippines:

[Constitution of June 30, 1876, extended to Cuba and Puerto Rico, April 7, 1881.]

IN SPAIN.

Date	Code	Books.	Titles.	Articles.	Volumes.
May 24, 1889	Civil Code	4	18	1976	1
Feb. 3, 1881	Civil Procedure	3	59	2182	1
June 17, 1870	Criminal Code	3	26	626	1
Sept. 14, 1882	Criminal Procedure	7	40	998	1
July 14, 1893	Mortgage Law	0	15	413	1
Aug. 22, 1885	Commercial Code	4	27	955	1
Aug. 24, 1888	Codigo Penal de la Marina de guerra	3	17	343	1
Sept. 27, 1890	Code of Military Justice......	3	49	750	1
Dec. 17, 1890	Organic Law of the Supreme Council of Army and Navy..	1	6	215	1

IN CUBA.

July 31, 1889	Civil Code.	Sept. 25, 1885	Civil Procedure.
May 23, 1879	Criminal Code.	Oct. 19, 1889	Criminal Procedure.
July 14, 1893	Mortgage Law.	Jan. 28, 1886	Commercial Code.

Autonomy extended to Cuba, November 25, 1897.

IN PUERTO RICO.

July 31, 1889	Civil Code.	Sept. 25, 1885	Civil Procedure.
May 23, 1879	Criminal Code.	Oct. 19, 1889	Criminal Procedure.
July 14, 1893	Mortgage Law.	Jan. 28, 1886	Commercial Code.

Autonomy extended to Puerto Rico, November 25, 1897.

IN THE PHILIPPINES.

July 31, 1889	Civil Code.	Feb. 3, 1888	Civil Procedure.
Sept. 4, 1884	Criminal Code.	Sept. 4, 1884	Criminal Procedure, to go into effect Jan. 1, 1888.
July 14, 1893	Mortgage Law.	Aug. 6, 1888	Commercial Code.

SPANISH-AMERICAN CONSTITUTIONS AND CODES.

[The Constitutions and many of the Codes have suffered amendments.]

ARGENTINE REPUBLIC.

Constitution of 1860.
Commercial Code of 1890.
Mining Code of 1887.
Compilation of Codes and Laws of 1888.

BOLIVIA.

Constitution of 1880.
Commercial Code of 1891.
Mining Laws of 1880–82.

BRAZIL.

Constitution of 1891.
Commercial Code of 1850.
Civil Code of 1891.
Mining Code of 1857.

COLOMBIA.

Constitution of 1886.
Civil Code of 1891.
Commercial Code of 1886–87.
Special Laws for Panama, 1886–89.
Registration of Foreign Corporations, Laws of 1888.
Mining Code of 1887.

CHILI.

Constitution of 1833.
Civil Code of 1856.
Commercial Code of 1865.
Mining Code of 1889.

COSTA RICA.

Constitution of 1871.
Commercial Code of 1853.
Mining Ordinances of 1830.
Compilation of Codes, 1887–88.

ECUADOR.

Constitution of 1884.
Civil Code of 1887.
Commercial Code of 1878.
Mining Laws of Spain and of 1886.

GUATEMALA.

Constitution of 1879.
Civil Code of 1877.
Commercial Code of 1877.
Mining Laws of 1882.

HONDURAS.

Constitution of 1894.
Land Laws of 1888.
Mining Laws of 1880–88.
Consolidated Laws of 1887.

MEXICO.

Civil Code of March 31, 1884.
Commercial Code of Sept. 15, 1889.
Mining Code of Nov. 22, 1884.

NICARAGUA.

Constitution of 1893.
Civil, Commercial and Criminal Codes, revised, and about to be adopted.
Mining Code of 1876.

PARAGUAY.

Constitution of 1870.
Civil and Commercial Laws, 1880–93.
Land Laws of 1885–92.

PERU.

Constitution of 1860.
Civil Code of 1851.
Commercial Code in Digest.
Mining Laws of Spain and of 1871.

URUGUAY.

Constitution of 1893.
Civil Code of 1895.
Mining Code of 1884.

VENEZUELA.

Constitution of 1893.
Commercial Laws of 1861–90.
Mining Code of 1891.

GENERAL INDEX.

[For continuation of General Index, see page 665.]

ALPHABETICAL INDEX TO CIVIL CODE.

[General index continued from page 606.]

www.ingramcontent.com/pod-product-compliance
Lightning Source LLC
LaVergne TN
LVHW091521200926
848483LV00002B/273
* 9 7 8 1 5 8 4 7 7 2 4 5 3 *